Readings in Intercultural Communication

Readings in Intercultural Communication

Experiences and Contexts

SECOND EDITION

Judith N. Martin

ARIZONA STATE UNIVERSITY

Thomas K. Nakayama

ARIZONA STATE UNIVERSITY

Lisa A. Flores

UNIVERSITY OF UTAH

Boston   Burr Ridge, IL   Dubuque, IA   Madison, WI   New York
San Francisco   St. Louis   Bangkok   Bogotá   Caracas   Kuala Lumpur
Lisbon   London   Madrid   Mexico City   Milan   Montreal   New Delhi
Santiago   Seoul   Singapore   Sydney   Taipei   Toronto

McGraw-Hill Higher Education

A Division of The **McGraw-Hill** *Companies*

2 3 4 5 6 7 8 9 0 DOC/DOC 0 9 8 7 6 5 4 3 2

Library of Congress Cataloging-in-Publication Data

Readings in intercultural communication / [edited by] Judith N. Martin, Thomas K. Nakayama, Lisa A. Flores.—2nd ed.
    p. cm.
  Rev. ed. of: Readings in cultural contexts. c1998.
  ISBN 0-7674-2716-5
  1. Intercultural communication.   2. Communication and culture.   3. Multiculturalism.   4. Ethnicity.   I. Martin, Judith N.   II. Nakayama, Thomas K.   III. Flores, Lisa A.   IV. Readings in cultural contexts.

GN345.6 .R43 2001
303.48'2—DC21   2001040330

Publisher, Nanette Kauffman; production, Publishing Support Services; manuscript editor, Darlene Bledsoe; design manager, Jean Mailander; text and cover designer, Claire Seng-Niemoeller; cover artist, Lauren Uram; manufacturing manager, Randy Hurst. The text was set in 9.5/12 Plantin Light by G&S Typesetters, Inc., and printed on 45# Scholarly Matte by R. R. Donnelley and Sons.

Text credits appear on a continuation of the copyright page, page 397.

www.mhhe.com

Contents

Preface

The field of intercultural communication continues to present us with great challenges. While there are some success stories in the political world of intercultural relations (e.g., Brazil, South Africa), there still remains the question of intergroup relations in the Middle East, the former Yugoslavia, and Indonesia. And each of us grapples with increasing diversity in our daily work and social lives, as industrial and technological advances bring us into contact with more people than ever before. A primary challenge is how to present intercultural communication scholarship in a way that helps students and professors to understand better the political interethnic relations and to improve the quality of intercultural friendship and work relationships.

Our goal in compiling these essays was to provide multiple perspectives in intercultural communication that are grounded in the everyday communication experiences of study: personal narratives, social science research, and critical analyses of popular culture texts, such as MTV or advertising. The essays in this collection range from the classic writings of E. T. Hall, Gerry Philipsen, and Geert Hofstede to more recent scholarship influenced by critical theory and cultural studies. The diversity of these readings creates an opportunity for students to deepen their understanding of intercultural issues.

We begin the book by presenting a dialectical framework that recognizes the complexities of intercultural communication and allows for multiple ways of understanding: through narrative, ethnographic studies, and textual and media analyses, as well as the more traditional social science reports. In addition to conceptual issues, many of the essays offer practical guidelines for meeting intercultural challenges faced in daily life.

Features

- The introductory material offers a broad unifying framework for integrating intercultural communication perspectives.
- The essays address practical as well as conceptual issues.

- A variety of essays are presented, from ethnographic accounts to narratives of everyday experiences, to analyses of cultural texts, to traditional social science reports.
- The essays offer insight into particular examples of intercultural communication in both domestic and international contexts.
- Author voices reflect a diversity of ethnicity, gender, and nationality.
- The essays are written in a tone and style that is accessible to students.
- Discussion Questions and Key Terms at the end of each essay help to launch classroom discussion on the relevant issues.

Highlights of the Second Edition Revisions

- While the essays still reflect a variety of perspectives, the emphasis is less on research and more on the practical aspects of intercultural communication.
- Essays were revised with a goal of making them more accessible and understandable to undergraduate students who may or may not be communication majors.
- New and revised essays include "Worldview, Religion, and Intercultural Communication," "Code-Switching: An Everyday Reality in Belgium," and "Being Chicana in a White World" (a personal narrative).
- Following the last article in each part, we have added new features:

  Activities for Skill Development, to assist professors in using the selected readings for more active learning in the classroom.

  A list of relevant Web sites, to help students further explore the issues presented in the essays.

  Additional Readings, to guide professors and students to related research that further explores various topics, issues, and questions.

Organization

We begin with essays that explore the basic concepts in intercultural communication. The first essay presents our integrative framework, which reflects and connects the diversity of perspectives and contributions in the field of intercultural communication. Other essays in this section explore basic definitions and foundational concepts, such as culture, perception, and worldview.

After establishing a foundation, we then focus on issues of identity. The essays in Part Two explore the multifaceted and dynamic connections among identity, culture, and communication. They focus on the overlaps and fluid aspects of ethnic, gender, race, class, and religious identities and offer practical insights from a variety of perspectives.

Part Three examines the importance of history in intercultural communication. The readings show how history influences various international and domestic communication settings in the United States, Europe, the Middle East, and Cyprus.

Essays in Part Four discuss language and its role in intercultural communication—how language can facilitate communication by language accommodation and code-switching, or how language can inhibit communication by reinforcing stereotypes. These essays also explore rules for speaking in specific communities, both international and domestic (e.g., public speaking by Native Americans and leave-taking in Colombia), and provide practical guidelines for resisting stereotyping based on language style and proficiency.

In Part Five, the essays explore cultural spaces and nonverbal communication practices by comparing nonverbal communication in European and American business contexts and print advertising in Korea and the United States. Other essays describe and analyze nonverbal practices in specific contexts: an American Indian gaming casino and a U.S. working-class neighborhood.

Part Six examines popular culture and intercultural communication, including the ways people consume and resist messages from television, movies, and sports. The essays also explore how popular culture influences our perceptions of other cultures and offer practical insights about how these perceptions can influence subsequent intercultural communication.

The essays in Part Seven discuss a variety of intercultural transitions—sojourns overseas, reentry shock on return, and the experiences of living "in-between" cultures, as immigrants or international adoptees. The essays also provide practical guidelines for easing transitions and living on cultural borders.

Part Eight focuses on intercultural relationships. These essays examine the role of culture in various kinds of relationships: family, work, friendship, and romance. The contributing authors offer ways to think about relationships as well as practical suggestions for developing intercultural relationships and meeting both the joys and challenges of these relationships.

The essays in Part Nine explore conflict, communication, and culture, offering cross-cultural comparisons of conflict management in both international and domestic settings. They provide practical guidelines for dealing with intercultural conflict and always offer insights on how mediated and international conflict can affect conflict on an interpersonal level.

Finally, Part Ten addresses ethical issues in intercultural communication. These essays provide ways to think about and understand ethical dilemmas in everyday life and offer practical guidelines for meeting ethical challenges.

Acknowledgments

First, we thank our editor, Holly J. Allen, for once again guiding us through the publishing process. She initiated the first edition and then patiently and insightfully provided guidance for revising and completing this second edition. Her help and friendship make publishing a joy (well, maybe manageable)! We also thank the contributing authors for their high-quality, conceptual essays. They met the deadlines in spite of their busy lives, and we are grateful to them.

We also want to thank our editorial assistants, Tamie Kanata and Sara DeTurk. Without their prompt and efficient work, this manuscript would never have been submitted on time. They worked independently and graciously, often under incredible time pressures and while juggling other tasks (such as taking comprehensive exams).

We owe a great deal to the reviewers: Terri Kelley Wray, George Mason University; Marjorie Jaasma, California State University, Stanislaus; Felecia Jordan-Jackson, Florida State University; Alan Hansen, State University of New York, Albany; Susan Strauss, Pennsylvania State University; Jennifer L. Willis-Rivera, Southern Illinois University; Susan Gibertz, Texas A&M University. They provided insightful, detailed, and very helpful comments. Their reviews helped us see the gaps that needed to be filled. Thanks to their comments, the essays in this book are more accessible, focused, and practically oriented.

Once again, to our partners, Ronald S. Chaldu, David L. Karbonski, and Marouf A. Hasian, Jr., as well as our colleagues, students, and friends, we owe thanks for support and understanding.

Contributors

James Baldwin (1924–1987) was an important U.S. writer who had a significant voice in racial issues, particularly in the late 1950s and 1960s. He grew up in Harlem and then moved to Paris; he later lived in both France and the United States. He was active in the U.S. civil rights movement. Many of Baldwin's works dealt with sexuality as well as racial issues. Author of many books, he is well known for *Go Tell It on the Mountain* (1953), *Notes of a Native Son* (1955), *Giovanni's Room* (1956), *Nobody Knows My Name* (1961), *Another Country* (1962), and *The Fire Next Time* (1963).

John R. Baldwin is an associate professor at Illinois State University. His research and publications focus on interethnic communication, intercultural and interracial relationships, and intolerance. He is currently researching cross-cultural and cross-disciplinary understandings of racism and sexual harassment.

Mary Catherine Bateson is the Clarence Robinson Professor of Anthropology and English at George Mason University. She has written on a variety of linguistic and anthropological topics and is the author of a memoir of her parents, Gregory Bateson and Margaret Mead, entitled *With a Daughter's Eye*. Her other books include *Peripheral Visions: Learning Along the Way* and *Full Circles, Overlapping Lives: Culture and Generation in Transition*.

Benjamin J. Broome is a professor of communication at Arizona State University, where he teaches intercultural communication, group design and problem solving, and conflict resolution. He has worked with numerous community groups and organizations in Europe, the Eastern Mediterranean, Mexico, and the United States, including several Native American tribes. His book *Journey Through the Greek Mosaic* (Intercultural Press, 1996) provides a guide to intercultural communication for Americans living, studying, working, and traveling in Greece. Recently, he lived and worked for more than two years in Cyprus as a Senior Fulbright Scholar, where he offered seminars, workshops, and training programs to groups of Greek Cypriots and Turkish Cypriots.

Donal Carbaugh is a professor of communication at the University of Massachusetts, Amherst. One of the leading scholars in cultural communication, his writings focus on the development of communication theory of sociocultural interaction integrating identity issues, forms of action, and emotional expression. His edited volume *Cultural Communication and Intercultural Contact* (1990) received the Distinguished Scholarship Award by the Speech Communication Association's International and Intercultural Communication Division.

Mary Jane Collier is a professor in the School of Communication at the University of Denver. Her research and teaching areas are cultural identity (national, ethnic, gender, class), intercultural communication competence and relationship development, and intercultural conflict management. Her work appears in international and national journals, and she is the editor of volumes 23–25 of the *International and Intercultural Communication Annual*. Currently, her research involves visiting international and local sites, investigating intercultural alliances, and public dialogue.

Leda Cooks (Ph.D., Ohio University, 1993) is an associate professor at the University of Massachusetts. Her teaching and research focus on the ways power, identity, community, and nation are communicated in a variety of contexts, ranging from instructional to interpersonal, to intercultural and computer-mediated contexts. Her most recent work looks at museums as sites of collective memory.

Frederick C. Corey is a member of the faculty of The Hugh Downs School of Human Communication and the associate dean of the College of Public Programs at Arizona State University. His research focuses on gay culture and performance studies.

Karen L. Dace is an associate professor of communication at the University of Utah. She has a joint faculty appointment in the Ethnic Studies Program and was recently appointed Associate Vice President for Diversity. Her research interests include intercultural communication and African American women's discourse.

Fernando Delgado is an associate professor of communication studies at Arizona State University West and is affiliated with the Hispanic Research Center at Arizona State University. His teaching and extensive publications focus on the politics of identity and representation in popular culture (sports, music, television, and film).

Carley H. Dodd is a professor of communication at Abilene Christian University. His nine books and numerous papers address many communication issues, including an emphasis on studying relationships from a variety of family systems and cultures.

Kristine Fitch is an associate professor at the University of Iowa. Her book *Speaking Relationally: Culture, Communication, and Interpersonal Connection* received the Gerald R. Miller Award for outstanding research in interpersonal communication in 1999. Her work centers around culture, persuasion, and personal relationships. She has taught and conducted research in Colombia, Finland, the UK, and Spain.

Lisa A. Flores (Ph.D., University of Georgia) is an associate professor of communication and ethnic studies at the University of Utah. Currently, she is serving as director of Chicana/o Studies and Coordinator of the Ethnic Studies Program. She writes and teaches in the areas of culture, Chicana/o studies, race, feminism, and rhetoric.

Anita Foeman received her Ph.D. from Temple University in 1982. Her area of specialty is organizational communication. Dr. Foeman's research is in the area of diversity in the workplace. She teaches a range of communication courses, including Intercultural Communication, Organizational Communication, and Public Speaking. She works with a range of organizations as eclectic as the Atlantic City Police Department and public school systems.

Etsuko Fujimoto is an assistant professor of intercultural communication at Southern Oregon University. She received her Master of Arts in Interdisciplinary Studies in Communication from Oregon State University. Her current research interests include negotiations, expressions, and representations of social and cultural identities, multiculturalism, and transnationalism.

Howard Giles (Ph.D., DSc, University of Bristol) is a professor of communication at the University of California, Santa Barbara, with affiliated positions in psychology and linguistics. His research interests include many areas of intergroup communication—intercultural, intergenerational, police-community relations. He is a past president of the International Communication Association and current president of the International Association of Language and Social Psychology.

Douglas R. Golden earned his B.A. in Rhetoric from the University of Illinois at Urbana-Champaign. He is currently completing his M.A. in Communication at Arizona State University. His research interests include intercultural communication and Jewish identity.

María Cristina González is Academic Dean and Co-Director of the Doctor of Ministry Program at the University of Creation Spirituality in Oakland, California, and an adjunct professor of communication at Arizona State University. Her work explores how social organization and culture constrain and enable communication and spiritual expression. She regularly takes graduate students on field courses to learn the "four seasons" methodology of ethnography and is active in grassroots Native American and Chicana/o community efforts.

Edward T. Hall is an internationally known anthropologist and author. He was a partner in Edward T. Hall Associates with his wife **Mildred Reed Hall.** This pioneering firm, founded in 1961, specialized in intercultural communication, providing lectures and consultations to international businesses, foundations, and government agencies. His most recent book is *West of the Thirties: Discoveries Among the Navajo and Hopi.* He co-authored with Mildred Reed Hall *Understanding Cultural Differences: Germans, French and Americans* and *Hidden Differences: Doing Business with the Japanese.* His earlier books—*The Silent Language, The Hidden Dimension, Beyond Culture,* and *The Dance of Life*—have been translated into 20 languages.

Marouf A. Hasian, Jr., is an associate professor of communication at the University of Utah. He is the author of *The Rhetoric of Eugenics in Anglo-American Thought.* His research areas include law and rhetoric, intercultural communication and postcolonial discourse, the rhetoric of science, and freedom of expression.

Michael L. Hecht is professor and department head at Pennsylvania State University, and he recently implemented a successful multicultural drug prevention program for adolescents.

Radha S. Hegde teaches in the Department of Culture and Communication, New York University. Her research interests lie in the area of globalization, postcolonial theory, and the study of transnational identities. Her recent work centers on global feminism and gender politics in South Asia. Her work has appeared in *Communication Theory, International and Intercultural Communication Annual, Communication Studies,* and *Women's Studies in Communication.*

Geert Hofstede is an Emeritus professor of organizational anthropology and international management at the University of Limburg at Maastricht, the Netherlands. He has conducted extensive research in the area of national and organizational cultures. His best-known books are *Culture's Consequences: International Differences in the Work-Related Values* (1980) and *Cultures and Organizations: Software of the Mind* (1991).

Mark C. Hopson (B.A., Western Michigan University) is a second-year master's student in the Department of Communication at Western Michigan University. His research interests include Black masculinities, African American male communication, and diversity-related issues.

Fred E. Jandt is a professor of communication studies at California State University, San Bernardino. His research interests are culture and conflict studies. His publications include *Intercultural Communication: An Introduction* (3rd ed., 2001) and *Win-Win Negotiating: Turning Conflict into Agreement* (1985), which is available in seven languages.

Min-Sun Kim is a professor in the Department of Speech at the University of Hawaii at Manoa. Her research interests include the role of cognition in conversational styles among people of different cultural groups. Her articles have appeared in many journals, including *Human Communication Research, Communication Monographs,* and the *Howard Journal of Communications.*

Young Yun Kim is a professor of communication at the University of Oklahoma in Norman. Her research activities address the role of communication in cross-cultural adaptation processes of immigrants, sojourners, native-born ethnic minorities, and employees of international organizations. Among her recent books are *Communicating with Strangers* with W. Gudykunst (McGraw-Hill, 1997) and *Becoming Intercultural: An Integrative Theory of Communication and Cross-Cultural Adaptation* (Sage, 2001).

Janis L. King is a professor of communication at Southwest Missouri State University, where she teaches rhetorical criticism, persuasion, women's rhetoric, and nonverbal communication. Her research focuses on women and/or Native Americans and the use of persuasion to present various perspectives during public conflict situations.

Judith N. Martin is professor of communication at Arizona State University. Her research and publications focus on intercultural communication and transitions, ethnic and racial identity, and communication competence.

Jacqueline M. Martinez is an assistant professor in The Hugh Downs School of Human Communication at Arizona State University. She received her Ph.D. from Southern Illinois University. She has taught at Purdue University, Babson College, and was a Chicana Dissertation Fellow in the Department of Chicano Studies at the University of California, Santa Barbara. She writes in the area of intercultural communication. She is the author of *Phenomenology of Chicana Experience and Identity: Communication and Transformation in Praxis* (Rowman and Littlefield, 2000).

Mark Lawrence McPhail is a professor and the department chair of communication at Miami University, Oxford, Ohio. His research interests include rhetorical theory and epistemology, contemporary race relations, discourse and power, and Eastern philosophy. His work has appeared in many journals, and he is the author of two books, *The Rhetoric of Racism* and *Zen in the Art of Rhetoric: An Inquiry into Coherence.*

Dreama G. Moon is an assistant professor in the Commmunication Department at California State University, San Marcos. Her research is focused at the intersection of culture, communication, and social justice. She has published essays on the discourse of Whiteness and race trading, passing as an intercultural practice, and the communication of classism.

Thomas K. Nakayama is a professor in The Hugh Downs School of Human Communication and the director of the Asian Pacific American Studies Program at Arizona State University. He received his Ph.D. from the University of Iowa. He writes in the areas of cultural studies, intercultural communication, and rhetorical studies, focusing particularly on issues of race, gender, and sexuality.

Teresa A. Nance is an associate professor of communication arts at Villanova University and is a member of the Africana Studies Program. Her areas of teaching and research include classroom communication and African American learning styles.

T. A. Niles is a doctoral candidate in communication in Arizona State University's Interdisciplinary Ph.D. Program. He is currently investigating relationships among communication, culture, and ethnic and racial identity.

Kimberly A. Noels is an assistant professor in the Department of Psychology at the University of Alberta, Canada. She received a doctoral degree in psychology from the University of Ottawa, Canada, and pursued postdoctoral studies at the Department of Communication at the University of California, Santa Barbara. Her research concerns the social psychology of language and communication processes, with a focus on intercultural communication. Her publications include articles on motivation for language learning, the role of communication in the process of cross-cultural adaptation, and intergenerational communication from a cross-cultural perspective. Her research has been recognized through awards from the Modern Language Association and the International Association of Language and Social Psychology.

Peter Ogom Nwosu is a professor of communication studies at California State University, Sacramento, and a nationally recognized contributor and consultant on intercultural training and development. He has co-edited two books, including *Transculture: Interdisciplinary Perspectives on Cross-Cultural Relations.* He is also editor of the *African Journal of Communication.*

Mark P. Orbe (Ph.D., Ohio University) is an associate professor of communication and diversity at Western Michigan University where he teaches in the Department of Communication and Center for Women's Studies. His research and teaching interests center on the inextricable relationship between culture, communication, and context.

Gerry Philipsen is a professor of speech communication at the University of Washington. He pioneered an area of scholarship known as cultural communication—ethnography of communication studies describing communication patterns of various speech communities.

Donald L. Rubin holds a joint appointment as a professor in the Department of Speech Communication and Language Education and in the Program in Linguistics at the University of Georgia. He teaches courses in intercultural communication and applied linguistics and also conducts training for international teaching assistants. He is currently the principal investigator for a large-scale assessment of study-abroad learning outcomes. Rubin's research focuses on various aspects of oral and written language variation and attitudinal responses thereto. He is the editor of *Composing Social Identity in Written Language* (Erlbaum, 1995).

Jean-Louis Sauvage (Ph.D.) teaches English at the Warocqué School of Business of the University of Mons-Hainaut in Belgium. After his doctoral thesis "Educational Software Program Designed to Improve English-Language Reading Skills of French-Speakers," his research in linguistics and computer science has continued. The use of multimedia is at the center of his research in developing reading-aid software. In addition, at the request of American sister universities and in the frame of student exchange programs, Jean-Louis Sauvage has started teaching European business culture to American students studying in Mons. He is the author of numerous articles, book chapters, and glossaries.

Ellen Seiter is a professor of communication at the University of California, San Diego. She investigates questions of gender, audiences, and media technology. Her latest book is *Television and New Media Audiences* (Oxford University Press, 1999). She is also the author of *Sold Separately: Children and Parents in Consumer Culture* (Rutgers University Press, 1993) and co-editor of *Remote Control: Television, Audiences and Social Power* (Routledge: 1989).

Shelley L. Smith is an education specialist at the University of Minnesota's Office of Preparing Future Faculty. She has been involved in international, intercultural, and diversity education as a teacher and trainer for 18 years in the United States and abroad.

Regina E. Spellers earned her doctorate degree from The Hugh Downs School of Human Communication where she is currently a faculty associ-

ate. Her research interests include ethnic identity, Black hair/body politics, and organizational socialization. Spellers also holds a Master's of Business Administration degree in international marketing.

Dolores Valencia Tanno is a professor in The Hank Greenspun School of Communication at the University of Nevada, Las Vegas. Her research has focused on intercultural communication and the ethics of research in this context. She has co-authored three books and has authored and co-authored articles in journals and anthologies. Dr. Tanno has been active in professional organizations and has served in many offices in the National Communication Association.

Jacqueline Taylor is a professor of communication and the director of the DePaul Humanities Center. She is the author of *Grace Paley: Illuminating the Dark Lives* (1990) and of various articles in the area of performance studies. Her recent work focuses on autobiographical performance. Her performance piece "On Being an Exemplary Lesbian: My Life as a Role Model" appeared in *Text and Performance Quarterly*. She is currently working on a memoir.

Stella Ting-Toomey is a professor of speech communication at California State University, Fullerton, where she teaches courses in intercultural communication, interpersonal conflict management, and intercultural communication training. She has published numerous books, chapters, and articles on the topics of intercultural facework, conflict styles, and conflict competence. Two recent books are *Communicating Across Cultures* and *Communicating Effectively with the Chinese*, with Ge Gao.

Kathleen Wong(Lau) is a doctorate student in The Hugh Downs School of Human Communication. Her research interests include ethnic, racial, class, and gender identity and intercultural communication, as well as multiculturalist policies and practices in higher education.

Gust A. Yep (Ph.D., University of Southern California, 1990) is a professor of speech and communication studies and of human sexuality studies at

San Francisco State University. His work focuses on communication at the intersections of race, ethnicity, class, gender, sexuality, and nationality. Dr. Yep's research has appeared in numerous interdisciplinary journals and anthologies. Recipient of a number of professional and community awards, he was the 1999 university-wide nominee for the U.S. Professors of the Year Award sponsored by the Carnegie Foundation.

PART ONE

Foundations of Intercultural Communication

In recent years, there has been a debate about the best way to approach the study of intercultural communication. Some experts think that the best way is to send out questionnaire surveys focused on discerning people's attitudes toward intercultural communication; for example, the surveys could ask people how they feel about other cultural groups or how they might change their communication to accommodate people who don't speak English as a first language. Other experts think that an ethnographic approach is the best; that is, they focus on communication patterns in one specific culture, using traditional anthropological methods. They may go into a new culture and through participation and observations try to understand its cultural and communication patterns. Some other experts think that a focus on popular culture (e.g., videos, the Internet, sitcoms, movies) can tell us a lot about how cultural groups are portrayed in a society and how intercultural communication works (or doesn't work). Still other experts believe that a focus on individual experiences told as a narrative can offer insights. For example, immigrants may tell their story of trying to adjust to a new culture while retaining aspects of their home identity. Such a story could teach us a lot about the process of culture shock and adaptation.

The first reading, "A Dialectical Approach to Intercultural Communication," provides a framework for understanding and integrating these various approaches to intercultural communication. We (Martin, Nakayama, and Flores) describe the dialectical approach as one that emphasizes the validity of many different approaches and the need to see the contributions of each. We identify three types of intercultural communication study—social science, interpretive, and critical—and show how each comprises a particular method and provides unique and complementary insights.

In the second reading, "Thinking about 'Culture' in Intercultural Communication," Dreama G. Moon describes the various ways in which culture has been defined in the field of intercultural communication. As she points out, each definition has implications for which groups are defined (or not defined) as being a distinct cultural group. She also helps us understand how definitions (and implications) change over the years. There is no "true" definition of culture.

In the final reading, "Worldview, Religion, and Intercultural Communication," we (Nakayama and Martin) describe broad belief systems that influence people's perceptions and form the foundation of many cultural groups. We also explore the contradictions of these belief systems and show how these differing patterns can lead to misunderstandings and intercultural conflict.

1 A Dialectical Approach to Intercultural Communication

JUDITH N. MARTIN, THOMAS K. NAKAYAMA, and LISA A. FLORES

We live in a world of increasing intercultural and international contacts. Sometimes these interactions are on an interpersonal level; sometimes they occur in organizational settings or political arenas. They are often facilitated by technological inventions such as jet travel, the Internet, and satellite transmissions of news events. The possibilities for intercultural communication are far greater than ever before. Yet, we know that these intercultural interactions include moments of conflict, friendship, hatred, romance, war, and an array of other experiences. The kinds of intercultural experiences that we face and the ways they occur often make intercultural communication a difficult field of study. It is not just interpersonal interaction, nor is it simply social interaction—it is quite complex indeed. Consequently, you need to think in more complex ways about intercultural interactions. There are no simple answers or easy items to memorize about any culture. Cultures are dynamic—as you are—and this ever-changing nature makes any attempt at static pieces of knowledge problematic.

A Dialectical Approach

Because of the dynamic nature of intercultural communication, we emphasize a *dialectical approach* to thinking about intercultural interaction. Many different kinds of dialectics have developed over thousands of years. Think about the judicial model, for example, in which the prosecution and the defense present the best cases they can from which the truth is to emerge. This dialectical relationship is rather oppositional. In many psychoanalytic models, however, the analyst and the analysand (patient) are not in an oppositional relationship, but rather in a helping, enabling dialectic. This text does not offer a comprehensive overview of these differing forms of dialectic; however, it does introduce you to dialectical ways of considering intercultural communication.

A dialectical approach emphasizes the *processual, relational, and contradictory* nature of intercultural communication. In other words, you will encounter many different kinds of intercultural knowledge. For example, some culture-specific information will tell you how closely people in that culture tend to stand to each other. Other studies will give you historical background that might help explain certain antagonisms felt toward and by members of that culture. These various kinds of knowledge need to be understood in relation to one another to help you better understand the culture you are studying.

A dialectical approach to intercultural interaction emphasizes the *processual* character of understanding. Cultures change and so do individuals. In this dynamic mixture, we cannot assume that someone has particular characteristics simply because he or she belongs to a certain culture. We change over our lifetime, and this dynamic nature of personhood needs to be considered in intercultural communication. The culture of the United States today is not the same as the culture of the United States in the 1950s or even in the 1970s. Many assumptions about gender, sexuality, race or ethnicity, age, and so forth have been drastically reconfigured. Thus, intergroup relationships need to be viewed dynamically. For example, terrorist activities, such as the bombing of the Federal Building in Oklahoma City, have forced us to reconsider how we think about terrorism, about the threat of White supremacy groups, and about the safety some of us feel in the U.S. culture. These changes have influenced U.S. culture, much as future changes will influence any culture as well.

A dialectical approach also emphasizes the *relational* rather than individual aspects and persons. In studying intercultural communication, the dialectical perspective emphasizes the relationship between

3

aspects of intercultural communication, and the importance of viewing these holistically and not in isolation. Can we understand culture without understanding communication and vice versa? Can we understand the conflict in the former Yugoslavia by only looking at the Serbian experience? Can we understand race relations in America without looking at the many different relationships among Blacks, Hispanics, Whites, and other groups?

The dialectical approach stresses the importance of relationship in intercultural communication encounters. Further, we cannot understand a relationship by only looking at two individuals' motivations, actions, and behaviors. A relationship has something unique that goes beyond the sum of two individuals. Intercultural communication scholar Muneo Yoshikawa (1987) describes this as the "dynamic in-betweeness" of a relationship—what exists beyond the two persons.

A more challenging aspect of the dialectical approach is that it requires holding two *contradictory* ideas simultaneously. This is contrary to most formal education in the United States. Most of our assumptions about learning and knowledge assume dichotomy and mutual exclusivity (e.g., multiple-choice and true/false tests). Dichotomies —good-evil, planets-earth, arteries-veins, air-water, man-animal—form the core of our philosophical, scientific, and religious traditions.

In contrast, a dialectical approach recognizes a need to transcend these dichotomies. This perspective is well known in Eastern countries and is based on the logic of *soku* (not-one, not-two). It emphasizes that the world is neither monistic nor dualistic (Nakayama, 1973, pp. 24–29). It is a way of seeing things as they are, recognizing the interdependent and complementary aspects of the seeming opposites (Yoshikawa, 1988, p. 187). For example, can we be wise and stupid at the same time? Of course. Can the strong also be weak? Of course; a strong tree branch, by bending and giving, doesn't break. Is it sometimes difficult to take a dialectical approach? Yes, but it seems very appropriate to studying intercultural communication because intercultural communication is about stepping outside normal frames of reference and trying to understand other worldviews.

Use a dialectical approach in understanding both the practice and the study of everyday intercultural communication. First, look at how to apply this approach to the practice of everyday intercultural communication.

The Dialectics of Intercultural Communication Practice

Communication scholar Leslie A. Baxter (1988) has identified three contradictory dialectic tensions that most of us recognize in relationships. For example, we sometimes feel the need to be both connected and autonomous in relationships with our parents and with others. We may also feel the need for novelty and predictability simultaneously, and the need to be open and yet private in our relationships. Six different dialectics come into play, taking into consideration the four building blocks of intercultural communication: culture, communication, context, and power (Figure 1).

CULTURAL-INDIVIDUAL DIALECTIC

Intercultural communication is both cultural and individual, or idiosyncratic—that is, you may have some behaviors not shared by anyone else, perhaps a unique way of wrinkling your nose or a unique way of using language. However, you may also share communication patterns with those who have shaped you (family) and with whom you share other cultural practices. For example, Judith, one of the authors, shares some language patterns with other Americans of Pennsylvania Dutch heritage, such as saying "Is the ice cream all?" when she means "Is the ice cream all gone?" She may also share some patterns with other women—a preference for hi-context (indirect) communication. She shares other communication patterns with other White people; for example, assuming that communication competence mainly involves being polite and nice and not thinking very often about issues of power in her interactions with others. And yet, her communication cannot be reduced to the sum parts of all her group memberships: gender, ethnicity, race, and so forth.

So in studying intercultural communication, we will sometimes talk about communication patterns cultural ———————— individual

personal ———————— social-contextual

differences ———————— similarities

static ———————— dynamic

present-future ———————— history-past

privilege ———————— disadvantage

FIGURE 1 • Intercultural Communication Dialectics

that are shared by particular groups (gender, ethnicity, etc.) and yet we always have to remember not to assume that group membership completely determines communication. This kind of rigid categorization leads to stereotyping.

PERSONAL-SOCIAL (CONTEXTUAL) DIALECTIC

This dialectic involves the role of context in intercultural communication. A dialectical perspective emphasizes the relationship between someone's personal characteristics and social, contextual behavior; that is, in some contexts we enact particular social roles that give meaning to our messages. For example, when lawyers, financial planners, or physicians communicate on specific topics, their messages may be interpreted in particular ways. In other contexts, messages may be interpreted differently.

As students and professors, we communicate in particular ways in classroom contexts, and our messages are interpreted in particular ways. Outside the classroom, in study group sessions, at football games, or at faculty meetings, we may communicate differently, expressing different aspects of ourselves. In understanding intercultural communication, we have to understand that we sometimes communicate as members of social groups, yet we also always communicate from our personal identities.

DIFFERENCES-SIMILARITIES DIALECTIC

A dialectical approach recognizes the importance of similarities and differences in understanding intercultural communication. Real, important differences exist between various cultural groups. Women and men do communicate differently in some contexts; so do Japanese and Americans. In real life, however, there are a great many similarities in human experience and ways of communicating.

There is a tendency sometimes to overemphasize group differences in intercultural communication—in a way that can set up false dichotomies and rigid expectations. Difference and similarity can coexist in intercultural communication interactions. For example, two men, one British and one Japanese, learn that they are going to be fathers. As men, they may share an initial joy and pride in parenthood, but differences in national culture, age, or religion might lead one to rejoice in the perpetuation of the family name while the other anticipates the father-child relationship. The cultural differences here may serve to complement the similarities and bring both men to a fuller appreciation of parenthood. Yet, consider another scenario: Israelis and Palestinians share a love for their holy city, Jerusalem. This similarity may be outweighed by the historical differences in meanings of Jerusalem so that the differences work in opposition. So, it is important to see how differences and similarities work in cooperation or in opposition.

STATIC-DYNAMIC DIALECTIC

The static-dynamic dialectic highlights the ever-changing nature of culture and cultural practices but also underscores the tendency to think about these things as constant. Some general cultural patterns remain relatively consistent over time, such as the emphasis in the United States on innovation, on liking things "new and improved." However, specific cultural practices, such as language, often vary substantially. For example, sociolinguists' descriptions of Black English or White counterculture language in the 1970s appear outdated when compared with contemporary language patterns. So thinking about culture and cultural practices as both static and dynamic helps us navigate through a diverse world.

PRESENT-FUTURE/ HISTORY-PAST DIALECTIC

A dialectic exists between the history-past and the present-future—that is, we need to balance an understanding of both the past and the present. Also, the past is always seen through the lens of the present. Consider the responses to Oliver Stone's film *Nixon*. The film was criticized because of the interpretation Mr. Stone made of (now) historical events and persons. Yet, as Mr. Stone pointed out, we are always telling our versions of history. How do we know what "really" happened in the first 100 years of U.S. history?

Understanding African American and White interaction in the United States is incomplete without understanding the history of slavery and the African diaspora. At the same time, contexts today are different from contexts 100 years ago. Many influential factors precede and succeed any intercultural interaction and give meaning to that interaction.

PRIVILEGE-DISADVANTAGE DIALECTIC

This dialectic concerns the role of power in intercultural communication. As individuals, we carry and communicate various types of privilege and disadvantage. These may be in the form of political preference, social position, or status. For example, if members of wealthy nations travel to less-wealthy countries, the intercultural interactions between these two groups will certainly be influenced by their differential in economic power. A colleague recounted a recent experience of being a U.S. tourist in Banff, Canada, and seeing many signs in upscale shops in Japanese rather than in English. She described how the Canadian shopkeepers seemed much more interested in interacting with Japanese tourists than with U.S. tourists.

Hierarchies and power differentials may not always be this clear. And people may be simultaneously privileged and disadvantaged, or privileged in some contexts and disadvantaged in others.

The question for us as we study intercultural communication is, How does understanding these dialectics change our approach to intercultural communication? We might also ask, How do we, as

scholars and practitioners of intercultural communication, use these dialectics in our daily intercultural interactions?

The dialectics themselves suggest that these questions are complicated, for as mentioned earlier, there are no easy answers. However, as an intercultural communicator, each of us can use our knowledge of these dialectics to guide our intercultural communication. One important thing to remember is that when we communicate across cultures, we can never just communicate with the individual. Instead, because we are always situated, to some degree, within our cultural identities, we bring those cultural identities to our interaction. Similarities, differences, power, context—they are always with us.

The Dialectics of Studying Intercultural Communication

This dialectical approach can also be extended to intercultural communication research, where there are many different ways to think about and study culture and communication. Some of the same dialectics discussed above also apply to intercultural research: Some intercultural communication researchers concentrate on identifying cultural differences; some seek similarities in communication patterns. Some think of culture and communication as fairly static entities; others see them as more fluid and dynamic. In addition, some scholars do qualitative analysis of poetry, folk tales, or media, while others gather quantitative data such as from survey questionnaires. Obviously, scholars disagree on the best way to study and understand intercultural communication.

This question of what counts as research knowledge is not just an academic debate because we all "do research" in informal ways. For example, we, the authors, might ask ourselves how we understand each other—across age, gender, sexual orientation, ethnicity. What kinds of knowledge about intercultural communication might help us understand each other? Television shows about Japanese or Pennsylvania Dutch culture? Results of surveys about male-female communication? Our experiences with other Japanese American, White, and Latino/a individuals? Studying the history of gender, race, and ethnicity in U.S. contexts? How we approach and answer these questions may influence what we know about each other, how we treat each other, and how or whether our relationship develops.

Additional dialectics having to do with research assumptions and methods are given in the three descriptions of intercultural communication research that follow. They illustrate three different ways to study and report on the issue of interethnic conflict. As you read these examples, think about which study is more appealing to you. What does each tell you about intercultural conflict? How does each study approach the dialectics discussed earlier?

The study in the first example attempted to discover if differences exist between the ways in which African American and White males and females deal with interpersonal conflict. A questionnaire about preferred styles of handling conflicts was completed by 123 Black and 180 White college students. It used a 30-item scale that measures three conflict communication styles: control, nonconfrontational, and solution oriented. Based on previous research, 12 hypotheses were posed. Results of the statistical analyses (MANOVA, and *t* tests) revealed that 4 hypotheses were supported, and 8 were not. The results showed that

1. Males, both Black and White, tended to use more indirect, nonconfrontational strategies than did females.

2. Black females, overall, tended to use slightly more direct, controlling conflict strategies.

3. White females, overall, tended to use more active solution-oriented conflict strategies (Ting-Toomey, 1986).

The study in the second example used ethnographic research methods (participant-observation, observation, interviews). The researchers spent a great deal of time observing and interacting with both Athabaskan and English speakers in northern Canada. Athabaskan language is related to many languages spoken by Native peoples in Canada and the United States. The researchers identified four differences in language use by Athabaskan and En-

glish speakers and concluded that these four differences often lead to intercultural misunderstandings and conflict:

1. *Presentation of self:* When first meeting someone, Athabaskans speak little, whereas English speakers talk a lot. When they know someone well and feel very comfortable, Athabaskans speak a lot; English speakers are more comfortable with silence.

2. *Distribution of talk:* In beginning conversations, the English speaker talks first; the Athabaskan rule is to wait. So when the two interact, the English speaker usually has control of the topic. Athabaskan speech has more and longer pauses. These differences in rules mean that an English speaker almost always has the floor, and an Athabaskan gets very little time.

3. *Information structure:* In English, information structure, or knowing how to interpret a statement, is shown by prosody (intonation, stress, tone of voice). For example, if you say "He told me so," it means something different from "*He* told me so." In Athabaskan, information structure is expressed by morphemes (suffixes or words at beginning or end of a phrase). When English speakers learn Athabaskan, they use stress and intonation; in speaking English, Athabaskans try to insert word endings to show emphasis. Both groups of speakers sound halting and confusing to the other group.

4. *Content organization:* Athabaskan organizes conversations and narratives in sections of twos and fours; English speakers, in threes. The result is that speakers sometimes feel they are out of synchrony with each other. English speakers feel Athabaskan stories are a little too long or points are irrelevant; Athabaskans feel that English speakers leave something out—the fourth part.

These differences in discourse rules often lead to stereotyping and conflict. Athabaskan speakers see English speakers as too talkative—always talking first, bragging, asking too many questions, interrupting. English speakers stereotype Athabaskans as being too silent, avoiding situations of talking, being too indirect, only wanting to talk to close acquaintances, and playing down their own abilities (Scollon & Wong-Scollon, 1990).

The study in the third example, which is grounded in critical theory, analyzes the centrality of land in dominant and Native American representations of Indians. The researcher's goal is to examine the ways land figures into political struggles of Native Americans. Beginning with a historical frame on discussions around land, the study traces two bodies of literature on Native Americans. The first, which comes predominantly from Western sources, exoticizes the relationship between Native Americans and land. Native American discourse, the second body of literature, offers a more complex picture of the importance of land to Native Americans. The researcher describes these contradictory discourses regarding Native peoples and their land:

> The political combat over land is wrapped in a complex of oppositional discourses, contradictory representations, and diverse cultural constructions. . . . The land is constructed in . . . narratives of dominance and survivance, historical and current simulations of the Indian by Native and North Americans.
>
> In contrast to the people who inhabited the expanse, the land itself was represented in early texts by romanticized images of Indians engraved on the landscape. While the Spanish were debating the ambiguous humanity of the Indians, the rough, earthy beauty of the new territory was symbolized by pairs of Indian men and women . . . framed in the exoticism of flora and fauna. . . . Images of the Princess and the squaw accommodate the colonial experience, the western expansion of settlement, and the development of the land over which we continue to struggle.
>
> Across Native America today, writing about the land reflects the differing experiences and practices of individuals and communities, even nations. But these differences are absorbed in an appeal to communality related to two distinct but intertwined cultural conceptions of the earth. . . . [S]urvival stories speak of land as a specific cultural construct articulated to the physical environment, an expanse of territory which locates the ideology, identity, and practice of a particular nation or community.
>
> With their small population and meager financial means, it is this ideological stance, this "difference," that distinguishes Native Americans in the minds of both Indians and others. . . . Indian resistance is cultural persistence; and it is voiced in strategies of direct and indirect opposition. . . . From this position, Indian "spiritness" asserts the promise of political autonomy, economic possibility, and cultural survival.
>
> The vague consciousness expressed in narratives of survival and dominance is not a paradigm for Native American cultural construction of the land. Indian discourses of the land affirm that space is cognitively and politically marked in metaphorical and real expressions of politics and ideology. (Valaskakis, 1996)

All three examples explore the notion of intercultural (interethnic) conflict, but in different ways. Which do you like the best? Why? Which seems to reveal the most about intercultural conflict? These examples represent three different kinds of scholarship. Each reflects different assumptions about culture, communication, and research goals and methods. Each takes a position with respect to the six dialectics discussed previously. So we can now extend our dialectical framework to include research dialectics (Figure 2).

Let's examine each dialectic, answering the following questions:

1. What is the goal of the researcher?

2. What is the relationship between culture and communication? (causal-reciprocal-contested dialectic)

3. What counts as knowledge? (reductionist-holistic dialectic)

4. What are the best methods for studying and reporting intercultural communication? (objective-subjective dialectic)

5. What is the researcher's view of intercultural communication practice—with respect to the six research dialectics?

SOCIAL SCIENCE RESEARCH

The first example is a good demonstration of social science study. The goal of this type of research is to describe and ultimately to predict, through hypotheses, conflict behavior. The hypotheses are usually drawn from previous research, and knowledge is

Social Science   Interpretive   Critical

Practice Dialectics

cultural ——————— individual

personal ——————— social-contextual

differences ——————— similarities

static ——————— dynamic

present-future ——————— history-past

privilege ——————— disadvantage

Research Dialectics

causal —— reciprocal —— contested

reductionist ——————— holistic

objective ——————— subjective

FIGURE 2 • Three Intercultural Communication Research Perspectives

accumulated in very systematic, incremental ways. Since only four hypotheses were confirmed in this study, a follow-up study may revise hypotheses, and either refine the theory or add another variable, or both. For example, perhaps conflict style depends on the type of conflict encountered.

In this type of research, culture and communication are often seen as two causal variables; that is, they are linked together in very explicit, causal ways. In this study, culture (ethnicity-gender) determines communication (conflict style). The hypotheses suggest that one's ethnicity or race and gender will determine one's preferred strategies for managing conflict. Black and White males and females use different strategies, as predicted by the theory and hypotheses.

What counts as knowledge? Knowledge is approached in a reductionist way—that is, the researcher breaks down communication and culture into specific, measurable variables (e.g., gender, conflict style). These variables are then measured and a causal relationship is established, often through statistical calculations.

What methods are used by social science researchers? The social science researcher emphasizes objectivity and tries to remain separate from participants in the research. In this example, the researcher mailed or distributed questionnaires to college students without knowing the people who participated in the study. These objective methods are similar to those used in psychology and sociology, such as survey questionnaires, observation, and standardized tests. After data are gathered, the analysis is often quantitative—that is, large numbers of individuals participate in the study and supply information that is then analyzed by statistical methods to establish quantitative relationships.

What is the best way to report knowledge? Usually in an objective, neutral manner. As seen in this example, the researcher tries to be as unbiased and objective as possible and often follows a set format for reporting research studies: theoretical background, research questions or hypotheses, methods, results, and discussion.

How do you think a social science researcher sees intercultural communication practice? Perhaps you can tell from this example that communication is studied as rather static, cultural, and personal; that is, we can learn something from a "snapshot" of communication behaviors that are assumed to be connected to the cultural background of individuals and are consistent in a variety of contexts.

To summarize, social science researchers generally emphasize cultural, static, personal, and present-oriented aspects of communication. They are often interested in identifying differences and not as interested in issues of power or privilege. Culture and communication are causally related, and research and research reporting emphasize objectivity.

INTERPRETIVE

The second example discussed earlier is interpretive research. The goal of interpretive researchers is generally to describe, rather than predict. Interpretive researchers usually see the relationship between culture and communication as a reciprocal one. Culture and communication are intertwined and dynamic. Culture is shaped through communication; communication is shaped and influenced by culture. They often look for patterns or regularities of communication, rather than universal or predictable relationships.

In the second example, the researchers describe different patterns of talk of Athabaskan and English speakers. They observed that different patterns of talk sometimes lead to conflict, but they did not begin their study with a prediction that ethnicity would produce certain kinds of talk or conflict.

What counts as knowledge? Information gathered in a more holistic and subjective way. Interpretive researchers emphasize the importance of seeing cultural communication in a holistic way; for example, beginning with general communication patterns of Athabaskan and English speakers. They did not approach their study with previously defined categories or variables. In terms of approaching and reporting research, interpretive researchers tend to be more subjective and qualitative—that is, they emphasize that getting close to people may provide unique insights not gained by more objective methods. Thus, many use ethnographic methods (borrowed from anthropology or sociolinguistics): participant-observation, observation, and interviews. As seen in the second example, conclusions about the Athabaskan and English communication patterns were arrived at after a long time of carefully observing and interacting with both Athabaskans and English speakers.

Another type of interpretive research is rhetorical analysis in which researchers might turn to films, television programs, newspaper articles, or even speeches from particular cultures to assess public images and representations of culture and intercultural communication. For example, a researcher might turn to *Star Trek* to find models of effective intercultural communication. Another possible study might involve analyzing newspaper accounts of a social issue, such as affirmative action, that would have implications for cultural interaction. Researchers are not involved in the subject of these studies, but they do approach the studies in a subjective, holistic mind-set.

Rhetorical scholars, then, might seek to uncover the rhetorical strategies used to mask or highlight culture. While they might rely on particular tools in their analysis (e.g., identifying metaphors), they do not explicitly predict what they will find. Instead, they are likely to let the findings emerge from the data.

Unlike this study, interpretive researchers often study communication patterns in one cultural group—rather than looking for cultural differences. They often prefer to do more in-depth analysis of communication rules in several contexts in one speech community. Contexts are important to the interpretive researcher.

To summarize, interpretive researchers are generally interested in individual similarities among or within a group of people; culture and communication are seen as dynamic and emerging. Understanding communication in context is very important. Like the social science researcher, interpretive researchers are not as interested in privilege-disadvantage dialectic. They approach research and report research in a more holistic and subjective way than do social science researchers.

CRITICAL

A third kind of scholarship shares many of the same assumptions as the interpretive, but the goal of the research is to produce societal change. In critical research, culture is seen as a site of struggle for various meanings. There is no easy or direct relationship between culture and communication—that is, there is no assumption that everyone in a cultural group will communicate in the same way. Rather, competing groups have competing meanings, and in those competitions the boundaries of cultures are negotiated.

In the third example, the researcher examined the various discourses and competing meanings for the relationship of Indians to their land. This complicated relationship can only be understood by examining the historical, political, and economic forces that affect understandings of culture, conflict, and communication. The example also illustrates the importance of locating power and resistance in intercultural interactions.

What counts as knowledge within this approach? Here, the material existence (or nonexistence) of a nation with specific land boundaries is only as significant as the meanings that are given to that nation. Knowledge is situated within cultural boundaries so that questions of proof or validity are recognized as specific cultural constructions of the definition of knowledge. As shown in our third example, a critical approach focuses on the communication texts where these meanings are located. In what ways are American Indians not simply Canadians or U.S. Americans? How do cultural texts portray them?

Critical researchers are also sensitive to which groups are more and less empowered to create these texts, whether on television or in movies, magazines, and newspapers. The notion of power here is crucial to understanding how these indigenous cultural groups are both manipulated and dominated by the dominant cultural groups. Power is also important in understanding how cultural groups resist meanings and maintain their own ways of understanding the world.

Critical methods are varied and frequently include analysis of media and other popular culture texts. The cultural discourses about "Indianness" are communicated through messages, and critical researchers often turn to these cultural texts. It is important, however, to note that critical researchers are also attentive to how these texts circulate in society, as well as the political, economic, and social differences between and among these cultural groups that form the foundation of much of this communication. A critical researcher does not assume that everyone can and does communicate from equivalent positions in society, nor that everyone is listened to in the same ways.

What are the best formats for reporting research? Narratives, stories, and dialogues that incorporate social statistics, such as data on hate crimes against certain cultural groups as well as income and educational differences, help us to better understand how these cultural texts are relevant in a given society. Critical researchers utilize a wide range of data and discourses to understand how intercultural communication is influenced by the social context in which it occurs. Thus, the forms for presenting critical research are quite varied and responsive to different ways of understanding different cultural texts and experiences.

To summarize, critical researchers are generally interested in individual experiences and similarities among or within a group of people, within the context of unequal relations of power. In this perspective, culture and communication are seen as dynamic and emerging, but also as contested. These contestations lead to empowering and disempowering different cultural groups in different ways. Critical researchers attempt to interpret and understand how this happens so that differing ways of intercultural communication can be undertaken to change contemporary ways of living and the attendant material conditions.

Understanding communication in context, particularly the macrocontexts (social, political, historical) is very important. Unlike social science and interpretive researchers, critical scholars are very interested in privilege-disadvantage dialectic. Like interpretive researchers, critical scholars approach research and report research holistically and subjectively.

Conclusion

Whereas most intercultural communication texts include one or two types of scholarship, we, the authors, believe that each of the three perspectives we discussed contributes something to the understanding of communication. Each represents one angle or one view of a very complicated topic—the intersections of culture and communication. Actually, it's more a matter of what each considers important. Most scholars would agree on the components of intercultural communication: culture, communication, context, power. But they would disagree on the relative importance of each, how they are interrelated, and the *best* methods for understanding intercultural communication.

Let's look more closely at what each kind of research contributes. *Social science research,* by taking "objective snapshots" of communication behavior, has helped us identify broad cultural *differences* in language and nonverbal behavior among various groups, as illustrated in the example of conflict styles of Blacks and Whites. This research has also helped us identify important variables, such as gender, ethnicity, and national culture, that influence and help us predict the intercultural communication process, both successes and failures. For example, scholars have identified factors that influence success in overseas sojourns as well as factors that determine how people accommodate their language in intercultural interactions.

Interpretive research, with an emphasis on *context,* has given us in-depth understanding of communication rules in very specific communities (e.g., Athabaskan and English). It shows us how communication often varies with context—within the same cultural community; for example, researchers have identified rules for speaking in places and contexts in working-class communities, for leave-taking in Colombian social contexts, and for Native American and White students in classroom contexts. Interpretive researchers concentrate on the shared communication rules, and their research helps us understand how communication, culture, and identity are dynamically and holistically intertwined.

Critical researchers have provided us with insights on the role of *power* in intercultural interactions, as well as the influence of historical, political, economic, and social forces on intercultural interaction. For example, critical researchers have examined the role of history in interracial interactions in the United States and in Arab-Israeli relations. They have also looked at how media images present contradictory messages about various cultural groups and how historical forces impact individuals' personal identity and development of interpersonal relationships across gender, ethnicity, and sexual orientation. Their research efforts are focused on understanding how power works, so that these power relations can be challenged for disempowered groups.

We can get a more complete picture of the complexities of intercultural communication by gleaning knowledge yielded from all three perspectives. While research is based on different and sometimes contradictory assumptions, taking a dialectical approach means living with some apparent contradictions and looking at intercultural communication from a variety of different angles.

References

Baxter, L. A. (1988). A dialectical perspective on communication strategies in relationship development. In S. W. Duck (Ed.), *A handbook of personal relationships* (pp. 257–273). New York: John Wiley & Sons Ltd.

Carbaugh, D. (1988). Comments on "culture" in communication inquiry. *Communication Reports,* 1, 38–41.

Hall, S. (1992). Cultural studies and its theoretical legacies. In L. Grossberg, C. Nelson, & P. Treichler (Eds.), *Cultural studies* (pp. 277–294). New York: Routledge.

Hofstede, G. (1984). *Culture's consequences.* Beverly Hills, CA: Sage.

Martin, J. N., & Nakayama, T. K. (1997). *Intercultural communication in contexts.* Mountain View, CA: Mayfield.

Nakayama, N. (1973). *Mujunteki, sosoku no ronri.* Kyoto: Hyakkaen.

Philipsen, G. (1992). *Speaking culturally: Explorations in social communication.* Albany: State University of New York Press.

Scollon, R., & Wong-Scollon, S. (1990). Athabaskan-English interethnic communication. In D. Carbaugh (Ed.), *Cultural communication and intercultural contact* (pp. 259–287). Hillsdale, NJ: Lawrence Erlbaum.

Ting-Toomey, S. (1986). Conflict communication styles in Black and White subjective cultures. In Y. Y. Kim (Ed.), *Interethnic communication: Current research* (pp. 75–88). International and Intercultural Communication Annual 10. Newbury Park, CA: Sage.

Valaskakis, G. G. (1996). Indian country: Negotiating the meaning of land in Native America. In C. Nelson & D. P. Gaonkar (Eds.), *Disciplinarity and dissent in cultural studies* (pp. 149–169). New York: Routledge.

Yoshikawa, M. J. (1987). The double-swing model of intercultural communication between the East and the West. In D. L. Kincaid (Ed.), *Communication theory: Eastern and Western perspectives* (pp. 319–329). New York: Academic Press.

Yoshikawa, M. J. (1988). Cross-cultural adaptation and perceptual development. In Y. Y. Kim & W. B. Gudykunst (Eds.), *Cross cultural adaptation: Current approaches* (pp. 140–148). International and Intercultural Communication Annual 11. Newbury Park, CA: Sage.

Key Terms

critical	methodology
culture	research
dialectic	social science
interpretive	

Discussion Questions

1. The authors identified six dialectics of intercultural communication practice. Can you think of other dialectics that might apply to intercultural interactions?

2. How might a dialectical perspective help us understand contemporary intercultural incidents,

for example, the different perceptions of Whites and Blacks toward the O. J. Simpson trial?

3. How does using these three approaches (social science, interpretive, and critical) provide a more comprehensive picture of intercultural interaction than any one approach?

4. If you were conducting intercultural communication research, which of the three approaches would you prefer? Why?

5. How might a critical researcher conduct an investigation of different conflict resolution styles used by Anglo Americans and Chicano(a)s? Would a critical researcher be interested in investigating this topic? If so, what kinds of methods might be used?

2 Thinking About "Culture" in Intercultural Communication

DREAMA G. MOON

I came to graduate study late in life. Having spent a number of years as an advocate for imprisoned women and men, then, later, for women and children terrorized in their own homes by domestic violence, I was anxious to learn more about the world of ideas in the hope that, through learning more, I could do more to help alleviate the dire situations of many people in the United States. As I had spent a lifetime engaged with thorny issues dealing with race, gender, social class, and power, I gravitated toward intercultural communication, seeing it as a venue in which to learn more about the possibility and varieties of cultural interventions. Having been a lifelong student of cultural politics, I was dismayed by the dominant way that "culture" was considered in intercultural communication. Moving in a world in which the visibility of poor people was under erasure through discourses on "welfare reform"; in which "ethnic cleansing" was a nice term for murder; in which, post–L.A. rebellion, Rodney King asked, "Can't we all just get along?" the unreflective approach to thinking about culture in intercultural communication was difficult to understand.

Culture is a complicated word because it has so many different meanings that we use in everyday life to communicate very different things. If someone says, for example, "She has no culture; she's so uncouth!" I know that culture in this sense refers to social class and manners. In this way, it is closely related to culture in "agriculture"—culture is a process, as in cultivation. Hence, we think about culture as cultivation when we tie education to culture. We read "great literature," listen to "classical music," and study "great artworks" in an effort to get culture. Now the meaning of culture has slid into "high culture," or the culture of the elite. It does not mean watching XFL, wrestling, or roller derby or listening to N'Sync, Christina Aguilera, or Brittany Spears. My point here is that culture has many meanings, but as one of the key terms in intercultural communication, it makes an enormous difference how we think about culture. It is important because the way we think about culture implies particular beliefs about cultural differences. For example, if culture refers to "nation," we might study differences in Belgian culture, Chinese culture, and U.S. culture, but overlook differences in social class, region, ethnicity, and even language within all of these cultures.

Let's look more closely at U.S. culture. How might we define what U.S. culture is? Is it the culture of White Americans who are well-to-do, live in gated communities, participate in soccer leagues, and shop at high-end malls? Who gets left out of this definition of culture, and why do their cultures matter less? Notice how this way of thinking about culture renders some cultures invisible. In other words, how we define culture does make a big difference in understanding intercultural communication and who benefits most from our work.

History of "Culture"

In an effort to understand how culture is utilized in intercultural communication, I decided to conduct a study of the field of intercultural communication from its inception in the 1930s to the present (the early 1990s) (see Moon, 1996). I gathered and read every article labeled "intercultural communication" listed in the *Index to Journals in Communication Studies Through 1990*. The so-called Matlon's *Index* is published by the field of communication's national professional association, the National Communication Association (at that time, called the Speech Communication Association), and served as a reasonable indicator of what was formally understood as intercultural communication research at the time. My search resulted in 102 journal articles. I was most curious to know if culture had always been defined as an ahistorical, acontextual variable in which it was seen as the cause of communication differences without any consideration of how we might think about that cause.

In my study, I discovered that the notion of culture had been defined differently in the past. Past research publications indicated the existence of a rich and varied tradition of the study of culture and communication in the United States. For instance, for the tumultuous 1970s when human rights were visibly on the social agenda, I found more than 50 studies that addressed the notion of culture in exciting ways. Culture was defined in many different ways, such as in terms of gender, race, and social-class identities. For example, Philipsen's (1975, 1976) work on how talk is used by working-class White men was groundbreaking in its focus on a group of people previously ignored. In a similar vein, Daniel (1970a, 1970b) published interesting examinations of cross-cultural communication between the affluent and the poor—something that had not been done before. In an era of tense interracial relations, Rich (1971) investigated how to improve classroom conversations among Black,

Chicano, Native American, and Japanese American students. Likewise, Colquit (1977), Sayer (1979), and Shuter (1979), in various ways, offered us insights into the ways in which communication differences play into social problems between Anglo and African Americans. These and other studies addressed important social issues of the time and were overtly concerned with the cultural politics of the day. Such studies encouraged us to think about social privilege, and how privilege and dis-privilege affect communication between groups. Moreover, they bring the idea of culture as unproblematically shared into question.

Not only were intercultural researchers more likely to address social challenges in their inquiry, but they were also more likely to "speak to," and critique one another's work and their implications. For instance, Whiting (1971) asked us to consider how researcher social-class bias might influence the ways in which we see and understand working-class communication styles. Similarly, Colquit (1977) interrogated the idea of "communication competence," suggesting that dominant notions of competence in the field were race-biased and privileged the communicative style of middle-class White Americans.

In addition, a series of studies expressed concern regarding the effects of new communication technologies and systems on indigenous cultures and developing countries (e.g., Grossberg, 1979; Katz, 1977; Lomax, 1977). In these and other ways, studies published during the 1970s were sensitive to, and engaged with, issues of power as they related to culture and cultural politics. Such inquiry encouraged researchers themselves to be more self-reflexive and sensitive to how their own biases might play out in their scholarship.

In my research, I found that things began to change in the field of intercultural communication around 1980. In an era of Reaganomics in the United States and Thatcherism in Great Britain, I observed a shift in scholarly interest from the United States and its social problems to the arena of international business. At this time, culture comes to be almost solely defined in terms of nationality (i.e., just check the appropriate box please!), and intercultural communication is conceived as predominantly an interpersonal interaction between individuals from different countries (often between U.S. American and Japanese persons). The underlying assumption in this work was that culture (i.e., nationality) denotes a certain homogeneity (or sameness) among members of nations, and a sense of shardness in the sense that people of the same country have cultural understandings, experiences, and behavior in common. Furthermore, there seemed to be emphasis placed on comparing cultures, in particular as related to specific communication variables such as uncertainty reduction. For example, during the 1980s, almost half of the 29 published journal articles dealt with cross-cultural tests of uncertainty reduction theory (e.g., Gudykunst, 1985; Gudykunst & Hammer, 1988; Gudykunst, Seung-Mock, & Nishida, 1985; Gudykunst, Sodetani, & Sonoda, 1987). Here the goal seemed to be the establishment of universal laws for understanding the issue of uncertainty and for reducing people's uncertainty.

Also in the decade of the 1980s, Gudykunst— then the most prolific intercultural communication scholar published in communication journals— outlines his "objectivist" approach to the study of intercultural communication, which, in some ways, is still with us. At that time, Gudykunst and Nishida (1989) argued that intercultural communication scholars should not be interested in culture per se, but rather should focus on how dimensions of culture, such as individualism or collectivism, affect a communication variable of interest such as information-seeking (i.e., U.S. Americans attempt to reduce the uncertainty experienced in interactions with culturally different others by seeking information in the form of asking direct questions). Based on the assumption that certain communication variables are universal (i.e., all peoples experience uncertainty and seek to reduce it), these types of studies had the effect of producing "intercultural rule books" based on blanket stereotypes of a society that one could then use to be successful in one's interactions with members of that society, especially as these interactions occurred in the context of international business. Such stereotypes were intended to differentiate the culture under study from "U.S. culture" (i.e., the U.S. culture is individualis-

tic; the Chinese culture is collectivistic). Kent Ono (1998) argues that this type of differentiation was intended to serve three purposes: "for arguing U.S. superiority, for providing inexperienced U.S. students . . . with tools for survival in the increasingly competitive world of business, and for providing quick fix solutions for students in introductory intercultural communication courses who envision, perhaps one day, communicating and interacting with the people under study" (p. 198). Ono went on to argue that these stereotypes do not hold up when put to the reality test and that they tend to offend and objectify people.

At the end of my investigation into the history of intercultural communication research, I began to reflect on how intercultural scholars might recover ideas from work done in the 1970s to create a broader intercultural communication inquiry in the new millennium. In particular, I was interested in how we might insert more complex notions of culture into our work. Despite critique from a number of intercultural scholars, the idea of culture as something shared, logically consistent, predictable, and historically transmitted from one generation to another is a common view still frequently used in intercultural communication research. I have found other ways of thinking about culture more useful in my own work.

Culture as a Contested Zone

One of the ways of thinking about culture I have found especially interesting is the idea of culture as a contested zone, which Martin and Nakayama (2000) discuss in the second edition of their textbook *Intercultural Communication in Contexts*. Martin and Nakayama note that many scholars have criticized intercultural research that "categorizes people and characteristics as set, unchanging, and unconnected to issues of gender, class, and history" (p. 61). Hannerz (1996) suggests that cultural processes are dynamic and fluid "organizations of diversity" that crisscross national and regional borders. This view of culture simultaneously acknowledges the overlapping nature (i.e., shardness) of various cultural realities within the same geographical space, while also recognizing that cultural realities always have some degree of difference. Thinking about culture as a contested zone helps us understand the struggles of cultural groups and the complexities of cultural life. It also aids us in coming to understand and consider various cultural realities and perspectives of the diverse groups that reside within any cultural space. If we define culture as a contested zone in which different groups struggle to define issues in their own interests, we must also recognize that not all groups have equal access to public forums to voice their concerns, perspectives, and the everyday realities of their lives.

In this definition of culture, we are already turning toward its connection to communication. Communication can be defined as the symbolic process by which we create meaning with others. In this sense, culture is not a static, fixed object, but is constantly being constructed and reconstructed through the various communication messages that struggle to become dominant. For example, cultural attitudes about women's right to vote have changed in the United States through the process of communication. Today, the dominant cultural attitude is that women should have the right to vote. This cultural attitude was not the dominant view a hundred years ago. So culture changes through the cultural struggles of various groups that utilize communication to change or retain cultural worldviews.

Thinking about culture in this way can be a little confusing, but as you think and talk about it, you may begin to be excited by this idea. Living in California, my students are able to point easily to examples of conflicting cultural realities and the material effects connected to adopting one view over another. For instance, in 2000, Californians grappled with competing ideas of "marriage" when we considered Proposition 22 and its exclusion of gay marital unions. There was a great deal of debate about how we as a people would conceive the notion of marriage—as a legal union between a male and a female versus one between two people who love each other. Various groups, including gay and lesbian and gay-friendly organizations and Christian groups, offered distinctly different cultural takes on the meaning of marriage. Although these views overlapped to some degree—all parties

seemed to uphold the idea and desirability of state-sanctioned love partnerships—the point of divergence concerned the sex makeup of marital couples. This example points both to how cultural meanings of marriage are shared, and to how culture is a site of struggle for contested meanings regarding the institution of marriage.

Clearly, this notion of culture as a site of struggle or a contested zone allows us to come to hear and perhaps appreciate the varieties of cultural experiences and views that make up what we understand as "America," and gives us a way of thinking about cultural politics that can point us in the direction of social change. Therefore, rather than believing in one cultural reality that is shared by all U.S. Americans, we are led to the idea of competing cultural realities that must be negotiated. These negotiations take place through communication.

Carey (1989) offers a wonderful way of thinking about the role and importance of communication in cultural life. He defines communication as a "symbolic process whereby reality is produced, maintained, repaired, and transformed" (p. 23). This notion of communication as constitutive of social and cultural reality is an important one. There are two important elements in the definition: the notion of communication as both *symbolic* and *processual*. To say that communication is symbolic means that the words we speak and the gestures that we use have no inherent meaning (Martin & Nakayama, 2000). In other words, there is no inherent connection between the word "dog" and Missy, my mother's Yorkshire terrier (who, of course, is a beloved member of the family!). The term dog could just as easily be said to indicate something else, such as food or an animal of labor. The meaning that we attach to the term dog (i.e., family member) is social (i.e., we agree upon its meaning) and culturally specific to the U.S. culture. The symbolic nature of communication can make for confusion when we assume that others share our cultural meanings. Many of the social debates of our time are really arguments about what things (should) mean. In using our earlier example, should marriage be linked to heterosexuality, or are there other ways of thinking about the meaning of marriage? Does the U.S. flag hold the same meanings for residents of Baghdad as it does for American citizens? Any sort of conversation, whether it be mediated or face-to-face, is likely to contain and elicit competing interpretations of the same symbols.

Given that links between symbols and their meanings must be forged or made rather than assumed, this helps us to see why communication is described as a process. In that symbols usually have more than one meaning, and that the meanings said to be attached to particular symbols are often very different, we begin to see how meaning is being constantly negotiated between groups and individuals. Very seldom are symbols understood in one way for time eternal; their meanings evolve and change. For instance, even though Proposition 22 passed in California, thus maintaining traditional ideas associated with the symbol "marriage," various groups within society continue the social conversation about marriage and its meanings. The meaning of marriage that gets adopted by many people or codified into law may very well change in the next 20 years. By changing meanings, we change the social world and our perceptions of how the world is (i.e., reality).

Popular Culture and Intercultural Communication

One arena into which intercultural communication scholars have ventured, taking along this provocative way of thinking about culture and communication, is that of popular culture. For many, media are important places for the study of intercultural communication. Stuart Hall (1981), a famous British cultural critic, argues that media produce "representations of the social world, images, descriptions, explanations, and frames for understanding how the world is and why it works as it is shown to work" (p. 35). He thinks that we can learn a lot about culture and cultural struggles by studying media texts. Likewise, Douglas Kellner (1995) maintains that the products of media culture provide materials out of which we "forge our very identities, our sense of selfhood, . . . our sense of class, of ethnicity and race, of nationality, of sexuality, of 'us' and 'them'"

(p. 5). So not only do media help us envision the world and human relations within that world, but they also help us imagine ourselves and others. The work of intercultural scholar vanDijk (1987) seems to confirm this idea. In his work, he found that much of what we know about "others" (i.e., groups we perceive as not like "us"), we learn from media. Many of us will never go to Uganda or meet a person from Uganda, but we may think we know something about Uganda and Ugandans. If we do not have direct experience, then we most likely have acquired our knowledge of Uganda and Ugandans through mediated forms of communication—books, television, the Internet, film, and so forth. This seems to suggest that media texts are important to consider in the study of intercultural communication, and are good places to focus on when taking a view of culture as a site of struggle and communication as constitutive of cultural reality.

Let's take a look at how we can utilize this notion of culture as a contested zone in the context of media by examining a current cultural struggle over the meanings of cultural icon Eminem, a White rapper who has received a fair degree of media attention since the release of his *Marshall Mathers* CD in May 2000. Due to some of the lyrics on this CD, Eminem has been accused of homophobia and misogyny. The announcement in the fall of 2000 regarding his scheduled appearance at the Grammy Awards with Sir Elton John, a White British gay rock star, triggered an uproar among gay and lesbian activist groups, anti–hate speech advocates, and general Slim Shady haters. Eminem seems to be at the center of a battle among competing cultural realities of free speech, artistic license, hate speech, hate-full behavior, and the connections between the latter two. As communication scholars, this debate should be of deep interest to us as it highlights a number of important issues related to communication. If we accept that media produce frames for understanding the world, ourselves, and our relations to others, then current cultural struggles being played out in media should warrant our attention. In addition, if we accept that it is through communication that cultural realities are produced, transformed, and maintained, then we begin to understand that Eminem is the most recent symbol of an ongoing debate about the types of social reality that certain communicative acts (such as hateful lyrics) can be argued to produce.

Will the Real Slim Shady Please Stand Up, Please Stand Up?

The media is one venue in which we learn about social reality and perhaps through which we can change social meanings. Media often reflect and take part in larger, ongoing social debates. In the case of Eminem, he is part of a larger debate about speech and its effects. There are many cultural discourses that we could draw upon in trying to grasp the meanings of Eminem. For instance, some see Eminem as a representative example of White supremacist, capitalist patriarchy—another wanna-be Vanilla Ice engaged in blaxploitation, making a buck by means of sensationalistic lyrics at the expense of marginalized groups such as gays and women (hooks, 1989). In this perspective, the corporate cooptation of rap has led to the construction of a very male-centered arena where the formula for a hit record is based on a problematic portrayal of masculinity: "fancy yourself a thug, pimp, or gangster, rhyme about jewelry, clothing, and alcohol, denigrate women in every conceivable way, and party and b. s. ad nauseam" (Powell, 2000, p. 66). Whereas it has become commonplace to espouse the old saw "sex sells" in this jaded climate, it is far more profitable to combine balling and bigotry (Goldstein, 2000). This particular representation of masculinity seems to work especially well for Eminem, a *White* rapper. For example, he is the first White artist in the history of rap to be widely played on rap radio stations in Black urban areas (Frammolino & Boucher, 2001). Thus, in rap, Black males and White males team up against bitches of all races in a brotherhood of bigotry in name of the Almighty Dollar (Goldstein, 2000). Eminem himself has overtly acknowledged this connection. In a recent life story of him that appeared in the *Los Angeles Times*, when a female former co-worker objected to the subject matter of his song "Kim," in which he fantasizes about killing Kim (also the name of

his former partner), he responded, "Yeah, but it will get me somewhere someday" (Frammolino & Boucher, 2001, p. 4). Here is one excerpt from the song "Kim": "Don't you get it bitch, no one can hear you?/Now shut the fuck up and get what's comin to you/You were supposed to love me!/ NOW BLEED BITCH BLEED . . . BLEED BITCH/BLEED . . . BLEEEED!" (Eminemworld, 2000).

For others, Eminem is portrayed as a "white-boy-rage" icon, representative of the recent discourse of the "angry white male" made popular in films such as *Falling Down* and *Fight Club* (Wilson-Smith & Deziel, 2000, p. 10). In an era of affirmative-action backlash, political correctness, and "reverse discrimination," Eminem symbolizes the anger of White males who see themselves as the new whipping post of multiculturalism. In the eyes of many suburban White male youths, he is a rebel, a man who "talks back" to discourses of multiculturalism and inclusion (Doherty, 2000). Byfield (2000) notes that Eminem "expresses the incoherent rage of today's disenfranchised young white male, using the art form of the black ghetto criminal class" (p. 4). Byfield reports that some people think that Eminem deserves respect for giving the "raging ambitions and hormones of young males a safe outlet" (p. 4). As one teen girl put it, "He's not scared of what people think about him. He does what he wants and doesn't care if people look down on him or anything. He has fun" (Crowe, 2001, p. 15). We have to ask what are the social and cultural implications of defining as "fun" lyrics such as "You faggots keep egging me on/Til I have you at knife point, then you beg me to stop/My words are like a dagger with a jagged edge/That'll stab you in the head whether you're a fag or les/Or the homosex, hermaph or a trans-a-ves/Pants or dress/Hate fags? The answer's yes . . ." (DeCurtis, 2000, p. 18). Do such communicative expressions create a hostile cultural environment for gays and lesbians? Is this a social reality about gay men that we wish to produce? These are important questions with which we as a society must grapple, and communication plays a vital role in this conversation.

For many, the controversy over the lyrics in Eminem's music is simply part of an ongoing debate regarding what should constitute free speech. For First Amendment proponents, artistic expression is a protected form of speech and artistic license makes acceptable art forms some might find objectionable. They suggest that the media is a site of entertainment, that people are capable of telling reality from fun, and that words have little relationship to, or effects on, what real people actually do. On the other side, many, including gay and lesbian rights advocates, see Eminem's lyrics as another example of hate speech that should be regulated. In this view, many oppose the social reality constructed by and through media, and argue that images and lyrics of hate are related to physical violence (i.e., hate crimes) against gays and lesbians and women. In short, they maintain that speech is connected to behavior. If media is a site from which we learn about others, what do these particular lyrics suggest to us to think and feel about gays, lesbians, and women?

The Gay and Lesbian Alliance Against Defamation (GLAAD) has been one of the leading voices of this side of the issue. Shortly after the release of Eminem's *Marshall Mathers* CD, the executive director of GLAAD issued this statement:

> The hatred and hostility conveyed on this CD have a real effect on real people's lives as they encourage violence against gay men and lesbians. At a time when hate crimes against gay people are on the rise, these epithets create even more bias and intolerance toward an entire community. The real danger comes from the artist's fan base of easily influenced adolescents who emulate Eminem's dress, mannerisms, words and beliefs. ("Musical gay bashing," 2000)

In this statement, GLAAD raises the issue of climate and how communication contributes to the construction of cultural climates in general.

Hate crimes are a source of concern for many in our society. Since 1991, we have seen an increase in the number of reported hate crimes each year, and a recent Gallup poll found that 70% of Americans favor stiffer penalties for hate crimes (Kalam, 2000, p. 593). In addition, a 2000 MTV survey of young adults found that nearly 90% of our young people believe that "racial, sexual orientation, religious, or gender discrimination is a serious problem facing our country today" (Hay, 2001, p. 2). Clearly, the seriousness of hate as a social issue is something on which many of us can agree. What is less clear is exactly which behaviors constitute hate. Some acts, such as those involving physical violence, are clear for many, while others involving words often elicit more disagreement.

critical

Conclusion

Coming to understand the role of communication and culture in thinking about the ramifications of the types of social realities that we create through media and other forms of interaction is not simple. The slippery nature of symbols does not allow us to answer such questions once and for all. Culture as a contested zone allows us to think and consider the various realities and interpretations available in the society. The idea of communication as constitutive of reality allows us to understand the central role of communication in deciding such matters as well as the social ramifications of those decisions.

References

Byfield, L. (2000, November 20). There are ways of silencing people like Eminem without even using a bullet. *Report/Newsmagazine (Alberta Edition), 27*(14), 4.

Carey, J. W. (1989). *Communication as culture: Essays on media and society.* Boston, MA: Unwin Hyman.

Colquit, J. L. (1977). The student's right to his own language: A viable model or empty rhetoric? *Communication Quarterly, 15,* 17–20.

Crowe, F. (2001, January 26). Is this man the new Wordsworth? *Times Educational Supplement, 4413,* 15.

Daniel, J. (1970a). The facilitation of black-white communication. *Journal of Communication, 20,* 134–141.

Daniel, J. (1970b). The poor: Aliens in an affluent society: Cross-cultural communication. *Communication Quarterly, 18,* 15–21.

DeCurtis, A. (2000, August 3). Eminem's hate rhymes. *Rolling Stone, 846,* 17–19.

Doherty, B. (2000, December). Bum rap. *Reason, 32*(7), 56–57.

Eminemworld. (2001). <http://www.eminemworld.com/mmlp16.html, lyrics to "Kim">.

Frammolino, R., & Boucher, G. (2001, February 21). Rap was Eminem's roots and road out of poverty. *Los Angeles Times*, pp. A1, 1.

Goldstein, R. (2000), July 18). Celebrity bigots. *Village Voice*, *45*(28), 37–40.

Grossberg, L. (1979). Interpreting the "crisis" of culture in communication theory. *Journal of Communication*, *29*, 56–68.

Gudykunst, W. B. (1985). The influence of cultural similarity, type of relationship, and self-monitoring on uncertainty reduction processes. *Communication Monographs*, *52*, 203–217.

Gudykunst, W. B., & Hammer, M. R. (1988). The influence of social identity and intimacy of interethnic relationships on uncertainty reduction processes. *Human Communication Research*, *14*, 569–601.

Gudykunst, W. B., & Nishida, T. (1989). Theoretical perspectives for studying intercultural communication. In M. F. Asante & W. B. Gudykunst (Eds.), *Handbook of international and intercultural communication* (pp. 17–46). Newbury Park, CA: Sage.

Gudykunst, W. B., Seung-Mock, Y., & Nishida, T. (1985). A cross-cultural test of uncertainty reduction theory: Comparisons of acquaintances, friends, and dating relationships in Japan, Korea, and the U.S. *Human Communication Research*, *11*, 407–455.

Gudykunst, W. B., Sodetani, L. L., & Sonoda, K. T. (1987). Uncertainty reduction in Japanese-American/Caucasian relationships in Hawaii. *Western Journal of Communication*, *51*, 256–278.

Hall, S. (1981). The whites of their eyes. In G. Bridges & R. Brunt (Eds.), *Silver linings: Some strategies for the eighties* (pp. 28–52). London: Lawrence and Wishart.

Hannerz, U. (1996). *Transnational connections*. London: Routledge.

Hay, C. (2001, January 20). Is anti-hate campaign contradictory to MTV? *Billboard*, *113*, 1–2.

hooks, b. (1989). *Talking back: Thinking feminist, thinking black*. Boston: South End Press.

Kalam, M. (2000). Recent legislation: Hate crimes prevention. *Harvard Journal on Legislation*, *37*, 593–605.

Katz, E. (1977). Can authentic cultures survive new media? *Journal of Communication*, *27*, 113–121.

Kellner, D. (1995). Cultural studies, multiculturalism, and media culture. In G. Dines & J. M. Humez (Eds.), *Gender, race, and class in media: A text-reader* (pp. 5–17). Thousand Oaks, CA: Sage.

Lomax, A. (1977). Appeal for cultural equity. *Journal of Communication*, *27*, 125–138.

Martin, J. N., & Nakayama, T. K. (2000). *Intercultural communication in contexts* (2nd ed.). Mountain View, CA: Mayfield.

Moon, D. G. (1996). Concepts of "culture": Implications for intercultural communication research. *Communication Quarterly*, *44*, 70–84.

Musical gay bashing doesn't sound so good. (2000, May 25). Gay and Lesbian Alliance Against Defamation Web site <http://www.glaad.org>.

Ono, K. A. (1998). Problematizing "nation" in intercultural communication research. In D. V. Tanno & A. González (Eds.), *International and Intercultural Communication Annual*, *21*, 193–202.

Philipsen, G. (1975). Speaking like a "man" in Teamsterville: Cultural patterns of role enactment in an urban neighborhood. *Quarterly Journal of Speech*, *61*, 13–22.

Philipsen, G. (1976). Places for speaking in Teamsterville. *Quarterly Journal of Speech*, *62*, 15–25.

Powell, K. (2000, October 9). My culture at the crossroads. *Newsweek*, 66.

Rich, A. L. (1971). Some problems in interracial communication. *Central State Speech Journal*, *22*, 228–235.

Sayer, J. E. (1979). The student's right to his own language: A response to Colquit. *Communication Quarterly*, *27*, 44–46.

Shuter, R. (1979). The dap in the military: Hand-to-hand communication. *Journal of Communication*, *29*, 135–142.

Shuter, R. (1990). The centrality of culture. *Southern Communication Journal*, *55*, 237–249.

vanDijk, T. A. (1987). *Communicating racism: Ethnic prejudice in thought and talk*. Newbury Park, CA: Sage.

Whiting, G. C. (1971). Code restrictedness and opportunities for change in developing countries. *Journal of Communication*, *21*, 36–57.

Wilson-Smith, A., & Deziel, S. (2000, November 6). "White-boy rap." *Maclean's*, 10.

Key Terms

communication	intercultural communication
contested zone	popular culture
culture	power

Discussion Questions

1. Why do you think that "culture" has so many different meanings in English? Can you think of some other ways that we use the word culture?

2. Why is it important to think about how we use the word culture when studying other cultures?

3. If you wanted to study another culture, how important is it for you to study that culture's popular culture? Give some examples of other cultures and popular culture.

4. Can you give some examples of how popular culture might influence the way that you view other cultures? For example, does *Baywatch Hawaii* influence how you view Hawaii?

5. If we view culture as a contested zone, does this mean that there is no agreement about what constitutes "American culture"? What are the advantages and disadvantages of that perspective?

3 Worldview, Religion, and Intercultural Communication

THOMAS K. NAKAYAMA and JUDITH N. MARTIN

Along with politics and sex, religion is often marked in U.S. American culture as one of the topics to be avoided in social conversation. Religion can be a divisive and explosive topic, as people often hold very strong feelings about their own religion and those of other people. Religious differences have tremendous implications for intercultural communication. Religion is a powerful force in marking cultural differences, which can lead to both intercultural conflict and intercultural cooperation. Even when not explicitly noted, religion may influence our attitudes about right and wrong and may influence our own behavior.

One of the reasons that religion is such a powerful force is that it is often an extension of an individual's deeply held values or worldview. However, it is also important to remember that while religious beliefs may appear to be simply a personal matter, these beliefs quickly move from the realm of the personal to the social. Religious differences, for example, can be an important influence in nationalist movements, as they demarcate cultural differences and differences in beliefs, attitudes, and values (witness the struggles in the former Yugoslavia). In this essay we first define what we mean by worldview, then describe the worldviews of the major religions.

Finally, we discuss some of the contradictions involving religion and intercultural communication.

Worldview

Every individual holds a set of values or beliefs about the way the world and human behavior *should be* (not necessarily the way things are). We acquire these values through interaction with the social environment and with various groups of individuals, first with family and people in the neighborhood, at school, at youth groups, at college, and so on. These sets of values reflect a sense of "oughtness." For example, in the United States, a commonly held value is that every person is equal in the eyes of the law. Yet we know that not everyone is treated equally: Those who are more attractive, or have more access to money and power, tend to be treated better individually and institutionally (in education, legal matters, etc.). Nonetheless, equality is something that Americans would strive toward, even though the reality may be contradictory to the ideal.

Cultural values cover many different aspects of society and together form an individual's worldview. How could we identify the most important cultural values that contribute to our worldviews? We could begin a list (e.g., equality, freedom, right to pursuit of happiness, individualism, etc.), but it would be hard to know when we've identified them all. Also, using this list approach makes it hard to compare values across cultures. For example, if people in the United States value freedom and equality, what do people with different values emphasize? Subjugation of others? So it is important in understanding other worldviews to be able to find a relatively neutral way to describe the worldviews of others.

One approach is to identify universal questions that all societies have to answer—for example, What is the relationship between humans and nature? One could then list a finite number of solutions: Humans control nature, nature controls humans, or humans should live in harmony with nature. Using this approach, one could identify the primary orientation of any given society on this particular value. Most people in the United States probably hold the value orientation that humans control nature. We control nature for our pleasure and needs (although some environmentalists would like a shift). We dam rivers, seed clouds, make snow when we need it for skiing, and so on. By asking these universal questions and identifying different cultures' responses to them, experts have identified a number of cultural values concerning social relations, orientation to time and authority, tolerance for uncertainty, orientation toward the supernatural, and the nature of human nature (Hofstede, 1997; Kluckhohn & Strodtbeck, 1961).

The interesting thing about the values that compose our worldview is that they are so fundamental, we don't often question them—they just seem normal. And others' cultural values may seem odd and/or wrong. For example, people in the United States are often outraged when they hear the rules that were instituted concerning women in countries such as Afghanistan, now under "traditional" Muslim rule: Women were ordered to stay off the streets unless dressed head to foot in traditional clothes, they were forbidden to work outside the home unless they could arrange to have no contact with men, and families were to paint their windows black so that no one could see the women inside (Fisher, 1999). The religious values that inspired these rules may seem wrong to many U.S. Americans and represent a cultural difference that's very hard to understand.

The important point here is that our worldviews influence the way we see and communicate with others. Our worldview is like a cultural "filter" or a perceptual "lens" that we use to see the world (Singer, 1998). When we (the authors, who hold a U.S. middle-class worldview) see Muslim women dressed in veils, walking quietly behind their husbands (or carrying a heavy load while the husbands carry nothing), our perceptual "lens" may cause us to think rather negatively about these women. This perception might lead to a negative communication situation if we were to engage these couples in communication. So our worldview often influences the way we think about and communicate with others.

What is the connection between these worldviews and religion? Sometimes worldview and religion are very closely connected. That is, the values we hold related to religion—ideas about God or ultimate reality, ideas about the origin and destiny of the world and of individual humans, a revelation or authority or mediation between the ultimate and humankind, and standards about what is expected of humans—may be explicitly stated in religious teaching (Ellwood, 1992). For example, the Ten Commandments from the Bible are used as guidelines today by many Christians and Jews. Other times, the connections between religion and worldview are less clear. For example, the influence of the Puritan settlers on U.S. society can be seen in the fact that U.S. Americans have rather conservative views about alcohol and nudity—something that many Europeans find rather prudish. This demonstrates the implicit influence of religion on worldview and perception—people in the United States who may not subscribe to Puritan or even Christian beliefs may still be influenced by that historical tradition and worldview.

How do the worldviews of the major religions of the world differ? It would be impossible to identify all the important religious worldviews today. However, we can draw some major contrasts in worldview among three groups of religions: (1) Western religions (Judaism, Christianity, Islam); (2) Eastern religions (Hinduism, Buddhism, Confucianism; and (3) the prehistoric and tribal religions (indigenous peoples of North America, Africa, Australia). According to the *World Almanac*, Christians make up 33% of the world population, Muslims 18%, Hindus 13%, Buddhists 6%, Jews 0.2%, Confucians 0.1% (Fisher, 1999). While there is tremendous variation among and within all these religions, there are some important similarities in worldviews. These similarities and differences illustrate the connection between worldview and religion and have important implications for intercultural communication.

Three important worldview distinctions differentiate the three groups of religions listed above: the nature of God or the conception of an ultimate reality; absolutism versus relativism; and the origin and destiny of the world and humans.

GOD OR ULTIMATE REALITY

Followers of Islam, Christianity, and Judaism—about half of the world's population—are monotheistic; that is, they believe in one God. They also believe that God started the universe, oversees it, and is responsible for it. They believe in a dualistic structure of life: God is out there and very separate from everyone else; life with God was good and humans are flawed images of God; the human responsibility is to obey God. And there are a number of "men of God" that are shared by Muslims, Jews, and Christians: Abraham, Isaac, and Jacob.

In contrast to the Western religions, about 30% of the world's population ascribes to the Eastern religions of Hinduism, Buddhism, and Confucianism, which are pantheistic—that is, there may be many gods, and deity can be in many places and in many forms. In original Hinduism (about 1000 B.C.E.), one of the oldest organized religions, there was only one god, Brahman, the Supreme Being, the one reality. This Supreme Being expresses itself in all that is, like a flame taking many shapes. However, in Buddhism, which developed about 500 B.C.E. in reaction to Hinduism, there is no authority figure. The same is true for Confucianism. In these traditions, religion starts not with God, but with humans; and gods reflect humans, so they too may be flawed. These religions are nontheistic; there is no split between humans and god. Sin doesn't exist; rather, the world is benign. The emphasis is on understanding self. In contrast to the dualistic framework of the Western religions, there is a less set structure for living a religious life; instead, there is an understanding that one should search self and society for answers (Ellwood, 1992).

While there is great variety among prehistoric and tribal religions, surviving indigenous peoples generally teach that all forms of life, all aspects of existence are spiritually interrelated. The land, the people, the animals, the weather, the unseen spirits, and the celestial bodies are all interwoven strands that form the great tapestry of life. The universe is a place inhabited by many spirits, some friendly, some not. There may be many gods and spirits; but there is usually a high god or a unifying force over them. For example, some American tribal people say that it is Grandmother Spider who continually weaves the cosmic web; other peoples have similar names for the great mysterious one who creates and interrelates all that is (Fisher, 1999, p. 31).

ABSOLUTISM VERSUS RELATIVISM

A second aspect of worldview that differentiates various religions concerns the degree to which the religion is seen as the *only* Truth. The Western religions hold to an absolutist framework, in that each religion is seen as the only true way. For Christians and Muslims, this has been demonstrated by a call to convert, and even conquer, other religious and cultural groups at various times throughout history. This tenet of absolutism has led many to believe that the rest of the world must be "saved," must be shown the true way at any cost. This worldview gives us some insight into historic intercultural clashes—for example, the Spanish Inquisition, and the subjugation of the Indians in the New World by European Christians. However, absolutism in Judaism has been interpreted differently and has not led to the same levels of proselytizing.

In contrast, in Eastern religions, religion is always relative to the situation, and ethics are what is absolutely desirable. While there has been some attempt to convert by traveling religious teachers, such as Bhaktivedanta Swami Prabhupada of the Hindu Hare Krishna movement, conversion attempts have never been on the scale of the zealous Christians and Muslims. The relativistic approach has also resulted in more tolerance and has led to more mixing of religions. In Japan, for example, it is not unusual for an individual to participate in rituals and celebrations of various religions.

The prehistoric and tribal religions would seem to fall under the relativistic framework, very similar to the Eastern religions in this respect. There is little emphasis on proselytizing or belief in the religion as being the one true way.

ORIGINS OF THE WORLD AND HUMAN BEINGS

The third aspect of worldview concerns the origin and destiny of the world and humans. In Islam, Judaism, and Christianity, everything is headed somewhere. There is a purpose to life and death, and there will be an accounting of how one has lived. For Christians and Muslims, the accounting will come after death (on the last day), and there will be eternal life or damnation for Christians, and reward or punishment in the Second Creation for Muslims. In Judaism, accounting is primarily in this life, and there is less emphasis on the afterlife. The implication here for cross-cultural clashes is obvious. A belief in the afterlife and eternal reward or damnation has led some Christians and Muslims to zealous evangelism of other peoples, "saving" them from eternal damnation (Ellwood, 1992).

In contrast, the Eastern religions tend to emphasize the circularity of life. For Hindus, the world and individuals go through endless cycles: the world through creation and destruction; the individual through countless lifetimes, which may include episodes in heavens and hells, finally transcending karma through God realization (Jain & Kussman, 2000). Similarly, for Buddhists, one eventually breaks through to attain the desired nirvana state (the void). Confucianism is vaguer on this point; there is no emphasis on an afterlife of creation, and the world originates from heaven and proceeds through interaction of yin and yang and five "principles or elements" and destruction (Ellwood, 1992).

In prehistoric and tribal religions, there was either no point of origin or the world was created by the gods or a high god who may subsequently have withdrawn from activity. Humans were often seen as children of gods or semi-divine primal parents. The destiny of the world was not clear, but humans were frequently said to go after death to another world, not unlike this world, and sometimes also to be reborn here in this world (Ellwood, 1992, p. 32).

Obviously, these great religions have very different worldviews concerning not only their view of God but also the origin and destiny of the world and individuals. What about the practices of these religions? Religions have traditionally set standards for acceptable behavior. What are some aspects of worldview that govern social norms and the expected behaviors toward others? Orthodox Judaism has a very precise set of laws governing many aspects of daily life. Christianity, based on New Testament teaching, encourages the ethics of love. Islam has social laws based on scripture and institutionalized custom, often derived from the exemplary life of the prophet Muhammad. Hindus have observed the Code of Manu, emphasizing social duties and the sacrifices of individual desires for the sake of order in society. Buddha prescribed doing good in religious and moral works in order to gain good rebirth. Confucianism emphasizes proper human relationships and group harmony. Let's look at each of these a little more closely.

Judaism Judaism, as a religion, minimizes formal theological doctrine; more important is adherence to the Jewish community, best expressed through practice—participating in Sabbath, festivals (high holy days and minor holy days), customs such as a strong respect for education, and a living sense of being part of the Jews' long history, which may include a sense of being an often-persecuted minority group. As in all religions, there is a wide range in degree of adherence to keeping the strict Sabbath or maintaining dietary laws (Fisher, 1999).

Christianity As a result of proselytizing, colonization, and conquest, Christianity is numerically the strongest religion in the world. As do most religions, Christianity comprises a great variety of contemporary expressions, about 21,000 different denominations (Fisher, 1999). The four major groups in order of size are Roman Catholicism, Protestantism, Eastern Orthodoxy, and Christianity-Indigenous mix (mostly found in South America and Africa). However, the underlying aim of all Christian sects is to seek to know God, to worship Him and to practice the ethics of love and service—based on teachings of Jesus as recorded in the New Testament portion of the Bible. Jesus' main commandment was to love God and fellow humans sincerely. The Christian God is merciful and forgiving to those who repent. Those especially blessed are the gentle in spirit, the sorrowful, the pure in heart, those who know they need God, who are merciful to others, and who make peace. Prayers should be private, good deeds should be done secretly, and the ultimate aim is to be included in the Kingdom of Heaven afterlife (Fisher, 1999).

Islam Like Christianity, the focus in Islam is on love for and fear of Allah (God). Believers should follow the example of the prophet Muhammad (unlike Christians' view of Jesus, Muhammad is not seen as divine) and the writings of the Qur'an. People who do not submit to Allah will be punished in the hereafter. In addition to observing prescribed social laws, five pillars of practice must be followed: (1) profession of the oneness of God and the messengership of Muhammad; (2) program of five daily prayers; (3) fasting (especially during the lunar month of Ramadan, when the Qur'anic revelations to the Prophet began); (4) charity—giving at least 2.5% to help balance differences in income within society; and (5) *hajj*, the pilgrimage to the holy city of Mecca at least once in one's life.

Hinduism Hinduism has been described as a religion of many contradictory beliefs and practices where its essential spirit seems to be "live and let live" (Jain & Kussman, 2000, p. 82). It is based on the belief that within the wholeness of the totality of existence, there are various levels of reality. Individual souls enter the world and pass through a sequence of bodies or life cycles until the state of consciousness or human form is attained and is now fully responsible for its behavior through the doctrine of karma—the moral law of cause and effect. There are four aims of human life: pleasure, wealth, righteousness, and liberation. The first three are

never ultimate goals, and the final aim is liberation. Tolerance is an important overriding element.

Buddhism Buddhism, a younger religion than Hinduism, focuses on the reality of worldly suffering and the skillful means to escape it. Followers of Buddha are to do good moral and religious works that will help them gain a good rebirth and eventually attain nirvana. One of the key precepts is the idea of *anatman*, or "no-self." Reflection on the idea of no-self provides an insight into the meaning of the Four Noble Truths and the Buddhist experience. These are the Four Noble Truths: (1) All life is suffering—not necessarily that life is always painful, but that there is something unsatisfactory and frustrating about life as lived ordinarily; (2) the reason for the inadequacy is that people always try to cling to things (objects, persons, ideas) that are partial and not fulfilling; (3) there is a state in which there is no suffering; and (4) there is a way to achieve this state.

The way to achieve this state is to realize the idea of no-self, that humans are not really separate *real* individuals, but collections of elements temporarily brought together and bound to break apart. To want to be a separate individual (and acquire fame, accumulate goods, or any other individualist aspirations) can only lead to disillusionment. The answer is to detach oneself from this hopeless task, to understand the nature of the mind, purify and retrain it—through meditation. The ultimate goal is to attain nirvana—a state of enlightenment, of egolessness, quietness, and bliss.

Confucianism Confucianism has endured as a basic social and political value system for over 2,000 years—500 years of the Yi dynasty in Korea, 250 years of the Tokugawa shogunate in Japan, and many dynasties in China (Yum, 2000). It is a philosophy of human nature that considers proper human relations as the basis of society. There are four principles: *jen* (humanism), *i* (faithfulness), *li* (propriety), and *chih* (wisdom or a liberal education).

Confucianism's emphasis on propriety (*li*) means that intermediaries are used even in personal relationships. The Confucian concept of *i* led to a strong distaste for purely calculated impersonal business transactions, so personal and public relationships often overlap. The emphasis is on cooperation, warm relaxed human relationships, consideration of others, and group harmony.

In comparing the important teachings of these world religions, there is one contrast that stands out—the Western religions tend to emphasize a personal, individual relationship with the ultimate being and stress the individual role in religious practices. In contrast, the Eastern religions tend to deemphasize the importance of self and stress social relationships, where individual achievement is less important; rather, cooperation, harmony, and tolerance are emphasized. This difference has important implications for intercultural communication. There are countless examples of misunderstandings between individual-centered people and persons who are more group-oriented.

It is easy to see how these religious beliefs and practices can be influenced by historical, political, and social contexts. For example, individualism as a tenet of Christianity was honed to an extreme by Europeans who came to the New World and needed to be self-reliant in subjugating a new and often hostile environment. The Yaqui Indians of Mexico and the southwestern United States had a strong belief in a Creator, in living in harmony with nature and others. These religious values were fused with the new religion of Catholicism that was forced on them. The Confucianism in China was influenced by the political regimes, by the Cultural Revolution in which religious sentiment was downplayed and religious practice outlawed.

A major contemporary influence on all religions has been globalization—the "shrinking" of the globe due to opportunities for rapid travel and interlinking of all people from all corners of the planet. Religious groups are no longer local pockets of homogeneity. Large-scale migration has occurred; for example, 2 million Muslims have migrated to the United States, with 50 Muslim mosques existing in Chicago alone; Tibetan Buddhist monks are scattered around the world; the Hinduism Forum of America Online is an electronic bulletin board with 5,000 postings (Fisher, 1999). This globalization

has led to many local variations of religions (e.g., American Buddhists following teachings of Deepak Chopra), what one expert has termed the "new geo-religious reality": "The map of the world in which we now live cannot be color-coded as to its Christian, Muslim, Hindu identity; each part of the world is marbled with the colors and textures of the whole" (Eck cited in Fisher, 1992, p. 14).

However, these new religious amalgams stemming out of globalization have also led to a contrary trend, fundamentalism. Some religious groups are trying to close their boundaries and return to a more traditional religious way. This has led to many intercultural clashes as the fundamentalists react against many aspects of modern life (pluralism, consumerism, materialism, and the stress on the equality of men and women). Fundamentalists have no room for ambiguity or relativism.

Religion, Culture, and Communication: Some Contradictions

As noted earlier, one of the major religions that has been exported around the globe is Christianity. Because of its dominance in the Western world, we often use the word "Christianity" synonymously with "religion." Of course, U.S. Americans know that all religions are not Christian, but when we hear someone say, "She's very religious," most of us assume that it means that she is very Christian. The spread of religions around the world does not mean that various cultures simply accepted any new religion. People around the world have negotiated many kinds of relationships to the religions to which they were exposed. Sometimes they embraced them, sometimes they rejected them, and sometimes they created a hybrid religion that mixed components of multiple religions. Let's explore some of the paradoxes that religion poses in the context of intercultural communication.

RELIGION AND CULTURAL IDENTITY

Religion is something that is intimately tied to many people's cultural identity. For example, Irish Catholics and Irish American Catholics often connect their Irishness to their religious identity. While all

Irish are not Catholic, and not all Catholics are Irish, there is a cultural identity that rests at the nexus of Irish and Catholic.

Chapter 5 of this reader focuses specifically on Jewish American identity. The complex relationship between religion and cultural identity is always contextual. The meanings of Jewish identity, like any other cultural identity, are tied up with the context in which it exists. So, for example, think about how being Jewish in the contemporary United States might be different from being Jewish in Spain during the Spanish Inquisition. Alan Dershowitz (1997), a Harvard law professor, has pondered over the changing context and its impact on Jewish identity. He fears that the new context will not sustain Jewish identity:

> Jews have faced dangers in the past, but this time we may be unprepared to confront the newest threat to our survival as a people, because its principal cause is our own success as individuals. Our long history of victimization has prepared us to defend against those who would destroy us out of hatred; indeed, our history has forged a Jewish identity far too dependent on persecution and victimization by our enemies. But today's most serious threats come not from those who would persecute us, but from those who would, without any malice, kill us with kindness—by assimilating us, marrying us, and merging with us out of respect, admiration, and even love. (p. 2)

Within shifting contexts, the meaning of and need for religious identity can change. In this case, Dershowitz argues that Jewish identity in a nonhostile environment has undercut the need for many Jews to retain Jewish identity. In contrast, the experience of Korean Americans is quite different. As minorities in the United States, they often feel a stronger need for a religious identity. Charles Ryu (1992), a Korean American minister, explains:

> In America, whatever the reason, the church has become a major and central anchoring institution for Korean immigrant society. . . . I think almost seventy to eighty percent of Korean Americans belong to church. And it becomes social evangelism. If those who had never considered themselves to be Christian want to be Korean, they go to church. (p. 162)

As Ryu further explains, the larger social context—that is, being a minority in the United States—increases the need for the refuge of the church. He says that the Korean American church is a major social place for Korean Americans:

> Your life revolves around the church. It could also become a ghetto in the sense of a Chinatown or a Koreatown. But at the same time, it can be a place, if done properly, where the bruised identity can be healed and affirmed, because living in American society as a minority is a very difficult thing. You are nobody out there, but when you come to church, you are somebody. The role of the black church in the civil rights era was the same thing. (pp. 162–163)

This contrasts sharply with the contemporary context faced by Jewish Americans. The role of the church and religion serves very different needs for the two different cultural groups. In this sense, then, cultural identity and religious identity can be very interconnected, which makes it difficult to separate them easily.

RELIGIOUS DIFFERENCES AND NATIONALIST DIFFERENCES

The relationship between nationalism and religious differences is sometimes complicated. Which one causes the other? In some ways, this question can seem like the proverbial chicken-and-egg question: Which came first? Let's look at the problematic here. We should ask ourselves why Irish in Ireland are mostly Catholic, and Irish in Northern Ireland are mostly Protestant. Or why the Dutch are largely Protestant and the Belgians mostly Catholic.

In both of these cases, the religious differences reflect nationalist differences, although it is difficult to know which is the cause and which is the effect. Prior to 1830, Belgium and the Netherlands were one nation called the United Netherlands. The religious differences were one very important cause for the split and eventual independence of Belgium from the Netherlands. Belgian social scientist Xavier Mabille (1997) explains, "For a long time, historians have considered liberal Catholicism . . . to have exercised an important influence in the unfurling of the events around 1830 in Belgium" (p. 94). But it is difficult to say if the religious differences caused the emergence of a separate national identity or were simply an effect of nationalist differences that emerged for other reasons.

Mabille points to other explanations for the Belgian nationalist sentiment, including economic class conditions. In other words, religious differences might lead to independence movements or they may be only one of the factors in the separation of nations. Intercultural conflicts that might arise can be due to religious differences, as in Northern Ireland or Palestine. The recent explosion that has reconfigured the former Yugoslavia is sometimes depicted as an ethnic conflict between Serbs, Croats, Bosnians, and Kosovars. At other times, these same conflicts can also be viewed as Christians against Muslims. But any of these conflicts cannot be easily connected to religious differences alone. Economic problems, among other issues, can also cause these intercultural conflicts.

RELIGIOUS DIFFERENCES ON THE INTERPERSONAL LEVEL

In dominant U.S. American culture, it is often considered impolitic to ask others about their religions. People are often concerned that religious differences might create obstacles in communication. However, sometimes people ask about religion for purely social reasons, as a way to begin conversation. John Reid (1990), a professor in North Carolina, explains the role of religion as a topic of socializing in the South that is not always understood by nonsoutherners:

> These things aren't simple. Take the question "What church do you go to?" Many newcomers find it offensive when brand-new acquaintances ask that. They assume it's the prelude to some serious witnessing, and it may be. On the other hand, it can also be just a conventional pleasantry, like "What do you do?" (a question Southerners sometimes find offensive) or "What's your sign?" (a question I always answer "No trespassing"). "What church do you go to?" can also be an insult, especially if the emphasis is on the word "you." Again, it depends. Migrants should just

recognize that they don't have a clue, and hope for the best. (p. 109)

While a humorous approach to dealing with cultural differences is often a good way to handle the potential conflicts that might arise, it is also important that we recognize the potential threat that religious differences might create for our cultural identities. If someone challenges our religious beliefs, they also challenge our cultural identity, as we noted earlier.

RELIGION AND COLONIALISM

We begin with a brief quotation from an obscure text written by a Christian missionary to French Indochina:

> We could cry out to a sleeping Church to awaken to her responsibilities. The task of carrying out Christ's Great Commission is far from finished. Too many are still playing at Missions. We are not praying enough, we are not giving enough, and we are not sending enough of our young people into the firing line. (Fisher, 1999, p. 11)

We used this quotation to draw attention to the role of religion in the historical spread of colonialism. It is not an accident that today many people in the Philippines, Latin America, Puerto Rico, and Guam are Catholic. But how did this happen?

Backed by powerful institutions, the spread of Christianity can hardly be overlooked as part of the colonial adventure. This historical legacy raises important questions about the relationship between the colonized peoples and the imported religion, Christianity. For example, in desiring to distance themselves from the dominant European ideologies, Chicano social movement discourses that embrace Aztlán [a Chicano homeland] do not simultaneously argue for distancing from Catholicism—despite its violent importation into Latin America. Steven Kaplan (1995), a professor of African studies and comparative religion, highlights the complexity of the relationship between colonialism and Christianity. He notes that there are other factors that complicate the spread of Christianity:

> Despite intensive Christian efforts all around the globe, the extent of positive response has varied

tremendously. While in some areas—including Latin America, Korea, the Philippines, and parts of sub-Saharan Africa—large numbers have converted to Christianity, [areas such as] India, China, Japan, Southeast Asia, and the Muslim Middle East have produced only a limited number of converts. (p. 1)

The ways that people have responded to the introduction of Christianity varied widely from one place to another, as indigenous religions have served differing functions around the world. Amidst the various rhetorics that constitute Christianity, it is important to avoid any simplistic approach to these discourses. As Todorov (1984) points out, on the one hand, Christian discourses were used to justify the domination, enslavement, and massacre of these "heathens" in the Americas. On the other hand, Christian discourses also invoke a sense of equality in which these Indians can be saved (pp. 160–163).

This ambivalence (and many others) appear throughout the Christian discourses, for example, Christianity as a universal religion versus Christianity as the special right of Europeans that empowers them to rule over these others. Christianity, like some other religions, contains seeds of tolerance and intolerance toward those who are of different religions. The tradition of intolerance is sometimes traced to the story of Moses who brought down the Ten Commandments and saw the people worshipping a golden calf. He denounced the worshipping of false idols, an act that has been used across the centuries to justify looking down on those who are not Christian. From this perspective, the introduction of Christianity serves a "civilizing" force. Josiah Strong, a 19th-century Congregationalist minister, explains: "The contact of Christian with heathen nations is awakening the latter to a new life. Old superstitions are loosening their grasp. The dead crust of fossil faiths is being shattered by the movements of life underneath" (1999, p. 220). He does not question his own worldview in which Christianity is correct and all other religions are outdated. Christianity also holds the seeds for tolerance as a part of its tradition.

John Locke (1632–1704), a 17th-century British philosopher, explains that tolerance is central to the true Christian:

Since you are pleased to inquire what are my thoughts about the mutual toleration of Christians in their different profession of religion, I must needs answer you freely that I esteem that toleration to be the chief characteristic mark of the true Church.

While Locke's notion of tolerance extends only to other Christians, these early seeds of tolerance are important to acknowledge. Thus, as Christianity spread around the world, at times it showed tolerance for the different cultures it encountered, and at other times it showed intolerance toward other cultures and religions. These contrasting faces of religion make it difficult to characterize in simple terms the role of religion in intercultural communication.

HYBRIDITY IN RELIGION

Our last point about religion is that it can be a moving target. Religions are dynamic worldviews that respond to different contexts in many ways. As the cultural needs of people change, in new contexts, religions change as well. In his fascinating study of Afro-Brazilian religion, French sociologist Michel Dion describes the complex religious practices that emerged from blending African slave religions with established Brazilian religion. This new blend, called Candomblé, is an example of hybridity. Dion (1998) explains: "Candomblé, an imaginary (re)-creation of Africa in Brazil by slaves and their descendants yields a notion of the world and religion that is completely opposite from the Western Christian vision, Catholic or Protestant" (p. 129). The worldview of this religion does not correspond to Western conceptions of religion. In many ways, this religion has survived by going underground and, at the same time, practicing Catholicism. Candomblé is not uniquely Brazilian, as it is also practiced in Africa, but its particular formation in Brazil is unique.

Conclusion

Religion is intertwined with culture and, therefore, cultural identity. As such, people can find it threatening to feel that this aspect of their cultural identity might be under interrogation. As we noted in this chapter, there are many different religious traditions that have very different orientations to spiritual understanding. These different orientations have led some religions, but not others, to emphasize spreading their religious beliefs.

While religious beliefs may seem to be a personal matter, these beliefs quickly move from the realm of the personal to the social. Religious differences, for example, can play an important influence in nationalist movements, as they demarcate cultural differences and differences in beliefs, attitudes, and values. It is also important to recognize the historical influences on religious beliefs. Filipinos, for example, are mostly Catholic because of the influence of Spanish colonialism. Yet, colonialism has not been entirely successful, as many areas of the world did not embrace Christianity despite the influence of European colonialism. Even in areas where the colonists might have believed their efforts successful, indigenous and underground hybrid religions may persist, as in the example of the Candomblé in Brazil.

References

Cole, W. O. (Ed.). (1996). *Six world faiths*. London: Cassel Publishers.

Deshowitz, A. M. (1997). *The vanishing American Jew: In search of Jewish identity for the next century*. New York: Touchstone.

Dion, M. (1998). *Mémoires de Candomblé: Omindarewa Iyalorisá*. Paris: Éditions l'Harmattan.

Ellwood, R. S. (1992). *Many people, many faiths* (4th ed.). Englewood Cliffs, NJ: Prentice Hall.

Fisher, M. P. (1999). *Religion in the twenty-first century*. London: Calmann & King, Ltd.

Hofstede, G. (1997). *Cultures and organizations: Software of the mind* (rev. ed.). New York: McGraw-Hill.

Huntington, S. P. (1997). *The clash of civilizations and the remaking of world order*. New York: Simon and Schuster.

Jain, N. C., & Kussman, E. D. (2000). Dominant cultural patterns of Hindus in India. In L. A. Samovar & R. E. Porter (Eds.), *Intercultural communication: A reader* (pp. 74–81). Belmont, CA: Wadsworth.

Kaplan, S. (1995). Introduction. In S. Kaplan (Ed.), *Indigenous responses to Western Christianity* (pp. 1–8). New York: New York University Press.

Kluckhohn, C., & Strodtbeck, F. (1961). *Variations in value orientations*. Chicago: Row, Peterson & Co.

Locke, J. (1996). *A letter concerning tolerance* (W. Popple, Trans. 1689). *Internet Encyclopedia of Philosophy.* <www.utm.edu/research/iep/text/locke/tolerat.htm> (Original work published 1689)

Mabille, X. (1997). *Histoire politique de la Belgique: Facteurs et acteurs de changement*. Brussels: Centre de recherche et d'information socio-politiques.

Reid, J. S. (1990). *Whistling Dixie: Dispatches from the South*. San Diego: Harcourt Brace Jovanovich.

Ryu, C. (1992). Koreans and church. In J. F. J. Lee (Ed.), *Asian Americans* (pp. 162–164). New York: New Press.

Singer, M. R. (1998). *Perception and identity in intercultural communication*. Yarmouth, ME: Intercultural Press.

Smart, R. (1988). Religion-caused complications in intercultural communication. In L. A. Samovar & R. E. Porter (Eds.), *Intercultural Communication: A reader* (5th ed., pp. 62–80). Belmont, CA: Wadsworth.

Smith, G. H. (1942). *The blood hunters*. Chicago: Moody Bible Institute.

Strong, J. (1999). Our country. In S. T. Joshi (Ed.), *Documents of American prejudice: An anthology of writings on race from Thomas Jefferson to David Duke* (pp. 212–222). New York: Basic Books. (Original work published 1885)

Todorov, T. (1984). *The conquest of America: The question of the other* (R. Howard, Trans.). New York: Harper & Row.

Yum, J. O. (2000). The impact of Confucianism on interpersonal relationships and communication patterns. In L. A. Samovar & R. E. Porter (Eds.), *Intercultural communication: A reader* (pp. 63–71). Belmont, CA: Wadsworth.

Key Terms

Buddhism	Judaism
Christianity	religious identity
Hinduism	worldview
Islam	

Discussion Questions

1. What is the relationship between worldview and religion?

2. How has your religious background influenced your values and worldview?

3. Religious conflicts have a long history around the world and continue even today. Why do you think that religion has caused so many conflicts, rather than preventing them?

4. Why do you think that religion is not simply something that individuals choose, but something that is tied up in other identities, such as national identity, ethnic identity, etc.?

5. If you were to change your religion, how would your family and friends react? Why.

Activities for Skill Development

1. Dialectic Exercise

One of the dialectics Martin, Nakayama, and Flores discuss in chapter 1 is the individual-cultural dialectic. In your intercultural experience, have you ever found yourself in a dilemma of this dialectic? Describe what happened and how it felt. How did you manage the tension? After this self-reflection, talk to a couple of your classmates and find out how they deal with this dialectic. Together, make a list of how to balance within the individual-cultural dialectic.

2. Tolerance vs. Acceptance

What do you think of the word "tolerance"? Should tolerance be a goal of intercultural communication? Are there any differences between tolerance and acceptance?

3. "American" Exercise

Think about what it means to be a U.S. American. Make a list of responses that come to your mind. Do you identify yourself as an American? If so, how did you learn to be an American? What have your parents/ caretakers, schoolteachers, people in your community, told you to be and to do? What activities, holidays, foods, songs, feelings, and so forth, do you associate with being an American? If you do not identify yourself as an American, where did you learn what an American is? Take notes of your reflections for a week, wherever you go and in whatever you do (e.g., shopping, watching TV, going out on a weekend). Then develop a 2- to 3-page essay to summarize your findings. Compare your essay to those of your classmates.

Web Sites

1. Check out a Web site of a major national or international newspaper (e.g., the *New York Times* <http://www.nytimes.com>, the *Christian Science Monitor* <http://www.csmonitor.com>, or the *Los Angeles Times* <http://www.latimes.com>). Do you find any news related to the dialectic approaches mentioned in chapter 1?

2. How can we expand our knowledge about religions through school education? Go to "Teacher Serve—Divining America: Religion and the National Culture" <http://www.nhc.rtp.nc.us:8080/tserve/dalinks.htm> and see what practical guidelines are offered for incorporating religious history in public school education.

3. Locate a Web site that "teaches" us about culture and communication. Does the Web site do a good job of presenting the information in a fair manner? Critique the Web site in terms of both the content and the approach it takes to discuss culture and communication.

Additional Readings

1. Alexie, S. (2000). Dear John Wayne. In S. Alexie, *The toughest Indian in the world* (pp. 189–208). New York: Atlantic Monthly Press.

2. Calloway-Thomas, C., Cooper, P. J., & Blake, C. (1999). Chapter 13: Becoming a competent communicator. In C. Calloway-Thomas, P. J. Cooper, & C. Blake, *Intercultural communication: Roots and routes*. Needham Heights, MA: Allyn & Bacon.

3. Yoshikawa, M. J. (1987). The double swing model of intercultural communication between East and West. In D. L. Kincaid (Ed.), *Communication theory: Eastern and Western perspectives* (pp. 319–329). New York: Academic Press.

PART TWO

Identity and Intercultural Communication

This part focuses on another very fundamental notion—identity—in intercultural communication. As individuals, as members of social groups and national cultures, we come to intercultural encounters with a wealth of experiences, beliefs, needs, and interests, all of which affect our intercultural communication with others. The complexities of our identities often mean that at particular times or in certain situations, aspects of our identities become either more or less important. Sometimes, we communicate from our gendered positions, speaking as women or men. At other times, our ethnic or racial identity may be important. Increasing numbers of people are living "in between" cultural identities. That is, they identify with more than one ethnicity, race, or religion. In intercultural situations, our identity positions shape our understanding of the world around us.

The essays in this section describe identity in various ways, from a fairly consistent set of categories to seeing identity as complex, dynamic, and socially constructed, having contradictory and competing aspects. Identity may be generational, gender-based, ethnic, racial, or religious, or any combination of these terms.

There are increasing numbers of biracial people in the United States, and Teresa A. Nance and Anita K. Foeman explore this identity in "On Being Biracial in the United States." They criticize the early deficit models of racial identity based on the ethnocentric notion that biracial individuals have to choose between their racial backgrounds and that the dominant racial background would prevail. They propose, instead, that biracial identity is socially constructed. To illustrate, they outline a three-stage communication model that shows how parents can help their children develop healthy biracial identities.

In "Jewish American Identity," authors Douglas R. Golden, T. A. Niles, and Michael L. Hecht emphasize the dynamic nature of identity and suggest that identities are created, maintained, and negotiated through communication. They note the ambiguity of U.S. Jewish identity—that it can be hidden, can be viewed as religious or ethnic, and can incorporate some views about the Holocaust. They suggest that Jewish identities are "layered": personal, enacted, relational, and communal. Their insights are gleaned from both media analysis and ethnographic interviewing.

Regina E. Spellers, in "Happy to Be Nappy: Embracing an Afrocentric Aesthetic for Beauty," traces the development of one important aspect of identity: self-image. She takes a more power-based approach. Using an Afrocentric framework, she recounts her own self-conscious struggle with and ultimate rejection of dominant U.S. knowledge claims about beauty. By example, she shows how minority individuals may develop a sense of self-image while recognizing the important influence of social, political, and historical forces.

We then turn to discussions of how individuals develop and juggle multiple, dynamic identities within social and political constraints. In "My Three Cultures: Navigating the Multicultural Identity Landscape," Gust A. Yep, an Asianlatinoamerican, describes in a personal story how he navigates and integrates his three ethnic heritages. He describes the internal conflicts (in his family relationships) and external conflicts (stereotyping, rigid expectations) that arise as identities are created and co-created in communication within social and political inequities. He gives suggestions for how negotiating identity from a minority position can be empowering and liberating.

The final reading explores the relationship between identity and prejudice. Jacqueline M. Martinez, in "Learning to See What I Was Never Supposed to See: Becoming Chicana in a White World," discusses the intersections of race, class, and identity. In telling her own personal story, she shows how identity can be shaped and constrained by prejudicial messages from other people.

4 On Being Biracial in the United States

TERESA A. NANCE and ANITA K. FOEMAN

These children have always been boxed and labeled, like they are goods, and damaged goods at that. Before it was words like half breed, half caste, mongrel, children with an identity conflict. Then the instructions came that they were black whether they feel it or not. It makes me so mad, they are both, not just black; we need new words to describe that identity, instead of just holding up placards and getting them to queue behind them.

("Choosing Sides," 1992, p. 14)

In the above quote, a Black social worker laments the bureaucratic convention that forces an "official" identity on biracial children. This lament highlights some of the communication issues and dilemmas experienced by biracial individuals. Who should decide ethnic and racial labels? What are the messages sent by society and the government to biracial individuals concerning their identity? What are the consequences when an individual's avowed identity is different from the label imposed by others? The answers to these questions are not easy and often reflect the interplay of race and power within our society.

Issues concerning biracial identity are becoming increasingly important as the biracial population in the United States grows. According to the article "Interracial Baby Boom" in *The Futurist* (1993), between 1968 and 1989, children born to parents of different races increased from 1% of total births to 3.4% (p. 54). Miller and Rotheram-Borus (1994) estimate that approximately 2 million multiracial people reside in the United States (p. 147).

For Black and White parents, births increased from 8,700 in 1968 to 45,000 in 1989. Births to Japanese and White parents have also increased. In fact, in the United States today, Japanese–White parents account for 39% more births than Japanese–Japanese parents. Similarly, between 1968 and 1989, births to Chinese–White parents more than tripled, from 1,000 to over 3,800.

As Susan Kalish (1992) of the Population Reference Bureau observes somewhat optimistically:

the upward trend toward more mixed births is a sign that the social meaning of race in the United States may be undergoing subtle shifts. It suggests that forces similar to those that softened the historical isolation of European ethnic immigrants over time may now be at work making somewhat more permeable the stubborn barriers of race. (p. 55)

This essay explores issues surrounding biracial identity formation and communication strategies that facilitate the development of a healthy biracial identity in children. There has been very little scholarship on biracial identity development and even less concerning the communication issues of biracial identity. This exploratory essay is part of a larger investigation of interracial families and is based on previous writing and our own experiences in multiracial families.

First, we discuss the social psychological mechanisms of identity formation and explore the meaning of race as an identity category in the United States today. We then describe the development of biracial identity. Finally, we relate what we understand to be the formative functions of communication in the process of positive self-development to the biracial child.

Identity Formation

Identity formation, especially among adolescents, has generated much interest and work since the renowned psychologist Erik Erikson (1968) proposed his eight stages of psychosocial development. Central to Erikson's development stages is the understanding that each phase involves a particular crisis that must be resolved before the person moves on to the next phase. Symbolic interactionists and communication theorists built on the foundation of Erikson's work. They stress that identities are not created by the self alone but are co-created through communication with others. Consequently, it is through interactions with significant others in our lives that we learn how to judge ourselves and others. We also learn from others how our social world is divided into categories and where we fit with respect to those categories, that is, to gender, race, and ethnicity (Hecht, Collier, & Ribeau, 1993).

While some of these lessons are taught intentionally, many lessons are simply deduced from everyday verbal, written, mediated, and nonverbal communication messages that are a part of our daily lives. And sometimes these messages conflict with how we see ourselves. The identity that we avow may not be the one that is ascribed to us by others. For example, biracial people are sometimes forced to place themselves in a category where they do not fit (Nakayama, 1997). As described in other readings in this book (see Yep, Martinez), ethnic, gender, and sexual orientation identity formation is a complex, communicative process.

Before describing how biracial identity is developed, let's examine how thinking about racial categories and identity has evolved in the United States.

The Social Construction of Race

Recent thought on race has shifted from an emphasis on physical characteristics to the social meanings of race. Contemporary theories suggest much of what we "know" is based on social myth rather than on scientific fact. Root (1992) calls the system we have for specifying race "simple and irrational" (p. 6). To better understand this charge, it is necessary to put the process of race-defining into a historical context.

During the early part of the 19th century, as the newly formed United States struggled to establish economic solvency, it was imperative that cheap forms of labor be readily available. Africans had been enslaved since the early part of the 17th century but did not accumulate in number until the 19th century. The Africans were "ideal" as slaves because in addition to their physical prowess and ability to withstand the heat, their skin color pro-

vided the necessary ingredient in the determination of race.

Long after the physical enslavement of African Americans ended, the cultural and economic enslavement continued. The popular myth that "one drop of Black blood made one an African American" can certainly be seen as derived from these old laws. The simple truth is that it's not really about blood at all. It's really about cultural dominance and power.

> People with no discernible African genotype or phenotype were regarded as Black on the basis of the fact that they had grandfathers or other remote relatives who were socially regarded as Black and they had no choice in the matter. . . . The boundaries were drawn in this manner to maintain an absolute wall surrounding White dominance. (Spickard, 1992, p. 16)

In many ways the one-drop myth can be seen as a means to concretize the boundaries between Black and White Americans. It makes sure that current labels, whether descriptively useful or not, are maintained so that a system that tends to oppress members without the correct label is also carefully maintained. Consequently, anyone accepting the one-drop rule means internalizing the oppression of the dominant group, buying into the system of racial domination (Spickard, 1992, p. 19).

The great irony here is that most scientists (biologists and physical anthropologists) acknowledge the essential commonality of all humans and see races as geographically and biologically diverging populations. Spickard (1992) states, "The so-called races are not biological categories at all; rather, they are primarily social divisions that rely only partly on physical markers such as skin color to identify group membership" (p. 17).

In other words, for scientists, there is more racially that unites us as human beings than separates us. The real issue is one of political control. The process of racial labeling starts with geography, culture, and family ties, and it runs through economics and politics to biology, and not the other way around. It has also led to the rather rigid dichotomization of racial categories—one is either White

Minority Identity[1]	Majority Identity[2]	Biracial Identity[3]
1. Conformity	1. Contact	1. Awareness of differentness and dissonance
2. Dissonance	2. Disintegration	2. Struggle for acceptance
3. Resistance/denial	3. Reintegration	3. Self-acceptance and assertion
4. Introspection	4. Pseudo-independent	
5. Synergetic articulation	5. Autonomy	

[1]Ponterotto & Pedersen, 1993
[2]Helms, 1990
[3]Kich, 1992

FIGURE 1 • Stages of Racial Identity Formation

or not White, and people often feel uneasy when they are unable to categorize individuals (Omi & Winant, 1994).

Racial Identity Formation

Given this historical context of racial categorization in the United States, it is not surprising that racial identity seems to develop differently for majority and minority members. While all young people pass through predictable phases of racial identity formation, minorities (e.g., African Americans, Hispanic Americans) develop racial awareness and identities earlier than Whites. This is the result of the imbalance of power and segregation in contemporary society. White children do not need to attend to the norms and values of minority groups unless they have direct exposure in their neighborhoods and schools. Minority children, however, are exposed to and compare themselves to White cultural norms through television, books, and other media (Miller & Rotheram-Borus, 1994, pp. 152–153).

How do we develop a sense of racial identity? And is biracial identity different from monoracial identity? As shown in Figure 1, minority identity formation usually involves an initial stage of conformity, of internalizing negative messages from society. This is followed by dissonance, then by a stage of positive, even superior feelings about race, and finally by a secure sense of racial identity where all races can be accepted and even appreciated

(Cross, 1978; Parham & Williams, 1993; Ponterotto & Pedersen, 1993).

In contrast, majority identity begins with unawareness of racial categories, then evolves to a passive acceptance of privilege in a racialized society, and may evolve to a stage of pseudo-independence and resistance to racist assumptions. Finally, it reaches an autonomy stage. The point is that the developmental process for monoracial adolescents (both majority and minority) follows a linear course, and the final identity is absolutely unambiguous (Miller & Rotheram-Borus, 1994).

For the biracial adolescent, however, the development of a biracial identity is not so easily understood. What roles are played by the child's self-identification, the family's attitudes, or society's label? Which racial group's label will have a more powerful influence on family and self-labeling? Society may rely on physical characteristics to assign identity, whereas the family may see bloodlines as most important. What happens when the child's self-label contradicts society's label (Miller & Rotheram-Borus, 1994, p. 151)?

Biracial Identity Formation

Glamour magazine replied to an anxious reader in 1955:

> Many colored men are fine people . . . but scientists do not yet know if it is wise for two such very different races as white and black to marry, for

sometimes the children of mixed marriages seem to inherit the worst characteristics of each race. ("Choosing Sides," 1992, p. 14)

THE DEFICIT PERSPECTIVE

Most of the early social psychological literature about biracial people in this country focused on the products of unions between Black and White parents. Biracial people were described as "marginal" people who lived tormented lives of self-doubt and social ostracism. As social outcasts, they existed between two different cultures and were not allowed into the social center of either racial group to become "whole" selves. Consequently, such peripheral social placement left them scarred and incomplete. They developed marginal personalities (Poston, 1990, p. 152). The belief was that the marginal person was destined to drift back and forth between two conflicting sets of values and lifestyles.

A closer look at this deficit model reveals it to be based on a truly ethnocentric framework. Implicit in each of the limitations is the assumption that the dominant culture is naturally better than the minority culture and that the essential struggle for all biracial individuals is to find a way to gain acceptance into the dominant culture. The deficit model does not recognize that the negative effects observed in biracial individuals may have been caused by the dominant culture's prejudicial attitudes and behavior and *not* by a defect caused by the race of one's parents.

CONTEMPORARY MODELS

As shown in Figure 1, more recent models of biracial identity development are less ethnocentric and differ somewhat from the monoracial models (Jacobs, 1992; Kich, 1992). A first stage is *awareness of differentness and dissonance,* where the child realizes that he or she is different from others and doesn't fit into a neat racial category. The child also becomes aware that others don't share the same self-perceptions. A second stage is the *struggle for acceptance,* in which the child deals with the ambiguity of identity and place. At this stage children openly experiment with and explore both cultures,

and they may intensify their struggles by actively and consciously choosing between cultures (Alexander, 1994; Herring, 1994). The third stage is *self-acceptance and assertion,* when the child is more self-expressive and less defensive, and has a more secure sense of self and a biracial self-concept.

It is important to note that biracial development is different from monoracial development in at least two ways. First, it is more ambiguous. That is, biracial adolescents may resolve their identity status in several ways, whereas models developed for monoracial people have a single end state—one has or has not resolved one's racial identity (Root, 1992; Miller & Rotheram-Borus, 1994). Biracial adolescents may identify with one group, both groups, or a new group (for example, biracial people), or they may accept community labels (Root, 1992).

Second, identity development is more cyclical than linear; there may be a cyclic reenactment of the three stages described above. As individuals mature, they may sometimes experience the same three phases with greater intensity and awareness (Herring, 1994, p. 179).

In direct contradiction to the earlier deficit model, some evidence suggests that biracial children may have advantages over monoracial children in that exposure to different cultural patterns increases both behavioral and cognitive flexibility. This flexibility facilitates the development of a multicultural identity. Biracial children who have been exposed to norms, values, and beliefs of both their heritage races may have bicultural identities as well as biracial status (Bennett, 1993; Ramirez & Castenada, 1974).

The Communication Game Plan

What are communication strategies that facilitate the development of a healthy biracial identity in children? First, what we know about biracial identity challenges us to think in new ways about racial identity development; static and dichotomous thinking about race is not useful. Second, we need to recognize that identity development occurs in the context of a racialized society. Because of U.S. history and our notions about race, society will often force a child to choose between the two heritage races, and depending on their physical characteristics, biracial children may face discrimination.

Kerwin et al. (1993) found that many of the parents of biracial children anticipated the fact that their children would confront racial discrimination. Not surprisingly, there was some difference between the White and Black parents' attitudes. The Black parent was the one who typically felt the need to prepare specifically for dealing with racial prejudice and bigotry (p. 225). Miller and Miller (1990) have argued that parents of biracial children best prepare themselves and their children for the challenge of coping with many of society's insensitivities by adopting a "minority orientation": "Without some orientation toward a minority agenda, a child cannot reconcile or cope with the conflict between African-American culture and majority culture or place this conflict in a relevant context" (p. 177).

Parents must teach their children how to recognize racialized language and situations and respond accordingly. Racial disharmony and polarization exists just as traffic exists. Responsible parents must inform their children about the dangers of living with racism just as they inform them about the dangers of living with cars.

Given that we know that children learn important lessons about who they are and how to behave from their interactions with others, and given the fact that ideas about race are socially constructed and not biologically preordained, we felt we needed to articulate a positive and proactive role that communication could play in this process. The following steps are languaged to relate to the experience of a developing child and are somewhat analogous to the three stages of biracial identity development shown in Figure 1.

Step One: Awareness

In this initial stage, parents of biracial children need to recognize the messages about identity and race that exist within their environment. These messages can be categorized as personal messages (the messages about identity coming from the immediate family and extended family members), social messages (those generated by significant others such as neighbors, schoolteachers, and religious and social groups), and mass media messages (those in readily available forms of mass communication such as television, radio, movies, newspapers, magazines, etc.).

PERSONAL MESSAGES

Parents of biracial children begin the process of heightening their children's perception of racial identity messages by locating the source of their own assumptions about race. We know that in dealing with other people, we often try to figure out the reason why people behave as they do. We first need to figure out our own attitudes and behaviors.

For example, it is important to discover if family members mirror the inequities of the broader social structure within the family. For example, are light-skinned children favored more than dark-skinned ones? Is the child with dark skin treated differently by immediate or extended family members? For example, the grandmother of one adopted biracial child treated her like a souvenir from Africa. In all families, issues of hierarchy and bonding patterns are established early on—and will be magnified if family members are also treated differentially by the larger society (Miller & Rotheram-Borus, 1994, p. 155).

Once people know their own positions and know that they are responsible for their own behaviors, they will impose that same standard of accountability on others as well. Consequently, when we try to make sense of the behaviors of others, we will seek to attribute a cause to an observed behavior.

According to this process, known in the communication literature as attribution, individuals can choose to assign cause to others' behaviors based on either external or internal causes. If we assume that circumstances or environment dictate behavior, then external causes are seen as the cause of the behavior. If, however, we understand that the person's behavior is uniquely his or her own, then we would conclude that internal reasons produced the behavior.

Race becomes problematic when added to the process of attribution, because race, in and of itself, is used as the cause and explanation of behavior. Statements such as "African Americans are natural athletes," "Asians work hard," and "White folks are smart and rich" reveal this problem. Other such race-based assumptions can include statements about perseverance, honesty, and beauty.

Within the context of family conversation, seemingly innocent statements and observations can be the source of identity difficulties for biracial children. For example, the uncle of one biracial little boy was heard to comment, "He'll be a great ballplayer someday because he'll be smart and strong!" Because the child's father is White and his mother is Black, the uncle's statement presumes that the child would be heir to the intelligence of his father's race and the athleticism of his mother's.

Parents need to hear these kinds of generalizations as disturbing and help their child (as appropriate to the child's age and maturity) hear both the complimentary explicit message and the dangerous implicit message of racial stereotyping. Given the comment made above, a parent could say to the child, "If you want to be a great athlete, you will have to work hard on your body and your mind to succeed."

SOCIAL MESSAGES

As children grow older and begin to move in social circles where parents are not always present, it becomes important that they learn to detect racialized "self-messages" on their own. For example, one parent reported that her 5-year-old daughter came home one day and recounted a playground conversation in which a little boy (who happened to be White) told her she couldn't be the queen. As the other children began to play, the little girl challenged the boy and asked why she couldn't be the queen. The boy explained simply that "queens are never Black."

The critical point in this story is that the little girl asked, "Why can't I be queen?" If she had simply accepted the roles as unequally distributed, she could attribute her being passed over for the part to any number of reasons. Because she asked the question, she brought the issue to the fore and allowed her mother, the teacher, and the boy's parents to deal with the issue.

We are not suggesting here that parents burden their children with heavy conversations about race, nor are we suggesting that parents make children

suspect everyone with whom they interact of being a closet racist. We are saying, however, that it is important to deal with conversations about race directly and honestly with an emphasis on recognizing the potential of the good and positive in every situation. An important aspect of the first stage of identity development is for the child to work through his or her awareness of racial issues and the dissonance of not belonging to one racial category (Jacobs, 1992).

When parents make race a natural part of their family dialogue, children are able to recognize and respond to comments and observations that are inappropriate. They will also know how to bring such statements to the attention of responsible adults who can provide assistance if needed.

MEDIA MESSAGES

Media messages need to be addressed as well. Helping children appreciate the ways in which other people provide them with messages about themselves that they may or may not accept is an especially important lesson for any biracial person to learn. When the son of one of the authors was watching the old television show *The Jeffersons,* he was perplexed by the term "zebra" used to refer to a biracial character on the show. Even after receiving an explanation that the term referred to the fact that the character had a parent who was Black and a parent who was White, the child concluded that the reference was "silly." It made no sense to him because zebras "are not people and they don't have a race." Clearly, he dismissed what he heard on television and recognized the comment as senseless.

Whether listening to irrational statements about race on situation comedies, or to well-meaning but condescending statements from a relative, the biracial child who has been made aware that such statements reflect the attitude of the language user and not some sort of "truth" is empowered to meet the challenge of living in our current racialized society.

Step Two: Coping

Learning to respond effectively to the racialized messages from the environment is the next step in the process as the child struggles for acceptance. It is important here for parents to understand the relationship between two important concepts: self-concept and self-esteem. Self-concept is the socially constructed image one has of oneself, and self-esteem is the value one has for oneself as well as one's perception of worth. As one's self-esteem rises and falls, the image one has of one's self is correspondingly influenced. It is certainly important for parents of all children to praise them and reinforce their overall self-concept. It is particularly important for parents of biracial children to monitor those aspects of their child's life that might influence the value the child holds for the "self" that may be grounded in race (Herring, 1994, p. 181).

Let's take the example of a biracial child (whose parents are White and Black) from a stable home environment, who has a relatively strong self-concept and is doing reasonably well in school. She sees herself as smart, athletic, and pretty well liked at the school. In a routine meeting with her guidance counselor, however, she is told that few Black students do well in an upper-level math course she has selected and that she might do better in a lower-level class.

In order for this child to cope with this challenge to her sense of self, her parents should provide her with the ability to understand that the guidance counselor's statement is an assumption about who she is and what she is capable of doing. The first step in helping children cope with damaging racialized messages is to instill in them a strong belief in their intrinsic worth. The children must believe that while they are not always perfect and will make mistakes, they are inherently good and worthwhile people.

Psychologist Jacobs (1992) describes four ways in which parents can help the biracial child develop a healthy self-esteem. First, they can *foster ego strength* by providing strong familial attachments. Ego strength is important for all children but especially important for the biracial child. Second, parents need to provide biracial children with a *biracial label* or a similar label (e.g., that their child belongs to the human race and color is not important).

Third, parents need to understand that their children's *racial ambivalence* is part of a normal developmental stage. More important, they should encourage children to verbalize racial thoughts and

feelings. It is very important in this stage that parents allow and encourage open discussions. In a society where race is not easily discussed openly and productively, the family may be the only place where the child feels safe to vent ambivalence or anger or both. Through verbalization, the child can find ways to channel anger and work through the developmental process (Gibbs, 1989).

Finally, to the extent that it is possible, parents should *provide a multiracial and multiethnic environment*. Recent evidence shows that positive intergroup relationships in the community contribute to high self-esteem of biracial children, while cross-racial tensions can lead to negative adjustment (Miller & Rotheram-Borus, 1994, p. 156). This type of environment not only contributes a great deal to the identity development of the child but can also provide communicative and emotional support for parents as well as children (Jacobs, 1992).

Given a starting point of "I know I'm an okay and worthwhile person," parents can work with their children to develop sets of appropriate responses. For example, in response to the situation outlined above, a younger child can be prepared to say, "Thank you for your suggestion. I'm not comfortable with what you are telling me now. I think my parents should probably continue this conversation with you." An older child may deal with the comment more directly by saying, "I am not comfortable with your comments and here's why. . . ."

In designing coping responses, biracial children and their parents should recognize the communication principle that meaning is not inherent in words or situations. Meaning is simultaneously created by people interacting with one another. When people communicate, they seek to create a common ground of understanding. Consequently, coping responses should acknowledge the response of the other and at the same time point out that some incongruency exists.

Many biracial students have developed their own repertoire of coping responses. For example, one young woman responded to the inevitable question "Are you Black or White?" with the response, "I'm 100% both." A well-meaning relative asked the parents of a biracial baby whether they thought the baby would have "good hair." The child's balding father quipped, "In this family, any hair is good hair!"

Children must learn to accept some messages, reject others, and ignore still others. Figuring out ahead of time the kind of responses to give in potentially negative situations gives children the confidence to face new and different situations with confidence.

Step Three: Emergence

Out of a strong sense of self, and a confidence that comes from understanding how labels are created and used, biracial children should reach a point of selecting and creating their own labels. As noted above, parents can offer the "biracial" label as a place to start. By doing this, parents are teaching their children that they should and can control the labels that categorize them. Children also learn that categories are created by people and are inherent in social life. This valuable lesson is a powerful one for all biracial people to understand.

One interesting feature of the emergence stage of this model is that the control of the stage shifts from the parent to the child. As Erikson (1968) described it, the primary developmental task of adolescents in Western culture is to establish their personal identity, of which racial identity is an important part.

Of course, the way in which this stage unfolds is directly related to the quality of the work done in the previous stages. From a communication perspective, in this stage biracial children become more self-expressive and less defensive or reactive. Both cultures are understood and valued. Biracial children can discern racialized messages from the environment, develop sets of appropriate responses, and create a place where they establish the ways in which they can define themselves (Herring, 1994; Jacobs, 1992). What makes this process so interesting is that the place the children define for themselves may not be the one initially envisioned by the parents.

One of the authors has a son named Jesse. He has attended university functions sponsored by African American faculty and students since he was a baby.

When Jesse was 8 years old, he talked to an engineering student who suggested that when he was old enough to attend the university, he should join an organization for Black engineers. Jesse thought about the suggestion and then shook his head and informed the engineering student that he couldn't join the group because he wasn't Black.

His mother was taken aback by his comment because she thought she had been diligent in helping Jesse and his brother craft their dual racial identity. As she was about to challenge Jesse's remark, she had another thought. She explained to Jesse that some people use the term Black to refer to African Americans.

When Jesse heard this, he started to shake his head again. With his hazel eyes, tightly curled light brown hair and tawny skin color, he concluded, "That's ridiculous, because I'm a White African American." Jesse's comment clearly indicated that he had figured out his place in our racialized society.

Jesse's mother also realized the simple truth that most parents of biracial children will never live the life of a biracial person. They can only prepare their children to live happy and productive lives and then watch from the sidelines to see how it all turns out. As children grow in age and experience, their ability to discern racialized messages, craft coping responses, and create communication space for themselves will also develop and change. The ultimate measure of any parent's success is the healthy and productive functioning of their children.

Summary

The issue of biracial identity development grows more important as the number of biracial children grows. Understanding the social construction of racial categories and the process of biracial identity formation is only the beginning. Parents of biracial children have the very real task of preparing their children to handle themselves in a racially troubled society. Working through the three stages of the communication process—awareness, coping, and emergence—provides parents and children with a method for beginning to address this serious but manageable situation.

References

Alexander, S. (1994). Vietnamese Amerasians: Dilemmas of individual identity and family cohesion. In E. P. Salett & D. R. Koslow (Eds.), *Race, ethnicity and self: Identity in multicultural perspective* (pp. 198–216). Washington, DC: MultiCultural Institute.

Bennett, J. M. (1993). Cultural marginality: Identity issues in intercultural training. In R. M. Paige (Ed.), *Education for the intercultural experience* (pp. 109–136). Yarmouth, ME: Intercultural Press.

Choosing sides. (1992, February 7). *New Statesman & Society, 5,* 14–15.

Cross, W. E. (1978). The Thomas and Cross models of psychological nigrescence: A review. *Journal of Black Psychology, 5*(1), 13–31.

Erikson, E. H. (1968). *Identity: Youth and crisis.* New York: W. W. Norton & Company.

Gibbs, J. T. (1989). Biracial adolescents. In J. T. Gibbs & L. N. Huang (Eds.), *Children of color: Psychological interventions with minority youth* (pp. 322–350). San Francisco: Jossey-Bass.

Hecht, M. L., Collier, M. J., & Ribeau, S. A. (1993). *African American communication: Ethnic identity and cultural interpretation.* Newbury Park, CA: Sage.

Helms, J. E. (1990). Toward a model of white racial identity development. In J. E. Helms (Ed.), *Black and White racial identity: Theory, research, and practice* (pp. 49–66). New York: Greenwood Press.

Herring, R. D. (1994). Native American Indian identity: A people of many peoples. In E. P. Salett & D. R. Koslow (Eds.), *Race, ethnicity and self: Identity in multicultural perspective* (pp. 170–197). Washington, DC: MultiCultural Institute.

Interracial baby boom: Ethnic lines blurring in the U.S. (1993, May–June). *Futurist, 27,* 54–55.

Jacobs, J. H. (1992). Identity development in biracial children. In M. P. P. Root (Ed.), *Racially mixed people in America* (pp. 190–206). Newbury Park, CA: Sage.

Kalish, S. (1992). Interracial baby boomlet in progress? *Population Today,* 1875 Connecticut Avenue, N.W., Suite 520, Washington, DC 20009-5728.

Kerwin, C., Ponterotto, J. G., Jackson, B. L., & Harris, A. (1993). Racial identity in biracial children: A qualitative investigation. *Journal of Counseling Psychology, 40*(2), 221–231.

Kich, G. K. (1992). The developmental process of asserting a biracial, bicultural identity. In M. P. P. Root (Ed.), *Racially mixed people in America* (pp. 304–317). Newbury Park, CA: Sage.

Miller, R. L., & Miller, B. (1990). Mothering the biracial child: Bridging the gaps between African American and white parenting styles. *Women and Therapy, 10*(1–2), 169–179.

Miller, R. L., & Rotheram-Borus, M. J. (1994). Growing up biracial in the United States. In E. P. Salett & D. R. Koslow (Eds.), *Race, ethnicity and self: Identity in multicultural perspective* (pp. 143–169). Washington, DC: MultiCultural Institute.

Nakayama, T. K. (1997). Dis/orienting identities. In A. González, M. Houston, & V. Chen (Eds.), *Our voices* (2nd ed., pp. 14–21). Los Angeles: Roxbury.

Omi, M., & Winant, H. (1994). *Racial formation in the United States from the 1960s–1980s* (2nd ed.). New York: Routledge.

Parham, T. A., & Williams, P. T. (1993). The relationship of demographic and background factors to racial identity attitudes. *Journal of Black Psychology, 19,* 17–24.

Ponterotto, J. G., & Pedersen, P. B. (1993). *Preventing prejudice: A guide for counselors and educators.* Newbury Park, CA: Sage.

Poston, W. S. C. (1990). The biracial identity development model: A needed addition. *Journal of Counseling and Development, 69,* 152–155.

Ramirez, M., III, & Castenada, A. (1974). *Cultural democracy, bicognitive development and education.* New York: Academic Press.

Root, M. P. P. (1990). Resolving "other" status: Identity development of biracial individuals. *Women and Therapy, 9*(1–2), 185–205.

Root, M. P. P. (1992). Within, between and beyond race. In M. P. P. Root (Ed.), *Racially mixed people in America* (pp. 3–11). Newbury Park, CA: Sage.

Spickard, P. R. (1992). The illogic of American racial categories. In M. P. P. Root (Ed.), *Racially mixed people in America* (pp. 12–23). Newbury Park, CA: Sage.

Stonequist, E. (1937). *The marginal man: A study in personality and culture conflict.* New York: Russell and Russell.

Wardle, F. (1987). Are you sensitive to interracial children's special identity needs? *Young Children, 42,* 53–59.

Key Terms

biracial	identity
coping strategies	race

Discussion Questions

1. What does it mean to say that race is a "social construction"? How do you define yourself racially? How comfortable are you with your definition?

2. Why were people of mixed racial heritage previously called "marginal"? How did that influence the way they were treated?

3. What advice do the authors give parents of biracial children to help them construct their own coping strategies? Take any one of the examples given in the section entitled "Step Two: Coping" and create your own response.

4. What makes "emergence" so difficult for parents of biracial children?

5 Jewish American Identity

DOUGLAS R. GOLDEN, T. A. NILES, and MICHAEL L. HECHT

I find it hard to identify myself as a Jew around other people. I don't wear a star or letter or anything. I'm not able to wear a kepah (yarmulke) because I'm a girl. Maybe I should wear a star, but once in school one of the girls asked the rabbi how to show people she was Jewish. He said she should take out her chain with the letter on it and wave it in people's faces. But I don't know, I just can't do that. Maybe I should. But when I'm in a bus I always get up and give an older person my seat.

—(Roiphe, 1981, p. 111)

This excerpt from an interview with an American Jewish teenager illustrates the saliency and problematic elements of her Jewish identity. From this small passage, her Jewish American identity is seen as a function of several different levels: how she feels about herself, how she wants others to regard her, how her actions represent her, and how she is connected to a certain community. Thus, "identity is both an individual and social construct emerging in a dialectic between the two" (Hecht, Collier, & Ribeau, 1993, p. 50). As a result of this dialectic tension, identity, often seen as an enduring trait, also possesses a dynamic quality. In the above situation, the teenager's self-concept and self-image, her relationships, the community with which she aligns herself, and her enactments in everyday life are continuously interacting to define a Jewish American identity.

The passage above also illustrates one of several characteristics that make Jewish American identity a problematic concept. The fact that she must find a way to symbolize her identity also shows her ability to "closet," or hide, her identity if she so desires and to answer for herself if, when, and how to express her Jewish American identity. Because she has no visible physical traits that define her as "Jewish," she can choose to show others that she is Jewish or she can also simply be an American or a teenage girl. Many Jews in America neither have visible "Jewish" characteristics such as a Jewish-sounding name nor choose to wear a traditional Jewish head covering; thus, revealing and concealing their Jewishness is a function of their Jewish identity. Weiss (1996), for example, admits: "I am a Chinese menu Jew; I pick and choose the values of my background that I wish to keep" (p. 27). In effect, being Jewish, like many other ethnicities in America, "has become a subjective identity, invoked at will by the individual" (Waters, 1990, p. 7).

The complex nature of Jewish American identity is compounded by the various ways of answering the basic question, Who is a Jew? In Jewish rabbinic law, the matrilineal principle answers that to be Jewish, one's mother must be Jewish. Also, through conversion, one can become Jewish. In recent years, however, the Reform Movement has adopted a nonlineal principle in which a child with one Jewish parent who is raised Jewish is considered Jewish.

This set of religious principles that define one as Jewish by *descent*, however, is only one means of determining who is a Jew. Being Jewish also may include the process of *assent* in which certain *chosen* strategies define one's Jewishness (Krausz, 1993). An embrace of modernism and individualism has transformed religious life to meet the needs of the individual (Meyer, 1990). Thus, instead of complying with the norms of a closed community of Jews, many Jewish Americans move toward considerations of what is meaningful for them as individuals. So, Jewish Americans now *choose* their way of being Jewish, whether it be through "believing in a Jewish God, embracing certain moral or social precepts, pursuing certain Jewish practices, pursuing Zionist [Jewish nationalist movement] activities, adopting a certain kind of persona or lexicon . . . , and so on" (Krausz, 1993, p. 273).

Jewishness-by-assent can be broken into religious and other cultural components. The former involves the degree of acceptance of one God and other beliefs connected with Jewish religious practices and observances; the latter focuses on an "identification with Jewish history" (Krausz, 1993), ancestry, and/or values, attitudes, and beliefs. In the premodern times some would argue that these elements were inseparable (Meyer, 1990). In contemporary America, however, we have seen a weakening of the religious component (e.g., understanding and participating in religious services), creating an increasing base of secular Jewry that has separated considerations of religion from considerations of group identification. The publisher's letter in a recent issue of *Davka: Jewish Cultural Revolution* poignantly illustrates this philosophy: "It does not matter if you have green hair, body piercings, or tattoos and feel more at home in a mosh pit than a *shul* [synagogue], wear a black caftan and dance your soul to ecstasy, or belong to all the possible lifestyles that lie between: you're a Jew and you belong" (Kaufman, 1993, p. 3). Thus, the unique intersection of religious and other cultural possibilities in Jewish America creates a problematic and ambiguous identity.

Another factor that adds to the ambiguous character of Jewish identity is the history of anti-Jewish discrimination and prejudice (anti-Semitism) throughout the world. Jewish people have a long history of victimization that is stored as a collective memory and often used to construct Jewish identity. Fein (1994) describes a Jewish identity that is constructed all too often as a reaction to the Holocaust:

> Why not intermarry? Because of Auschwitz. Why not assimilate? Because too much Jewish blood has been spilled. We may march behind the star of David, but it is the swastika that urges us on. . . . Our slogan is not a blessing, but a curse: "Never again!" (p. 10)

The Holocaust remains a "constant background factor . . . affecting the way Jews see themselves and the way they perceive their relationship to the non-Jewish world" (Simon, 1989). Also, Jewish American history is marred by the presence of anti-Semitic barriers that confined Jews to certain occupations and excluded them from mainstream corporate management (Sacks, 1994). The Jewish American response to anti-Semitism has been as diverse as the types of Jewish identities in America. Some Jews have internalized stereotypes and become "what the group labeling them as Other has determined them to be" (Gilman, 1986, p. 12). Others see anti-Semitism as something that obligates them to strengthen ties with the Jewish community or religion, or both (Fein, 1994).

To reiterate, as a result of the ability to closet one's Jewish identity, the complexities of defining one's Jewishness, and a history of anti-Semitism, Jewish identity has been shown to be an ambiguous and dynamic process that is difficult to pinpoint. The aim here is to view Jewish American identity and its idiosyncrasies through the lens of a communication perspective.

Communication Theory of Identity

The Communication Theory of Identity states that "identity is 'stored' within individuals, relationships, and groups and is communicated between relational partners and group members" (Hecht et al., 1993, p. 166). Four "locations," or layers, have emerged as perspectives for understanding identity. These four (sometimes competing, sometimes complementary) layers illustrate identity as being problematic as they push and pull each other toward adopting a number of different identities. The *personal layer* focuses on one's self-cognition, spiritual self, self-concept, and sense of well-being. The *enactment layer* deals with how messages express identity. The *relational layer* deals with how one's identity emerges through one's relationships with others and how relationships themselves possess their own identities. Finally, the *communal layer* involves an identity that is shared among a certain group of people or a particular community. A community possesses its own identity and represents the shared identities of its members. These frames of identity can work together or create dialectical oppositions (Hecht et al., 1993).

The premise of the communication theory of identity is that interaction is central to the identity process. Several propositions show how communication and identity shape each other.

- Identity is formed, maintained, and modified through social interaction.
- Identity influences interaction through shaping expectations and motivating behavior.
- Identity is enacted in social interaction, and the conditions of interaction influence identity enactments.
- Identity is an individual and social event.
  (Hecht et al., 1993)

In essence, communication shapes identity while identity shapes communication. When the four layers of identity are considered simultaneously, the formation of identity can be seen as a negotiation or conversation between and among the individual, the enactments, the relationship, and the community or any combination of the four.

Through our own research interpreting a Jewish media image and an ethnographic study of a Jewish fraternity along with examples drawn from published ethnographies and interviews, we will illustrate the emergent and dialectical processes of Jewish American identity. First, we will explore Jewish identity from each of the four layers of identity; then, we will illustrate how these four layers intersect in the identity process.

PERSONAL JEWISH IDENTITY

"As a characteristic of the individual, identity has been known as self-concept or self-image and provides an understanding of how individuals define themselves in general as well as in particular situations" (Hecht, 1993, p. 79). Although personal identity resides within the individual, the personal layer does not exist independently of the other three layers. Personal Jewish identity, therefore, emerges from and with other influences such as one's community, relationships, actions, and other identities (e.g., gender and occupation). The Jewish American identity of any given individual is a process that is also situationally emergent (Collier & Thomas, 1988; Hecht et al., 1993) and is a source of expectations and motivations (Hecht, 1993; Hecht et al., 1993).

Various studies indicate that personal identity also influences how individuals interpret mass communication, and how meaning is created differently by individual viewers of television shows, movies, or news programs (Wolfe, 1992). In our own study of Jewish American viewers' reactions to certain themes on the *Northern Exposure* television show, we found that different interpretations were attached to the themes, images, and narratives of the show. For example, some perceived Joel's Jewishness and his identity as a New Yorker as inseparable, while others saw the two characteristics as distinct aspects of Joel's identity. One Jewish New Yorker we interviewed said that "one almost assumes that the East Coast tradition is a Jewish tradition . . . and *Northern Exposure* illustrates that." A small-town Wisconsin Jew, however, resented the portrayal and felt that Joel's enactments did not accurately portray Jewish characteristics. The variety of interpretations illustrates that Jewish identity and images and interpretations of Jewish identity are neither universally shared nor monolithic. Each American Jewish person creates his or her own Jewish identity through the interaction of various layers and unique experiences, and uses this identity to interpret the social world.

An interesting process that relates to the interpenetration of the personal layer and other layers is the internalization of stereotypes. When stereotypic communal images are internalized as personal identity, it is often called "Jewish self-hatred" or "Jewish anti-Semitism" (Gilman, 1986). Gilman has characterized Jewish self-hatred as a result of American Jews' acceptance of the Jewish stereotypes generated by non-Jewish Americans. This occurs as a product of assimilation: "The more one attempts to identify with those who have labeled one as different, the more one accepts the values, social structures, and attitudes of this determining group, the farther away from true acceptability one seems to be" (pp. 2–3).

This process helps to shape one's personal identity, but is a product of an interaction with other layers. Bershtel and Graubard (1992) interviewed several self-hating Jews. One woman in this collection expressed that "[my family was] always talking about problems and moaning and whining. That is Jewish to me: whining. And I whine to this day, and I hate it" (Bershtel & Graubard, 1992, p. 9). Thus, this woman dislikes that she is a whiner (personal layer), but that she connects whining with being Jewish is a product of a stereotype that was formulated by the group to which she is trying to assimilate (communal layer).

JEWISH AMERICAN ENACTED IDENTITY

Not only is identity a property of the individual, but it is also found in communication. "Identities are enacted in social interaction through communication and may be defined as those messages" (Hecht, 1993, p. 79). When enacting Jewish customs, practices, and observances, one is expressing values, affirming beliefs, and reinforcing fundamental commitments and rejections that connect one directly with elements of group identity. The enactment layer of identity thus allows us to view the emergent quality of Jewish identity through Jewish actions (or nonactions).

Studies of Jewish identity have closely examined the enactment layer as an indicator of one's individual Jewish identity. These studies have consistently focused on such formal enactments as ritual behavior, formal organizational participation, Jewish

social ties, and charity giving (Medding, Tobin, Fishman, & Rimor, 1992). Furthermore, Medding et al. point out that certain situations and events in one's life bring Jewish identity to a conscious level. Choosing a marriage partner, the birth and raising of a child, decisions about raising children, and reactions to prejudice are all occasions in which Jewish identity can emerge through the choices made and their subsequent enactments. These enactments usually occur in coordination with the other three identity layers. On a relationship layer, for example, a couple can choose to send their child to a Jewish day school. On a personal layer, one can wear a Star of David. Through these enactments, Jewish identity is both experienced and expressed.

One particular episode of *Northern Exposure* illustrates how identity emerges through one's enactments: Joel Fleishman's uncle dies, and Joel promises his aunt that he will find a *minyan* (a quorum of 10 Jewish men needed to say certain prayers) so he can say the *Kaddish* (memorial prayer) for his uncle. The townspeople of Cicely then work together to find 9 more Jews for Joel. During the search, Joel doubts that Buck, one of the "recruits," was Jewish, so he asks him to say the *Shema* (a prayer that most Jews know). Buck recites the prayer, thereby enacting a Jewish identity. The members of Cicely discuss other enactments, such as displaying a sense of humor, using a particular last name, or being smart, as possible indications that a person is Jewish. Other episodes present Joel's argumentative style and his dour demeanor. In these cases, Jewish identity is attributed through certain enactments characterized (perhaps stereotypically) as Jewish.

The *Northern Exposure* episodes show how identity emerges through the enactments of an individual; however, communal groups can be the source of enactments as well. For example, in a study of an all-Jewish fraternity at a large Southwest university conducted by Golden (1996), communal identity was explored through the fraternity's enactments. One of the members mentioned that:

> We do get involved in Hillel [the Jewish student union] because we want some of their guys to

become our members. . . . So, like we volunteer our services as ushers at the High Holy Day services, we put together a Passover Seder, and we do some philanthropies with them. (p. 34)

Through the fraternity's communal enactments of volunteering at High Holy Day services and doing other activities and rituals with the Jewish student union, a Jewish identity emerges.

The fraternity's enactments illustrate that how an individual or organization chooses to act or not to act is a function of Jewish identity. This includes engaging in behaviors that disclose or mask one's Jewish identity. One of the authors, for example, has remarked to another, "You don't have to let others know you are Jewish!" As illustrated by the young woman on the bus who expressed concern about identifying herself as a Jew around other people, the fact that Jewish Americans often cannot be identified by their physical appearance alone allows those who may not want their "Jewishness" to be known to closet, or hide, their identity. Closeting one's membership in a particular group is not uncommon within groups that have been stigmatized, discriminated against, or otherwise oppressed. Within some African American communities, this phenomenon has been called "passing," and many individuals with names that indicate membership in other stigmatized ethnic groups have changed their names to sound more "American."

Hiding one's group membership when one internally acknowledges being a member of the group may represent an *equivocation,* or compromise, of one's identity and, in effect, one's self. Such a compromise ultimately is the result of apprehension about the consequences of having one's group identity known or the result of holding negative attitudes, beliefs, and feelings about one's own group. Feelings of apprehension are often present because of a historical stigma attached to one's identity and the negative consequences (e.g., verbal and physical abuse) suffered by individuals who share that identity. In some cases, however, although there may be little fear of negative consequences, individuals may choose to hide their identity because they have accepted negative evaluations of their group. In either

case, one is likely to experience discomfort and self-doubt, because the possibility always exists that one might be "found out" and criticized by both in-group and out-group members.

JEWISH AMERICAN RELATIONAL IDENTITY

The relational layer focuses on identity as mutually constructed in social interaction (Hecht, 1993): "People define themselves in terms of their relationships" and "the relationships, themselves, take on identities" (p. 80). A person, therefore, can retain personal identity while also participating in the negotiation of a shared relational identity (e.g., marriage, groups of friends, and families). The relational level is about who associates with whom and how this association contributes to the construction and enactment of identity. From certain relationships a Jewish identity can emerge.

A couple is an excellent context to explore the relational layer of identity. From the beginning of a relationship between two Jewish people, a Jewish relational identity may be created through the negotiation of the personal identities of the individuals and the enactments of the couple. Did they meet through a Jewish organization? Do they go to Synagogue together (if at all)? Did they have a traditional Jewish wedding? Do they send their children to Jewish day school? Do they belong to Jewish groups? In part, the way these questions are answered both reflects *and* constitutes the couple's Jewish identity.

When one parent is not Jewish, these questions become more problematic. In a study of Jewish identity and intermarriage, Medding et al. (1992) found that in a mixed marriage, "the likelihood of creating an unambiguous Jewish identity [in the household] . . . is virtually nil" (p. 37). Although some intermarried couples make a conscious decision to have a Jewish family (i.e., send their children to Jewish day school and celebrate exclusively Jewish holidays), a vast majority of these intermarried households incorporate aspects of both traditions. Examples of the latter include having a "Hanukah bush" or sequentially celebrating Hanukah and Christmas to combine a family's Christian and Jewish heritages. Mixed-marriage households often create permeable boundaries between what is Jewish and what is not.

Relationships between Jewish and non-Jewish partners are the norm on television. More often than not, Jewish male characters have romantic relationships with non-Jewish women on prime-time television (Pearl & Pearl, 1993). Programs such as *L.A. Law, thirtysomething, Mad About You,* and *Northern Exposure* all portray relationships in which Jews and non-Jews are paired together. In the television drama *thirtysomething,* Michael Steadman, a Jewish baby boomer, and his non-Jewish wife, Hope, are unable to decide whether to have a Jewish ritual circumcision for their newborn son. Ultimately, their decision to have the ceremony is a "public declaration" of the family's Jewish relational identity (Pearl & Pearl, 1993).

JEWISH AMERICAN COMMUNAL IDENTITY

The communal layer enables us to explore identity as "something held by a group of people which, in turn, bonds the group together" (Hecht, 1993, p. 80). On this layer, identity emerges from groups and networks. Jewish organizations, religious movements, and the media are all sites in which Jewish identity can be viewed on the communal layer.

The above-mentioned fraternity, for example, possesses a communal Jewish identity. This identity, in turn, creates communally held expectations. Thus, a commonly understood expectation of the fraternity is that all the members are Jewish. The idea of Jewish membership is salient in the myths of the fraternity, which has implications for how the members as a collective and as individuals present themselves to Jewish and non-Jewish underclassmen. Golden (1996) gives the following description of how a member of the fraternity recruits (or rushes) students on campus:

> So he (a fraternity member) comes up with certain questions like, "What are you doing for the holidays?" and if they (recruits) don't say Rosh Hashanah or Passover or the High Holy Days, or

something like that, then he'll actually say "what are you doing for such and such [Jewish] holiday?" and if they act whimmed, (i.e., confused) that means that they are not Jewish and then he pretty much gives the cold shoulder. (p. 19)

Although the recruit does not need to observe Jewish laws or holidays or even know much about Judaism, a fundamental knowledge of Jewish American life and a Jewish self-identification are necessary to become a member. Thus, the fraternity's communally held Jewish identity is enacted (giving "the cold shoulder") in recruiting and is reflected in the expectations of its members.

Television is also an excellent setting in which to explore the communal layer of Jewish identity. "Since the beginnings of television, Jewish themes and characters have been a steady element in popular television shows, from dramas and situation comedies to miniseries and made-for-TV movies" (Pearl & Pearl, 1993, p. 25). As the Jewish community, for many, no longer plays the same role it used to in the formation of Jewish identity, those who do not belong to a strong traditional Jewish community learn and gain insight about Jewish traditions, the Jewish community, and Jewish life from nontraditional sources such as television shows and other forms of mass media. Thus, television has some interesting implications for the formation and enactment of a Jewish communal identity.

Pearl and Pearl (1993) discuss a number of studies that have demonstrated that TV depictions are often absorbed and emulated by viewers and have the potential to affect viewers' behaviors, attitudes, knowledge, and understanding of the world. Although Hawkins and Pingree (1981) have pointed out that television probably does not shape culture, their research has shown that television does make a contribution to the creation of social reality. Pearl and Pearl (1993) illustrated the significant impact that television has on Jewish identity by claiming that an expertly done episode of *The Wonder Years* that dealt with a Bar Mitzvah had a positive effect on Jewish youngsters and their views of Jewish rituals. *Northern Exposure* also shows rituals, discusses Jewish theology, and portrays characteristic

Jewish personality traits. These presentations, there-fore, can impact the identities of Jewish American viewers.

Television programming not only contributes to the shaping of social reality but is also an enact-ment of communal identities and beliefs. The writ-ers, producers, directors, and actors on a television program enact and perpetuate communal percep-tions of Jewish identity when they create a television show. Many of the characters found on television shows are projections of those who create them. Sy Dukane, a coproducer of *The Home Court,* noted that the Jewish main character was a natural charac-ter for him and his partner to write about and stated that "we were also writing from our own experi-ences. . . . We're both Jewish, and so it was easier to do that" ("In the Spotlight," 1995, p. 4). Thus, the salient issues within the Jewish community are made visible through Jewish portrayals on televi-sion. Intermarriage, assimilation, and ritual portray-als are therefore salient off the screen and on. Prell (1992) has said that "the power of these cultural representations does not lie in their accurate de-scriptions, but in their ability to synthesize the feel-ings and the anxieties about living in American so-ciety" (p. 22).

The state of Israel, itself, is a problematic aspect of communal identity for some. Do Jews, particu-larly American Jews, accept Israel's policies and cel-ebrate its break with historical victimization? Many American Jews have no identification with Israel as a part of their Jewish identity, whereas other American Jews use Israel as a basis for their Jewish identity.

INTERPENETRATION OF FRAMES

As illustrated by this discussion of Jewish American identity, identity is a process that incorporates the personal, the relationship, the enactment, and the communal levels. These four layers should be un-derstood as interpenetrating and inseparable. Each layer only serves as a method to focus on identity in a variety of contexts. For example, one's personal identity feeds off one's relations while at the same time the individual contributes to a relational iden-tity. The boundaries between these two layers are fluid and undefined. Where does one's personal identity end and a relational identity begin?

An illustration of the interpenetration of the four levels concerns intermarriage. One's personal Jew-ish identity creates motivations and expectations that help to decide whether one will pursue intimate relations only with Jews. Over 50% of American Jews have non-Jewish spouses. On a personal level, this reflects the feelings one has toward Jewish law, the beliefs one has concerning a multicultural America, and the saliency of one's Jewishness. In part, a re-lational identity reflects the individual identities of each person in the relationship. Also, the identity of the relationship (i.e., as a mixed marriage) is created through the enactments of the couple. Fi-nally, the identity of the relationship is a function of the pressures of the Jewish community. Some Jew-ish communities choose to marginalize intermarried couples, while others seek to reach out to them. Thus the couple's relational identity is drawn from a negotiation of personal identities, the enactments of the couple, and the input of the community(ies) to which they belong(ed).

The frequency with which Jewish Americans are intermarrying also recreates Jewish communal identity. "The 1.3 million gentile spouses and the children of these intermarried couples are radically changing the anatomy of the Jewish community and blurring the lines of who exactly is a Jew" (Bei-ser, 1996, p. 26). Mixed marriages are a reality in America and are portrayed as normal on the me-dia. These images, viewed and understood as the norm by many Jewish Americans, help to create personal expectations and motivations for Jewish Americans. Thus, the phenomenon of intermar-riage can be seen as an identity issue that is a func-tion of all four levels of identity.

Conclusion

This essay discusses Jewish American identity. In it we apply the Communication Theory of Identity (Hecht, 1993) to examine personal, enacted, relational, and communal identities and the interpenetration of these four layers. We have attempted to unpack some of the problematic elements of this identity group without imposing stereotypical constructions. The diversity among Jewish Americans is great, and it is impossible to understand the process of Jewish identity as one type of person, action, relationship, or community.

One of the problematic elements of Jewish American identity is Jewish Americans' phenotypically White appearance. They can "pass" as White—they are often "racially" grouped this way—and many would self-identify this way. Jews can, and often do, claim the benefits of "Whiteness," although Jews are typically among the top-five hate-crime victim groups, and one can find active and virulent anti-Semitism on the Internet. Faced with potential censure and discrimination, afforded the opportunity to assimilate or pass, challenged by the demands of religious and cultural practice, do Jewish Americans maintain their Jewish identities, closet these identities, or change them? What effects do these identity processes have? Does closeting equivocate or compromise one's identity? If a Jewish American chooses not to enact that identity when he or she perceives it to be salient and appropriate, does this influence that person's sense of self? How?

It was our goal in this essay to provide an introduction to Jewish American identity and raise questions about this community and identity groups in general. How well does our knowledge of Jewish Americans apply to Jews worldwide; to other American identity groups? Is the closeting of Jewish American identity similar to that of gay men and lesbians? What do Jewish Americans perceived to be "passing" have in common with members of other groups perceived to be passing? One thing is clear: Jewish Americans share a unique history that weaves together factors such as religion, persecution, minority status, ghettoization, and liberation. Jewish American culture has evolved through immigration, the Holocaust, the creation of Israel, and the emerging American middle class. So we end with a question: Who are Jewish Americans, and what can we learn about and from them?

References

Beiser, V. (1996, September 6). Intermarried with children. *Jerusalem Report, 7,* 26–30.

Bershtel, S., & Graubard, A. (1992). *Saving remnants: Feeling Jewish in America.* New York: Free Press.

Collier, M. J., & Thomas, M. (1988). Cultural identity: An interpretive perspective. In Y. Y. Kim & W. B. Gudykunst (Eds.), *Theories in intercultural communication* (pp. 99–120). Newbury Park, CA: Sage.

Fein, L. (1994). *Smashing idols: And other prescriptions for Jewish continuity.* New York: Nathan Cummings Foundation.

Gilman, S. L. (1986). *Jewish self hatred: Anti-Semitism and the hidden language of the Jews.* Baltimore: Johns Hopkins University Press.

Golden, D. R. (1996). *What's so Jewish about a Jewish fraternity? Interpreting Jewish communal identity.* Unpublished manuscript, Arizona State University.

Hawkins, R. P., & Pingree, S. (1981). Using television to construct social reality. *Journal of Broadcasting, 25,* 347–364.

Hecht, M. L. (1993). 2002—A research odyssey: Toward the development of a communication theory of identity. *Communication Monographs, 60,* 76–81.

Hecht, M. L., Collier, M. J., & Ribeau, S. (1993). *African American communication: Ethnic identity and cultural interpretations.* Newbury Park, CA: Sage.

In the spotlight. (1995, September). *Jewish Televimage Report, 5,* 3–4.

Kaufman, A. (1993, Spring/Summer). Publisher's letter. *Davka: Jewish Cultural Revolution, 1,* 3.

Krausz, M. (1993). On being Jewish. In D. Goldberg & M. Krausz (Eds.), *Jewish identity* (pp. 264–278). Philadelphia: Temple University Press.

Medding, P. Y., Tobin, G. A., Fishman, S. B., & Rimor, M. (1992). *Jewish identity in conversionary and mixed marriages.* New York: American Jewish Committee.

Meyer, M. (1990). *Jewish identity in the modern world.* Seattle: University of Washington Press.

Pearl, J., & Pearl, J. (1993). All in the Jewish family: Understanding, utilizing and enhancing images of intermarriage and other Jewish family relationships on popular television. *Journal of Jewish Communal Service, 69,* 24–39.

Prell, R. E. (1992). The begetting of America's Jews: Seeds of American Jewish identity in the representations of American Jewish women. *Journal of Jewish Communal Service, 69,* 4–23.

Roiphe, A. (1981). *Generation without memory: Jewish journey in Christian America.* New York: Linden Press.

Sacks, K. (1994). How did Jews become white folks? In S. Gregory & R. Sunjek (Eds.), *Race* (pp. 78–102). New Brunswick, NJ: Rutgers University Press.

Simon, H. (1989). *Jewish identity: A social psychological perspective* (2nd ed.). New Brunswick, NJ: Transaction Publishers.

Waters, M. C. (1990). *Ethnic options: Choosing identities in America.* Berkeley: University of California Press.

Weiss, P. (1996, January 29). Letting go. *New Yorker,* 24–33.

Wolfe, A. S. (1992). Who's gotta have it? The ownership of meaning and mass media texts. *Critical Studies in Mass Communication, 9,* 261–276.

Key Terms

closeting	Jewish identity
communal identity	layers
enacted identity	personal identity
equivocation	relational identity
intermarriage	

Discussion Questions

1. Golden, Niles, and Hecht discuss intermarriage as a situation in which all the layers of identity interact. What other examples can you think of in which several layers interact?

2. What does the essay tell us about the role of communication in the process of identity?

3. The essay suggests that there are a variety of ways to enact Jewish identity. If one has a Jewish mother, belongs to several Jewish organizations, and knows Hebrew, but also is a practicing Buddhist, what can we say about this person's Jewish identity?

4. The essay discusses the process of internalizing stereotypes. How does this process play out within other ethnic/racial/gender groups?

5. Golden, Niles, and Hecht explain that Jewish Americans can choose to engage in behaviors that disclose or mask their Jewish identity. Is this different for other identity groups? What are the implications of having this choice?

6 Happy to Be Nappy!
Embracing an Afrocentric Aesthetic for Beauty

REGINA E. SPELLERS

Her beauty cannot be measured with standards of a colonized mind darker than blue
her blackness unblemished her features are broad and striking. . . .

—Me'Shell N'Degeocello

Beauty is in the eye of the beholder. Beauty is only skin deep. But who is the beholder? And whose skin can be beautiful? For women of color in the United States, this is a very critical question. It is a question that has the potential to transform one's self-concept and reconfigure one's identity. In this essay, I utilize my own personal narrative to illustrate how a critical investigation of the creation, ac-

ceptance, and maintenance of dominant knowledge claims about beauty can lead to a paradigm shift—a different way of viewing the world than previously encountered. Specifically, I interrogate how one takes an Afrocentric worldview and moves from valuing mainstream standards of beauty to embracing a conception of beauty that evolves from one's personal ideology. Race, class, gender, sexuality, and, I argue, beauty are social constructs that are salient in American culture. This paper interrogates the degree to which beauty has been sociopolitically constructed in the United States and how as a text, the corporeal can be used to resist the dominant interpretation of female beauty. As performance studies scholars Carol Simpson Stern and Bruce Henderson (1993) suggest,

> In many ways, the body has become a kind of text, or even a set of texts, that we remake not only as we grow up physically and go through puberty and other physical stages but also as we reflect on and engage in psychological and sociopolitical dimensions of experience. (p. 317)

Central to understanding how we co-create social constructs is the idea that through self-awareness and self-conscious struggle we can control the degree to which social constructs influence how we act and think. In this paper I share my experiences of experimenting with different ways of styling my hair. My personal story is interwoven with a discussion of three theoretical frameworks that guide my analysis of dominant knowledge claims about beauty: the idea that one's personal story impacts his or her perception of reality, that individuals co-create their reality, and that telling one's personal story can be empowering. Finally, I offer an Afrocentric framework that provides a way to deconstruct existing standards of beauty.

Roots

On my vanity table in my bedroom sits a picture of me when I was 5 years old. This photograph was taken on picture day, one of the highlights of a kindergartner's life. I am wearing a new dress, and my hair is neatly styled in two ponytails with Shirley Temple curls dangling about my shoulders. No doubt, my mother's beautician had "pressed" my hair for the occasion. "Pressing" is a technique that can be hazardous to your health. If the person styling your hair has a slip of hand, you can be burned. If the hot comb is left too long in your hair, your hair can be burned. If you flinch during the process of getting your hair pressed, you can be labeled tenderheaded.

My heart goes out to the tenderheaded child. Being tenderheaded in the Black community means that you cannot withstand the pull of your hair through the hot comb; that your scalp cries out in agony when the relaxer meets your naps; that tight braids strain your scalp so much that your eyes want to pop out of your head. Your mama, or whoever does your hair, scolds you, rolling her eyes in disbelief, "You have the nerve to be tenderheaded with this thick head of hair full of naps? Shame on you!"

And you feel ashamed. You learn how to detest the natural kink of your hair. You never marvel at the rich coarseness of its texture. You do not say, "I am happy to be nappy." Instead, you come down with a bad case of blonde ambition. You desire hair that is longer, bouncier, straighter, and shinier than your own. You invest in potions and lotions, gels and pomades that hold the unspoken promise of good hair; pretty hair; Indian-looking hair, baby hair, kinda curly/kinda straight hair, hair like a White person's hair; hair that is anything but nappy. You convince yourself that it is absolutely necessary to get your hair chemically treated on a regular basis in order to have beautiful, healthy hair. Good hair. You get your hair dyed, fired, and laid to the side in an effort to suppress the natural kinky, nappy curl of your hair. You are not convinced that Black is beautiful. You do not say, "I am happy to be nappy." Shame on you. Shame on me.

The first theoretical framework in this essay suggests that personal stories can give insight into how people construct their lives (Madison, 1993). Social constructs evolve out of culture. My experience of race, class, gender, sex, ethnicity, and identity may be different from your experience. I am a woman of color. Like the theme suggested in Lorraine Hansberry's (1969) play, I am young, gifted, and Black. My experiences of reality as a Black woman are shaped by the time and place of my birth, my social networks, my gender, and among other things, my race and ethnicity. Taken together, all of these factors make up my story. We all have a story. However, in traditional social science research, some histories and herstories are given prime-time status, whereas other stories—my story—the stories of the everyday lived experience of Black women in the United States, are often marginalized (James, 1997). This means that I do not often hear my story. Communication scholar Sidney Ribeau (1997) writes that "these omissions separate the academic world from the realities students encounter in daily life and see on television and film" (p. 23).

In her book entitled *Black Feminist Thought: Knowledge, Consciousness and the Politics of Empowerment,* Patricia Hill Collins (1991) investigates why the Black female experience in the United States tends to be a neglected area of inquiry in the social sciences. She suggests that "maintaining the invisibility of Black women and our ideas is critical in structuring patterned relations of race, gender, and class inequality that pervade the entire social structure" (p. 5). Silencing the stories of marginalized groups aids in the creation of a dominant discourse. By studying personal stories, the tendency to naturalize one's experiences of reality as a universal experience of reality becomes minimized and we come to understand that there are different ways of knowing. The personal story presented in this paper interrogates dominant knowledge claims about beauty that may give insights into what it means to be Black and female in America.

The practice of silencing certain voices in traditional social science research is only one way dominant discourse is created. Often when the experiences of marginalized groups are discussed, they are framed in opposition to the experience of dominant groups, which functions both to marginalize racioethnic groups and center Whiteness as the dominant paradigm. The result is what Collins (1991) calls either/or dichotomous thinking: us/them, right/wrong, Black/White. By conceptualizing phenomena in an oppositional framework, the articulation of difference becomes polarized and equated with claims of superiority/inferiority. She also argues that images of the Black woman as "the Other" provide ideological justification for race, gender, and class oppression:

> Finally, because oppositional dichotomies rarely represent different but equal relationships, they are inherently unstable. Tension is resolved by subordinating one half of the dichotomy to the other. Thus whites rule Blacks, men dominate women, reason is thought superior to emotion in ascertaining truth, facts supersede opinion in evaluating knowledge, and subjects rule objects. The foundations of a complex social hierarchy become grounded in the interwoven concepts of either/or dichotomous thinking, oppositional difference, and objectification. (p. 70)

One way to subvert the practice of framing marginalized discourse in opposition to dominant discourse in traditional social science research is to tell our stories in our voices (e.g., González, Houston, & Chen, 1997). Centering marginalized discourse in an autonomous framework rather than a framework of opposition emancipates us from dichotomous thinking and suggests that difference has utility and meaning.

Black Barbie

Although I was not tenderheaded, I did have long, thick, nappy hair. Reflecting on the different techniques I employed to style my hair, I can now see that there were periods in my life where I unconsciously defined my appearance in relationship to Eurocentric standards that value a particular kind of external beauty. By the time I reached high school, I had graduated from my press-and-curl days and now had a permanent relaxer or a perm. I had traded the inconvenience of having to endure the hot comb every 2 weeks to instead having to "touch up" my perm every 6 to 8 weeks at the salon. Like pressing, a perm also straightens the natural kink of my hair. In between salon visits, I would style my own hair. Learning to do my own hair took some practice. I struggled with techniques to get my hair as straight and shiny as possible without damaging it. Eventually, though, after religiously reading Black hairstyle magazines and getting advice from other Black women, I developed a beauty ritual that, albeit time consuming, resulted in the bouncy shiny curls I so desired. I could flip and bounce my hair with the best of them. I was Black Barbie.

The second framework that guides this essay assumes that individuals actively construct their reality. Berger and Luckman (1967) argue that we create social constructs, and in turn, we are created by them (James, 1997, p. 46). Viewing race as a social construct, sociologists Omi and Winant (1994) argue that the manner in which racial categories are defined and utilized in the United States is linked to economic and political changes within a society and that one can trace how race is socially constructed in the United States by conducting a sociopolitical analysis of history. They cite the experience of

Blacks in the United States to illustrate their claim that the sociopolitical history of this country is characterized by a legacy of oppression. During the period in U.S. history when Black Africans were enslaved here, having dark skin was associated with being inferior, and in turn, this definition became a way to justify slavery. As described by John Hope Franklin (1995):

> The presence of persons of African descent, almost from the beginning had helped whites to define ethnicity and to establish and maintain the conditions by which it could be controlled. If their color and race, their condition of servitude, and their generally degraded position did not set them apart, the laws and customs surrounding them more than accomplished that feat. . . . It was not enough for Americans, already somewhat guilt-ridden for maintaining slavery in a free society, to exclude blacks from American society on the basis of race and condition of servitude. They proceeded from that point to argue that Negroes were inferior morally, intellectually, and physically. (p. 28)

Particular meanings, stereotypes, and myths that compromise racial ideology can be linked to specific historical moments and continuities. The system of racial meanings established in the United States is based on the practice of one group asserting power over other groups in order to justify control of economic resources (Omi & Winant, 1994).

Ruth Frankenberg (1993) describes how, in her study of the social construction of Whiteness in the United States, social constructs serve to marginalize certain groups: "given male domination within white culture, the 'protection' or 'salvation' of white women and their supposedly civilized sexuality has been the alibi for a range of atrocities from genocide and lynching to segregation and immigration control" (p. 76). The association of inferiority with certain phenotypical features also played an important role in the U.S. government's extermination policy of American Indians, the anti-Chinese movement in California prior to World War II, and the establishment of detention camps for Japanese Americans on the West Coast of the United States during World War II. These historical examples illustrate that race is socially constructed and how, as a social construct, defining certain racial groups as inferior serves to position the dominant group as being superior.

Stern and Henderson (1993) argue that social constructs also have material consequences:

> . . . As long as we live in a racist society, the concept of race will continue to be important; we may envision a world in which this concept has disappeared, but until then, we need to confront its meaning in the lives of those people whose bodies are constructed along racial lines.
>
> In America, the issue of race has centered most consistently and devastatingly on the lives of African-Americans, in large part, of course, to their enslavement for economic purposes from the colonial period to the end of the Civil War and their continued economic disadvantage today. In recent years, more attention has been paid to the racism practiced historically . . . against . . . Native Americans, Hispanic-Americans, and Asian-Americans. In fact, so potent a concern is racism that the term *people of color* has been coined to provide an umbrella description for all those groups who have experienced oppression because they are not members of the dominant European-American or "white" culture. (pp. 324–325)

Investigating epistemological standpoints that are rooted in dominant knowledge claims (for example, about aesthetics) encourages discussion about how this particular way of seeing impacts members of nondominant groups.

Nap Attack

For members of marginalized groups, constructing identity in a racist environment can be a complex and difficult task. The challenge is to positively reconstruct one's self-image within the context of a system of racial domination. Although I do not position myself, as the title of Marlon Riggs's film suggests, the judge of what "Black is and Black ain't," I do struggle daily against the subtle seduction of images that suggest my brown skin, my nappy hair, my full lips are not beautiful. Cultural studies scholar bell hooks (1992) describes how being subjects of and subjected to a European gaze creates the potential for Blacks to internalize racism:

Opening a magazine or book, turning on the television set, watching a film, or looking at photographs in public spaces, we are most likely to see images of black people that reinforce and reinscribe white supremacy. Those images may be constructed by white people who have not divested of racism, or by people of color/black people who may see the world through the lens of white supremacy-internalized racism. (p. 1)

Learning to value self involves investigating ways in which one has embraced practices and ideologies that promote self-hatred.

Starting my first real job in a large corporation, I wanted a new executive look that encompassed a new hairstyle. Ponytails were fine for bad hair days (which for me usually meant that I was having a nap attack—the natural kink and curl of my hair rebelled and resisted all of the mechanisms designed to suppress it), but I needed a style that was polished and sophisticated. Still perming my hair, I decided to cut my hair in a short bob. Although the style gave me peace of mind (I no longer debated over how to wear my hair), I grew tired of the beauty ritual my permed hair required. I wanted simplicity. I wanted low maintenance. Braids were an option because the upkeep was minimal. A braided style required a beauty ritual but not an extensive one. But, I wondered, is this style for me? Will I be viewed as unprofessional/too ethnic/too Black? I agonized over these questions and sought advice from other Black women and men working in white-collar corporate America. They spoke from experience. The consensus was that wearing braids would probably be frowned upon in a work environment where the values of the corporate culture are synonymous with the values of the dominant culture, but that you also have to be happy. Happy? Happy. Happy to be nappy.

Closely related to the second framework, the third framework that guides this essay stems from a personal sense of purpose, of empowerment, legacy, and resilience. In the legacy of Marsha Houston (1992) and so many other scholars who often write with a keen sense of purpose, I am writing for my life. I am telling my story because if I do not, who will? Alice Walker (1983) expresses how having a sense of purpose guides her work:

In my own work I write not only what I want to read—understanding fully and indelibly that if I don't do it no one else is so vitally interested, or capable of doing it to my satisfaction—I write all the things that I should have been able to read. (p. 13)

While my own personal story is unique, it can also have relevance for others. This is echoed by Navita Cummings James (1997):

[N]o one story is so unique or idiosyncratic that it cannot provide us insight into the overall human experience. One of the most powerful ways to gain an understanding of "the other" (e.g., a person from a culture other than one's own) is to hear or read the story of "the other" in his or her own words. (p. 47)

Like these scholars, I am also motivated to tell my story, hoping that as a member of a marginalized group that has historically been oppressed in America, I may give critical insights into the experience of oppression.

I cannot, however, separate thought from action. The very act of telling my story is one of resistance. In my experience, publicly speaking about internalized racism in the Black community, particularly of the struggle of believing Black to be beautiful for ourselves, is taboo. It is painful to speak of how one's race is represented in the mass media knowing that some of the negative stereotypical images were created by members of our community. bell hooks (1992) suggests that it is also painful to articulate this issue of representation because to do so one must not only critique how Whiteness has been centered as the dominant paradigm, but also interrogate how one has played a role in sustaining this position:

To face these wounds, to heal them, progressive black people and our allies in struggle must be willing to grant the effort to critically intervene and transform the world of image making authority of place in our political movements of liberation and self determination (be they anti-imperialist, feminist, gay rights, black liberation, or all of the above and more). If this were the case, we would be ever mindful of the need to make radical intervention. We would consider crucial both the kind of images we produce and the way we critically write and talk about images. And most important, we would rise to the challenge to speak that which has not been spoken. (p. 4)

By centering our stories, in our voices, even when our stories are about how we see ourselves aesthetically, we become empowered. We open up a space for healing. We create an opportunity for our stories to be heard and to be meaningful in a context that has traditionally negated their significance.

Free Your Mind, the Rest Will Follow

I am presently a long way from my press-and-curl days. My once-shoulder-length hair is now cut into a short Afro. Today, I am happy to be nappy. For me, being happy to be nappy is a state of mind that allows me to feel liberated, to understand that I have the right to define who I am and that this definition is ever changing. My past experiences experimenting with different hairstyles is part of a journey that I do not regret. They have brought me to a place where I understand that there is value in the self-conscious struggle that often results from the discrepancy between how we define ourselves and how we are defined by others. Given that there is a dynamic contrast between how we see ourselves and how others see us, how is it possible to resist conceptions of self that promote self-hatred while at the same time engage in the process of reconstructing our identity?

One solution is through the process of decolonization, which challenges us to rethink our acceptance of images that support and maintain our oppression and promotes the conscious effort to reject nonaffirming images of self. bell hooks (1992) suggests that the complex process of decolonization is a critical, difficult, and painful process for all colonized people, in particular for Black folks in America. It is critical for colonized individuals because the practice of exalting Whiteness as the ideal negatively impacts their self-identity (p. 3). It is difficult to achieve because America is a White supremacist society in which marginalized and nonmarginalized people are still shackled to the promise of mainstream success (p. 17). It is a painful process be-

cause it forces you to see the wounds of your self-hate; "often it leaves us ravaged by repressed rage, feeling weary, dispirited, and sometimes just plain old brokenhearted" (p. 4).

Images, deeply woven with ideology, determine not only how we think about others but how we think about ourselves. Learning to resist dominant knowledge claims about beauty is an ongoing process. Equating beauty with being White, blonde, young, thin, and having blue eyes has material consequences for all women. White American females who judge their appearance from a Eurocentric standard of beauty also fall victim to dominant knowledge claims about beauty (Collins, 1991, p. 79). I propose, however, that while the dominant perspective on who can be beautiful in American society is destructive for all women, it has additional dire implications for women of color. Any attempts to meet these dominant beauty standards require women of color not only to remake themselves but to denounce and negate their personal value. Writing on this subject, Collins suggests that "African-American women experience the pain of never being able to live up to externally defined standards of beauty—standards applied to us by white men, Black men, and, most painfully, one another" (p. 80). Negative images of Black women serve to reinforce dominant ideology about beauty:

> From the mammies, Jezebels, and breeder women of slavery to the smiling Aunt Jemimas on pancake mix boxes, ubiquitous Black prostitutes, and ever-present welfare mothers of contemporary popular culture, the nexus of negative stereotypical images applied to African-American women has been fundamental to Black women's oppression. (p. 7)

Resisting the temptation to internalize these and other negative images of self requires self-conscious struggle.

The pain of being subjugated to a gaze that seeks to dominate and colonize can often lead to denial:

> Many black folks refuse to look at our present condition because they do not want to see images that might compel them to militancy. But militancy is an alternative to madness. And many of us are entering the realm of the insane. Like

Pecola, in Toni Morrison's *The Bluest Eye,* black folks turn away from reality because the pain of awareness is so great. Yet it is only by becoming more fully aware that we begin to see clearly. (hooks, 1992, p. 6)

It is through decolonization and self-conscious struggle that one begins the journey to heal the wounds of self-hate and emancipate oneself from the prison of a colonized mind. Through the act of self-definition, one begins the journey of a changed consciousness, which becomes a way of transcending images that limit the view we have of ourselves. This change can be empowering.

Behold the Quiltmaker

Redefining beauty is a crucial step in deconstructing social constructs that value and uphold one group while simultaneously devaluing and degrading another group(s). Constructing a definition of beauty that simply suggests what was good is now bad and what was bad is now good, however, does not adequately challenge the existing dichotomous framework characteristic of dominant ideology. As Collins (1991) suggests,

> But proclaiming Black women "beautiful" and white women "ugly" merely replaces one set of controlling images with another and fails to challenge how Eurocentric masculinist aesthetics foster an ideology of domination. Current standards require either/or dichotomous thinking: in order for one individual to be judged beautiful, another individual—the Other—must be deemed ugly. Accepting this underlying assumption avoids a more basic question concerning the connection among controlling images, either/or dichotomous thinking, and unequal power relationships. (p. 88)

What is required, then, is a perspective that not only deconstructs existing standards of beauty but also emancipates beholders of beauty from judging who can and cannot be beautiful based on external or ornamental qualities or both.

Afrocentric theory is such a perspective. It provides a means to deconstruct and redefine existing standards of beauty. A central assumption in Afrocentric thought is that of centeredness. The Afrocentric idea "is a strategy to seek one's centrality or

one's human agency from the fringes or the periphery. . . . [I]t rejects the notions and practices of hegemonic or alleged universal tendencies and practices of a given paradigm" (Bekerie, 1994, pp. 136–137). For this reason, this perspective has important implications for deconstructing and redefining existing standards of beauty. As the leading proponent of Afrocentricity Molefi Kete Asante (1995) writes, "Our aim is to open fields of inquiry and to expand human dialogue around questions of social, economic, historical, and cultural concern. . . . Our methods are meant to establish a clear line of discourse that may be followed by others" (p. 3). Afrocentricity provides a framework that can be utilized by all to center their discourse in a particular cultural context. Bekerie (1994) argues that

> Afrocentricity is an intellectual pursuit that endorses humanistic mission. This mission is pursued by first affirming our own humanity. It is pursued by defining and naming phenomena that emanate from our own experience. . . . Afrocentric theory is a theory of being a subject. It is about exercising one's agency. It is a theory that seeks to empower, free the mind, and ring the bell of harmony. (p. 148)

Theorizing about beauty from an Afrocentric orientation provides an alternative to the dichotomous way in which this social construct has been traditionally conceptualized.

Patricia Hill Collins (1991) and others offer quiltmaking as an example of an Afrocentric feminist aesthetic for beauty.

> . . . African-American women quiltmakers do not seem interested in a uniform color scheme but use several methods of playing with colors to create unpredictability and movement (Wahlman & Scully, 1983, in Brown, 1989, p. 922). For example, a strong color may be juxtaposed with another strong color, or with a weak one. Contrast is used to structure or organize. Overall, the symmetry in African-American quilts does not come from uniformity as it does in Euro-American quilts. Rather, symmetry comes through diversity. (Collins, p. 89)

The emphasis on diversity, rather than either/or conceptualizations of beauty, creates a space for all women to be beautiful. As Collins suggests,

The Afrocentric notions of diversity in community and functional beauty potentially heal many of the oppositional dichotomies inherent in Western social thought. From an Afrocentric perspective, women's beauty is not based solely on physical criteria because mind, spirit, and body are not conceptualized as separate, oppositional spheres. Instead, all are central in aesthetic assessments of individuals and their creations. . . . Moreover, participation is not based on conformity but instead is seen as individual uniqueness that enhances the overall "beauty" of the group. Using such criteria, no individual is inherently beautiful because beauty is not a state of being. Instead beauty is always defined in a context as a state of becoming. (p. 89)

The pieces of cloth once deemed scrap become useful when taken together as a whole. The quiltmaker is the beholder of beauty and utilizes her creativity to self-define that which is beautiful.

Conclusion

I have tried to show how one's personal story gives insight into how we construct our identity and how our identity is socio-politically constructed. As socially constructed in the United States, gender (Frankenberg, 1993), race (Martinez, 1995), age, class, and beauty have significant material consequences. The process of decolonization suggests that individuals must take an active role in reconstructing themselves within particular cultural contexts. hooks (1992) argues that "all whites (as well as everyone else within white supremacist culture) have learned to over-value 'whiteness' even as they simultaneously learn to devalue blackness" (p. 12). A critical examination of how we, as co-creators of this interpretation of dominant ideology, can decolonize our minds, has critical implications for subverting dichotomous thinking. Investigating dominant knowledge claims about beauty requires a critical examination of the beholder of beauty—those who possess the power to define who is beautiful. Rejecting controlling and oppressive images of Black womanhood often requires self-evaluation. Through self-conscious struggle, we critically examine who we were, who we are, and who we are becoming.

References

Asante, M. (1995). *Malcolm X as a cultural hero.* Trenton, NJ: Africa World Press, Inc.

Bekerie, A. (1994). The four corners of a circle: Afrocentricity as a model of synthesis. *Journal of Black Studies, 25,* 131–149.

Berger, P. L., & Luckman, C. (1967). *The socialization of reality.* Garden City, NY: Anchor Books.

Brown, E. B. (1989). African-American women's quilting: A framework for conceptualizing and teaching African-American women's history. *Signs, 14,* 921–929.

Collins, P. H. (1991). *Black feminist thought: Knowledge, consciousness and the politics of empowerment.* New York: Routledge & Chapman and Hall.

Frankenberg, R. (1993). *White women, race matters: The social construction of whiteness.* Minneapolis, MN: University of Minnesota Press.

Franklin, J. H. (1995). Ethnicity in American life: the historical perspective. In A. Aguirre & D. Baker (Eds.), *Sources: Notable selections in race and ethnicity* (pp. 24–32). Guilford, CT: Dushkin Publishing Group.

González, A., Houston, M., & Chen, V. (1997). *Our voices: Essays in culture, ethnicity, and communication* (2nd ed.). Los Angeles: Roxbury Publishing Company.

Hansberry, L. (1969). *To be young, gifted and black.* New York: Signet.

hooks, b. (1992). *Black looks: Race and representation.* Boston: South End Press.

Houston, M. (1992). The politics of difference: Race, class, and women's communication. In L. F. Rakow (Ed.), *Women making meaning* (pp. 45–59). New York: Routledge.

James, N. C. (1997). When Miss America was always white. In A. González, M. Houston, & V. Chen (Eds.), *Our voices: Essays in culture, ethnicity, and communication* (2nd ed., pp. 46–51). Los Angeles: Roxbury Publishing Company.

Madison, D. S. (1993). "That was my occupation": Oral narrative, performance, and Black feminist thought. *Text and Performance Quarterly, 13,* 213–232.

Martinez, E. (1995). Beyond black/white: The racism of our time. In A. Aguirre & D. Baker (Eds.), *Sources: Notable selections in race and ethnicity* (pp. 79–90). Guilford, CT: Dushkin Publishing Group.

N'Degeocello, M. (1993). Untitled. *On Plantation lullabies* [CD]. New York: Maverick.

Omi, M., & Winant, H. (1994). *Racial formations in the United States from the 1960s to the 1990s.* New York: Routledge.

Ribeau, S. (1997). How I came to know "In self-realization there is truth." In A. González, M. Houston, & V. Chen (Eds.), *Our voices: Essays in culture, ethnicity, and communication* (2nd ed., pp. 21–27). Los Angeles: Roxbury Publishing Company.

Riggs, M. T. (Producer/Director), & Atkinson, N. (Co-Producer). (1994). Black is, black ain't. [Video]. Available from California Newsreel, 149 9th Street, San Francisco, CA 94103.

Stern, C. S., & Henderson, B. (1993). *Performance: Texts and contexts*. White Plains, NY: Longman Publishing Group.

Walker, A. (1983). *In search of our mother's gardens*. New York: Harcourt Brace Jovanovich.

Wahlman, M., & Scully, J. (1983). Aesthetic principles of Afro-American quilts. In W. Ferris (Ed.), *Afro-American folk arts and crafts* (pp. 79–97). Boston: G. K. Hall.

Key Terms

Afrocentric	marginalize
decolonize	social construct
ideology	

Discussion Questions

1. Spellers discusses dominant discourse and marginalized discourse in terms of how beauty is conceptualized in the United States. Can you think of other dominant knowledge claims that may conflict with the experience of members of marginalized groups?

2. The author views the body as text. How does this inform our understanding of communication?

3. Can one's personal story be viewed as scholarship?

4. Spellers's essay suggests that we are co-creators of our identities. Who or what co-creates our identity with us?

5. What does this essay tell us about diversity? How is diversity defined in this essay?

7 My Three Cultures
Navigating the Multicultural Identity Landscape[1]
GUST A. YEP

[We] cannot enter the struggle as objects in order later *[emphasis in the original] to become human beings.*
　　　　　　　　　　　　　　　—Paulo Freire

I am Asianlatinoamerican.[2] Although I have never been to China, I am racially what my parents describe as "100% pure Chinese." During my formative years, we lived in Peru, South America, and later moved to the United States. I learned to speak Chinese first, mainly to communicate with my grandmother, a traditional Chinese woman who rarely ventured beyond the boundaries of the Chinese community in Lima. I then learned to speak Spanish in school in Peru, where we lived until I finished high school at the age of 15. I started learning English when I came to the United States to attend college. After completing my doctorate, I started my university teaching career in Los Angeles, California, and I am currently teaching in San Francisco and residing in the city with my two Pomeranians, Tyler and Dino. I am trilingual (English, Spanish, Chinese) and I speak all three languages with a slight accent. I used to be concerned about the accent in my speech, but in recent years I have adopted a different attitude: My accent might simply be an indication that I probably speak more languages than my conversational partner. I "look Asian American," yet at times my Latino culture is most prominent in some communication settings. I strongly identify with all three cultures, and they are more or less integrated into this complex entity that I label as my "multicultural self." Such integration,[3] however, is an ongoing process. In this essay, I explore how I negotiate this multicultural identity in my daily communication experiences. More specifically, I discuss (1) the nature of identity, (2) the co-creation and re-creation of my identity in everyday encounters, and (3) the negotiation of identity as a liberation process.

The Nature of Identity

Broadly defined, identity is a person's conception of self within a particular social, geographical, cultural, and political context. Identity gives the individual a sense of self and personhood and an intepretive frame of experience (Hecht, Collier, & Ribeau, 1993). Identity is abstract, complex, multi-dimensional, fluid, and amorphous (Cupach & Imahori, 1993). People have multiple identities—ethnic, racial, occupational, socioeconomic, sexual, gender, and relational—which Cupach and Imahori describe as "interconnected cultural identities" (p. 114).

Collier and Thomas (1988), consistent with Geertz's (1973) conceptualization of culture as historically transmitted systems, define cultural identity as "identification with and perceived acceptance into a group that has shared systems of symbols and meanings as well as norms/rules for conduct" (p. 113). Sarup (1996) further notes, "identity is a construction, a consequence of a process of interaction between people, institutions and practices" (p. 1). In short, cultural identity is a social construction that gives the individual an ontological status (a sense of "being") and expectations for social behavior (ways of "acting").

Cultural identity can be characterized as political, fluid, and nonsummative. First, cultural identity is political (Appiah, 1996; Harvey, 1993; Moraga, 1983; Sarup, 1996; Thornton, 1992). Cultural identity separates individuals on the basis of ingroup-outgroup differences. Appiah (1996) elaborates, "if other people organize their solidarity around cultures different from ours, this makes them, to that extent, different from us in ways that matter to us deeply" (p. 39). Such contrasting loyalties are necessarily associated with political power. Citing Ernesto Laclau's work, Sarup (1996) maintains that

> the relations between groups are constituted as relations of power; each group insists on its difference on the basis of the exclusion and subordination of other groups. . . . If the oppressed is defined by its difference from the oppressor, such a difference is an essential component of the identity of the oppressed. But in that case, the latter cannot assert its identity without asserting that of the oppressor as well. (pp. 59–60)

A dominant group, to maintain its status in the hierarchy, will seek to keep others in lower positions. One powerful way to accomplish this is through discursive practices.

"Why won't you just be like everybody else?" is a remark that I have often heard directed to people of color or to other people who do not conform to the "norm." Underlying this seemingly innocuous remark are cultural conceptions of power and privilege. Who is this entity called "everybody else"? It is the dominant group who determines who and what is normal or deviant, desirable or undesirable, right or wrong, successful or unsuccessful, beautiful or ugly, human or subhuman, native or alien, us or them. Being like "everybody else," the identification to the dominant group, takes on a natural appearance, remains unnamed and unquestioned, and therefore disguises and hides power relations between the oppressor and the oppressed. For people of color (or other marginalized groups), "being like everybody else" is a double bind: Regardless of how we attempt to be like the dominant group, our very presence would almost automatically label us as the "other." This assimilationist view directs the marginalized person to try harder and harder to adhere, obey, and follow the rules of the dominant group—rules that he or she can never fully and completely participate in creating.

For an individual with a multicultural identity, this can be a site of multiple tensions. People who are multicultural and multiracial are often expected to choose and privilege one aspect of their background over others, and such tension can be manifested externally or internally or both. Thornton (1992) notes that while some multiracial individuals are demanding political representation through the creation of a unique census category, others are concerned about losing political power associated with their primary racial identity. He cites the example of an African American/Native American man who believes that a distinct multiracial category will dilute African American political representation. For Moraga (1983), this tension is both external and internal. As a fair-skinned Latina lesbian, she describes her struggle with her own internalized racism ("light skin is better"), classism ("feeling superior to poor and uneducated Mexicans"), and heterosexism ("heterosexuality is better"), which eventually propelled her to political activism.

Being monoracial and multicultural, my own experience with my multicultural identity has brought about internal and external conflicts. As a child in a Chinese family, I was expected to always listen to my parents, never question their authority, and never demand an explanation for their actions toward me. My primary duty was to excel in school and consequently, I was expected to do school-related work every day, year-round. I never had a weekend to relax or a summer to play. Being about a full school year ahead in my math, I questioned my father one summer day about the purpose of doing school work every day when all my friends were having fun. He was surprised that I questioned him. After giving me an explanation, he told me in Chinese, "You are becoming like a white ghost" (which can be translated into English as "You are becoming 'too Westernized'"). Although I felt like saying that I have never lived anywhere but the West, I could not think of further upsetting my father.

I have also experienced external conflicts with my multicultural identity. Although I always introduce myself as multicultural during my first class meeting with students, some inevitably express that they are very glad to have an "Asian professor teaching communication courses." These students seem to be genuinely delighted to have an Asian role model. Given that both Asians and Latinos are underrepresented in the communication discipline, I sometimes feel that I am not properly representing the Latino part of me. Although I have become more comfortable with the persistent internal and

external tensions associated with my multicultural identity in recent years, I am always mindful of them in my everyday interaction.

Second, cultural identity is fluid (Martin & Nakayama, 1997; Sarup, 1996). In other words, one's cultural identity is ever evolving, growing, and changing. It is never static; as Sarup (1996) notes, "identity [has] to do not with being but with becoming" (p. 6). I have experienced—and will continue to experience—many subtle and profound changes in my multicultural identity. I still recall my attempts to repress my Chinese identity during my adolescent years. Whether this was a product of adolescent rebellion against parental insistence that I should be Chinese above all else or a sense of identification with my Latino peers or a fascination with my new American culture seems immaterial. During my college years, I slowly started reembracing the Chinese in me. I started having a deep appreciation for Chinese philosophy, wisdom, and the hardships that many Chinese have endured in foreign lands. I became interested in my family story—why and how they left China during the Communist Revolution. I also became fascinated by how Asian Americans give voice and legitimacy to their own experiences through oral histories and literature.

Third, cultural identity is nonsummative (Cupach & Imahori, 1993). In other words, one's cultural identity is not a simple addition of the component parts of one's cultural background. To put it another way, one cannot get a complete sense of my multicultural identity by simply adding my Chinese, Latino, and American parts. I am more than the sum of those individual parts. The combination of my experiences, values, beliefs, and perceptions in all three cultures constitutes a new gestalt, a fluid entity that I describe as my "multicultural self." This can be observed when I speak to my family over the telephone. We usually start our conversation in one language (usually Chinese), then I would start speaking English and Spanish, and in a few minutes we have a phone conversation using all three languages. Typically, when I speak Chinese with my parents, I feel more like a child and would often behave differently than an independent and free-thinking adult. I switch to English when I have something serious to discuss and to Spanish when I have strong emotions to express. However, I cannot say that those cultural parts of me only "come out" when I speak in that language, for I have directly and openly disagreed with my parents in Chinese, expressed my love for them in English, and discussed my plans to redesign my home in Spanish. My identity transcends the boundaries of those individual cultural components.

The Co-creation and Re-creation of Identity

Cultural identities are co-created and re-created in everyday interaction. In other words, we create our identities with those individuals with whom we interact (co-creation) and in the context of specific communication episodes and encounters (re-creation). The process of co-creation and re-creation of identity can only occur through *dialogue*. Freire (1970) writes:

> Dialogue is the encounter between [people], mediated by the world, in order to name the world. Hence, dialogue cannot occur between those who want to name the world and those who do not wish this naming—between those who deny others the right to speak their word and those whose right to speak has been denied them. (p. 69)

Put in another way, co-creation of identity cannot occur when there is an attempt on the part of one of the communicators to, consciously or unconsciously, dominate the other physically or symbolically. This process of domination between oppressor and oppressed is, in Freire's terms, "by prescription." He further maintains that "every prescription represents the imposition of one individual's choice upon another, transforming the consciousness of the person prescribed to into one that conforms with the prescriber's consciousness" (p. 29). Genuine co-creation of identity becomes difficult when asymmetrical power relations exist.

In my daily encounters, I have experienced numerous instances in which the other interactant attempted to prescribe a label, an identity for me. A long time ago, when I was involved in a play for a church fundraiser, the director demanded, "Show your Oriental anger!" I first thought that I did not hear him correctly. I was completely dumbfounded when he repeated the same command. I objected to the label "Oriental" and I was not sure what "Oriental anger" was. Finally, I uttered, "I do not understand you. . . . How does anger come to have a derogatory ethnic label? Is it supposed to be different from your (an older man's) anger, a woman's anger, or some other form of anger?" I then proceeded to tell him that if we were going to work together, we needed to come up with labels that were comfortable and agreeable to both of us. He did not understand.

Although this process of prescription is not always necessarily a conscious or a malicious one, we need to be mindful of it and its potential harm. When we allow this process to occur, we are tacitly choosing to participate in a transaction as *objects*—not subjects (in the above example, I would not have been an active agent in the communication but rather a passive fulfillment of whatever characteristics, attributes, and expectations the director had of an "Oriental" and his particular brand of anger, "Oriental anger"). In other words, we are not affirming our humanity as free agents with a capacity and potential to create, to construct, to wonder, and to venture when we are reduced to the status of objects or things (Freire, 1970). To put it differently, *both* interactants are responsible for this process of identity creation. If one prescribes, the other needs to be aware that unless the prescription is resisted and the transaction redefined (in the same example above, I reclaimed my subject position, in the end, by negotiating the terms of interaction that were acceptable to both of us), a true co-creation of identity cannot occur.

Freire's (1970) notion of prescription resonates with Cupach and Imahori's (1993) concept of "identity freezing." They maintain that identity freezing occurs when one interactant imposes an objective and public identity (like a stereotype, whether positive or negative) on the other (Cupach & Imahori). For example, if I tell an Asian student that she must be good with numbers (presumably a positive stereotype), I am freezing her identity and prescribing our relationship. With this example, I also want to point out that prescription and identity freezing are not necessarily restricted to intercultural encounters but are applicable to intracultural relations as well.

As I indicated earlier, to co-create and re-create identities, we need to participate in the process, in Freire's (1970) terms, "as subjects of the transformation" (p. 108). When someone tells me, "You are not a typical university professor," I often ask what they mean by the statement. In the process, we usually uncover some stereotypical attributes of university professors that I do not possess (I do not smoke a pipe; I do not have gray hair [yet]; I am not absentminded) and some stereotypical qualities that I do possess (I am nearsighted; I am constantly reading; I am nerdy). I usually follow up this discussion with another question, "What does it mean to you that I am not a 'typical university professor'?" This usually prompts a discussion that allows both of us to co-create and re-create ourselves as we develop a greater sense of connectedness and understanding of each other's perception of self and interpretive frame of reference.

Fundamental in dialogue or dialogical action is cooperation. Freire (1970) further notes that cooperation "can only be achieved through communication" (p. 149). In other words, communication is intrinsic to the process of co-creation and re-creation of one's cultural identity. Another example appears to be in order. I have been a member of the La Raza Caucus of the National Communication Association (NCA) since I was a graduate student. As the name might indicate, the primary focus of the La Raza Caucus is on Chicano(a) and Latino(a) culture and communication, and most members are of Latin descent. Although some members of the caucus attempted to prescribe, or "freeze," my Asian identity, most welcomed my presence. We entered the dialogue as subjects mutually defining our unique cultural identities. Through communication, we have achieved, over the years, a great sense of understanding, fondness, and familiarity with each other, and I became the first Asianlatinoamerican to serve as chair of the caucus.

The Negotiation of Identity as a Liberation Process

Negotiating identities is a process involving both parties. Freire (1970) describes this as a "process of liberation" (p. 28) in which both oppressor and oppressed find freedom.

Because of my multicultural identity, I have felt, at times, that "I am neither here nor there." Although San Francisco is a city characterized by a rich cultural, ethnic, social, gender, and sexual diversity, I sometimes feel like a foreigner in the crowded streets of Chinatown or Clement (another predominantly Chinese populated area), the congested streets in the Mission (a predominantly Latino district), or the busy streets in the Marina (a predominantly affluent Euro American area). For many Chinese Americans, I am "not quite Chinese." For many Latinos, I am "not quite Latin." For many Euro Americans, I am "a person of color." This view of marginality, of "otherness," is one of isolation, invisibility, alienation, and deprivation.

Otherness represents the undesirable, degraded, exiled, suppressed, deviant, disenfranchised, and incongruous elements of the "ideal order." As I stated earlier, otherness and the ideal order must exist together for they are the opposing extremes of a dichotomy. Dichotomies, according to Sarup (1996),

> are exercises in power and at the same time their disguise. They split the human world into a group for whom the ideal order is to be erected, and another which is for the unfitting, the uncontrollable, the incongruous and the ambivalent. (p. 9)

If I were to subscribe to this view of otherness, I would have automatically accepted a less privileged subject position.

I endorse another view of marginality. Marginality may also be conceptualized as resembling Turner's (1990) notion of liminality, a threshold or space "in between" states. He further elaborates, "The attributes of liminality or of liminal personae ('threshold people') are necessarily ambiguous, since this condition and these persons elude or slip through the network of classifications that normally locate states and positions in cultural space"

(p. 147). Reminiscent of Turner's notion of liminality, hooks (1990) maintains that marginality is a "space of radical openness" (p. 149). Although such space is never a safe place, hooks argues that it is necessary to locate oneself there to find alternatives, envision possibilities, and create a future. In other words, marginality can be a position and place of resistance to the dominant power. Citing her earlier book *Feminist Theory: From Margin to Center*, hooks further explains her view of marginality as a site of radical possibility:

> To be in the margin is to be part of the whole but outside the main body. . . . Living as we did—on the edge—we developed a particular way of seeing reality. We looked both from the outside in and from the inside out. We focused our attention on the center as well as on the margin. We understood both. . . . This sense of wholeness . . . provided us with an oppositional worldview—a mode of seeing unknown to most of our oppressors, . . . [and] strengthened our sense of self and solidarity. (p. 149)

This view of marginality is empowering and liberating. Negotiating one's identity from the cultural margins can allow us to see things from both the center and the margins—a perspective that those who attempt to prescribe labels for us simply do not have.

Although the margins are our sites of resistance and survival, Trinh Minh-ha (1995) cautions that if we reclaim the margins "as our exclusive territory, [the oppressors] happily approve, for the divisions between margin and center should be preserved, and as clearly demarcated as possible, if the two positions are to remain intact in their power relations" (p. 216). To challenge these power relations, she calls for the work of displacement. Minh-ha further elaborates, "by displacing, it never allows this classifying world to exert its classificatory power without returning it to its own ethnocentric classifications" (p. 216). The active creation and re-creation of our own identities are acts of displacement.

Summary and Conclusions

In this essay, I have explored the political, fluid, and nonsummative nature of cultural identity. I maintain that cultural identities are co-created and re-created in interaction only when dialogue, cooperation, and communication—not prescription or identity freezing—exist between interactants. I also argue that negotiation of identity from the margins—and engaging in acts of displacement—can empower us to enter the dialogue as subjects rather than powerless objects or prescribed labels.

Notes

1. The title invokes James Clifford's (1992) notion of travel and traveling identities. Smith and Katz (1993) argue that "travelling provides a means for conceptualizing the interplay among people that are no longer so separate or inaccessible one to the other. Travel . . . suggests social, political and cultural identity as an amalgam, the intricacy of which defies the comparative simplicity of 'identity'" (p. 78). However, I do not intend to imply a "spatial essentialism"—that is, the view that multicultural identities are fixed in absolute spaces. I am suggesting quite the contrary: a landscape metaphor to indicate that "multicultural identity spaces" are fluid and constantly evolving terrains with ever changing colors, fragrances, shapes, and sizes. I dedicate this essay to my parents.

2. I am using this label to imply an integration of my three cultures. This term places all three cultures together without separation, division, or hyphenation that might imply disconnection between them. Further, I do not intend to suggest that my multicultural identity is linear and hierarchical—Asian, then Latino, and finally American—as the label might appear to indicate. Such a label is a limitation of language.

3. The term "integration" is used here to indicate union, connection, and unification. However, I do not claim that such integration is necessarily harmonious and free of tension. In fact, I argue that tension is vital in the process of self-definition, identity negotiation, and personal liberation.

References

Appiah, K. A. (1996). Identity: Political not cultural. In M. Garber, R. L. Walkowitz, & P. B. Franklin (Eds.), *Fieldwork: Sites in literary and cultural studies* (pp. 34–40). New York: Routledge.

Clifford, J. (1992). Traveling cultures. In L. Grossberg, C. Nelson, & P. Treichler (Eds.), *Cultural studies* (pp. 96–116). New York: Routledge.

Collier, M. J., & Thomas, M. (1988). Cultural identity: An interpretive perspective. *International and Intercultural Communication Annual, 12*, 99–120.

Cupach, W. R., & Imahori, T. T. (1993). Identity management theory: Communication competence in intercultural episodes and relationships. *International and Intercultural Communication Annual, 17*, 112–131.

Freire, P. (1970). *Pedagogy of the oppressed.* New York: Continuum.

Geertz, C. (1973). *The interpretation of cultures.* New York: Basic Books.

Harvey, D. (1993). Class relations, social justice and the politics of difference. In M. Keith & S. Pile (Eds.), *Place and the politics of identity* (pp. 41–66). London: Routledge.

Hecht, M. L., Collier, M. J., & Ribeau, S. A. (1993). *African American communication: Ethnic identity and cultural interpretation.* Newbury Park, CA: Sage.

hooks, b. (1990). *Yearning: Race, gender, and cultural politics.* Boston: South End Press.

Martin, J. N., & Nakayama, T. K. (1997). *Intercultural communication in contexts.* Mountain View, CA: Mayfield.

Minh-ha, T. T. (1995). No master territories. In B. Ashcroft, G. Griffiths, & H. Tiffin (Eds.), *The post-colonial studies reader* (pp. 215–218). London: Routledge.

Moraga, C. (1983). La güera. In C. Moraga & G. Anzaldúa (Eds.), *This bridge called my back: Writings by radical women of color* (pp. 27–34). New York: Kitchen Table Press.

Sarup, M. (1996). *Identity, culture and the postmodern world.* Athens, GA: University of Georgia Press.

Smith, N., & Katz, C. (1993). Grounding metaphor: Towards a spatialized politics. In M. Keith & S. Pile (Eds.), *Place and the politics of identity* (pp. 67–83). London: Routledge.

Thornton, M. C. (1992). Is multiracial status unique? The personal and social experience. In M. P. P. Root (Ed.), *Racially mixed people in America* (pp. 321–325). Newbury Park, CA: Sage.

Turner, V. (1990). Liminality and community. In J. C. Alexander & S. Seidman (Eds.), *Culture and society: Contemporary debates* (pp. 147–154). New York: Cambridge University Press.

Key Terms

cultural identity   negotiation of identity
identity freezing   otherness
liminality   power
marginality

Discussion Questions

1. Yep's essay starts with Paulo Freire's quote "[We] cannot enter the struggle as objects in order *later* to become human beings." How does the essay explain and illustrate this quote?

2. Yep suggests that we have multiple identities. What does he mean? What types of identities do you have when you are communicating with someone from the same culture? Someone from a different culture?

3. Yep observes that power is inherent in relations between groups. How is power manifested in those relationships? How is power related to "otherness"? How is power related to identity?

4. How are cultural identities co-created and re-created? Describe a communication situation in which you co-created and re-created your own identities. Describe a situation in which your identity was prescribed by the other communicator.

5. Yep presents two views of marginality. How are they similar? Different?

8 Learning to See What I Was Never Supposed to See

Becoming Chicana in a White World

JACQUELINE M. MARTINEZ

For many years, from the time I was a child until my early adulthood, I considered myself basically "White."[1] I grew up in the postal districts known as Northridge and Chatsworth, in the northwest part of the San Fernando Valley, which lies about 35 miles northwest of downtown Los Angeles. My family lived in a cozy six-bedroom ranch-style home with a three-car garage, swimming pool, large country kitchen, formal dining room, and two fireplaces. My father was a successful business executive and we lived an economically comfortable life. The idea that racial or ethnic discrimination existed in the United States was so foreign to me that I might have thought mentally unstable anyone who offered such a point of view. I find it incredibly ironic that I grew up in an era of U.S. American history when some of the most important political and social battles over racial and ethnic discrimination were fought, yet I have no memory from that time of any awareness of these issues as they were confronting us as a nation. I don't recall seeing, much less knowing, a single Hispanic, Black, or Asian among my cohorts during my elementary school years. As I was growing up from the mid-sixties to the mid-eighties in The Valley, I had every reason to naively follow along with the U.S. American cultural values of equality, individualism, future-centered thinking, and can-do pragmatism. Everything around me encouraged me to think that I was White, and that whatever social or cultural differences were carried in my family's history were irrelevant. I was raised to believe that success in life

was a matter of personal determination, that cultural history was irrelevant to my life, that the past was not important, and that learning how to be a responsible and mature individual was what growing up was all about.

Skin Color, Language, and the Markings of Difference

Despite the overwhelming presence of cultural and social messages that encouraged me to think of myself as White, there were certain signs, some subtle and some obvious, that didn't allow me to remain totally ignorant of my Mexican American cultural heritage and what that heritage signified within U.S. American culture. Perhaps the earliest and most obvious of these signs was a very simple question that I recall being posed to me: "Do you speak Spanish?" I remember being a very little girl, dressed up in Sunday clothes, standing outside the church after services, adults talking. One adult leaned down, smiled broadly, and asked me if I spoke Spanish. Always, for as long as I can remember, the question, "Do you speak Spanish," follows the Anglo-other's recognition of my surname. At first, my answers were simple: "No." But the pervasiveness of the question communicated something very important that was in direct contradiction to the messages that predominated in my "White" childhood. In the absence of ever being able to address questions concerning my Mexican American cultural identity directly, I learned that being named Martinez meant being Mexican, meant speaking Spanish. From a very young age, and without being consciously aware of it, I learned that because I didn't speak Spanish, I wasn't a real Mexican. The power of cultural messages is that they are often conveyed

---

[1] This essay is a re-presentation of many of the issues discussed in *Phenomenology of Chicana Experience and Identity*, 2000, and should be referred to for a full discussion of the social, historical, and political implications of personal history.

without any obvious source.[2] I couldn't pinpoint exactly where I got the message from, but I got it loud and clear. Real Mexicans speak Spanish and live in barrios.

My first direct social confrontation with issues of race and racism came in the mid-seventies when the Los Angeles Public School System instituted busing so that African American kids could attend schools in The Valley. I was a student at Nobel Jr. High School in Northridge. When Black students from the "inner-city" of Los Angeles (no one really cared enough to actually name the places or talk about the histories of the communities where the students came from) were bused to Nobel, we had no way to avoid the knowledge that busing was about redressing social inequities in education. But despite the obviousness of the issues, I cannot recall a single interpersonal or small group conversation concerning anything having to do with Black students being bused to our school. There were never any conversations in which we were invited to talk, or listen to our peers talk, about the experience of encountering each other. There was never any context, formally in the materials we studied in class, or informally by the way we interacted outside of class, to assist us in living through this encounter with our African American peers. The strongest memory I have is of hearing a rumor one day that there was going to be a White versus Black fight after school. The fight never materialized, but it is clear that talk of fighting was the only socially available language through which we could articulate the encounter with the Black students. Culturally, and in the absence of any other discourse, the speech of *White-to-Black* race relations is a speech of defending what is "ours," of fighting a dangerous enemy, of destroying the Other, of war. If there was a sense that it was right for the students to be bused to our school, there was never any argument made as to why it was correct. No one broached the question as to how the Los Angeles Public School System had become segregated in the first place. There was no formal or informal consideration of the economic

and political histories that result in urban racialization and ghettoization. I don't recall the history of race or ethnicity in the United States ever being a topic of study in my primary education. In the absence of these kinds of discourses, the White students responded with the racist attitudes carried in culture since the Europeans first set foot in the "new world." It is ironic that busing, seen as a partial remedy to the injustices perpetuated by racist attitudes and their accompanying racist institutional practices, becomes for the students living out the fact of busing policies, simply another place where racist divides are themselves perpetuated. I doubt that any of the students who lived in Northridge ever came to know anything personally about any of the Black students with whom we attended school. Cultural messages about race had the power to sustain themselves even when interpersonal learning was made possible by direct contact. In that time and that place, the Black students were clearly the Other, and by virtue of my not being one of them, I was White.

I was able, for the most part, to ignore issues about race and racism as it was related to my experience with African Americans. But I could not ignore those issues when I came in contact with other Mexican Americans in The Valley. I knew that the postal district of San Fernando, which was located in the northeast part of The Valley, was generally identifiable as the barrio, as "low-rider" territory where the predominantly Mexican American community was economically poor, youth were in gangs, kids were streetwise, and thus the social signs of criminality dominated. I didn't actually know that the crime rate was higher in San Fernando. Instead, I just had a clear sense—reinforced by everything in my cultural world—that this was true. Then there was also the postal district of Reseda, right next to Northridge, which we came to call "little Mexico," where I saw what I assumed were illegal aliens living crowded into one-bedroom apartments, standing on the street corners looking to deal in drugs. Of course, the easy availability of drugs in "my" part of town didn't dissuade me from believing that the drug problem was especially bad in Reseda and San Fernando—a belief encouraged within the cultural milieu in which I lived. I attended Chatsworth High School. Even the name evokes for me the sense I had unconsciously during my years there—that we

---

[2] See Reusch and Bateson (1951/1987) for a comprehensive theory concerning the relationship between cultural messages and personal perception.

were all that was right and good in the world. There were a few other Hispanics and African Americans at Chatsworth, but everything about that place discouraged any critical thinking about race, ethnicity, or cultural heritage.

It was through my high school softball team that I got my largest glimpse of those who bore the social markings of Mexican American. Our team traveled to various other high schools in The Valley, and playing at San Fernando High gave me my greatest exposure to the socially recognizable stereotypes that my family's class standing allowed me to escape. Traveling to San Fernando High forced me to ask questions about what it means to encounter people who were the more marked Mexican Americans, the ones who spoke Spanish, the low-riders, the girls with their big hair and white eyeliner, the guys with their hair slicked back and shirts buttoned at the top, sharp and ironed all the way down—the ones who came from the barrios. I felt a vague sense of commonality with these marked others, yet I encountered them through a whole series of recognized differences having to do with class, lifestyle, and language. I didn't know what zoot suit or *pocho* (a Mexican American who is too "white" or Anglicized) was. I knew these students were different from me, but not in the same way that the Black students were different. Unlike my experience with Black students, I couldn't separate myself from the students I encountered at San Fernando High.

I recall the time I was traveling with my summer league softball team to Arizona. The summer league teams were much more diverse in membership, so each team had players from all over The Valley. Our pitcher and star player, Deede, was like the marked others I had encountered at San Fernando High. Between games, several members of our team ended up in one of our motel rooms having a pillow fight. I cornered Deede, poised myself aggressively toward her, and pulled my pillow back in preparation for a full-force blow upon her. Being fairly low on the hierarchy of this team, my cornering of Deede was quite a statement of presence and power. She looked startled, but stopped my attack in its tracks by saying, "That's the Mexican in you." It was a moment that fueled the subtle recognition of my Mexican American ancestry that I had experienced all my life. Yet in all of these encounters with Mex-

ican Americans—seeing them on the street corners in Reseda and taking the school bus down to San Fernando High—I had no concrete way to pose questions about myself and them. What was my connection to them? What did these differences mean? Growing up in the environment I did, I had no way to actually ask those questions. I had no means of pursuing possible answers. Instead, they remained all around me, confronting me here and there like being tapped on the shoulder then turning to find no one there. Rooted as I was in that middle-class suburban White environment that dominated my Southern California life, these questions seemed to have a life of hovering, never real, only surreal.

Privilege Revealed

It really wasn't until I came out as a lesbian that an opening emerged through which I could think critically about what I was raised to believe. I had always been a "tomboy," but that never led me to question my heterosexuality. In fact, in my late teens I made it through two friendships—one with a woman who told me she was bisexual and she thought I might be lesbian, and another with a gay man who asked me directly if I was lesbian—with my heterosexuality firmly intact. I didn't have any negative feelings about people being gay; I just knew that it wasn't me. I dated men and had what I think were probably very typical male-female late adolescent relationships. But when I was in my early twenties, I met a woman in college, my same age, and I suddenly realized that I had a very strong sexual attraction to her. At that moment of realization, I could look back and see how I had been a lesbian all along. I knew immediately that the only thing that prevented me from discovering my lesbianism was a very powerful and pervasive set of cultural messages that precluded me from recognizing what had been within me all of my life. I began to think very critically about the social and cultural environment in which I grew up, and I began to wonder what other parts of myself had been hidden by the norms of the cultural environment in which I lived.

I began reading voraciously and thinking critically. Among the materials I read was the now famous collection of essays that deserves credit for opening the view of so many to issues of race, class, sexuality, and cultural history in the United States: *This Bridge Called My Back,* edited by two Chicana lesbians, Cherríe Moraga and Gloria Anzaldúa. Many times I had the experience of reading various essays in that book and finding them so overwhelming that I had to push myself away, take a step back and just breathe, as I felt the deeply significant ideas they were presenting reverberate throughout my body. One essay in particular, "La Güera," by Moraga, named aspects of my experience so powerfully that my so strongly conditioned identity as "White" began to tremble and break.

But what would come in its place? I didn't grow up speaking Spanish. My middle-class lifestyle allowed me to avoid knowing anything about the realities of people who grow up with Mexican cultural heritage close at hand. I didn't see any difference between my private family home life and the mainstream of U.S. American culture. I had spent much more time with my grandparents and cousins on my mother's mostly Anglo side of the family than with relatives on my father's Mexican side. Though not dark-skinned, I have inherited subtle hints of my mestizo and Native American ancestry. Even as a young girl, I could see my almond-shaped brown eyes, high cheekbones, and dark features. Like so many U.S. Americans, my family was fond of making references to "the pure-blood Tennessee Cherokee" who was my maternal grandfather's great-grandmother. It is so obvious to me now that White American interest in things "Indian" is limited only to those things that serve the interests of Euro American culture. We knew about the Cherokee in our family, the story goes, because we thought we might be entitled to some money generated by oil found on a reservation. Never did we have any interest in Native American culture, history, or the experience of this "pure-blood" ancestor of ours. I see now how insulting U.S. American culture is toward Native American cultures.

History, Memory, and the Emergence of Cultural Identity

I grew up making frequent visits to my maternal grandparents' home in Lucern Valley, in the desert of Southern California. The desert has always been a magical place of unlimited beauty for me. I saw this as a child. It was my maternal grandmother who opened this view for me. And it is she who gets the credit for allowing me to look in the mirror and see myself as not White. It wasn't that I considered myself Native American or Mexican in the cultural sense, but that I knew I was not just a White person, that I had a heritage that was of a different world than my growing-up world. This was a difference that was not always perceptible to me, and even when perceptible, not clear-cut. It also coincided with the notion I developed through my maternal grandmother that there was a spiritual power to my ancestry connected to the desert and a certain kind of magical existence that transcended the ordinary facts of my day-to-day life. My grandmother was a deeply spiritual woman, and though she often evoked the name of Jesus Christ, she was spiritual in a no-man kind of way. I never associated her spirituality with church or buildings or the image of Christ crucified. I associated her spirituality with the desert—incomprehensibly beautiful, the earth, the magic of a desert sunset. After dinner, walking with my grandmother, holding her hand as she swung her arms vigorously in front and behind her shouting for all the earth and sky to hear, "Oh, Joy, Oh Joy, Oh Joy," in a continuous refrain. My grandmother has always known that I'm an Indian. I grew up, it seems, telling her stories about my past life as an Indian. She knew my stories to be true, and she always nurtured my belief in a spirit world that lives in the earth and sky, far beyond this ordinary world we live in. Though I have no recollection of telling my grandmother these stories, the spirit world that she helped me to live in has always been so very real for me; the desert, a deeply spiritual place.

As a very young girl, I was always very proud of my name "Martinez." I knew it made me different—something to do with Mexico. In my childhood imagination it meant "great people," "proud warriors," "fighting spirit." I don't know where I got this, except from my maternal grandmother's encouragement and my father's very quiet and determined way. I began thinking about my father's life and wondering if—despite that everything about my cultural environment discouraged it—there were any traces of his Mexican American cultural heritage in my own life. He has always been mostly silent about his childhood, but one of my most prominent memories is his rare but impactful story-telling about the poverty within which he grew up. Short and to the point, left with no word to follow, his stories always confused me.

My paternal grandmother was visiting us once when I was a little girl. She was making beans and tortillas for us. As she spread the beans out on the table, carefully sorting out the chunks of dirt and small rocks from the beans, my father told me how he remembered her doing that when he was a little boy, except that as the family sat around that table sorting the dirt from the beans, they looked at all the food they had for the week. As they sat around the table, my father and his brother and sister knew that that was all the food they had.

When I was very young, we went to visit some relatives in Santa Ana, the occasion of a wedding or birthday, I think. Everyone spoke Spanish, and there were all kinds of foods I didn't recognize but saw my father eat knowingly. Mexican music, dress, and decorations were all around. Years later, my father told me how those relatives in Santa Ana used to laugh and make fun of him because his family was so poor. But after he had moved to California, worked his way through UCLA, and was earning a very good living as a corporate manager, these relatives invited him to their parties and celebrations. These stories told me that being poor, more than being Mexican, was the condition by which one suffered discrimination.

I sensed something about my father's suffering that told me it was dangerous to ask for explanations. Both he and his mother were stiff-lipped, straight-backed—we didn't talk about the past. Being poor and Mexican was something we couldn't talk about. It was something hidden, dangerous, evil. As I was growing up, I learned never to ask questions. It was only as an adult that I could begin to pose questions to my father about his own childhood and life experience. He tells me that he saw blatant discrimination as he was growing up. As kids, he and his younger brother and sister could swim in the public swimming pool on Sunday evenings only—they cleaned the pool on Monday. Certain "Anglo only" barber shops were off limits to my father and his two siblings. But he also says that the social markers he noticed most were class markers. He says that for every Anglo kid who acted in dis-

criminatory ways toward him, there were other Anglo kids who didn't. At the same time, he saw a certain disrespect for self and others carried out in the actions of some of the people around him. He says that he felt that there was more discrimination within the Mexican American community than from the Anglo community—a perception certainly encouraged by the norms of U.S. American culture.

American Dreams and the (Dangerous) Promise of Assimilation

To become "anglicized" was to have greater freedom from the negative stereotypes that hound those who come from heavily marked ethnic and racial communities where economic resources and access to education are limited. My father determined, from a very young age, I think, that his children would not have to suffer the burdens that he did. He naturally gravitated toward those opportunities that would give him greater access to economic and educational opportunities. He enlisted in the navy because the G.I. Bill would help him pay for college. He majored in business, not because of an intellectual interest, but because that would give him access to the kind of corporate management position that would allow him to provide for his family in the way he desired. And, he stopped speaking Spanish.

The American Dream of upward social mobility provides hope that if you are born poor, you do not have to remain poor, that your children might be better off than you were. Hope is an important thing. If you believe in the dream, believe in yourself, manage to get education, and have a good bit of luck, you may indeed find yourself advancing up the socioeconomic scale of U.S. American society. Yet this is just one scenario of how the American Dream works. There is a sinister side as well. The mere existence of the dream legitimates that there will always be those who have not achieved it; it authorizes the notion that those who have not made it up the socioeconomic scale deserve to be at the bottom. And it removes social accountability to even the most horrifically poor, destitute, and socially isolated communities within society. The pervasiveness of the American Dream in the psyche of

U.S. American culture creates a whole series of double binds for those living in poverty, with poor education, surrounded by the most virulent racist stereotyping and the inevitably self-deflating encounters with mainstream U.S. American culture. In this way, the American Dream authorizes the existence of incapacitated communities where life is defined by fighting daily battles for basic survival. In such an environment, the simple but profound achievement of one's sense of personal human dignity becomes a crucial measure of success, albeit a success unrecognized within the narrow terms of the American Dream. I am the daughter of a man who, thanks to his parents' own sense of human dignity, made it out of poverty's often deadening grip on self-respect, and who was then fortunate enough to make it out of the economic conditions that keep people locked into chronically impoverished and otherwise constrained communities.

My father's determination to succeed directed him into the belly of an Anglo world. He became fully integrated into the Anglo world because that was where the possibilities for success lay. Although fully bilingual as a child, my father's movement into the Anglo world closed the space for his Mexican-mestizo cultural difference to be explicitly embraced or carried to his children. This aspect of my family heritage points to the essential racism of an assimilationist culture. People who are marked as a racial Other are encouraged to transcend racial discrimination and prove themselves within the false universal proposed by the dominant culture. Upon so doing, the dominant culture points to the successfully assimilated as an example that others should follow. The fact that such success results in the erasure of the racialized Other's cultural difference is barely noticed by the dominant culture, and never actually called into question as a violence perpetuated against people and their histories.

Becoming Chicana

It has been through a process of interrogating the very terms and conditions though which I was discouraged from considering myself anything other than White, that I have finally come to a place where I can embrace myself as a Chicana. I have dedicated myself personally, and as a professional academic, to understanding how race, ethnicity, and cultural history are and are not respected within the mainstream of U.S. American culture. I have forged connections with women from other non-White racial and ethnic backgrounds, and I have participated in dialogues with people of all backgrounds on these very important issues confronting U.S. American culture and society. Even still, I encounter many perplexing situations in my everyday life. I find that I am often "Whited" by acquaintances and colleagues who assume that because I lack many of the stereotypical signs of Mexican American, that I am a fully assimilated White person. Such circumstances are always uncomfortable for me and leave me in a bit of a quandary. What do I say? Do I insist that they recognize me as a Chicana and a woman of color? If I do, I end up becoming the subject of the conversation and I am put in the uncomfortable position of either trying to make myself fit their stereotype by talking barrio Spanglish (impossible for me to do, although I am sure they are expecting it) or having to explain exactly how I consider myself a Chicana. It is a no-win situation for me. There is a kind of racism that gets expressed in these circumstances, but it is not the kind of racism that we normally expect. The ironic part is that despite their (especially White "progressive" feminists) assertions of support on issues of racism, they themselves are unwilling to hear the critiques I make with regard to their own thinking, speaking, and acting. I am all too aware that I've been tokenized for my name and have therefore served the interests of White racism. I have found that many White "progressive" feminists get especially upset when I refuse to support the interests of White racism.

I went to graduate school and became a professor in large part so that I could live those parts of myself that have been erased within the mainstream of U.S. American culture. All of my studies, my reading, writing, and speaking are part of that effort to gain access to those parts of my cultural heritage that have been erased in my life, and to create space for others who experience similar erasures. This is not an abstract effort—it is a concrete effort of struggle in which I engage every day. Yet, in my own experience, there are very few White academics working on issues related to race and racism who are actually interested in and capable of addressing these issues as they emerge in our daily interactions as teachers and colleagues. The classroom spaces for discussions of these sorts are therefore even more limited. And this at a time when there is nothing that we need more. I have spent most of my life trying to become smarter about racism and cultural erasure in the hope that I may be part of a successful effort to counter the very powerful social norms of U.S. American culture that would have all of us become "White-washed" and ignorant of the complex histories of the non-Europeans who have been so central to the building of this country. Here is where I find a rarely recognized violence perpetuated against racial and ethnic minorities in the United States: In large part, the United States is the country and culture it is because of the many Native, Mexican, and African Americans who have been a part of it forever. Yet rarely do any of us get beyond the deeply powerful messages of mainstream U.S. American culture that homogenizes our complex histories, and actually come to know and appreciate how the presence of so many different people from so many different cultural backgrounds has enriched our culture and heritage. It is time that we all begin to reflect on the ways in which U.S. American culture has made us ignorant of the lives of so many people and how it continues to encourage us to erase the histories of those of us who are non-White.

References

Martinez, J. M. (2000). *Phenomenology of Chicana experience and identity: Communication and transformation in praxis.* Lanham, MD: Rowman and Littlefield Press.

Moraga, C. (1983). "La güera." In C. Moraga & G. Anzaldúa (Eds.), *This bridge called my back: Writings by radical women of color* (pp. 27–34). New York: Kitchen Table: Women of Color Press.

Moraga, C., and G. Anzaldúa. (1983). *This bridge called my back: Writings by radical women of color.* New York: Kitchen Table: Women of Color Press.

Ruesch, J., & G. Bateson. (1987). *Communication: The social matrix of psychiatry.* New York: W. W. Norton & Company. (Original work published 1951).

Key Terms

American Dream	Mexican American
Chicana	race
identity	racism

Discussion Questions

1. Martinez identifies equality, individuality, future-centered thinking, and can-do pragmatism as central to U.S. American culture. How do these cultural ideals affect her coming to know about her Mexican American cultural heritage?

2. How does Martinez illustrate the power of cultural messages to dominate even when there are opportunities for direct communication among peers?

3. How is sexuality important in Martinez's process of "becoming Chicana"?

4. What is the relationship between Martinez's Native American and Mexican American cultural heritage? What role does each play in her "becoming a Chicana"?

5. Martinez says that U.S. American culture is insulting to Native American cultures. How so?

6. How does the American Dream figure into Martinez's process of "becoming Chicana"?

Activities for Skill Development

1. Social Identity Awareness

Adapted from an activity in Bailey W. Jackson's Social Issues in Education class, under the aegis of the Social Issues Training Project (now the Social Justice Education Project). Dr. Jackson is currently the Dean of the School of Education at the University of Massachusetts at Amherst.

As a class, generate a list of social group categories, such as gender, race, and economic class. Individually, list these on a sheet of paper and add any others that you find personally important to the way you see yourself and are treated in society. Then, for each category, identify your own avowed identity, and to what extent, or in what situations, each identity gives you power in society. Next, reflect on the following questions and discuss them with a partner:

- Which identities are you most aware of on a day-to-day basis? Why?
- Which ones are visible to others? Are there any that others misattribute to you?
- Which, if any, have you chosen, and which ones might change over time?
- Which ones give you a strong sense of self, pride, or community?
- Are there any that make you ashamed? That make you angry about the way members of your group are treated by others?
- If possible, identify one social group you belong to that gives you power in society, and one that does not. For each one, try to remember the first time you became aware that (a) you were a member of that group, and (b) there were others who were different from you.

2. Interaction with Others: How Diverse Is Your Life?

Developed by Gene Richardson, a volunteer facilitator for the "Tempe Talks" diversity dialogue program, Tempe, Arizona. Used by permission of Mr. Richardson.

Between class sessions, observe the people with whom you interact on a daily basis. With whom do you live, work, attend class, and socialize? Who else do you greet in your neighborhood or residence hall? With whom do you interact while shopping, exercising, going out to eat, and attending to other weekly tasks or events? Keep a log of the people you greet, including the following information about each person:

- role/relationship to you
- race/ethnicity
- age
- gender
- any other visible social identities

What do you notice about the diversity of your network? Are you satisfied with it, or would you like to expand it? How might you go about diversifying your social network?

3. Let's Go Swimming

Alternatives to Violence Project (1982). *Manual, Second Level Course.* New York: Alternatives to Violence Project, Inc.

As a class, divide into three groups: testers, waders, and plungers, according to which label best characterizes you. Once in your groups, make lists of attributes that you would assign to each group, including your own. Then describe how you think members of the other groups might describe you. Once all three groups are finished, share your perceptions of each group. Then compare assumptions you had about each of the other groups' perceptions. Discuss together

- Where do stereotypes come from? How are they disseminated and perpetuated?
- What effects do they have on communication? On identity?

Web Sites

1. Go to <http://www.aclu.org> and explore some of the civil rights issues and related court cases addressed by the American Civil Liberties Union. How do these controversies reflect intercultural relations in the United States?

2. Who are "Irish Americans"? Why did the Irish come to America? Find answers to these questions, as well as information about genealogy, Irish music, and famous Irish Americans at "The Irish in America: Long Journey Home," <http://www.pbs.org/wgbh/pages/irish/>.

3. What is biracial identity? Check out *<http://www.geocities.com/Athens/Oracle/1103/>* for definitions, statistics, and legal issues regarding interracial marriage, adoption, and other related topics.

Additional Readings

1. Anzaldúa, G. (1990). La conciencia de la mestiza: Towards a new consciousness. In G. Anzaldúa (Ed.), *Making face, making soul/Haciendo caras* (pp. 377–389). San Francisco: Aunt Lute Books.

2. Edelman, S. M. (2000). To pass or not to pass, that is the question: Jewish cultural identity in the United States. In M. W. Lustig & J. Koester (Eds.), *AmongUS: Essays on identity, belonging, and intercultural competence* (pp. 33–40). New York: Longman.

3. Tanno, D. (2000). Names, narratives, and the evolution of ethnic identity. In A. González, M. Houston, & V. Chen (Eds.), *Our voices: Essays in culture, ethnicity, and communication* (pp. 25–28). Los Angeles: Roxbury.

PART THREE

History and Intercultural Communication

Many different kinds of histories influence intercultural communication. Asking parents and grandparents about family history and origin is one way that people come to understand who they are. Another basis for cultural identity comes from the ways in which different cultural groups understand the past. Think about what significance the Holocaust, Hiroshima and Nagasaki, the O. J. Simpson trial, the Oklahoma bombing, or the Stonewall incident has for different cultural groups. In what ways are these historical events important in the construction and maintenance of various cultural identities?

Intercultural communication experts have only recently focused on how history influences intercultural interaction. Yet, we know that any historical event can have many different interpretations and meanings for many different cultural groups. These various interpretations have important implications for understanding cultural group identity and intercultural communication. Collective memories and cultural interpretations of history are central in our understanding of cultural differences in attitudes, beliefs, values, and behaviors. For example, events such as the Gulf War have no single meaning across cultures, but instead have different cultural and historic accounts. What was seen by many U.S. Americans as a victory against a demented tyrant was seen by people of Iraq and many other countries as a valiant struggle of a little country (Iraq) against a powerful and strong aggressor (the United States). These different perceptions influence communication between Americans and Iraqis is at a very individual level.

In addition to recognizing the multiple meanings of historical events, it is also important to recognize the need for broader knowledge of global histories. We can no longer afford to ignore the histories of any place or people.

As we see more signs of the technological global village, we realize the limitations of our historic knowledge. In order to understand intercultural communication, we must understand more about the various ways in which different cultural groups in the present understand the past.

This part of the book is not intended to give a comprehensive understanding of the past; instead, it is designed to help us see how we might think about the past. The essays expand our knowledge of history and its implications for intercultural communication. They address both the idea of competing histories and the gaps in knowledge of history.

The first three essays focus on the intersection of domestic and international histories. In "Stranger in the Village," writer James Baldwin recounts his experience of living in a tiny Swiss village whose inhabitants had never seen an African American before. He uses this experience to explore the unique historical contexts of race relations in the United States. He points out that the United States, unlike Europe, was founded on the oppression of Africans and that the histories and destinies of African Americans and Whites in the United States are inextricably intertwined. Baldwin explores how these histories present challenges and opportunities for intercultural communication among all peoples of the United States.

"Crossing an Irish Border" is about Irish Americans, cultural identity, illegal immigration, and sexual difference. In this essay, Frederick C. Corey uses the metaphor of the border as a way of examining social and personal territory. Like many European Americans in the United States, his family has an unclear understanding of how they came here. He questions his own family's telling of their history and his own relationship to Ireland and the United States.

In "Migrations across Generations," Kathleen Wong(Lau) examines how Asian American immigrants sometimes retain an identity from the host country over generations that bears little relationship to contemporary life in the "old country." She explores how this "imagined community" and the heterogeneity in the Asian American community affects communication across generations. She points out that immigrant identity can only be understood in relationship to historical, economic, and political forces.

The final essay focuses on the impact of conflicting interethnic histories in an international context—Turks and Greeks in Cyprus. In "Views from the Other Side," Benjamin J. Broome recounts how the contrasting Greek- and Turkish-Cypriot perspectives and history reveal the dynamic relationship between external forces of media and family influences and the personal fears and ideas about the conflict. From his own extensive experience and ethnographic research, he provides background to understand the importance of history in understanding contemporary conflicts and in determining the future for Cyprus.

9 Stranger in the Village

JAMES BALDWIN

From all available evidence no black man had ever set foot in this tiny Swiss village before I came. I was told before arriving that I would probably be a "sight" for the village; I took this to mean that people of my complexion were rarely seen in Switzerland, and also that city people are always something of a "sight" outside of the city. It did not occur to me—possibly because I am an American—that there could be people anywhere who had never seen a Negro.

It is a fact that cannot be explained on the basis of the inaccessibility of the village. The village is very high, but it is only four hours from Milan and three hours from Lausanne. It is true that it is virtually unknown. Few people making plans for a holiday would elect to come here. On the other hand, the villagers are able, presumably, to come and go as they please—which they do: to another town at the foot of the mountain, with a population of approximately five thousand, the nearest place to see a movie or go to the bank. In the village there is no movie house, no bank, no library, no theater; very few radios, one jeep, one station wagon; and, at the moment, one typewriter, mine, an invention which the woman next door to me here had never seen. There are about six hundred people living here, all Catholic—I conclude this from the fact that the Catholic church is open all year round, whereas the Protestant chapel, set off on a hill a little removed from the village, is open only in the summertime when the tourists arrive. There are four or five hotels, all closed now, and four or five *bistros,* of which, however, only two do any business during the winter. These two do not do a great deal, for life in the village seems to end around nine or ten o'clock. There are a few stores, butcher, baker, *épicerie,* a hardware store, and a money-changer—who cannot change travelers' checks, but must send them down to the bank, an operation which takes two or three days. There is something called the *Ballet Haus,* closed in the winter and used for God knows what, certainly not ballet, during the summer. There

seems to be only one schoolhouse in the village, and this for the quite young children; I suppose this to mean that their older brothers and sisters at some point descend from these mountains in order to complete their education—possibly, again, to the town just below. The landscape is absolutely forbidding, mountains towering on all four sides, ice and snow as far as the eye can reach. In this white wilderness, men and women and children move all day, carrying washing, wood, buckets of milk or water, sometimes skiing on Sunday afternoons. All week long boys and young men are to be seen shoveling snow off the rooftops, or dragging wood down from the forest in sleds.

The village's only real attraction, which explains the tourist season, is the hot spring water. A disquietingly high proportion of these tourists are cripples, or semicripples, who come year after year—from other parts of Switzerland, usually—to take the waters. This lends the village, at the height of the season, a rather terrifying air of sanctity, as though it were a lesser Lourdes. There is often something beautiful, there is always something awful, in the spectacle of a person who has lost one of his faculties, a faculty he never questioned until it was gone, and who struggles to recover it. Yet people remain people, on crutches or indeed on deathbeds; and wherever I passed, the first summer I was here, among the native villagers or among the lame, a wind passed with me—of astonishment, curiosity, amusement, and outrage. That first summer I stayed two weeks and never intended to return. But I did return in the winter, to work; the village offers, obviously, no distractions whatever and has the further advantage of being extremely cheap. Now it is winter again, a year later, and I am here again. Everyone in the village knows my name, though they scarcely ever use it, knows that I come from America—though, this, apparently, they will never really believe: black men come from Africa—and everyone knows that I am the friend of the son of a woman who was born here, and that I am staying in their chalet. But I remain as much a stranger today as I was the first day I arrived, and the children shout *Neger! Neger!* as I walk along the streets.

It must be admitted that in the beginning I was far too shocked to have any real reaction. In so far as I reacted at all, I reacted by trying to be pleasant—it being a great part of the American Negro's education (long before he goes to school) that he must make people "like" him. This smile-and-the-world-smiles-with-you routine worked about as well in this situation as it had in the situation for which it was designed, which is to say that it did not work at all. No one, after all, can be liked whose human weight and complexity cannot be, or has not been, admitted. My smile was simply another unheard-of phenomenon which allowed them to see my teeth—they did not, really, see my smile and I began to think that, should I take to snarling, no one would notice any difference. All of the physical characteristics of the Negro which had caused me, in America, a very different and almost forgotten pain were nothing less than miraculous—or infernal—in the eyes of the village people. Some thought my hair was the color of tar, that it had the texture of wire, or the texture of cotton. It was jocularly suggested that I might let it all grow long and make myself a winter coat. If I sat in the sun for more than five minutes some daring creature was certain to come along and gingerly put his fingers on my hair, as though he were afraid of an electric shock, or put his hand on my hand, astonished that the color did not rub off. In all of this, in which it must be conceded there was the charm of genuine wonder and in which there was certainly no element of intentional unkindness, there was yet no suggestion that I was human: I was simply a living wonder.

I knew that they did not mean to be unkind, and I know it now; it is necessary, nevertheless, for me to repeat this to myself each time that I walk out of the chalet. The children who shout *Neger!* have no way of knowing the echoes this sound raises in me. They are brimming with good humor and the more daring swell with pride when I stop to speak with them. Just the same, there are days when I cannot pause and smile, when I have no heart to play with them; when, indeed, I mutter sourly to myself, exactly as I muttered on the streets of a city these children

have never seen, when I was no bigger than these children are now: *Your* mother *was a nigger.* Joyce is right about history being a nightmare—but it may be the nightmare from which no one *can* awaken. People are trapped in history and history is trapped in them.

There is a custom in the village—I am told it is repeated in many villages—of "buying" African natives for the purpose of converting them to Christianity. There stands in the church all year round a small box with a slot for money, decorated with a black figurine, and into this box the villagers drop their francs. During the *carnaval* which precedes Lent, two village children have their faces blackened—out of which bloodless darkness their blue eyes shine like ice—and fantastic horsehair wigs are placed on their blond heads; thus disguised, they solicit among the villagers for money for the missionaries in Africa. Between the box in the church and the blackened children, the village "bought" last year six or eight African natives. This was reported to me with pride by the wife of one of the *bistro* owners and I was careful to express astonishment and pleasure at the solicitude shown by the village for the souls of black folk. The *bistro* owner's wife beamed with a pleasure far more genuine than my own and seemed to feel that I might now breathe more easily concerning the souls of at least six of my kinsmen.

I tried not to think of these so lately baptized kinsmen, of the price paid for them, or the peculiar price they themselves would pay, and said nothing about my father, who having taken his own conversion too literally never, at bottom, forgave the white world (which he described as heathen) for having saddled him with a Christ in whom, to judge at least from their treatment of him, they themselves no longer believed. I thought of white men arriving for the first time in an African village, strangers there, as I am a stranger here, and tried to imagine the astounded populace touching their hair and marveling at the color of their skin. But there is a great difference between being the first white man to be seen by Africans and being the first black man to be seen by whites. The white man takes the astonishment as tribute, for he arrives to conquer and to convert the natives, whose inferiority in relation to himself is not even to be questioned; whereas I, without a thought of conquest, find myself among a people whose culture controls me, has even, in a sense, created me, people who have cost me more in anguish and rage than they will ever know, who yet do not even know of my existence. The astonishment with which I might have greeted them, should they have stumbled into my African village a few hundred years ago, might have rejoiced their hearts. But the astonishment with which they greet me today can only poison mine.

And this is so despite everything I may do to feel differently, despite my friendly conversations with the *bistro* owner's wife, despite their three-year-old son who has at last become my friend, despite the *saluts* and *bonsoirs* which I exchange with people as I walk, despite the fact that I know that no individual can be taken to task for what history is doing, or has done. I say that the culture of these people controls me—but they can scarcely be held responsible for European culture. America comes out of Europe, but these people have never seen America, nor have most of them seen more of Europe than the hamlet at the foot of their mountain. Yet they move with an authority which I shall never have; and they regard me, quite rightly, not only as a stranger in their village but as a suspect late-comer, bearing no credentials, to everything they have—however unconsciously—inherited.

For this village, even were it incomparably more remote and incredibly more primitive, is the West, the West onto which I have been so strangely grafted. These people cannot be, from the point of view of power, strangers anywhere in the world; they have made the modern world, in effect, even if they do not know it. The most illiterate among them is related, in a way that I am not, to Dante, Shakespeare, Michelangelo, Aeschylus, Da Vinci, Rembrandt, and Racine; the cathedral at Chartres says something to them which it cannot say to me, as indeed would New York's Empire State Building, should anyone here ever see it. Out of their hymns and dances come Beethoven and Bach. Go back a few centuries and they are in their full glory—but I am in Africa, watching the conquerors arrive.

The rage of the disesteemed is personally fruitless, but it is also absolutely inevitable; this rage, so generally discounted, so little understood even among the people whose daily bread it is, is one of the things that makes history. Rage can only with difficulty, and never entirely, be brought under the domination of the intelligence and is therefore not susceptible to any arguments whatever. This is a fact which ordinary representatives of the *Herrenvolk,* having never felt this rage and being unable to imagine it, quite fail to understand. Also, rage cannot be hidden, it can only be dissembled. This dissembling deludes the thoughtless, and strengthens rage and adds, to rage, contempt. There are, no doubt, as many ways of coping with the resulting complex of tensions as there are black men in the world, but no black man can hope ever to be entirely liberated from this internal warfare—rage, dissembling, and contempt having inevitably accompanied his first realization of the power of white men. What is crucial here is that, since white men represent in the black man's world so heavy a weight, white men have for black men a reality which is far from being reciprocal; and hence all black men have toward all white men an attitude which is designed, really, either to rob the white man of the jewel of his naïveté, or else to make it cost him dear.

The black man insists, by whatever means he finds at his disposal, that the white man cease to regard him as an exotic rarity and recognize him as a human being. This is a very charged and difficult moment, for there is a great deal of will power involved in the white man's naïveté. Most people are not naturally reflective any more than they are naturally malicious, and the white man prefers to keep the black man at a certain human remove because it is easier for him thus to preserve his simplicity and avoid being called to account for crimes committed by his forefathers, or his neighbors. He is inescapably aware, nevertheless, that he is in a better position in the world than black men are, nor can he quite put to death the suspicion that he is hated by black men therefore. He does not wish to be hated, neither does he wish to change places, and at this point in his uneasiness he can scarcely avoid having recourse to those legends which white men have created about black men, the most usual effect of which is that the white man finds himself enmeshed, so to speak, in his own language which describes hell, as well as the attributes which lead one to hell, as being as black as night.

Every legend, moreover, contains its residuum of truth, and the root function of language is to control the universe by describing it. It is of quite considerable significance that black men remain, in the imagination, and in overwhelming numbers in fact, beyond the disciplines of salvation; and this despite the fact that the West has been "buying" African natives for centuries. There is, I should hazard, an instantaneous necessity to be divorced from this so visibly unsaved stranger, in whose heart, moreover, one cannot guess what dreams of vengeance are being nourished; and, at the same time, there are few things on earth more attractive than the idea of the unspeakable liberty which is allowed the unredeemed. When, beneath the black mask, a human being begins to make himself felt one cannot escape a certain awful wonder as to what kind of human being it is. What one's imagination makes of other people is dictated, of course, by the laws of one's own personality and it is one of the ironies of black-white relations that, by means of what the white man imagines the black man to be, the black man is enabled to know who the white man is.

I have said, for example, that I am as much a stranger in this village today as I was the first summer I arrived, but this is not quite true. The villagers wonder less about the texture of my hair than they did then, and wonder rather more about me. And the fact that their wonder now exists on another level is reflected in their attitudes and in their eyes. There are the children who make those delightful, hilarious, sometimes astonishingly grave overtures of friendship in the unpredictable fashion of children; other children, having been taught that the devil is a black man, scream in genuine anguish as I approach. Some of the older women never pass without a friendly greeting, never pass, indeed, if it seems that they will be able to engage me in conversation; other women look down or look away or rather contemptuously smirk. Some of the men drink with me and suggest that I learn how to ski— partly, I gather, because they cannot imagine what I would look like on skis—and want to know if I am married, and ask questions about my *métier*. But some of the men have accused *le sale nègre*— behind

my back—of stealing wood and there is already in the eyes of some of them that peculiar, intent, paranoiac malevolence which one sometimes surprises in the eyes of American white men when, out walking with their Sunday girl, they see a Negro male approach.

There is a dreadful abyss between the streets of this village and the streets of the city in which I was born, between the children who shout *Neger!* today and those who shouted *Nigger!* yesterday—the abyss is experience, the American experience. The syllable hurled behind me today expresses, above all, wonder: I am a stranger here. But I am not a stranger in America and the same syllable riding on the American air expresses the war my presence has occasioned in the American soul.

For this village brings home to me this fact: that there was a day, and not really a very distant day, when Americans were scarcely Americans at all but discontented Europeans, facing a great unconquered continent and strolling, say, into a marketplace and seeing black men for the first time. The shock this spectacle afforded is suggested, surely, by the promptness with which they decided that these black men were not really men but cattle. It is true that the necessity on the part of the settlers of the New World of reconciling their moral assumptions with the fact—and the necessity—of slavery enhanced immensely the charm of this idea, and it is also true that this idea expresses, with a truly American bluntness, the attitude which to varying extents all masters have had toward all slaves.

But between all former slaves and slave-owners and the drama which begins for Americans over three hundred years ago at Jamestown, there are at least two differences to be observed. The American Negro slave could not suppose, for one thing, as slaves in past epochs had supposed and often done, that he would ever be able to wrest the power from his master's hands. This was a supposition which the modern era, which was to bring about such vast changes in the aims and dimensions of power, put to death; it only begins, in unprecedented fashion, and with dreadful implications, to be resurrected today. But even had this supposition persisted with undiminished force, the American Negro slave could not have used it to lend his condition dignity, for the reason that this supposition rests on another: that the slave in exile yet remains related to his past, has some means—if only in memory—of revering and sustaining the forms of his former life, is able, in short, to maintain his identity.

This was not the case with the American Negro slave. He is unique among the black men of the world in that his past was taken from him, almost literally, at one blow. One wonders what on earth the first slave found to say to the first dark child he bore. I am told that there are Haitians able to trace their ancestry back to African kings, but any American Negro wishing to go back so far will find his journey through time abruptly arrested by the signature on the bill of sale which served as the entrance paper for his ancestor. At the time—to say nothing of the circumstances—of the enslavement of the captive black man who was to become the American Negro, there was not the remotest possibility that he would ever take power from his master's hands. There was no reason to suppose that his situation would ever change, nor was there, shortly, anything to indicate that his situation had ever been different. It was his necessity, in the words of E. Franklin Frazier, to find a "motive for living under American culture or die." The identity of the American Negro comes out of this extreme situation, and the evolution of this identity was a source of the most intolerable anxiety in the minds and the lives of his masters.

For the history of the American Negro is unique also in this: that the question of his humanity, and of his rights therefore as a human being, became a burning one for several generations of Americans, so burning a question that it ultimately became one of those used to divide the nation. It is out of this argument that the venom of the epithet *Nigger!* is derived. It is an argument which Europe has never had, and hence Europe quite sincerely fails to understand how or why the argument arose in the first place, why its effects are so frequently disastrous and always so unpredictable, why it refuses until today to be entirely settled. Europe's black possessions remained—and do remain—in Europe's colonies, at which remove they represented no threat whatever to European identity. If they posed any problem at all for the European conscience, it was a problem which remained comfortably abstract: in effect, the black man, *as a man,* did not exist for Europe. But in America, even as a slave, he was an inescapable part of the general social fabric and no American could escape having an attitude toward him. Americans attempt until today to make an abstraction of the Negro, but the very nature of these abstractions reveals the tremendous effects the presence of the Negro has had on the American character.

When one considers the history of the Negro in America it is of the greatest importance to recognize that the moral beliefs of a person, or a people, are never really as tenuous as life—which is not moral—very often causes them to appear; these create for them a frame of reference and a necessary hope, the hope being that when life has done its worst they will be enabled to rise above themselves and to triumph over life. Life would scarcely be bearable if this hope did not exist. Again, even when the worst has been said, to betray a belief is not by any means to have put oneself beyond its power; the betrayal of a belief is not the same thing as ceasing to believe. If this were not so there would be no moral standards in the world at all. Yet one must also recognize that morality is based on ideas and that all ideas are dangerous—dangerous because ideas can only lead to action and where the action leads no man can say. And dangerous in this respect: that confronted with the impossibility of remaining faithful to one's beliefs, and the equal impossibility of becoming free of them, one can be driven to the most inhuman excesses. The ideas on which American beliefs are based are not, though Americans often seem to think so, ideas which originated in America. They came out of Europe. And the establishment of democracy on the American continent was scarcely as radical a break with the past as was the necessity, which Americans faced, of broadening this concept to include black men.

This was, literally, a hard necessity. It was impossible, for one thing, for Americans to abandon their beliefs, not only because these beliefs alone seemed able to justify the sacrifices they had endured and the blood that they had spilled, but also because these beliefs afforded them their only bulwark against a moral chaos as absolute as the physical chaos of the continent it was their destiny to conquer. But in the situation in which Americans found themselves, these beliefs threatened an idea which, whether or not one likes to think so, is the very warp and woof of the heritage of the West, the idea of white supremacy.

Americans have made themselves notorious by the shrillness and the brutality with which they have insisted on this idea, but they did not invent it; and it has escaped the world's notice that those very excesses of which Americans have been guilty imply a certain, unprecedented uneasiness over the idea's life and power, if not, indeed, the idea's validity. The idea of white supremacy rests simply on the fact that white men are the creators of civilization (the present civilization, which is the only one that matters; all previous civilizations are simply "contributions" to our own) and are therefore civilization's guardians and defenders. Thus it was impossible for Americans to accept the black man as one of themselves, for to do so was to jeopardize their status as white men. But not so to accept him was to deny his human reality, his human weight and complexity, and the strain of denying the overwhelmingly undeniable forced Americans into rationalizations so fantastic that they approached the pathological.

At the root of the American Negro problem is the necessity of the American white man to find a way of living with the Negro in order to be able to live with himself. And the history of this problem can be reduced to the means used by Americans— lynch law and law, segregation and legal acceptance, terrorization and concession—either to come to terms with this necessity, or to find a way around it, or (most usually) to find a way of doing both these things at once. The resulting spectacle, at once foolish and dreadful, led someone to make the quite accurate observation that "the Negro-in-America is a form of insanity which overtakes white men."

In this long battle, a battle by no means finished, the unforeseeable effects of which will be felt by many future generations, the white man's motive was the protection of his identity; the black man was motivated by the need to establish an identity. And despite the terrorization which the Negro in America endured and endures sporadically until today, despite the cruel and totally inescapable ambivalence of his status in his country, the battle for his identity has long ago been won. He is not a visitor to the West, but a citizen there, an American; as American as the Americans who despise him, the Americans who fear him, the Americans who love him—the Americans who became less than themselves, or rose to be greater than themselves by virtue of the fact that the challenge he represented was inescapable. He is perhaps the only black man in the world whose relationship to white men is more terrible, more subtle, and more meaningful than the relationship of bitter possessed to uncertain possessor. His survival depended, and his development depends, on his ability to turn his peculiar status in the Western world to his own advantage and, it may be, to the very great advantage of that world. It remains for him to fashion out of his experience that which will give him sustenance, and a voice.

The cathedral at Chartres, I have said, says something to the people of this village which it cannot say to me; but it is important to understand that this cathedral says something to me which it cannot say to them. Perhaps they are struck by the power of the spires, the glory of the windows; but they have known God, after all, longer than I have known him, and in a different way, and I am terrified by the slippery bottomless well to be found in the crypt, down which heretics were hurled to death, and by the obscene, inescapable gargoyles jutting out of the stone and seeming to say that God and the devil can never be divorced. I doubt that the villagers think of the devil when they face a cathedral because they have never been identified with the devil. But I must accept the status which myth, if nothing else, gives me in the West before I can hope to change the myth.

Yet, if the American Negro has arrived at his identity by virtue of the absoluteness of his estrangement from his past, American white men still nourish the illusion that there is some means of recovering the European innocence, of returning to a state in which black men do not exist. This is one of the greatest errors Americans can make. The identity they fought so hard to protect has, by virtue of that battle, undergone a change: Americans are as unlike any other white people in the world as it is possible to be. I do not think, for example, that it is too much to suggest that the American vision of the world—which allows so little reality, generally speaking, for any of the darker forces in human life, which tends until today to paint moral issues in glaring black and white—owes a great deal to the battle waged by Americans to maintain between themselves and black men a human separation which could not be bridged. It is only now beginning to be borne in on us—very faintly, it must be admitted, very slowly, and very much against our will—that this vision of the world is dangerously inaccurate, and perfectly useless. For it protects our moral highmindedness at the terrible expense of weakening our grasp of reality. People who shut their eyes to reality simply invite their own destruction, and anyone who insists on remaining in a state of innocence long after that innocence is dead turns himself into a monster.

The time has come to realize that the interracial drama acted out on the American continent has not only created a new black man, it has created a new white man, too. No road whatever will lead Americans back to the simplicity of this European village where white men still have the luxury of looking on me as a stranger. I am not, really, a stranger any longer for any American alive. One of the things that distinguishes Americans from other people is that no other people has ever been so deeply involved in the lives of black men, and vice versa. This fact faced, with all its implications, it can be seen that the history of the American Negro problem is not merely shameful, it is also something of an achievement. For even when the worst has been said, it must also be added that the perpetual challenge posed by this problem was always, somehow, perpetually met. It is precisely this black-white experience which may prove of indispensable value to us in the world we face today. This world is white no longer, and it will never be white again.

Key Terms

Africa	rage
America/American	slavery/slaves
Black/negro	stranger
Europe	West, the
history	White (man, people)
identity	

Discussion Questions

1. What exactly does Baldwin mean by the phrase "Stranger in the Village"? Have you ever experienced that feeling of strangeness? When? Where?

2. In much intercultural literature, there is talk that as a world, we are moving toward a "global village." What does Baldwin's essay tell us about our progress toward that global village?

3. As Baldwin recounts his experiences of strangeness, he notes that the people in the village did not mean to be unkind even when the children shouted *"Neger!"* and when people suggested he let his hair grow long and make it into a coat. And yet, as he tells the story, he is also clear about the fact that he did feel pain, in spite of the intentions of the villagers. This question of the role of intentionality persists in intercultural communication. How can we reconcile misunderstandings across cultures that are not intentional? Or, do we need to?

4. According to Baldwin, how has U.S. history shaped Blackness and Black identity? What does Baldwin's essay tell us about the influence of history on today's daily experiences?

5. How are Baldwin's experiences of his identity as an African American man in the United States different from his experiences as a Black man in the Swiss village? How do the different historical experiences in Switzerland and the United States affect his different sense of himself and his different experiences of being Black?

10 Crossing an Irish Border

FREDERICK C. COREY

In 1967 I was confirmed under the name of Joseph. This name was not my choice. We were at a Holy Confirmation rehearsal, in a combined class of fourth- and fifth-grade boys, and my brother Bob and I were in line. Sister Mary Stevens announced that today we would practice with our names. I raised my hand, and when called upon, I said, "Sister, I have not yet selected my Holy Confirmation name." "Well, blow me down said Popeye," Sister bellowed. "How many of you have not yet selected a name?" A slew of us raised our hands, and Sister was aghast. She swung her arm and marched down the aisle, pointing to each of us in succession, "John. Joseph. John. Joseph," until she reached the end. My brother Bob became John. The names lacked distinction. My oldest brother's name is John Joseph. He was confirmed during the era of the Singing Nun, and he selected Dominique.

Joseph. I never intended to be Joseph, just as I never intended to work "in the field." I was trained as a literary critic. I can scan a poem with the best of them, excavate a metaphor, and trace a symbol to its rhizome. I took an interest in fieldwork when, on my first sabbatical, I decided to conduct an ethnographic study of gay men in Irish pubs (Corey, 1996). I am still intrigued by the metaphor of "fieldwork": the comparison between research and the earth, between a cultural space and a pasture suitable for tillage. The metaphor appears to have its roots in farming. The researcher enters the field to see how things grow, develop, endure a life cycle. The metaphor has its limits, though, for fieldwork does not always embody the simplicity, serenity, or charm so often associated with pastoral life. Joseph, quite by chance, was no farmer. He was a carpenter. He built things.

Many contemporary writers are fieldworkers and carpenters. Although they do visit the pastures and watch things grow, they also labor in the shop, building things. They till, cultivate, and fertilize. They carve, sand, level, curve, and design little bureau drawers in which to hide ideas, such as old

rings from ex-lovers. Contemporary writers herd sheep, build doors, turn the soil, and get splinters. Are the metaphors yet exhausted? Contemporary writers—the postmodern crew—are strong like the fieldworker, clever like the carpenter. They can make things fit like the carpenter and make things bloom like the fieldworker. But wait: The postmodernist is also the cartographer, the person who maps the terrain, excavates the topography of discourse, and traces the landscape of cultural identity. A fieldworker, a carpenter, and a cartographer. The postmodern writer is a busy person.

This is an essay about Irish America, cultural identity, illegal immigration, and sexual difference. This is where we are going. How we are going to get there is quite another matter. I have a story to tell, but I want to place this story in the context of communication theory. The problem is, no one theory seems to be a good fit; so I will borrow several theoretical concepts, put them together, and build a place for my story. Here, I am like a carpenter.

The idea of building a theoretical framework to analyze a communication event is not new. In his book *Democracy in an Age of Colonization,* Deetz (1992) advocates an integrative analytical approach in communication studies (p. 66). Integrating theoretical constructs gives the communication scholar an opportunity to "reveal a stream with many forces that provide many new channels to cut, cross, and bridge" (p. 6). In the same spirit, Allport (1979) argues that critical questions may not be answered with one theoretical approach, that there "is no master key. Rather, what we have is a ring of keys, each of which opens one gate of understanding" (p. 208). Some people, some very wise people, might well disagree with the principle of integrating theoretical concepts, and some might say that the concepts I am about to mix do not mix well.

For better or worse, I do not know, but in this essay I have blended principles of social constructionism, personal narrative, autoethnography, literary criticism, cartography, and fieldwork. From Eve

Kosofsky Sedgwick (1985, 1990) I borrow ideas on how to engage in a subversive reading of desire as it is constructed in literary discourse. In his famous analyses of the history of sexuality, Michel Foucault (1976/1978, 1984/1985) argues well for the contextualization of desire, and a series of writers (e.g., Greenberg, 1988; Halperin, 1995; Stein, 1990) followed with cogent discussions of sexuality as a social construction. Although I acknowledge the debates over the social constructionism (see, for example, Mohr, 1992) and believe in a biological foundation of sexuality, I lean toward the belief that sexuality-as-cultural-practice is constructed through social discourse. My interests in the construction of sexuality, literary discourse, and questions of identity have led me toward autoethnography (Crawford, 1996), or the (re)placement of myself in the cultural texts I analyze. Autoethnography is a blending of the autobiography and the study of a people; in this case, I blend my own story with the literary and cultural texts of Irish in America. Crawford (1996) writes: "Autoethnography orchestrates fragments of awareness—apprehended/projected and recalled/reconstructed—into narratives and alternative text forms which (re)present events and other social actors as they are evoked from a changeable and contestable self" (p. 167). Such evocations may be more suited to an entire book, certainly, but in this essay I can address some central themes of silence and speech, sexuality, and immigration. Finally, I turn to Deleuze and Guattari (1991/1994), Browning (1996), and Bell and Valentine (1995), from whom I borrow principles of territorialization, geography, and the mapping of discourse. In short, I pledge my allegiance not to a flag that symbolizes a traditional theoretical perspective, but to the winds that destabilize that flag.

"We are not Irish," my mother would say, "we are American. Now, go do your homework." St. Patrick's Day was never a celebration at our house. The day would come and go with barely a notice. No hats, no green beer, no sing-alongs. Not until I spent a sabbatical in Ireland did I see just how Irish I was in habit and attitude. There was the food, of course, the beef stews, roasted chickens, simple salads, and the habit of heating dinner plates in the oven before serving. But there were also the quirks of everyday life: spending an inordinate amount of energy decorating the most unattractive corner in the backyard, attending to the front door of the house no matter how wretched the rest of the house appeared, treating the local library or bookstore like a community center, and telling stories that weave from point to point without ever having any point at all.

On a lark, I spent a week in a tiny town called Dingle, in County Kerry, on the western shores of Ireland. I took to riding my bike out to Slea Head, a breathtaking jolt of earth set against the Atlantic Ocean. One day I watched the blue sky disappear within seconds, and suddenly the fog was so thick I could not find my bicycle. I was unnerved as I groped through the thickness of the beach. When at last I found my bike, I started to make my way across what I thought was the road. I stumbled upon a shepherd, an old man with a dog at his side, and I asked him which way was the town. "What you need is a pint," he said. "You won't make it to the town you won't." I tried anyway. Lost, not knowing which way was anywhere, I found myself in Dunquin. In the distance, I saw the silhouette of a large building and at my feet a small sign saying THE GREAT BLASKET CENTER. I made my way to the building.

The fog was beginning to roll away, but I decided to stay in the museum until I could see clearly the way back to Dingle. I would learn about the Blasket Islands, some remote chunks of land deserted by their final 21 residents in 1953 (Mac Conghail, 1987; Thomson, 1988). Some photographs on a gallery wall caught my eye. I walked directly to the photographs and studied the two men, looking dashing and sporty, and then a photograph of one of the men, alone, with a wispy look on his face, and a caption stating the photo was of Maurice O'Sullivan, taken by his "good friend, George Thomson." This photograph captivated me at numerous levels. The photograph looked for all the world like a photograph in my parents' scrapbooks, and although all photographs from the 1920s look similar, this one was particularly familiar. The guy looked like a relative, with the same cheeks, same jaw, same pose, same attitude. I would never know who he looked like. He may have looked like a Gratton, one of my mother's uncles, maybe Joseph, who was born around 1878, or Henry, who worked for an electric company and was electrocuted, or Howard, who simply "had no progeny." Howard. All I know of Howard is that he left no progeny. The men in the photographs looked like boyfriends is what they looked like. I know boyfriends when I see them.

The next day I went to the local library and read about "the boyfriends" for hours. Maurice O'Sullivan was a writer, and he is best known for his autobiography, *Twenty Years a-Growing.* My gay radar, or gaydar, as we say, went off when I saw the introduction by E. M. Forrester, and as I read the book, I discovered yet another Irish custom, an indirection of discourse that simultaneously spoke eloquently of the truth yet never named the unmentionable. The two men loved each other. When O'Sullivan met Thomson in 1923, O'Sullivan was tending sheep. The sun, he writes, "was yellowing in the west and a lark singing above. Indeed, little bird, you have me beguiled, said I to myself. Just then the earth shook beneath me" (O'Sullivan, 1933, p. 220). The two men became the closest of friends, spending all of their time together, but they were faced with a dilemma: O'Sullivan had plans for America, but Thomson was English, a scholar with a career in Britain. Eventually, Thomson persuaded O'Sullivan to move to Dublin to join the police force. When O'Sullivan was admitted to the Civic Guard, Thomson said, "you have made your white coat" (p. 283), an Irish phrase that is said to a woman when she finds a husband, meaning "you are settled for life."

I proceed with caution as I venture into the discursive territory of the relationship between O'Sullivan and Thomson. I make no claims that the two men were lovers in the way two men might be lovers today. In her discussions of love between men, the literary critic Eve Kosofsky Sedgwick (1990) writes about homosexuality in the English novel:

> "Modern sexuality" and hence modern homosexuality are so intimately entangled with the historically distinctive contexts and structures that now count as *knowledge* that such "knowledge"

can scarcely be a transparent window onto a separate realm of sexuality but, rather, itself constitutes that sexuality. (p. 44)

I do not take what I know today and assume that O'Sullivan knew what I know, or that he viewed sexuality in a way similar to the way I view sexuality. Rather, I engage in a dissident reading of the text (Sinfield, 1994) and forsake the assumption that the two men are heterosexual. I read the novel looking for signs of the (in)visible homosexual-heterosexual binary, of the unspeakable border dispute. Irish culture constitutes the backdrop for my interpretation.

The scenes in *Twenty Years a-Growing* are tender and affectionate, but never explicitly sexual. We never enter the bedroom. When O'Sullivan arrives in Dublin, Thomson meets him at the train station. They go to Thomson's flat. They close the bedroom door at 4:00 in the morning, and, one sentence later, open the door at 11:00 with "the two of us awake, talking and conversing" (p. 273). *You can take me to the bedroom door,* my mother would say of sex in movies and novels, *but you don't need to take me inside the bedroom. Just leave the door closed.* How to map the discourse of the unspoken? Irish law would have prevented any discussion of same-sex desire. Part One Section Two of the Censorship of Publications Act forbade literary discussions of "sexual immorality or unnatural vice," and as John Broderick, an Irish writer born in 1927, observes, "the Irish are pathological about homosexuality. . . . it was one of the things that was absolutely unspeakable and which they would never admit to" (quoted in Carlson, 1990, p. 46).

Once a year, in cities such as Boston and New York, gay men and lesbians do battle with the Ancient Order of Hibernians to be included in the St. Patrick's Day parade. Gay men and lesbians want to march under a banner that identifies their sexuality, and the Ancient Order of Hibernians refuses, usually with the argument that it is not possible to be Irish *and* gay or lesbian. The parade organizers, who are named well, express genuine bafflement. They do not understand how someone could be Irish *and* gay or lesbian, and the basis of their argument has far less to do with the pope than some might imagine. The pope merely serves as "expert testimony." The essence of the problem is that same-sex desire in ancient Hibernia—the literary word for Ireland—did not exist as discourse. Queer desires were unspeakable. Contemporary Ireland now boasts some of the most liberal laws in all of Europe (Rose, 1994), and Irish gays and lesbians are mapping new terrains of sexual discourse (Dublin Lesbian and Gay Men's Collectives, 1986; Finnegan, 1994; O'Carroll & Collins, 1995; Pettitt, 1996). But the Ancient Order of Hibernians are not contemporary. They are a preservation of historical discourse. Their journey from Ireland to America constitutes a transportation of epoch.

While in Cork, I took a day trip to the port city, Cobh, and tried to imagine what it must have been like when my ancestors left Ireland. I had never given the emigration much thought, and certainly the topic was never discussed when I was a child. The details are sketchy at best: They left during the famines, probably around 1850, and landed in what was then British North America and is now Canada. They probably landed in Gross Ile and one by one made their way through the provinces to northern Michigan and Wisconsin. The path is vague. Discourse has obscured the map. The names I know: Corey, Sullivan, Nichol, Gratton. My great-grandmother, Josephine Sophia Ramesbotham, was born in Chatham, New Brunswick, in 1854, and she met my great-grandfather, Patrick Scott Gratton, a farmer, through her occupation. She taught English. When they moved to the United States is a mystery. There are no records of the move because *all of the records were destroyed in a terrible church fire.* My mother does not know for certain if her mother, Flora Gratton, was born in the United States. "She was very proud of being American," my mother tells me, "and resented any questions at school about her children's nationality. We were instructed to answer always that we were American. When the Irish hoopla would start around St. Patrick's Day, she would say, 'I wonder if Ireland is so great why we are all here?'" When I raised my eyebrows over this rather incredulous story, my mother assured me that not once has the possibility of illegal immigration ever been raised, and I was being overly sus-

picious. Two weeks later, my mother told me that over lunch she asked Bishop Harrington what he thought, and he said that there were a lot of church fires, Faith, a lot of church fires. Wink. The luck of the Irish.

My father's family, by contrast, is completely American, and to suggest otherwise is an affront to the family name. My great-grandfather fought in the Civil War, for goodness sake, and received from President Lincoln a plot of land in Chelsea, Michigan. Nana had relatives in Belfast, and my father's father had a drinking problem, so we never talked about him. That my father was born in Canada was a matter of chance, nothing more, and when we crossed the border between Detroit and Windsor for a day trip or a vacation, we were to sit in the back of the station wagon and not say a word. Not one word. "All American citizens," my father would say. Once, the border guard asked about the place of birth. "The United States," my father said. This was the only time I have known my father to lie outright.

A border is deceptive. How is it possible to lie through deception? My father was an American soldier in World War II. Why should he have to explain his birth to the border patrol? He is of the Irishmen who "defined themselves not only as Americans but as Americans of a superpatriotic kind" (Shannon, 1963, p. 132). Would not a discussion of birthplace excavate an unnecessary historical discourse of the Irish and their border instabilities? The onset of "Wisconsin Fever" and "Michigan Fever" brought the laborers from New Brunswick to the United States, often by way of Maine (Fitzgerald & King, 1990). The Irish, then, who were British subjects, crossed the Atlantic, landed in Canada, migrated to the United States, reentered Canada, and found their way back to the United States. Borders were for crossing, and perhaps my father, like the United States census takers of the 19th century, considered a person Irish only if that person were *born* in Ireland. Information about the descendants of the Irish, particularly those with ties to Canada, is unreliable at best, and more accurately lost (Fitzgerald & King, 1990; McDonald, 1954/1976).

"Borders are," writes Batten (1996) of the poetry of Paul Muldoon, "troublesome in Ireland"

(p. 175). There is the border between Northern Ireland and The Republic, between English and Irish law, between the colonizer and the colonized. There are the borders between Catholic and Celtic traditions, the patriarchy and matriarchy, censorship and the Irish devotion to literature. The Irish poet has a way with words, yet has been silenced. Batten writes,

> At the borders of the linguistically competent self, the self colonized by the Law, metaphors cross easily from self to world, and vice versa, precisely because no checkpoints are required along a border that appears to guarantee a private self and a public world. (pp. 174–175)

What of the border between heterosexuality and homosexuality? In the time of Maurice O'Sullivan, no Irish word for homosexual existed. The Irish words for same-sex desire—*homaighneasach* for men and *Leispiach* for women—were not established until the 1970s, and the etymologies of these words are based not in the Irish language but in the Greek, suggesting that not only the words but their ideas are imports. There were English words, such as buggery or inversion, but no Irish words. How could Maurice O'Sullivan have been *homaighneasach*? The word did not exist. Thomson, like a character out of an English novel, outgrew his affection for O'Sullivan. He returned to England, took a wife, established a career and a name as a scholar (Enright, 1988). How very English. As for O'Sullivan, he too took a wife, but his career as a police officer never took off, never became his "white coat." He tried to write a second book but failed.

O'Sullivan did not commit suicide. He drowned in the placid waters off Salthill, a holiday beach just north of Galway.

In their discussion of what they call "geophilosophy," Deleuze and Guattari (1991/1994) write that "thinking takes place in the relationship of territory and the earth" (p. 85). We may well never know the geophilosophy of sexuality on the Blasket Islands, and we will never know what O'Sullivan was thinking as he drowned in the waters off Salthill. I shall never know what my father was thinking when he told the border police he was born in the United States, but now, as an adult, I have the tools to interpret relationships between what people say and where people are, between beings and borders. The line between the United States and Canada is a river, the Detroit River, and it is a friendly, albeit murky, crossing. The Detroit River is a fluid moment in the history of national identity. The border is a "plane of immanence" (Deleuze & Guattari, 1991/1994, pp. 35–60), which is not entirely unlike the border between silence and speech. I have 5 siblings, 36 first cousins, and the good Lord only knows how many relations on the historical plateau of the earth. I am the only homo. Or, more aptly put, I am the only one to cross the hetero-homo border and claim a queer identity. I am going to say something, but I do not want to be quoted out of context, and I do not want to be conveniently misunderstood: I was born heterosexual. On the map of my Irish Catholic history, all roads were built of the discourse of heterosexuality. I turned off that road and followed a road I knew to be a truer, more honest road. I crossed a border. I spoke the words, "I am gay." Are there now or have there ever been any gays or lesbians in my family? I have my suspects, but such suspicions constitute dangerous territories. I shall say nothing of Jessica, who was born in 1927. Jessica did not want to be a girl, says my mother, because men had more career options. Jessica had a Ph.D. in biology and was a research scientist. Jessica never married. I shall say nothing of the photographs of men who send my gaydar into high alert, and I shall say not a word, not one word, about the priests. Let us say simply this: If there were any gay men or lesbians, *all of the records were destroyed in a terrible church fire.*

When I deterritorialize my own map, I am able to view the history of my terrain as "the set of conditions, however recent they may be, from which one turns away in order to become, that is to say, in order to create something new" (Deleuze & Guattari, 1991/1994, p. 96). Throughout this essay, I have explored "borders" as the conditions from which I turn as I move through questions of identity. These borders are deceiving and deceitful. The border between gay and straight is a discursive territory, disturbed by language and culture, silence and speech, censorship and literature. The border between Irish and American is also a discursive territory, disturbed by fact and fiction, memory and history, truth and the essence of truth. The line between gay and straight, like the line between Irish and American, is not an absolute, but rather an ongoing construction. The line is shifted, altered, shaved, and nurtured. My ancestors created "something new," an American identity, by blurring the lines of immigration.

I, too, create "something new" when I interface the autobiography with ethnography. When I tell my own story and place that story against the portrait of a people, I bring history to the moment and ground my identity. I accomplish this construction of a "newness" through "various stories of vicarious truths" (Crawford, 1996, p. 168), and a modest attempt to map the discourse of the unspoken. Maurice O'Sullivan could not have written about a sexual desire for his "good friend." In Irish culture, such a desire would have been unspeakable. My ancestors could not have talked openly of illegal immigration, for this, too, would have been unspeakable. What, then, to make of my scandalous discourse? I offer the possibility of O'Sullivan as a queer. I offer a possibility of illegal immigration. I depolice the border of the silence surrounding sexual desire in Irish culture, and I interrogate the crossing of the Canadian-American border by my ancestors. I build a place for discourse, for talk of possibilities, disturbing as such discourse is to an Irish pattern of denial. My awareness is evoked from this changeable and contestable self, within a changeable and contestable culture.

We can learn not to deny our own sexual desires, and we can learn how to venture into the silences—the unspoken terrains—of the cultures from which we come. When we tell our stories against the cultural backdrops that nourish those stories, we transcend self-indulgence and contribute to a rewrite of the governing, cultural narrative (Corey, in press). That is, the personal narrative interrupts social discourse. My claims of desire disturb discursive assumptions of heterosexuality, and through the personal narrative, the body of the self, which has been colonized by cultural law, is policed not by a border patrol, but by the capacities of language. A story, then, is rooted in cultural norms, but through language, a storyteller is able to construct a form of

identity, reshape memory, sand a rough moment, curve a straight line, or build a bureau of clandestine drawers in which to hide things, things such as a place of birth, a line of flight, an undeveloped thought, or the pleasure of a name.

References

Allport, G. W. (1979). *The nature of prejudice* (Rev. ed.). Reading, MA: Addison-Wesley.

Batten, G. (1996). "He could barely tell one from the other": The borderline disorders of Paul Muldoon's poetry. *South Atlantic Quarterly, 95,* 171–204.

Bell, D., & Valentine, G. (Eds.). (1995). *Mapping desire: Geographies of sexualities.* New York: Routledge.

Browning, F. (1996). *A queer geography: Journeys toward a sexual self.* New York: Crown.

Carlson, J. (1990). *Banned in Ireland: Censorship and the Irish writer.* London: Routledge.

Corey, F. C. (1996). Performing sexualities in an Irish pub. *Text and Performance Quarterly, 16,* 146–160.

Corey, F. C. (in press). The personal: Against the master narrative. In S. J. Dailey (Ed.), *The future of performance studies: The next millennium.* Annandale, VA: Speech Communication Association.

Crawford, L. (1996). Personal ethnography. *Communication Monographs, 63,* 158–170.

Deetz, S. (1992). *Democracy in an age of colonization.* Albany: SUNY Press.

Deleuze, G., & Guattari, F. (1994). *What is philosophy?* (H. Tomlinson & G. Burchell, Trans.). New York: Columbia University Press. (Original work published 1991).

Dublin Lesbian and Gay Men's Collectives. (Eds.). (1986). *Out for ourselves: The lives of Irish lesbians and gay men.* Dublin: Women's Community Press.

Enright, T. (1988). George Thomson: A memoir. In G. Thomson, *Island home: The Blasket heritage* (pp. 117–150). Wolfeboro, NH: Brandon.

Finnegan, B. (Ed.). (1994). *Quare fellas: New Irish gay writing.* Dublin: Basement Press.

Fitzgerald, M. E., & King, J. A. (1990). *The uncounted Irish in Canada and the United States.* Toronto: Meany.

Foucault, M. (1978). *The history of sexuality. Volume I: An introduction* (R. Hurley, Trans.). New York: Random House. (Original work published 1976)

Foucault, M. (1985). *The history of sexuality. Volume II: The use of pleasure* (R. Hurley, Trans.). New York: Random House. (Original work published 1984)

Greenberg, D. F. (1988). *The construction of homosexuality*. Chicago: University of Chicago Press.

Halperin, D. M. (1995). *Saint Foucault: Towards a gay hagiography*. Oxford: Oxford University Press.

Mac Conghail, M. (1987). *The Blaskets: A Kerry island library*. Dublin: Country House.

McDonald, G. (1976). *History of the Irish in Wisconsin in the nineteenth century*. New York: Arno. (Reprint of doctoral dissertation, Catholic University of America, published by the Catholic University of America Press, Washington, DC, 1954)

Mohr, R. D. (1992). *Gay ideas: Outing and other controversies*. Boston: Beacon.

O'Carroll, I., & Collins, E. (Eds.). (1995). *Lesbian and gay visions of Ireland: Towards the twenty-first century*. London: Cassell.

O'Sullivan, M. (1933). *Twenty years a-growing* (M. L. Davies & G. Thomson, Trans.). New York: Viking.

Pettitt, L. (1996). G(ay)uinness is good for you. *South Atlantic Quarterly*, 95, 205–212.

Rose, K. (1994). *Diverse communities: The evolution of lesbian and gay politics in Ireland*. Cork, Ireland: Cork University Press.

Sedgwick, E. K. (1985). *Between men: English literature and male homosexual desire*. New York: Columbia University Press.

Sedgwick, E. K. (1990). *Epistemology of the closet*. Berkeley: University of California Press.

Shannon, W. V. (1963). *The American Irish*. New York: Macmillan.

Sinfield, A. (1994). *Cultural politics—queer reading*. Philadelphia: University of Pennsylvania Press.

Stein, E. (Ed.). (1990). *Forms of desire: Sexual orientation and the social constructionist controversy*. New York: Garland.

Thomson, G. (1988). *Island home: The Blasket heritage*. Wolfeboro, NH: Brandon.

Key Terms

autoethnography	mapping
fieldwork	personal narrative
gay	sexuality
immigration	social constructionism
Irish	

Discussion Questions

1. In what way is "coming out of the closet" similar to "crossing a border"?

2. What are some of the relationships between language and identity? Is it possible for a person to be homosexual if no word exists to describe such a love?

3. The author claims that when we tell our stories against the cultural backdrops that nourish these stories, we transcend self-indulgence and contribute to a rewrite of the governing, cultural narrative. Do you agree or disagree?

4. If being homosexual is not part of Irish tradition, should lesbians and gay men be allowed to participate in the traditional St. Patrick's Day parade?

5. What are some of the borders you have crossed?

11 Migration Across Generations
Whose Identity Is Authentic?

KATHLEEN WONG(LAU)

In many movies and popular novels by Asian Americans, particularly Chinese Americans Amy Tan and Maxine Hong Kingston, Chinese Americans are portrayed as struggling with issues of identity that stretch across generations and centuries of traditional Chinese thought and values (Kingston, 1976; Tan, 1989). The younger generation is seen to struggle with the conflicting conservative immigrant traditional values of Chinese Confucianism and the individualistic values of U.S. Americanism. Though these fictional models may be informative about some American-born Chinese, they are indicative of a shrinking proportion of Chinese Americans. The 1990 U.S. census reports 37% of Asian Americans were native-born Americans, compared to 92% of the general population. For Chinese Americans the number of native-born Americans is only 30.7% (Min, 1995). The characters of these popular novels may give some insight about the experiences of American-born children of Chinese immigrants who immigrated from the 19th century through the 1960s. These immigrants came mostly from rural areas of southern China through the port of Hong Kong at a time when rural Chinese culture was imbued with Confucian values, especially in regard to family structures (Sodowsky, Kwan, & Pannu, 1995). The cultures of these countries have been preserved in the minds and subsequent practices of immigrants, seemingly frozen at the time of immigration (Anderson, 1983).

This phenomenon of preserving ethnic cultural practices has been common among all immigrants throughout the migrant history of the United States (Anderson, 1983; Ignatiev, 1995). One still finds Italian American neighborhoods in Boston and Polish American neighborhoods in Chicago (Takaki, 1993). Immigrants preserve their identities and cultural practices in an effort to survive in a hostile society where dominant cultural values often conflict with traditional values and economic opportunities

are scarce. Immigrants often pool economic resources and experiential knowledge, help one another find employment, learn to negotiate bureaucracy, learn English, find familiar foods, and celebrate familiar holidays. Immigrants also learn to avoid becoming victims of unscrupulous employers, landlords, and others who may take advantage of new arrivals (Wei, 1993). Many Asian American communities have created these immigrant communities as primary landing places for new immigrants, who ultimately move to Asian American suburbs or predominantly White suburbs once social and economic security are attained (Fong, 1994). Often immigrant communities in the United States have preserved practices over generations that are rarely even practiced by their cohorts in the home country, as these countries have continued to modernize since the time of an individual's immigration and absence.

Thus we have the incongruous phenomenon of Greek American cultural experts going back to Greece to play traditional Greek songs, perform traditional Greek dances, and cook traditional Greek dishes during festivals designed for U.S. Americans. Many of these cultural practices may be unfamiliar to their Greek hosts except in stories passed down from grandparents. The following quote is from a recent Greek immigrant who teaches Greek folk dance and music in the United States to Greek Americans:

> Greeks in Greece are currently interested in disco and fashions from Milan. There is a new form of music called urban music, which is like traditional Greek music and disco. I think Greek Americans whose ancestors immigrated to America generations ago are usually quite shocked when they get there. (personal interview with anonymous participant; July 1994)

The experience of my parents returning to Hong Kong in 1980 for the first time in 20 years after their immigration to the United States illustrates a similar clash of conceptions of "Chinese" culture across the recent history of their own lives. The cosmopolitan capitalistic Hong Kong they encountered upon their arrival shocked and saddened them. Hong Kong resembled Manhattan more in its values than it did the Chinese city they remembered in their young adulthood. My mother had stated, "Now I feel as if I truly belong nowhere. When I am here [Hong Kong], I feel so American. When I am home in America, I feel so Chinese." The Chinese values she had so carefully preserved for her children and family now seemed to exist only among the group of Chinese American immigrants whom we saw several times a month and at special holidays back home in the United States—thousands of miles away from Hong Kong and Asia.

The following quotes illustrate how markedly different my mother's experiences are from those of recent Chinese American immigrants in the 1990s. The first quote is from a conversation that my husband and I had with my young immigrant cousin about his difficulty in adjusting to living with us in the United States. The second quote is from a conversation I had with my parents that same week. These examples caution us about the complexity of what it means to be of Chinese descent in America across migration waves:

> ABCs [American-born Chinese] are so old-fashioned. You are young, but it is like you live in old Chinese history books—you are SO old-fashioned and strict! You celebrate August Moon festival. You know how to make wonton and potstickers. Only poor people cook. You have money, but you order white rice in fancy restaurants. How embarrassing! *I can't believe you are Chinese.* Chinese are supposed to be "tight," you know, good dressers, good in business, "tight" cars, go out to eat all the time, cell phones. (cousin, personal conversation, 1995)

> Chinese people are honorable people. We respect our elders, value family, cherish children, and we are honest. Chinese people look at what is inside a person, not focus on smooth talk and nice dress like Americans [White Americans] do. I don't trust them [Hong Kongese]. They are upper crusty. . . . All they care about is money and buying things,

nice cars, clothes, watches—spend money. They are supposed to take care of those less fortunate in society, be thrifty. *They aren't very Chinese.* (parents, personal conversation, 1995)

Race, Ethnicity, and Identity

Whose identity is more Chinese or Chinese American? Whose is more authentic? To choose one or the other is a grave mistake. Identity is fluid and shaped through experience. Identity formation arises in interaction and is a function not only of the individual and his or her relation to the ethnic or racial group but of that group's place in the wider social setting (Rosenthal, 1987). In intercultural communication, communicative interaction at the individual as well as group level is the focus of study in identity formation. Intercultural communication is an overall encompassing term. In recent literature in intercultural communication, communication has come to include everyday discourse in conversations, mediated discourses in textbooks, news media, popular culture, advertising, and other types of communication. Thus the conversations we have, the movies we watch, and the books we read all serve to mediate our identity formation. We, in turn, impact the identity formation of others by our everyday discourses and our influence on the media and popular culture.

From this standpoint, the relationships within ethnic and racial groups are more complex than what appears on the surface. Questions of identity, ethnicity, and race often become confusing and complex. The popular media, the press, and even scholars often interchange race and ethnicity or combine these concepts with a slash using "race/ethnicity" rather than selecting one or the other. Students often ask, "What is the difference between race and ethnicity?" The reason for this confusion is that concepts of both race and ethnicity include notions of social construction and identity formation. Though for many centuries we believed that race was biologically based, we now know that the notion of race is really the result of the social process of grouping people we *believe* to be different based on what we *perceive* are inherent genetic immutable differences. The process has been described as *racializing* (Goldberg, 1993). In anthropology and many of the social sciences, the traditional concept of ethnicity is based on the notion of collective cultural practices that are part of the socialization of groups in specific isolated geographical communities.

In the present political and social context, concepts of race and ethnicity become further entangled when groups appropriate either or both of these notions for similar political resistance. Individuals may often base their identity and group formation to specifically resist being discriminated against based on others' beliefs of racial or ethnic inferiority. As a result, we often connect specific ethnic practices with specific racial groups. However, in the previous examples of Greek Americans and Hong Kong Americans, traditional concepts of race and ethnicity in and of themselves provide little explanatory power for the phenomena in these instances of intercultural and intracultural interaction. How would one describe Greek American or Chinese American ethnicity in these instances? It would be helpful to develop a framework for understanding a more dynamic way of looking at racial and ethnic identity formation. The following section examines a framework in the specific instances of Asian American identity formation with implications for more widespread application of these concepts.

Frameworks for Asian American Identity

In intercultural communication literature Asian Americans are often described as possessing characteristics of a specific ethnic (Chinese American, Japanese American, Indonesian American) or racial (Asian or Pacific Islander) group. There is a long list of characteristics such as collectivism, face-saving, filial respect, and preference for uncertainty reduction. These characteristics are believed to originate from traditional beliefs based in Confucianism rooted in the Asian continent. Although these characteristics may prove true for a portion of U.S. Americans of Asian descent, they are not representative for many Asian Americans.

Asian Americans are a heterogeneous group, speaking many different languages in addition to English, each incomprehensible to another. Asian Americans practice many different religions, ranging from the Christianity of Chinese American Baptists to Buddhism, Hinduism, and Islam (Sodowsky et al., 1995). Asian American immigrants also arrive from Asian countries that have had centuries or decades of national and ethnic conflict. These conflicts have resulted in wars and hostilities, many of which still exist in Asia. Asian Americans may trace their ancestors to differing regions, decades, and centuries—each with its own unique values, historical relations, and cultural practices.

It is easy to accept, given evidence, that all ethnic groups are heterogeneous. We must be cautious, however, that knowledge of heterogeneity doesn't encourage us to only make longer lists of ethnic characteristics. The common frame used to understand Asian Americans in social science is to provide a large overarching laundry list of characteristics or dimensions of ethnic identity. These identities describe class, gender, and cultural practices as characteristics of ethnic groups influenced by the culture of the country of origin, not as effects of *ethnic and racial formation across time, generations, regions, and countries.* It is more productive and informative to conceptualize Asian American identity as the ever changing effects of individual and group experiences of migration, of historical contact with other Asian groups, other people of color, and White U.S. Americans. These effects are complex, involving the formation of beliefs about social status, economic status, institutions, the home country, relationship of the United States to the outside world, and preservation of cultural values.

THE DIASPORA AND IMAGINED COMMUNITIES

Metaphors of the *diaspora* and of the *imagined community* are helpful for examining ethnic and racial identity. A diaspora is the dispersion of a minority group of people among a majority group beyond the borders of the minority's homeland. The notion of imagining a community describes the ways in which all people construct a collective community to which they identify and belong. Beliefs about nationalism, patriotism, and what it means to be a U.S.

American are constructed this way. For example, a Nebraskan using communication through the stories she tells constructs an imagined community of Nebraskans from a specific location with specific beliefs. She constructs this community even though she may not know all Nebraskans or even a significant percentage of them. Yet she identifies herself as part of this community and shares common stories about what it means to be Nebraskan. She imagines that other Nebraskans are in the diaspora in the greater United States, having come from this community even though the neighborhood she left in childhood may be unrecognizable today.

Similarly, immigrants often preserve and incorporate dimensions of their cultural practices in the diaspora, often constructing their ethnic identity around beliefs and memories of cultural values and practices that existed in their home country at the time of immigration. As waves of immigrants arrive over many generations from countries that experience tremendous global, political, cultural, and technological change, we find that these imagined communities often clash even as different waves of immigrants arrive from the same locale in Asia. Notions of "authentic" ethnic identity in ethnic communities in the United States create much intracultural friction, especially between American-born and immigrant communities.

In this framework of ethnic formation, who represents the Chinese American perspective, much less the Asian American perspective? Chinese communities struggle with differences across class, relations to technology, cultural history, traditional legacies, and traditional family hierarchies. In July 1997 Hong Kong will revert back to Communist China from the United Kingdom; as a result, many Chinese emigrants from Hong Kong have already immigrated to the United States and other countries. Many are descendants of Chinese who immigrated to Hong Kong decades ago after fleeing the Communists. As China fires missiles over Taiwan to encourage its "One China Policy," we can see how complicated and fraught with conflict the development of an ethnic Chinese American identity can be. Although non-Chinese others may see you and communicate to you as being simply Asian, Asian American, Chinese American, or Chinese, you may

see yourself as being ethnically Taiwanese American, or Hong Kongese American, distinct from Chinese Americans who trace their ancestral home to mainland China. The difficulties of identity formation are even more problematic when labeling assumes that every Asian-looking person is Chinese, or more derogatory terms such as Oriental or Chink.

These dynamics with the larger White communities can create great tensions for many ethnic minorities in the United States, where communities struggle with tremendous differences not only with the larger dominant White majority, but also within their own ethnic communities on how to handle this seeming effort to lump people of Asian descent together. The following is an example of the ambivalent situation a Korean American student faced when encountering a well-meaning White colleague:

> A White woman acquaintance at my university pulled me aside and in a serious voice announced that she understood what I had been talking about all these months about ethnicity and race. "I saw the movie *The Joy Luck Club* with my husband over the weekend. I feel so close to you now, like I understand you so much better! Chinese women are so lucky to have relationships with their mothers with such deep emotions!" I felt confused and speechless and didn't know where to begin. In addition to the fact that I am not Chinese American, I wondered what in the world this woman and her husband have fantasized about my life and family relations based on this Hollywood movie.
> (G. Kim, conversation in a graduate seminar class, 1994)

Under these circumstances, ethnic minorities often create a larger, more strategic *political identity* such as "Asian American identity." This imagined community is one in which individuals are unified in their beliefs about being similarly discriminated against and share similar histories of struggle in the diaspora of Asians in the United States. In many ways the community is one of strategic racial formation designed to recognize and resist racial oppression. It is this process of political identity formation that allows for Asian Americans and Pacific Islanders to encompass the same diasporic community regardless of the extremely complex and sometimes problematic histories of languages and conflict in home countries. It is this same process that allows for Asian American Pacific Islanders to form coalitions with other groups of color to fight common causes of discrimination and stereotyping often based on perceptions of race.

Consider the experience I had while attending a recent regional academic communication conference in a large hotel in the American Pacific Northwest: I am in the hotel restaurant and walking to my table to sit with my colleagues. Although I am dressed in typical professional conventioneer clothing and am wearing a conference name tag, I am grabbed twice by unfamiliar White communication professors who demand that I seat them. One White male professor grabs my upper arm tightly and barks, "I said, Clear my table!"

My experience is eerily similar to those experienced by Cornel West, bell hooks, Gloria Anzaldúa, Ronald Takaki, Maxine Hong Kingston, and other scholars of color in similar professional settings, where White people that you know generally exhibit a level of respect and genuine friendship and those that you don't know are likely to racialize you and stereotype you to be one of "the help."

What does it mean to be Chinese, Chinese American, and Asian American in the United States in the 1990s? There is not now, nor has there ever been, an easy or stable answer. Trying to pinpoint and understand what ethnic and racial identity means in the United States is like shooting at a moving target. I am an American-born woman of Chinese descent, born of working-class immigrant parents in the United States. The experiences of the Korean American graduate student and myself illustrate the different ways in which the identities of people of Asian descent can be very complex and at times very problematic even in academia. To some White colleagues I can be different things: a Chinese American woman with deep secrets about her past, or a laborer in food service, or one of the thousands of people of color who clean our offices, maintain our campuses, and serve our food. These colleagues shape their perceptions of my identity not by who I am as a Chinese American, but by assigning simplistic ethnic and class characteristics based on their own perceptions of my physical appearance, my

race, my Chineseness and Asianness. This process is racialization, or racial stereotyping. My own perception of my identity is often in shockingly sharp conflict with how others perceive and assign my identity.

Being an Asian American means being faced with the difficult dilemma of constantly having to contradict preconceived ethnic and racial stereotypes of Asians and Asian Americans, or of letting these stereotypes pass, knowing that they will continue to be imposed on others. It means being wary that one's whole identity does not become merely a reaction to these stereotypes, while recognizing that these struggles are a part of the formation of my identity as an American. These struggles are part of my imagined community of fellow strugglers. Though I do not know Cornel West, bell hooks, or Maxine Hong Kingston personally, we all share a sense of community through our writings and through our ethnic and strategic racial identity formation.

This formation of a collective identity is not without its problems. Asian Americans struggle with relationships with other people of color in the United States. For an Asian American, identifying as a person of color who is concerned about the core issues of social and economic empowerment for marginalized people can often mean having to take an uncomfortable look at racial, social, and economic privilege in relationship to the status of other ethnic American groups. For example, during a university class for gifted students of color that I taught in 1996, a session on Asian American/African American conflict became heated as a discussion about Asian immigrant entrepreneurship in African American communities unfolded. Students began taking sides, which left some Asian and Asian American students questioning their own loyalties to their own ethnic and racial group against their solidarity with African American students in a joint struggle to improve the lives of all marginalized people. "Why do I feel pressured to choose? Can't I be Asian American AND a person of color?!" an exasperated Chinese American woman asked me.

Many Asian Americans who immigrated to the United States after 1965, with the exception of refugees, emigrated largely from urban areas of Asia.

Unlike their predecessors who arrived from poor rural farming areas with little money and resources, many recent immigrants arrive with advanced college degrees and investment capital. Most Americans—including Asian Americans—are unaware that through changing immigration criteria, the federal government has encouraged the immigration of this class of affluent merchants in order to bolster the American economy (Ikemoto, 1995; Min, 1995; Sodowsky et al., 1995). Many recent Asian American immigrants arrive with little understanding of American class dynamics, especially in regard to racial dynamics. They may not understand their actions in the context of racial formation in the United States and may still be struggling with their own ethnic and racial identity here. The media, as we saw in the simplistic portrayals of Korean merchants and African American residents of Los Angeles after the Rodney King verdicts, does not assist immigrants or the public at large in understanding the complex, problematic, and tragic race relations in the United States that go well beyond whether Korean Americans and African Americans have conflicting communication styles and disparate economic opportunity (Ikemoto, 1995).

Intercultural communication should not and cannot study Asian American communication in isolation from the historical, social, political, economic, and racial dynamics of the peoples of the United States and of the larger world. Examining ethnicity and race within the framework of the diaspora and imagined communities can help us understand the complexities and challenges of intercultural and intracultural communication. We must use this framework to examine identity as a process, as an effect of discourses about racial and ethnic formation that stretches across continents, history, generations, governments, and peoples. Using the metaphors of diaspora and imagined communities, we can examine the discourses that we use or are exposed to that both help us and hinder us in shaping notions of community. These communities should be viewed as fluid and ever changing as new immigrants arrive, new generations are born, new alliances are formed, old alliances are broken, and events such as wars and conflicts and other common concerns arise around the world.

References

Anderson, B. (1983). *Imagined communities*. London: Verso.

Fong, T. (1994). *The first suburban Chinatown: The remaking of Monterey Park*. Philadelphia: Temple University Press.

Goldberg, D. T. (1993). *Racist culture: Philosophy and the politics of meaning*. Oxford: Blackwell.

Ignatiev, N. (1995). *How the Irish became white*. New York: Routledge.

Ikemoto, L. (1995). Traces of the master narrative in the story of African American/Korean American conflict: How we constructed "Los Angeles." In R. Delgado (Ed.), *Critical race theory: The cutting edge* (pp. 305–315). Philadelphia: Temple University Press.

Kingston, M. H. (1976). *The woman warrior: Memoirs of a girlhood among ghosts*. New York: Alfred A. Knopf.

Min, P. G. (1995). *Asian Americans: Contemporary trends and issues*. Thousand Oaks, CA: Sage.

Rosenthal, D. A. (1987). Ethnic identity development in adolescents. In J. S. Phinney & M. J. Rotheram (Eds.), *Children's ethnic socialization: Pluralism and development* (pp. 156–179). Newbury Park, CA: Sage.

Sodowsky, R. G., Kwan, K. L. K., & Pannu, R. (1995). Ethnic identity of Asians in the United States. In J. Ponterotto, J. M. Casas, L. A. Suzuki, & C. M. Alexander (Eds.), *Handbook of multicultural counseling* (pp. 123–154). Thousand Oaks, CA: Sage.

Takaki, R. (1993). *A different mirror*. Boston: Little, Brown.

Tan, A. (1989). *The joy luck club*. New York: G. P. Putnam's Sons.

Wei, W. (1993). *The Asian American movement*. Philadelphia: Temple University Press.

Wong, K. S. (1993). Our lives, our histories. In D. Shoem, L. Frankel, X. Zuniga, & E. Lewis (Eds.), *Multicultural teaching in the university* (pp. 87–94). Westport, CT: Praeger.

Key Terms

Asian American
  identity
diaspora
identity

imagined communities
intercultural
  communication
migration

Discussion Questions

1. Wong(Lau) uses the metaphors of the diaspora and imagined communities. Using these concepts, discuss examples of diasporic formation and

imagined communities on your campus. How would these considerations impact your communication in these groups?

2. In communication literature, especially in intercultural literature, the concept of context in the shaping of communication is often emphasized. This essay helps us understand the importance of looking at the experience of migration in identity formation. What other types of contextual considerations could be relevant? Discuss your own experiences.

3. What does Wong(Lau)'s essay suggest about the possible ways in which people may identify with the terms "Asian American," "Chinese American," or "people of color"? Discuss these terms using the concepts of race and ethnicity.

4. What types of communication discourses are out there about Asian Americans and specific eth-

nic Asian Americans? Identify the source and the message. How might these discourses impact the identity formation of Americans of Asian descent? How might they impact Americans of non-Asian descent?

5. Discuss the power of communication in identity formation and community formation. In what ways do groups persist in maintaining diasporic communities over time? Start with larger imagined national and regional communities such as the United States, the South, and New England and move to smaller, more specific ones. Where did you learn about these regional and ethnic characteristics, even if you haven't had contact with these communities? What does this tell us about intercultural communication?

12 Views From the Other Side
Perspectives on the Cyprus Conflict
BENJAMIN J. BROOME

Introduction

During the past 2½ years, I have lived and worked on the eastern Mediterranean island of Cyprus, which is the legendary birthplace of Aphrodite, the ancient goddess of love and fertility. Unfortunately, there are few signs today of Aphrodite's legacy, as the country is engaged in a long-standing conflict that has resulted in the physical division of the country between two ethnic communities, the Greek Cypriots and the Turkish Cypriots. I was in Cyprus as a Fulbright Scholar, offering seminars, workshops, and training programs in communication and conflict resolution. I worked in both communities and in a bicommunal setting with individuals of all ages, professions, and political persuasions. My initial goal was to introduce concepts and skills that might help members of the two com-

munities work together more productively. In the process of offering these programs I became a third-party facilitator for bringing members of the two communities together across a dividing line that has proven to be even stronger than the Berlin Wall.

The Cyprus conflict has become one of the most protracted international disputes of modern times. Almost immediately after Cyprus gained its independence in 1960, intercommunal violence started between the Greek Cypriots and the Turkish Cypriots, who at the time were living in mixed or neighboring villages and towns. Disputes over changes in the constitution led to the withdrawal of the Turkish Cypriots from the government in 1963, and violent clashes later that same year resulted in the formation of Turkish Cypriot enclaves scattered throughout the island. United Nations peacekeeping troops were brought in to help prevent further bloodshed. Unrest between the two communities continued, however, and in 1974 a coup against the Cyprus government, staged by the military dictatorship of Greece, led to intervention by Turkish troops. Thousands of Greek Cypriots were forced from their homes and businesses in the northern part of the island, and almost all Turkish Cypriots fled their homes in the southern part of Cyprus and were resettled in the north. This resulted in ethnic partition of the island, enforced to this day by the heavy military presence of the Turkish army. United Nations peacekeeping forces patrol a buffer zone that divides the island across the middle from west to east. In spite of continuous diplomatic activity mediated by the United Nations, the United States, Great Britain, and the European Union, no settlement of the Cyprus conflict has been reached in over 22 years of negotiations.[1]

Although Turkish Cypriots and Greek Cypriots speak different languages and follow different religions, they share many common cultural characteristics, the results of over 400 years of living together on a small island. Their social values, their lifestyles, their traditional crafts, and many of their songs and dances are similar. They have a large shared vocabulary, and they have much in common in their communication style—both speak a dialect of their respective languages, and these dialects share common rhythmic patterns. Both Greek Cypriots and Turkish Cypriots feel connected to the island in similar ways, and they face similar difficulties when they travel to their respective "motherlands," Greece and Turkey. Even in their physical characteristics they are difficult to distinguish. On many occasions I have shown photos of bicommunal groups to outsiders, and it was impossible for them to indicate the ethnic background of the participants. Even Cypriots themselves usually cannot identify members of the other community by physical appearance alone.[2] Yet the mental pictures that each holds of the other and of the past are totally different. There are few places in the world where two communities living in a single geographical area who share so much in common are so far apart on issues that divide them.

One of the primary factors contributing to the stalemate in Cyprus is the almost total lack of contact between the two communities. Although it is never easy to deal with conflict situations, it becomes even more difficult when there is no direct communication between the parties involved. Without an exchange of ideas and perceptions, negotiation and compromise are unlikely, and it is impossible for relationships of trust and empathy to develop.[3] Although the avoidance of communication is sometimes a conscious choice of the conflicting parties, the Greek Cypriot and Turkish Cypriot communities in Cyprus are trapped in a situation where communication is actually prohibited or very tightly controlled. Almost all forms of direct interaction are nearly impossible because of the absence of normal communication links between the two communities—only with the help of third parties such as the United Nations can residents contact each other via telephone, mail, or personal visits, and there is almost no business exchange between the two communities. During the past 30 years, the primary images each has developed of the other have come through the mass media, the education system, and political propaganda. The forced separation has created a gap that will make it very difficult to find a solution to this tragic conflict.

The de facto partition of Cyprus has meant that a generation of Turkish Cypriots and Greek Cypriots have grown up without knowing anyone from the other community. Many of these people are now university students, and they have very different perspectives about the conflict on their island and distorted perceptions of each other. Most important, they hold very different beliefs about what must be done to resolve the conflict. This article gives an account of these seemingly incompatible realities, as they are described by the younger generation. It presents two letters, each addressed to you, a person who lives outside Cyprus and who may not be familiar with the situation. The letters come from Cypriot students—one from a Greek Cypriot university student living and studying in the Greek Cypriot–administered part of the island, one from a Turkish Cypriot university student living and studying in the Turkish Cypriot–administered part of the island.

In these letters, the authors try to explain their understanding of the Cyprus conflict, as they have learned about it from their family, in their school, and from the media. Neither of the letters was written by a single person; rather, each one is based on numerous discussions I have had with students in Cyprus during the past 2 years. Most of the students are undergraduates at universities in their respective communities, in some cases studying only a few kilometers from each other but living in very different worlds. Of course, students hold a variety of views about the Cyprus situation, so as you read these letters keep in mind that any particular Cypriot student may disagree with some of the points. Nevertheless, each letter represents a composite of attitudes and views that are widespread throughout the respective communities.

As you read the letters, note the similarities and differences in the two points of view. The Cyprus issue is very emotional for all those involved, making it difficult for anyone caught up in the conflict to listen to the other. At the end of this article I provide a brief analysis of the two perspectives. Before reading my comments, ask yourself if there is any possibility of bridging the differences between the two communities. What do you think are the primary obstacles to building empathy? Can you find common themes upon which empathy might be built? Do you believe it is possible for the two individuals to understand each other?

A Greek Cypriot's View of the Cyprus Conflict[4]

Hello, my fellow student. I am glad to know that you are interested to learn something about the conflict in my beautiful but tragic country, and I will do my best to explain the situation to you. I don't know if you have heard much about Cyprus, but I am sure that you learned many things in your school about Greece because it gave the world the concept of democracy and provided the basis for all of Western science, art, medicine, and philosophy. Well, Cyprus has been part of the Greek world for more than 3,000 years, and if you visit my island you will see all the ancient Greek temples and other archeological sites. We have been speaking the Greek language here since the earliest Greeks arrived, just after the Trojan war described by Homer, the great poet of antiquity. Of course, we have endured many conquerors since that

time, but none of them have been able to take away our language and culture. We were subjugated by many empires, including the Romans, the Franks, and the Venetians, but we suffered the most under the Turks, who invaded our island over 400 years ago and kept us under their yoke for over 300 years.

When the Turks were ruling Cyprus they sent many soldiers and farmers here, who settled in many of our villages and towns. Today these people make up the Turkish Cypriot population, who comprise about 18% of the total. These newcomers to our island speak a different language (Turkish) and follow a different religion (Islam). We Greek Cypriots are very hospitable, however, so we used to get along quite well with the Turkish Cypriots. Most of them learned to speak Greek, and we lived together in harmony as good neighbors. After Turkish rule ended in the late 1800s, we became a British colony. The Turkish Cypriots stayed, and we let them keep their lands, houses, and businesses.

Although the British made some positive contributions to the island, particularly in improving our roads and other means of communication, they wouldn't let us join with Greece, our mother country, to whom we felt we belonged (at least at that time). The British wanted to keep us as their colony, but eventually we managed to get rid of them, thanks to our heroic EOKA (or freedom) fighters. Unfortunately, we were not able to achieve our goal of union with Greece, but we became an independent country, the Cyprus Republic, in 1960. However, our constitution was drawn up by outsiders, and it was very unfair, giving too much power to the Turkish Cypriots who were only 18% of the population. We tried to make it work, but the Turkish Cypriots were always blocking legislation, making it impossible for the government to function effectively. When we wanted to introduce some changes that would make the system more workable, the Turkish Cypriots decided to stop participating in the government. This happened near the end of 1963, and although I don't know much about what took place, I remember there were troubles that occurred when Turkish Cypriot terrorists killed some people. After that, the Turkish Cypriots chose to abandon their homes and villages and live together in areas they controlled. I guess they felt safer there, although they had nothing to fear from us. In any case, life went back to normal for a while.

Unfortunately, Turkey started getting involved in Cyprus around this time, and things took a turn for the worst. I think that Turkey was behind the Turkish Cypriots leaving the government and convinced them to be afraid of us. You see, Cyprus is only about 60 kilometers from the Turkish coast, and the expansionist plans of Turkey have always called for takeover of Cyprus. Turkey was waiting for the right opportunity, and it tried to create trouble several times. In 1974 we Greeks gave it the excuse it needed. There was a military dictatorship in Greece at the time, and it overthrew our government, installing its own leader in Cyprus in place of our democratically elected president. We were too weak to do anything about it, even though no one liked what happened. In any case, Turkey immediately sent in an invasion force to take over Cyprus, claiming it was intervening to protect the Turkish Cypriots.

When the Turkish army came, it was a savage and barbaric onslaught against a defenseless people. The army killed innocent civilians, raped the women, burned our forest, stole valuable icons. We put up a brave resistance, but the Turks had too many soldiers, tanks, and airplanes. We didn't stand a chance. The army landed on the north coast, and as it advanced, the soldiers forced all the Greek Cypriots from their homes and businesses, turning them into refugees within their own country. The Turks took many prisoners, and 1,619 of them are still missing. Finally the army stopped and drew a line across the middle of Cyprus, dividing the island into the north and south. After chasing all the Greek Cypriots from the northern part, the army took all the Turkish Cypriots and moved them to the north to live in our homes. In the end, it was a very effective job of ethnic cleansing.

My own family suffered greatly at the hands of the Turks. My father's brother was killed trying to defend against the invasion, and the son of my mother's sister was taken prisoner. We have never found out what happened to him. Our family came from a beautiful village on the north coast called Lapithos, in the Kyrenia district. My mother's family had lived there for generations, and we had a beautiful house and many orchards of cherry and almond trees. The view from our village was the best in Cyprus, since you could see all along the coast of the beautiful Mediterranean, while behind you were the magnificent forested slopes of the Pendedactylos mountains. There were some beautiful churches in Lapithos, with famous icons and centuries-old paintings, all of which were stolen by the Turkish army. When the Turks came, we had to leave quickly. We had no time to

pack anything. Everything was left behind, including all the wonderful lace and tablecloths my mother had made and even the photos of my parents' wedding. Now some Turkish military officer or some settler from Anatolia is probably living in our house, and who knows what condition it is in.

It was not easy to overcome the loss inflicted upon us by the Turks. My father and mother had three children, and they had to live in tents for many months before they could find a suitable house. I was born just after they found an apartment. Fortunately, my father worked for a bank in Kyrenia, so he was able to keep his job by transferring to another branch in Paphos. So we slowly recovered, in spite of the pain from the loss of my uncle and the tremendous anxiety about the fate of my cousin. Some of my friends were not so fortunate—they lost all means of supporting their families.

In spite of all that has happened to us, and in spite of the way the media reminds us daily of the losses we suffered, I never learned to hate the Turkish Cypriots. I have always known that it was the Turkish army that created all the trouble, and I am sure that if we could get rid of the army, we could live in peace with the Turkish Cypriots. Although most of my friends are more fanatic, my parents are peace-loving, and they have always said only kind things about Turkish Cypriots. My grandfather used to have many Turkish Cypriots working for him, especially during the time of the year when the fruit was ripening and the land needed working. We paid them well, and they always brought us things, such as the nice sweets made from the green almonds. My grandfather was one of those who learned to speak Turkish, so all the Turkish Cypriots liked him a lot.

I am worried, however, because the Turkish Cypriots are being taught a lot of propaganda about us, and I am not sure if the new generation will think of us so positively. I feel sorry for the Turkish Cypriots, because they have to live daily with the Turkish army, and I don't think they like the soldiers any better than we would. More disturbing is the fact that so many of them are leaving Cyprus and going to England or Canada because their economy is so poor and there are no job opportunities for them. It's ironic that they took the best part of Cyprus and yet they are in such bad condition. Turkey doesn't really care about the Turkish Cypriots, and the illegal regime of Denktash has brought in tens of thousands of uneducated farmers from Anatolia who are Islamic fanatics. Soon we won't have any Turkish Cypriots left in Cyprus, just a bunch of settlers that we could never live with.

Now the Turkish Cypriots have declared an illegal state in which they have their own pseudopresident and pseudoparliament. Everyone knows there is no democracy, and their leader, Mr. Denktash, is intent on keeping his power by maintaining the division of Cyprus. They talk about peace, but it is clear that they don't mean it. The Turkish army occupies nearly 40% of my island and doesn't intend to give up any of it. I'm afraid that Turkey wants the whole island and is just looking for the right excuse to continue the invasion. Lately, the Turks have been engaging in many provocative acts to create trouble. Our side has responded with restraint, but I'm sure that one day war will break out and we will lose everything and have nowhere to go.

In order to bring about a settlement to the Cyprus problem, the United States has to exert a lot of pressure on both Turkey and Mr. Denktash. Our side has compromised so much over the years, and yet there has been no movement from their side. The Turkish army continues its occupation of our country, even though there have been many United Nations Security Council resolutions calling for its withdrawal. I don't understand why countries such as the United States are willing to send in their armies to throw Saddam Hussein out of Kuwait but won't do anything about the illegal occupation of our country. Somehow, Turkey has become the "pet" of the Western world, and it can get by with anything. The whole international community ignores the blatant violation of human rights by Turkey, and the rest of the world doesn't seem to care that so much injustice exists right here in Europe. There can never be real peace in Cyprus until the Turkish army leaves, the settlers are expelled, and we Greeks are allowed to go back to our homes. Even though I was not born at the time, I have strong images of our home, and I believe that one day I will be able to return.

Well, I hope I haven't depressed you with my description of the situation in Cyprus. Myself, I am not very optimistic about the future. I live every day with the fear of another invasion. I really hope for a solution soon, because I know that both we and the Turkish Cypriots will be better off in a united Cyprus. Sometimes I come home and find my mother crying because she can see the Pendedactylos but cannot go there. She wants to visit her mother's grave and put flowers there. She goes every Sunday to church and prays for the day when she can go home again. It re-ally hurts me to see the pain in her heart, and I hope that before she finishes her life, she is able to live again in her own house.

A Turkish Cypriot's View of the Cyprus Conflict[5]

Greetings from Cyprus. It is a great honor to accept your invitation to explain a few things about the situation in this troubled place we call home. You probably think that Cyprus is a Greek island, and you may be surprised to learn that I speak Turkish, worship in a mosque (occasionally), and travel often to Turkey. I've never been to Greece, although I hope I can visit there someday. Unfortunately, the world understands very little about Cyprus and even less about the Turkish population of our little island. When I go abroad and tell people I am from Cyprus they always say something to me in Greek or ask something like "How is Zorba (or Zeus or some other Greek character)?" I find this very offensive, although I can forgive them because I know it is not their fault. The blame must be put on the Greeks and Greek Cypriots, who have managed to create many problems for this little island by spreading the myth that it belongs to Greeks. I apologize for starting off on such a negative tone, but you must understand that my people have suffered much in the past 40 years because of the Greek Cypriots, and I cannot escape these feelings.

The Turkish presence in Cyprus goes back to 1571, when the island became part of the Ottoman Empire and a population of Turks were brought to settle here and help the island grow and develop. At that time Cyprus was ruled by the Venetians, who subjugated the Orthodox Christian population and tried to convert them to Catholicism. The residents of the island welcomed the Ottomans as liberators, and the Orthodox church was given a great deal of autonomy and independence. In fact, it became an important part of the Ottoman administration, responsible for taking care of the affairs of the Christian population. The freedom and prosperity brought to the residents of Cyprus by the Ottomans was similar to that brought to other lands that became part of the Ottoman empire—the Ottomans were the first rulers to take a multicultural approach in the administration of vast territories. As Turkish Cypriots, we are proud of our Ottoman heritage and the many contributions our ancestors made to art, science, engineering. In

Cyprus their influence is everywhere—in the design of houses, in the traditional clothing styles, in the music and dance, in the handicrafts, and in the foods we eat. We remained part of the Ottoman Empire until 1925, when we became a British colony. I should point out that England had actually governed the island from 1878, after the initial breakup of the Ottoman Empire, until Cyprus gained its independence in 1960. In any case, it is important to remember that the Turkish population has been in Cyprus for more than 400 years, before the first English settlers came to North America, and that for most of that time we were the ruling class.

The current troubles started in the 1950s, when Cyprus was still a British colony. The Greek Cypriots tried to achieve what they call *enosis*, or union, with Greece—in essence to become a Greek island, like Crete or Rhodes. If you see what happened to the Turkish population of those islands when they became part of Greece, you will understand why the Turkish Cypriots did not want *enosis*—it would have meant the end of our existence. In fighting for *enosis*, the Greek Cypriots told us to stay out of the way, that it was their business and that we shouldn't worry because they would take care of us. Even while they were fighting against the British, there were several killings and even some massacres of Turkish Cypriots, so it is easy to see how they meant to "take care of us." Of course, the Greek Cypriots were not the only culprits, because the British were following their normal policy of "divide and rule," which helped turn us against each other. Actually, there were quite a lot of good Greek Cypriots who helped us and were very friendly as neighbors. But they let the extremists get away with destroying the relations between us. They should have stopped them while they had the chance, because now too many minds have been poisoned.

When Cyprus achieved independence in 1960, the constitution created a partnership between the Greek Cypriots and the Turkish Cypriots. Although it was not a completely equal sharing of power, there were certain guarantees built in to the system to ensure that the Turkish Cypriots, who were much fewer in number, would not be completely dominated by the Greek Cypriots. As you might expect, the Greek Cypriots did not like this system, and they set about trying to destroy it from the very first moment. Even though the constitution specifically ruled out the possibility of any kind of union with another country, the Greek Cypriots began immediately trying to find a way to continue their campaign for *enosis*. The

EOKA movement started again, and the Turkish Cypriots suffered almost immediately. In fact, the Greek Cypriots created the "Akritas Plan," which called for the extermination of Turkish Cypriots. Apart from that, they made it difficult for Turkish Cypriots to travel abroad, to get loans, to build businesses, and in other ways to live as full citizens of the Cyprus Republic. We were constantly harassed when we tried to travel from one place to another for work, to visit relatives, and even to get medical attention. We were treated as second-class citizens from day one.

In 1963 we were thrown out of the government by the Greek Cypriots. They tried to change the constitution from a partnership to a Greek Cypriot state in preparation for another attempt at *enosis*. In December of the same year, they began to implement the plan to exterminate the Turkish Cypriots, and we had no choice but to flee our homes and villages and gather in enclaves where we could protect ourselves. We left everything behind and became refugees in our own country. The Greek Cypriots looted our houses and sometimes would not allow basic supplies to come through to the enclaves. We had no work and no place to live that we could call our own. In some cases we were sleeping 20 people to a room, for months on end. It was a terrible existence. We began to hope that Turkey would come to our rescue. Before this, we had never felt that close to Turkey, but now we were forced by the Greek Cypriots to look to our motherland for protection.

Finally, in July of 1974, the Greek Cypriots went too far. They used military force to overthrow their own leadership and installed a known terrorist in power who could be a puppet of Greece. The Turkish prime minister went to Great Britain, one of the three guarantor powers of the independence of Cyprus (along with Greece and Turkey), and asked for intervention to prevent this illegal takeover. When Britain refused to take action, Turkey had no choice but to come to our rescue. It had shown great restraint several times during the previous 10 years, but it decided to act this time. Turkey feared additional massacres of Turkish Cypriots if it waited any longer, so on July 20 it began the rescue operation aimed at protecting the Turkish Cypriots and restoring the independence of the Cyprus Republic. War is never a pretty sight, and many people on both sides were killed. Many brave Turkish soldiers died while trying to protect us from the Greek Cypriots, who were intent on carrying out further massacres. It was decided that the only viable solution was to divide Cyprus into two zones, one administered by the Turkish Cypriots and the other by the Greek Cypriots. So we again had to give up our homes and become refugees. Almost all the Turkish Cypriots fled to the north part of Cyprus, and the Greek Cypriots decided to go to the south. A border was drawn across the middle of Cyprus, and at last the Turkish Cypriots felt safe and ready to start a new life.

My own family suffered so much from the Greek Cypriots between 1963 and 1974, and life has not been easy for us since that time. We had a beautiful house in a small village near Polis, one of the loveliest parts of the island. The sea there is so calm and clean, and there are wonderful wildflowers everywhere. In 1963 we had to abandon our house because of the threats by the Greek Cypriots, and even though we returned from time to time, we spent most of the next 10 years crowded together at my aunt's house in a nearby village, protected by sentries. I was not born until after the events of 1974, but I have heard so many stories from all my family, so the events between 1963 and 1974 seem very real to me. When the coup happened in 1974, my father, who was well respected in both communities, was shot by some Greek Cypriots belonging to EOKA, for no reason other than that he was a Turkish Cypriot. Fortunately, he survived, but we became refugees again, leaving the area where my parents' ancestors had lived for generations. We left everything behind and went by bus, under the protection of the United Nations, to our new home in Lapta (what the Greeks used to call Lapithos). Because our family had been well-off, we were given a nice house, but because it was not ours, we had a hard time getting used to living there.

Because of all the things that have happened, I don't know if we can ever live together with the Greek Cypriots again. Although many people from the older generation hate the Greek Cypriots, I don't personally have anything against them. We have to move beyond the past and never allow it to repeat itself. However, the only solution is to live separately, at least for one or two generations. When I hear my parents talk about the Polis area, I know they miss it, even though they have no desire to return to their former homes and face the difficulties and dangers of living among the Greek Cypriots.

In any solution the most important thing is our security, both physical and social. There is always the danger of attacks by Greek Cypriot extremists, and

given the record of the United Nations in other places around the world, the only force we can count on for protection is the Turkish army. I know the Greek Cypriots don't like this, but they have to face reality and understand that the Turkish Cypriots will never agree to a solution that does not guarantee their security. However, security is more than protection from physical attack. Since 1974 we have been able as a community to build up our own institutions and forms of government. Before 1974, we were just second-class citizens under the Greek Cypriots. It takes time for a community like ours to break out of a past in which we were so suppressed, so we still have many problems, and we are more dependent on Turkey than we would like. But if we have enough time, I know we can overcome these difficulties and feel proud of ourselves and what we have accomplished.

The primary obstacle to our development as a community is the extreme isolation we face in the world. The Greek Cypriots have managed to turn almost everyone against us, and they have placed an economic and diplomatic embargo against us that makes it almost impossible to develop our economy or our ties with other countries. They have managed to trick the world into viewing them as the sole legal representative of Cyprus, even though it should be obvious that we have no voice in their government. No one will trade with us or establish diplomatic ties because they are afraid they might upset the Greeks. I don't understand how the Greeks became such "darlings" of the western Europeans and the Americans. I think most of it has to do with the fact that we are Muslims, and the Christian world is not ready to accept us, in spite of their talk about tolerance and cooperation. I face this isolation every time I travel. I have to use the Turkish passport rather than my own, and because there are no international embassies on our side, I have to get my visas from Istanbul. My father's business does not qualify for any of the loan programs that the Greek Cypriots have access to from the European Union, and even the local chapter of the Rotary Club cannot belong to the international bodies because it is considered "illegal." We are always referred to as the "pseudostate" or the "illegal regime." This kind of treatment only hardens our attitudes, and I worry about how the young people like myself will ever develop a desire to make peace with the Greek Cypriots. Unfortunately, most of us won't stay in Cyprus after we finish our education, because there are few opportunities for meaningful jobs. The Greek Cypriots have pushed us away with their embargoes and the political isolation they have imposed on us, and soon the only people left in the north will be the hard-line politicians and the poor farmers coming here from Anatolia.

I'm sorry if I confused you with so many details, but the Cyprus situation is very complex. I am not very hopeful about the possibility for working things out in the near future, but I hope that someday I will be able to cooperate with the Greek Cypriots. Every day I wonder if the Greek Cypriots will start another war. They are buying so many arms and making constant talk about fighting. They won't stand a chance against the Turkish army, but if war comes, we will all suffer. My parents are getting older now, and the anxiety they have felt for the past 30 years gets stronger all the time. I hope that before they leave this earth, they can feel the peace in their hearts that comes from not having to worry about the possibility of war, harassment by Greek Cypriots, or becoming refugees again.

An Analysis of Conflicting Views

It is difficult to read these two letters without feeling some degree of hopelessness about the situation in Cyprus. Indeed, if you focus on the differences in *content* of the two letters, they seem so far apart that you must wonder if there is any possibility for a peaceful settlement to the conflict. The Greek Cypriots see the 1974 events as the starting point of the conflict, whereas the Turkish Cypriots see the 1963 events as the most crucial. The Greek Cypriots refer to 1974 as an invasion of the Turkish army, but the Turkish Cypriots refer to it as a peace operation. The Greek Cypriots believe that the two communities lived together happily before the division, and the Turkish Cypriots remember their unpleasant treatment as a minority. The Greek Cypriots believe that the island is undeniably Hellenic in character, and the Turkish Cypriots emphasize the Ottoman influence. The Greek Cypriots see the use of an economic embargo and political isolation of the Turkish Cypriots as the only way to force concessions, but the Turkish Cypriots see these as part of a continued attempt to push them off the island. The Greek Cypriots seek complete freedom of movement and settlement within the island, whereas the Turkish Cypriots seek a self-administered area with

a great deal of autonomy. The Greek Cypriots vehemently insist on the withdrawal of all Turkish troops from the island, and the Turkish Cypriots insist that the troops are required for their protection. The Greek Cypriots demand a return of their homes and property in the north, but the Turkish Cypriots have little or no desire to go back to their homes in the south. The list of differences could continue ad infinitum. One could easily conclude that there is no possibility for empathy to develop.

Unfortunately, the points listed above are exactly where the disputants get bogged down in their attempts to negotiate with one another—they focus exclusively on the content and fail to discuss aspects of the *process* that are holding them back. If we examine the two letters from a more analytical perspective, it becomes clear that both of the writers are trapped by a similar manner of approaching the events, and it is this approach—not the different views on the subject—that prevents empathy. Specifically, the letters illustrate five major barriers to empathy:

1. *One-sided interpretation of history.* It would be misleading to suggest that anyone can be completely objective about the past, but the deliberate distortion of history to serve primarily political purposes creates unnecessary division and presents a serious obstacle to reconciliation. The writers of both letters are very selective in their memory of past events, and their description of these events is far from objective. For example, the Greek Cypriot emphasizes the long history of Hellenic influence in Cyprus and totally ignores the positive contributions of the Ottoman period. In the current school curriculum of the Greek Cypriots, the Ottomans are portrayed as barbaric tyrants who treated the Greek-speaking population as slaves. Most accounts of this period clearly show that the Ottomans gave a great deal of autonomy to the Christians, putting mechanisms in place that allowed the Orthodox church to become very powerful in running the affairs of the island. The church was much better off under the Ottomans than under the Venetians or other previous conquerors. The Turkish Cypriot emphasizes the massacres by the EOKA militia during the 1950s and 1960s but

does not point out that a similar organization created by the Turkish Cypriots (called TMT) was guilty of equally hideous crimes. Many reports document that TMT instigated killings of their own people and then placed the blame on EOKA in order to generate greater fear of the Greek Cypriots among the Turkish Cypriots. These examples are typical of the way in which the past has been distorted beyond recognition by the educational systems and political propaganda of both sides. Such one-sided interpretations of historical events push the two communities further apart and allow little room for healing processes.

2. *Negative portrayals of the other.* It is difficult to share a small geographical area with someone you don't like, respect, or otherwise consider as your equal, and it is especially difficult if the other is considered your enemy. Both the Greek Cypriot and Turkish Cypriot paint a negative image of each other. The Turkish Cypriot description is especially harsh, portraying the Greek Cypriots as suppressors and murderers. Although there is acknowledgment of the "good Greek Cypriots," the overall image is one of extremists intent on exterminating the Turkish Cypriots. Historically, it is true that the Turkish Cypriots suffered a lot at the hands of Greek Cypriots, and even though the majority of the population was not directly involved in committing acts of violence, it took no steps to prevent the extremists from carrying out their deeds. However, most Greek Cypriots feel a degree of warmth toward the Turkish Cypriots, even if this warmth is sometimes condescending. At first glance it might seem that the Greek Cypriot was less negative in the portrayal of the Turkish Cypriots, especially given the reference to the kindness of Turkish Cypriot neighbors and their affection for the grandfather. However, it becomes clear upon closer examination that the Turkish Cypriots are not viewed with respect or equality. In the mind of the Greek Cypriot, Turkish Cypriots occupy a minority status and should not expect to be treated as equals. Their proper role is seen as workers and laborers for the more prosperous Greek Cypriots. Such images of the other do not make it easy to enter into productive negotiations about issues that divide communities.

3. *Placement of blame on the other.* It is rare that full responsibility for a problem can be attributed solely to one party. In Cyprus the case can be easily made that both parties share the blame equally (along with Turkey, Greece, the U.K., and the United States). Yet each of the letter-writers places almost full blame for the situation on the other. The Greek Cypriot claims that the troubles of 1963 started when Turkish Cypriot terrorists killed people; however, most international reports state that Greek Cypriots started the troubles. Similarly, the Greek Cypriot implies that the Turkish Cypriots created the constitutional crisis by withdrawing from the government; but most people outside of Cyprus recognize that it was the Greek Cypriot attempt to take away Turkish Cypriot rights that left the Turkish Cypriots no choice but to withdraw. Although some acceptance of responsibility is acknowledged for the role of the coup, the Greek Cypriot focuses almost exclusively on the expansionist policies of Turkey and the resulting invasion. There is no mention of the guarantor rights under the 1960 constitution that Turkey declared in carrying out its intervention. Similarly, the Turkish Cypriot lays primary blame for the current troubles on the *enosis* movement but does not acknowledge the current strong movement among Turkish Cypriot officials toward *enosis* with Turkey. The Turkish Cypriot blames the Greek Cypriots for enforcing an economic embargo against their products but never brings up the failure of Turkey to heed numerous United Nations resolutions calling for the prompt withdrawal of Turkish troops from the island. This kind of blaming places each of the parties in a defensive position, causing each to focus on attacking the other rather than acknowledging its own responsibility for creating and maintaining the situation. Such blaming actions quickly spiral into a mutually destructive exchange of accusations, making it impossible for the two sides to consider concessions to the other.

4. *Mistrust of the other.* No relationship can last long without the existence of mutual trust. Lack of confidence in the intentions of the other leads to continuous questioning of each other's motives. It is clear that each of the letter-writers is suspicious of

the motives of the other's community. This is particularly true for the Turkish Cypriot, who believes that the Greek Cypriots will take the first opportunity they find to continue their attempt to dominate and suppress the smaller Turkish population. The Greek Cypriot is convinced that Turkey is waiting for the right time to take over the whole island. Both sides are caught in a vicious trap, with one afraid to live without the protection of the Turkish army and the other living each day in fear of further attack by this same army. Even more serious, each side doubts the sincerity of the other about wanting an agreement. Each believes that the other is gaining positive benefits from the current situation and stands only to lose if the conflict ends. Such mistrust leads to continuous posturing by both sides, resulting in a game of exaggerated demands and resistance to backing off first for fear that one will take advantage of the other.

5. *Unwillingness to make offers of friendship toward the other.* No deadlock can be broken until one side or the other makes the first conciliatory gesture. If each side maintains a hard-line stance, it offers no way for the other to take positive steps that might relax the situation and lead to a positive climate for negotiation. In this case, it is not so much what one or the other says or does as it is what they *fail* to say or do. Although each of the letter-writers hints of possible cooperation, neither offers suggestions that might help defuse the tension. Each is afraid of taking the first step toward building confidence. The Greek Cypriot is waiting for the Turks to withdraw their troops and allow the Greeks to return to their homes, and the Turkish Cypriot is waiting for the Greek Cypriots to lift the embargoes and other restrictions. In order for fruitful discussions to take place between the two sides, each needs to offer an opening toward peace, a window in which a future could be built together.

Is Empathy Possible?

The dismal picture created by the students' letters does not become any more optimistic with the process analysis just completed. At first glance, the existence of the barriers in combination with the in-compatible positions seems to create an impossible situation. However, an awareness of these barriers offers hope for improving the situation. In conflicts where so much divides the parties, it is not always advisable to enter into direct discussions about the contentious issues. These discussions will almost certainly fail, as negotiations have failed numerous times in Cyprus. It is more productive to encourage different ways for the two sides to view each other and to communicate with each other. Each needs to develop a less one-sided view of history, to construct more positive perceptions of each other, to learn to accept responsibility for its own community's mistakes, to build a greater sense of trust, and to create ways of breaking the deadlock by taking steps toward the other. Only by overcoming these barriers can they develop a relationship characterized by genuine trust and empathy.

In both of the letters, the writers provided a small but significant opening on which to build a positive relationship. The Greek Cypriot expressed hope for a solution in the near future, and the Turkish Cypriot expressed hope that it will be possible to cooperate in the future with the Greek Cypriots. These hopes can provide an entry point for working together to overcome some of the prejudices and biases in their attitudes toward each other. As part of my work in Cyprus, we started a group of university students composed of over 50 individuals from each community who were willing to come together in a bicommunal setting for the purpose of learning about one another. Prior to our workshops, most of these students had never met anyone from the other community. They came in with a variety of attitudes toward the other community and a range of perspectives about the Cyprus problem. Through our meetings, these students began to overcome most of the barriers illustrated in the letters. By listening to one another, each learned more about how the history of the conflict is seen by the other side. Through their interactions, they gained more positive perceptions of one another. By discussing the effects of various events on each community, they took significant steps toward recognizing how their own community had contributed to the current situation. In working together on common projects, they slowly started the process of trust building.

Finally, by accepting one another as partners in the struggle for peace, they started thinking about ways to express friendship across the buffer zone that divides them. Of course, this group has a long way to go, but it has taken a giant leap toward reconciliation.

Fortunately, the student group is only one of many such bicommunal groups that are now operating in Cyprus.[6] Groups of young business leaders, young political leaders, educators, management trainees, women, journalists, policy leaders, and citizens from all walks of life are participating in workshops and seminars in which they attempt to overcome the obstacles to building peace on their island. Our experience has shown that under the appropriate conditions and using an appropriate methodology, groups can move beyond the barriers described above and develop a stronger basis for working together in the future.[7] Without such work, the two communities are destined to move further apart and remain forever trapped in a cycle of mistrust and misunderstanding.

Notes

1. For helpful descriptions of the Cyprus conflict, see Attalides (1979), Bahcheli and Rizopoulos (1996), Hitchens (1984), Markides (1977), Koumoulides (1986), and Stearns (1992).

2. On several occasions we have been able to schedule bicommunal meetings outside the buffer zone. When we have coffee together in the afternoon or eat lunch or dinner together, we often ask the owner of the coffeehouse or restaurant to tell us which members of the group are Greek Cypriot and which are Turkish Cypriot. The man's usual response, after a quick look at the group, is to throw up his hands and shake his head, saying that it is impossible to make the distinction. During a recent visit by a bicommunal student group to each community leader's office, it was clear that both Mr. Clerides and Mr. Denktash have the same problem.

3. I use the term "empathy" in the relational sense rather than in the psychological sense of the term. That is, I believe that empathy is a characteristic of the relationship between individuals rather than something that one person has for another. Viewed in this manner, empathy does not develop simply through the efforts of one person to understand another. Instead, it requires communication between individuals in a climate characterized by a willingness to learn. See Broome (1993) for a more complete description of relational empathy and its role in resolving difficult conflict situations.

4. For a more complete exposition of the Greek Cypriot point of view, see Clerides (1988). Also write to the Press and Information Office of the Republic of Cyprus, Nicosia, Cyprus.

5. For a more complete exposition of the Turkish Cypriot point of view, see Denktash (1988). Also write to the Press and Information Office of the "Turkish Republic of Northern Cyprus" in Lefkosa, Mersin 10, Turkey. Volkan (1979) provides a psychological analysis of the Cyprus conflict that helps explain many of the Turkish Cypriot fears toward the Greek Cypriots.

6. A written description of my initial work in Cyprus with peace-building groups is contained in a report that is available for the cost of copying and postage. Write to Anna Argyrou at the Cyprus Fulbright Commission (P.O. Box 4536, Nicosia CY1385, Cyprus) and ask for a copy of *Designing the Future of Peace-Building Efforts in Cyprus: Report of Design Workshops with the Conflict Resolution Trainers during 1994 & 1995*, initially written in January 1996 and updated throughout the year.

7. Many of these groups are using a problem-solving and design methodology called "interactive management," described in Broome and Keever (1989) and Broome and Chen (1992).

References

Attalides, M. A. (1979). *Cyprus: Nationalism and international politics*. Edinburgh, UK: Q Press.

Bahcheli, T., & Rizopoulos, N. X. (1996, Winter). The Cyprus impasse: What next? *World Policy Journal*, 27–39.

Broome, B. J. (1993). Managing differences in conflict resolution. In D. J. Sandole & H. van der Merwe (Eds.), *Conflict resolution theory and practice: Integration and application* (pp. 95–111). Manchester, UK: Manchester University Press.

Broome, B. J., & Chen, M. (1992). Guidelines for computer-assisted group problem-solving: Meeting the challenges of complex issues. *Small Group Research*, 23, 216–236.

Broome, B. J., & Keever, D. B. (1989). Next generation group facilitation: Proposed principles. *Management Communication Quarterly*, 3, 107–127.

Clerides, G. (1988). *My deposition* (Vol. 1). Nicosia: Alithia Publishing.

Denktash, R. R. (1988). *The Cyprus triangle*. New York: Office of the "Turkish Republic of Northern Cyprus."

Hitchens, C. (1984). *Cyprus.* New York: Quartet Books.

Koumoulides, J. T. A. (Ed.). (1986). *Cyprus in transition: 1960–1985.* London: Trigraph.

Markides, K. C. (1977). *The rise and fall of the Cyprus Republic.* New Haven, CT: Yale University Press.

Stearns, M. (1992). *Entangled allies: U.S. policy toward Greece, Turkey, and Cyprus.* New York: Council on Foreign Relations Press.

Volkan, V. (1979). *Cyprus—War and adaptation.* Charlottesville: University Press of Virginia.

Key Terms

bicommunal	Cyprus conflict
communication barriers	empathy
conflict	Greek Cypriot
content-process	Turkish Cypriot

Discussion Questions

1. This essay emphasizes how the lack of direct communication between parties over long periods of time creates obstacles toward efforts to resolve protracted conflicts. Do you believe this is always the case, or can you think of situations where the absence of contact can make problem solving easier?

2. The two letters contained in this article show that a great divide exists between Greek Cypriots and Turkish Cypriots. Do you think that differences of this magnitude exist between any cultural groups in the United States?

3. Broome suggests that it is more productive to focus on changing the form of communication between parties in conflict than to allow disagreements about issues to lead to a stalemate. How difficult do you think it is for parties to de-emphasize content and focus on process?

4. The five major obstacles to empathy illustrated in the letters could make any conflict situation more resistant to resolution. How might they be applied to conflicts with which you are familiar (either intergroup or interpersonal)?

5. At the end of his article, Broome mentions several bicommunal groups in Cyprus that are meeting regularly. He implies that through their interactions, they are overcoming the five major obstacles to empathy. What are some of the activities such groups might use to accomplish this aim?

Activities for Skill Development

1. Family History

Interview one of your family members, especially an older person, and ask the following questions: Where did your ancestors originally come from? Why did they relocate? Did your family surnames change? If so, why? What is your preferred ethnic identification? Also, what and how did you learn about your ethnicity? What are your experiences of discrimination?

2. "Different Versions" Exercise

Choose one historical event or person (e.g., Civil War, Thomas Jefferson, Christopher Columbus) and develop a list of different versions of knowledge associated with the history. Which version did you learn in school? Do you think it is important to learn different sides to history (hence, "histories")? What suggestions would you make to develop well-grounded historical consciousness?

3. Policy Exercise

Imagine that you, as an intercultural communication expert, have been asked to analyze the lingering effects of slavery in the United States. You have been commissioned by the federal government to recommend strategies in regard to reparation for past wrongs. Research a variety of positions, as well as ways in which governments have addressed similar issues pertaining to discrimination and persecution of U.S. American Indians, German Holocaust victims, and Black Africans in Zimbabwe and South Africa. Write brief position papers outlining your recommendations and share your thoughts with your classmates.

Web Sites

1. Are you well informed of the Black history? Check out the Black History Project by the Christian Science Monitor at <*http://www.csmonitor.com/atcsmonitor/specials/bhmonth/index.html*> and learn more about the Black history, from both U.S. and non-U.S. perspectives.

2. Want to learn more about world cultures and histories? Visit Professor Richard Hooker's "World Civilizations" course offered at Washington State University, <*http://www.wsu.edu:8080/~dee/WORLD.HTM*>. Browse through it and think about how learning about human histories helps us deepen our understanding of intercultural communication.

Additional Readings

1. Edelman, S. M. (2000). To pass or not to pass, that is the question: Jewish cultural identity in the United States. In M. W. Lustig & J. Koester (Eds.), *AmongUS: Essays on identity, belonging, and intercultural competence* (pp. 33–40). New York: Longman.

2. Morris, R., Sanchez, J., & Stuckey, M. E. (2000). Why can't they just get over it? In M. W. Lustig & J. Koester (Eds.), *AmongUS: Essays on identity, belonging, and intercultural competence* (pp. 134–147). New York: Longman.

3. Nakayama, T. (2000). Dis/orienting identities: Asian Americans, history, and intercultural communication. In A. González, M. Houston, & V. Chen (Eds.), *Our voices: Essays in culture, ethnicity, and communication* (3rd ed., pp. 13–18). Los Angeles: Roxbury.

PART FOUR

Language and Intercultural Communication

Language can serve to strengthen community and cultural identity; it can also be a source of misunderstanding and an obstacle in intercultural interaction. The essays in this part explore various aspects of language used in intercultural encounters—from very specific sociolinguistic features, such as accent, to broad language use across contexts. These essays show how language can be predicted to influence or reflect attitudes, or both, or how it can be studied as rituals that are intimately and reciprocally linked to cultural norms and identity.

The first two essays seek to explain and predict language use. In "Communication Accommodation in Intercultural Encounters," Howard Giles and Kimberly A. Noels describe how speakers adapt their language in intercultural interactions. These authors predict how and when individuals will seek to diverge or converge in their communication with others; that is, in some intercultural contexts individuals try to speak more (or less) like the person with whom they are speaking. They stress the important role language plays in cultural (e.g., ethnic) identity and point out that under certain conditions, individuals will try to minimize difference and converge with or "mirror" the other speaker's tone, rate, accent, and so forth. In some encounters, however, speakers will emphasize cultural difference and diverge in speech, particularly when power inequities exist.

In "Help! My Professor (or Doctor or Boss) Doesn't Talk English," Donald L. Rubin describes a common problem—when accent affects perceptions and leads to stereotyping. He presents a typical U.S. college interaction, between international instructors and college students, but also provides examples from health care and business interactions. Rubin shows how, in each case, that accent or *perceptions* of accent can result in "listening

115

barriers." He bases his conclusions on a series of objective data-based studies and then gives practical suggestions for overcoming the tendency to negatively stereotype on the basis of accent.

In another education example, Donal Carbaugh explores the contrasts between Native Americans and White communication rules in U.S. classroom contexts. In "'I can't do that' but I 'can actually see around corners,'" he describes the communication among the Blackfeet, which emphasizes listener-active silence more than public speaking skills. He shows how the Blackfeet communication patterns are in direct contradiction to typical demands of U.S. classrooms, where public speaking is a highly valued skill. Carbaugh illustrates how these different communication patterns reflect deeply held beliefs and values. Using conclusions based on personal experiences and ethnographic interviews, he suggests that teachers should carefully consider what they are asking Native American students (and other cultural groups) to "undo," and outlines what each group might learn from the other.

"A Ritual for Attempting Leave-Taking in Colombia," by Kristine Fitch, focuses on a specific language pattern in an international context. She analyzed conversations that took place between hosts and guests at social occasions and argues that in these social gatherings, special relationships, or *vínculos,* are formed. These relationships lead to particular ways of saying good-bye. Fitch shows how these language rituals, as cultural expressions, serve to strengthen interpersonal relationships in social contexts.

Finally, Jean-Louis Sauvage, in "Code-Switching: An Everyday Reality in Belgium," describes from personal experience what it is like to live in a country with a complicated history that led to the presence of three different language groups: Dutch-speaking Flemish, French-speaking Walloons, and German speakers. He explains the various ways and contexts in which code-switching (changing languages in midconversation) occurs. He also points out the challenges and the joys of being bilingual and able to code-switch, emphasizing that in spite of difficulties, learning a foreign language opens doors to other cultures, other worlds, and, ultimately, the hearts of other people.

13 Communication Accommodation in Intercultural Encounters

HOWARD GILES and KIMBERLY A. NOELS

When members of two cultural groups come together, they often have to make choices about whose communication system to use and how much to accommodate each other. Consider backpackers in a European youth hostel at the end of a day on the road. Travelers from the four corners of the world, including Germans, Israelis, Australians, South Africans, Iranians, Americans, and Japanese, come together in the common room to prepare their meals. They discuss the details of their latest adventure, share their impressions of the city in which they have arrived, and seek advice on the next place to visit. How will they communicate? What language will serve? For those who can speak each other's language, how will they decide which linguistic code to use? The process of negotiating these decisions and their behavioral implications is the concern of the theory covered in this chapter, Communication Accommodation Theory (CAT). We will begin with a discussion of the importance of language for interethnic relations. The fundamental tenets of CAT will then be outlined, including the notions of convergence and divergence, followed by a consideration of some recent research findings.

The Importance of Language in Intercultural Relations and Communication

Despite the complexities of negotiating a language for intergroup communication, few scholars have investigated language behaviors and processes in intercultural encounters. This is surprising given worldwide prominence of language issues in intercultural interactions, and particularly in conflict-ridden interactions (Clément, 1996). Consider the following examples.

The official language of the Ottoman Empire, which had been in use for over 400 years, was sup-pressed in 1922 in an effort to promote a modern version of the language. It was felt that this linguistic change to modern Turkish would discourage identification with the old empire and encourage linguistic identification with central Asia. Elsewhere, in an attempt to distinguish their language from Serbo-Croatian, Macedonian writers in Yugoslavia began to incorporate words and grammatical structures used in rural areas in an effort to develop a new standard of the language. This attempt to change the language occurred at the same time as Macedonians strove for a separate Macedonian republic in Yugoslavia.

During the 1976 Soweto riots in South Africa, many Blacks and Whites were killed. These riots occurred at a time when Blacks were protesting the White government's insistence that the Afrikaans language be used in the education of Black students. As expressed by Black leaders,

the situation has unearthed the innermost frustrations of Black people which were hidden from the outside world. Although there is a prevalent belief in some quarters that Afrikaans as a medium of instruction was not a direct positive factor in these riots, this is not so. Afrikaans was forced down Black students just as much as the Trust Land Act, pass laws, and migratory labour. (reported in *The Times* [London, June 23, 1979], cited in Giles & Coupland, 1991, p. 95)

As a symbol of White domination and oppression, Blacks most certainly perceived the enforced use of Afrikaans in the school system as an abhorrent and inexcusable attack on their social identity.

More recently in Canada, concerns over cultural autonomy and language maintenance threaten to divide Canadians. In a 1995 provincial referendum, 49% of the Quebec population voted to remove themselves as a province from Canada, a percentage only slightly less than the 51% who decided to stay in Confederation. This concern over cultural maintenance centers to a large extent on linguistic issues: The Quebec government passed legislation requiring that commercial signs be printed primarily in French and that French be the primary language of instruction for most non-French-speaking immigrant children (Lemco, 1992).

Finally, concern over language issues remains an important facet of ethnic relations in the United States. In response to the diversity of languages spoken in some areas, many states have declared English as their official language. These movements are also evident at the federal level. Identity issues have often centered in these debates, for those who are both for and against official language policies. For instance, Republican House Representative Norman Shumway (1992) wrote

> [English] has been the "glue" which has held us together, forging strength and unity from our rich cultural diversity. From our earliest days, despite our melting pot inheritance, English has been the language in which we expressed the goals, objectives, ideals, principles and duties of our form of government. It is the language in which the Declaration of Independence and the Constitution are written. . . . And in my view, it is the primary language in which our government should continue to function. (pp. 121—122)

Elsewhere, in opposition to an officially monolingual society, columnist Montaner (1992) writes

> "We quarrel, are jealous, love, and hate with certain words, with certain tones, with certain inflections of the voice learned in childhood and adapted to a given set of gestures that also cannot be transported into another language. . . . We cannot do without our own tongue without brutally mutilating our individual consciousness. . . . If this is so, is it reasonable to ask millions of human beings to do without this fundamental part | of their lives solely so that others are not inconvenienced . . . ? (p. 164)

WHY IS LANGUAGE SO IMPORTANT FOR INTERETHNIC RELATIONS?

According to Giles and Coupland (1991), there are at least three reasons: Language is often a criterion for group membership, it is a cue for ethnic identity, and it is a means of facilitating ingroup[1] cohesion.

There are different criteria for membership in an ethnic group, including ancestry, physical features, religion, and so on. Most ethnic groups also have a distinct language or dialect, and the ability to use this language may be necessary for group membership. To illustrate, there was a common saying in Hispanic communities in the southwestern United States in the 1970s: "A Mexican American who can't speak Spanish should choke on his chili beans!" Even when there are clear and distinctive criteria for ethnic group membership, such as skin color, an ethnic language variety often remains a critical attribute. When he met his African "brothers" in Sierra Leone, one African American member of the Peace Corps was surprised and dismayed when they called him *oyimbo* (White man) because of his standard American English and behavior (Hancock, 1974).

Language has been shown to be an important aspect of ethnic identity, more important even than cultural background for many social groups, albeit not for all. For instance, Smolicz (1984) argued that Dutch people in Australia did not consider language to be central to their identity, although Polish and Greek people did. Taylor, Bassili, and Aboud (1973) found, however, that some French Canadians felt closer to an English Canadian who spoke French than to a French Canadian who did not. In a similar vein, Clément, Gauthier, and Noels (1993) examined Franco Ontarian adolescents who spoke French most often or English most often. Their results showed that although both groups learned French as their native language, Francophones who spoke primarily English identified less strongly with the Francophone group and more with the Anglophone group than did those who spoke primarily French. For many groups, then, the language used is closely connected to feelings of ethnic identity.

Language is also important for ensuring within-group cohesion. Kim (1988) suggests that the linguistic code, as one of the primary media through

---

[1]The term "ingroup" refers to the group to which the individual belongs. The term "outgroup" refers to any group to which the individual does *not* belong.

which the daily activities of human affairs are conducted, can well be described as a carrier of culture. By sharing a common language for communication, individuals also share a common manner of interacting in the social world. Moreover, this shared commodity carries symbolic value: Fishman (1977) suggests provocatively that language "can become the ultimate symbol of ethnicity, since in expressing, referring to, and evoking something else in addition to itself, it becomes valued in itself" (p. 25). Naturally enough, people are very emotionally attached to this ethnic symbol, so much so that ethnic group members using a language and speech style other than that of their group may be labeled cultural traitors by fellow group members. Indeed, recent Internet graffiti from the United States on the Punjab Usenet group (cited by Sachdev, 1995) illustrates how important language may be for within-group solidarity: "To any Punjabi out there, whether you are a Hindu, Muslim, or Sikh. If you speak Hindi or Urdu instead of Punjabi, you are a serious disgrace to your culture and you shouldn't call yourself a Punjabi!" (p. 175).

At the same time, it is important to note that members of an ethnic group need not speak the language so long as they have it available; indeed, "ethnicity is frequently related more to the symbol of a separate language than to its actual use by all members of a group" (De Vos, 1975, p. 15). Gaelic, Welsh, and Breton are all examples of languages that are not spoken by the majority of those who identify with their respective groups, but that are nevertheless highly valued as aspects of ethnic identity. Moreover, De Vos argues that, even without a distinct language, "group identity can . . . be maintained by minor differences in linguistic patterns and by style of gesture" (p. 16). For example, many immigrants may speak their host language, but with a distinctive accent and with words and phrases borrowed from their own ethnic tradition, culture, and religion. In a similar way, many Australians are reexamining the influence of American and European traditions on Australian culture and are considering the nature of a distinctive Australian identity. In an article about the Australian Renaissance ("Ockerism") in the *London Observer Review* (June 27, 1976), language was considered to be a central aspect of this issue:

Americanization of the language is much more significantly pervasive than the high incidence of skate-boards and roadside fast food parlors. . . . The American invasion of the Australian stomach was always on the cards. But the invasion of the language is less easy to laugh off. (cited in Giles & Coupland, 1991, p. 100)

Language is hence often important for intercultural relations because (1) it serves to classify people as members of a particular ethnic group, (2) it is important for their identity as an ethnic group member, and (3) it can be used to emphasize solidarity between ingroup members and to exclude outgroup members from ingroup transactions.

Communication Accommodation Theory

Having established that language behaviors have diverse and complex implications for interethnic relations, we move now to consider how it is that communicators fashion their self- (and also group) presentations via language. The framework used to describe and explain these communicative behaviors is Communication Accommodation Theory (CAT). According to CAT, we are motivated to use language in different ways to achieve a desired level of social distance between ourselves and our listener. Each of us often accommodates verbally and nonverbally to others—and is aware of others accommodating to us (or *not*, as can be the case) on many levels. Such experiences are common in settings such as the classroom, the courtroom, business and commerce, and so forth. To illustrate, referring to the travelers in the youth hostel described in the introduction, an American traveler from Georgia may use a standard U.S. American accent (such as the accent used by television anchorpersons on national television) while talking with a fellow-traveler from Vermont. Upon returning home to Georgia, he may switch back to the accent more typical of that part of the country. It may even be argued that there are no occasions in which we do not adjust our language style to take into account what we believe to be the perspective of the person with whom we are interacting.

There are many kinds of accommodative acts, many reasons for accommodating, and many consequences arising from accommodation. In the following sections, the fundamental strategies of convergence and divergence and their complexities are addressed first. We then examine the synchrony between speakers' intentions and actual behavior, and listeners' interpretations. Finally, we consider how social beliefs, such as stereotypes and norms, guide accommodation, although not always in ways that lead to successful interactions.

CONVERGENCE AND DIVERGENCE

Convergence can be defined as a strategy whereby individuals adapt their communicative behavior on one or a number of linguistic, paralinguistic, and nonverbal features in such a way as to become more similar to their interlocutor's behavior. Among the many communicative behaviors that may be modified are languages and dialects, and characteristics found within language groups, such as speech rate, pauses, utterance length, phonological variants, smiling, and gaze. Although most studies have been conducted in the West and in English-language settings, convergence on temporal, phonological, or language-switching dimensions has been noted in many different languages, including Hungarian, Frisian and Dutch, Hebrew, Taiwanese Mandarin, Japanese, Cantonese, and Thai (see sources in Giles, Coupland, & Coupland, 1991).

As suggested earlier, motives for converging vary widely. Certainly, converging to a common linguistic style can improve the effectiveness of communication (Gallois, Giles, Jones, Cargile, & Ota, 1995)—the similarity in speech styles between interlocutors has been associated with predictability (Berger & Bradac, 1982) and intelligibility (Triandis, 1960). Another motive that has received considerable attention since the inception of the theory (Giles, 1973) is the desire to gain approval from one's interlocutor. The premise is that the more similar we are to our interlocutor, the more he or she will like us and the better able we will be to gain social rewards from them. Indeed, convergence is generally associated with more positive evaluations (Bourhis, Giles, & Lambert, 1975). This tendency, however, may be constrained by several factors that are discussed later in this essay.

Divergence refers to the way in which speakers accentuate speech and nonverbal differences between themselves and others. Divergence is designed to emphasize distinctiveness from one's interlocutor, usually on the basis of group membership. Following the premises of Tajfel's (1978) Social Identity Theory, CAT maintains that individuals categorize the social world into groups, and derive a part of their identity and self-esteem (called "social identity") from groups to which they belong. Assuming that people are motivated to maintain self-esteem, they will tend to differentiate their own group from other groups, provided they are pleased to belong to that group.

Consistent with the idea that people will try to differentiate themselves linguistically from others when their social identity is strong, Bourhis and Giles (1976) designed an experiment to demonstrate the use of accent divergence among Welsh people in an interethnic context. The study was conducted in a language laboratory where people who placed a strong value on their national group membership and its language were learning the Welsh language (only about 26% of Welsh people at that time, as now, could speak their national tongue). During one of their weekly sessions, Welsh people were asked to help in a survey concerned with second language learning techniques. The questions in the survey were presented to them verbally, in English, in their individual booths by a very English-sounding speaker, who at one point arrogantly challenged their reasons for learning what he called a "dying language with a dismal future." As expected, the informants diverged by broadening their Welsh accents when replying to the perceived threat to their ethnic identity, compared to emotionally neutral questions asked earlier. Moreover, some informants began introducing Welsh words and phrases into their answers. One Welsh woman did not reply for a while, and then was heard to conjugate a pejorative verb gently into the microphone.

A phenomenon similar to divergence is *maintenance,* in which a person continues in his or her original speech style, in spite of the convergence or divergence of the interlocutor. Maintenance is often evaluated in the same way as divergence (Bourhis, 1979).

FIGURE 1 • Some Increasing Variants of Convergence and Divergence
(*Source:* Adapted from Giles, Bourhis, and Taylor, 1977.)

FURTHER DISTINCTIONS IN CONVERGENCE AND DIVERGENCE: DIRECTION, DEGREE, AND MUTUALITY OF ACCOMMODATION

The complementary nature of convergence and divergence is summarized in Figure 1. Individuals may speak the language of the outgroup with no trace of an accent, such that they can pass as a member of that group, or they may affect a slight to heavy accent to hint at their ingroup origins. Alternatively they may maintain their original language but speak more slowly to help the outgroup member understand. Finally, they may completely diverge (i.e., show no convergence) by using the ingroup language at the usual speed used by native speakers. One might accommodate on one feature, such as accent, but at other times on multiple features, for example, by adjusting word choice and speech rate in addition to accent. Moreover, convergence (or divergence) on some features of a language does not imply that there will be convergence (or divergence) on all features.

Accommodation is not a one-way process. As outlined in Figure 2 (p. 122), within a communicative episode, each interlocutor can converge, diverge, or maintain, although not necessarily to the same extent as the partner. When accommodation is approximately equal for both partners, it is said to be symmetrical. At other times one partner may converge or diverge to the greater or lesser extent, or fail to react (i.e., maintain), or behave in a contrasting manner. This is called asymmetrical accommodation. Thus, although convergence and divergence are complementary concepts, they can both occur in a communication episode and in different ways for each interactant. Moreover, as complex as accommodation is, its complexity is amplified further when one considers how speakers interpret their own and their listeners' intentions subjectively.

OBJECTIVE, SUBJECTIVE, AND PSYCHOLOGICAL ACCOMMODATION

There are several levels on which accommodation phenomena can be investigated. The previous discussion focuses on objective accommodation, that is, on actual communicative behavior, as assessed through direct observation of linguistic exchanges in an interaction. The examination of accommodation, however, is not restricted to this behavioral level, but includes, perhaps more interestingly, an examination of the intentions of speakers and the perceptions of listeners. These latter two levels are termed psychological and subjective accommodation, respectively. A speaker's intention is often consistent with actual behavior, but this need not always be the case. For example, referring back to the example in the introduction, one of the American travelers may decide to adopt a Spanish accent in order to accommodate a Spanish fellow-wanderer. This accent may not, however, truly represent the Spanish speaker's accent or in any way correspond with an actual Spanish accent. Similarly, speakers may converge to their listener objectively, but the intent behind this convergence may not be to indicate intimacy with the listener but to exclude the listener from the language group. For instance, Woolard (1989) reports of a language norm in Spain to the effect that Catalan should only be spoken between Catalans, such that Castillian speakers who

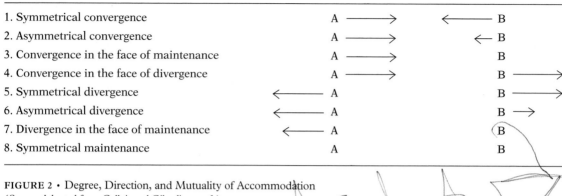

FIGURE 2 • Degree, Direction, and Mutuality of Accommodation
(*Source:* Adapted from Gallois and Giles [in press].)

attempted to speak Catalan would likely receive a reply in Castillian. In an empirical examination of correspondence between speakers' intentions and their actual behavior, Thakerar, Giles, and Cheshire (1982) examined student nurses in conversations with their supervisors. Contrary to objective measures that indicated that their behavior became less similar to the supervisors', the nurses maintained their behavior did not change.

Subjective accommodation refers to the listener's interpretation of the speaker's act. Like psychological accommodation, subjective accommodation does not necessarily correspond with objective behavior. Returning to the example of the interaction between the Spanish and English speakers, the Spanish speaker may not be familiar enough with English to notice that the English speaker has altered his or her language or may not recognize the change as a shift to a Spanish accent. Similarly, even if the change in behavior is perceived, the Spanish speaker's interpretation may not be consistent with the English speaker's intention—the Spanish speaker may see it as a rude joke, as mimicry of his or her imperfect English. In a similar vein, Giles and Smith (1979) varied convergence on three linguistic characteristics—pronunciation, speech rate, and message content—and found that convergence on any one level was viewed positively but that convergence on all three levels was viewed negatively. Thus, in spite of the greater similarity that objective convergence implies, the listener may not interpret this behavior as actually indicating greater intimacy.

OPTIMAL LEVEL OF ACCOMMODATION: STEREOTYPES AND NORMS

The mismatch between objective accommodation on one hand, and psychological and subjective accommodation on the other, implies that interactants have some notion of an optimal level of accommodation (Giles & Smith, 1979); that is, speakers and listeners have beliefs and expectations that act as guidelines for what is appropriate and acceptable accommodation behavior. Two such guidelines are stereotypes regarding outgroup members (and their level of communicative competence) and beliefs about the appropriate norms regarding language use.

Stereotypes Stereotypes about characteristics of outgroup members are often associated with expectations about how they will respond in a social encounter. Returning to the interaction between the American and Spanish travelers, the American may expect Spanish people to be emotional and sociable, and alter his or her behavior to become similarly expressive and outgoing. Using the stereotype as a guideline for communication, the American may risk offending the travel-weary Spaniard, who in fact sees such behavior as boisterous and intrusive. In this scenario, the American could be said to over-accommodate the Spaniard. Other expectations regarding characteristics and behaviors of outgroups may similarly affect convergence. For instance, the person who thinks that his or her interlocutor could not reasonably be expected to be fluent in the speaker's language may not see divergence or maintenance in a negative light. In line with this notion, Simard, Taylor, and Giles (1976) found that nonconvergence on the part of the interlocutor that was the result of linguistic incompetence was viewed less negatively than nonconvergence that was perceived to be the result of a lack of effort.

Norms In addition to stereotypes regarding outgroup members, norms regarding language use can also influence the extent of convergence and divergence, and the manner in which these accommodation phenomena are evaluated. According to De-Ridder, Schruijer, and Tripathi (1992), when two groups coexist in a society for a long period of time, they establish norms for how members from the two groups should interact with each other. Extending this idea to the realm of language, these norms may constrain the extent to which one can converge or diverge. For instance, Bourhis (1991) found that despite the fact that the French-speaking population was a majority in provincial government offices in New Brunswick, Canada, both Anglophones and Francophones reported using English more often than French when interacting across language groups. Moreover, regardless of the level of English competence, Francophones were more likely to converge to English, even when the English speaker was a subordinate employee. The same was not true of English speakers, who usually maintained their use of English even when interacting with French-speaking superiors. Thus, intergroup norms for language use overrode the importance that demographic representation could have had in affecting patterns of language use. Adherence to norms may also moderate our impressions of others. Simard, Taylor, and Giles (1976) found that when attempts to converge were perceived as a reaction to situational pressures forcing them to converge, convergence was viewed less positively than when it was seen as an attempt to reduce intercultural distance between the two speakers.

A pervasive norm is that individuals will converge to the language of the group with greater ethnolinguistic vitality, who often speak what is termed the standard or prestige variety of a language. Ethnolinguistic vitality refers to the power of a language group, in terms of its demographic representation, institutional support in areas such as government and education, and social prestige (Giles, Bourhis, & Taylor, 1977). Thus, all other factors being equal, it would be expected that Latinos converge to English speakers in the United States, Francophones converge to Anglophones in Canada, and Turkish speakers converge to German speakers in Germany. This straightforward hypothesis is complicated by the fact that different dialects may compete as a standard language. To illustrate, although French remains a prestigious language in Tunisia since France's attempt to colonize that country up until the 1940s, Tunisian Arabic is widely accepted as a marker of "real" Tunisians. Lawson-Sako and Sachdev (1996) investigated convergence, divergence, and code-switching in Tunisian pedestrians who were randomly approached by either Arab Tunisians or White Europeans who asked for directions to the local post office. Half of the pedestrians were asked for directions to the post office in Tunisian Arabic and half in French. The researchers expected that a Tunisian confederate asking for information in Tunisian Arabic would receive a reply in Tunisian Arabic, and a European would receive one in French. Although respondents generally converged to the language of the researcher, they were more likely to converge if the request was presented in Tunisian Arabic. They were more likely to use code-switching strategies or to diverge if addressed in French. Thus, despite the prestige of French, Tunisians were likely to signal their distinctiveness from their former colonizers.

Further complexities are evident when one considers that different dialects may have varying appeal for different groups of people. For instance, Al-Khatib (1995) explains that although Modern Standard Arabic may be the standard dialect in Jordan, the urban variety of Jordanian Arabic is also highly regarded, albeit more so by women than by men. In an investigation of the impact of interlocutor sex on linguistic accommodation, Al-Khatib examined the use of phonological variants of the two dialects by speakers on a phone-in radio show. As expected, men were more standardized in their linguistic behavior, and women were less standard-ized and more urbanized.

The importance of gender in determining ad-herence to different linguistic styles is further illus-trated in a study by Willemyns, Gallois, Callan, and Pittam (in press). Undergraduates applying for a job as a research assistant received two interviews, one from an interviewer who spoke in a broad Aus-tralian English accent and one from an interviewer who spoke in a cultivated accent. Male applicants diverged from cultivated-accented females, partic-ularly if they identified with the broad accent. As pointed out by Willemyns and his colleagues, this is consistent with the premises of CAT that the stronger a person's loyalty to their language, the more he or she will emphasize distinctiveness be-tween groups. Women, however, did not change their accent, suggesting that they are more accom-modative than men.

In addition to considering intergroup norms, situa-tional norms may further affect the extent and eval-uation of language use. For instance, in the study by Willemyns et al. (in press), applicants used broader accents when talking with the broad-accented in-terviewer than when talking with the cultivated-accented interviewer. There was, however, no evi-dence of convergence to the cultivated-accented interviewer. The authors suggest that possibly the formal nature of the interview situation primed the applicants to speak with as cultivated an accent as possible. Depending on the formality of the situa-tion, convergence and divergence may be more or less positively viewed. Coté and Clément (1994) presented students with hypothetical interactions between a Francophone and an Anglophone. In less intimate, task-oriented settings, Anglophone inter-locutors who used English were evaluated less fa-vorably than those who used French; but in intimate situations, the language used by the Anglophone interlocutor did not affect their evaluations. The authors suggested that in intimate situations, expec-tancies regarding appropriate language behavior may be more relaxed and flexible than in task-oriented situations. Thus, the positivity of conver-gence may be situationally bound.

Epilogue

This essay has focused on the importance that lan-guage has in intercultural relations. It suggested that language helps to categorize, symbolize, and give coherence to cultural groups. Because language is often an important aspect of ethnic identity, how we use it can emphasize how closely we identify with the people with whom we interact, so that by con-verging our linguistic style to others', we generally wish to indicate closeness, and by diverging in our linguistic style, we generally imply distance. Space precludes a discussion of many other issues ad-dressed by CAT, such as accommodative strategies at the discourse level or greater elaboration of the is-sues of under- and overaccommodation, but more extensive treatments can be found elsewhere (e.g., Gallois et al., 1995; Gallois & Giles, in press; Giles & Coupland, 1991; Giles et al., 1991). The present discussion does suggest, however, that satisfying communicative exchanges may require a delicate balance of convergence to demonstrate willingness to communicate, as well as divergence to promote a healthy sense of group identity (see Cargile & Giles, 1996).

We have seen that interactants have expectations regarding the optimal level of convergence and di-vergence, expectations that may be based on stereo-types about outgroup members and norms for in-tergroup interactions and situationally acceptable behavior. Individuals' linguistic choices may cor-respond with their intentions and with listeners' in-terpretations, but there is oftentimes a mismatch between these aspects of accommodation. In inter-cultural interactions, it is not difficult to imagine the potential for miscommunication that can result if interactants do not share common assumptions about group characteristics and appropriate inter-group behavior across different situations.

It is also important to note that CAT's utility in explaining intercultural relations extends beyond the microinteractions discussed here, to more ma-crolevel ones, including issues of language learning, language maintenance and shift, and creolization. With its attention to intergroup communication strategies, CAT can readily be applied to other intergroup settings, such as encounters between genders, across generations, and between people who are physically challenged and those who are not. However CAT is applied, the perspective emphasizes that intercultural communication or communication in general is often not so much about the exchange of referential information as it is about social connectedness and the negotiation of social identities.

References

Al-Khatib, M. (1995). The impact of interlocutor sex on linguistic accommodation: A case study of Jordan radio phone-in programs. *Multilingua, 14,* 133–150.

Berger, C. R., & Bradac, J. J. (1982). *Language and social knowledge.* London: Edward Arnold.

Bourhis, R. Y. (1979). Language in ethnic interaction. A social psychological approach. In H. Giles & B. Saint-Jacques (Eds.), *Language and ethnic relations* (pp. 117–141). Oxford: Pergamon.

Bourhis, R. Y. (1991). Organizational communication and accommodation: Toward some conceptual and empirical links. In H. Giles, J. Coupland, & N. Coupland (Eds.), *Contexts of accommodation* (pp. 270–303). Cambridge: Cambridge University Press.

Bourhis, R. Y., & Giles, H. (1976). The language of intergroup distinctiveness. In H. Giles (Ed.), *Language, ethnicity, and intergroup relations* (pp. 119–135). London: Academic Press.

Bourhis, R. Y., Giles, H., & Lambert, W. E. (1975). Social consequences of accommodating one's style of speech: A cross-national investigation. *International Journal of the Sociology of Language, 6,* 55–72.

Cargile, A. C., & Giles, H. (1996). Intercultural communication training: Review, critique, and a new theoretical framework. In B. R. Burleson (Ed.), *Communication yearbook, vol. 19* (pp. 385–423). Thousand Oaks, CA: Sage.

Clément, R. (1996). Prologue: Social psychology and intergroup communication. *Journal of Language and Social Psychology, 15,* 222–229.

Clément, R., Gauthier, R. M., & Noels, K. A. (1993). Choix langagiers en milieu minoritaire: attitudes et identité concomitantes. *Canadian Journal of Behavioral Science, 25,* 149–164.

Coté, P., & Clément, R. (1994). Language attitudes: An interactive situated approach. *Language and Communication, 14,* 237–251.

DeRidder, R., Schruijer, S. G. L., & Tripathi, R. C. (1992). Norm violation as a precipitating factor of negative intergroup relations. In R. DeRidder & R. C. Tripathi (Eds.), *Norm violation and intergroup relations* (pp. 3–38). Oxford: Clarendon Press.

De Vos, G. (1975). Ethnic pluralism: Conflict and accommodation. In G. De Vos & K. Romanucci-Ross (Eds.), *Ethnic identity: Cultural continuity and change* (pp. 5–41). Palo Alto, CA: Mayfield.

Fishman, J. A. (1977). Language and ethnicity. In H. Giles (Ed.), *Language, ethnicity, and intergroup relations* (pp. 15–58). London: Academic Press.

Gallois, C., & Giles, H. (in press). Accommodating mutual influence in intergroup encounters. In M. Palmer (Ed.), *Mutual influence.* New York: Guilford.

Gallois, C., Giles, H., Jones, E., Cargile, A. C., & Ota, H. (1995). Accommodating intercultural encounters: Elaborations and extensions. In R. Wiseman (Ed.), *Intercultural communication theory* (pp. 115–147). Thousand Oaks, CA: Sage.

Giles, H. (1973). Accent mobility: A model and some data. *Anthropological Linguistics, 15,* 87–109.

Giles, H., Bourhis, R. Y., & Taylor, D. M. (1977). Towards a theory of language in ethnic group relations. In H. Giles (Ed.), *Language and intergroup relations* (pp. 307–348). London: Academic Press.

Giles, H., Coupland, J., & Coupland, N. (Eds.). (1991). *Contexts of accommodation: Developments in applied sociolinguistics.* Cambridge: Cambridge University Press.

Giles, H., & Coupland, N. (1991). *Language: Contexts and consequences.* Pacific Grove, CA: Brooks/Cole.

Giles, H., & Smith, P. M. (1979). Accommodation theory: Optimal levels of convergence. In H. Giles & R. St. Clair (Eds.), *Language and social psychology* (pp. 45–65). Oxford: Blackwell.

Hancock, I. F. (1974, Spring/Fall). Identity, equality, and standard language. *Florida FL Reporter, 49–52,* 101–102.

Kim, Y. Y. (1988). *Communication and cross-cultural adaptation.* Clevedon, Avon: Multilingual Matters.

Lawson-Sako, S., & Sachdev, I. (1996). Ethnolinguistic communication in Tunisian streets: Convergence and divergence. In Y. Suleiman (Ed.), *Language and identity in the Middle East and North Africa* (pp. 61–79). Richmond, Surrey: Curzon Press.

Lemco, J. (1992). Quebec's "distinctive character" and the question of minority rights. In J. Crawford (Ed.), *Language loyalties: A source book on the official English controversy* (pp. 423–433). Chicago: University of Chicago Press.

Montaner, C. A. (1992). "Talk English—you are in the United States." In J. Crawford (Ed.), *Language loyalties: A source book on the official English controversy* (pp. 163–165). Chicago: University of Chicago Press.

Sachdev, I. (1995). Predicting Punjabi linguistic identity: From high to low in-group vitality contexts. *International Journal of Punjab Studies, 2,* 175–194.

Shumway, N. (1992). Preserve the primacy of English. In J. Crawford (Ed.), *Language loyalties: A source book on the official English controversy* (pp. 121–123). Chicago: University of Chicago Press.

Simard, L., Taylor, D. M., & Giles, H. (1976). Attribution processes and interpersonal accommodation in a bilingual setting. *Language and Speech, 19,* 374–387.

Smolicz, J. J. (1984). Minority languages and the core values of culture: Changing policies and ethnic response in Australia. *Journal of Multilingual and Multicultural Development, 5,* 23–41.

Tajfel, H. (Ed.). (1978). *Differentiation between social groups.* London: Academic Press.

Taylor, D. M., Bassili, J. N., and Aboud, F. (1973). Dimensions of ethnic identity: An example from Quebec. *Journal of Social Psychology, 89,* 185–192.

Thakerar, J. N., Giles, H., & Cheshire, J. (1982). Psychological and linguistic parameters of speech accommodation theory. In C. Fraser & K. R. Scherer (Eds.), *Advances in the social psychology of language* (pp. 205–255). Cambridge: Cambridge University Press.

Triandis, H. C. (1960). Cognitive similarity and communication in a dyad. *Human Relations, 13,* 175–183.

Willemyns, M., Gallois, C., Callan, V. J., & Pittam, J. (in press). Accent accommodation in the job interview: Impact of interviewer accent and gender. *Journal of Language and Social Psychology.*

Woolard, K. A. (1989). *Double talk: Bilingualism and the politics of ethnicity in Catalonia.* Stanford, CA: Stanford University Press.

Key Terms

accommodation
- linguistic accommodation
- objective accommodation
- optimal level
- overaccommodation
- psychological accommodation
- subjective accommodation

Communication Accommodation Theory
convergence
divergence
ethnolinguistic vitality
ingroup
intergroup differentiation
maintenance
outgroup
Social Identity Theory
underaccommodation

Discussion Questions

1. Drawing from your own experience, what might be the implications of CAT for learning a second language? Using the constructs of convergence and divergence, discuss how well an individual might learn a second language and how often he or she might be inclined to use it.

2. As pointed out in this essay, CAT can be applied in a variety of intergroup contexts (e.g., intercultural, intergenerational, intergender, etc.). Consider how CAT might be useful in describing interactions between grandparents and their teenaged grandchildren. How does the application of the theory in this context differ from the intercultural context—or does it?

3. Reflect on your travels to other areas where people do not speak your native language. How did you decide on which language to use to speak with the people from that country? Was the reaction of those people to your language choice positive, neutral, or negative? How would CAT explain why this reaction happened?

14 Help! My Professor (or Doctor or Boss) Doesn't Talk English

DONALD L. RUBIN

On his way to the first meeting of his Introduction to Business Accounting class, marketing major Greg Hanover[1] was feeling that familiar sickly sweet sensation in the pit of his stomach—half anticipation and half fear—that always accompanied him during the first week of class. As he approached the classroom, he saw his friend Barbara Coleman, another junior in marketing, hovering just outside the doorway. Greg and Barbara had taken two classes together last year, and they would occasionally get together to study before an exam.

"Hey," called Greg, "looks like the dynamic duo is back together again to fight the Battle of Accounting this fall. Let's go do it, partner."

"Hey, Greg! Awright!" Then, with her smile waning, Barbara continued, "But I don't know about this here accounting class. I just can't risk getting a bad grade in it. I need at least a B."

"Well, it's a required class; you've got to take it anyway, so we'll just bust our chops and do it. Right? I mean it may not be the most exciting stuff, but we'll do okay, and really I can see that you kinda need this stuff."

"It's not that. Have you looked to see who's teaching it?"

Barbara motioned with her head for Greg to glance into the room. The instructor was standing at the podium, looking over some notes, shuffling papers until the official start of class period. Barbara rolled her eyes and raised her eyebrows.

"Yeah, so, it's some TA. You always get graduate students teaching these intro classes. So what?"

"I'm sorry," Barbara said with finality in her voice, "I just can't go through another killer class with a teacher who doesn't speak English. I mean, math is not my best subject. So at least I need a guy who can speak the language when he's doing problems at the board. This summer I took stat from this Chinese guy. And I mean he was smart and everything I guess, but geez I couldn't understand a word he said. And everybody in the class

was the same way. Some of them even went to the department chair to complain. Most people just stopped going because they could learn just as much on their own. I even went to the tutor and everything—but that lady was from some damn place too and it was just as hopeless with her. I mean, I was lucky I even got a D in that class. So I said, from now on I'm not going to take any more classes from foreigners."

"So what are you gonna do?" asked Greg.

"I'm going to the section that's scheduled for 3:20 this afternoon and see who's teaching it. I might have to move my work schedule around, but it'll be worth it to me even if I have to take a closing shift one or two days a week. I just can't take another class from a guy who can't talk English. And if the teacher for that 3:20 class is another one of them, I dunno. . . . I gotta go. See ya! Good luck, sucker."

"Hey," Greg called after Barbara, "you've still got my number? Let me know what you find out about that afternoon class, okay? Give me a call!"

International Instructors on U.S. Campuses

Many readers will find that the preceding conversation between Greg and Barbara strikes a familiar chord. It is an instance of what communication researcher Nagesh Rao (1995) has called the Oh No! syndrome. In one survey (Rubin & Smith, 1988), more than two out of every five students reported that they had withdrawn from a class or switched classes when they found that their teacher was a non-native speaker of English.[2] Nearly three out of five agreed with Barbara in the vignette above and attributed a poor grade in at least one class to

---

[1] All names used in this chapter are fictional. The incidents are not.

[2] Some institutional data (Norris, 1991; Oppenheim, 1996) suggest that students actually "vote with their feet" when they encounter international teaching assistants much less frequently than their survey responses indicated.

the poor communication skills of an international instructor.[3]

It's an ever more common scenario. The number of international instructors in U.S. colleges and universities is on the rise. Already by 1987 40% of the junior faculty teaching mathematics at U.S. institutions had received their own degrees overseas (Smith, Byrd, Nelson, Barrett, & Constantinides, 1992). Less than a decade later, nearly one third of *all* graduate teaching assistants (i.e., faculty-in-training across all disciplines, not just the math-intensive fields) at some major universities were not native speakers of English (Oppenheim, 1996). In a number of math-intensive fields such as computer science and physics, well over half the doctoral candidates who are qualifying to teach at the college level are not U.S. citizens. In large universities, the student who graduates without ever encountering an international instructor is rare indeed; many have encountered four or more international instructors in four years of college (Fox & Gay, 1994; Plakans, in press; Rubin & Smith, 1988).

Ethnolinguistic Minority Speakers in Positions of Authority

The growing internationalization of the college professoriate is just one case of a broader social trend regarding ethnolinguistic minorities in the United States. In the past, ethnolinguistic minorities in this country almost always occupied subservient social strata—disproportionately undereducated, politically powerless, economically exploited. To be sure, ethnolinguistic minorities more often than not continue to occupy underclass positions in the United States. But as this nation moves toward greater infusion of cultural heterogeneity throughout its various sectors and strata, the phenomenon of ethnolinguistic minority speakers in positions of relative

authority or power becomes increasingly frequent. Thus, as we have seen, it is now commonplace on most North American college campuses for Chinese or Arab or Latino instructors to occupy positions of relative authority over mainstream Anglo students (i.e., the teacher's institutional authority over the student).

A parallel situation occurs in the health care context. Increasing numbers of physicians are internationals, many of whom do not speak standard American varieties of English. As a rough correlate of national and ethnolinguistic diversity among the ranks of physicians, the American Medical Association estimated that 21.4% of all U.S. physicians licensed in 1990 were international medical graduates, perhaps a quarter of whom were U.S. citizens (Roback, Randolph, & Seidman, 1992). Between 1970 and 1992, the number of international medical graduates practicing in the United States increased 132% (U.S. Department of Commerce, 1994). Apparently these physicians are subject to the same sort of Oh No! syndrome as are international instructors. As evidence, consider the following introduction to a letter to advice columnist Abigail Van Buren:

> Dear Abby: So many physicians today seem to be of foreign extraction. I have no problem with that, if one can understand them. However, my gynecologist's new partner is Asian, and I often leave his office wondering what he has told me. . . .
> ("Patient Irked by Doctors with Accents," 1990, p. E2)

Another parallel situation emerges in employment contexts, in which upper-level managers of multinational corporations are often non-U.S. nationals, often not speakers of mainstream North American Englishes. For example, in 1989, within just the relatively isolated state of Georgia, Japanese trade officials estimated that about 200 manufacturing and commercial establishments maintained Japanese national management teams to supervise U.S. workers (Rubin, DeHart, & Heintzman, 1991). The not uncommon antipathy of mainstream North Americans toward Japanese managers was the premise of the popular 1980s comedy film *Gung Ho*. Here too, then, we see ethnolinguistic minorities in positions of power. In complex but increas-

---

[3] The perception of students that international instructors damage their grades does not generally comport with actual institutional data. On average, students who enroll in class sections taught by international teaching assistants do just as well on examinations (Jacobs & Friedman, 1988) and on final course grades (Norris, 1991) as students who are taught by U.S. teaching assistants.

ingly common social dynamics such as these, how do listeners evaluate the speech patterns of such speakers?

Some Dimensions of Language Variation

Before we proceed much further discussing linguistic stereotypes, it is necessary to describe exactly who is subject to such stereotyping. I am going to label these speakers by means of an admittedly clumsy—but I think informative—acronym. I will call them NNSMNAEs. The acronym stands for the mouthful, "Non-Native Speakers of Mainstream North American Englishes." We need to use this acronym as a consciousness-raising device. It reminds us that no one group or nationality owns the English language. It reminds us that we tend to judge a speaker's English language skills to be wanting mainly when that speaker's style fails to match our own. And it reminds us that the lines of demarcation between who counts as a standard English speaker and who is linguistically deviant can be fuzzy indeed.

Consider, for example, Chakravathi ("Chaki") Ghoshal. Chaki is a graduate teaching assistant in educational psychology. To look at him, he is clearly a person of color, and behind his back, at least one Anglo student has referred to him as a "sand nigger." Chaki's English is marked by language features that set him apart from North American speakers. For example, he pronounces the consonant "v" like the sound /w/ (e.g., "a wery big book"). Occasionally, his sentence structures sound odd, though not technically ungrammatical (e.g., "The question, it is not so very difficult were you to break it down"). Chaki grew up in a household in which English was spoken most often, with Hindi spoken mainly in the presence of his grandparents. He attended a school in which most academic subjects were taught in English from first grade. His own undergraduate college education in Bombay was conducted entirely in English. And yet when he first taught at a U.S. college, a delegation of students complained that Chaki was "a foreigner who can't speak English." To the contrary, Chaki *is* a native speaker of English, but

the variety of English he speaks is an Indian English (Kachru, 1970). To accuse Chaki of not being a native English speaker is both an insult to him and an embarrassment for his accusers. The accusation also maligns the marvelous breadth and flexibility of the English language.

The United States receives large numbers of immigrants and sojourners from nations such as Jamaica in the Caribbean, Nigeria in central Africa, and Guam in the Pacific, as well as India and Pakistan in South Asia. Many residents of these nations speak English as their native languages, but they are not the same varieties of English one typically hears in Nebraska or Connecticut. They speak what have become known as "world Englishes." It is important to appreciate that just because one does not speak a North American English, one may still be wholly proficient in a world English. U.S. students who would like to grab a share of the emerging global economy would be wise to become comfortable at least in world Englishes (if not in some second or third language), the *lingua franca* for communication of international trade and technical information.

Consider now the case of Hilda Estrada-Jackson. Hilda teaches an introduction to art history. Her mother is from a Puerto Rican background, though she grew up in New York City, as did Hilda. Hilda's father is African American, also a native New Yorker. Although Hilda can conduct rudimentary conversations in Spanish ("restaurant Spanish" her cousins in Puerto Rico call it), not much was really spoken in her home. Indeed, much of the Spanish Hilda did hear at home and on the streets of East Harlem was a kind of hybrid "Spanglish." When Hilda lectures or answers a student question, her sentence structure is quite standard, but her pronunciation marks her as culturally different from her students. She may say something that sounds a little like /Chew gunna halfta figyo that out yosef, my fren/.

Hilda feels that students challenge her credibility and authority more vociferously than they challenge her Anglo colleagues. She suspects that her students prejudge her to be academically inept (at least until they take her first exam!) because they stereotype her based on her skin color and her language patterns. Clearly Hilda is a native speaker of North American English, but it is not a *mainstream* language variety like that of most of her students.

Finally, meet Li Wen Shu, a laboratory assistant in the nutritional science department. Wen Shu is a native speaker of Cantonese. He started learning English as a high school junior. (Prior to that time English was not a frequently taught language in the People's Republic of China, and even afterward, most language teaching materials and models came from the British Council.) He has been living in the United States for 6 years now, always choosing to room with a North American roommate, so as to improve his English skills. While he knows much current slang, he still misses the allusions of many common sayings and cliches such as "bone tired" or "easy as pie." Like many second language speakers, he has difficulty recognizing when people are joking around or being sarcastic in English, and he long ago abandoned any hope that English speakers would appreciate his own attempts at a light-hearted tone. Wen Shu has become quite proficient in English, but he may never quite master native English speaker patterns. Thus his speech will always mark him as "foreign."

We see, then, that deviations from mainstream North American English patterns can derive from various sources and can be manifest in a variety of ways. NNSMNAEs may mark their "otherness" by means of nonstandard pronunciation (what linguists call "phonology"), different ways of forming words ("morphology"), different choices and uses of words ("lexicon" and "semantics"), or variant sentence structures ("syntax").

One source of language interference that especially troubles mainstream listeners relates to the way language is used in social contexts ("pragmatics"). For example, a teaching assistant may say "Now it is the time for your question" rather than "Does anyone have any questions before we move on?" Students may perceive this teaching assistant as gruff or rigid, and perhaps they will not feel comfortable voicing the questions that are on their minds. In truth, this instructor may care a great deal about student learning but simply has not quite mastered North American norms for inviting inquiry (Myers, 1994).

Another type of language interference that seems to deeply affect listeners' impressions of NNSMNAEs pertains to the category of "prosody." Prosody refers to features that overlay words, such as stress and sentence intonation. Prosody gives our speech rhythm, melody, and emphasis. In typical Mainstream North American English (MNAE) declarative sentences, we drop our voices at the ends of sentences, and we usually do not stress each syllable equally. To mention but one example, in contrast, it is common for native Mandarin Chinese speakers to violate these MNAE patterns for prosody. As a result, it can seem to some North American listeners as if the Chinese speaker of English is shouting or scolding. Indeed, some studies conclude that prosody exerts more impact than even vowel and consonant pronunciation on listeners' judgments of speaker proficiency (see review in Munro & Derwing, 1995).

Linguistic Stereotyping

Some of the earliest and most influential research on how a speaker's language variety can trigger listeners' stereotyped evaluations was conducted in the 1960s in Quebec (for a comprehensive review of language and attitude research, see Bradac, 1990). Researchers wanted to determine how listeners in that ethnolinguistically fractious setting would react to speakers solely on the basis of language choice— French vs. English. But the researchers knew that listeners react not only to *group* identities deriving from language choice, but also to *idiosyncratic* personality factors signaled by such highly individual vocal cues as voice quality (nasal, resonant, etc.) and pitch (high or low). They therefore developed the "matched guise technique" (Lambert, Hodgson, Gardner, & Fillenbaum, 1960), which has served ever since as a methodological mainstay of language and attitude research. Matched guise research uses a speaker who is competent in more than one language variety to produce speech samples. When comparing reactions to, for example, a French speech sample and an English speech sample produced by the same speaker, researchers can be confident that any measurable differences in listener attitude are due solely to the contrasting language varieties.

Using the matched guise technique in the French Canadian context, researchers found that listeners formed very strong impressions of speakers based on very brief speech samples. The sociopolitical climate in Quebec has changed considerably since those studies were conducted (see for example Guimond & Palmer, 1993), but at that time, Francophone Québécois constituted a distinct underclass, whereas Anglophone Quebecers controlled most financial and governmental resources. Language attitudes paralleled this social stratification. When listeners heard a speaker talking in French, they judged the speaker to be less intelligent and less capable than when the very same speaker spoke in English. These linguistic stereotypes were similar for both Anglophone and Francophone listeners, leading to the conclusion that many French speakers in Quebec suffered from a kind of "linguistic self-hatred." Perhaps of greatest concern was the impact of language attitudes in educational settings. Teachers judged French-speaking children to have lower scholastic potential than their English-speaking peers. Teachers tended to give a low grade to a composition attributed to a French-speaking child, while the very same composition attributed to an English-speaking child received a higher grade (Seligman, Tucker, & Lambert, 1972).

Inspired by these studies of language and attitude in French Canada, U.S. researchers began to consider whether similar processes contributed in particular to stereotyped interracial perceptions. Not surprisingly—but still sad to say—it was found for example that Spanish-accented speakers suffered at job interviews. When listening to a Spanish-accented guise, personnel officers judged a job applicant eligible for a janitorial job, whereas the same person speaking in a MNAE might be judged management trainee material (de la Zerda & Hopper, 1979).

In school settings, educators were trying to understand why children who spoke Black English Vernacular (BEV) tended to achieve more poorly than children who spoke MNAEs. There are no barriers to learning inherent in BEV grammatical structure (Labov, 1972). Instead, teachers' linguistic stereotypes may contribute to student failure. When teachers hear students speaking BEV, they may expect those students to be less intelligent and less academically oriented. These teacher expectations can become self-fulfilling; that is, teachers may give less assistance and encouragement to the BEV speakers, and hence over time those children do indeed become academically less skilled than MNAE speakers (Williams, 1976). Thus the nonstandard language variety is not itself the cause of student failure, but teachers' reactions to that language variety may contribute to failure in school. Even when there is no linguistic basis for judging a student, if a teacher determines that a student belongs to an ethnolinguistic minority group, that teacher may *perceive* more nonstandard features in the student's language and devalue the student's school achievement accordingly (Pichè, Rubin, Turner, & Michlin, 1978).

The "Foreign Teacher Problem"[4]

The case of NNSMNAE college instructors is the obverse of these earlier studies of teacher expectancy and language attitudes. Here we have students judging their teachers rather than the other way around, teachers who are "others" vis-à-vis the dominant culture, and a curious power dynamic

---

[4] I place the phrase "foreign teacher problem" in quotes because I want readers to think about the implications of each of its terms. The term "foreign" itself carries negative connotations (the term "international" is more neutral) because it conveys the sense that a person so labeled is like an invading body, not to be embraced by the society, but eventually to be isolated and expelled. Moreover, the salient issue may or may not be the instructor's overseas birth. Britishers or Canadians are not generally regarded as part of the "foreign teacher problem"; their particular international status might even be seen as an advantage in a teacher. On the other hand, U.S.-born teachers of Latino backgrounds cannot legitimately be called "foreign," yet they very likely are included in the "problem." And briefly, interrogate the nature of the term "problem" here. Why should a teacher with a broad background and multilingual ability be defined as a "problem"? If there were a "problem," to whom does it rightfully belong—to the international instructors or to the U.S. students? Who is in the best position to fix any such "problem"?

wherein teachers would surely possess high authority were it not for the compromising impact of their ethnolinguistic identities.

Negative reactions to "foreign" teachers are legion. College newspapers, as well as the wider circulation press, periodically investigate or editorialize about the "problem." Typical is this lead article from the *St. Louis Post Dispatch:* "For some college students, the classes taught in the ivory tower sound more like something out of the tower of Babel. They say they can't understand—much less learn from—some of the foreign graduate students teaching their classes" (Casmier, 1993, p. 1). State legislators and regents have in many instances joined the chorus decrying "foreign" instructors' inadequate teaching skills (Monoson & Thomas, 1993).

The overwhelming complaint is that "foreign" teachers lack sufficient English proficiency. They are too hard to understand. Their lectures are incomprehensible, they fail to understand students' questions, and in any event their responses to student questions are just as undecipherable as are the lectures that caused the confusion in the first place. Students who are frustrated by their NNSMNAE instructors usually give up on their teachers and seek other information resources—other classmates or bearing down with the textbook—or else they just plain give up (Fox & Gay, 1994; Plakans, in press).

Universities across the United States have responded to student, legislative, and administrative complaints with programs to "remediate" instructors' English skills (see review in Smith et al., 1992). Usually these programs are targeted to graduate student teaching assistants (TAs), perhaps in part because it is politically more expedient to dictate requirements for graduate assistants than for full-fledged faculty members. While initially focusing on strictly linguistic skills such as pronunciation and classroom vocabulary, these TA testing and remediation programs have evolved so that they now address a wide range of instructional skills—for example, how to formulate good test questions, how to write a clear syllabus, how to conduct a lively discussion, even how to appreciate cultural diversity among U.S. undergraduates. In fact, these "foreign" TA workshops are the kinds of training experiences that would be of benefit to *all* college teachers, regardless of experience and regardless of ethnolinguistic background.

Stereotyping in the Perception of NNSMNAE Instructors

If these language "remediation" programs have the felicitous outcome of improving NNSMNAEs' teaching skills, perhaps that is fine. But just how justified are they? Are NNSMNAE instructors really so difficult to understand? No doubt some NNSMNAE instructors do lack adequate English skills and should never be thrust to the front of a classroom. But all of our prior knowledge about linguistic stereotyping suggests that we had better look carefully at any accounts that attribute blame only to those who diverge from the ethnolinguistic mainstream.

First, let's ask by what criterion we should be judging the English language proficiency of NNSMNAEs. The bottom line in evaluating the speech performance of any teacher ought to be intelligibility and comprehensibility. Can the instructor be understood? Comprehensibility and intelligibility are not the same as subjective judgments of speech accentedness or foreignness. In one study (Munro & Derwing, 1995), college students rated a set of tape-recorded speech samples as highly accented—even some speech that (unknown to them) was produced by MNAE speakers. On the other hand, when those same students listened to those very same speech samples on another occasion, they comprehended the speech quite well. Just because you think an individual speaks with a strong accent does not mean you can't understand that person.

Next, let's consider the validity of our judgments of speech accentedness. A number of studies suggest that many U.S. students cannot distinguish between accents from different nationalities (e.g., between native speakers of British English and Malaysian; see Gill, 1994). Also, U.S. students aren't very acute in distinguishing different degrees of accentedness (e.g., between highly and moderately Chinese-accented English; see Rubin & Smith, 1988). I believe that each of us has a sort of "threshold of foreignness." When we feel (for reasons that are not fully understood) that a speaker's accent falls beyond some limit of tolerable divergence from MNAE, we perceptually lump that speaker together with other NNSMNAE speakers. In effect, we write off the speaker as just one more incomprehensible "foreigner."

Now we are ready to see how these perceptual processes operate in our judgments of NNSMNAE college teachers (summaries of relevant research can be found in Rubin, 1992, and in Smith et al., 1992). We know from end-of-term course evaluation data that international instructors are generally judged to be poorer teachers than their U.S.-born colleagues. Students regard NNSMNAE instructors as relatively less approachable, less enthusiastic, less interpersonally attentive, and less fair.

These perceptions of NNSMNAE instructors can be influenced by a variety of factors. Some of these factors are indeed instructionally relevant. For example, instructors with stronger English proficiency (as independently measured) or those who use personal anecdotes to help convey information fare relatively well. But judgments of language proficiency and teaching competence are also susceptible to factors that should be extraneous. For example, the nationality of a speaker (e.g., Sudanese vs. Italian vs. Iranian in one research study) or attributed institutional status (professor vs. TA) can affect students' reactions to the very same speech sample (Brown, 1992). A student's own background and experience also influence his or her impressions of NNSMNAE teachers. Students with liberal arts majors seem to be more tolerant than agriculture students (Fox & Gay, 1994; Plakans, in press). Students in more advanced classes register more positive evaluations than students in introductory ones (Oppenheim, 1996).

Students' stereotyped expectations of NNSMNAE teachers are foregrounded in a series of studies in which I have been involved. In these studies, for example, students who thought an instructor (whether international or U.S. born) was physically attractive generally had more positive perceptions of the instructor's accent and teaching competence. (This is adding insult to injury for those of us who resemble Gene Hackman more than Robert Red-

ford!) More to the point of this story about ethnolinguistic identity, student judgments of instructors were not sensitive to *actual* differences in degree of accentedness. However, judgments of instructors were affected by listeners' *perceptions* of accentedness. Teachers whom students *heard* speak with a strong accent—regardless of the reality of those accents—received relatively poor ratings.

In addition, students' perceptions of the cultural "otherness" of the teacher exerted equally strong impact. Specifically, the degree to which students saw a teacher as more Asian-like and less Caucasian-like negatively influenced their evaluations of that teacher. These findings are consistent with others that examine how students on predominantly White campuses perceive Black teachers (Hendrix, in press).

To explore how students respond to the very ethnicity of NNSMNAE instructors—apart from any language differences—I devised a very simple experiment.[5] Students heard a lecture tape-recorded by a MNAE speaker (a speech teacher from central Ohio). In one condition the students were shown a slide of an Asian face, and told that this was the face of the instructor to whom they were listening. In the other condition they were shown a Caucasian face. When students thought they were listening to an Asian, they perceived the instructor to speak with a marked accent—that is, students *heard* a "foreign" accent just because they were looking at an Asian face. Even more distressing, students recalled significantly less information when they thought they were listening to an Asian. They found the Asian's speech to be less comprehensible than the Caucasian's, even though in reality *it was the very same MNAE speech*. This is about the clearest possible evidence of stereotyped expectations in operation. One expects an Asian instructor to be incomprehensible, and so one in fact comprehends less.

Why are U.S. undergraduates so likely to harbor distorted perceptions of NNSMNAE teachers? Perhaps students have heard college folklore conveying horror stories about "foreign" teachers, and this

---

[5] This study has now been replicated and extended, with similar results. This gives me a degree of confidence in its conclusions.

creates high levels of anxiety. This anxiety throws up an "affective filter" that prevents students from listening accurately. We do know that direct experience with NNSMNAEs can dispel that tendency to distort. Students who have had relatively large numbers of classes from NNSMNAEs can comprehend accented speech with greater accuracy, and their attitudes toward NNSMNAEs are less negative.

This pattern of results, incidentally, is generally consistent with findings regarding NNSMNAEs in other professional or higher status settings. In the case of Japanese managers in a sales organization, for example, U.S. listeners had relatively positive attitudes when they judged the manager to be speaking with a MNAE accent. Even when the manager was in fact using a "Japanese-typical" persuasive strategy, listeners regarded him positively, as long as they mistakenly thought that his persuasive strategy was American-like (Rubin et al., 1991). In the case of South Asian physicians, U.S. listeners did a poor job of discriminating a moderate Indian accent from a stronger one. But when they *believed* they were listening to a South Asian, they found this doctor to be cold and unsympathetic. They did not like this person. Interestingly, though, in terms of medical competence, U.S. patients were not uncomfortable with the expertise of a "foreign" doctor. Their comprehension was not measurably impaired by listening to a NNSMNAE physician, but that is because their overall comprehension of the medical topic was so poor even when listening to an identified MNAE speaker, that it could hardly have been made any worse (Rubin et al., in press).

Strategies for Dealing with Linguistic Stereotypes

I do not believe that you or I or anyone else is a "bad person" for harboring linguistic stereotypes. Stereotyping is inevitable and in fact has some adaptive value for us. What I do believe is that we must all acknowledge and explore our stereotypes and then figure out how to deal with those stereotypes so that we can treat people in an equitable fashion, according to their merits rather than according to our expectations.

In the case of NNSMNAE instructors, their merits—if we allow ourselves to come to know

them—are likely to be rather impressive. In many countries, the proportion of the population with access to higher education is less than a tenth of the U.S. norm (about 45% of the U.S. adult population has had at least some college course work). A college graduate from one of these nations, therefore, must possess extraordinary qualities. And then imagine the degree of competence and dedication it takes for one of these overseas graduates to function at a U.S. university level (even if not perfectly) in a second language! College students in the United States are indeed fortunate to be able to draw upon the intellectual elite from across the planet.

In order to capitalize on the invaluable resource that NNSMNAE teachers—or physicians or corporate managers—represent for us in the United States, we need first off to accept that successful intercultural communication occurs when *both* parties in an interaction make efforts to accommodate each other. To be sure, many NNSMNAEs can use improvement of their English language and instructional communication skills, and we can be grateful that so many universities have initiated instructional development workshops for that purpose. At the same time, members of the mainstream host culture also need to accommodate. In fact, when we consider which parties are under the least stress in U.S. culture, which have the greatest degree of discretion and choice in their behaviors, and which have the most to gain from a successful classroom interaction—it makes sense to think that MNAE speakers might do a sizable share of the accommodating in these encounters.

A number of experts have laid out principles for effective intercultural communication behaviors in general (see, for example, review in Martin, 1993), and for effective student-teacher intercultural interactions in particular (e.g., Fox & Gay, 1994; Plakans, in press; vom Saal, 1987). From these, we can extract some concrete recommendations for MNAE-speaking students (or patients or workers) to take responsibility for effective communication with NNSMNAE instructors (or doctors or bosses):

• *It's okay to talk about language and cultural differences.* Most sojourners from another culture are delighted to have a chance to speak about the customs with which they grew up. The trick is to avoid putting the other on the defensive, as if you are attacking the person for being different. But if you approach the subject of cultural differences as a curious, open-minded ethnographer, you might be able to say such things as, "I see. In your college classes in Japan, the lecturer made a point of never making eye contact with students? And you all saw that as a sign of the teacher's credibility? That's pretty strange to me because in the United States. . . ."

• *Respond empathically.* Put yourself in the shoes of an instructor who is trying to function in a second language and culture, whose interpersonal support system may reside thousands of miles away, and who feels "on the line" to prove competence every time that person stands in front of your class. What would you want and need to hear were you in such a position? Perhaps you'd like to hear someone acknowledging your efforts—and occasionally your successes. Perhaps you'd like to hear someone commiserating with you about shared problems. You might find yourself saying things like, "You must find it incredibly frustrating having students wandering in and out of class the first week of the term. The registration situation at this stupid university is outrageous. I bet you've had problems yourself getting into some of your graduate courses. . . ."

• *Focus on what you can understand rather than on what you miss.* Exact recall of information in a typical academic lecture is actually fairly low, even when the teacher is a speaker of MNAE. And besides, most lectures contain a degree of redundancy. You should not be put off if not every word your instructor is saying is intelligible to you. Work on getting the gist. If the topic makes sense to you, congratulations. You're comprehending. If it doesn't make so much sense, see the following advice about listening actively.

• *Listen actively.* In the United States, we often expect a speaker to take the lion's share of responsibility for clarity. We tend to blame the speaker's inadequacies for communication failure. We expect our teachers to be explicit about the significance of some topic in class or about course assignments. In other cultures, however, it can actually be rude to speak too explicitly. Listeners are given credit for making sense and are expected to draw their own conclusions. That is just one reason why it is important for students to ask questions, to paraphrase, and to check perceptions with NNSMNAE instructors. But you'll need to do so in a way that does not come across as challenging your teacher's authority. Take ownership of your questions. You might find yourself saying something like, "This idea of a standard error of measurement is a little confusing to me, and I want to make sure I understand how it's different from a plain old standard deviation, which we talked about a couple of weeks ago. Here's what I understood you to be saying about that. . . ." In some cultures, students do not ask questions in the middle of class; they wait until afterward or for the privacy of the instructor's office hour. You might want to visit your instructor during office hours of the first week of class. Ask the instructor if it's okay for you to ask questions during the lectures. If negotiated in this manner, your instructor might be very pleased to have you as a classroom ally.

• *Take a stand against prejudice.* A class is a kind of culture unto itself. It has a set of characteristic norms and values and communication practices, just like a larger culture. In some classroom cultures, a norm of intolerance toward NNSMNAEs begins to take root when the first student says "Oh no!" and the second student rolls her eyes and the third student slams his book and the fourth student mutters under her breath. If you don't stand up and turn this behavior around, it will escalate, and only the most skilled teacher will be able to keep the classroom climate from utterly deteriorating. Talk to your fellow students in the hallway during class break. You might find yourself telling them, "Give this prof a break. What are you tearing her down for before she even gets started?" Get together with another like-minded student in the class and make conscious efforts to give the teacher positive, public feedback during class (you can do this without being too soupy). If despite your efforts the prejudice expressed in the class becomes too virulent, have the courage to find institutional channels for complaining against those who would sabotage your learning.

• *Don't panic. Be patient.* Many of the studies cited in this chapter point to the same conclusion. When we expose ourselves to NNSMNAE speech, and have positive expectations about doing so, we gradually accommodate to it. We become more effective listeners. This is a tremendous benefit for anyone who intends to function at top potential in a multicultural-multilingual nation and in an interdependent global community. It is a benefit that extends beyond what you learn or do not learn about the subject matter of a particular class. It is a benefit lost to those who throw up their hands and walk out of any situation in which they encounter a NNSMNAE.

Remember Barbara Coleman from the scenario that opened this chapter? Pity her.

References

Bradac, J. J. (1990). Language attitudes and impression formation. In H. Giles & W. P. Robinson (Eds.), *Handbook of language and social psychology* (pp. 387–412). New York: Wiley.

Brown, K. (1992). American college student attitudes toward non-native instructors. *Multilingua, 11,* 249–265.

Casmier, S. (1993, April 25). English debate renews. *St. Louis Post Dispatch,* 1, 9.

de la Zerda, N., & Hopper, R. (1979). Employment interviewers' reactions to Mexican American speech. *Communication Monographs, 46,* 126–134.

Fox, W., & Gay, G. (1994). Functions and effects of international teaching assistants. *Review of Higher Education, 18,* 1–24.

Gill, M. M. (1994). Accent and stereotypes: Their effect on perceptions of teachers and lecture comprehension. *Journal of Applied Communication Research, 22,* 348–361.

Guimond, S., & Palmer, D. L. (1993). Developmental changes in ingroup favouritism among bilingual and unilingual Francophone and Anglophone students. *Journal of Language and Social Psychology, 12,* 318–351.

Hendrix, K. G. (in press). Student perceptions of the influence of race on professor credibility. *Howard Journal of Communications.*

Jacobs, L., & Friedman, C. (1988). Student achievement under foreign teaching associates compared with native teaching associates. *Journal of Higher Education, 59,* 551–563.

Kachru, B. (1970). Some style features of South Asian English. In K. Goodwin (Ed.), *National identity.* London: Heinemann Educational Books.

Labov, W. (1972). *Language in the inner city.* Philadelphia: University of Pennsylvania Press.

Lambert, W., Hodgson, R., Gardner, R., & Fillenbaum, S. (1960). Evaluational reactions to spoken languages. *Journal of Abnormal and Social Psychology, 60,* 44–51.

Martin, J. N. (1993). Intercultural communication competence: A review. In R. L. Wiseman & J. Koester (Eds.), *Intercultural communication competence* (pp. 16–32). Newbury Park, CA: Sage.

Monoson, P. K., & Thomas, C. F. (1993). Oral proficiency policies for faculty in U.S. higher education. *Review of Higher Education, 16,* 127–140.

Munro, M. J., & Derwing, T. M. (1995). Foreign accent, comprehensibility, and intelligibility in the speech of second language learners. *Language Learning, 45,* 73–97.

Myers, C. L. (1994). Question-based discourse in science labs: Issues for ITAs. In C. Madden and C. Myers (Eds.), *Discourse and performance of international teaching assistants* (pp. 83–102). Alexandria, VA: TESOL.

Norris, T. (1991). Nonnative English-speaking teaching assistants and student performance. *Research in Higher Education, 32,* 433–448.

Oppenheim, N. (1996, April). *Undergraduate learning from nonnative English-speaking teaching assistants.* Paper presented at the Annual Meeting of the American Educational Research Association, New York.

Patient irked by doctors with accents. (1990, May 11). *Atlanta Journal and Constitution,* E2.

Pichè, G. L., Rubin, D. L., Turner, L. J., & Michlin, M. L. (1978). Effects of nonstandard dialect features in written compositions on teachers' subjective evaluations of students and composition quality. *Research in the Teaching of English, 12,* 107–118.

Plakans, B. S. (in press). Undergraduate experiences with and attitudes toward international teaching assistants. *TESOL Quarterly.*

Rao, N. (1995, May). *The Oh No! syndrome: A language expectation model explains initial encounters between U.S. undergraduates and foreign teaching assistants.* Paper presented at the International Communication Association convention, Albuquerque, New Mexico.

Roback, G., Randolph, L., & Seidman, B. (1992). *Physician characteristics and distribution in the U.S.* Chicago: American Medical Association.

Rubin, D. L. (1992). Nonlanguage factors affecting undergraduates' judgments of nonnative English-speaking teaching assistants. *Research in Higher Education, 33,* 511–531.

Rubin, D. L., DeHart, J., & Heintzman, M. (1991). Effects of accented speech and culture-typical compliancegaining style on subordinates' impressions of managers. *International Journal of Intercultural Relations, 15,* 267–283.

Rubin, D. L., Healy, P., Zath, R., Gardiner, T. C., & Moore, C. P. (in press). Non-native physicians as message sources: Effects of accent and ethnicity on patients' responses to AIDS prevention counseling. *Health Communication.*

Rubin, D. L., & Smith, K. A. (1988). Effects of accent, ethnicity, and lecture topic on undergraduates' perceptions of nonnative English-speaking teaching assistants. *International Journal of Intercultural Relations, 14,* 337–353.

Seligman, C. R., Tucker, C. R., & Lambert, W. E. (1972). The effects of speech style and other attributes on teachers' attitudes toward pupils. *Language in Society, 1,* 131–142.

Smith, R. M., Byrd, P., Nelson, G. L., Barrett, R. P., & Constantinides, J. C. (1992). *Crossing pedagogical oceans: International teaching assistants in U.S. undergraduate education.* ASHE-ERIC Higher Education Report No. 8. Washington, DC: George Washington University School of Education and Human Development.

United States Department of Commerce. (1994). *Statistical abstract of the United States 1994.* Washington, DC: United States Printing Office.

vom Saal, D. R. (1987). The undergraduate experience and international teaching assistants. In N. Chism (Ed.), *Institutional responsibilities and responses in the employment and education of teaching assistants: Readings from a national conference* (pp. 267–274). Columbus: Ohio State University Center for Teaching Excellence.

Williams, F. (1976). *Explorations in the linguistic attitudes of teachers.* Rowley, MA: Newbury House.

Key Terms

accented speech
ethnolinguistic minorities
instructional communication
intercultural competence
international instructors
language and attitude research
linguistic stereotypes
listening (active)
managers
matched guise technique
non-native speakers
physicians

Discussion Questions

1. In the scenario that begins this essay, the students make a whole string of inferences about the instructor on the basis of very limited information. How does this process of attribution work? Can you think of instances outside the classroom where these attribution processes also occur? Have you ever been the object of attributions that others have made about you on the basis of very limited information?

2. The author uses a very imposing label, "nonnative speakers of mainstream North American Englishes" (NNSMNAE). Do you agree that this label is useful? What is included and what is excluded by each of the modifiers? For example, why does the author say "North American Englishes"? Why not just "*American* English," or just plain "*English*"?

3. The essay proposes that effective communication is the responsibility of both speaker and listener. According to the essay, listeners sometimes are obliged to work extra hard to understand a speaker. Do you agree with this position? Is this what you learned in your basic public speaking class? Exactly what is the obligation of the listener to the speaker in intra- and intercultural contexts?

4. The essay describes some research in which potential patients regard NNSMNAE physicians to be as competent as U.S. mainstream physicians. Still, they did not like the "foreign" doctors. Can you think of some situations in which you have had these ambivalent feelings about groups of individuals? That is, you admire certain qualities in members of this group but dislike others.

5. At the end of the essay, you are challenged to stand up against expressions of prejudice among your peers. Have you ever heard a friend make a snide or disparaging remark about NNSMNAEs? What did you do in that situation? Do you really see any point in following the charge that this essay gives you?

15 "I can't do that!" but I "can actually see around corners"
American Indian Students and the Study of Public "Communication"

DONAL CARBAUGH

"I can't do that!" The young woman was talking to me in my office about a required speech to be delivered in a public speaking course. The first assignment involved preparing and delivering a five to seven minute speech that demonstrated a basic process or principle. We had been going over—in class and now again in my office—some of the possible tactics one might use to design and produce such a speech when her hands trembled, her eyes watered, and with her head bowed she exclaimed forcefully through clenched teeth, "I can't do that!"

I remember vividly her highly intense emotional response. In fact, her reaction was so intense that I began immediately to search for possible reasons for her expressed difficulties, so I could help formulate possible and productive courses of action for her. While it took years for me to eventually understand even some of her concerns, some of the meanings in her exclamation that she "can't do that," we nonetheless worked hard together, for hours, to prepare for the delivery of her first speech—which turned out to be a very painful event for everyone involved, especially her.

The young woman in this opening story is Ms. Mina Running Eagle, a member of the Blackfeet Indian Nation which is centered upon a reservation in Montana, USA.[1] Over the next semesters and years of my teaching, I had occasion to contact several Blackfeet students in communication classrooms. Not all, nor even most were like Mina, but in her reaction we can eventually hear parts of the Blackfeet culture at work. After giving some time to reading about the Blackfeet, making their acquaintance, and learning some of their ways through observing and being with them, I came to a somewhat better understanding of Ms. Mina Running Eagle, and of what she was "up against" in her university course in public communication. Her exclamation of "I can't do that!," now over 16 years old, carries enduring meanings, and with the passing of time assumes newer meanings for me.

In this essay, I hope to show how I came to some understanding of Mina's exclamation by exploring the cultural forms of communication surrounding this required university course. By reflecting in this essay upon this event with Ms. Running Eagle, and similar others, I will demonstrate a complexity of cultural features that are involved in these and similar communicative events, and thus suggest what reflecting upon them can contribute to our critical understanding and practice of communication. I hope readers' teaching and understanding of communication will benefit, as mine has, by reflecting upon the use of diverse cultural forms of communication in settings of education, and in other human institutions.

Blackfeet "Communication"[2]

My grandparents taught me: The people lived in harmony with nature. The animals were able to speak. Their understanding of communication was far more advanced than from today's standards.

—Leon Rising Wolf

Some Blackfeet people, like Leon Rising Wolf, upon some occasions, use a cultural model of "communication" that presumes, *sui generis,* a patterned way of living. A primary mode of this "communication," from the Blackfeet view, is what might be called a "deeply communicative silence," a listener active form of non-verbal co-presence in which all is presumably interconnected. Mr. Leon Rising Wolf, a Blackfeet "blood" (i.e., a full-blooded Blackfeet) introduced that form of "communication" above, as something he was taught by his "grandparents," and discussed it further in this way: you are "able to communicate spiritually and physically . . . you are in tune with something long enough, to a point that you know it inside-out." His main examples of this cultural form consisted of detailed descriptions of "communicating with animals and spirits," "because when you're able to communicate with the animals [and spirits], you actually live that life, and you try to live that life every day."

This Blackfeet model of "communication," when realized, involves a scene of "harmony," of silently connective co-presence, a nonlinguistic togetherness in which one is knowingly integral to and communing with the actual persons, animals, spirits, and things with which one dwells. This is both an ideal for "communication" that is especially apparent in some special Blackfeet ceremonies (e.g., sweat lodge rituals), and, it is a desirable condition of "every day" communicative action. For this kind of "communication" to be forceful in social living, it presumes (and thus recreates) an unspoken consensus of interconnection that is largely non-verbal and non-linguistic, yet shared and publicly accessible, if one just listens.

This cultural model of "communication" creates a special significance for nonlinguistic channels of messages, and an important duty for communicants as listeners. Participants in this communication must therefore become active *listeners,* and observers of that which they are already a part. Mr. Rising Wolf described this ever-watchful form of "communication" in this way.

It's the hardest thing to concentrate on
   what you really believe in
It's the hardest thing to listen
It's one of the hardest things I think human
   beings have
   is to listen

And actually listen and hear what they listen to
   Not listen and then make up their own mind
      of what they heard
   Which is pretty common today
But to actually listen.
   And you start hearing the spirits talking

And they communicate with people like
   Bigfoot, the eagle,
   elk, deer, the rocks, water

When these spirits come in
   you can feel, or
   you can hear those spirits. And
   you can feel them doing things to you.
Say if an eagle came in
   you could feel the breeze of that wing as he
      flies by
   you can feel it when he comes and puts his
      head by you
Same with an animal that has hair
   you can feel the hair
   you can feel the difference in hair too
      if you're born in the mountains
         been around mountains
         been around animals
   you've always touched the animals, so
   you can tell the difference
   you can close your eyes and
   you can almost say
      this is a dog
      this is a deer
      this is an elk
So you can tell that
   in the ceremonies.

By going through those there
   it rejuvenates your spiritual, spirituality
      and your rebirth of your confidence in
         who you are
      and that it's still alive and strong
      and no matter how far back East in
         some city
      you might be
   you know that nature and the
      communication
      between the animals and man is still
      there.
   it makes you feel spiritually strong
      to the point that you just want
      to jump with cheer and joy.

And you go back to your city life with that energy.

Mr. Rising Wolf's words point to a dimension of experience that is itself not a verbal event, but a real spiritual and physical event in which a person can (and should) participate, in which the meanings of interconnective living are constantly being re-created, if one listens and observes properly. This is a most valued event, a scene of Blackfeet "communication," that can be sought and realized not primarily through verbal interaction, but through actively listening amidst a silent co-presence.[3]

This form of communication can be alluded to with a rather quick verbal ellipsis. A middle-aged Blackfeet male, Mr. Perry Weasel, invoked this cultural form of "communication" with these few words, as he told me about his grandfather: "He was a superb communicator," then later, "he very rarely verbally talked, but there was just always a sense of knowing. His communication had a great effect on me as a child." The grandfather embodied and taught "superb" Blackfeet communication, not mainly through his words, but with a nonlinguistic "sense of knowing."

Using—what I now understand to be—this mode of communication, a Blackfeet boy gave what one fellow student called a "mesmerizing" seven minute public communication (i.e., a "public speech"). His presentation consisted of actively and artfully maneuvering "nunchakus" for his "speech." The only verbal portion of his "speech" consisted of only three words, spoken once about midway through the presentation (i.e., "like an eagle").

In these comments and actions, a primary mode of Blackfeet communication is being culturally invoked, and signified. It involves a kind of listener active, participant co-presence within shared activities, with each activity (e.g., Leon Rising Wolf's words, Perry Weasel's grandfather, the nonverbal "speech") demonstrating a kind of Blackfeet non-linguistic "communication." Through this mode, the Blackfeet are saying something about people being already connected (or seeking a holistic connectedness), about people, spirits—and ancestors—being an inherent part of this grand picture, about natural features and animals being figured into this interconnected realm, with all of this providing a cultural scene of Blackfeet "communication." A primary mode of some Blackfeet communication is thus to "communicate spiritually and physically" through a listener-active silence with a cultural premise (a belief and value) of this mode

being the inheritance of a holistic world of intricate interconnections.

This means of communicative living is difficult for Blackfeet to sustain in some institutional settings, yet it is also a means of coping with that very difficulty. As Leon Rising Wolf puts it:

> After I finish school here I go back [home, to the reservation]
> to regenerate my knowledge
> to regenerate my spiritual beliefs
>   myself
> by going to the sweats and start communi-
>   cating again
>   with the animals and the way of life
>   around you
> the frustration, the turmoil, the confusion
>   of everything is gone
>
> Y'know, you've got a clear mind and a clean body
>   you can think
>   you can see a lot better
>   you can actually see around corners
>   you can actually feel things happen
>   when they actually happen
>
> So today I use my Indian ways to help me
>   communicate
>   in the Whiteman's world and travel
>   through it.

While "school" had created "frustration," "turmoil," and "confusion," "communicating" the Blackfeet way enabled Mr. Rising Wolf to "think," "see," and "feel" "a lot better," to the point that he could "see around corners." By tuning into the non-linguistic "way of life around" him, he was able both to "regenerate" his "knowledge" and "beliefs," and to "travel through" "the Whiteman's world."

For Blackfeet people who hold to this primary mode of connective co-presence, verbal "speaking" and "speaking in public" assumes a secondary status or mode. To "speak" in public, literally to say words while in the presence of many others, is an important skill for some in the tribe to master. In fact, speaking well is a valued art, as we will see shortly. But it is also risky as a social action. To speak publicly is to risk severing or tearing the actual or preferred interconnections among people, and to risk rippling the communal waters from which every member of the tribe draws sustenance. Part of the risk also results from stepping into a very weighty social position: it is to be one who can and should take such a performative risk; it is to be one who has been apprenticed in the proper form for this public, verbal action; it is to be one who is known by the community to be so apprenticed and so skilled; it is to be one whose speaking others can trust, for to speak is to carry (not necessarily only positive) repercussions for the community and the interconnected world. "Speaking in public" is thus to activate a secondary mode of communication that is risky both as a form of social action and weighty as to its social position.

For Blackfeet people, the social position associated with speaking in public is most typically, but not exclusively, an elder male.[4] As noted, to be one who can so speak is to be one of the proper social rank including one who has been tutored for years in proper public speaking. The risk of speaking, however, is magnified when in the presence of certain audience members, especially when with "outsiders" and "elders." Mr. Jon Moore, a professional, highly educated (i.e., Ph.D.) middle-aged Blackfeet male who "enjoys speaking to kids," discussed the special context created when "older people" are in his audience: "I don't like to talk in front of older people. Subconsciously, I get a feeling of inadequacy, not up to par with everyone else, fear that you might tread on waters you shouldn't tread on because you're not as experienced as someone in the crowd." To do so is, for Mr. Moore, to insinuate yourself into a place where you do not quite fully belong. Presumably, those best equipped to speak are those who have been a part of this world the longest, are properly "in tune" with it, and have been properly trained to speak about it. As another Blackfeet put it: "If you speak out, you subject yourself to criticism," with this criticism coming most likely from those deemed most knowledgeable and skilled at public speaking, the elders of the tribe.

To speak, then, implies that one is presuming a particular social position, but further, that one is conducting a weighty social action. Why? Because the act itself involves pulling something out of the interconnected realm and giving it verbal attention. This is intrinsically a risky action, in that what one extricates from the interconnected realm is poten-

tially (through the interconnective premise) a part of everyone's shared world, and that speaking about it invokes a knowledge that is the special province of "the elders." Speaking then presumes that one has stepped into a revered social position, that one has command of knowledge requisite to that social position, that one has the exercised ability to indeed speak about this in the presence of the present others, and that what one is verbalizing might—in varying degrees—be already known to everyone present.[5]

Those best equipped for public speaking are also those most socially interconnected (i.e., the elders). As an elder, one incurs the obligation to embody and transmit communal ways, and, when appropriate, to speak for other members of the community. This is an important ability because "speaking for others" in this way is a way of properly vocalizing the concerns of others in some communal affairs. That Blackfeet are prominently members of the familial community is evident with the wide use of a popular form of address—"nixokoawa," or "my relations"—which expresses this presumed collective membership, and indicates possible access of each to the others, including the elders who can speak for them. Important to emphasize here is that the elder, in the performance as a vocalizer for others, is speaking not just for himself or herself but is speaking carefully and artfully as a member of an already interrelated community. The basic premise for such speaking is the inter-related whole of which each is an integral part. The specific focal concern being expressed by the individual who is speaking thus plays the concerns of individuals within this largely familial and communal premise. Through this process of elders being vocalizers for and with others, all active members of the interconnected Blackfeet people—including all others who are not elders—are presumably involved in communal, or tribal affairs, whether being the explicit vocalizer or not.[6]

These modes of Blackfeet "communication" rely upon, and in turn recreate deeply held cultural values. Some of these are the nurturing of the tribal heritage and natural geography, which are especially associated with tribal ancestors (especially "grandparents"), events (e.g., "traditional encampments," sweat lodge ceremonies), and the unspoken system of interconnections that precedes and encompasses any one sentient being, thing, or event. Related values involve modesty (deferring to the difference of each other, and a reverence for the whole) and stability (continuity of belief and value across time) with particular tribal members deemed a small and relatively unimportant part of this rather durable and holistic, "spiritual and physical" picture. Within this communal scene, persons and relations are erected upon a valuing of, and respect for social difference, with the society, and public speaking itself being at times a performance of social differences based upon individual autonomy, age, and gender.

In summary, Blackfeet "communication" is designed upon a primary mode of listener-active silence and its associated premise of interconnectedness. Figured upon this premise, the secondary mode of verbal speaking in public is deemed risky as a social action (because it might violate the presumed interconnectedness), and presumptuous as to social position (in that one steps into a highly respected position presuming one can so act by speaking). The secondary mode of verbal speaking relies upon and invokes social positions of difference with elder males being the traditional public vocalizers. These modes of communication and the cultural life they express reflect a valuing of heritage, nature, modesty, stability, and respect for differences in social positions.

"The Whiteman's Communication"

The alternate model of communication that Mina Running Eagle had contacted in her course in public communication could be called a "whiteman" or "white people's" model, this being the way it is characterized by the Blackfeet. Note that here, with this cultural model, the primary mode of communication is not a listener-active silence, but verbal speaking. The "white people's" primary mode of action is verbal and is based at least partly upon these "other" cultural premises: Speaking makes something public that was heretofore private, personal, or internal; Speaking helps create (or con-

struct) social connections among those who were presumably different or separate; and, Connecting through speech is the principal way a society is made, and made to work. From the "white people's" view, the primary mode of communication is verbal speaking, with this mode being important for the actual "constructions" of personal, social, and societal life (Carbaugh, 1988).

A secondary mode of communication in the "white people's" system is silence. Communicative silence is figured upon the primary mode of verbal speaking and its premises. Silence plays upon the primary mode, however, by risking its negation, or by signaling the absence of the very premises that are presumably being activated in "white people's" actions of verbal speaking. Silence as a communicative action can mean, to "white people," a negation of one's personal being (as in "the silent treatment"), a failure to "connect" with others in "relationship," and a sign that social institutions have been ruptured or broken or corrupted (e.g., "a conspiracy of silence"). Without speaking, and with silence, one can hear (or feel) being amplified not an interconnectedness as among the Blackfeet, but a separateness, and disconnectedness that is present between presumably different individuals or peoples. Silence, then, is a prominent way to accentuate the different, separate, and even disconnected states of affairs which are so often presumed as a basis for many public American (i.e., multicultural) events and scenes.

For the Anglo speaker, the primary mode of verbal speaking is associated not with a special role of "elder," but with the prominent and common social position of "citizen." Speaking in public, as a political and legal (i.e., constitutional) matter, is a performative possibility for everyone. The action of speaking in public is an essential part of being a citizen, and this action is codified and cultivated in the nation's legal codes. As a citizen, one is entitled to "speak in public," and given this "right," one can (and should) exercise it—and permit it to be exercised—rather "freely." The role of "citizen," from the vantage point of the primary mode of speaking, then, is not erected fundamentally upon social differences between the members of the society, but is erected upon a political premise of commonality among all members of the nation of the United States of America.

Because speaking is available to all citizens, and because it can be used to construct personal lives and social organization, one can use speaking as a means both to gain access into society, and to better one's place within that society. This Anglo belief—and the attendant, deeply felt necessities for construction and progress—it is crucial to recognize, is not a natural state of human beings, but is a belief that has been *created,* partly through this cultural conception of speaking. Further, it is being actively (re)created each time the political position of "citizen" is being connected with the primary expectation for verbal participation, and all of the typical cultural premises associated with that expectation (i.e., verbal participation as the necessary means of constructing, and bettering individual, social, and socio-political life). Some of the values associated with this belief system are upward mobility (that one can and should do better than one's current lot in life), change (that one should be different or "grow" beyond one's present state or lot in life), and progress (that movement and change is necessary for betterment and improvement). These values are often operationalized at a personal level, leading "the whiteman" to articulate and assert the values of change and uniqueness (that individuals are psychologically different, and should aspire to become better and different as a person).

The "white person's communication," then, relies upon a primary mode of oral speaking, with this being the means through which personal, social, and socio-political life is "constructed." The secondary mode of silence plays upon this primary mode and is a prominent way of signifying the absence of, or negating the possibility for personal, social, and socio-political life. The quintessential social position associated with verbal speaking in public is the role of "citizen" which is erected upon a common political model of "individual rights" among the nation's members. Anglo "communication," designed this way, reflects and recreates beliefs about the separateness of individuals as well as the optimism of constructing a personal yet com-

munal life, while valuing upward mobility, change, progress, and uniqueness.

Intercultural Dynamics in the Classroom

With the benefit of these different cultural understandings of communication, we might now better understand Ms. Mina Running Eagle's comments, and the larger situation in which she found herself. What was she saying, when she said, "I can't do that!" What exactly was it that she couldn't do?

The general, "whitepeople's" logic of the classroom assignment to which Mina responded could be put this way: As a citizen of this country, you will be required to speak in public, and you yourself can benefit from so speaking. Thus, learning to speak in public is essential to your general liberal arts education. In this class, the first assignment requires you to speak for about 5–7 minutes. You will verbally inform the class about a topic of your choice, one that is important to you, but also one that is important to

TABLE 1 • Summary Of Blackfeet and "Whiteman's" Models of Communication in a Classroom Setting

	BLACKFEET	"WHITEMAN"
Primary Mode:	Silence →	Speaking →
Cultural Premise:	Listener-active, Interconnected	Speaker-active, Constructive
Secondary Mode:	Verbal Speaking →	Silence →
Cultural Premise:	Risky, Rupture	Division
Social Position:	Differences by gender and age	Commonality, equality
Typical Speaker:	Elder Male	Citizen
Cultural Persona:	Relational Connection	Unique individual
Values:	Nature, heritage, modesty, stability	Upward mobility, change, progress

this class, or this community today. In your speaking, you will not only display what you know about the topic, but also you will help construct a sense of that topic for your audience. This was the task before her.

From Mina's point-of-view, she had a different, or additional cultural frame-of-reference which competed for her allegiance, and with which she reacted to the assignment. Perhaps this, her interpretation, reflected—as another Blackfeet put it—a deeply "subconscious," "physical and spiritual" worldview or ethos. From this, Mina's view, the assignment was creating a social position of "public speaker" which was foreign to her and her place in her communal ways. Incoherent social expectations were being created for her as the assignment asked her, a young female adult, in effect, to speak publicly, and thus to step into the traditional position of being an elder male. With regard to the age dimension of this speaking role, she was too young and had no experience or training or at this point even desire to become an elder who would or could so speak. With regard to the gender dimension of this speaking role, she had of course no real physical or cultural experience. Public actions of speaking would (and should) come, if at all, much later in her developmental and cultural scheme of things. In effect, the course was addressing her as one who must perform in a social position that she respectfully reserved for "elders," especially "elder males."

With regard to her "communication" activities, she had been watching and "listening" carefully in class. She knew she was being asked to perform verbally (in her secondary mode), and she also knew that her verbal performance was to be witnessed by an audience that included two types of people—"whitepeople" and an older male teacher—cultural *persona* that were culturally salient to her, and to whom she felt public speaking was deeply inappropriate. To speak to this public was, to her, both inappropriate and incredible. From her cultural frame of reference, this presented a real problem, for she was being required to "talk" in public, to do so to people who were different and knew more than her, and further to do so in a scene which to her was very disconnected from her past, thus removing traditional sources of knowledge she had been taught to

recognize and use. Further, she was being asked to perform through a communicative mode that was secondary to her. This kind of communication, itself, even for an elder male, is risky. To act this way, at so young an age, as a female, to this group of "whitepeople" including an older man, from whom she was culturally disconnected, all of this was nearly incomprehensible and dearly anxiety provoking for her. As a middle-aged, very successful, public *male* Blackfeet figure put it: "when I was younger, I used to get sick when I'd have to speak." Imagine how Mina felt.

We could summarize the sense of confusion and violation that the assignment created for Mina by formulating at least these conflicting, cultural messages: (1) About what was deemed proper in a learning environment: Mina was caught between Blackfeet demands to be a respectful listening student and "the whitepeople's" expectation that she be a verbally active student; (2) About what was deemed sensible as social organization: She was caught between her Blackfeet status as a young adult female and "Whitepeople's" expectations that treated her as a "citizen," with this role of "citizen" placing her incredibly, from her Blackfeet view, in the position of a male elder; (3) About "communication": She was caught between Blackfeet demands to utilize the primary, proper connective silence rather than the "whitepeople's" expectations to utilize, what was to her, a secondary, presumptuous verbal performance; (4) About attitudes toward the audience: She was caught between her Blackfeet heritage that taught her to respect differences in people based on age and gender and thus remain observant, rather than enact the "whitepeople's" citizen role and speak out; and (5) About the values that should be operative in this scene: Mina felt both the Blackfeet imperative to exercise proper modesty and respect for self, scene, and others, and the "whitepeople's" apparent requirement to exercise a productive verbal efficacy. Because she was being asked (required) to be, what she considered to be, inappropriately verbally active, incredibly an elder role, improperly speaking to an audience she did not know but whom she knew included "whitepeople" and a male teacher she wanted to respect, and because she thought the assignment required her to be not only rude but someone whom she was not and could not be, she exclaimed: "I can't do that!"

Beyond Mina's particular position, we could summarize the generally operative intercultural dynamics in this classroom in this way: In public speaking, "whiteman's" model presumes a common role of citizen, and a primary mode of speaking, which is erected upon beliefs about the separateness of individuals and thus the necessity to verbally construct life. Such "constructions" are often guided by the values of upward mobility, change, and progress. From the Blackfeet point-of-view, setting the educational scene in this way puts undue emphasis upon a secondary mode of communication (i.e., verbal activity), and strips the social scene of its deepest resources (i.e., the interconnected cosmos), its proper persona (i.e., elders), and its most valued features (i.e., of heritage, modesty, and respect for differences in gender and age). Entirely supplanted in this scene is the more primary Blackfeet mode of traditional communication (which to "whitepeople" can symbolize not affirmation and holism but negation and division) and the proper beliefs about persons, social positions, tribal living, and values associated with these.

Culturally Situated, Critical Reflections

In the contemporary world that we [Native Americans] deal with, we have an understanding of all the other religions, different types of language and cultures. Then when we try to communicate, say, with the people around us, or the people we're working with, it's really hard to do because (pause) of a lack of understanding of other Ind- of other people. Where a white person, wh- I don't know. (long pause) a confusion will really set in because white people don't understand the Native American.

—Leon Rising Wolf

What is an ethnographer's responsibility when confronted with situations like these, as in some scenes of education when a female American Indian student exclaims, "I can't do that!"? Or, when a male American Indian student gives a seven minute "speech" of three spoken words? Or, similarly, when Blackfeet males come to one's office and "speak for" a Blackfeet female?

I think we should, first of all, educate ourselves about such moments of communication, and be sure we recognize if, and when, and how, there are cultures at work in them. For each educational context, and for each peopled place, there will be cultural views of communication operating. Perhaps for some, a verbal channel is deemed valuable and very constructive; it is used as a way for each to exercise fundamental rights of each human being. Teaching and learning this channel is highly valued by them, for it can carry great force in their common political life. Failing to engage the verbal channel can lead, from this vantage point, to missed opportunities, continued oppression, even social disorganization. For others, from another view, a nonverbal channel is deemed valuable and interconnective; it is a way of inhabiting an already inhabited world. Teaching and learning this channel is highly valued, for it keeps one "in tune" with "physical and spiritual" life. Failing to learn and exercise the nonverbal channel can lead, as some Blackfeet have said, to "elimination," "confusion and turmoil." As teachers, researchers, and citizens, we should be vigilant and cautious when the former "white" view requires the Blackfeet to speak up verbally and be heard, even (especially?) under the guise of "participatory democracy," for the demand itself supplants that which it seeks to understand and include. From the other angle of vision, if the Blackfeet were to make a demand, it might be for us to watch and listen, to be respectful and modest of that which we are all a part, especially when in the presence of something to which we are not yet attuned, like a deep cultural difference. The latter suggestion seems forcefully pertinent today, because it is too often "talked over," especially when our expectations are built upon narrow conceptions of "communication" and "democracy," with the accompanying imperative that all voices speak-up and be heard.

Ethnographic studies of intercultural communication can help us understand how different cultural orientations relate to practices of living like these, in and out of the classroom. They can help us understand the complexity and depth of perplexity created in some intercultural encounters, as when one sees great value in speaking up, participating and being heard, while the other sees value in remaining quiet, for so much goes (and should go) without saying. Knowledge as this is necessary if we are to understand, and critically reflect upon intercultural relations of each with the other.

In situations of education like the ones between the "White" teacher and the Blackfeet students, we must get to know better what our students are doing when they communicate. We must know who we, as teachers, are teaching, and the depth (when there is depth) of what we, therefore, are dealing with as we teach. In the process, we can come to know better what we are doing as teachers, only as we understand better what we are attempting to "undo" in our students. Only by knowing what we are attempting to un-do, can we better appreciate what our brand of education (and communication) is doing.

In turn, we must reflect upon what we, ourselves, are presuming as we teach, such as the beliefs and values we presume about speaking and learning. In time, we can then come to know better what at least some of our students are up against.

As with Mina and her teacher, so too for others can the paths of cultural reflection lead to mysterious places, including a critical distance from one's own familiar ways. By taking some time to walk and watch with each other, then, perhaps, we can design our actions—theories, practices, tools—with the intelligence of both in mind, knowingly creating our lives within the variety of available cultural views, helping each along our various ways. Proceeding in this way, giving each its proper due, suggests diagnosing our social ills, and designing elegant solutions for them, not by distributing some general critical manual for proper social and cultural and communicative conduct, but by carefully exploring the actual worlds of people and practices in particular places. So placed, situated in scenes of actual living, within cultural and communicative processes, we can then remain vigilantly watchful and cautious, so we do not—by championing our own way—mindlessly "eliminate" that which we failed to understand.

In the wake of the French Revolution, Vicomte de Chateaubriand expressed a similar thought when reflecting upon what others considered to be the perhaps quaint or obsolete mysteries of their day: "There is nothing beautiful, pleasing, or grand in life, but that which is more or less mysterious. The most wonderful sentiments are those which produce impressions difficult to be explained. . . . It is a pitiful mode of reasoning to reject whatever we cannot comprehend." Perhaps Leon Rising Wolf opens the door to a similar, under-appreciated "beautiful, pleasing, or grand" mystery with his comments about "the communication between the animals and man," since communicating this Blackfeet way can "make you spiritually strong to the point that you just want to jump with cheer and joy." Failing to learn from these "difficult to be explained" impressions, from the delightful cultural mysteries others' lives present for our own, would be pitiful indeed.

Notes

1. The selection of name for these people is not without some complication. The people of concern here are one of "the Blackfoot Confederacy" that consists of five tribes: the North Blackfoot, the Bloods, The North and the South Piegans and the Small Robes, the latter being exterminated by smallpox and warfare. What were the South Piegans are now called the Blackfeet, referring to the only tribe located in Montana, the others being in Canada. However, this version of history is written in English, and stands rather uneasily beside one inscribed in the Blackfoot or "Siksika" language. According to a Blackfeet: "In the Blackfoot language, the term Blackfeet is seldom, if ever, used to describe the American tribe. The name Blackfeet is an exclusively English term. The Blackfoot language name of the tribe is Amskapi Pikuni, or South Piegans. Pikuni derives from an old form meaning, 'Spotted Robes'" (Darrell Robes Kipp, 1993, p. 5). Because Robes Kipp goes on to use "Blackfeet" in his English writings, because this usage was adopted by my informants, and because this is the typical way of referring to these people in English, I select this usage. The Blackfeet reservation consists of four different governmental districts: Browning, Heart Butte, Seville, and Old Agency. Most of my consultants and observations are centered in Browning, with a few from Heart Butte.

2. The cultural models of communication summarized here are based upon earlier works with the Blackfeet (i.e., Carbaugh, 1993) and other Americans (e.g., Carbaugh, 1988). The larger project of which this essay is a part involves additional chapters, one exploring Blackfeet views of "education," another a comparative analysis of Native American peoples' views of speaking, teaching, and learning, and a third that explores the implications of these views for a communication theory of language, culture, thought, and reality. Following the Blackfeet, I use the terms "Whiteman" and "White people" as a cultural term to characterize prominent patterns in America today. Following Philips (1983, p. 16), I also use the term Anglo as a way of referring to traditions of communication that derive from an English heritage (see also Philips, 1983, p. 16). There is no easy way to refer to these patterns, yet perhaps they are best identified as "prominent American" in that they are prominent in many scenes of America today, and are thus used by—or expected of—people with various heritages (racial, ethnic, or cultural). Exactly how such patterns play into these various scenes is an ongoing topic of my own research.

3. Mr. Rising Wolf's story is of course a verbal narration. What it narrates, however, or points to, is a kind of cultural "communication" that is not itself verbal. The event he narrates is deeply communicative but it is not itself a linguistic or verbal event. It is a "spiritual and physical" connection among things, beings. That it takes linguistic communication or a verbal narrative to describe that non-linguistic event, should not imply that the event being narrated, itself, is linguistic or verbal. This further underlines the importance of learning this kind of "communication" through watching, listening, and observing, through direct involvement in it, rather than through a secondary verbal discussion about it.

The crucial role of "listening" is apparent in a recent reflection upon the Cultural Survival group's State of the People Tour, a tour designed to educate audiences of violations in indigenous groups' rights around the world. In summarizing the tour, from "an indigenous person's point-of-view," Marchell Wesaw (1994, p. 1) wrote: "Each solution, if it is to be an effective solution, must come from a finely tuned listening. Indigenous communities know what is best for themselves."

4. The skill of speaking well, its association with elder males, and its use in disputes has deep historical roots in Blackfeet culture. One historian of the Blackfeet, when writing about the Northern Plains Indians during the late 17th century noted as much: "Each band was led by a chief selected for his generosity, bravery and ability to speak well. Chiefs decided band movements and resolved internal disputes" (Bryan, 1985, p. 56).

Speaking in public however is just one activity within a whole cultural system of practice. That system, as a way of living, according to Beatrice Medicine (1994) derives from an equitable gender arrangement. She discusses American Indians prior to contacting the "Whiteman": "In most precontact societies, native women shared equally with men in social, economic, and ritual roles. Most ethnographic accounts (for the Plains culture area) emphasize the dynamic, dyadic interplay of both genders in the ongoing enterprise that allows indigenous societies to exist" (Medicine, 1994, p. 67). She goes on to review some of the deleterious consequences to indigenous people of contacting the "Whiteman's" educational (see below) and legal systems. She concludes somewhat optimistically by noting that now, over one third of the "seven hundred American Indian and Alaska Native lawyers" educated since the 1970's are women. Whether and how these changes—adaptations to the "Whiteman's" world—pervade traditional Indian modes of communication, and the resulting conceptions and arrangements of gender roles in American Indian societies, needs investigated. For example, in 1985, Myrna Galbreath became "one of the few Blackfeet women to be elected to a tribal leadership position" (Bryan, 1985, p. 71). Whether Blackfeet (and other peoples) deem this event to be culturally significant and if so, how so, needs further attention, especially focusing on the role of communication in executing such a position (e.g., as a woman in an elected position of tribal leadership).

5. The possible exception to this is a speech about "oneself." A Blackfeet consultant explained that the "easiest speech to give is a speech about oneself." Presumably such a speech lays no claims to knowledge beyond oneself and is thus less featured in, but perhaps no less a part of the interconnected realm. The relation between Blackfeet models of person, "self," verbal speaking, and the listener active realm of "communicating with the animals and life around you," warrants much further attention. See Percy Bullchild (1985).

6. The importance and prominence of this elder speaking role is apparent in an advertisement for "The second annual Blackfeet Community College Traditional Encampment." Its first words are: "Join the elders and Blackfeet Community College for the second annual encampment. The elders will share knowledge and wisdom in the following areas: approaching an elder for assistance or knowledge . . . story telling by elders and traditional people." From the "Official publication for the town of

Browning and the Blackfeet Reservation," *Glacier Reporter,* July 6, 1989, p. 8.

Author's note: I express deep thanks to the Blackfeet people who gave me the gift of their time and words. Parts of this essay were presented at the Ethnography of Communication Conference in Portland, Oregon, August, 1992; at a forum on Discursive Psychology, Oxford, England, October, 1992; at the Applied Linguistics Conference on the Intercultural Communicator, Tampere, Finland, November, 1992; at the Institute for Psychology, Innsbruck, Austria, March, 1993; and at the University of Massachusetts Conference on Ethnography and Qualitative Research in Education, June, 1994.

References

Basso, K. (1990). "To give up on words": Silence in Western Apache culture. In D. Carbaugh (Ed.), *Cultural communication and intercultural contact* (pp. 303–320). Hillsdale, NJ: Lawrence Erlbaum Associates, Inc.

Berry, W. (1990). *What are people for?* San Francisco: North Point Press.

Bryan, W., Jr. (1985). *Montana's Indians: Yesterday and today.* Helena: Montana Magazine, Inc.

Bullchild, P. (1985). *The sun came down: The history of the world as my Blackfeet Elders told it.* San Francisco: Harper & Row.

Carbaugh, D. (1988). *Talking American.* Norwood, NJ: Ablex.

Carbaugh, D. (1990). The critical voice in ethnography of communication research. *Research on Language and Social Interaction, 23,* 262–282.

Carbaugh, D. (Ed.). (1990). *Cultural communication and intercultural contact.* Hillsdale, NJ: Lawrence Erlbaum Associates.

Carbaugh, D. (1993). Cultural pragmatics and intercultural competence, *The competent intercultural communicator: AFinLA yearbook 1993.* (Ed. by L. Lofman, L. Kurki-Suonio, S. Pellinen, and J. Lehtonen) *Publications de l'association Finlandaise de linguistique appliquée, 51,* 117–129.

Darnell, R. (1988). The implications of Cree interactional etiquette. In R. Darnell & M. Foster (Eds.), *Native North American interaction patterns* (pp. 69–77). Hull, Quebec: Canadian Museum of Civilization.

Deetz, S. (1992). *Democracy in an age of corporate colonization: Developments in communication and the politics of everyday life.* Albany: State University of New York Press.

Kipp, D. R. (June 1993). The Blackfeet: A Native American perspective," *Montana Magazine, 119,* 4–11.

Medicine, B. (Winter 1994). North American indigenous women and cultural domination. *Cultural Survival Quarterly, 17,* 66–69.

Philips, S. U. (1993). *The invisible culture: Communication in classroom and community on the Warm Springs Indian Reservation.* Prospect Heights, IL: Waveland.

Powell, R., & Collier, M. J. (1990). Public speaking instruction and cultural bias. *American Behavioral Scientist, 34,* 240–250.

Scollon, R., & Scollon, S. (1981). *Narrative, literacy, and face in interethnic communication.* Norwood, NJ: Ablex.

Sousa, A. (1994). *An "observation" of "participation": Interaction between Cheyenne Americans and Anglo-Americans.* Paper prepared for Communication 514: Social Uses of Language, University of Massachusetts, Amherst.

Weider, L., & Pratt, S. (1990). On being a recognizable Indian among Indians. In D. Carbaugh (Ed.), *Cultural communication and intercultural contact* (pp. 45–64). Hillsdale, NJ: Lawrence Erlbaum Associates, Inc.

Weider, L., & Pratt, S. (1993). The case of "saying a few words" and "talking for another" among the Osage people: "Public speaking" as an object of ethnography. *Research on Language and Social Interaction, 26,* 353–408.

Welch, J. (1987). *The death of Jim Loney.* New York: Penguin.

Wesaw, M. J. (Winter 1994). Mind over matter: Reflections on the State of the Peoples Tour. *Cultural Survival Quarterly, 17,* 1.

Key Terms

Blackfeet	silence
communication style	Whiteman's model
public speaking	

Discussion Questions

1. How does listener-active silence as expressed by the Blackfeet differ from listening as experienced by most White people?

2. What are some similarities between the Blackfeet and the Whiteman's model of communication?

3. Donal Carbaugh used ethnographic research methods (observations, interviewing) in this study.

What are other methods a researcher could use to investigate this same topic?

4. What are some communication strategies that White people might use in order to communicate effectively with Blackfeet people?

5. Can you think of other groups of students in U.S. college classrooms for whom public speaking may be a very unusual and difficult situation?

 ## 16 A Ritual for Attempting Leave-Taking in Colombia

KRISTINE L. FITCH

Today's urban Colombians live in an interpersonal world centered on connectedness and relationships. Persons are, according to Colombians, first and foremost sets of bonds (*vinculos*) to other people. This world view contrasts sharply with North Americans', which focuses primarily on individuality and freedom of choice (e.g., Carbaugh, 1988; Slater, 1970; Bellah et al., 1985). The pervasiveness and power of this Colombian idiom of human union can be heard in countless instances of interpersonal discourse.[1] For example, confidence is often expressed in the importance of influential "connections," through whom persons may expect to transcend virtually any law or institutional regulation to achieve a goal. In a related vein, Colombians devote significant attention to development of relationships with service providers with whom they must deal on a regular basis, such as auto mechanics, hair stylists and shopkeepers. They explain the investment of time and energy involved in forming such connections as a preference for service *relationships* over service *encounters*. That is, they believe that business should ideally be conducted with persons one has an established relationship with, rather than with strangers.

A final illustration of the importance Colombians attach to connectedness is the frequency with which the desirability of developing romantic relationships is commented upon in terms of the group memberships of the potential partners. Individual dispositions are rarely talked about as significant determiners of whether a relationship is likely to "work out." Instead, the compatibility of each individual's important relational circles is discussed: Their social and occupational parity, their regional origin, their political affiliation, etc. Assertions are frequently made to the effect that, if those networks were sufficiently similar, any individual discord could be resolved. If they were not, tremendous difficulty would befall the couple regardless of how well the two of them might get along. For that reason, unions considered undesirable by friends or family members are verbally discouraged, and more direct intervention to disrupt the relationship is commonplace.

These examples illustrate the point of Colombian connectedness in a way which is consistent with much traditional ethnographic practice. But the mission of Michael Moerman's *Talking Culture* (1988) is to lessen reliance on reasoning from this kind of data, drawn from interviews and/or the researcher's field notes. The examples given above would not, in his view, constitute sufficient evidence for a claim about Colombian interpersonal ideology. Moerman urges, instead, that ethnographers draw on everyday conversation, produced spontaneously and recorded (presumably) unobtrusively. Examination of the sequential organization of such conversation would enable a closer view of the culture, less distorted by the ethnographer's own cultural understanding of the nature of the world and of persons. Conversation analysis as a centerpiece of ethnographic method provides a way to ground cultural claims in recordings and transcriptions which are "'out there' on the page for analyst and reader to encounter, cite, be responsible to, and make sense of according to explicit conversation analytic procedures" (Moerman, 1988, p. 33).

This paper follows Moerman's lead by presenting a conversational enactment of a leave-taking ritual which is, I will argue, an archetype for Colombian spoken life in a sense similar to the way that *dugri* speech expresses an essential element of Israeli *sabra* culture (Katriel, 1986). It is drawn from audiotaped, naturally-occurring conversation recorded in Colombia in 1987. The purpose of analyzing this conversation is both to describe a conversational sequence which performs a symbolic activity among Colombians during leave-taking from social gatherings, and to elucidate what ethnographic information may (and may not) emerge from conversation analysis. Beyond celebrating the importance of Moerman's proposal for the practice of conversation analysis in ethnography, I hope to demonstrate that in this speech pattern, an interpersonal ideology is revealed which revolves around the crucial importance of human connectedness, over and above individual desires.

Taking Leave

The participants in this conversation are two brothers of the bride, hosts (H1, H2) at a wedding reception held in their home, and a friend of the groom who is a guest (G) at the reception. The three have spoken only briefly, if at all, earlier in the evening.

1 G: Me voy.   I'm leaving.
2 H1: ¿Se va? ¿Por qué?   You're leaving? Why?
3 G: La tarjetica decía   The little card [wedding
        muy <u>claramente</u>   invitation] said very
        que de 7 a 10 y ya   <u>clearly</u> that [the reception
        son las 10:30.   would last] from 7 to 10
                                         and now it's 10:30.
4 H2: Pero que <u>va</u>, yo   But so <u>what</u>, until
        hasta las cinco y
        media de la mañana   five thirty in the morning
        [   ]   [   ]
5 G: heh heh heh   heh heh heh
6 H2: estoy aquí=   I'll be here=

7 G: =Pero me tengo   =But I have to <u>go</u>=
        que <u>ir</u>=
8 H1: =Hmf, que se   =Hmf, that you have
        tiene que ir. Y por   to go. And <u>why</u>.
        que.
9 G: Porque vivo   Because I live
        <u>le   jos</u>   <u>far</u> away
        [   ]   [   ]
10 H2:   Pero   But that
        no impor::ta   doesn't <u>matter</u>
11 H1: Hmf. Dizque me   Hmf. Says he's going.
        voy. Asi no   Just like that, I'm going
        más, me voy   [   ]
        [   ]
12 G: heh heh   heh heh
        ha ha ha ha   ha ha ha ha
          (.3)   (.3)
        Pero es que tengo   But it's that I have to go
        que salir a coger   catch a <u>bus</u>=
        <u>bus</u>=
13 H2: =No, no, luego le   =No, no, later
        lle vamos   we'll take you
        [   ]   [   ]
14 H1:   <u>To</u>:me se   <u>Ha</u>:ve
        otro traguito   another little drink
        mano   brother
        [   ]   [   ]
15 H2:   o se va   or you can go with
        con Alberto   Alberto who lives out
        que vive por alla y   there and has a car . . .
        tiene carro . . .

This conversation begins with G initiating leave-taking. His intention is questioned. He responds, and the response is challenged. He repeats his intention, which is questioned again; offers another account, which is denied; and offers another, different account, which is also denied. Much like Moerman's example (1988, p. 23; transcript p. 127), the participants in this episode are divided into two "teams." G is a guest, whose expressed intention is to leave the party. H1 and H2 are hosts, whose apparent intention is to keep G at the party awhile longer. H1 and H2 were successful in this aim; G stayed at the party for another hour.

From the tenacity with which H1 and H2 deny G's reasons for needing to leave, and the number of alternatives to his leaving that they propose, it might seem as though they particularly enjoy or desire his company. But the fact is that, because G is a friend of the groom rather than the bride (their sister), they have met him only briefly earlier in the reception, if at all. They persistently ask, "Why?" when G announces that he must leave:

1	G:	Me\ voy.	I'm leaving.
2	H1:	¿Se va? ¿Por qué?	You're leaving? Why?
.			.
.			.
.			.
7	G:	=Pero me tengo qui ir	=But I have to go=
8	H1:	=Hmf, que se tiene que ir. Y por que.	=Hmf, that you have to go. And why.

Additionally, they negate the accounts he offers for why leave-taking is appropriate at that moment:

3	G:	La tarjetica decía muy claramente que de 7 a 10 ya son las 10:30.	The little card [wedding invitation] said very clearly that [the reception would last] from 7 to 10 and now it's 10:30.
4	H2:	Pero que va, yo hasta las cinco y media de la mañana	But so what, until five thirty in the morning
6	H2:	estoy aquí=	I'll be here=

H2 even mimics G's announced intention, by repeating in his dismissal of G's excuse the intonation with which the excuse was offered:

9	G:	Porque vivo le jos [ ]	Because I live far away [ ]
10	H2:	Per o no impor::ta	But that doesn't matter

Although G has reminded them that the invitation said the reception was expected to last from 7 to 10 p.m. and that it is now well past 10, H2's mimicry suggests that leave-taking at that moment is a ludicrous action, which may even be an affront to the hosts.

Despite the frequency of vigorous negation and denial, the sequence does not evoke a confrontive or tense atmosphere. G laughs in turns 5 and 12 as his accounts are denied. On both occasions his laughter is preemptive, suggesting that he sensed the point that was about to be made and was amused by it.

A noteworthy feature of this conversation is that there are few pauses, and considerable overlap and latching. The two "teams" seem to be working closely together to bring something off. Because G's oft-repeated intention is to leave the gathering, that "something" seems akin to terminal exchanges that close conversations generally (Schegloff & Sacks, 1984). Schegloff and Sacks point out that some types of conversational tasks require particularly close ordering of utterances, to assure that a desired successive utterance type is eventually produced. Encounters and closings, they argue, are such tasks.

The transcribed fragment is not, however, the termination of an ongoing conversation. It is virtually the *entire* conversation, preceded only by eye contact between G and the brothers and followed by trailing-off attempts from H1 to secure "another little drink" for the guest.

Additionally, H1 and H2's comments on G's intention, and their refusals of his accounts, challenge G's competence to decide when to leave. Their challenges range from very general ("But that doesn't matter," turn 10) to specific ("you can go with Alberto who lives out there," turn 15, when in fact H1 and H2 have no way of knowing where G lives). In Labov and Fanshel's (1977) terms, they deny G's readiness to leave as being an A event (one that can only be known by the speaker, as opposed to B events, which may be known by both speaker and hearer). By hinting that leave-taking at that moment would be offensive, H1 and H2 reframe G's departure from something that affects primarily, or only, himself into an action which has an impact on them as well. If he follows through on his announced intention, he will insult/hurt/deprive them of something they are willing to engage in verbal battle to preserve.

The two teams seem to be engaging in a sequence which has, as its logical ultimate objective, the guest's departure. Why, then, are apparently strenuous objections offered to his going?

A candidate answer to that question is that this leave-taking is an instance of a conversational routine, similar to the telephone openings described by Hopper (1989). That is, it could be that the hosts respond to announced intentions to depart with objections because that expectation has arisen through years and generations of Colombians interacting. This kind of leave-taking has become so habitual that it is only remarkable in its absence.

There is no question that this episode fits neatly into grooves worn deep into Colombian social interaction. The pattern of:

1. G announces intention
2. H1 or H2 asks for account
3. G gives account
4. H1 or H2 denies account and/or offers alternative

is repeated twice (turns 1–6 and 7–10). A partial third repetition occurs in turns 12–15 as G recycles step 3 and again receives step 4 in response, this time from H1 and H2 almost in chorus. As noted earlier, the exchange is produced rapidly, almost without pause. There is a finely tuned syncopation of turns here. Even though the participants have not met, they seem to experience little difficulty coordinating the steps of a leavetaking sequence. They have never "talked" this route before; or have they?

Examination of 11 leavetaking episodes, transcribed from tape recordings or written down from memory, shows a consistent pattern of exchange. The pattern is close to the one identified in the conversation transcribed above:

1. Guest(s) announce intentions to leave, sometimes thanking host(s) for invitation.
2. Host asks why guest is proposing to leave and protests timing of departure (it's early yet, you just got here, your companion is still having fun).
3. Guest repeats intention to leave and/or offers account for needing to leave.
4. Host rejects account and/or suggests alternative (wait until this song is over and we'll call you a taxi; have one more drink; ten minutes and X will go with you or take you home, etc.)

In slots 2 and 4, hosts have a third option, which is to introduce a new topic, suggesting that departure is inappropriate until the new conversational business is concluded. In those cases, the guests' announcements that they are leaving act as possible pre-closings (Schegloff & Sacks, 1984). That is, they offer an opportunity for closing (in this case leavetaking) which may be taken as opportunities to bring up an "unmentioned mentionable." As Schegloff and Sacks point out,

> The opening that a possible pre-closing makes for an unmentioned mentionable may thus result in much more ensuing talk than the initial mentionable that is inserted; for that may provide the occasion for the "natural occurrence" of someone else's mentionables in a fitted manner. It is thus not negative evidence for the status of (such utterances) as possible pre-closings that extensive conversational developments may follow them. (1984, p. 80)

This type of exchange is repeated with minor variations, perhaps several times, until someone changes the subject or engages the guest or host in some other activity. Leavetaking occurs after some time has elapsed after the initial attempt, and three or more exchanges of this type often precede departure. The fact that so many instances of leavetaking followed a similar sequence of assertion/denial suggests that an identifiable closing exchange sequence exists among Colombians.

Of the 11 recorded instances, on only two occasions did the guests actually leave after the first performance of the *salsipuede* ritual. I also observed or was told about three occasions when guests left social gatherings without engaging in the ritual at all. Both actions (leaving after the first round of goodbyes, and leaving without saying goodbye) were evaluated as rude or incompetent, i.e., deficient performances of the act of leavetaking.

This leavetaking episode thus reflects a structure similar to that claimed as universal to conversational closings by Schegloff and Sacks. It is so familiar to the participants precisely because it follows a routine that all of them, as competent members of the interpersonal world, have engaged in countless times before.

More importantly than the conversational problem of drawing interaction to a close, however, a task central to Colombian interpersonal ideology is performed here. Much in the way that *dugri* speech celebrates *sabra* toughness through straightforward communication among Israelis (Katriel, 1986); this sequence constitutes "connection" talk among Colombians. Exploration of the task performed, and discovery of its cultural significance, are elucidations which must go outside of any naturally occurring conversation or collection of instances. That inquiry, in other words, requires examination of the cultural context in which the interaction took place.

The Communication Ritual of *"Salsipuede"*

Colombians, and probably other Latin Americans[2] engage in the kind of conversational exchange exemplified by the instance reported here virtually every time they depart from a social gathering. The purpose does not seem to be to thank the host. Often (as in this conversation) no word of thanks is uttered in the course of the interaction. This type of exchange is confined to social gatherings; it does not occur after business meetings, at the end of telephone conversations, or when family members leave for work in the morning. The native term for the action performed is *"despedirse,"* to say goodbye. Saying goodbye requires two teams of at least one person each, representing the host(s) or organizer(s) of the event and the guest(s) or attender(s). Although the exchange presented earlier was a good-natured series of contradictions and denials, the sequence itself is not merely a pro forma pre-sequence to taking leave. I tried countless times, with utmost sincerity and determination, to leave social gatherings at what seemed to me to be reasonable hours, and found it often was impossible to actually escape until much later than I wanted. Colombians tell with rueful laughter of similar experiences, so that it was not merely a marker of non-native incompetence that I was unable to break away sooner.

My initial reactions on such occasions were anger and confusion. Hosts and organizers seemed quite comfortable denying my own and my companions' experience of the moment (e.g., I'm tired, I've had enough of your company, it's a long way home) to insist we stay longer. I was puzzled about why they did so when they hardly knew me/us. In

the case above, the hosts had not said two words to G during the course of the gathering, but then vehemently opposed his leavetaking. Confusion about this eventually motivated me to carry a tape recorder to several social events (including this wedding reception) and turn it on as I was about to leave.

Through interviews with Colombians, I came to understand that the worst thing that could happen at any social gathering, regardless of how well hosts and guests might or might not know one another (or like each other) was taking leave without engaging in the kind of conversational sequence presented earlier. The American pattern of

GUEST: Well, we must be going.
HOST: Oh, so soon? Well, thanks for coming.

would be a sign in Colombia of boredom, even antagonism, on the part of the host. Having observed on numerous occasions the sequential pattern in the transcript above of the guest's "departure" from the wedding reception, I came to call it the *"salsipuede"* (leave if you can) ritual. The term *salsipuede* is drawn from a popular dance tune from the 1970's, in which "Salsipuede" is the name of a most agreeable, friendly small town. The general flavor is one of nostalgia, as if the singer had departed with difficulty, and with many fond memories of wonderful times spent there. The term struck me as appropriate, because guests' attempts to pull themselves away from parties met with such resistance from their hosts. From their end, guests seemed to accompany their expressed desires to leave with an apparent willingness to stay, as though the ambience of the party exerted an attraction far stronger than their needs to get up the next morning.

Presented with the term *"salsipuede,"* Colombians immediately recognized the kind of leavetaking behavior it connoted. Nonetheless, *salsipuede* is an ethnographer's borrowing, not a native term for a commonplace interactional event. The *lack* of a native term does not, however, in itself call into question the cultural significance of the action. Katriel and Philipsen (1981), for example, describe "communication" as a cultural ritual among certain Americans, proposing that essential features of American interpersonal life are captured in the term "communication." When their subjects described the episodic sequence of "communication," however, they referred to the action with different native phrases such as "sit down and talk," "work out problems," or "discuss our relationship" (1981, p. 310). Although they used different words to refer to the events than did the ethnographers, the subjects had identifiable expectations for the ritual of "communication." In a similar sense, Colombians shared expectations for leavetaking episodes at parties that reflected common beliefs about relationships, even though they did not attend to those episodes so consciously that a specialized term had evolved to describe them.

The episode presented earlier may, like "communication" among Americans, appropriately be described as a ritual for several reasons. First, the moves which constituted the speech event of announcing intentions to leave, and having those intentions met with spirited opposition, were performed in similar ways on 11 occasions detailed in my fieldnotes, three of which were also captured on audiotape. This repetitive quality suggests that whatever function is performed by the exchange, it is a function recognized by most or all Colombians and performed in similar ways across dissimilar contexts.

Another reason that the term "ritual" seems appropriate to the event described earlier is its close fit with Philipsen's (1987, p. 250) definition of ritual as a form of cultural communication: A "structured sequence of symbolic acts, the correct performance of which constitutes homage to a sacred object." The moves which constitute the *salsipuede* ritual may be viewed as symbolic in that they take place in roughly the same manner and intensity regardless of the nature of the relationship between participants. That is, hosts are expected to vigorously oppose guests' departure from social events whether or not they have a sincere interest in the guests' remaining. Even when hosts and guests barely know one another and have not interacted during the course of the event, as was the case in the conversation transcribed here, a relationally significant moment is botched if the *salsipuede* ritual is not performed when the guests first attempt to depart.

The sacred object to which tribute is paid by this ritual is the *vínculo:* the relationship formed, symbolically or concretely, during the social event. When Colombians share a meal, a drink, an evening of song and poetry, or an afternoon of sandlot soccer, an interpersonal bond forms between the participants. The native term for such a bond is *"vínculo"* (literally: tie), a central symbol in the Colombian ideology of personal identity. Persons are, according to Colombians, first and foremost conjunctions of ties to other people. Beyond their individual uniqueness, persons are much more crucially defined by to whom, and how profoundly, they are connected to others. It follows that individuals (or pairs of individuals) are not supposed to leave a social event simply because they, *as* individuals, are ready to go. Some affirmation that a relationship has been formed or maintained must occur, and that affirmation may be accomplished by denying guests' needs or even rights to leave.

In this context, social events take on a much greater importance for Colombians than they do for North Americans. Many occasions commemorated by Americans with phone calls or a card, such as Mother's Day and anniversaries, are celebrated with social gatherings by Colombians. Social events in Colombia are, from my observation, rarely only half-social (such as working lunches or gatherings convened for purposes of "networking"), nor are guest/host roles ever ambiguated (as with potluck meals, progressive dinners, bring-your-own-bottle or no-host cocktail hours). When Colombians socialize, they do so lavishly, relative to the socioeconomic status and age of the hosts. Social events are significant because of the sacredness of the *vínculos* (interpersonal ties) that are formed and maintained in that context. The importance of those bonds is reaffirmed in the *salsipuede* ritual.

Interpersonal bonds are important for all of the reasons suggested at the beginning of this essay. Through contacts with appropriately powerful others, one may transcend institutional regulations to achieve almost any goal. Everyday tasks of life are accomplished far more quickly and reliably if one has developed a *vínculo* with the service provider. One's choices about the future, including friends and spouse, will affect those persons with whom strong *vínculos* already exist, so that comment and even intervention in those decisions is to be expected from the other parties.

Notes

1. The data on which this essay is based are reported more fully in Fitch (1989), drawn from ten months' fieldwork in Bogotá, Colombia in 1987.

2. I have not encountered data on interpersonal communication patterns in other Latin American countries that would allow for a systematic comparison. The similarities of history and tradition among Colombia and its close neighbors, such as Ecuador, Venezuela and certainly Panama, are so extensive that I am sure the pattern and beliefs I describe here are not unique to Colombians. Yet it seems appropriate to describe this as a "Colombian ritual" because all of the data were collected in Colombia, among Colombians; and because of the current lack of data that would allow for comparison with other countries in the region.

References

Bellah, R., Madsen, R., Sullivan, W., Swidler, A., & Tipton, S. (1985). *Habits of the heart: Individualism and commitment in American life.* Berkeley: University of California Press.

Carbaugh, D. (1988). *Talking American: Cultural discourses on Donahue.* Norwood, NJ: Ablex.

Fitch, K. (1989). Communicative enactment of interpersonal ideology: Personal address in urban Colombian society. Unpublished Ph.D. dissertation, University of Washington, Seattle.

Hopper, R. (1989). Speech in telephone openings: Emergent interaction vs. routines. *Western Journal of Speech Communication, 53,* 178–194.

Katriel, T. (1986). *Talking straight: "Dugri" speech in Israeli Sabra culture.* Cambridge: Cambridge University Press.

Katriel, T., & Philipsen, G. (1981). "What we need is communication": "Communication" as a cultural category in some American speech. *Communication Monographs, 48,* 301–317.

Labov, W., & Fanshel, D. (1977). *Therapeutic discourse: Psychotherapy as conversation.* New York: Academic Press.

Philipsen, G. (1987). The prospect for cultural communication. In L. Kinkaid (Ed.), *Communication theory: Eastern and Western perspectives* (pp. 245–254). New York: Academic Press.

Schegloff, E. A., & Sacks, H. (1984). Opening up closings. In J. Baugh & J. Scherzer (Eds.), *Language in use* (pp. 69–99). Englewood Cliffs, NJ: Prentice-Hall.

Slater, P. (1970). *The pursuit of loneliness.* Boston: Beacon Press.

Key Terms

Colombia	leavetaking
ethnography	social relationships

Discussion Questions

1. How does this *"salsipuede"* leavetaking ritual in Colombia reflect an important Colombian cultural value?

2. What leavetaking rituals do you and your friends engage in? Do these rituals vary from context to context (social vs. task)?

3. To what extent does Fitch's characterization of the typical North American leavetaking ritual hold true for all cultural groups in the United States?

4. Why is *"salsipuede"* leavetaking in Colombia described as a "communication *ritual*"?

5. How might a critical researcher approach this study of communication rituals?

17 Code-Switching
An Everyday Reality in Belgium
JEAN-LOUIS SAUVAGE

Prologue

When asked to write a paper about code-switching, I realized that as a French-speaking Belgian, and regardless of my educational background (as a linguist!), I was de facto considered as someone who must know something about languages. Indeed, someone living in a country credited with trilingualism can be expected to have a sound grasp of code-switching. While code-switching can be easily defined as changing communication systems and languages, it offers a glimpse into the complexity of Belgium. It is like squaring the circle, however preposterous this sounds. It might not seem that difficult to describe such a small country, as Belgium is about the size of the U.S. state of Maryland. This seemingly innocent observation brings us to the heart of the difficulty: Is Belgium a country such as France or Germany or the United States?

Code-Switching

When you start a sentence in one language and finish it in another, you change languages. Linguists call this "code-switching." This switch does not have to occur in the middle of a sentence. You also switch codes when, being a native speaker of language X, you answer the phone in language Y.

In my opinion, the following cases should be taken into consideration:

- Two native speakers of language X intersperse it with a dialect of language X or with bits of another language.
- Two native speakers of language X use language Y when speaking together.
- A native speaker of language X (also speaking language Y) and a native speaker of language Y (also speaking language X), use the one language after the other in the same sentence or in the same act of speech.
- A native speaker of language X (also speaking language Y) resorts to language Y when speaking to a native speaker of language Y (not knowing language X).

As in the case of Belgium, location (i.e., where the languages are used) is also a parameter that is key to the problem.

A corollary issue resulting from this discussion is, Why do people switch languages? I do not think this is an irrelevant question. If it is easy to understand why a native speaker of language X (knowing language Y) uses language Y when speaking to a native speaker of language Y who does not have a clue of language X, what about the other cases?

Belgium: A Multilingual Country?

Geographically, Belgium is bordered by the Netherlands to the north, by the North Sea to the northwest, by Germany and Luxembourg to the east, and by France to the south. Belgium is divided into two distinct geographical regions: a fairly flat, fertile farmland area to the north and west; and a hilly, wooded region, the Ardennes, to the south and east. The country is crossed by two main rivers coming from France, the Scheldt (Escaut) and the Maas (Meuse), which flow into the North Sea via the Netherlands.

Historically, Belgium is a very young nation. It became a separate and independent state in 1830. There is no history of Belgium as such before this date. Studying the history of Belgium prior to its independence amounts to examining the past of its neighbors. Everyone who studied Latin or the history of the Romans has heard of Julius Caesar defeating the Belgae tribes of northern Gaul around 57 B.C.E. When the Roman Empire collapsed in the

5th century, Germanic tribes settled in the northern, sparsely populated plains of the country. As a result, a Germanic-speaking population (the Flemings) prevailed in the north while the Gallo-Romans of the south spoke a Romance language, a variety of Latin, that was later to become French (may my colleagues in this field condone this *very* simplistic summary!). Belgium has ever since been fractured along this age-old European great divide between the Germanic north and the Romance south, a division expressed in the constant regional bickering between Dutch-speaking Flanders and French-speaking Wallonia. There is even a small community (0.7%) of German speakers in the east. Because of their neutrality in the "conflict" between the 60% of Dutch speakers and the 40% of French speakers, the German-speaking Belgians call themselves "the best Belgians of all."

According to Richard Hill (1997),

> The best way to understand Belgium is to imagine a Belgian road junction. Four drivers coming from four different directions, none of them giving way. One of the cars contains the Flemish, the second the Walloons, the third the Brussels Community and the fourth the German-speakers from the *Ostkantone*. They all meet in the middle, but they don't crash. They simply block one another's way, including their own. (p. 141)

Linguistically, Dutch, French, and German are spoken in three unilingual places (for lack of a more precise word, see Fitzmaurice's definitions infra). Dutch and French are spoken in a bilingual place (Brussels), and French and German are spoken in a place nevertheless considered as unilingual *die Ostkantone*. The Constitution of 1830 envisaged a strong centralized national government; neither regions nor language communities were recognized. Initially, Belgium was unilingual, and French was the official language. Gradually, the equal status of Dutch came to be acknowledged and its use legally permitted. The language laws of 1932 implemented the idea of language regions and a "linguistic frontier." In practice it resulted in two major unilingual regions, with the native language principle being restricted to Brussels.

These laws are very complicated. They have nevertheless built up a reputation of having enabled the populations living in Belgium, whatever their size, to live in peace. Minorities in the former Yugoslavia are said to be very interested in these laws. At this stage, it is worth pointing to John Fitzmaurice's *The Politics of Belgium: A Unique Federalism* (1996). You will find in this book the ins and outs of Belgian federalism. The following excerpt, in my opinion, will help you better understand the linguistic and political issues at stake:

DEFINITIONS

Regions are a geographic concept and *communities* are a cultural/linguistic concept. There are three regions in Belgium:

> *Flanders,* consisting of four Flemish provinces (Antwerp, Limburg, East Flanders, and West Flanders);

> The *Walloon region,* consisting of the four traditional Walloon provinces (Hainaut, Liège, Namur, and Luxembourg) and part of Brabant (basically the *arrondissement* of Nivelles); and

> The *Brussels region* consisting of 19 *communes* (municipalities).

There are three communities in Belgium. They do not have a geographic competence as such, but are responsible for linguistic and cultural policy, education and so-called personalisable matters (health, social provision) for speakers of French, Dutch, and German. Given the application of the territorial principle, their "territory" in effect covers the areas in which their language is spoken and for the French and Flemish communities in bilingual Brussels as well.

> The *Dutch-speaking community* consists of all Dutch-speakers in the Flemish provinces and Brussels. The Flemish region and community have been fused and, though deriving their competences from separate articles of the Constitution (59 *bis* and 107 *quater*) have only one set of institutions and are seen as one unit.

> The *French-speaking community* consists of all French-speakers in the Walloon provinces, part of Brabant, and Brussels.

The *German-speaking community* consists of 70,000 German-speakers living in the Eupen-Malmédy-Sankt Vith area near the German border.

The *Brussels region.* Some community matters in the capital are handled by the Brussels regional executive and council, split into its two linguistic components.

The now small French-speaking minority living in Flanders, outside Brabant, belongs to no community at all. The official language of Flanders is Dutch, but is often referred to as Flemish—Flemish being a series of Dutch dialects spoken in Flanders. Dutch-speakers are referred to either as *"Nederlandstalige"* or *"Vlaamstalige."* However, the official name of the Flemish community is *"De Vlaamse Gemeenschap."*

—John Fitzmaurice, *The Politics of Belgium,* 1996, pp. 122–123

As can be imagined after considering all these intricacies, there are many forms of code-switching in Belgian everyday life.

Forms of Code-Switching

Two native speakers of language X intersperse it with a dialect of language X or with bits of another language.

1. *With a Dialect*   Dialects enjoy a different status whether you are in Flanders or in Wallonia. Even if using a dialect of the official language meets the same needs in both the north and south of the country (whatever their cultural differences, people are the same everywhere!)—intimacy, secrecy, complicity—the way they have been treated is different. Remember that at the start Belgium was a unilingual country, French being the official language. And so, speaking a dialect in Flanders was in fact speaking a kind of "illegal" language, Dutch in this instance. It was a political act. Even if this is no longer the case, dialects are still used by many Flemings, which is often a nightmare for Dutch-learning Walloons who do not understand them. So "contumacy" could be added to intimacy, secrecy, and complicity.

In Wallonia, the situation is different. Walloon was considered vulgar. Schoolchildren were punished when they spoke Walloon. Here is a description of how I personally behave—linguistically—in everyday life:

I only speak Walloon to my father. I never spoke Walloon to my (now deceased) mother. She would have considered this as very rude.

I rarely speak Walloon to any persons having a high social status. But I do use Walloon when I speak to people of a lower social status, most of the time hoping they will understand me better and they will appreciate that I can adapt to their level.

I sometimes use a Walloon word or expression in my French when I think it enables me to better explain what I mean.

I never speak Walloon with my son, considering that it is more useful for him to know French correctly. To tell the truth, I cannot say this without feeling a pang of remorse.

And if I may add something as a linguist, I like Suzanne Romaine when she quotes Max Weinreich's dictum "a language is a dialect with an army and a navy" (1994, p. 14).

2. *With Bits of Another Language*   This is performed by many people in Belgium who intersperse their French or their Dutch with borrowed words or phrases from other languages, particularly English expressions. This is not necessarily because of snobism, for example, I want you to realize I know some English; or because of fashion, for example, everything (however negative sometimes) coming from the United States is warmly welcome. Regardless of the efforts of European terminology banks, many English words are used because of the lack of a proper equivalent in French or in Dutch. Many Belgian computer scientists, for example, learn and use the English computer terms as they become familiar with new hardware and software, because these terms are available before French and Dutch equivalents.

Often, many Belgians use "bilingual" expressions without knowing it. Let's look at some examples of how languages can become intertwined. Everything used in the Belgian army (shoes, uniforms, etc.) is referred to as ABL. This is not a brand name, it just means *Armée Belge/Belgish Leger* (*leger* meaning *army* in Dutch). This French-Dutch combination is one way to mix languages.

Another way to borrow words from another language is to incorporate them into the common vocabulary. For example, the median strip between the right and left lanes of a highway is normally referred to in French as *le terre-plein central.* In French-speaking Belgium it is called *la berme centrale,* from Dutch *berm. Berme* exists as a loan word from Dutch in French and has an entry in the French dictionary *Le Petit Robert,* but under another definition.

Sometimes words are borrowed to give a little twist to the meaning. When ministers holding key positions, such as interior, defense, foreign affairs, and so on, are summoned to Brussels by the prime minister, the French-speaking press reports that the *kern* (cabinet) is in a meeting. *Kern* is Dutch for "core" as in "hard core."

Two native speakers of language X use language Y when speaking together. This sounds crazy and it is. Except at school, where language teachers are supposed to develop conversation skills as a priority, why would two native speakers of the same language want to communicate in another language? "Make them speak" is the slogan chanted by everybody, including language teachers. If it is reasonably easy to motivate language learners to try to understand phone calls (listening comprehension skill), to read instructions (reading comprehension skill), and to write letters (writing skill), for some of them it is inconceivable to resort to a foreign language when speaking to a fellow native speaker. I have acquired considerable experience in taking French-speaking students to English-speaking countries: Even the most taciturn ones become very talkative when they are in the real situation, in other words, when they are motivated to speak English.

A native speaker of language X (also speaking language Y) and a native speaker of language Y (also speaking language X), use the one language after the other in the same sentence or in the same act of speech. This happens mostly in bilingual places, that is, where two languages are known

and used. Although bilingual situations exist around the world, Brussels is one such place where native French speakers frequently encounter native Dutch speakers. Code-switching here is more than just a sudden impulse to communicate in another language. There are many elements to be mulled over. Consider the following situations:

a. X wants to be kind to Y and show him he can speak Y's native language, however imperfectly. Whatever language used, it does not matter between two people appreciating—maybe unawarely—"this social move toward the other."

b. X wants to speak Y's native language, but his knowledge of the language is limited in given sectors. For example, my house was built by a contractor who sometimes resorted to Flemish subcontractors. One of these subcontractors was the electrician. I spoke Dutch to him but had to use French words when I referred to technical notions that I did not completely understand even in French. This was not a problem for the electrician, who knew these terms in Dutch as well as in French but would have been unable to explain them to me in French.

c. Sometimes, X and Y will switch to one language in particular because they only know the terms needed in one specific field in this language that happened to be the language of their education in this area. For example, as a paratrooper in the army, my military training was (at my request) in Dutch. At the end of my training, there were many military terms with which I had become familiar but was totally unable to translate into French.

A native speaker of language X (also speaking language Y) resorts to language Y when speaking to a native speaker of language Y (not knowing language X). This is an everyday situation for many Belgians, particularly in the workplace. Trade represents 50% of Belgium GDP. Approximately 76.5% of goods "made in Belgium" are exported abroad. Buyers—in other words, the people having money—impose their native languages in commercial transactions. Code-switching is forced on

Belgians who have to cope with monolingual (or pretending to be so) commercial partners. The latter expect their respective native languages to be spoken correctly, and subsequently, Belgian employers in the private sector require their personnel to have a high level of knowledge of potential buyers' native languages. When graduates in management of the Warocqué Business School (in the Francophone university where I teach) apply for a job, they have to go through a lot of interviews in English, Dutch, and possibly a third or even a fourth language. This is largely due to the "take it or leave it" principle in a country where the unemployment rate is still close to 8.6%.

Code-Switching: The Bottom Line

THE NEGATIVE OR TRAGIC SIDE

Having to cope with different languages is very often a burden for many Belgians. You can be a brilliant student in management but fail your language examinations. You, Mr. X, can be a most gifted and talented politician, but you will never become a federal prime minister in Belgium if you do not have some command of Ms. Y's language. Nevertheless, it does not mean you have to speak or pronounce the other's language perfectly. This is why the French laugh at the way we Belgian Francophones are supposed to speak French, that is, with a strong Flemish accent; they think (or pretend to think) all of us speak French like our Flemish ministers.

THE TRAGICOMIC SIDE

A strike by high school teachers stopped in Flanders because the Flemish-speaking prime minister had promised *snoepgoed* (sweets), a metaphor that was honestly meant as a solace. Unfortunately, it was translated awkwardly (some say on purpose) into *biscuits,* a word that can have very negative connotations in French. You buy biscuits for your dog—*biscuits pour chien.* When you are in the army, *le biscuit militaire* is part of your combat ration. It is as hard as stone and could not possibly be translated into English as a "military cookie"!

When, a few days after the catastrophe in Chernobyl, the amount of nuclear radiation reached the threshold considered as critical by Belgian legislation, cows had to be put back in their stalls in Flanders but not in Wallonia. The measure should have been the same, but being worded in two different languages, the interpretation resulted in two opposite reactions. Hence the importance in matter of law to have a unique reference text. This would be much easier, but it is totally impossible to implement in a country where three national languages are considered equal.

When there is a general election in France, the French community (French people living in Belgium) can vote in the various French consulates scattered all over Brussels and Wallonia. Each time, Belgian radio and TV announcers bend over backward to explain to Belgian Francophones that this "French community" (*communauté française*) has nothing to do with the "French-speaking community" wrongly or maliciously called *Communauté Française* instead of *Communauté Francophone.* The English translation "French-speaking Community" denotes exactly what it is. This is not entirely innocent in the Kingdom of Belgium (some would say there must be something rotten in it).

THE POSITIVE OR COMIC SIDE

Belgium is considered by the whole planet as a trilingual country, which is not entirely true, but it is very useful for its image as the capital of the European Union. If it were trilingual, there would not be "linguistic bickering" in Belgium. Anyway, having to learn foreign languages has probably made Belgian people more tolerant toward foreigners. Many Belgians will try to help, even in poor English (or Dutch, or French), in whatever way they can, so long as, for some of them, the persons they help do not belong to the other Belgian community! A Finn speaking French in Flanders and Dutch in Wallonia will be assisted as long as he first explains he is from Finland.

Learning foreign languages opens the door to other cultures, to other worlds, and gives you a shortcut to the hearts of native speakers of the language studied. From a very pragmatic point of view, it enables you to penetrate foreign markets and to land contracts. This is something the founders of the Warocqué Business School understood at the turn of the 19th century when they imposed Chinese into the curriculum of what was then called "commercial engineering." As a result, Belgium, this tiny country in that salad of nation-states aiming to become as united as possible in the European Union, built a major part of the Chinese railway system. As a side note, history has it that such a "salad" is sometimes called a *macédoine* (after Macedonia) in French. And though it can be litigious at times, this Belgian *macédoine* works peacefully.

Epilogue

Having to learn so many foreign languages, independent of their fields of specialization, is a real encumbrance for many Belgians, and for Europeans more generally. But as Europeans we have to come to terms with the burdensome heritage of the past.

Through the Erasmus program, the European Union provides grants to help students spend one year in another country of the union. Knowledge of English, the new *lingua franca* of Europe, and of one "proximity" language (i.e., the native language of a neighboring country) is going to be part of every EU student's curriculum. This is the only way for Europeans to talk to each other, to understand each other, to learn about _____ ifferences. If I understand why mar_____ not learn foreign lar_____ why some U.S. Am_____ of student exchange _____ ot urge their students _____ n- roll in non-English _____ es. May the followin_____ ce them: Knowing y_____ ill help you secure his loyalty. This arg_____ am afraid, will have more weight than the cultural argument in a world where the number-one value is money. But why not imagine how the two can be compatible!

References

Fitzmaurice, John. (1996). *The politics of Belgium: A unique federalism.* London: Hurst & Co. Publishers.

Hill, Richard. (1997). *We Europeans.* Brussels: Europublications.

Romaine, Suzanne. (1994). *Language in society.* Oxford: Oxford University Press.

Key Terms

Brussels region
code-switching
Communauté Française
De Vlaamse Gemeenschap
dialects
Dutch-speaking community
Flanders
Flemings
French-speaking community
German-speaking community
linguistic frontier
Wallonia
Walloons

Discussion Questions

1. In this essay, Jean-Louis Sauvage discusses the status of dialects and languages in Belgium. For example, he notes that he does not speak Walloon to his son and considered it rude to speak it to his mother. He also notes some remorse in not teaching his son Walloon. Why do you think he might feel remorse? How are dialects different from languages?

2. Sauvage gives you a lot of information about the relationship between the various languages in Belgium, along with their relative populations. While French was once the official language of the Belgium, there are now three official languages—each with their own region. What is the relationship between languages and the people who speak those languages?

3. While many Belgians can speak Dutch and French, why might they choose to speak one and not the other?

4. Brussels is a bilingual region in which Dutch and French are officially used. Do you think that language tensions in this region are heightened or lessened by having people negotiate which language they will use?

5. Belgians are forced to learn other languages. Sauvage argues that this is an asset for their nation, as multilingualism is an economic advantage. Do you think that U.S. Americans see the value of multilingualism for economic reasons? Why or why not?

Activities for Skill Development

1. Labels

Make a list of labels that are sometimes used to refer to you (e.g., guy, chick, WASP, Jew, teenager). Identify the ones you find offensive and the ones you find positive or neutral. Then discuss your responses (and the reasons behind them) with a small group of other students. Share your conclusions with the whole class.

2. Englishes

Generate a list of "Englishes" (e.g., British English, Asian Indian English, Pidgin English, American English, Black English, U.S. regional variations, and those shared by speech communities such as fraternities, prisoners, accountants, or musicians). Then identify (a) how much prestige or status you think each form of English has among Americans; (b) how many "Englishes" you can speak; and (c) in what contexts you might use each one. Compare your impressions with those of your classmates.

3. Speech Rituals

Between class meetings, observe the speech events that go on around you. These might include greetings, friendly conversations, course lectures, sales pitches, and comedy show monologues. Make a list of the rituals you observe, and choose one for close analysis. See how many rules you can identify for the speech event you choose. For example, a job interview might include the following "script": The interviewer first greets the interviewee, who then stands up to shake hands with the interviewer. Both parties state their names and say, "Hello, it's nice to meet you." The interviewer then invites the interviewee into a private office and offers him or her a seat. The interviewee says, "Thank you," and waits for the interviewer to ask a question. . . .

Web Sites

1. Linguist George Lakoff argues that our thoughts and perceptions are shaped by metaphors, and that it is impossible to communicate abstract ideas with-out them. Lakoff and his colleagues have analyzed a wide variety of metaphors used in American English, many of which reveal very interesting elements of U.S. American culture. Check out his Web site at *<http://cogsci.berkeley.edu>*.

2. Can computers do effective translation between languages? Many linguists argue that since meaning is specific to speech communities, many concepts cannot be translated directly from one language to another. What do you think? Try it out at *<http://www.freetranslation.com/>*.

3. Is Ebonics a language? Do a Web search for "Ebonics" and review some of the pages that come up. Compare and contrast their views on related linguistic and political issues.

4. What do you think about English-only laws? Bilingual education in schools? Check out current legislative efforts on these and related issues at *<http://ourworld. compuserve.com/homepages/ JWCRAWFORD/>*.

Additional Readings

1. Philipsen, G. (1990). Speaking "like a man" in Teamsterville: Cultural patterns of role enactment in an urban neighborhood. In D. Carbaugh, *Cultural communication and intercultural contact* (pp. 11–26). Hillsdale, NJ: Lawrence Erlbaum Associates.

2. Gangotena, M. (2000). The rhetoric of *La Familia* among Mexican Americans. In *Our voices: Essays in culture, ethnicity, and communication* (pp. 72–83). Los Angeles: Roxbury.

3. Katriel, T. (1990). "Griping" as a verbal ritual in some Israeli discourse. In D. Carbaugh, *Cultural communication and intercultural contact* (pp. 99–118). Hillsdale, NJ: Lawrence Erlbaum Associates.

PART FIVE

Cultural Spaces and Nonverbal Communication

Part Five focuses on nonverbal aspects of intercultural communication. National cultures are often diverse and heterogeneous, and within cultures there are many different norms and rules about how to communicate, norms and rules that are largely influenced by nonverbal cultural contexts or spaces. Cultural groups develop and share communication practices that can sustain cultural identity and strengthen group unity. However, at the same time, these same communication norms and rules can prevent inter-group interaction.

These essays show how cultural practices may strengthen a community but also have competing and contradictory meanings in these cultural locations. In a classic essay, "Key Concepts: Underlying Structures of Culture," Edward T. Hall and Mildred Reed Hall describe cultural spaces and practices of various national groups. They identify broad cultural (national) differences in patterns of nonverbal communication, focusing specifically on high-low context information, use of personal space, and monochronic-polychronic approaches to time. They suggest that the particular pattern of nonverbal behavior (e.g., monochronic or polychronic) dominant in any society influences other aspects of communication behavior.

Leda M. Cooks's essay takes a very different approach to nonverbal behavior. In "Foxwoods Casino and the (Re)presentation of Native American Identity," she analyzes photographs and other cultural artifacts in a Native American gambling casino in Connecticut. Cooks takes issue with E. T. Hall's broad generalizations about cultural space and practices. She emphasizes the importance of historical background in leading to contradictory images of Native Americans. In the casino, images of the "warrior savage" (e.g., cocktail servers wearing loincloths and feathers) are prominently displayed along with a museumlike collection of tribal artifacts. Her analysis shows the contradictory interpretations that can be given to nonverbal practices.

Min-Sun Kim's "A Comparative Analysis of Nonverbal Expressions as Portrayed by Korean and American Print-Media Advertising" is similar to the Halls's approach to nonverbal practices. Kim predicts (and finds) differences between nonverbal behaviors portrayed in magazine advertising in the United States and Korea—in facial expression, hand and arm gestures, body exposure, touch, and male-female communication. She concludes that although there is a great deal of similarity in advertising due to global media influence, national differences in norms for nonverbal behavior still exist.

The last essay in this part, "Places for Speaking in Teamsterville," describes the cultural practices of a very specific community—a working-class White neighborhood near Chicago. In this classic study, Gerry Philipsen analyzes the rules for speaking in various locations in the community—the neighborhood, the street, the corner, and the front porch. He finds that each location is the speaking domain for specific groups (e.g., young men in the street, women on the porch, etc.). Philipsen's conclusions are based on months of participant observation and involvement in the community.

18 Key Concepts
Underlying Structures of Culture

EDWARD T. HALL and MILDRED REED HALL

Culture Is Communication

In physics today, so far as we know, the galaxies that one studies are all controlled by the same laws. This is not entirely true of the worlds created by humans. Each cultural world operates according to its own internal dynamic, its own principles, and its own laws—written and unwritten. Even time and space are unique to each culture. There are, however, some common threads that run through all cultures.

It is possible to say that the world of communication can be divided into three parts: *words, material things,* and *behavior.* Words are the medium of business, politics, and diplomacy. Material things are usually indicators of status and power. Behavior provides feedback on how other people feel and includes techniques for avoiding confrontation.

By studying these three parts of the communication process in our own and other cultures, we can come to recognize and understand a vast unexplored region of human behavior that exists outside the range of people's conscious awareness, a "silent language" that is usually conveyed unconsciously (see Edward T. Hall's *The Silent Language*). This silent language includes a broad range of evolutionary concepts, practices, and solutions to problems which have their roots not in the lofty ideas of philosophers but in the shared experiences of ordinary people. In the words of the director of a project on cross-cultural relations, understanding the silent language "provides insights into *the underlying principles that shape our lives.*" These underlying principles are not only inherently interesting but eminently practical. The readers of this book, whether they be German, French, American, or from other countries, should find these principles useful at home and abroad.

Culture can be likened to a giant, extraordinarily complex, subtle computer. Its programs guide the actions and responses of human beings in every walk of life. This process requires attention to everything people do to survive, advance in the world, and gain satisfaction from life. Furthermore, cultural programs will not work if crucial steps are omitted, which happens when people unconsciously apply their own rules to another system.

During the three years we worked on this book, we had to learn two different programs for our office computer. The first was quite simple, but mastery did require paying close attention to every detail and several weeks of practice. The second was a much more complex program that required weeks of intensive practice, hours of tutoring, and days of depression and frustration when "the darn thing didn't work." Learning a new cultural program is infinitely more complicated and requires years of practice, yet there are many similarities in the learning process.

Cultural communications are deeper and more complex than spoken or written messages. *The essence of effective cross-cultural communication has more to do with releasing the right responses than with sending the "right" messages.* We offer here some conceptual tools to help our readers decipher the complex, unspoken rules of each culture.

Fast and Slow Messages: Finding the Appropriate Speed

The speed with which a particular message can be decoded and acted on is an important characteristic of human communication. There are fast and slow messages. A headline or cartoon, for example, is fast; the meaning that one extracts from books or art is slow. A fast message sent to people who are geared to a slow format will usually miss the target. While the content of the wrong-speed message may be understandable, it won't be received by someone accustomed to or expecting a different speed. The

165

problem is that few people are aware that information can be sent at different speeds.

Examples of Fast and Slow Messages

FAST MESSAGES	SLOW MESSAGES
Prose	Poetry
Headlines	Books
A communique	An ambassador
Propaganda	Art
Cartoons	Etchings
TV commercials	TV documentary
Television	Print
Easy familiarity	Deep relationships
Manners	Culture

Almost everything in life can be placed somewhere along the fast/slow message-speed spectrum. Such things as diplomacy, research, writing books, and creating art are accomplished in the slow mode. Buddha, Confucius, Shakespeare, Goethe, and Rembrandt all produced messages that human beings are still deciphering hundreds of years after the fact. Language is a very slow message; after 4,000 years, human beings are just beginning to discover what language is all about. The same can be said of culture, which incorporates multiple styles of "languages" that only release messages to those who are willing to spend the time to understand them.

In essence a person is a slow message; it takes time to get to know someone well. The message is, of course, slower in some cultures than in others. In the United States it is not too difficult to get to know people quickly in a relatively superficial way, which is all that most Americans want. Foreigners have often commented on how "unbelievably friendly" the Americans are. However, when Edward T. Hall studied the subject for the U.S. State Department, he discovered a worldwide complaint about Americans: they seem capable of forming only one kind of friendship—the informal, superficial kind that does not involve an exchange of deep confidences.

Conversely, in Europe personal relationships and friendships are highly valued and tend to take a long time to solidify. This is largely a function of the long-lasting, well-established networks of friends and relationships—particularly among the French —that one finds in Europe. Although there are exceptions, as a rule it will take Americans longer than they expect to really get to know Europeans. It is difficult, and at times may even be impossible, for a foreigner to break into these networks. Nevertheless, many businesspeople have found it expedient to take the time and make the effort to develop genuine friends among their business associates.

High and Low Context: How Much Information Is Enough?

Context is the information that surrounds an event; it is inextricably bound up with the meaning of that event. The elements that combine to produce a given meaning—events and context—are in different proportions depending on the culture. The cultures of the world can be compared on a scale from high to low context.

A high context (HC) communication or message is one in which *most* of the information is already in the person, while very little is in the coded, explicit, transmitted part of the message. A low context (LC) communication is just the opposite; i.e., the mass of the information is vested in the explicit code. Twins who have grown up together can and do communicate more economically (HC) than two lawyers in a courtroom during a trial (LC), a mathematician programming a computer, two politicians drafting legislation, two administrators writing a regulation. (Edward T. Hall, 1976)

Japanese, Arabs, and Mediterranean peoples, who have extensive information networks among family, friends, colleagues, and clients and who are involved in close personal relationships, are high-context. As a result, for most normal transactions in daily life they do not require, nor do they expect, much in-depth, background information. This is because they keep themselves informed about everything having to do with the people who are important in their lives. Low-context people include Americans, Germans, Swiss, Scandinavians, and other northern Europeans; they compartmentalize their personal relationships, their work, and many aspects of day-to-day life. Consequently, each time they interact with others they need detailed background information. The French are much higher on the context scale than either the Germans or the Americans. This difference can affect virtually every situation and every relationship in which the members of these two opposite traditions find themselves.

Within each culture, of course, there are specific individual differences in the need for contexting—the process of filling in background data. But it is helpful to know whether the culture of a particular country falls on the high or low side of the scale since every person is influenced by the level of context.

Contexting performs multiple functions. For example, any shift in the level of context is a communication. The shift can be up the scale, indicating a warming of the relationship, or down the scale (lowering the context), communicating coolness or displeasure—signaling something has gone wrong with a relationship. In the United States the boss might communicate annoyance to an assistant when he shifts from the high-context, familiar form of address to the low-context, formal form of address. When this happens the boss is telling the subordinate in no uncertain terms that she or he has stepped out of line and incurred disfavor. In Japan moving the direction of the context is a source of daily feedback as to how things are going. The day starts with the use of honorifics, formal forms of address attached to each name. If things are going well the honorifics are dropped as the day progresses. First-naming in the United States is an artificial attempt at high-contexting; it tends to offend Europeans, who view the use of first names as acceptable only between close friends and family. With Europeans, one is always safe using a formal form of address, waiting for the other person to indicate when familiarity is acceptable.

Like their near relations the Germans, many Anglo-Americans (mostly those of northern European heritage) are not only low-context but they also lack extensive, well-developed information networks. American networks are limited in scope and development compared to those of the French, the Spanish, the Italians, and the Japanese. What follows from this is that Americans, unless they are very unsophisticated, will feel the need for contexting, for detailed background information, any time they are asked to make a decision or to do something. The American approach to life is quite segmented and focused on discrete, compartmentalized information; Americans need to know what is going to be in what compartment before they commit themselves. We experienced this in Japan when we were asked on short notice to provide names of well-placed Japanese and Americans to be participants in a small conference. Like most prudent Americans, we were reluctant to provide names until we knew what the conference was about and what the individuals recommended would be expected to do. This seemed logical and reasonable enough to us. Nevertheless, our reluctance was read as obstructionist by our Japanese colleagues and friends responsible for the conference. In Japan the mere presence of certain individuals endows the group and its activities with authority and status, which is far more important than the topic of the conference. It is characteristic of high-context, high-information societies that attendance at functions is as much a matter of the prestige associated with the function as anything else. This in turn means that, quite frequently, invitations to high-level meetings and conferences will be issued on short notice. It is taken for granted that those invited will eschew all previous commitments if the meeting is important enough. As a general rule Americans place greater importance on how long ago a commitment was made, on the agenda, and on the relevance of the expertise of different individuals to the agenda. (For an in-depth discussion of the Japanese, we refer the reader to the authors' *Hidden Differences: Doing Business with the Japanese,* in the reading list.)

Another example of the contrast between how high- and low-context systems work is this: consider a top American executive working in an office and receiving a normal quota of visitors, usually one at a time. Most of the information that is relevant to the job originates from the few people the executive sees in the course of the day, as well as from what she or he reads. This is why the advisors and support personnel who surround the presidents of American enterprises (as well as the president of the United States) are so important. They and they alone control the content and the flow of organizational information to the chief executive.

Contrast this with the office of virtually any business executive in a high-context country such as France or Japan, where information flows freely and from all sides. Not only are people constantly coming and going, both seeking and giving information, but the entire form and function of the organization is centered on gathering, processing, and disseminating information. Everyone stays informed about every aspect of the business and knows who is best informed on what subjects.

In Germany almost everything is low-context and compartmentalized. The executive office is both a refuge and a screen—a refuge for the boss from the distractions of day-to-day office interactions and a screen for the employees from continual supervision. Information communicated in the office is not shared except with a select few—the exact antithesis of the high-information cultures.

High-context people are apt to become impatient and irritated when low-context people insist on giving them information they don't need. Conversely, low-context people are at a loss when high-context people do not provide *enough* information. One of the great communications challenges in life is to find the appropriate level of contexting needed in each situation. Too much information leads people to feel they are being talked down to; too little information can mystify them or make them feel left out. Ordinarily, people make these adjustments automatically in their own country, but in other countries their messages frequently miss the target.

The other side of the coin when considering context level is the apparent paradox that high-context people, such as the French, want to see *everything* when evaluating a *new* enterprise to which they have not been contexted. Annual reports or tax returns are not enough. Furthermore, they will keep asking until they get the information they want. Being high context, the French are driven to make their own synthesis of the meanings of the figures. Unlike Americans, they feel uncomfortable with someone else's synthesis, someone else's "bottom line."

Space

Every living thing has a visible physical boundary—its skin—separating it from its external environment. This visible boundary is surrounded by a series of invisible boundaries that are more difficult to define but are just as real. These other boundaries begin with the individual's personal space and terminate with her or his "territory."

Territoriality

Territoriality, an innate characteristic whose roots lie hundreds of millions of years in the past, is the act of laying claim to and defending a territory and is a vital link in the chain of events necessary for survival. In humans territoriality is highly developed and strongly influenced by culture. It is particularly well developed in the Germans and the Americans. Americans tend to establish places that they label "mine"—a cook's feeling about a kitchen or a child's view of her or his bedroom. In Germany this same feeling of territoriality is commonly extended to all possessions, including the automobile. If a German's car is touched, it is as though the individual himself has been touched.

Space also communicates power. A corner office suite in the United States is conventionally occupied by "the brass," and a private office in any location has more status than a desk in the open without walls. In both German and American business, the top floors are reserved for high-ranking officials and executives. In contrast, important French officials occupy a position in the *middle*, surrounded by subordinates; the emphasis there is on occupying the central position in an information network, where one can stay informed and can control what is happening.

PERSONAL SPACE

Personal space is another form of territory. Each person has around him an invisible bubble of space which expands and contracts depending on a number of things: the relationship to the people nearby, the person's emotional state, cultural background, and the activity being performed. Few people are allowed to penetrate this bit of mobile territory and then only for short periods of time. Changes in the bubble brought about by cramped quarters or crowding cause people to feel uncomfortable or aggressive. In northern Europe, the bubbles are quite large and people keep their distance. In southern France, Italy, Greece, and Spain, the bubbles get smaller and smaller so that the distance that is perceived as intimate in the north overlaps normal conversational distance in the south, all of which means that Mediterranean Europeans "get too close" to the Germans, the Scandinavians, the English, and those Americans of northern European ancestry. In northern Europe one does not touch others. Even the brushing of the overcoat sleeve used to elicit an apology.

THE MULTISENSORY SPATIAL EXPERIENCE

Few people realize that space is perceived by *all* the senses, not by vision alone. Auditory space is perceived by the ears, thermal space by the skin, kinesthetic space by the muscles, and olfactory space by the nose. As one might imagine, there are great cultural differences in the programming of the senses. Americans to some extent and Germans to a greater extent rely heavily on auditory screening, particularly when they want to concentrate. High-context people reject auditory screening and thrive on being open to interruptions and in tune with what goes on around them. Hence, in French and Italian cities one is periodically and intrusively bombarded by noise.

UNCONSCIOUS REACTIONS TO SPATIAL DIFFERENCES

Spatial changes give tone to communication, accent it, and at times even override the spoken word. As people interact, the flow and shift of distance between them is integral to the communication process. For example, if a stranger does not maintain "normal" conversational distance and gets too close, our reaction is automatic—we feel uncomfortable, sometimes even offended or threatened and we back up.

Human beings in the course of a lifetime incorporate literally hundreds of spatial cues. They imbibe the significance of these cues like mother's milk, in the context of their own culture. Just as a fragrance will trigger a memory, these cues and their associated behaviors release unconscious responses, regulating the tone, tempo, and mood of human transactions.

Since most people don't think about personal distance as something that is culturally patterned, foreign spatial cues are almost inevitably misinterpreted. This can lead to bad feelings which are then projected onto the people from the other culture in a most personal way. When a foreigner appears aggressive and pushy, or remote and cold, it may mean only that her or his personal distance is different from yours.

Americans have strong feelings about proximity and the attendant rights, responsibilities, and obligations associated with being a neighbor. Neighbors should be friendly and agreeable, cut their lawns, keep their places up, and do their bit for the neighborhood. By contrast, in France and Germany, simply sharing adjacent houses does not necessarily mean that people will interact with each other, particularly if they have not met socially. Proximity requires different behavior in other cultures.

Time

Life on earth evolved in response to the cycles of day and night and the ebb and flow of the tides. As humans evolved, a multiplicity of internal biological clocks also developed. These biological clocks now regulate most of the physiological functions of our bodies. It is not surprising, therefore, that human concepts of time grew out of the natural rhythms associated with daily, monthly, and annual cycles. From the beginning humans have been tied to growing seasons and were dependent on the forces and rhythms of nature.

Out of this background two time systems evolved—one as an expression of our biological clocks, the other of the solar, lunar, and annual cycles. These systems will be described under the headings "Time as Structure" and "Time as Communication." In the sections that follow we restrict ourselves to those manifestations of time that have proved to be stumbling blocks at the cultural interface.

MONOCHRONIC AND POLYCHRONIC TIME

There are many kinds of time systems in the world, but two are most important to international business. We call them monochronic and polychronic time. Monochronic time means paying attention to and doing only one thing at a time. Polychronic time means being involved with many things at once. Like oil and water, the two systems do not mix.

In monochronic cultures, time is experienced and used in a linear way—comparable to a road extending from the past into the future. Monochronic time is divided quite naturally into segments; it is scheduled and compartmentalized, making it possible for a person to concentrate on one thing at a time. In a monochronic system, the schedule may take priority above all else and be treated as sacred and unalterable.

Monochronic time is perceived as being almost *tangible:* people talk about it as though it were money, as something that can be "spent," "saved," "wasted," and "lost." It is also used as a classification system for ordering life and setting priorities: "I don't have time to see him." Because monochronic time concentrates on one thing at a time, people who are governed by it don't like to be interrupted. Monochronic time seals people off from one another and, as a result, intensifies some relationships while shortchanging others. Time becomes a room which some people are allowed to enter, while others are excluded.

Monochronic time dominates most business in the United States. While Americans perceive it as almost in the air they breathe, it is nevertheless a learned product of northern European culture and is therefore arbitrary and imposed. Monochronic time is an artifact of the industrial revolution in England; factory life required the labor force to be on hand and in place at an appointed hour. In spite of the fact that it is *learned,* monochronic time now appears to be natural and logical because the great majority of Americans grew up in monochronic time

systems with whistles and bells counting off the hours.

Other Western cultures—Switzerland, Germany, and Scandinavia in particular—are dominated by the iron hand of monochronic time as well. German and Swiss cultures represent classic examples of monochronic time. Still, monochronic time is not natural time; in fact, it seems to violate many of humanity's innate rhythms.

In almost every respect, polychronic systems are the antithesis of monochronic systems. Polychronic time is characterized by the simultaneous occurrence of many things and by a *great involvement with people.* There is more emphasis on completing human transactions than on holding to schedules. For example, two polychronic Latins conversing on a street corner would likely opt to be late for their next appointment rather than abruptly terminate the conversation before its natural conclusion. Polychronic time is experienced as much less tangible than monochronic time and can better be compared to a single point than to a road.

Proper understanding of the difference between the monochronic and polychronic time systems will be helpful in dealing with the time-flexible Mediterranean peoples. While the generalizations listed below do not apply equally to all cultures, they will help convey a pattern:

MONOCHRONIC PEOPLE	POLYCHRONIC PEOPLE
do one thing at a time	do many things at once
concentrate on the job	are highly distractible and subject to interruptions
take time commitments (deadlines, schedules) seriously	consider time commitments an objective to be achieved, if possible
are low-context and need information	are high-context and already have information
are committed to the job	are committed to people and human relationships
adhere religiously to plans	change plans often and easily
are concerned about not disturbing others; follow rules of privacy and consideration	are more concerned with those who are closely related (family, friends, close business associates) than with privacy

MONOCHRONIC PEOPLE	POLYCHRONIC PEOPLE
show great respect for private property; seldom borrow or lend	borrow and lend things often and easily
emphasize promptness	base promptness on the relationship
are accustomed to short-term relationships	have strong tendency to build lifetime relationships

THE RELATION BETWEEN TIME AND SPACE

In monochronic time cultures the emphasis is on the compartmentalization of functions and people. Private offices are soundproof if possible. In polychronic Mediterranean cultures, business offices often have large reception areas where people can wait. Company or government officials may even transact their business by moving about in the reception area, stopping to confer with this group and that one until everyone has been attended to.

Polychronic people feel that private space disrupts the flow of information by shutting people off from one another. In polychronic systems, appointments mean very little and may be shifted around even at the last minute to accommodate someone more important in an individual's hierarchy of family, friends, or associates. Some polychronic people (such as Latin Americans and Arabs) give precedence to their large circle of family members over any business obligation. Polychronic people also have many close friends and good clients with whom they spend a great deal of time. The close links to clients or customers create a reciprocal feeling of obligation and a mutual desire to be helpful.

POLYCHRONIC TIME AND INFORMATION

Polychronic people live in a sea of information. They feel they must be up to the minute about everything and everybody, be it business or personal, and they seldom subordinate personal relationships to the exigencies of schedules or budgets.

It is impossible to know how many millions of dollars have been lost in international business because monochronic and polychronic people do not understand each other or even realize that two such different time systems exist. The following example illustrates how difficult it is for these two types to relate:

> A French salesman working for a French company that had recently been bought by Americans found himself with a new American manager who expected instant results and higher profits immediately. Because of the emphasis on personal relationships, it frequently takes years to develop customers in polychronic France, and, in family-owned firms, relationships with customers may span generations. The American manager, not understanding this, ordered the salesman to develop new customers within three months. The salesman knew this was impossible and had to resign, asserting his legal right to take with him all the loyal customers he had developed over the years. Neither side understood what had happened.

These two opposing views of time and personal relationships often show up during business meetings. In French meetings the information flow is high, and one is expected to read other people's thoughts, intuit the state of their business, and even garner indirectly what government regulations are in the offing. For the French and other polychronic/high-context people, a tight, fixed agenda can be an encumbrance, even an insult to one's intelligence. Most, if not all, of those present have a pretty good idea of what will be discussed beforehand. The purpose of the meeting is to create consensus. A rigid agenda and consensus represent opposite goals and do not mix. *The importance of this basic dichotomy cannot be overemphasized.*

Selected References

Hall, E. T. (1959). *The silent language.* Garden City, NY: Doubleday.

Hall, E. T. (1976). *Beyond culture.* Garden City, NY: Doubleday Anchor Books.

Hall, E. T. (1987). *Hidden differences: Doing business with the Japanese.* Garden City, NJ: Anchor Press/ Doubleday.

Key Terms

high context   polychronic
low context   space
monochronic   time

Discussion Questions

1. What kind of misunderstandings could occur between high- and low-context people?

2. What are some suggestions you might give to people who work together who have different orientations to time?

3. What are some common English sayings that reflect a monochronic time orientation (e.g., time is money, a stitch in time saves nine)?

4. What advice would you give French international students about time management at a U.S. university?

5. Would you characterize your communication with people whom you've known for a long time as more low-context or more high-context?

---

19 Foxwoods Casino and the (Re-)presentation of Native Identity

LEDA M. COOKS

Framed against a clear sky, the lone tree on a prominent knoll represents Mashantucket, the "much-wooded land" where the Pequots hunted and kept alive their identity as an independent people. . . . The fox stands as a reminder that the Pequots are known as "the fox people."

—Promotional pamphlet for Foxwoods Casino

The promotional pamphlets and commercials advertising the Foxwoods Casino in Ledyard, Connecticut, use the slogan "Gaming In Its Natural State." "Gaming" in this instance means gambling: slot machines, roulette tables, bingo, Baccarat, Keno, racing, Blackjack, craps, and Pai Gow poker. In other contexts, gaming is often the verb used to describe the activity of hunting, the activity that once provided the Pequots with sustenance and survival on this very land. Thus, gaming here takes on several meanings that are of great importance in understanding both the history of the Pequots and the complex cultural spaces that make up Foxwoods Casino.

The irony of their present wealth, acquired through casino gaming as opposed to the gaming that provided their livelihood for thousands of years,

is not lost on the Pequots. However, the fact that Foxwoods is the wealthiest and the largest casino in the world has little to do with the luck and chance often associated with gambling. The Pequots are, first and foremost, survivors. They lost almost all of their land and their people and have fought for centuries to get it back.

Understanding the meaning and importance of land in Pequot history is essential to comprehension of the complex cultural symbols that went into the design and structure of the casino. In one enormous space—including two hotels, a shopping mall, both a smoking and a nonsmoking casino, several restaurants, a bingo parlor that seats 3,200, a cinetropolis (city of specialty theaters)—are representations of indigenous culture, imperialistic images of the warrior savage, and re-creations of colonial New England. These images (and others discussed throughout this essay) point to the complexities of a postmodern Native identity: romanticized and racialized, neither oppressive nor empowering, but negotiated in certain moments and in ways that have served to make the Pequots wealthy. And, along with this wealth, to make them arguably the most (in)visible tribe in the world.

This chapter examines the cultural spaces where the multiple notions of gaming come together to signify the complexity of Native identities.[1] In the process, it seeks to raise the issues complicating traditional notions of a unidimensional and static cultural space. Traditional representations of marginalized or indigenous cultural space fail to recognize the complexities of dynamics that racialize, ethnicize, or romanticize identities for consumption of the dominant culture. Space itself is thus a social construction that reflects the dynamics of power in cultural stories.

This essay also examines the junctures at which diverse stories about cultural space come together. In doing so, it suggests movement from a functionalist perspective of space toward a more complex understanding of the spaces in which cultural meanings are created. Borrowing from social constructionist and critical perspectives, the chapter looks at the negotiation of dominant and marginalized identities at work in particular works of art, architecture, statues, and the tribal mascot. It does this by interweaving dominant cultural stories about the history of the Pequots and notions about their indigenous identity with representations of such at work in the particular artifacts and spaces of the casino.

To begin to understand the interplay among spaces, symbols, and stories about cultural identity, we should first assess the overall layout of the casino and the placement of walls, windows, lighting, shops, casinos, restaurants, bingo parlors, and so forth within it. The casino is located several miles into the reservation and sits isolated from residential or commercial areas. Only one two-lane road leads to and from the casino, and this approach provides visitors with a view of a giant self-contained city— almost spaceshiplike in structure. As you enter Foxwoods, you enter into a world that easily overwhelms the senses: bright neon lights, clanging bells, masses of people everywhere. The gaming rooms are primarily lit by the neon of the slot machines; the low ceilings provide little overhead lighting and there are no windows. This lack of overhead lighting in the immense gaming rooms makes them seem to go on forever. All of these structural arrangements

(along with the absence of clocks) combine to produce an effect of timelessness well known among casino designers. Many people interviewed at Foxwoods for this study reported feeling as though they had lost track of the passage of time while in the casino area.[2] Although Foxwoods promoters often remark that it is one of the only casinos that has windows, the windows are located in the mall area of the casino, not in the gambling areas. The effect of such spatial design is both to create the effect of escaping time and to keep the senses so overwhelmed with the high-pitched and high-paced world of fantasy (and addiction) that real-world concerns become irrelevant.

The mall area of Foxwoods, while totally enclosed, is designed to create the effect of being outside (the man-made "natural state" of gaming). The ceilings are very high, and atriums throughout the mall display artificial and real plants hanging from wrought iron archways and planters along the walls. The iron arches and other fixtures are painted aquamarine and mauve—colors that signify the Pequot tribe. Large disks with designs of vines and flowers painted on them hang from the iron bars. On the other side of the mall are false storefronts that give the impression that one is walking through a small town in colonial New England. One of the false fronts looks like an old fire station, another a lithograph shop, and yet another—in an interesting re-creation of local colonial history—the "Mashantucket Town Hall." Behind the other false fronts of colonial houses are expensive specialty stores that sell dominant cultural representations of Native Americans (fringe-and-moccasin-wearing plastic dolls for $400) or artifacts that have been appropriated and commercialized as indicative of all tribes, regardless of their origin. Leather jackets with fringe, jackets with colorful Navajo designs, moccasins, wind catchers, blankets, and wood flutes are sold along with imported clothing from Third World countries in South America, Africa, and Asia.

Above these specialty boutiques are Disney-like displays of colonial U.S. history. These animated and mechanized figures act out scenes from 17th-century coastal New England: In one a wife chastises her husband for staying out all night; in another a captain asks passersby to sign up on his whaling ship; in another a young woman talks with her father. The irony of these scenes is, of course, that they represent certain symbols that are active in dominant cultural stories of New England history. All the figures are White, all are dressed in colonial garb, and none tell us anything about the oppression suffered by the tribe on whose land we stand. These animated "historical displays" are at odds with the other cultural "decor" of Foxwoods—the Hollywood and commercialized representations of Native Americans, the Vegas-style casinos and gaming rooms, and the high-tech cinetropolis/virtual reality area.

At the center of the mall area is a warrior statue that serves as its focal point. The warrior is made of glass that glows and changes colors. Aiming a bow toward the sky (or in this case the roof of the atrium), he stands amid fountains of water. He speaks every hour on the hour as thunder claps, lasers shoot from his bow, and water shoots out of the fountains. Statues of Native American warriors, women, and children are scattered throughout the casino—but none are in positions of prominence and certainly none are as large or as grandiose as the glass statue. These statues are of Indians far removed from the Pequot tribe. None have the facial structure, hair, or skin that are indicative of the Mashantuckets, and many of the costumes are representative of Plains warriors.

Near the statues, walking in and out of the restaurants, lounge, and gaming areas are other pseudo-Pequots. These "Indians" are cocktail servers (White women) in Native costume. They are wearing low-cut tops and mini-loincloths and have headbands and feathers in their hair. Although they are not statues, these women are perhaps equally objectified. They are moving mannequins, adornments to the farce of representation. These symbols play to the stories, colonial and colonized, of warriors frozen in time—warriors with feathers in their hair, who wear loincloths and live in tepees—of women who remain colonized by historical stories in which they are not actors but objects of men's actions.

Although the casino could arguably be said to represent more about gambling culture than Pequot culture, it stands on Pequot land and is filled with representations (Hollywood, Disney, and otherwise)

of Native American peoples and artifacts. What, then, about these spaces can lend further insight into the numerous and seemingly contradictory meanings that inhabit this cultural space?

As mentioned previously, traditional theories about cultural space are useful as a frame for understanding the varying functions of space; however, they are limited in that they cannot account for the dynamics of social interaction, which constantly (re)create the variety of cultural meanings active here. In other words, space and culture are created through language, through the stories people tell about what they mean and thus who they are. There are numerous possibilities for cultural stories, depending on who is telling the stories, where the stories are being told, who the audience is for these stories, and the time in which the storytelling takes place (at what historical juncture). What becomes important then are the ways cultural spaces are (re)created through language and the narrative construction of history. The following section looks at the space of the casino from the standpoint of the social construction of stories around gaming.

Space and Gaming as a Social Construction

This section tells three stories of gaming that both reflect and deflect the cultural spaces of the casino. Language or, more specifically, a word such as gaming refuses a closed interpretation, a single meaning that is complete in and of itself. Thus, the word gaming as used by the Pequots to advertise Foxwoods Casino (Gaming In Its Natural State), draws meaning from the past history of the Pequots as hunters and survivors, even as it points us toward other referents—gaming as gambling or as identity at play (in images and cultural signifiers that represent and negate the Native American identity). Each reading points to the difficulty of directly representing cultural identity through space in a society where spaces no longer signify cultural locations.

GAMING: WAMPUM AND WARRIORS

The stories of the past are always present in cultural spaces. Archeological evidence suggests that Pequot culture dates back thousands of years; however, the earliest European account of the tribe dates back to 1614, when a Dutch explorer reported the presence of the tribe. At that point the Pequots were already heavily involved in the production of wampum, the currency for trading in the fur industry.[3] Because of their ideal location (the Pequots controlled the area from Long Island Sound to the lower Connecticut River) and their reputation as the main producers of wampum in the area, the Pequots were targeted by the English and Dutch colonists. In 1637 the settlers invaded the Pequots, burning their villages, killing their leader, and killing or enslaving most of the population. Throughout the 17th and 18th centuries, the Pequots were granted small parcels of forest and swampland (from 500 to 1,000 acres), which were always repossessed by colonists who wanted the land for farming. In 1667 the Pequots were awarded the dubious distinction of being the first Native reservation in the English Colonies and received 3,000 acres of primarily rock and swampland.[4] They refused to move from their coastal home near present-day Noank until 1712, when the town of Groton legislated their land for the English colonists. At that time the Pequots were forced to move to the Ledyard Reservation—to the land where they are today.

By the late 18th century, their 3,000 acres had dwindled to approximately 300 and the Pequots, having been once again dispossessed of their land, were widely dispersed throughout New England. Some were sold into slavery in the West Indies; others were indentured to their English conquerors; some worked on whaling ships and still others worked on mills and farms.[5] By the 1960s the few acres (approximately 213) of remaining reservation land were maintained by two female tribal elders who used their guns and their settlement deeds to resist territorial encroachment from the state as well as from the local hunters. In 1973 Richard (Skip) Hayward took over as the leader (chair) of the newly created tribal council. Under his leadership, the tribe has received federal recognition and progressed from selling maple syrup to running bingo games, and it now owns the largest casino in the world. The tribe now offers extensive social and health services for its members and invests in local communities through charitable donations. In the late 1980s the tribe established the Mashantucket

Pequot Archeological Project, which has functioned to locate and recover lost graves and artifacts and, in the process, document land since lost to the state government.[6]

Even as they were forced to assimilate into local communities to survive, the Pequots fought to hang on to their cultural values and traditions. Perhaps it is because of their struggle for centuries to retain their tribal lands that the concepts of land and survival continue to be central values in Pequot culture. According to many historians, archeologists, and anthropologists working with the Pequot community on the museum, casino, and projects such as land reclamation, the genocide of 1637 is still very much a part of the present Pequot cultural story. Hauptman (1990) goes so far as to note that "[t]he ways in which the Pequots, who are always conscious of the War of 1637, commemorate this tragedy, interact with both their Indian and non-Indian neighbors and build the modern day community are similar to other experiences after genocide" (p. 71). Hauptman further comments that the geographical location of the Pequot Reservation—only 10 miles from the Mystic Fort site of the 1637 massacre—and the nearby Mohegan and Narragansett tribes who, along with the British, "enslaved and nearly annihilated them in the seventeenth century" (p. 77), serve as a constant physical reminder of a tragic past.

The Connection Between History, Identity, and Cultural Space Cultural spaces are infused with the past, markers of identity that are creative and created through historical events and experiences. Comparing Native and western European notions of history, Deloria (1994) comments that

> American Indians hold their lands—places—as having the highest possible meaning, and all their statements are made with this reference point in mind. Immigrants review the movement of their ancestors across the continent as the steady progression of basically good events and experiences, thereby placing history—time—in the best possible light. When one group is concerned with the philosophical problem of space and the other with the philosophical problem of time, then the statements of either group do not make much sense when transferred from one context to the other

without the proper consideration of what is taking place. (pp. 62–63)

The experience of tragedy and the struggle to reclaim their land and, in doing so, their existence, are part of the contemporary spaces of the Pequots. While many non-native peoples talk about the reservation as land "granted" the Mashantuckets, the Pequots are quick to point out that the tribe received a land "settlement" and not a land "grant." The difference between the two words, while seemingly trivial to an outsider, is of great significance to the Pequots. The phrase "land grant" ignores the fact that the Pequots were the original settlers of coastal Connecticut, forced off their land through invasion and legislation, and assumes that the land was donated as a social service by the U.S. government. Here again, cultural space and representation are intimately connected with language. Who employs the words and phrases that characterize ownership of this space shape the ways in which a culture is legitimized or marginalized. As such, the casino is a location invested with historical and cultural meanings that represent the (in)visibility of the Pequot people.

The Warrior The Pequots call themselves the fox people, and history shows that they were skilled hunters and warriors. They were known by surrounding tribes and traders as a fiercely aggressive and independent people. Today the notion of the warrior is very much a part of Pequot identity, although some confusion exists about what it means to embody that idea. As Kate Abril (1996) described it,

> there are warriors. And warriors aren't just soldiers. They are people trying to do the right thing—which oftentimes gets confused even by the warriors. But then it can be with any missionary too. It gets too focused on principle rather than on relationships . . . on accumulation versus giving away—those are often contradictory ideas that get Indians in trouble. . . .[7]

This notion of Mashantucket history—that the Pequots were warriors and hunters—is perhaps represented to visitors in the giant warrior statue that is the focal point of the mall area of the casino.

Although such representations harken back to the early Hollywood stereotypes of Indians-with-feathers-in-their-hair-who-live-in-tepees, they are an effective way of making visitors aware of whose land they are on as they gamble. But the irony of the warrior statue is that it plays into the racism that continues to plague the modern-day Pequots, for not only are they most definitely not loin-clothed warriors living in tepees, their skin color is not representative of the dominant Indian stereotype.[8] The warrior statue serves to make visible a powerful image of the tribe that conforms to the stereotype of the dominant culture while it perpetuates the Pequots' invisibility.

> It [the excavation of the mass graves] became a powerful experience. The artifacts and everything that was buried with them were so gorgeous. . . . And I can remember Loretta, Skip's aunt, looking at them. And she's a real tough old lady. She had tears in her eyes and she said, "And they call us savages. How could savages make anything that beautiful?" And they were beautiful. Like something out of Egypt.
> —Interview with Kate Abril, past museum coordinator and PR director for Mashantucket Pequots, September 4, 1996

Wampum and Other Artifacts One of the driving forces in the design of the casino was the historical significance of wampum, Pequot basketry, and the tribal artifacts uncovered in burial sites around Connecticut. The aquamarine and mauve colors throughout the casino came from the colorful costumes and artifacts unearthed in the excavations of the Long Pond and other digs in the late 1980s. The shell design that signifies wampum can be seen in various areas of the mall, and representations of Native artifacts are scattered throughout the atrium and waterfall area. Until recently, Foxwoods contained the largest collection of Native artifacts in New England.[9] However, the designs and artifacts that represent Pequot and Native American history are located away from the gaming and other entertainment areas and are not easily accessible to visitors. The artworks display price tags and names of artists but give no information about origin or cultural significance.

The centrality accorded to the more gaudy Indian stereotypes is neither an accident nor the design of some architect unfamiliar with Pequot culture. All of the design work in the casino was discussed in tribal council meetings and had to pass council in order to be approved. The meetings were often 5 or 6 hours long and were in most cases a formality, but according to one source, they produced a sense that the tribe was involved collectively in the building of the casino:

> Everyone was complaining about the long hours and the meetings, and all the kids were getting into trouble because the parents weren't around as much. But on the whole it was exciting. Walking through the casino and seeing the building . . .[10]

The importance of the tribe's involvement in both the excavations and the design of the casino is that they were part of a larger process of re-creating and re-presenting Pequot identity to the dominant culture. As part of the process of legitimizing the tribe to gain federal recognition and status, and as part of the survival (often in very physical terms) of a culture, gaming takes on the meaning of the Pequot as hunter, as warrior, and, most important, as survivor.

GAMING AS GAMBLING: A NEW VERSION OF AN OLD GAME

Gambling has a long history among Native Americans and is associated with spiritual and ritual traditions. Numerous Native American tribes played dice games long before European settlers arrived, but the games had different meanings and functioned quite differently than they do today. Pasquaretta (1994) observes that "unlike Euro-American games of chance which function as secular rituals and foster acquisitiveness, individual competition and greed, traditional Native American games of chance are sacred rituals that foster personal sacrifice, group competition and generosity" (p. 698). Most early games of chance were offerings to the gods and helped to enhance community with singing and good-natured joking. As Mourning Dove comments: "All gambling required good sportsmanship. It was shameful for poor losers to grieve. They would get no sympathy."[11] Although scholars such as Vizenor and Pasquaretta argue that perhaps the contrast between the high-stakes Vegas-

style gambling that promotes materialism and competitiveness and the early games that promoted community signals the last phase of Native American assimilation, the Foxwoods Casino can be seen as a business venture that functions to support institutions and communities that have revitalized Pequot culture.

Still, the gambling story is more complex than simply indigenous forms of gambling (and thus indigenous culture) lost to the competitive and greedy world of contemporary casinos. The conceptualization and design of the casino reflect both the big business of gambling addiction and the big business of exoticizing culture. Designers and architects involved in the building of the casino went to Las Vegas and to Epcot Center for inspiration, and one source who worked closely with the tribe observed that the casino reflected Hayward (the tribe's leader): "One side of his family is Mashantucket Pequot and the other D.A.R. [Daughters of the American Revolution]. This was Skip's vision."

Addiction as Big Business Since its opening day over 4 years ago, the casino has never shut down. It remains open to gambling 24 hours a day, 7 days a week. The state of Connecticut requires that 1-800-gambling posters and pamphlets (for gambling addiction support groups) be displayed prominently in front of each of the slot rooms. Next to the signs are automatic teller machines that take credit cards. "Wampum clubs" located near the entrance to the gaming rooms offer credit. Although seemingly contradictory on the surface, the message is consistent with other messages surrounding success and addiction in a late capitalistic society. Advertising creates and then supports a culture of excess; then social and governmental institutions offer support services for the unfortunate addicted. The message is that money can buy you everything—success, good looks, good health, and, at Foxwoods, even culture.

Certainly, the Pequot tribe has grown wealthy from their venture into the industry. Yet economic wealth and cultural wealth take on vastly different meanings in terms of (re)creating cultural traditions and of assimilating into the dominant society. The dominant culture as well as other tribes in the northeastern United States see Pequot identity as being most closely associated with gambling and wealth. In the media, issues around gambling and around the plight of Native Americans in the United States most certainly invoke the Pequots. The Mashantuckets have been hired as consultants to tribes and corporations building casinos around the world. The tribe was featured on the popular prime-time news show *60 Minutes* and in cover stories in *Money* and *Fortune* magazines. Local and national news stories on Native Americans and casinos highlight the controversy around gambling in general: Gaming is the big business of addiction. All view Indian culture from a dominant perspective that highlights the ethics of gambling and the impact on local communities over stories about tribal survival and the decimation of tribal culture. Another frequent focus of news stories is the use and abuse of blood quantum as a marker of Indianness and a ticket to free land and health care.

These stories contribute to the contemporary narrative of Native American gaming from a dominant cultural perspective. Because "recognizable Indians" (i.e., those who wear loincloths and have feathers in their hair) no longer pose a threat to White settlers—and Native identity is developed scientifically through the measurement of blood—popular culture needs a new signifier for a different kind of savage. The success of tribal casinos has given rise to images of the new Indian who feeds off the addictions of the poor and the socially disadvantaged.

GAMING AS SOCIOACUPUNCTURE[12]: THE SPACE OF IMAGINATION

The final story of gaming is that of the Pequots as players in a carnival of ironic and contradictory images of Native identity. The giant glass warrior with his bow raised to the sky rotates on the stage. Thunder claps and he changes colors; he speaks, although his voice is lost amid the din of clanging slot machines. Cocktail waitresses with feathers in their hair and dressed in sexy pseudo-loincloths serve beverages to clientele who gamble in a fantasyland of money. Venders throughout the casino sell Pequot

Reservation t-shirts and sweatshirts along with key chains and other souvenirs of a visit to the exotic space of Pequot land.

Revisiting the Mall Geographic space as representative of both culture and history becomes irrelevant in the space of imagination. Any customer at Foxwoods with enough money—or credit—can buy the spaces of history and culture. The Pequots as capitalist entrepreneurs contribute to the decimation of local cultures in favor of the global Indian— the universal savage—through the marketing of this representation. A consumer buying Native art buys it because of its decorative function as an exotic artifact. Certainly, reproductions of artifacts are marketed for this function: The Indian doll for $400 is made in China, the leather jackets with fringe on them (certainly a Hollywood creation) now represent all Native American cultures divorced from the historical spaces they inhabit. The mall is the new global cultural space. Indeed, even the mall specialty stores located in the casino on the Pequot Reservation contain artifacts that represent other Native cultures as their own. All cultural spaces can be collapsed for the purposes of buying and selling—and what is exotically primitive to the colonizers are now the artifacts of the colonized.

Reconfiguring Time and Space as Native Culture Much like the clockless, timeless space of the casino, the history of Native peoples has been characterized by space, not time. Tune Browne, speaking at a conference on tribal identities at U.C. Berkeley, noted that the photographer who captured his image in Native "costume,"

> removed the clock, colonized the culture games and denied us our time in the world . . . [the photographer] paid us for our poses; it was hot then, but he wanted us to wear leathers to create the appearance of a traditional scene, his idea of the past. . . . We never saw the photographs then and never thought that it would make a difference in the world of dreams, that we would become *his* images. (cited in Vizenor, 1990, p. 90)

That these images of the past, snapshots created to capture the time of the space of Native history and identity, have become part of national memory merely validates dominant images of Native identity. To legitimize themselves as "real" Indians to the governments and people that captured their land and their culture, Native Americans had to reinvent themselves as the images created and contained in photographic images. The Pequots are by no means exempt from this game of "playing Indian." The images that they construct to represent Indianness are satirical, not shameful. The irony is not lost in translation; it is part of a (re)created tribal identity, an identity that cannot be divorced from a history of domination and the current circumstances that dictate their legitimacy as marginalized peoples.

Browne (cited in Vizenor, 1990) explains that satire is "not social ridicule as a form of social control . . . but satire from magical connections with the oral tradition . . ." (p. 91). Satire is socioacupuncture, a process that puts the "facts" of Native identity and existence into play:

> Socioacupuncture reverses the documents, deflates data, dissolves historical time, releases the pressure in captured images, and exposes the pale inventors of the tribes. . . . Lyman tells us that [the photographer] set out to construct a "photographic monument to a vanishing race." Not so, it was the photographer who would have vanished without our images to take as captured families. (p. 91)

Gaming at Foxwoods is definitive of socioacupuncture; the images validate the White imagination while the Pequots work behind the scenes. The Pequots are the ultimate marketers of a global culture; all cultural spaces meld into one Mall Mecca where they are sold as souvenirs. Here, displaced and marginalized people sell "exotic" artifacts to those who long to be diasporic peoples, to be marginalized because it isn't trendy to be mainstream.

Here, also, perhaps Native peoples work to imagine different possibilities, to conceive of identities not completely captured and defined by White words and White science. As N. Scott Momaday said: "We are what we imagine. . . . Our very existence consists in our imagination of ourselves. . . . The greatest tragedy that can befall us is to go unimagined" (cited in Vizenor, 1990, p. 96).

Conclusion

This essay has sought to examine the space of culture as a social construction. Although the functions and uses of space in Foxwoods Casino were discussed in descriptive terms, to more fully comprehend the complexities of identities as they are bound to the spaces of culture, the notion of space as a social and cultural construction was examined through three narratives about gaming. From these narratives of warriors, wampum, land, survival, gambling, irony, and contradiction we can see that the meaning of space emerges in and through its interpretation. The notable difference in understanding cultural space from this vantage point is that space and culture cannot function apart from the language we use to construct it. Thus, communication is central to the process of cultural interpretation.

What also becomes important in this analysis is the role that power plays in the dynamics of interpretation. The viewpoint espoused in this essay indicates White/dominant culture and cultural spaces even as it points to other ways of knowing and thinking about space as history and identity. Cultural space includes the negotiated places where imperialist and colonized stories are in conflict *with* and determinate *of* the indigenous and creative knowledges that characterize modern Pequot identities. The fox people play games; they set up uneasy coalitions of power. They are the new warriors, with a new kind of dice game and wampum made in Malaysia.

Notes

1. I use the plural form of identity to connote the idea that identities themselves are social constructions and thus cannot be separated from the social context in which they are "identified." It follows then that communication (both verbal and nonverbal) is central to any understanding of culture and cultural space.

2. Fifteen people were interviewed in the mall area of the casino. They were asked whether this was their first time at the casino, where they came from, and what their reactions were to the general atmosphere of the gaming rooms and the mall area. They were also asked what they

knew of the Pequots and whether they had seen the statue and other artifacts around the casino.

3. Wampum are small tubular columella beads that are woven into chains, bracelets, necklaces, and belts. White and purple wampum beads came from grinding down the inner pillars or columellas of rare northern whelks (white) or hard-shell clams (purple). The use of wampum as currency has a long history among the coastal Indian tribes that predates the arrival of European explorers. The Europeans (Dutch, British, Portuguese, and French) discovered the value of the beads through the process of fur trading; the Iroquois were said to value wampum more than any of the other valuables the traders could produce (Ceci, 1990).

4. Silberman, 1991, 35.

5. De Forest, 1964, 423–425.

6. Silberman, 1991, 36.

7. Interview 1. Teacher of Native American Studies at Mohegan Community College.

8. The fact that many Pequots appear "darker" than the stereotypical Native American is a significant dynamic in their history and current identity that is not addressed in academic discussions of culture. As their wealth and visibility through business ventures increases, so too does the racism and imperialist sensibility with which people mark them as neither White nor Indian, neither conqueror nor "legitimately" conquered.

9. The new Mashantucket Pequot Museum is currently under construction.

10. Interview with Kate Abril, September 1, 1996.

11. Mourning Dove, 1990, 102–103.

12. The inspiration for the concept of socioacupuncture, according to Edward Vizenor (1990), is Tune Browne, who "never wore beads or feathers or a wristwatch; he never paid much attention to time or to his image until he became an independent candidate for alderman" (p. 88).

References

Abril, K. (Sept. 4, 1996). Personal interview.

Ceci, L. (1990). Native wampum as a peripheral resource in the seventeenth-century world-system. In L. M. Hauptman & J. D. Wherry (Eds.), *The Pequots in southern New England: The fall and rise of an American Indian nation.* Norman: University of Oklahoma Press.

De Forest, J. W. (1964). *History of the Indians of Connecticut from the earliest known period to 1850.* Hamden, CT: Anchor Books.

Deloria, V. (1994). *God is red: A native view of religion.* Golden, CO: Fulcrum Publishing.

Hauptman, L. M. (1990). The Pequot war and its legacies. In L. M. Hauptman & J. D. Wherry (Eds.), *The Pequots in southern New England: The fall and rise of an American Indian nation* (pp. 69–80). Norman: University of Oklahoma Press.

Mourning Dove. (1990). *Mourning Dove: A Salishan autobiography* (J. Miller, Ed.). Lincoln: University of Nebraska Press.

Pasquaretta, P. (1994). On the Indianness of bingo: Gambling and the Native American community. *Critical Inquiry, 20,* 694–714.

Silberman, N. A. (1991). Pequot country. *Archeology, 44,* 34–39.

Vizenor, E. (1990). *Crossbloods: Bone courts, bingo and other reports.* Minneapolis: University of Minnesota Press.

Key Terms

casino	Native
culture	Pequot
gambling	space
gaming	

Discussion Questions

1. What is the relationship between symbols and stories? Who participates in symbol creation?

2. Who are the storytellers in this essay? Who are the audiences? Does anyone "own" a particular cultural story?

3. The author makes the point that spaces cannot directly represent cultural identities. Do you agree or disagree? Are there some spaces that might signify cultural locales? If so, where?

4. What, in Cooks's view, can language tell us about the naming of cultural identities and spaces?

5. From the quotes from Tune Browne, what role do you think photography has played in establishing a cultural identity and cultural space for Native peoples?

6. What symbols stand out to you in each of the three stories told in this essay? Do you think that these are important symbols to the Pequots? Why or why not?

20 A Comparative Analysis of Nonverbal Expressions as Portrayed by Korean and American Print-Media Advertising

MIN-SUN KIM

Relationship Between Advertising and Culture

A persistent debate continues about whether advertising in non-Western countries reflects primarily the indigenous culture or Western culture. It is the purpose of this study to shed further light on this issue.

Nonverbal Expressions as Cultural Context

Print advertising usually consists of verbal and nonverbal messages. According to Millum (1975, p. 24) nonverbal messages are clear at a glance, facilitate conscious recall, and carry subconscious messages most effectively. Research has strongly suggested that major cultural differences are invested in nonverbal behaviors, because they are basic *core* values that are slow to change. Eisenberg and Smith (1971) argued that, as the symbols of language are structured into tight patterns, a *grammar* of nonverbal body language comes into being. Every culture has its specific set of *display rules* as to how and when its members may express themselves (Ekman, 1973). For instance, *boundary* is an important concept relating to people's mode of behavior. It refers to the way that people in a given culture cognitively divide up their worlds into separate areas. Cultures define boundaries temporally (days, microseconds), geographically (states, cities), and in terms of personal space (Arabs stand close to converse, whereas Americans stand three to four feet apart). Boundaries can be rigid (India's caste system) or flexible (America's egalitarian society) (cf. Durgee, 1986, p. 38). Watson and Graves (1966) found that Arabs confront each other more directly when conversing

than do Americans, sitting closer to each other, and looking each other more squarely in the eye. Likewise, traditional Japanese culture requires two individuals to stand no closer than the distance permitting the customary bow (Kunihiro, 1980).

Nonverbal expressions of advertising models such as gestures, facial expressions, and postures are symbolic representations of cultural values. Goffman (1979) specifically examined ways in which men and women are pictured in advertisements. He found that women smile more often and more expansively than do men; and, similarly, men tend to be located at higher levels than women, symbolically confirming sexual stereotypes. Expression is considered to be socially learned and socially patterned. We take for granted our own modes of expression until we see them compared to those of another culture (i.e., nationality, ethnicity, or gender). Insights into the American mode of advertising expression and the fundamental cultural values by which the mode is influenced can be obtained by comparing American advertising to that of another culture.

Framework of the Study

The disagreement among researchers regarding the relationship between advertising and culture might be traced to the lack of a clear definition of *societal culture*. Most studies (Madden, Cabellero, & Matsukubo, 1986; Norman, 1965; Singh & Huang, 1962; Unwin, 1974) concentrate on differences and consistencies in the form of advertising expression—format, creative style, and information level—across cultures. Rarely is the relationship between advertising and culture studied in depth. For a fundamental understanding of the issue, a

181

clear identification of the major values of a culture is essential, followed by a comparison of those values with the cultural content of advertising.

The importance of visual images in advertisements as a cultural parameter has not been studied comprehensively. It is through the influence of culture that people learn to communicate nonverbally. Cultures differ in their manner of encoding nonverbal messages. The culturally defined nonverbal patterns of communication, therefore, constitute indispensable parameters for analyzing culture. Some studies (e.g., Choe et al., 1986) have dealt with facial expressions in advertising, but few have focused on such pictorial displays as gestures, degree of body exposure, tactile communication, and eye behavior.

This study seeks to determine (a) whether nonverbal expressions of models in Korean and American advertising are related to their cultural orientation, (b) whether nonverbal expressions in advertising are influenced by the gender of the models and the products being advertised, (c) the possible influence of product categories on nonverbal expressions of both Korean and American advertising models, and (d) how far, if at all, Korean advertising values have converged with those of the West.

Communication Patterns of Korean and American Culture

Although generalizations about entire cultures and their communication patterns are difficult and dangerous to make, nonetheless, it is possible to observe and report cultural differences. The ways Koreans and Americans communicate are based mostly on their basic philosophies. Korean perception of communication is anchored in Buddhist philosophy, which is characterized by the inarticulate or prelinguistic process of the mind (Yum, 1987): Truth must be gained without trying and in every spoken truth the unspoken has the last word; words are approximations, sometimes helpful, sometimes misleading (Oliver, 1962, p. 143). In Western culture, however, people believe that words

do, in fact, mean what they say. Aristotle insisted that clarity is the first virtue of good style (Oliver, 1962, pp. 142–143).

. . . For purposes of this study, we limit the nonverbal aspects of culture mainly to facial expressions, hand and arm gestures, tactile communication, degree of body exposure, and communication between the sexes.

FACIAL EXPRESSIONS

Everyday experience suggests that smiling is one of the most common nonverbal signals used for communication among humans. According to Ekman and Friesen (1971, pp. 124–129), happiness, generally indicated by a smile, is one of six human emotions said to be universally present and understood. Whereas a smile of happiness may be a universal expression, cultural, contextual, and personal influences can affect its meaning and frequency, as well as degree of expansiveness. Research has shown that general cultural rules about smiling (for example, frequency and expansiveness) are learned, and are significant in social interaction (Morse, 1982; Kraut & Johnston, 1979). Traditionally, Koreans are trained not to show their emotions. Because nonverbal expressions are associated mostly with the projection of emotional states, Koreans tend to avoid expressive nonverbal actions. Most Koreans do not, even in joyous humor, shout, laugh loudly, clap hands, jump up and down, tap the shoulders, embrace, or dance. Koreans who are angry try not to express their anger outwardly (Yim, 1970, p. 214). Among strangers, neutrality of expression is the rule in Korean culture. Adults, especially men, are not expected to smile frequently; it is a sign of weakness.

HAND AND ARM GESTURES

Hand and arm movement is another form of culture-specific expression. Clearly, there are differences among cultural groups as to what are considered appropriate frequency and style of hand and arm gestures. Whereas some people gesture broadly and often, others do so narrowly and seldom (Eisenberg et al., 1971, p. 100). A study of Waxer (1985), comparing nonverbal displays of emotion in American and Canadian television game show contestants, showed that American females use their hands more than do the Canadian females. In the Eastern view, adults who use many gestures when they speak are thought to be childish, because repression of overt bodily expression connotes self-control (Ramsey, 1984, p. 148). On the other hand, Western culture is likely to use strong expressive gestures to convey messages. One's ability to communicate is measured by his or her verbal and nonverbal expressive skills. These differences are assumed to be carried into nonverbal expressions used in print-media advertising illustrations.

TOUCHING

Tactile communication is an important nonverbal expression that defines and differentiates cultural values. It is measured by the degree and extent of touch employed by people in the process of communicating with each other (Watson & Graves, 1966). Different cultures attach different meanings to distance and touch, consequently displaying different amounts and kinds of spatial behavior. Like Hediger (1961), who divides animal species into *contact type* and *distant type*, Hall (1963, p. 1005) deals with *contact* and *non-contact* cultures. In contact culture, touch is common and acceptable as part of everyday life. Consequently, social members in that culture interact more closely with one another and touch one another more than do members of the noncontact group. The contact group is composed of Arabs, Latin Americans, and Southern Europeans; Asians, Indians, Pakistanis, and Northern Europeans make up the noncontact group.

Southeast Asians do not ordinarily touch during a conversation, especially one between opposite sexes, because many Asian cultures adhere to norms that forbid public display of affection and intimacy. Pares (1985) offered her impressions on the relationship between sexes:

Contact between the two groups (men and women) seems to be slight: communication, be it serious or light-hearted, is confined to the immediate circle who, almost invariably, are of the same sex. To a Korean this doubtless seems proper and normal, but to a Westerner . . . the apparent indifference of sexes to each other can be somewhat disturbing. (p. 38)

One of the five harmonies of Confucian philosophy, the division of sexes still affects relationships between men and women. Even in modern times, embracing and kissing in public, winking at others, or engaging in intimate touch are regarded as uncivil (Yim, 1970).

EYE BEHAVIOR

The adage "eyes are the window of the soul" reflects the importance of eyes as a gauge of emotion (Watson, 1970, p. 48). Gaze, or visual behavior, refers to an individual's looking behavior, which may or may not be directed at another person. Mutual gaze refers to two interactants looking at each other, usually in the region of the face (Knapp, 1978, p. 276). Eye behavior also varies according to social norms. Hall (1963, p. 1012) mentioned some cross-cultural differences in eye contact. Navahos, for instance, are taught not to gaze directly at another person during a conversation. Watson (1970) performed the most extensive study of cultural differences in gaze. Subject dyads consisting of foreign students were observed conversing in their native language. A coding system for gaze behavior showed that Arabs, Latin Americans, and Southern Europeans focused their gaze on the eyes or face of their conversational partner. In contrast, Asians, Indians, Pakistanis, and Northern Europeans tended to show *peripheral gaze* (indirect gaze, oriented toward the other without looking directly at the face or eyes) or no gaze at all. Interestingly, no relationship has been found between gaze behavior and time spent overseas, suggesting that gaze patterns are unlikely to change with environmental social influence.

The Confucian tenet of division of the sexes is symbolically represented in Koreans' perception of direct eye contact among people of different ages or sex. In Korea, direct eye contact among unequals connotes competition, constituting an inappropriate form of behavior. On the other hand, Americans expect direct eye contact when they talk to each other. Many Americans think a person who shuns eye contact is shy or lacking in self-confidence.

CLOTHING AND DEGREE OF BODY EXPOSURE

The forms of nonverbal expressions discussed so far, such as facial expressions, hand and arm gestures, and tactile communication, involve bodily movements. Not all nonverbal communication is carried out with such signals. Cultural norms and values are also projected through style of dress. The way one dresses may represent "deep-seated psychic intentions" (Eisenberg & Smith, 1971, p. 105). Dress style hints at our self-image and the image we seek to project to others. Clothing is an important nonverbal parameter in conveying messages. The Japanese, whose culture is based upon group-centered identification, are notorious for uniformity in clothing: the stereotypical *salaryman* (businessman) wears a dark suit, dark tie, shiny black shoes, and company lapel pin. Japanese tourists baffle their foreign hosts with their uniformity in dress, buying habits, and group spirit, doing everything together in the same way (Condon & Yousef, 1975, p. 138).

The degree of body exposure in dress styles indicates some values of a cultural group. Each culture has its own understanding of which parts of the body may be exposed or should be covered, and of the significance of bodily display to social acceptance (Pares, 1985, p. 56). Because degree of body exposure is related to the function of clothes in matters of propriety and attraction, cultural norms and values in relationships between people determine the parts and degree of body exposure of societal members. In traditional Oriental philosophy, people have their place in nature as well as in society. Indeed, their social roles are as important as their roles as individuals. Manner, dress, etiquette, and behavior all assume considerable significance. The desire for propriety and the interest in social appearance have produced a tradition of the clothed, rather than

unclothed, treatment of the human form in Korea (Pares, 1985, pp. 57–59).

In contrast, Americans have a higher tolerance for body exposure than Koreans. For instance, bared shoulders, legs, and backs are acceptable. However, American tolerance for body exposure is not uniform. The fundamental attitudes in Western Christian society toward nudity, shaped by its equation with sinfulness and by the Greco-Roman appreciation of the human form as the measure of nature, have engendered a tension and vitality that go far in explaining the Western preoccupation with the nude form (Pares, 1985, p. 57).

Although social rules governing nonverbal expressions in Korea are changing as a result of close and frequent contact with foreign countries, particularly the United States, the foundations of traditional values that gave rise to display rules remain.

Methodology

The research design used in this study was content analysis, which involves critical analysis of the advertising illustrations in terms of the parameters previously defined. In accordance with this technique, the study analyzes the manifest nonverbal parameters portrayed in Korean and American advertising illustrations.

To make advertisements comparable across cultures and to obtain a wide range in readership, two general interest magazines and one women's magazine published in each of the two countries were selected. The magazines targeted for the general audience were *Time* and *Newsweek* (American), and *Shin-Dong-Ah* and *Wol-Gan-Choson* (Korean). The two women's magazines were *Good Housekeeping* (American) and *Yeo-Sung-Jung-Ang* (Korean). The magazines dated from January 1985 through December 1986.

The magazines used in this study were weeklies and monthlies. For the weekly magazines, the following issues were selected: (1) the first weeks' issues of January, May, and September; (2) the second weeks' issues of February, June, and October; (3) the third weeks' issues of March, July, and November; and (4) the fourth weeks' issues of April, August, and December. For the monthly magazines, every other month's issues were included. The procedure used in sampling the weekly and monthly magazines was designed to minimize any weekly or seasonal variations that might affect advertising content. This sampling procedure yielded 118 issues (May 1986 and September 1986 were not available for *Yeo-Sung-Jung-Ang*).

The criteria for selecting advertising illustrations were as follows:

1. Only full-page or double-page ads were used. Such illustrations can clearly portray nonverbal expressions and are easier to analyze than smaller ones.

2. Only advertisements that contained both adult males and females as main characters were included, because such ads portray real-life social interaction, showing the cultural value orientations of a given society more readily than single-sex ads. Family scenes with children were excluded.

A total of 400 ads from the six magazines were analyzed to provide a clear picture of nonverbal expressions presented and were considered to be an adequate number to satisfy the objectives of the study.

OPERATIONAL DEFINITION OF NONVERBAL EXPRESSIONS

Five nonverbal parameters were selected because they were considered to describe fully and to differentiate nonverbal expressions in advertising illustrations of the magazines. Categories of these parameters range from very conservative to highly expressive.

Facial Expressions Facial expression was measured through categories of smiling, which were derived primarily from Kraut's and Johnston's (1979, p. 1542) smiling feature classification: (1) neutral face or blank expression (very conservative), wherein the mouth is relaxed; (2) hint-of-smile (conservative), which is characterized by corners of the mouth being turned up with the lips together, or the mouth being relaxed with lips slightly parted; (3) half-smile (expressive), wherein corners of the mouth are turned up and lips are parted to show teeth; and (4) full-smile (highly expressive), in which corners of the mouth are turned up and upper and lower teeth are parted.

Hand and Arm Gestures Hand and arm gestures were classified as (1) nonuse (very conservative), wherein arms and hands are held downward, or wrists are raised; (2) narrow use (conservative), wherein movements of hands are limited to below the elbow area; (3) mild use (expressive), in which hands are raised above the elbow but below the shoulder line; and (4) broad use (highly expressive), in which hands are raised above the shoulder line.

Degree of Body Exposure This category provides for the degree and kind of body exposure, including (1) nonexposure (very conservative), describing the models who show only face, neck, hands, lower arms, and areas below the knee; (2) slight-exposure (conservative), which includes exposure of the upper arm, knee, and cleavage; (3) half-exposure (expressive), describing models who expose their thighs and shoulders; and (4) full-exposure (highly expressive), showing chest, belly, back, or total nudity.

Tactile Communication Tactile communication was measured by the degree of touching between male and female models: (1) nontouch (very conservative), which does not involve any type of bodily contact; (2) shoulder-to-shoulder touch (conservative), wherein models stand side-by-side touching each other's shoulder; (3) moderate touch (expressive), wherein models are shown holding hands, shaking hands, touching a shoulder by hand, locking arms, patting on the back, and touching chest-to-shoulder; and (4) intimate touch (highly expressive), which includes embracing, face-to-face hugging, hugging from the back, caressing, face-to-face touching, and kissing.

Communication Between the Sexes Through Eye Behavior The analysis of communication between men and women was based upon the type of visual contact between them: (1) noncommunicative (very conservative), wherein models do not gaze at each other, rather they look down or gaze into space; (2) indirectly communicative (conservative), in which models look at a third object, having the other person within the field of vision; (3) one-way communicative (expressive) defined as only one—either male or female—model gazing at the other; and (4) highly communicative (highly expressive), in which both male and female models focus directly on each other's eyes.

PRODUCT CATEGORIES

In addition to these nonverbal parameters, the types of products advertised were also coded. It was assumed that the types of products might induce a different degree of nonverbal expression in advertising illustrations. Product categories were classified into primary goods and secondary goods. The criterion for the classification was how basic were the needs those products served. Primary goods include clothes, food, and household goods such as televisions, refrigerators, furniture, and telephones. Secondary goods include cosmetics, jewelry, beer, liquor, cigarettes, and services such as banking, insurance, resorts, hotels, and transportation.

Discussion of Findings

RELATIONSHIP BETWEEN NONVERBAL EXPRESSIONS AND CULTURAL ORIENTATION

. . . A significant relationship between nonverbal expressions shown by advertising models and their cultural orientations was found to exist. The findings generally support the expectation that Korean

models use more conservative, traditional modes of nonverbal expression than do the American models. On the other hand, the American models reflect their open cultural values, showing more expansive nonverbal expressions than do the Korean models.

Hypothesis 1.1 A significant difference in the frequencies of facial expressions between the American and Korean models was noted. . . . the greatest difference between the two cultural groups was in the full-smile category (highly expressive). . . . The general pattern shows that Korean models were less expansive in facial expressions than their American counterparts.

Hypothesis 1.2 Analysis of the relationship between hand and arm gestures and culture . . . shows . . . differences in the hand and arm gestures between the American and Korean advertising models were striking, with the majority of the American models showing wide, open hand use, while the Korean models remained passive, rarely using exaggerated hand or arm gestures (most of the Korean models with broad hand usage were teenagers).

Hypothesis 1.3 The results of the analysis of the degree of body exposure . . . illustrate that the American models showed a greater degree of body exposure than the Korean models. . . . American models scored fairly high percentages of body exposure in all three categories: slight-, half-, and full-exposure (19.3% combined). On the other hand, only 10.4% of the total Korean models were classified under these three categories.

Hypothesis 1.4 This hypothesis was analyzed through the type of touch that occurred between male and female models. . . . there is a strong relationship between the degree of expression in the touching behavior of Korean and American couples shown in ads and their cultural orientation. . . . Overall 58.3% of the 181 Korean couples were depicted as not involved in any type of bodily contact (nontouch/very conservative), while only 45.9% of the American couples were thus shown. Among other categories, American advertising models showed fairly high percentages . . . in the intimate touch (highly expressive) category as contrasted with relatively low percentages . . . among Korean models. American models showed more intimate and closer bodily contact than Korean models; touching by Korean models tended to be limited to hand contact.

Hypothesis 1.5 Degree of nonverbal expression through communication between the sexes was analyzed through eye behavior between males and females shown in advertising illustrations. The findings . . . illustrate that advertising does reflect the cultural orientations of the two countries. . . . Thirty-two percent of the American couples were classified in the highly communicative category (highly expressive—couples looking at each other), compared to only 13.9% of the Korean models in that category. On the other hand, more Korean couples . . . were classified in the noncommunicative category (couples not looking at each other) than were their American counterparts. . . .

RELATIONSHIP BETWEEN NONVERBAL EXPRESSIONS AND GENDER OF MODELS WITHIN CULTURAL GROUPS

The relationship between nonverbal expressions and gender was analyzed on the first three parameters; namely, facial expressions, hand and arm gestures, and degree of body exposure. The results of the analysis yield strong support for gender differences in nonverbal expressions within cultural group, except for hand and arm gestures as shown by American models.

Hypothesis 2.1 In comparing facial expressions between Korean male and female models . . . , more Korean females fell into half-smile (expressive) and full-smile (highly expressive) categories than did their male counterparts. On the other hand, male models portrayed neutral faces . . . more often than did females. . . .

American female models also had higher percentages in half-smile (expressive) and full-smile

(highly expressive) categories than did American male models. . . . The results of this analysis demonstrate that facial expressions of advertising models depend upon the gender of the models in each culture. . . .

Hypothesis 2.2 . . . Korean female models were more conservative in hand use than Korean male models (44.8% vs. 31.4%). Examined in more detail, Korean males were depicted more frequently with broad use of their hands . . . than were the Korean female group. . . . In the case of American advertising models . . . , interestingly enough, the American female models exhibited a far higher percentage of broad use . . . than did their male counterparts. . . .

Hypothesis 2.3 . . . Korean female models exposed their bodies more frequently than did Korean male models in all three exposure categories (slight-, half-, and full-exposure). . . . There were also highly significant differences between American male and female models and degree of body exposure. . . . the American female models show relatively higher percentages in all three exposure categories (slight-, half-, and full-exposure) than do male models. . . .

RELATIONSHIP BETWEEN NONVERBAL EXPRESSIONS AND PRODUCT CATEGORIES WITHIN CULTURAL GROUPS

The results of the comparison between product categories and nonverbal expressions shown by Korean advertising models demonstrate that only female facial expressions, female hand and arm use, and communication between the sexes were dependent upon the types of products advertised. . . . None of the other nonverbal parameters yields strong differences across primary and secondary products. In terms of facial expression, . . . Korean female models showed a higher score (13.5%) in the full-smile classification for primary goods such as clothes and food, while only 7.1% for secondary goods. . . . As to hand and arm use, Korean female models showed far more broad use . . . in primary goods than in secondary goods. . . .

In the case of American advertising models, only facial expression was dependent upon the product categories advertised among five nonverbal parameters. . . . The most striking difference in male facial expression across product categories was found in the full-smile classification, where American male models scored 31.3% for primary goods ads, but only 9.8% for secondary goods. . . . It was also found that the female models followed almost the same trend as their male counterparts: more full-smile classifications in primary goods ads, and more neutral face classifications in secondary goods. All the other parameters, such as hand and arm use, degree of body exposure, touch, and communication between the sexes, yielded no significant relationship between product categories advertised and models' nonverbal expressions.

In sum, among the five nonverbal parameters, only that of facial expression was dependent upon the product categories advertised in both American and Korean advertising models: regardless of culture, more models fit the full-smile classification in primary goods ads and the neutral face classification in secondary goods ads.

Discussion

It was found that the five nonverbal expressions were important cultural parameters, which served as determinants of the different cultural orientations in Korea and America. The cultural parameters effectively describe and differentiate nonverbal expressions between Korean and American models. The findings show that nonverbal messages transmitted by models in Korean and American magazine advertisements are generally reflective of their cultural orientations. Korean models tended to smile less frequently, use their hands and arms less frequently, and expose their bodies less frequently than did American models, thus reflecting each culture. Male and female models in American advertising tended to touch each other more frequently

and look at each other more frequently than their counterparts in Korean magazines.

Regarding gender differences, female models in both countries smiled more and exposed their bodies more frequently than did their male counterparts. These findings conform to the social norms of both societies. As far as these two cultural parameters are concerned, gender differences seem to be similar regardless of the cultural setting. In terms of hand and arm use, Korean female models showed less expressive hand gestures than their male counterparts, as was expected. For American models, however, the trend was the opposite: female models showed a far higher percentage of broad use of hand and arm gestures than did males. These findings somewhat limit cross-cultural generalizations or stereotypes of males using relaxed gestures (open, expansive, and frequent use of arms) and females using tense hand gestures (narrow and infrequent use of arms).

Another important finding is that facial expressions vary across product categories in both Korean and American advertising illustrations. Different products may require different degrees of facial expression, because models in both countries had more full-smile classification in primary goods ads and more neutral face classification in secondary goods ads. For primary goods, models try to show product satisfaction through smiling expressions, while for secondary products they strive to create a mood that does not necessarily require a full smile.

THEORETICAL IMPLICATIONS

The foregoing literature has revealed that there are three basic arguments about the relationship between culture and advertising. The first begins with the premise that advertising primarily reflects the unique indigenous culture, be it Western or non-Western. To prove this argument, the cultural content of advertising in Korea should contain primarily Korean elements of expression, and, likewise, in America, American elements. Consistent with this position, nonverbal expressions shown by models in Korean and American magazine advertisements were found to be highly related to their cultural orientations. Korean models tend to be more conservative than expressive in nonverbal modes, such as facial expression, body exposure, touch, hand and arm gestures, and eye behavior, than do American models.

The second position declares that advertising in non-Western countries is not a product of those cultures, but is primarily Western in character. This position is clearly negated by the results of the study. The findings obtained in the content analysis show that Korean advertising primarily reflects its own cultural values rather than Western values, at least in the context of nonverbal expressions.

The third position asserts that advertising in non-Western countries does not reflect solely the indigenous cultures, but a mixture of those cultures with some selected Western cultural traits. These researchers have reported the trend of countries to move toward a global, predominantly Western culture. This position is not consistent with the current data. Nonverbal expressions shown by Korean advertising models still basically reflect their indigenous cultural traits.

To summarize, the results of this study are consistent with the first position, which claims that advertising reflects primarily the indigenous culture, be it Western or non-Western. The strong relationship between advertising and cultural orientation observed in the present study may be due, in part, to the focus on nonverbal behaviors, which are fundamental core values that are hard to change. People's unconscious nonverbal cues are truer than their conscious verbal cues. Thus, nonverbal cues may constitute deeply hidden messages that are less susceptible to foreign influence. Advertising and culture can have a symbiotic relationship in the sense that culture influences advertising, which, in turn, engenders a way of life that becomes a part of that culture (cf. Marquez, 1973). Future research should examine how, with increasing interdependence among nations, nonverbal expressions shown in advertising change over time.

The major concern of this research is the cultural aspect of advertising. Advertising has an overt function—to sell things; however, the inner structures of advertising communication bear important cultural meanings and connotations that must be uncovered in order to make clear the full meaning of advertising messages. In the United States, the study of advertising communication has occurred mostly within a paradigm shaped primarily by the interests of the business community and defined as *consumer behavior* (Schultze, 1981, p. 371). This paradigm emphasizes consumer demographics and advertising appeals. Advertising communication should be studied in a broader cultural context in order to improve our understanding of international advertising.

PRACTICAL IMPLICATIONS

International marketers are often faced with the problem of whether, and to what extent, they should alter their advertising messages from one country to another (see Britt, 1974; Hornick, 1980; Munson & McIntyre, 1979; Ricks, Arpan, & Fu, 1974; Whitelock & Chung, 1989). Multinational companies that market their products on a worldwide basis are faced with the decision of whether to standardize their messages across countries, or to individualize their messages in each country. Traditionally, it has been more or less accepted that nationalistic differences prevented the use of similar copy and themes on a multinational level (Ryans, 1969). However, the apparent success of various companies, including Coca-Cola and Exxon, with its "Tiger" campaign, along with the benefits of using a standardized approach, are leading other companies to examine the feasibility of universal advertising themes (see Whitelock & Chung, 1989). Advertising standardization is not a simplistic concept and should be considered in terms of degree of uniformity rather than in absolute terms (see Peebles, Ryans, & Vernon, 1978). In general, however, the findings suggest limitations to the universal approach to advertising, because significant differences in nonverbal expressions exist between nations. One may suspect that a foreign model would be permitted to violate local norms; however, use of foreign models in Korean advertising was almost nonexistent. Overall, the current findings suggest that expressive nonverbal cues shown by American advertising models may be less effective in Korea because their appeal runs counter to Korean cultural values.

In the past, language was considered to be an important constraint to advertising standardization and posed the most difficult obstacle to universal standardization of advertising messages (Thackray, 1985). Incorrect translation of an advertisement into clumsy or embarrassing wording can cause adverse reactions (e.g., Nova means "no go" in Spanish). Similar problems often arise from failure to understand nonverbal idioms in a culture. Domestic success is no guarantee of predictable performance in a different environment (Ricks et al., 1974). Different nonverbal idioms may render many businesses' normal procedures inapplicable or untransferable.

There seems to be little doubt that culture plays an important role in the perception and use of advertising. Certain fundamental differences across cultures make imperative the use of sensitized advertising appeals when advertising abroad. Ricks et al. (1974) found that most international advertising blunders occur because of a failure to understand the foreign culture and its social norms. The importance of having an adequate cultural sensitivity on the part of advertising practitioners involved in international operations may be the major determinant in the success of an international business venture. It is particularly cogent for them to scrutinize and choose the correct cultural expectations in which advertising will appear. Only when the cultural rules of different cultural groups are identified will advertisers be able to get across their messages, reach the hearts and minds of the targeted group, and successfully promote their products in a foreign market.

References

Britt, S. H. (1974). Standardizing marketing for the international market. *Columbia Journal of World Business, 9*, 39–45.

Choe, J.-H., Wilcox, G. B., & Hardy, A. P. (1986). Facial expressions in magazine advertisements: A cross-cultural comparison. *Journalism Quarterly, 63*(1), 122–126, 166.

Condon, J. C., & Yousef, F. (1975). *An introduction to intercultural communication.* New York: Bobbs-Merrill.

Durgee, J. F. (1986). Richer findings from qualitative research. *Journal of Advertising Research, 26*(4), 36–44.

Eisenberg, A. M., & Smith, R., Jr. (1971). *Nonverbal communication.* New York: Bobbs-Merrill.

Ekman, P. (1973). Cross-cultural studies of facial expression. In P. Ekman (Ed.), *Darwin and facial expression: A century of research in review.* New York: Academic Press.

Ekman, P., & Friesen, W. V. (1971). Constants across cultures in the face and emotion. *Journal of Personality and Social Psychology, 17*(2), 124–129.

Goffman, E. (1979). *Gender advertisements.* Cambridge, MA: Harvard University Press.

Hall, E. T. (1963). A system for the notation of proxemic behavior. *American Anthropologist, 65*, 1003–1026.

Hall, P. M., & Hewitt, J. P. (1973). The quasi-theory of communication and the management of dissent. In M. H. Prosser (Ed.), *Intercommunication among nations and peoples* (pp. 530–540). New York: Harper & Row.

Hediger, H. (1961). The evolution of territorial behavior. In S. L. Washburn (Ed.), *Social life of early man* (pp. 34–57). Chicago: Aldine.

Hornick, J. (1980). Comparative evaluation of international versus national advertising strategies. *Columbia Journal of World Business, 21*, 9–17.

Knapp, M. L. (1978). *Nonverbal communication in human interaction.* New York: Holt, Rinehart & Winston.

Kraut, R. S., & Johnston, R. E. (1979). Social and emotional messages of smiling: An ethological approach. *Journal of Personality and Social Psychology, 37*, 1539–1553.

Kunihiro, T. (1980). Personality structure and communication behavior: A comparison of Japanese and Americans. In W. von Raffler-Engel (Ed.), *Aspects of nonverbal communication.* Lisse, Swets, and Zeitlinger.

Madden, C. S., Cabellero, M. J., & Matsukubo, S. (1986). Analysis of information content in U.S. and Japanese magazine advertising. *Journal of Advertising, 15*, 38–45.

Marquez, F. T. (1973). *A comparative analysis of culture and the cultural content of print-media advertising in the Philippines and Thailand.* Unpublished doctoral dissertation, The University of Wisconsin, Madison.

Millum, T. (1975). *Images of women: Advertising in women's magazines.* Savage, MD: Rowman & Littlefield.

Morse, C. (1982). College yearbook picture: More females smile than males. *Journal of Psychology, 110*, 3–6.

Munson, J. M., & McIntyre, S. M. (1979). Developing practical procedures for the measurement of personal values in cross-cultural marketing. *Journal of Marketing Research, 16*(1), 48–52.

Norman, G. R. (1965). *Advertising as a reflection of national character in the United States and Great Britain.* Unpublished master's thesis, The Pennsylvania State University, University Park, PA.

Oliver, R. T. (1962). *Communication and culture: The problem of penetrating national and cultural boundaries.* Springfield, IL: Charles C. Thomas.

Pares, S. (1985). *Crosscurrents: Korean Western culture in contrast.* Seoul, South Korea: Seoul International Publishing House.

Peebles, D. M., Ryans, J. K., & Vernon, I. R. (1978). Coordinating international advertising. *Journal of Marketing, 42,* 28–34.

Ramsey, S. (1984). Double vision: Nonverbal behavior East and West. In A. Wolfgang (Ed.), *Nonverbal behavior: Perspectives, applications, intercultural insights* (pp. 139–167). New York: C. J. Hogrefe.

Ricks, D. A., Arpan, J. S., & Fu, M. Y. (1974). Pitfalls in advertising overseas. *Journal of Advertising Research, 14,* 47–51.

Ryans, J. K. (1969). Is it too soon to put a tiger in every tank? *Columbia Journal of World Business, 4,* 69–75.

Schultze, Q. J. (1981). Advertising, culture, and economic interest. *Communication Research, 8,* 371–384.

Singh, P. N., & Huang, S. (1962). Some socio-cultural and psychological determinants of advertising in India: A comparative study. *Journal of Social Psychology, 57,* 113–121.

Thackray, J. (1985, November). Much ado about global advertising. *Newsweek:* Special Marketing Section.

Unwin, S. J. F. (1974). How culture affects advertising expression and communication style. *Journal of Advertising, 3*(2), 24–27.

Watson, O. M. (1970). *Proxemic behavior: A cross-cultural study.* Hawthorne, NY: Mouton de Gruyter.

Watson, O. M., & Graves, T. D. (1966). Quantitative research in proxemic behavior. *American Anthropologist, 68,* 971–985.

Waxer, P. H. (1985). Video ethology: Television as a data base for cross-cultural studies in nonverbal displays. *Journal of Nonverbal Behavior, 9*(2), 111–120.

Whitelock, J., & Chung, D. (1989). Cross-cultural advertising: An empirical study. *International Journal of Advertising, 8,* 291–310.

Yim, S.-C. (1970). Customs and folklore. In S.-S. Lee et al. (Eds.), *Korean studies today: Development and state of the field* (pp. 199–220). Seoul National University: Institute of Asian Studies.

Yum, J. O. (1987). Korean philosophy and communication. In D. Kincaid (Ed.), *Communication theory: Eastern and Western perspectives.* New York: Academic Press.

Key Terms

advertising	Korea
cross-cultural comparisons	nonverbal communication

Discussion Questions

1. How do the philosophy and religious beliefs in Korea influence nonverbal behavior? Do you think religious beliefs in America influence nonverbal behavior?

2. Kim investigated the effects of nationality and gender on nonverbal behavior. What are other factors that may influence nonverbal behavior?

3. Based on Kim's findings, how would television advertising in Korea differ from television advertising in the United States?

4. How might a critical researcher conduct a study of print advertising in Korea and the United States?

5. How might Kim's findings be different if the analyzed advertisements were from different magazines (e.g., *Ebony, Rolling Stone*)?

21 Places for Speaking in Teamsterville

GERRY PHILIPSEN

The significance of speaking as a domain within a culture varies across speech communities. Not only do bearers of different cultures speak differently one from another but, more importantly, they hold different assumptions about the value, purposes, and significance of speaking as a mode of human experience. Like religion, politics, and law, so speech, the principal medium of creating meanings in social interaction, itself holds different meanings for the various peoples whose views of the world afford it a place.

This essay reports in part the meanings which speech has in a community I labeled Teamsterville. It builds upon a previous essay[1] by developing further my answers to two questions: When the people of Teamsterville look out on the world or conjure up some image of it, what does the world look like to them, and what do they envision as the place of speaking within it? Does Teamsterville's view of the situated appropriateness of speaking implicate something about the meaning and significance of speaking to its people? Answers to such questions, in this study and others like it, provide the descriptive materials from which to construct a theory of the place of speaking in cultures.

Attention to at least the most salient and accessible features of Teamsterville's outlook on speaking was facilitated by using Hymes' schema of components of speech events.[2] The idea behind using schematic components such as "participants," "topic," or "setting" is that they are, singly or in combinations, devices for discovering native inter-

pretations about speaking. The assumption is that since natives use such conceptual devices as frames, places, or features for discovering and ordering cultural interpretations about speaking, the investigator can use these devices to accomplish roughly the same thing, albeit for different purposes. For example, a number of studies show that much of a person's culture—his shared, tacit knowledge—is organized in terms of social identities,[3] and other work suggests that components such as topic and setting also serve as organizing features in cultural world views.[4]

Previously I used one of these situational features in reporting on how Teamstervillers view the place of speaking in social life. That report focused on the native view of *who* may appropriately use speech and in what situations. That view is very sensitive to speaking as an instrument for creating social meaning by virtue of either using it or refraining from its use in the context of specific social identity relationships. For example, when a Teamsterville boy talks brashly to a man, the boy implicitly violates a social boundary. For the man to respond with talk implicitly confirms that the boundary is weak; in contrast, nonverbal threats or physical retaliation reestablish the social boundary by warning the boy to "keep his place" and by affirming the man's place in the social hierarchy. In this view of the personae who dwell in the world and of the activities by which they most convincingly enact specific roles, speech is located both situationally and functionally.

A Teamsterville outlook on settings or locales also informs native understandings about speaking

[1] Gerry Philipsen, "Speaking 'Like a Man' in Teamsterville: Culture Patterns of Role Enactment in an Urban Neighborhood," *QJS*, 61 (1975), 13–22.

[2] Dell Hymes, "Models of the Interaction of Language and Social Life," in *Directions in Sociolinguistics: The Ethnography of Communication*, ed. John J. Gumperz and Dell Hymes (New York: Holt, Rinehart, and Winston, 1972), see particularly pp. 58–71.

[3] Roger M. Keesing, "Toward a Model of Role Analysis," in *A Handbook of Method in Cultural Anthropology*, ed. Raoul Naroll and Ronald Cohen (Garden City, New York: The Natural History Press, 1970), pp. 423–453.

[4] See Susan U. Philips, "Acquisition of Rules for Appropriate Speech Usage," *Georgetown University Monograph Series on Languages and Linguistics*, 2 (1970), 77–94.

as a situated mode of social activity. In addition to the personae which the culture marks for speaking "parts," the culture also marks particular scenes for occasions of talk. There are no labeled conversation areas or orators' arenas in the community, but its world view includes social boundaries, scenes, and scenes within scenes which refer to everyday stages upon which a particular kind of dramatic action may unfold. The native view of settings, and of the activities they most appropriately realize specifies, among other things, places for speaking, and in turn that specification permits an inference about the place of speaking in Teamsterville.

"Place" is used here in several senses but each contains various ideas of location, such as a position in a social hierarchy, a physical setting, or the niche which is properly occupied by a thing, person, or idea. In the latter sense one speaks not only of things but also of people and ideas as having a place "in the scheme of things." A place can also be regarded as a perspective from which one discovers or explores a subject by the use of mental images. "Place," then, may simultaneously suggest notions of social, physical, perceptual, and heuristic location.

The phrase, "places for speaking in Teamsterville," uses each of these senses of the word "place." Although this paper locates speaking in social and physical space, primarily it locates speech in the community's culture. Teamsterville's outlook on the occasioned uses of speaking suggests that a sense of place—at once both hierarchical and physical—is a "major unifying perception"[5] in its cultural world view; a perception which creates shades of meaning and interpretation regarding speech as an instrument of communication and social life. Accordingly, two features of place, personae and scene, are perspectives which have special relevance for exploring Teamsterville's images of the world, and for thereby discovering where its people locate speech in their cultural scheme of things.

Four Teamsterville place concepts form a simple taxonomy of culturally defined places for speaking. Each is labeled by a native place term, and is defined

in terms of the kind of setting to which it refers, the personae whose presence in it create a scene, and how the scene-personae configuration creates an occasion for talk. Scene, personae, and talk thus are interwoven aspects of the design I use in reporting Teamsterville places for speaking, "the neighborhood," "the street," "the corner," and "the porch."

Places for Speaking

A sense of neighborhood has a deep and compelling significance to the dwellers of Teamsterville. The sociospatial boundaries which residents perceive as "the neighborhood" make up the largest region within which it is considered most appropriate and in which it is most "natural" to engage in talk, and the residents think of these boundaries as co-extensive with a particular style of speaking which is characteristic of the community and to which its residents should conform. Definitions of neighborhood as scene, then, relate to native judgments about when to talk and ways of speaking, and both kinds of judgment are linked to a native view of place.

Every resident readily and emphatically identifies "the neighborhood" and defines it very insistently in terms of specific streets and blocks. Residents are equally insistent that they "know everybody around here," i.e., within the boundaries they perceive. Field observation and questioning of informants reveal that the boundaries reported vary considerably from person to person, and that the "we know everybody" assertion is not literally true. But the very specific definition and the insistent assertion suggest that a resident defines "the neighborhood" by reference both to physical setting ("around here") and to the particular people who make up his network of friends, associates, and acquaintances ("everybody") within it.

The physical boundaries of the neighborhood frame a scene for sociable interaction. For most residents these boundaries are the outer perimeter beyond which they do not socialize. In the course of my interviews of them, few Teamsterville men or women reported that they had participated in social events during the previous year with anyone who lives more than ten blocks from their home. Their reports of speaking practices, which observation

[5] The phrase is from Walter J. Ong, "World as View and World as Event," *American Anthropologist*, 71 (1969), p. 635.

confirmed in most cases, indicate a pattern of overt behavior, but what is more important here is that the reports suggest a local preference for talking within, not without, the perceived physical boundaries. Teamstervillers view the physical neighborhood as the largest scene within which talk is appropriately a focus of activity.

Within the physical neighborhood a Teamsterviller can be in the presence of people whom he defines as intruding into his social world. The physical boundaries are therefore supplemented by social boundaries which define "everybody"—the roster from which may be drawn appropriate personae for talk. Specifically, the ethnicity and residence of a potential interlocutor—his social and physical place—are salient variables in decisions to mark an occasion as appropriate for speaking. A visitor to the neighborhood, if he is so bold as to intrude into semiprivate regions (which include, among other places, "the street"), must be placed by the resident in terms of ethnicity and residence before a conversation can comfortably proceed. Once a stranger is so located, talk might be relatively free, depending on the kind of person he is. "The hillbillies" and "the Mexicans" live within the neighborhood boundaries but do not, in the eyes of the long-term white residents, really "belong" there. These groups should, in the view of the people I studied, "keep in their place" by living elsewhere and socializing among themselves. They are not, as a rule, appropriate partners for talk. Finally, there are those people who live in the neighborhood and whose ethnicity fits one of the traditional categories but whose ethnicity is different from one's own. Germans, Italians, Poles, and Lithuanians, among others, now talk to each other, but in the past these neighborhood groups had been relatively isolated from each other physically and socially, and there is still a sharp sense of difference between them. These persons include some people in the other groups in the term, "everybody," yet they still can visualize an image of "the neighborhood" as people of like ethnicity sharing a street or block, and it is that scene in which talk most appropriately and naturally has its place.

The unusually strong relationship of social to physical place is no accident. In the nineteenth century Teamsterville's first residents established tightly segregated patterns of residence and association along ethnic lines. The residents, who were new or relatively new immigrants, settled in row houses on a block or street peopled by their countrymen, and ethnicity was a pervasive determinant of interaction, association, and residence. Today the patterns born of ethnicity are altered but not totally replaced. Even though a person's street address is no longer a perfect guide to his ethnicity, many streets and blocks are still associated with a particular ethnic group. Parents still forbid their children to play in a particular place because it is an "Italian [Polish, etc.] block." Ethnicity and locality thus are at least partially interchangeable as organizing devices, criteria by which the Teamsterville resident selects from among the many social experiences available to him those which appropriately call forth speaking as a mode of activity.[6]

In addition to locating occasions of speaking within the boundaries of "the neighborhood," Teamstervillers also locate on a scale of social worth the style of speaking they associate with the neighborhood. Awareness of their own speaking style as one distinct from others is reflected in their readily reported assessment, consistent across informants, that their speech is inferior to the Standard English of middle class people, e.g., people who live on "the north side" (of Chicago), but superior to the speech of, respectively, "hillbillies," "Mexicans," and "Negroes." They respect and resent the speech of people who have a better control of Standard English than they do, are insecure about their own speech outside of neighborhood contexts, and find reassurance in what they perceive to be the deficiencies of "Negro" speech. Thus Teamsterville judgments of locale, socioeconomic standing, and conformity to accepted standards of speaking are correlated—Teamstervillers see themselves as be-

_____

[6] For other treatments of neighborhoods much like Teamsterville as "urban villages," see Herbert I. Gans *The Urban Villagers: Group and Class in the Life of Italian-Americans* (New York: The Free Press, 1962); Gerald D. Suttles, *The Social Order of the Slum: Ethnicity and Territory in the Inner City* (Chicago: Univ. of Chicago Press, 1968).

ing sandwiched between the richer, linguistically superior whites of the north side of town and the poorer, linguistically inferior blacks who live to the south of Teamsterville.

Awareness of a linguistic norm and the concurrent belief that one's own speech is substandard can create what Labov calls "linguistic insecurity."[7] This in turn can lead to attempts at correction, even hypercorrection, the practice of speaking so carefully as to betray a deliberate attempt at compensation. Teamstervillers do not attempt or value correction or hypercorrection, and cultural interpretations linking speech behavior with native attitudes about social and physical place may account for suppression of attempts at change. On the one hand, the awareness of a linguistic norm that Teamstervillers do not measure up to serves to heighten a positive affective awareness of community patterns, providing a kind of unity in adversity, in which the local deviation from Standard English functions as a defining attribute of membership in "everybody around here." On the other hand, a resident who changes his speech to be more like Standard English is seen as symbolically attempting to leave the neighborhood. His deviation from local usage is interpreted as an inappropriate assertion of upward mobility, an assertion which is, like other attempts at rising in the world, resented by those who do not make such efforts. One informant revealed a significant Teamsterville image when he described the neighborhood as a big crawfish barrel from which everyone tries to crawl out and in which everyone resents those few who succeed in reaching the top.

Teamstervillers believe that in order to maintain their status as one of the "everybody" they should not significantly modify their speaking style so as to deviate from local patterns. Changes in speech are easily noticed, so speech is therefore a means by which a person can signal his desire either to move upward on the social scale or to affirm his commitment to the norms of his present group. Teamsterville reactions to two prominent people provide a

neat illustration of this dual possibility. Speech style is a principal factor verbalized in positive evaluations by Teamsterville teenagers of the television program "All in the Family," based on the lives of a New York City family which lives in a neighborhood much like Teamsterville. The day after Jean Stapleton won an Emmy award for her performances on the show, a group of Teamsterville girls expressed their strong approval of the show and the award. They were, however, keenly disappointed to learn that in real life Jean Stapleton talks differently from the character she portrays on television, i.e., she sounds "real sophisticated." On the other hand, a Teamsterville resident can succeed in the eyes of the world and yet not be resented by his neighbors. I asked one informant why it is that a particular local politician could be so successful and still enjoy the almost reverent adoration of his Teamsterville neighbors. The informant replied, in a tape recorded interview, "Well, see, he doesn't scare anybody because he speaks lousy English. I mean he has rotten pronunciation. And he has, y'know, he murders the American language, the way most of us do, so we know he's one of us, he's just like us."[8]

A college student, responding to a question about his own speech, spoke for himself and other Teamsterville residents when he said that he feels insecure in a university or other "middle class" setting because he grew up in an "illiterate, poor neighborhood." The informant said he is reluctant to change his speaking habits because that would alienate him from his friends in the neighborhood. Few residents face the dilemma articulated by the informant, for they live their lives amidst friends and neighbors who constitute the network of people known as "the neighborhood," and among these people speech is viewed as a resource for signaling one's similarity to his friends and for confirming his loyalty to them and their shared values. Thus it is

---

[7] William Labov, *The Social Stratification of English in New York City* (Washington, D.C.: Center for Applied Linguistics, 1966), p. 477.

[8] The same politician mentioned by the informant once sought, upon the recommendation of a political advisor, to undertake speech lessons from a professor of speech at Northwestern University. At the end of the first lesson, the politician said, "I'm sorry, Doc, if I talked the way you want me to they'd laugh me out of the neighborhood." I am indebted to Glen E. Mills for this information.

that a Teamsterviller's sense of neighborhood is a lens through which he locates speech, socially, physically, and hierarchically.

"The neighborhood" is the most macroscopic concept which Teamstervillers use to distinguish places in general from places for speaking. They supplement their view of places for speaking with several other place concepts which "the neighborhood" subsumes. The most important supplementary concept is "the street," which as physical location refers to all outdoor areas in the neighborhood, but particularly to streets, sidewalks, and porches. "Everybody" participates in street life. A street is, however, considered primarily a man's rather than a woman's territory. Men spend more time in the street and have access to more of it than women do. It is used as a general setting for sociability among neighborhood residents. Although it legally is public territory, residents do not treat it merely as such; street territory as physical setting can be a scene in Teamsterville because people actively socialize there, and outsiders who walk or drive on sidewalks or streets often are felt to be intruding on at least semiprivate territory.

The nature of front porches, the physical design of the neighborhood, and the density of population facilitate the use of the street as a social setting. Porches are open and in most cases flush to the ground; they are small, usually about six feet square. One porch is near enough to another that neighbors can converse and at the least are mutually visible. People socialize in front of, not behind, their houses; they visit on front porches but not on back porches, perhaps because the latter look out on alleys and hold garbage cans. There are few back or side yards. A typical street has twenty-four buildings on one side (with a very small space between each building), each building has two or three flats (one flat per story), and flats house an average of 3.4 people. On one side of a typical block, then, there are about 160 people who are potential users of that block's porches, sidewalk, and street. There are about seven to ten people available for interaction in and around each front porch stoop.

An upper middle class suburb contiguous to the northern boundary of Chicago is an instructive

contrast to Teamsterville. There friends visit inside houses or in back yards where there is a patio, a large fenced yard, and a garden. Visitors are usually from outside a ten block radius. Only one family lives in each building, with an average of 2.95 people per household. A resident can enter his home by driving in the alley to his garage and walking from the garage door to enter the house by the back door, without exposure to his neighbors. Adults do not socialize in front yards, and certainly not on front porches. In short, there are relatively few residents per block and they preserve privacy and avoidance patterns.[9]

It is as part of the general physical layout that the street can be understood to be a significant setting in Teamsterville. Sociable speech is conducted in a relatively public region, the street, where people are available to each other because of the physical design of the community. Add to this the facts of population density and the relative absence of air conditioning, and one can picture people spilling out in the street in summer. When outdoors, people frequently congregate at porches and corners, and Teamstervillers share a view of what personae and what speech activity are appropriate to those two places.

"The corner" is an outdoor setting, at or near a street corner, which a particular group of boys marks as its regular meeting place and as its "turf," which is to say that a corner is the territory of boys or young men who are long-time friends and associates. For some men the neighborhood tavern becomes a surrogate for a street corner, so "corner personae" can include men of all ages beyond early adolescence with the scene shifting from corner to tavern in early adulthood. "The corner" in the broad sense is the principal scene where members of a group of males converse. Group members promote extensive sociability among themselves and define sharp boundaries between themselves and non-members. Accordingly, talk is an appropriate

---

[9] Demographic data are from Evelyn Kitagawa and Karl Taeuber, *Local Community Fact Book, 1960* (Chicago: Univ. of Chicago Press, 1963).

focus of activity "on the corner," but not elsewhere, and talk has value as social currency among corner personae but not with others.

A particular corner has social significance for a Teamsterville boy not only because that corner is where the boy's most important social activity occurs, or where he meets the group with which he has deep feelings of loyalty and identification, but also because there is more than a casual association of scene with personae. Youths express their group membership in terms of place references: they describe themselves as "Wallace [Street] Boys," "The Spirits of 32nd [Street]," "the 33rds," etc. They write the street name on their clothing, and they paint the street name on neighborhood buildings.[10] Accordingly, where a boy "hangs" influences how others see him and how he sees himself—it is a significant attribute of his persona. A boy feels at home, in the "right place," at his corner, and that has special significance in a neighborhood in which "keeping your place" both physically and hierarchically is an extremely compelling *topos*. Thus one boy summarized the corner's significance to him in saying, "Where you hang is your turf—you won it and it's yours."

One corner boy said that his group did not allow Mexicans to enter its turf but that others could pass through without incident. The boy's group does not define Mexicans as part of "the neighborhood," even though Mexicans live within the physical boundaries. This illustrates that a stranger's entry into another group's turf is considered a challenge to the claimants' control of their territory. Frequently such an intrusion prompts a fight. On the other hand, if a boy enters the turf of people he knows, even if he does not "belong" there, he is allowed safe passage because he is part of "everybody" around there. Thus, to walk only where one

is known ensures peaceful relations even with unfriendly groups. Because the presence of a stranger in alien territory can lead to fighting, residents value both staying where one "belongs" and knowing everybody.

Where a boy "hangs" is not only his turf but is also the social context he marks as most appropriate to speaking occasions, and this association of speech with a particular context has significance for understanding the Teamsterville boy's outlook on speaking. At the corner, the boy acquires a highly developed appreciation for loyalty to and familiarity with his identity-matched fellows, and an equally sharp sense of the importance of the social and physical boundaries which insulate his group from outsiders. The corner boy's place for speaking is therefore relatively impermeable by interlocutors who do not share his background of meanings and experiences; and, on the other hand, the boy sees the world outside his place as a context not appropriate to activity which has speech as its focus. A consequence is a heightened appreciation for speech which (1) by its form emphasizes the boy's similarity to others in his group and sets him apart from those outside, and (2) is highly dependent for its meanings upon a context of shared experience. In short, the cultural meanings attached to places for speaking imply a preference for what Bernstein calls a "restricted" mode of speaking (in which the speaker does not make verbally explicit his meanings and in which speech does not serve as a mode for expressing the personal uniqueness of the speaker), and a relative de-emphasis of what he calls speaking in the "elaborated" mode (speaking which is verbally explicit and which serves to make public the unique motives, feelings, ideas, etc., of the speaker).[11]

Since women are denied full use of the street, they use front porches. The front porch of a house

---

[10] The use of public walls for culturally significant writings is, of course, not new. For an interesting example of another contemporary setting, see Herbert Kohl, "Names, Graffiti, and Culture," in *Rappin' and Stylin' Out: Communication in Urban Black America*, ed. Thomas Kochman (Urbana: Univ. of Illinois Press, 1972), pp. 109–133.

[11] Basil Bernstein, "Social Class, Language, and Socialization," in *Language and Social Context*, ed. Pier Paoli Giglioli (Harmondsworth, Middlesex, England: Penguin Books, 1972), pp. 173–78. For the classic treatment of corner groups in a white, working class neighborhood, see William Foote Whyte, *Street Corner Society: The Social Structure of an Italian Slum* (Chicago: Univ. of Chicago Press, 1943).

is not exclusively a woman's territory, but it has special significance for the Teamsterville woman. Although the street is in general a setting for sociability, not every means of participation in street life is sanctioned for women. In the local view, the woman's place is in the kitchen and the home, the man's in the street and the outside; and Teamsterville men and boys report neighborhood boundaries which are more extensive than those reported by girls and women. The negative sanction on certain types of female street interaction is reflected in patterns of child rearing. Girls are not allowed outside of the home without permission. They are carefully supervised and must account for their whereabouts at all times. Teamstervillers believe that strict control in raising a girl is the only alternative to overpermissiveness, which brings many negative sanctions. How, then, is a woman or young girl to participate in the social life of the neighborhood? The front porch serves as a link between street and home, as a place in which a Teamsterville woman can appropriately participate in social life. An adult woman, who has lived in Teamsterville all her life, reported that in winter she hardly sees anyone, but "in summer the whole block opens up" and everyone congregates on or around front porches.

"The porch" is a place at or near the front porch of a house, the physical porch usually being only a stoop or a few steps. "Everybody" uses the porch. It is a principal setting for sociability, particularly for young children and for women of all ages. Its use also facilitates a person's entry into neighborhood life, serving as a link between home and street. Although I had previously been aware of the front porch as a gathering place, and had participated in front porch conversation, its deep cultural significance first became apparent to me by accident. I asked an informant about who is and who is not socially active in the neighborhood, as a way of eliciting the characteristics of socially accepted people. The informant mentioned an attorney who was minimally accepted but not active in the round of block sociability. After several minutes of persistent but unproductive questioning about how the man could become more socially active if he so wanted, the informant answered with a note of exasperation and finality that the man could never be fully ac-

cepted because he did not have a porch. Later work with other informants indicates that the front porch is used for extending invitations to talk and as a place for launching one's own participation in neighborhood social life. The consequences of having a front porch might appear negligible. However, an understanding of the function of the front porch in Teamsterville suggests ways of introducing oneself in the neighborhood, of initiating sociability, and of receiving such initiations from others.

Fieldwork as Intercultural Communication

When a person seeks to understand speech behavior in a community whose culture is alien to him, the possibility of misunderstanding is high. Upon hearing that I was studying "Communication in Teamsterville," a middle class visitor to the neighborhood remarked, "There is no communication in Teamsterville," for this outsider believed that because he heard little talk where he expected it, there was none. Richard Sennett, a student of middle class mores and manners, wrote that when middle class people want to feel they are socializing in a warm, personal way they seek out "intimate and small places, the most powerful being their own homes."[12] Real entertaining is sheltered by the house walls and limited to those invited within. Teamsterville's taxonomy of places for speaking suggests a very different model from that of middle class or white collar America: Teamstervillers have a strong appreciation for sociability in such "public" places as neighborhood, street, corner, and porch. Indeed, these are the kinds of places for speaking they value most. An implication is that one should discover where people talk in order to acquire anything but a culture-bound understanding of a people's speech behavior.

Teamsterville's criterion for marking a place for speech is different from that of some other communities. An upper middle class living room is a place for talk, and men and women, adults and children,

---

[12] Richard Sennett, *The Uses of Disorder: Personal Identity and City Life* (New York: Vintage Books, 1970), p. 76.

are appropriate personae for conversation there. Even relative strangers can be welcome; note that a host is anxious if a visitor does not participate in the round of talk and often a host deliberately encourages a reticent guest to speak. In Teamsterville, by contrast, the living room is not popular as a setting for talk. Rather, settings are popular which exclude those of different sex or social position and where outsiders would not be present to participate. In Teamsterville it is the presence of such identity-matched personae in a location traditionally set aside for sociability among them, to the exclusion of others, that marks a place for speaking. The search, then, should not end with the discovery of speaking locations but should uncover what, in the native view, makes a place fitting for talk.

In the present study the question of places invariably became, upon analysis, one of personae and of the scenes most appropriate for gatherings of particular personae. In other words, talk is not a focus of activity merely because of the setting. A gathering of Mexican and Italian boys on the same corner is an occasion for careful visual scrutiny as one group quietly passes through the other's turf, but to make it an occasion for talk would be to invite trouble. Similarly when an outsider walks into a corner tavern he changes the occasion from one of loud frequent talk to one of near-perfect silence. On the other hand, a person comes to have a particular persona through participating in activity which is inextricably bound up with particular locales. One becomes part of the "everybody" by being from "around here." An adolescent girl can be excluded from the round of talk because she lives a block away from other participants in a conversation. A boy becomes a corner boy because he spends time on a corner and "his" corner is, to him and others, a significant aspect of his persona. The two schematic components, scenes and personae, were not in this study discretely separable. The outsider who uses situational components heuristically, as means for discovering a pattern in native judgments about talk, should be prepared to find that in accounting for cultural data in any given case, the components are interdependent.

Teamsterville data suggest that the major settings and occasions a people mark for speaking are im-portant to understanding a culture pattern of speaking. It would, for example, be difficult to discern the significance of the front porch to Teamsterville ways of speaking if the investigator could not see its use and meaning as part of a larger pattern of setting and speech behavior in the community, a pattern which interrelates concepts of neighborhood, street, corner, and porch. Furthermore, discovering that pattern enables an investigator to explain symbolic behavior other than speaking which might otherwise be inexplicable. For example, Teamsterville place concepts were helpful to me in explaining one neighborhood practice which at first struck me as quite puzzling, the display of bowling trophies in funeral parlor windows.

A Teamsterville funeral parlor is, like a Teamsterville tavern, not so much an impersonal public setting as it is an intimate, familiar, private setting. It is not the setting for a brief service followed almost immediately by a trip to the cemetery; rather, there is a wake, which is attended by many people throughout the day and evening. A family chooses a funeral parlor along socially patterned lines, following the preference of their social circle within their parish. The funeral parlor owner is, in many cases, a resident of the neighborhood, a person who is an acquaintance, if not a social intimate, of the mourners. Thus the funeral parlor is a place for the meeting of friends and relatives as well as for the expression of sympathy.

For the funeral parlor, symbolic participation in the life of the street is an important rhetorical strategy, one aim of which is to create a scene appropriate to the funeral parlor's activities, and the display of a bowling trophy is a tactic in this strategy. The trophy faces *into the street,* not into the building, as is true of the small military figures which were, at the time of the research, displayed in many Teamsterville homes which had a family member in the military service. The funeral parlor businessmen and the residents display the trophies to people in the street, the front window serving not only as a boundary marker but also as a channel through which to announce locally-valued information, and through which to participate in the life of the street, a life whose focus is the expression of solidarity and of interaction with a close-knit peer group.

A bowling trophy in the window of a funeral parlor creates an effect which is wholly consonant with local patterns of symbolic expression of neighborhood solidarity. It is significant to local passersby. It communicates that the displayer values a popular peer group activity in the neighborhood, bowling, and that the displayer is therefore very much a part of neighborhood life. A bowling trophy in the window symbolically links the inside region of the funeral parlor with the outside regions of street and corner and thus serves the rhetorical end of creating an impression that the funeral parlor is an appropriate place for its principal activity, meetings at which friends express solidarity and support. So viewed, as symbolic participation in neighborhood street life, the bowling trophy in the window is neither tasteless indelicacy nor queer custom but a fitting display in its context. In order to see it thus, one must use the Teamsterville perspective on places for speaking.

Conclusions

When Teamstervillers look out on the world their perception of it is shaped by a finely developed sense of place. They see boundaries, social and physical, where others do not, and this vision serves as a major unifying perception in their world view. The centrality of place in the cultural outlook is reflected in a strong concern for locating people in social-physical space; in a view of places as locales whose boundaries rightly enclose and shelter some people and deny entry to others; and in a pervasive concern that oneself and others know and stay in the proper place both hierarchically and physically.

Speech, of course, is an object of that world view, and speaking as a mode of human experience takes on a culturally distinctive meaning when viewed from Teamsterville's perspective. Speaking is a focus of activity in social relationships and in physical settings which have sharp boundaries that insulate the participants from interaction with those not matched to the relevant identity attributes. Speech is seen as an instrument of sociability with one's fellows, as a medium for asserting communal ties and

loyalty to a group, and serves—by its use or disuse, or by the particular manner of its use—to signal that one knows one's place in the world.

One feature of "place" in Teamsterville is the settings in which the world view locates speaking. These settings are significant not merely as physical locations, as the blocks and boundaries which define a neighborhood, as particular streets, or as the corners and porches which dot the streets. The world view associates these places with certain people and thus "imbues the landscape with social meaning."[13] These are the scenes in which speaking has a place in Teamsterville life, and these scene-personae configurations, because of the kinds of talk they invite, create for the resident of the community a cultural awareness of speaking. Thus by attending to the settings the community marks for talk, one can discover a lens through which to see not only the community's places for speaking but also the particular way in which its people understand that, in human affairs, talk has its place.

Key Terms

ethnicity   social identity
neighborhood   speech

Discussion Questions

1. Philipsen describes how speaking serves cultural ends in Teamsterville. Can you think of other contexts in which speaking serves cultural ends?

2. Philipsen suggests that we know little about the cultural values placed upon speaking in contemporary America. What other cultural spaces would you explore to find these cultural differences?

3. Philipsen's essay helps us understand that there are many different ways of speaking in the United States. If we are so diverse, is there a rec-

---

[13] Philip K. Bock, *Modern Cultural Anthropology: An Introduction* (1969; rpt. New York: Alfred A. Knopf, 1974), p. 175.

ognizable or identifiable U.S. American way of communicating? Who "owns" this type of communication?

4. What does Philipsen's essay suggest about how language helps create cultural spaces and cultural boundaries? Can we learn to speak in cultur-

ally appropriate ways in order to gain access to and acceptance in cultural communities?

5. What does Philipsen's essay tell us about the role of class in culture? of race and ethnicity? of gender? of age?

Activities for Skill Development

1. Cultural Space Exercise

Interview a classmate (preferably someone you have not yet spoken with), and ask the person to describe one particular cultural space (e.g., a neighborhood or a region) where she or he grew up. Ask the following questions:

- Where was the place?
- Was the place culturally diverse? Who lived there (racial, ethnic, class compositions)?
- Did people of different cultural backgrounds live together harmoniously, or separately?
- What has the particular place meant to you? Did it influence the way you view yourself and others today?

2. Etiquette Expert

Write an "etiquette guide" explaining how to show "respect" in the following situations:

- You are visiting your instructor's office during his/her office hours.
- You are meeting your significant other's (partner, boyfriend, girlfriend, fiancé, etc.) parent(s).
- You are a guest at a wedding ceremony.

Describe your behaviors as precisely as possible. How overtly or subtly would you express your intent? Then, share your responses with your classmates. How do your behaviors vary by context or relationship? How might other cultural groups show respect in a similar context?

3. Silent Observation

Observe the use or avoidance of silence in your interactions with others. Take note of silence (a) in your classes, (b) in conversations with friends, and (c) at home with your family. How long might it last? What does it convey? How does it feel? How does silence differ from one context to another?

Web Sites

1. What images do you associate with the word "Harlem"? Have you met anyone from the community? Visit HarlemLive <*http://www.harlemlive.org/*> and check out the Harlem Youth's voice on its Internet publication.

2. Have you heard of "Little Tokyo," a Japanese American community located in Los Angeles? Go to the Web site <*http://www.janet.org/janet_little_tokyo/ ja_little_tokyo.html*> and feel a sense of the community through the list of activities, location map, and related links to Japanese American culture.

Additional Readings

1. Basso, K. (1990). To give up on words: Silence in the Western Apache culture. In D. Carbaugh (Ed.), *Cultural communication and intercultural contact* (pp. 303–320). Hillsdale, NJ: Lawrence Erlbaum.

2. Anderson, P. A. (1999). *Nonverbal communication: Forms and functions*. Mountain View, CA: Mayfield.

3. Morris, D. (1994). *Bodytalk: The meaning of human gestures*. New York: Crown Trade Paperbacks.

Popular Culture and Intercultural Communication

The essays in this part emphasize the place of popular culture in understanding intercultural communication. Popular culture, from movies and television shows to sports and music, can be an important arena for intercultural interaction. In our personal lives we engage with popular culture on a daily basis. In many industrialized societies, there is almost no escape from the influence of popular culture. Although we can negotiate our consumption of some popular culture—by not watching particular television programs or movies, or by refusing to buy and read certain magazines or newspapers—we cannot entirely avoid it.

From advertisement to music to sports, popular culture surrounds us. This means that we need to consider the ways in which our knowledge and perception of other groups is shaped by popular culture. How are cultural groups portrayed in popular culture? For example, images of the United States seen in movies overseas may influence social attitudes toward U.S. citizens. Some cultural groups within the United States are portrayed very negatively or very minimally in popular culture. How does this affect intercultural encounters with these groups?

The following essays examine the cultural implications of popular culture, showing how it can be instrumental in shaping images of racial and ethnic groups and how it can contribute to the invisibility of particular groups. They also help us understand how we can use popular culture to think about interpersonal, social, and even international intercultural relations.

In "Cultural Differences in the Perceptions of Sports Mascots," Janis L. King addresses an issue that has plagued, perplexed, and confused many: Is the use of Native Americans as sports mascots problematic? King follows a campaign to end this use and analyzes the persuasive strategies used—trying to educate non-Indians about these racist practices and the disrespect shown by imitating and appropriating native religious and cultural practices. She then explains why the campaign ultimately failed. She identifies the role of power, especially that power held by team owners and fans, as central in the continued use of Native American mascots.

We then move to television. Ellen Sieter, in her essay "Different Children, Different Dreams: Racial Representations in Advertising," looks at issues of representation in advertising. She argues that U.S. advertising, and especially advertisements with children, perpetuate notions of racial divisions by emphasizing White-Other differences in ads. She shows how the notion of Whiteness is construed as normal and tied to the American Dream, while non-Whites are marked as "different." Sieter concludes that more attention should be given to the ideological underpinnings of representations of race and ethnicity in advertising.

In "Looking at the Front Door: Exploring Images of the Black Male on MTV's *The Real World*," Mark P. Orbe and Mark C. Hopson discuss how African American men were portrayed in the *The Real World* TV series. Orbe and Hopson found that although the producers/directors chose a diverse group of young people each season to live together in a different city, they also tended to select Black men whose personas were likely to evoke tension and they used selective editing to create characters that perpetuated negative stereotypes. Through an analysis, the authors identify common themes: The Black men were portrayed as angry, emotionally unstable, a violent threat, and sexually aggressive.

In "*The Siege* and American Media Portrayals of Arabs and Moslems," Marouf Hasian Jr. explores some media portrayals of Arabs and Moslems in Anglo American popular culture. Through a rhetorical analysis of *The Siege*, Hasian argues that this film perpetuates the stereotyping of Arabs and Moslems as potential terrorists or the exotic Other. This essay illustrates how even well-meaning producers and actors can inadvertently recirculate negative portrayals that denigrate marginalized communities.

22 Cultural Differences in the Perceptions of Sports Mascots
A Rhetorical Study of Tim Giago's Newspaper Columns

JANIS L. KING

Every fall, two sporting activities, baseball's World Series and professional football, draw public attention. But it was not until the fall of 1991 that these received media coverage for something other than the actual games. With the Atlanta Braves reaching the World Series and the Washington Redskins' winning record came attention to their mascots.

Native Americans protested the use of names and rituals that ridiculed Native American traditions. One person who publicly voiced opposition was Tim Giago, the editor-in-chief and publisher of *Indian Country Today*. There are three purposes for studying Giago. The first is to discuss the strategies employed in arguing that sports teams should discontinue the use of words, mascots, dress, objects, caricatures, and actions that pertain to Native Americans. The debate about mascots and regalia is a continuing exigence. Native Americans again protested at the 1995 World Series when the Atlanta Braves and Braves fans' infamous tomahawk chop, tom-toms, and turkey feathers met the Cleveland Indians and Chief Wahoo, with his huge nose and wide grin. Giago (1996) continues to write concerning Native Americans allowing their "proud name to be dragged through the mud" (p. A4). Second, this study seeks to analyze cross-cultural rhetoric that has many audiences—Native American and non–Native American. More rhetorical situations are developing that require one piece of persuasion to be designed for many cultures; consequently, differences in culture and perceptions need to be addressed. And third, this study illustrates the use of Smith and Lybarger's (1996) suggestions in reconstructing Bitzer's (1968, 1980) rhetorical situation.

In order to complete this discussion, 11 of Tim Giago's columns ("Notes From Indian Country") will be examined. These articles date from September 25, 1991, to August 11, 1993. All appeared in *Indian Country Today* (formerly *The Lakota Times*), a weekly newspaper founded in July 1981, and were made available for syndication through the Knight-Ridder Tribune News Service. The text is not edited or changed based on the potential audience. It is estimated that at least 200 non-Indian newspapers reprint the columns each week, with the possibility of about 1,000 newspapers if all subscribing to the service did use their reprint option (A. Little Eagle, personal communication, December 9, 1996). As the 1991 World Series ended, Giago (1991c) wrote that his columns were developed to be "sound, intelligently made and educational" (p. A4). In addition, as a good editorial writer, he created a dialogue or debate that would make people want to comment.

A reconstructed model of a rhetorical situation will serve as the guide in discussing Giago's columns. In 1968, Lloyd Bitzer wrote about rhetorical situations in which the situation "calls the discourse into existence" (p. 2) and that consisted of three components: the exigence, "an imperfection marked by urgency" (p. 6) or reason to persuade; the rhetorical audience, "those persons who are capable of being influenced by discourse and of being mediators of change" (p. 8); and a set of constraints, "beliefs, attitudes, documents, facts, traditions, images, interests, motives" (p. 8). After several scholars critically responded to this initial discussion, Bitzer (1980) revised his original concept. But Smith and Lybarger (1996) believed that he still maintained a "bias against the social construction of reality" (p. 201) and that he did not acknowledge situations as a collection of perceptions that made the situation more subjective and less controlling than the objective, linear concept that Bitzer conceived. Smith and Lybarger employed some of Bitzer's revisions to extend the model of the rhetorical situation into the complex postmodern world. The reconstructed model then allowed for multiexigences that may be real as well as created by the rhetor; multiaudiences that may be capable of altering the situation though not necessarily in the same ways; and multiconstraints that develop from the many perceptions of the audiences. These multicomponents explained why a piece of rhetoric succeeds with one of the audiences but does not remove incongruity between the perceptions of the rhetor and those perceptions of another audience.

In each calendar year of this study, Tim Giago wrote about his exigences, his need to persuade. He (1991b) wrote:

> Isn't it amazing when things I have been writing about for years suddenly are given a national focus. . . . The media has centered its attention on whether the sham rituals and painted faces in the stands at Braves' baseball games border on racism. In our minds (Indians) it does, . . . (p. A4)

A week later, after being on a radio talk show, Giago (1991c) extended his discussion to answer the question, Why now?

> A common question was, "Why are Indians jumping on this issue all of a sudden when they haven't said anything all of these years?" The fact of the matter is, we have been saying something all of these years but no one was listening, . . . It all came to a head when the Atlanta Braves won the pennant and then went on to the World Series. Out of the woodwork, on national television, many of us saw for the first time the now infamous "tomahawk chop." (p. A4)

So why are Native Americans upset? Millions of television viewers in the United States as well as other countries are seeing non–Native Americans ridiculing and making light of Indian dress, songs and chants, dance, and sacred traditions.

A year later, Giago (1992a) simply stated: "Well, another football season has just begun and this is my annual column about mascots. The battle isn't so uphill anymore" (p. A4) because Indians' concerns are receiving national media coverage. And by February 4, 1993, he simply noted that "Indians as mascots has been an issue with most American Indians for many years. . . . It has just become public knowledge over the past two years when the

national media finally focused on our complaints" (p. A4). Racism, ridiculing Indian religious and sacred traditions, and Indians as mascots provided the reasons for Giago's attempts to convince team owners and fans who did not (and still do not) see the use of Indian mascots as a problem. In addition, Giago had to address Native Americans who did not view the mascot issue as a problem or who were manufacturing and selling Indian regalia to the sports teams as well as Native Americans who supported Giago's position and were picketing at games. Consequently, his persuasive commentaries had to be developed with many audiences in mind.

The articles contained several arguments to convince fans and team owners to discontinue the use of Indian mascots and regalia. Giago's comments centered around two topics: discrimination based on and insensitive to skin color and insensitivity to religion. The primary strategy that he used in organizing and presenting these arguments was to educate individuals. Giago (1991a) provided examples of new team names to illustrate the offensiveness and unlikelihood of the use of stereotypes associated with different races and cultures:

> Just think of the pageantry the [San Francisco] Forty Niners could add to their half-time show if their team was the "Yellowskins." A mascot dressed as a mandarin could leap about the infield while the fans in the stands could paint their faces yellow, wear long pigtails, and attempt to sing ancient Oriental songs while bashing a giant gong. . . . "Redskin" fans see nothing wrong in waltzing about wearing feathers, toting imitation Pipestone pipes, beating miniature drums, sporting painted faces, and conducting themselves in other bizarre ways that insult the traditions, culture and spirituality of the First Americans. . . . Suppose the Washington Redskins . . . did change their names to "Blackskins." Would the fans in the stands feel comfortable painting their faces black, wearing Afro wigs and otherwise carrying out stereotypical activities that are supposedly characteristic of blacks? Not on your life. . . . (p. A4)

Giago (1991c) later continued the analogy when he discussed his participation on a radio talk show:

> One lady called and said she was a Cub Scout leader and she often has her Cubs dress up as In-

dians so they can get the feel of being a part of another culture. I asked her if she also had them paint their faces black, wear African attire, and learn to say "B'wana." Utterly horrified she said, "Why of course not. That would be insulting to black people." (p. A4)

Giago's educational approach in showing that people would not dress up and act like other minorities should have made team owners and fans more sensitive to Indian concerns. If fans would not dress up as other minorities because it would be offensive, then the same should hold true for American Indians. But the persuasion did not succeed. Fans stuck turkey feathers in their hair and performed humorous versions of acts and gestures. Team owners did not change names or mascots. Giago, consequently, took a different approach in 1993.

Interpretation of words and symbols often creates problems cross-culturally because of differences in perceptions. In a column entitled "What's in a word? Racism," Giago (1993b) educated readers about the meaning of the word "redskin":

> The word "redskin" comes to us from the slang of the early, white hunters and trappers. When a bounty was placed upon Indians, the hunters and trappers brought in their grisly trophies of scalps, ears, scrotums, and the severed breasts of Indian women along with their other pelts. They would say, "Here's a beaver skin, raccoon skin, ermine skin and this here one's a redskin." (p. A4)

How many White fans would have a similar reaction to the term "whiteskins" if their ancestors had been hunted and skinned for money and for extermination? Giago wanted the fans to understand the history of the word "redskin" and the negative connotation the word has for American Indians.

If arguments pointing out racism and word etymology would not work, perhaps a plea and examples of a religious nature would make team owners and fans more understanding of Native American objections. Giago (1991b) called the various activities performed by a team mascot and the fans "sham rituals" and suggested that these performances were "direct attacks upon the spirituality (religion) of the Indian people" (p. A4). He then employed an anal-

ogy using the New Orleans Saints as a way to show a comparison between religions:

> For instance, suppose Saints' fans decided to emulate Catholicism as part of their routine. What if they carried crosses, had a mascot dressed up like the Pope, spread ashes on their foreheads, and displayed enlarged replicas of the sacramental bread of Holy Communion while drinking from chalices filled with wine? (1991b, p. A4)

He referred to the Christian Bible and the proverb "Do unto others as you would have them do unto you." He (1991b) ended his comparison by asking "Would God-fearing Christians use sports mascots that would insult the Jewish people, Muslims, Buddhists, Shintoists, Hindus or any other minority religious group?" (p. A4). By referring to the religions of team owners and fans, Giago hoped to change people's perceptions so that consequently they would understand the reasons for Indians' objections to current practices of not only the Atlanta Braves and Washington Redskins, but also the Cleveland Indians and Kansas City Chiefs.

Giago (1993c) continued his religious comparison referring to the Fighting Irish of Notre Dame, the Celtics of Boston, and the San Diego Padres:

> The "Irish" were named from the inside by Jesuit priests who were themselves Irish. The Celtics were also named from within. The avid fans of these teams do not jump up and down in the stands pretending to be Irishmen or Celtics. They also do not insult the religion or the spirituality of the Irish or Celts. . . . No, the Padres' fans do not make fun of a religious order in supporting this team. They do not dress up as priests or use religious symbols and artifacts to enhance their mascot. . . . It's the things the fans do not do that makes the world of difference. (p. A4)

Giago (1993c) then completed the comparison when he reviewed the activities of fans for teams with Indian mascots:

> However, the fans do dress up like Indians, they do paint their faces in Day-glow paint and stick turkey feathers in their hair. They do attempt to sing what they believe to be Indian war chants, and they do use a deadly weapon, the tomahawk, to make threatening gestures. (p. A4)

If fans do not do these acts for teams based on various religions and ethnic groups, then they should not perform acts based on American Indian religions.

By 1993 some university and college teams had changed their names and mascots to eliminate the use of Indian images and objects. But no professional team had made any effort. Giago published a letter that he had written to Ted Turner, the owner of the Atlanta Braves, in response to Turner's comments that he did not see any problems with the use of Indian clothing, objects, and chants. Giago (1993a) explained the meaning of a feather:

> At the end of the ceremony [Sun Dance], most of the other participants gave the boy [only 8 years old] an eagle feather. The eagle, a messenger between the people and *Wakan Tanka* (God), is sacred. Its feathers bestow honor and wearing its feathers on your head lifts your thoughts from the earth to a sacred place. . . . Feathers are given only at times of great honor—a graduation, a naming ceremony, after saving someone's life or after serving honorably in the defense of this nation. . . .
> We all know that the easiest way to destroy someone's pride in something is to make light of it, to belittle it, to insist that it is not important. Just as you and your fans insist that mimicking of Indians and Indian ways is only for sport and should not offend. (p. A4)

Giago used instruction about the meaning of the feather as a way to convince Turner and fans to make changes based on religion. This completed his strategy of illustrating racism, language and meanings, and religious ridicule.

Giago (1993d) summarized his arguments developed to convince non–Native Americans to change the mascots:

> American Indians are a living, breathing, vital race of people. One hundred years ago, when colleges and high schools began to use Indians as mascots for their sporting teams, America as a whole believed Indians were about to become extinct. But that never happened. The original idea was to honor a dying race. (p. A4)

But this is no longer the case (Giago, 1996). Native Americans are here and many are offended by Indian mascots and by fans who ridicule Indians' beliefs, religions, and traditions.

Giago's messages were designed to use common beliefs and values (discrimination is bad; respect people's religions; do unto others) that could assist in readjusting team owners' and fans' perceptions and make the exigence real to them. Only when this audience perceived the mascots as a problem would change occur. But these people were not the only audiences that he had to address in his columns. Native Americans composed another element of the reading audience.

In the same articles Giago also educated Native American audiences. Native Americans who were protesting at the games already viewed the exigence as real and only needed Giago's ideas as further reinforcement that they were correct in their actions. Giago's comments served to unify and encourage them. But Giago needed a more pragmatic style when addressing the other two Native American audiences. One such group felt that the mascot issue was not a major concern and that there were far more serious problems to solve, such as drug and alcohol use, poverty, and suicide. The other Native American audience consisted of those who manufactured and sold cheap versions of Indian regalia and objects. Giago used religion, profiteering, and long-term effects on children in educating these groups.

On October 23, 1991, Giago called the various things that fans perform as imitation Indians "sham rituals" (p. A4), including "wearing of feathers, smoking of so-called peace pipes, beating of tom-toms, fake dances, horrendous attempts at singing Indian songs, the so-called war whoops, and the painted faces" (p. A4). He claimed that these actions were "direct attacks upon the spirituality (religion) of the Indian people" (p. A4). Religion and tradition are extremely important in Native American cultures, so reminding those who felt that there was no problem about the religious significance served to change the perceptions of the uncommitted.

A week later Giago (1991c) wrote about the Eastern Cherokees who were manufacturing tomahawks for the Atlanta Braves. He noted that a group from the Eastern Cherokees had been on CNN and had discussed the money that they were making. Giago described this interview: "This little charade by the Eastern Cherokee was used by many white callers to support their ignorance and bigotry. Profiteering isn't peculiar to the white race" (p. A4). This line of argument was continued in an editorial entitled "We are humans, never mascots" (1991), which argued,

> We must consider those Indian people who would profit at the expense of their own culture and spirituality by selling sacred artifacts to tourists or to professional sporting teams as traitors to their own kind. We can think of no other way to phrase this. . . . Surely there are other items these profiteers can sell that will not be used to degrade or insult us. (p. A4)

Giago's ("We are humans," 1991) last appeal concerned Princess Pale Moon, an imitation "Indian" who sings at Redskins games played in Washington, D.C., and fans' pre-game behavior. The editorial stated that Native Americans protesting outside of the stadium were being spat upon by both White and Black fans arriving at the game and that this action is "a situation all grassroots Indians should find intolerable" (p. A4). The final plea appeared at the end of the editorial: "We must stand together as Indian people to bring this disgraceful use of our heritage and our race to promote fun and games for black and white sports fans to an end. These racial slurs and insults must cease!" (p. A4). The editorial attempted to change perceptions of the two Native American audiences so that they would believe the exigence to be an imperfection that must be changed.

The following year Giago (1992a) referred to a petition presented to the federal government that was initiated by seven well-known and respected Native Americans. By using "experts," Giago attempted to convince other Native Americans that they, too, should support the elimination of Indians as mascots. A couple of the names on the petition (Vine Deloria, Jr., and Manley Begay, Jr.) would be known to some people who are not Native Americans, but all of the petitioners would be more credible to Indians. Giago wrote:

> "Those guys" took a look at seven Washington Redskin trademarks and said, "Whoa!" The old war horse Vine Deloria, a man active in Indian affairs for more than 30 years, saw a fly in the ointment. The federal government cannot issue

federal trademark registrations on matters that are offensive or disparaging. . . . The petition found these trademark names to be "pejorative, derogatory, denigrating, offensive, scandalous, contemptuous, disreputable, disparaging and racist." (p. A4)

Giago (1993e) used an expert later when he discussed Native American Ben Nighthorse Campbell, a United States Senator from Colorado. Campbell attempted to get Jack Kent Cooke, owner of the Washington Redskins, to change the name of the team by introducing legislation concerning Cooke's desire for federal land for a new stadium and by comparing the name "Redskins" to "'prairie nigger'" (p. A4). Perhaps the use of experts' perceptions of the mascot issue would cause Native Americans to view the exigence in the same way.

In October, Giago (1992b) wrote a column in response to his appearance on the *Oprah Winfrey Show*. Giago suggested that selling products that demeaned Indians was affecting the self-esteem of Native American children. He concluded:

> There are always those Indians who are out of step with the majority. They call whenever I do a radio talk show and say, "I'm part Cherokee (or Chippewa, or Aztec) and I don't mind being a mascot." Every time this has happened, the caller has always admitted to having been raised in a totally white environment, never living on an Indian reservation, and having lost all touch with their heritage. And yet, these are the people the media turns to when pointing out that some Indians don't mind being used as mascots. (p. A4)

Giago clearly discredited these Native Americans as well as the media because these spokespersons have a White person's perception of the exigence rather than an Indian perception. It was hoped that Native Americans would change their perceptions of these spokespersons.

In addition, Giago (1993d) compared the Indian struggle over the mascot issue to the beginning of the Civil Rights movement in the 1950s and 1960s when Rosa Parks refused to give up her bus seat to a White person:

> Educating America has also included educating some of our own people. Indians, like any other ethnic group, can become conditioned to bending

to the will of the majority. Please recall that it wasn't that long ago when white America was singing about the happy and contented "darkies" lolling about the little cabin floor. . . . The process of educating the non-Indian means educating some of our own people at times. (p. A4)

Giago concluded by reinforcing the need not only to educate Whites in general and team owners in particular but also to reach those Indians who were not supporting the protest.

Two questions need to be answered to evaluate Giago's columns: (1) Why use the strategy of education? and (2) Did Giago's strategy work in changing perceptions and eliminating Indian sports mascots?

First, the strategy of education allowed Giago to use one column to reach all audiences because the lack of knowledge about the demeaning and denigrating nature of the teams' mascots applied to the various reading audiences. Giago (1992a) wrote that "it has always been a matter of educating the masses. I've always believed that if white and black people knew why we objected to being used as mascots, they would understand" (p. A4). Giago believed that readers, once informed, would alter their beliefs and subsequently want to change patterns of behaviors.

Second, the educational strategy was an ideal choice because it allowed Giago to address the issue of Native Americans joining together to protest in a unified manner. To restore unity was very important because internal division created only confusion. If Native Americans did not see the mascots as a concern, why should non–Native Americans perceive them as a problem? By reminding Native Americans about religious traditions, the meanings of the feather, songs, and drums, and by using respected Native Americans as support for his ideas, he forced these two nonsupporting audiences to address and rethink their decisions.

The second question of importance to this discussion is whether Giago succeeded in his persuasion. All of the changes in the use of Indian mascots have been at the high school and university levels. Stanford University now has the cardinal as a mascot and St. Johns University is no longer referred to as the Redmen. But no professional sports team has made any attempt to change the names or items sold at the stadiums. Fans of these teams still dress as Indians and perform imitation rituals. Ignorance and a lack of understanding still prevail. The only indication of some success in reaching a team owner is with Ted Turner. One of Turner's cable networks produced several made-for-television movies about Indians of the past (Geronimo, the Iroquois Confederacy, and Crazy Horse) using Native American actors. The Braves, however, are still the Braves and the tomahawk chop is still part of fan ritual at games.

The educational strategy with team owners and fans who ultimately control the language and actions did not work. Why did pointing out racial insults, redefining terms, and an appeal to religious insensitivity fail? The answer is found in Smith and Lybarger's postmodern description of a rhetorical situation.

Smith and Lybarger (1996) identified two questions that come out of the complexity of multiple exigences and audiences and the resulting constraints as the rhetor attempts to achieve congruence with the many audiences: (1) "Is the speaker's assessment of an exigence the same as the audience's?" and (2) "Did the speaker make adjustments for differences with audience regarding the perception of and felt interest in an exigence?" (p. 210). Giago perceived the sports mascots as a problem but his non–Native American audience did not. Consequently, as Smith and Lybarger noted, Giago had to create an exigence for this group. He attempted this creation by pointing out (1) the discrimination in using Native Americans as mascots when Whites would never do such a thing with other ethnic or religious groups, (2) the religious ridicule associated with attire and actions, and (3) the meanings of certain names and actions. But Giago failed in this creation of an exigence because he did not make adjustments for the different perceptions and did not take into consideration the felt interests of the non-Indian audience. Native Americans raised in their tribal heritages, such as Giago, have different perceptions from non–Native Americans and even Native Americans raised in a White European-based culture. Native Americans with a strong heritage viewed fans' actions as ridiculous and almost sacrilegious, whereas non–Native

Americans believed that these actions honored those who demonstrated courage and perseverance in the face of adversity and enemies. Giago did not deal with this "honor" perception; consequently, non–Native Americans, who believed that they were representing courageous behavior, did not change their perceptions, and thus would not see the exigence as real.

In addition, Giago ignored the felt interests of the non–Native American audience. He did mention African Americans and Asian Americans in one of the early columns and may have made the few fans of these racial groups more sensitive to the exigence, but team owners and the majority of the fans are White. And it is these individuals who have the power to eliminate the mascots, clothing, and actions. Giago did not provide any interests to which the owners and fans could relate. He did not address the financial factors, including profit losses, that team owners and players would incur by changing mascots and creating new artifacts to sell to fans. Most of the fans have not had their civil rights denied or ridiculed; therefore, they have no direct experience with discrimination or lack of recognition or both. These individuals, thus, are not able to transfer abstract beliefs and values to real-life felt interests. They have not experienced the same "life" and, consequently, do not have similar perceptions and worldviews. Those with the money (team owners) and those in the majority (White fans) are traditionally, in the American culture, the ones with the power to change the exigence. In this case, the exigence has no power for the non–Native Americans because it is not perceived. Giago did not deal with the interests of this group, which resulted in no changes in perceptions. The groups remained in a fragmented stage.

Based on this essay's study, there are a few suggestions for intercultural communication. First, rhetors must include factors that relate to the various audiences' perceptions and felt interests in order to create congruence with each group. Although the ideal would be to have distinct pieces of rhetoric for each audience, this is not practical in today's media coverage. Second, the education strategy should work well for others if various perceptions are included because it tends to make people less defen-

sive. But information must be provided that appeals to the felt interests of all audiences. Third, rhetors must recognize which audiences truly have the power to make changes and then make the exigence "real" for these groups by modifying their perceptions and including their interests. If the rhetor's purpose is to modify or remove the exigence, the rhetor in a postmodern world must reach congruence with those who have societal power, a factor that Smith and Lybarger did not deal with specifically. Fourth, in many instances of intercultural persuasion, rhetors ignore, intentionally or unintentionally, the lack of agreement in perceptions. Rhetors of any race or culture involved in intercultural communication must deal with worldviews other than their own. To fail to recognize this means persuasion and communication will not succeed.

References

Bitzer, L. F. (1968). The rhetorical situation. *Philosophy and Rhetoric, 1*, 1–14.

Bitzer, L. F. (1980). Functional communication: A situational perspective. In E. White (Ed.), *Rhetoric in transition: Studies in the nature and uses of rhetoric* (pp. 21–38). State College: Pennsylvania State University Press.

Giago, T. (1991a, September 25). Pigskin mascots: A seasonal insult. *The Lakota Times*, p. A4.

Giago, T. (1991b, October 23). Mascots, spirituality and insensitivity. *The Lakota Times*, p. A4.

Giago, T. (1991c, October 30). Ignorance adds insult to injury. *The Lakota Times*, p. A4.

Giago, T. (1992a, September 16). Keeping looking over your shoulders, you "R———-s." *The Lakota Times*, p. A4.

Giago, T. (1992b, October 15). Tuning into an important topic on a talk show stage. *Indian Country Today*, p. A4.

Giago, T. (1993a, February 4). Waiting for reply from broadcaster Ted Turner. *Indian Country Today*, p. A4.

Giago, T. (1993b, March 10). What's in a word? Racism. *Indian Country Today*, p. A4.

Giago, T. (1993c, May 5). *Denver Post* still doesn't get it. *Indian Country Today*, p. A4.

Giago, T. (1993d, June 23). Pepsico stand against mascots is the right one baby—uh-huh! *Indian Country Today*, p. A4.

Giago, T. (1993e, August 11). Racist cartoons: We are not amused. *Indian Country Today,* p. A4.

Giago, T. (1996, December 16–23). Seminoles allow proud name to be dragged through the mud of Florida State football field. *Indian Country Today,* p. A4.

Smith, C. R., & Lybarger, S. (1996). Bitzer's model reconstructed. *Communication Quarterly, 44,* 197–213.

We are humans, never mascots. (1991, November 13). *The Lakota Times,* p. A4.

Key Terms

exigence	perception
felt interests	racism
mascots	rhetor
naming	rhetoric
Native American	sports

Discussion Questions

1. King's essay suggests that one piece of rhetoric may have many audiences of different cultural backgrounds and with different concerns. What other rhetorical situations exist that involve such audiences?

2. King uses Giago's columns to illustrate how exigences may be real to one cultural group but must be created for another cultural group. Can you think of other social contexts or issues in which this creation must occur?

3. What suggestions for change would you give to Mr. Giago in order to make his columns more "real" for non–Native American audiences?

4. What does King's essay tell us about cultural perceptions? Can a person of one cultural background really understand the perceptions of a person from a different culture?

5. In King's essay, names and the various perceptions associated with the names cause conflict for those involved. Can you think of other intercultural situations, such as generational differences, in which naming may be one of the factors in the conflict?

23 Different Children, Different Dreams
Racial Representation in Advertising[1]
ELLEN SEITER

Advertisers like to use children—and not only in advertisements for toys and diapers. Babies are attention grabbers; they are especially good at catching the eyes of women consumers who so often constitute the target market. Perhaps most important for the cautious advertiser, children rarely offend. Picturing children allows advertisers to call up rich, cherished associations: nostalgia, love, the fullness of the future, the comfort of home, the pleasures of family life. The use of children is a way to suggest many of the values that advertisers routinely associate with their products: newness, innocence, energy, rejuvenation, mildness, happiness, protection. Increasingly, corporate image advertising draws on images of children to suggest kindness, responsibility, benevolence, and the ordinariness of their concerns.

———

Symbolic connotations aside, there is nothing innocent about the use of children in advertising. Each infant crawling across the screen carries a heavy load of ideological projections. The scene in a commercial for Luv's diapers of a blonde girl tempting a boy with an apple juice bottle is typical of the gender projections found in children's advertising. The regal infant, white-skinned and dressed in white, picnicking with mom and dad beside the tennis court, expresses "Cadillac style" and the assurance of lifetime affluence. Our common sense notions of childhood are tied up with ideas about social Darwinism, genetics, inheritance, nature vs. nurture. Children so often grow up to fulfill the status quo that the representation of children is especially good at "naturalizing" social relations, by making unequal destinies seem inevitable. After all, boys so often grow up to be boys. For the blonde blue-eyed laughing boy, advertisements project dreams of power and success. For the dancing, light-skinned Black girl no such future is ever envisioned.

Most families on series television are upper middle class; poor and working-class children appear to us only on news and tabloid shows, where their stories of victimization mark them off—as though members of another nation entirely, as of the Third World—from the beautiful, happy faces of the advertisements. Overall, people of color are usually represented through the frame of "problems," which is why they are seen more often on the news. Television so often portrays suffering children as Black and Hispanic that it has been hard for the white middle class in the 1980s to comprehend the fact that staggering numbers of mothers and children who live in poverty are white.

The Geography of Whiteness

Let me begin with a discussion of white babies in mass-market advertising and by calling attention to those advertisements where children of color never appear. Tessa Perkins has argued that you must look at stereotypes of dominant groups to understand the latent content of stereotypes of oppressed groups. Positive, laudatory stereotypes about white men, for example, may be as persistent as pejorative stereotypes of Black women. The association of reasoned authority with white men is as strong as the association of heightened sexuality with Black women. Positive stereotypes are as important as negative ones in defining the field of what the media communicate to us about race. As Hazel Carby has put

it, "Stereotypes only appear to exist in isolation while actually depending on a nexus of figurations which can be explained only in relation to each other" (Carby, 1987, p. 20).

Dreams of a great and inevitable destiny begin at infancy for whites as seen in print advertising. Their preciousness is underscored by allusions to their future economic value. A Johnson advertisement shows a bare white buttocks under the headline, "One day this little bottom may sit on the board of directors. Today it needs Johnson's." (The girl's version of the advertisement reads "One day this soft hair may be colored and permed," across the forehead of a blonde, blue-eyed girl in extreme close up: a typical example of the strenuous gender identification of all children in advertisements.) "Power Play" reads the bold headline over a picture of a blonde, grimacing boy ruggedly dressed in flannel shirt, jeans and thermal undershirt; as he drives his *Power Wheels*. Playskool advertises "Alphie II My First Computer," with a picture of a red-haired boy, gazing directly into the camera, above the line "We've got a Genius for Making Learning Fun." In a two-page advertisement for the Socrates "Educational Video System," a smiling blonde boy holds up his test with an A plus marked prominently in red; the opposite page reads, " 'Pay attention to the young and make them just as good as possible'— Socrates." The preoccupation with children's intelligence and achievement spills over into all product categories: "Kids are brighter than they used to be" promises Vivid bleach, above three fashionably dressed and smiling white kids.

One of the most common stereotypes of white infants and small children in advertising is the go-getter. The go-getter is not a stereotype available for the representation of Black children, who tend to be shown in advertising as passive observers of their white playmates. If Black children were pictured in the same aggressive postures used for white boys, the available stereotype with which they are likely to be associated by whites is the "pushy" Black or the hoodlum. Thus the same set of behaviors, descriptively speaking, can be negatively or positively evaluated in racial stereotypes.

When I began looking for children in commercials, I was struck by the remarkable stability of images of white children, how often blondes were cast in commercials, and how similar they all looked. It is because "a dominant group's position is relatively stable and unproblematic" that images of blonde children seem to have remained largely unchanged for a century (Perkins, 1979, p. 148). It is very difficult for whites to see how whiteness *as a norm* informs all media representation, "as if it is the natural, inevitable, ordinary way of being human," Richard Dyer explains (Dyer, 1988, p. 44).

> "White is not anything really, not an identity, not a particularizing quality, because it is everything—white is no color because it is all colors. This property of whiteness to be everything and nothing, is the source of its representational power. . . ." (Dyer, 1988, p. 45)

This is why it is easy to pick out children of color in advertisements, but harder to see their absence in all-white commercials. The perspective of whiteness makes it impossible to see difference within minority groups. Overwhelmingly, advertisers use a single Black to signify "minority," while whites are portrayed as endlessly varied, individual, even quirky and idiosyncratic.[2] Advertisers utterly fail to register the tremendous range of differences *among* Hispanics, *among* Blacks, *among* Asians, *among* American Indians.

"The invisibility of whiteness," writes Richard Dyer, "masks whiteness itself as a category." One of the most opaque masks of whiteness is the code of "nostalgia." Norman Rockwell's illustrations made a comeback in 1989 commercials to sell breakfast cereal and station wagons, and they offer a good example of the representation of whiteness as innocence. Rockwell's work epitomizes many aspects of the nostalgic myth of America: small town, parents and children together, naughtiness in boys, flirtatiousness in girls, the institutions of school, church, Boy Scouts—everyone is white.

The classroom is a favorite location for the nostalgia motif. The set design—bathed in yellow light, flag in the front of the class and globe on the teacher's desk—places the classroom in a mythical and decidedly pre-integration past. This is made explicit in a US West commercial where the music classroom of the past (bathed in soft white light, resembling an illustration from Laura Ingalls Wilder's *Little House on the Prairie*) gives way to the "modern" classroom where the music teacher, an Asian woman, instructs via a video monitor. It is the white girl, center frame, who performs for the teacher. The Asian girl seated next to her listens silently, politely.[3] In a commercial for Eggo waffles, the classroom is visually the same as the room in the US West "flashback," and again every face is white. A boy gets up in front of the class to explain his "invention"—he has remodelled his toaster to prevent his brother from stealing his waffles—displaying the smartness and ingenuity of young white boys.

When television commercials are set in the home, in the domestic sphere, we can predict with certainty that only white children will be shown. Whenever commercials take place at the kitchen table, or on the front porch, whites are pictured alone. White children may be pictured with Black children playing in public (albeit in a restricted set of locations, as I shall describe below) but whenever the parents or grandparents are present, if the space is personal, intimate, familial, scenes are totally segregated by race. Children of color are orphaned on television commercials, excluded from the loving grasp of parents, restricted to token membership in a peer group, relegated to the status of "neighborhood kids" as Mattel named one of its multi-racial ensembles of dolls.

Exploration and Discovery

Commercials targeted directly at children, those shown during Saturday morning television, for example, differ in important ways from general-market commercials featuring children in the cast. Adults are only rarely present, and parents are subjected to various forms of rebellion—even humiliation. In a Cornflakes commercial, a redhaired girl sits at the kitchen table refusing to speak to her mother—she answers by holding up signs, "Yes" and "No" in a strategy to persuade her mother to let her eat grown-up cereal—Cornflakes. In another advertisement, a boy of six or seven sneaks up on his father quietly reading the paper on the porch, and snaps his picture (with a camera available through proof of purchase seals) at the very moment the father's toupee blows off.

. . . White boys are always cast as the adventurous, courageous "explorers"; while children of color are either excluded altogether, or are represented as passive, primitive, and ignorant. In a Nestle's Quik cartoon, two children in search of a schoolhouse, accompanied by a rabbit and polar bear as their guides, suffer an avalanche, then head into a diner for a spot of hot chocolate. A smiling Eskimo, so much a caricature that his eyes are drawn by straight lines, speechlessly and smilingly serves them. Silent, smiling, and in the background, this is the only Native American child I found on contemporary television commercials from 1988–1990. After drinking their Quik, the rabbit frightens the polar bear who runs through the wall of the igloo. The huge hole in the wall reveals to the now happy children that the school is within sight. In another version of the Quik advertisement, the scene is a space ship and all the child astronauts are white. The same is true of the junior explorers used for the "Dinosaur Hunt" for Chef-Boy-Ar-Dee and for the Chips-Ahoy "Expedition." In a mixture of horror and adventure genres, a group of children who are camped out in the "Fun Fruits Forest" tell ghost stories and "discover" Sunkist Fun fruits as skeletons and monsters jump out at them. One of the four children is a Black boy. He is once again seen only in long shot, our view of him partially obscured as he dances in the background.

Fanciful "exotic" adults populate live action advertisements also. In a Honeycomb commercial, the white children are visited by a magical strong man genie: a well-muscled shirtless Black man, turbanned, covered with jewelry. He is shot in extreme close up to emphasize his huge size, and he appears and disappears according to the children's whim. An inscrutable Asian man, "The Wisdom Tooth," recommends Crest toothpaste. An Indian man sings in English about potato chips baked by "Pequenos Keebleros," animated Keebler elves. In a commer-

cial for trash bags, a group of aged American Indians watch over children dressed in scouting uniforms as they pick up trash on a hillside. In close up, the chief nods approvingly then literally "vanishes," optically dissolving from the picture. "Leave the land as you found it," is the voice over's message. Thus, minority adults are relegated to the roles of supernatural companions and helpers, playing roles very similar to those of animated animal figures. Their representations are fixed in "orientalist" fairy tales (Said, 1978). Again, we need only re-cast these advertisements with a middle aged white man in any of these parts to recognize the racial problematic implicit in these images.

Together on Saturday Morning

A spot that launched the Nabisco cookie, Teddy Grahams, typifies the representation of white and black children together. This commercial, in thirty and fifteen second versions, has had a great deal of air play, both on Saturday morning and in the "early fringe" weekday slots. It has been shown hundreds of times during many different time periods, during and outside of Saturday morning. Three adult-sized Teddy Bears sing a version of Elvis's "Teddy Bear" ("I wanna be your Teddy Graham"). They perform on a glittery stage, wearing fashion sunglasses and holding microphones. Three children join them on stage: a white boy and girl and a black boy. (The children syntagmatically represent the three varieties of teddy grahams, chocolate, vanilla and cinnamon). As the children pop up behind the white piano that one of the bear musicians plays, eat cookies, and crowd into the spotlight, the Black boy is partially obscured from view by the piano or nearly pushed out of the frame by the other kids.

This commercial exemplifies many of the rules which seem to govern the representation of children of color in Saturday morning commercials. First, they are always outnumbered by whites. Most often three children are pictured—two whites and one African-American (white boy in center, Black boy on left, white girl on right, as in the Teddy Grahams commercial). Children of color are pictured singly on commercials, if at all. The minority child is seen left screen—the least dynamic portion of the frame according to design theory. The Black child is not given a speaking part and is seen mainly in group shots with white children, only once alone and never in facial close up. Like most Black models, the boy has been directed to smile broadly and act clownish, manic. (Sadness, frustration, or complaint are the prerogatives of whites.) These rules govern the representation of children in commercials across a broad range of advertising styles and narratives.

Through casting, advertising glorifies white features, "good hair," light skin. Black feminists have described the oppressiveness of this beauty standard: to look as much like whites as possible. Toni Morrison has described a child's point of view in *The Bluest Eye* (Morrison, 1970). This tyranny of physical type is strongest in the representation of Black girls. When advertising the most feminine toys: baby dolls, modelling clay flowers, kitchens, toy commercials use white models. When girls are really being middle-class girls—wearing long hair and traditional, pastel dresses, playing with dolls and flowers—they are always *white* girls. This is an extension of the taboo against representing children of color in the domestic space. Commercials such as those for "Bouncin' Babies" and "Fantastic Flower Basket" are typical of this genre. Merchandising as well as advertising excludes Black girls from the most strictly gender-coded types of play. An exception here is Mattel, which markets Black and Hispanic product lines extensively. In television commercials for a new "Style Magic," one African-American and two white girls appear together. Here the girls marvel over the voluptuous curly blonde hair of Barbie. It is unusual that the Black girl is given the largest speaking part, exclaiming over the fun of Barbie, enthusiastically describing her attributes. But the Black version of the doll is seen only in long shot, and is never admired or played with by the Black girl. In the final shot, the Black girl stands behind a seated white girl, fixing her hair.

Typically, advertisements express a hierarchy of race relations. White children are always the stars, African-American children the bit players. The superiority of white children is reinforced through visual composition and through gestural codes. Erving Goffman has noted how characters' "placement relative to one another will provide an index or mapping of their presumed *social* position relative to one another" (Goffman, 1976, p. 26). A four page advertisement for the Today's Kids series features four different pieces of play equipment: On the first page, five children of different ages direct their attention to various "activity centers" on the circular "Busy Center." Only the Black child has his back to the camera, his face turned away. On the second page girls play with the stove, the play phone, the vanity of the "Sweetheart Playhouse." Seven children appear, all of them white, with long curly hair. On the third page, the Merry-go-Round features three children playing. Again, it is the blonde children who smile and look directly into the camera, while the Black child has turned his head so that his face is completely out of view. Finally, on the last page, three boys play "All Star Basketball," and the Black boy is shown full face. His two white playmates are somewhat blurred as they go up for a shot but, they are twice the size and twice the age of the Black child.

Black children are routinely granted the authority of a privileged relation to sports and music. For example, Black children appear in nearly all the advertisements for infant sports shoes, thus emphasizing their presumably "inborn" athletic ability. A television commercial for Apple Jacks uses a rap soundtrack and a basketball game to envision the "teamwork" of whites and Blacks playing together. One of the Black boys makes the final slam dunk of the cereal box at the end: the only starring role repeatedly offered to Black boys. In a commercial for "Pocket Rockers," top-forty singles on miniature cassettes, a Black girl is given center stage, flanked by her white playmates as they dance down the street. Achievement in sports and in music are obviously a proud and valuable aspect of Black culture. But in advertising they are distorted because they appear not as aspects of culture but as innate, natural talents. They are the only arenas for achievement and ambition allowed Black children.

To understand the significance of this, we must return to the representation of white children. Cultivation of learning and creativity are the qualities advertisers associate with white children. It is especially significant that toy advertising that makes particular claims for developing creativity has only white actors. The commercial for Ohio Art's ZAKS (a lego-like building toy) features a rap soundtrack: but only whites play in the advertisements. The same is true of the new series of PlayDoh commercials. McDonald's has run a couple of Saturday morning advertisements where the link to the future is made explicit. In the first, "Report Card," a group of children is seen at school opening their report cards. The white children have a range of reactions—joy, excitement, fainting, grief. But the single Black boy is seen opening the card and rapidly closing it, in a quick shot in which his reaction is open to a variety of readings (shock? relief?). The kids then head off to McDonald's to recuperate. The Black boy joins them at the table, but he is seen only from the back in an over-the-shoulder-shot. A second advertisement, "Big Dreams," features a group of children discussing what they want to be when they grow up. A girl says, giggling, "I want to be a lawyer, or maybe a fashion designer." A song describes three of the dreams in flashback/fantasies—to be a dancer, rock-n-roller, rodeo rider. When we cut back to the scene at the table, two Black girls are briefly shown, moving in and out of frame, slightly out of focus.[4] They are not given speaking parts. The range of possibilities discussed by the kids: from Aerospace engineer, to Electrocardiogramtechnologist, are the province of the white kids. "Tomorrow belongs to you," advertising tells white children over and over again.

———

Advertising is one discourse that negotiates these contradictions; it must be seen as part of a complex of messages that children receive, along with school, religion, family, and so on.

———

The search for "positive images" is limited by ideology, a set of relations which include hierarchies based in class and gender. The work of the Burrell agency certainly offers more desirable images of African-American children than those offered in white advertisements. But the efforts of minority agencies are circumscribed by ideology and by the worry over offending white audiences. In focusing on the family in these commercials, they both answer and replicate the dominant media construction of minorities as a "problem." Since the Moynihan report of the 1960s, the media have explained the problem with Blacks as deriving from the absence of the father and the female-headed household (the Black matriarch). As many Black sociologists and feminists have explained, this thesis, which has been remarkably durable as an ideological construct, denies the possibility that Black poverty is created through white economic privilege (hooks, 1981, pp. 51–86). The history of slavery, the grossly inferior public education system, and employment discrimination vanish and the Black family is the source of the problem. These commercials "answer" the negative Black images produced by whites by picturing the Black middle-class family—with father present. But the terms of the representation are the same; we simply have the positive rather than the negative version of the stereotype. These issues have been heard in the debate over the *Cosby* show, the object of great suspicion (by white leftists) and wonder (by industry workers) because of its enormous popularity with whites and Blacks. While it has "normalized" the Black family, *Cosby* has been vigorously attacked for its upper-middle-classness, its materialism, its conspicuous consumption, its adoption of conventions from white family sitcoms (see Miller, 1988).

The Burrell commercials do what advertising does best: provide celebratory, utopian, unabashedly sentimental pictures of the family. They are important as an intervention, as an antidote, to the white advertising I have described here. But there is no such thing as a free lunch. The African-American community has had to badger McDonald's to purchase advertising time on Black-owned stations. Their huge profits are substantially due to Black consumers (and to Black employees). These "best" images of the Black family advertise a product indisputably dangerous to a community at risk of high blood pressure and heart disease.

———

Postscript: Studying Stereotypes

Many advertisers treat minority consumers no better than Columbus treated the Indians centuries ago. The comparison is apt because media audiences today are indeed, like the Indians, an economic colony, exploited and disregarded by a dominant group with little interest in their culture. The press and trade journals report that advertisers are paying increasing attention to minority audiences through target marketing. But when we consider advertising on network television and popular magazines it becomes clear that most advertising is for the general market, that is, for whites. To complain of stereotyping in advertising is to raise the two issues that Todorov discusses: the hierarchical representation of characters in advertisements, in which whites are always favored, and the erasure of difference, the incessant reworking and repetition of white values, scenarios, beliefs, and images, ideology.

Notes

1. This paper is based on a book chapter from *Sold Separately: Aspects of Children's Consumer Culture*. Winchester, MA, and London: Unwin Hyman, forthcoming.

2. Jews are an ideologically crucial exclusion here. Whiteness is Christian, usually WASP. One of the marks of anti-semitism is the obliteration of Jews from advertising images. Totally assimilated Jews do appear on some popular dramatic television shows, such as *LA Law* and *thirtysomething*.

3. Since the 1940s, Asians have been represented as a "Model Minority," a stereotype that is defined primarily by the fact that Asians are seen as different from and more desirable than African-Americans. Asian children usually conform to this model minority stereotype. Currently, the model minority stereotype seems to be undergoing a process of re-evaluation, and is now taking on the negative connotations of "drudge." The Asian student as drudge is seen as an "unfair" competitor with white college students (see Fong, 1989).

4. This imitation documentary style (handheld camera, imperfect framing, loss of focus) is frequently used to pan quickly past children of color. It is a way of signalling their presence, while "accidentally" passing them over.

References

Carby, H. (1987). *Reconstructing Womanhood: The Emergence of the Afro-American Woman Novelist*. New York: Oxford.

Dyer, R. (1988). "White." *Screen 29*(4), 44–65.

Fong, C. (1989). "The Model Minority and Shifts in the images of Chinese Americans, 1800–1930." Unpublished Ph.D. dissertation, University of Oregon.

Goffman, E. (1976). *Gender Advertisements*. New York: Harper and Row.

hooks, b. (1981). *Ain't I A Woman: Black Women and Feminism*. Boston: South End Press.

Marchand, R. (1985). *Advertising the American Dream*. Berkeley: University of California Press.

Miller, M. C. (1988). "Cosby Knows Best." *Boxed In*. Evanston: Northwestern University, pp. 69–78.

Morrison, T. (1970). *The Bluest Eye*. New York: Washington Square Press.

Perkins, T. E. (1979). "Rethinking Stereotypes." *Ideology and Cultural Production*. Eds. Michele Barrett, et al. New York: St. Martin's Press, pp. 135–159.

Said, E. (1978). *Orientalism*. London: Routledge & Kegan Paul.

Simpson, P., Ed. (1987). *Parents Talking Television*. London: Comedia.

Spivak, G. (1988). *In Other Worlds*. New York: Routledge.

Todorov, T. (1984). *The Conquest of America: The question of the other*. Trans. Richard Howard. New York: Harper and Row.

Key Terms

advertising stereotypes
race relations Whiteness
representation

Discussion Questions

1. What does Seiter mean by the "geography of Whiteness"? What other examples in popular culture contribute to this geography of Whiteness?

2. Seiter argues that Whiteness is invisible. In what ways is it invisible?

3. How does understanding the representations of Whiteness help us understand the representations of other ethnic groups?

4. Seiter argues that different characteristics are attributed in advertising to Whites and non-Whites. What are these different characteristics, and what are some possible implications of this differentiation for intercultural communication?

5. In what ways does advertising help us negotiate social meanings of race and ethnicity?

24 Looking at the Front Door
Exploring Images of the Black Male on MTV's The Real World
MARK P. ORBE and MARK C. HOPSON

In early 1992, the viewing public was introduced to MTV's newest form of innovative television programming—a series that promised to bring the real-life experiences of a diverse group of young people (18–25 years old) into the homes of millions. *The Real World* is described by the creator/producer as a show about "real people, undirected, sharing their lives" (Huriash, 1996, p. C25). The premise of the show is simple: MTV chooses seven individuals, representing diverse backgrounds, to reside rent-free in a house for 3 months while every aspect of their lives is taped by a multitude of cameras. The result is a Generation X fishbowl of sorts, a representation of American culture viewed by 60 million people in 52 countries every week, and a cult hit for MTV (Sakurari, 1996). Other popular "docudramas"—such as *Road Rules, Survivor, Making The Band,* and *Big Brother*—soon followed and continue to attract record-breaking numbers of viewers.

For many viewers (and scholars), one of the most intriguing aspects of these shows is the cultural diversity of each cast. In this regard, MTV's *The Real World* provides a glimpse into the social relations based on race/ethnicity, gender, sexuality, class, and religion. As each season approaches, the anticipation about cast members and house dynamics builds to the point where the focus of the initial episode is the front door of the house. Who will be in the house this year? How will this selectively diverse group of young people get along? Who will play what role? What drama(s) will define this season? Each season begins as seven new cast members enter through the door of their new house, and consequently ends when each exits through the same avenue. The focus of our essay is what occurs between these two points; specifically, we are interested in exploring how African American men who enter the *"Real World"* are portrayed on the show. How are their "characters" developed through the editing process—one that selectively narrows 3–5 months of video footage into approximately 11 hours of "reality"?

Earlier research (Orbe, 1998) analyzed the early portrayals of African American men on the first six seasons of *The Real World.* This analysis critiqued images of (1) Kevin, a 25-year-old writer/part-time teacher from Jersey City, New Jersey, who appeared on the first season in New York City; (2) David, a stand-up comic from Washington, D.C., who was part of the second season filmed in Los Angeles; (3) Mohammed, a cast member from the third season (San Francisco), who is a 24-year-old musician/singer; and (4) Syrus, a 25-year-old self-defined "playa" from Sacramento who appeared on the sixth season located in Boston.

In this essay we reexamine the previous critique of images presented for three additional African American male cast members who appeared in the seventh, eighth, and ninth seasons of *The Real World*. In short, we analyze media depictions of (1) Stephen, a student from U.C. Berkeley who was raised as a Black Muslim but converted to Judaism, from the Seattle cast; (2) Teck, a 22-year-old PK (preacher's kid) from Peoria, Illinois, who attended a HBCU (historically Black college university) before joining the Hawaii cast; and (3) David, from the New Orleans cast, who is a 4.0 student from the South Side of Chicago. (In order to differentiate "Davids," we use David [LA] and David [NO].) We analyze the images associated with these African American men in order to see if earlier stereotypes for Black men on the show were perpetuated, challenged, or altered. In short, then, this essay includes the most recent depictions of African American men and the ways they have appeared on *The Real World*.

Using Semiotics to Understand the Signifying Process

Semiotics is a methodological tool that can be used to study popular culture images. Semiotic analyses, like the one by Orbe and Strother (1996), can help us understand how hegemonic meaning is created for images of people of color in the mass media. According to Eco (1976), meaning is created and maintained when a signifier (or set of signifiers) is (are) closely associated with a particular concept, idea, or identity. For instance, in the United States, the Nike (Swoosh) symbol has no inherent meaning. However, over time—and through much media exposure—we have come to associate this symbol with certain signifiers (sports, athleticism, excellence, quality, etc.). The process of association is so powerful that some advertisements currently don't even show any references to athletics; they simply flash the logo, knowing that the audience will make the connection.

In our analysis, we use semiotics to try to understand how Black men on MTV's *The Real World* were associated with certain behaviors in ways that made it seem like these things were natural for all African American men. Our next sections spell out our interpretation of Black male signifiers on the show and explain how these impact the larger societal stereotypes that exist. At this point, it is important to understand that the insights contained in this essay summarize, as well as extend, earlier research that critiqued representations of black masculinity on *The Real World* (Orbe, 1998; Orbe, Warren, & Cornwell, 2001). While different interpretations are possible, we argue that the signifiers associated with Black men on the show reflect general stereotypes found in all aspects of U.S. popular culture.

Black Male Signifiers on *The Real World*

Given the seven African American male cast members across nine seasons of *The Real World,* many opportunities existed to display the great diversity of Black men in the United States. However, our analysis reveals the presentation of several signifiers that legitimized a general social fear of Black men. We illustrate how these African American male cast members have been represented as inherently angry, emotionally unstable or unpredictable or both, a violent threat, and sexually aggressive.

THE BLACK MALE AS INHERENTLY ANGRY

Throughout the course of each *Real World* season, viewers are provided with a brief window into the worlds of each cast member. Several common themes emerge when investigating the lived experiences of Black male cast members. We learn that most have come through a tough inner-city life and survived several hardships (i.e., being raised on welfare, not having a relationship with one's father, avoiding gangs, or other urban-related problems). In this context, the African American male is situated as well versed in the harsh realities of life lessons generally, and of a racist society specifically. Gradually, viewers are prompted to generalize that these sets of experiences help fuel an inherent anger in these men.

Through limited exposure to the African American men on *The Real World,* viewers are given some insight into the source that fuels Black male anger. This image is constructed through "diagnosis" by non–African American cast members, and most often comes from instances when the African American male cast members strive to educate the others on "what it's like to be a Black man in America." In each season, we see the familiar attempts of the lone Black man in the house to enlighten his roommates (and subsequently the television viewers) as to the various problems that Black men face on a daily basis. In this regard, other members of the house learn—some, for the first time—the impact that societal stereotypes have on African American men (e.g., being harassed by police in areas where they do not "belong"). Some cast members downplay the expression of African American men, citing similar struggles and hardships in their own lives (Dace, 1994). In different instances, we see these attempts to educate take a variety of forms. Kevin uses his poetry, confrontation of others, and less volatile means such as posting provocative thoughts on a bulletin board. David (LA) uses rap lyrics and his comedic talents to drive home some issues. Syrus uses metaphors during "teachable moments" to enlighten his housemates (e.g., discussing the negative connotations of the color Black using a casual pool game). In one way or another, all of the Black men on *The Real World* share varying yet similar sides and shades of themselves with others.

While these interactions served as a means to educate non–African Americans about the experiences of African American men living in an inherently racist country, they also seem to contribute to the credibility of the angry Black male stereotype. The attempts to enlighten others seemed to be taken by the other cast members as additional evidence for existing stereotypical images of African American men. From a critical viewer/researcher's perspective, this appeared especially true with non–African Americans as seen in their interactions with their Black male housemates. For instance, in one particularly intense conflict involving Kevin and Julie (a European American woman), she accuses him of "having a lot of misdirected anger." In another interaction, a male housemate attests that "all he knows of Kevin is a pattern of aggressive behavior." David (LA) experiences similar responses from the Los Angeles cast. Irene, a Los Angeles deputy sheriff, articulates her fear of David (LA): "He has something up inside of him that's building and building and building." The "something," it is inferred, that Irene and others sense is the Black man's raging reaction to a history of oppression in the United States. In the eyes of other cast members, the presence of this inherent anger is so problematic that several openly discuss the feasibility of removing some of the Black men (most notably Kevin, Syrus, and David [NO] from the show. In one season, David (LA) is forced to leave the house midseason. In another, Stephen is diagnosed by other cast members and *required* to undergo anger management counseling in order to remain in the house.

THE BLACK MALE AS EMOTIONALLY UNPREDICTABLE OR UNSTABLE

In each season, a few positive examples of how African American men are adapting to the tensions of living in a racist society are provided; these include Kevin's poetry and radical politics, David's (LA) comedy, and the musical outlets used by both Mohammed and David (NO). However, what is foregrounded for the viewers are the unpredictable ways that Black men deal with their internal feelings. Some seem to shut themselves down and isolate themselves from others in the house. While all of the African American male cast members exhibited this strategy, it seemed especially true for Kevin, Mohammed, and David (NO). Others, however, were seen exhibiting a wide range of behaviors that appeared to have no rhyme or reason. In certain instances, they were open and honest with their feelings; in others, they were shown "losing it" or "blowing up" with little warning. Across many of the seasons, cast members expressed a genuine fear that the anger of Black men would be "misdirected" at "innocent" bystanders. This was even articulated for Mohammed—whose demeanor was a picture-perfect model of serenity, control, and nonviolence—when a fellow cast member called him a "bitch." The point is that the signifier of being emotionally unpredictable was associated with all African American male cast members regardless of other personal characteristics or past behaviors.

Without question, this was most apparent in an analysis of Stephen's behavior during an episode when one of his female housemates (Irene) was leaving the Seattle show for medical reasons. Given that he was represented as caring and sensitive (albeit somewhat emotionally unstable) through earlier episodes, no one would have predicted his actions when Irene insinuated that he was homosexual. His first reaction was to call her a bitch and simulate a masturbating motion. Then he retrieved a stuffed animal that he had stolen from her and threw it in the ocean as she watched. As Irene tried to leave, Stephen chased down the car that she was in, opened the door, and, to the dismay of everyone around them, smacked her in the face. The lesson is undeniable: No matter how sensitive and caring African American men may appear, it is impossible to predict how they might behave in any given situation.

The signifier that African American men are emotionally unpredictable or unstable or both is not limited to the ways in which they deal with an inherent anger. As illustrated with the example of Stephen, it is also associated with the next signifier: the Black male as violent threat. The same could be said for the final theme: the Black male as sexually aggressive. In other words, the ways that African American male cast members express their sexuality is divergent and unsystematic. For instance, sexual desire may be exhibited through spontaneous displays of nudity, as evidenced by David's (LA) urge to pull his pants down in front of others, Teck's streaking in different contexts, or David's (NO) desire to strip for his female housemates. It is also seen in the ways that African American men fulfill their sexual needs (e.g., Syrus's multiple partners, David's [LA] fascination with masturbation, or David's [NO] preoccupation with bringing strippers to the house). Black male sexuality is also displayed in more aggressive ways—most notably in

the context of rape in the LA and Boston seasons (discussed in great detail in the section on page 224). Most relevant to the point here, however, is that African American men are signified as emotionally unpredictable in terms of how they express themselves. Given the other signifiers revealed in this essay, this element is increasingly problematic.

THE BLACK MALE AS A VIOLENT THREAT

As shown thus far, images showing reason for a justified societal fear of Black men are clearly maintained across *The Real World* seasons. Consequently, we hear cast members revealing their fear of potential violence of Black men with so much internal rage. In fact, several non–African American cast members confidentially (to one another or within the context of the "confessional room") explain their discomfort around Black men who, they believe, clearly have great *potential* for violence. Interestingly, comments taken from different seasons appear hauntingly consistent in the ways that this fear is expressed. For instance, Julie, a European American woman in New York stated

> I really like Kevin . . . and could never deny that. I respect him a lot, and I think that he is really intelligent and has a lot of important things to say. . . . That doesn't mean that I ever want to be alone with Kevin again . . . in my life. I will never be comfortable, and don't really understand how I can expected to be.

Others, most often European American women, talked about their feelings of being "unsafe" and "uncomfortable" as long as the African American men were present. Sometimes it was the physical persona (David's [NO] muscular physique or Syrus's athletic build) that appeared to fuel a sense of discomfort. Other times, it was the possibility—despite how remote—that a violent outburst might occur. It is difficult to understand these perceptions of African American men given that other cast members were clearly more physically violent in their behaviors. Their actions are obviously interpreted as situational and not indicative of a larger pattern. However, African American male behaviors are not perceived in the same way as their non-Black counterparts—even in the absence of *any* violent tendencies.

Take, for example, an interaction between Syrus and his Boston housemate, Montana. Throughout the show, the pair had numerous disagreements about different issues, but none contained any threats of violence. Interestingly, however, in the confessional room Montana shared her fear of violence when discussing a disagreement about a late-night phone call.

> I thought that [Syrus] came across a little strong last night . . . I got the idea that [he] was about to hit me . . . He can apologize until the cows come home, and I can say, "fine, I accept your apology," . . . but I'm not going to forget what happened. In the back of my mind, that will always be there.

Montana's fear of Syrus becoming physically violent is especially telling given that he is extremely easy-going, nonconfrontational, and nonviolent throughout the show. What appears to be happening, at least as we see it, is that specific cast members unconsciously tap into long-established stereotypes in framing their current perceptions of Kevin, David (LA), Mohammed, Syrus, Stephen, Teck, and David (NO). Then, based on these underlying stereotypes, cast members—most often European American women—work to persuade others to adopt their interpretation of certain behaviors enacted by African American men. Regardless of the different personal characteristics, a similar sign is invoked: Black men represent a violent threat.

Even when the possibility for violence is slim—and relatively less than for any other person—cast members perceive a potential for violence as central in their interactions with Black men. For example, in two different instances, Julie and Kevin (NYC cast) are involved in a conflict in which she makes her fear of him apparent by asking him if he is going to physically harm her. In one scene, Julie asks Kevin, "Why are you getting so close? Why are you getting so emotional? What are you going to do, hit me?" Kevin attempts to explain how proximity and emotional expressiveness are culture specific; Julie's response is to passionately argue: "It's not a Black-

White thing!" Kevin then gives consciousness to the larger question in the minds of those who recognize the subtle influence that stereotypes have in this interaction when he confronts her perception by asking, "Do you assume that because I'm a Black man that I'm going to hit you?"

THE BLACK MALE AS SEXUALLY AGGRESSIVE

The final signifier/stereotype involves the sexual aggression associated with Black men. This is made a subtle trait with several of the African American male cast members (i.e., Kevin's disclosures about his sexual fantasies in response to a lighthearted discussion on issues prompted by a "book of questions"), but it is highlighted for others. For instance, at least four of the Black men on *The Real World* were represented as having enormous sexual appetites. Such is certainly the case with Teck, who is presented as having several one-night stands, including one with a stripper. Similarly, David (NO) speaks openly about his sexual desires, spends a significant amount of time entertaining strippers, and overtly "hooks up" with several women while in New Orleans. The most memorable of these relations occurs when he has intercourse with a woman while his (virgin) roommate lies awake in the adjacent bed. David (NO) later states that he does not know the woman's name, and that there is no "shame in his game." David's (NO) philosophy is similar to Syrus's perspective of women ("Women are like potato chips . . . you can't have just one"). Furthermore, concerns regarding Syrus's sexual freedom to pursue a variety of women are dangerously increased during the third episode when cast members (and viewers) learn that Syrus was accused of rape while in college. Regardless of Syrus's guilt or innocence, the producers of the show have chosen to portray him as a sexually aggressive Black man, who potentially may use rape to satisfy his sexual needs.

Whereas some Black men's sexual appetites were distinct traits in the creation of their *Real World* personas, David's (LA) sexuality was signified in a more subtle, yet equally powerful manner. David (LA) is a comedian, always joking and "playing the fool" for the camera, but he sexualizes his behaviors as he jokingly discusses his love of masturbation and other sexual acts. His playful joking with housemates becomes more serious during one episode when a prank between he and Tami, an African American woman, escalates into a heated conflict. In the most replayed LA episode, David playfully attempts to pull the blanket off of Tami, who is in her bed for the night and wearing only her panties and bra. For a couple of minutes, there is a lighthearted struggle; this drastically changes when David continues to try to pull the blanket off of Tami as she gets up to take a phone call. The latter part of the interaction is filled with screams of "STOP! DON'T! DAVID, STOP!" from both Tami and Beth (a European American woman). The line has clearly been crossed when Tami escapes to the bathroom, throws on a robe, and immediately begins to retaliate against David. The following excerpts illustrate the conversation that ensued:

DAVID: You guys were laughing, giggling, playing—

TAMI: You can take off your pants in front of the camera, but I am not like that. It was NOT funny, okay?

DAVID: Here, hey, here you go . . . I'll take off my clothes [drops his pants to his ankles exposing himself]

IRENE [calls from the bedroom, where she is still in bed]: I'll call the police and scream rape!

BETH: We should file charges against him. . . .

Once again, accusations of rape are associated with the behaviors of a Black man. Even within the context of a nonsexual interaction, the concept is powerfully represented and becomes even more intense as Beth confronts David directly:

DAVID: You're going to press charges for me pulling a cover off of her??? For playing??? You guys were on the floor screaming [mocking their playful tone] "Stop . . . stop . . ."

BETH: Yeah, and that is what a rapist says too—

DAVID: Rape??? This hasn't anything to do with rape!

BETH [imitating a rapist]: Yeah, you wanted it, baby . . .

DAVID: I didn't try to rape—this hasn't nothing to do with rape!

BETH: No means no, okay?

DAVID: Wait a minute . . . who? . . . when? You're taking this too far; I wasn't going to rape the girl . . . I was playing . . . I was just pulling the blanket.

The power of a European American woman conjuring up images of the Black male rapist is not lost on David, who obviously recognizes the power of such accusations. "In the old days," he tells the group, "I would be hung. Because a woman said rape . . . not rationally hung, just hung." Based on the women's fears, he is asked to leave the house (and subsequently is replaced on the show).

Conclusion

Black images have been filtered through the racial misconceptions and fantasies of the dominant White culture, which has tended to deny the existence of a rich and resilient Black culture of equal worth (Dates & Barlow, 1990). Consequently, these images remain in a constant state of degeneration, particularly for the Black male (Berry, 1992; Bogle, 1994; Smith, 1993). Generalizations of Black men often include symbols of violence, anger, sexual aggression, and unpredictable behavior that reinforce existing negative stereotypes. Such is the case with *Real World* images. In general, the mass media serve as the tool for promoting these misconceptions to the larger society. At this point, it is important to understand that while the drama on *The Real World* features a number of stereotypes for other groups, the depictions of African American men are more crucial given the lack of balanced images in the media. Given the history of media images (Bogle, 1994; MacDonald, 1992), portrayals of African Americans are never neutral. Each image, according to Elise and Umoja (1992), "advances or retards the struggle for self-determination and empowerment" (p. 83).

According to the creators/producers of *The Real World*, the characterizations of African American men (as well as others) on the show feature "real people, undirected, sharing their lives" (Huriash, 1996, p. C25). However, it is questionable whether these occurrences, constructed and edited for the purpose of entertainment, constitute real life. Furthermore, this analysis argues that the cast on *The Real World* is assembled around a combination of race, class, gender, and power issues. It is through these issues that images of the cast members are constructed. Calling attention to specific symbols associated with the *Real World* Black male, we identify limitations of his character, personality, and overall participation. We argue that negative symbols are not associated with other cast members and do not bind them in the same way. Although questions have been raised regarding the authenticity of shows like *The Real World* (Orbe, 1998), it becomes a moot point when considering that images are presented and subsequently consumed as real-life experiences. Additionally, scholars report the extreme perpetuation of stereotypes within society as a result of connecting stereotypical images in media with our everyday interactions (Kellner, 1995). Others have documented the severity of these historical depictions, revealing that "a grossly distorted public image of Black Americans was being persuasively etched into the American mind" (Watkins, 1994, p. 55). Hence, image is everything. In this essay, we emphasized the need to examine the signs, symbols, and fear-evoking codes linked to Black males on *The Real World* and in other media contexts. Our desire is to create a critical awareness among media consumers in the subtle, and not-so-subtle, ways that media images shape our perceptions of others (Gray, 1995).

As discussed earlier, *The Real World* has great potential to provide representations of Black men that extend beyond stereotypes and reflect the rich diversity of their life experiences. However, nine seasons after its introduction, *The Real World* has yet to reach that potential. Instead, minimal efforts have been made to eliminate a mass-mediated process that serves to negate the Black male or otherwise requires his one-dimensional character to speak for all Black men. We believe that the representations of African American men on *The Real World* extend a long history of problematic media portrayals of mi-

crocultures in the United States. Previous portrayals of these groups in science and society have been relatively insignificant and have adversely affected its members, particularly Black men. Consequently, identity issues constrict or expand the Black man's self-knowledge and his relationships with others (Jackson, 1997).

In conclusion, we are left awaiting future *Real World* seasons and wondering what type of African American male "characters" will walk through the door that leads directly to our living rooms. Will the production team continue to select Black men whose personas are the most likely to evoke tension, and use selective editing to create "characters" that people love to hate? Or will future cast members illustrate the great diversity of African American men in the United States and, in doing so, assist in dispelling existing negative stereotypes? Furthermore, how will these individuals be perceived? Will they be stereotyped as soon as they enter through the door? Isolated within a house that forces them to walk out the door in order to get any type of support during their stay? Or will they simply be forced to leave? We, like millions of viewers across the world, continue to wait, watch, and wonder.

References

Berry, V. T. (1992). From *Good Times* to *The Cosby Show:* Perceptions of changing televised images among Black fathers and sons. In S. Craig (Ed.), *Men, masculinity and the media* (pp. 111–123). Newbury Park, CA: Sage.

Bogle, D. (1994). *Toms, coons, mulattoes, mammies, and bucks: An interpretive history of Blacks in American films.* New York: Viking Press.

Dace, K. L. (1994). Dissonance in European American and African American communication. *Western Journal of Black Studies,* 18(1), 18–26.

Dates, J. L., & Barlow, W. (1990). *Split image: African American in the mass media.* Washington, D.C.: Howard University Press.

Eco, U. (1976). *A theory of semiotics.* Bloomington: Indiana University Press.

Elise, S., & Umoja, A. (1992). Spike Lee constructs the new Black man: Mo' better. *Western Journal of Black Studies,* 6, 82–89.

Gates, H. L. (1992). TV's Black world turns—but stays unreal. In M. L. Andersen & P. H. Collins (Eds.), *Race,* class, and gender: An anthology* (pp. 310–316). Belmont, CA: Wadsworth.

Gray, H. (1995). *Watching race: Television and the struggle for "Blackness."* Minneapolis: University of Minnesota Press.

Huriash, L. J. (1996, July 10). Surreal world. *Fort Lauderdale (Florida) Sun-Sentinel*, p. C25.

Jackson, R. L. (1997). Black "manhood" as xenophobe: An ontological exploration of the hegelian dialectic. *Journal of Black Studies, 27*(6), 731–750.

Kellner, D. L. (1995). *Media culture.* New York: Routledge.

MacDonald, J. F. (1992). *Black and white tv: Afro-Americans in television since 1948.* Chicago: Nelson-Hall.

Orbe, M. (1998). Constructions of reality on MTV's "The Real World": An analysis of the restrictive coding of Black masculinity. *Southern Communication Journal, 64*, 32–47.

Orbe, M., & Strother, K. (1996). Signifying the tragic mulatto: A semiotic analysis of *Alex Haley's Queen*. *Howard Journal of Communications, 7*, 113–126.

Orbe, M., Warren, K. T., & Cornwell, N. C. (2001). Negotiating societal stereotypes: Analyzing *The Real World* discourse by and about African American men. *International and Intercultural Annual, XXIII*, 107–134.

Sakurari, S. H. (1966, July 17). *The Real World* is hell. *Salon*, 16–19.

Smith, S. (1993, November). *From the junkman to the garbage man: The evolution of the African American male in the Black situation comedy*. Paper presented at the annual meeting of the Speech Communication Association, Miami, FL.

Watkins, M. (1994). *On the real side: Lynching, lying, and signifying, the underground tradition of African American humor that transformed American culture, from slavery to Richard Pryor*. New York: Simon & Schuster.

Key Terms

African American men

media stereotypes

MTV's *The Real World*

reality-based television

semiotics

Discussion Questions

1. One image of African American men portrayed on *The Real World* is that of unpredictability and anger. Given that this show is not marketed exclusively to African Americans, why do you think that non–African Americans might want to view African American men in this way?

2. The image of African American men as sexually aggressive has a long history in the United States, including lynchings, accusations of rape, and other historical legacies. Do you think that David (LA) uses this image to his advantage? Or is he trapped in it?

3. Viewers can be active in how they watch any television show. Do you think that viewers of *The Real World* buy into these images of African American men? Or do they resist them?

4. If you were to be cast on *The Real World*, what stereotypes and images do you think that you would have to deal with? What images would viewers already have about your social group?

5. Do you think that the way this program is structured increases or decreases the use of stereotypes? Do the other cast members invoke these stereotypes in commenting on their housemates?

25 *The Siege* and American Media Portrayals of Arabs and Moslems

MAROUF HASIAN, JR.

In 1998, a group of Hollywood actors and producers completed *The Siege*, another film that invited audiences to imagine what life would be like if the U.S. government had to deal with internal terrorism, kidnapping, and "Moslem" fundamentalism. For more than a hundred years, Arabs and Moslems living in both England and the United States have had to deal with such stereotyping, but what made *The Siege* even more controversial than similar films was the way in which promoters tried to package it as anti-racist. Much of the action in the film was centered around the activities of FBI agents—including one Lebanese operative—who were trying to stop Arab terrorism in America. The movie "opens with President Clinton on television in the wake of the Somalia bombing, warning that 'America takes care of its own,' intercut with video footage of the devastating Federal Building in Oklahoma" (Hollings, 1999, p. 54). By the end of the movie, audiences have witnessed the deaths of hundreds of innocent bystanders in the United States, civil authorities have trouble maintaining authority, and the president eventually has to authorize the use of martial law. The implied message: Do something about internal and foreign terrorism today, or risk an apocalyptic future filled with Arab or Moslem terrorists.

As one might imagine, not everyone considered this movie to be an innocent form of entertainment. There were many critics who worried that this cinematic representation was simply going to reinforce many of the preexisting negative stereotypes of Arabs and Moslems that already circulated within U.S. popular culture. Jack Shaheen, professor emeritus of broadcast journalism at Southern Illinois University, noted that some of these problems come from the fact that such movies "take the lunatic fringe" and make them "represent the majority. . . . It would be like showing that every Catholic is an I.R.A. member, or every Jew was a member of the Kach party" (quoted in Goodstein,

1998, p. 20). Protesters around the country picketed *The Siege* when it opened (Stack, 1998, p. C-3). The American-Arab Anti-Discrimination League issued a statement claiming that the movie was "insidious, incendiary and dangerous" (Zwick, 1998, p. A-29). Detractors claimed that more than $70 million had been spent making a film that did nothing to help the images of Arabs, Arab Americans, or Moslems living in the United States (Barnes, 1998, p. B-3).

Defenders of the movie responded by noting that critics were simply trying to whitewash the fact that terrorism is a real danger to Americans, both here and abroad. As Zwick (1998) explained:

[I]f "The Siege" engenders a dialogue on ethnic stereotyping, on terrorism, on the increasingly cloudy legal landscape between personal rights and the public interest, then it will have accomplished far more than I might ever have imagined for a Hollywood thriller. Movies about aliens and asteroids can't offend anybody, but neither do they try to hold up a mirror to unattractive aspects of our country. (p. A-29)

Instead of apologizing for the movie, or making significant changes in the script, some defenders claimed that this was a very complex film that helped with social reform and consciousness raising. For example, Muravchik (1999) averred:

Half of the 36 terrorist organizations mentioned in the report [*Patterns of Global Terrorism*], moreover, are Muslims. . . . This is not to suggest that terrorism is endemic ethnically to Arabs or doctrinally to Islam. But it does underline the fact that terrorism has enjoyed a prevalence and acceptance in the Muslim Middle East that has no parallel elsewhere. . . . Those protesting *The Siege* seem to think a complete ban on the subject of Middle Eastern terrorism will do the trick, but as long as the reality endures, nothing is likely to dispel the image in people's minds. (pp. 58–60)

Just whose "reality" this represented was never clarified. Nor did we hear much about the complex nature of Middle Eastern affairs. The line between "real" terrorism and cinematic representations of that reality was completely blurred as promoters of the film continued to defend its authenticity and its social importance. Even reporters who tried to be fair to both sides in the controversy, such as Waxman (1998), claimed that "*The Siege* mirrors the real-life story of fundamentalists who tried to blow up the World Trade Center" (p. A-18.)

This essay provides a rhetorical analysis of *The Siege* that looks at how the film and the conversations around it give us an index for measuring how White U.S. Americans think about Arab and Islamic communities. Do observers see *The Siege* as pure entertainment, or do they take in the lessons that are being taught about martial law, Islamic "fundamentalism," and the trustworthiness of Arab Americans? Do films such as this help us demythologize some of our ethnic misconceptions, or do they reproduce the very stereotypes they purport to critique?

To help answer such questions, this essay is divided into three major sections: The first part provides a basic context for the study by looking at prior cinematic imaging of Arabs, Arab Americans, and Moslems. The second part looks at how *The Siege* enters into this conversation. A concluding section summarizes the implications of this debate for America's popular culture.

A Rhetorical History of America's Media Representations of Arabs, Arab Americans, and Moslems

There is little question that our stereotyping of Arabs and Moslems comes to us with much ideological baggage. As Goodstein (1998) explains, these representations of "terrorists and villains" are "only the latest in a long line of ethnic groups and nationalities cast in stereotypical bad-guy roles, from American Indians to Germans to Japanese to African Americans to Russians" (p. 17). Over time, we experience changes in our political and economic alliances, and new enemies must be found to

help justify the choices that we make in a variety of domestic and international situations. Dawson (1999), a writer for the Manchester *Guardian*, lamented the ways in which *The Siege* seemed to be the type of movie needed when the "Russians unsportingly withdrew from the Cold War" (p. T-8).

Obviously, this was not the first time that either Arabs, Arab Americans, or the followers of the Islamic religion had been cast in a negative light. Rehman (1992) once observed:

> All three commercial television networks and public television services have consistently portrayed Arabs and Muslims as aggressive, violent, primitive, and unreasonable people. This is not only true of fictional materials but also of news programs and documentaries about Muslims and Arabs. Negative stereotyping is found in situation comedies such as MASH to docudramas such as The Death of a Princess to news documentaries about desert life. A survey of recent years of TV programming reveals that ten stereotypes have been established. Some of these broad and erroneous generalizations are:
> All Arabs are extremely wealthy.
> OPEC consists of Arab nations.
> Muslims condone slave trading.
> Arabs are polygamous and have many wives and large harems.
> Arabs are rulers of kingdoms.
> Muslim nations have primitive and severe laws.
> Muslims are violent and war-loving.
> All Palestinians are terrorists.
> Arab families are self-destructive.
> Muslims are the enemies of the world's peace-loving peoples. (p. 40)

These stereotypes were not only symbolic constructs created by members of the media—they have also been produced by ordinary citizens and leaders. For example, Judeo-Christian narratives about the Crusades are filled with characters such as Saladin, who helped the Moslems reconquer Jerusalem, a place considered to be only temporarily occupied by foreign interlopers who belonged to heathen religions.

Before the term "Middle East" was invented in 1902 (Adelson, 1995, p. xiii), much of this region between Egypt and Iraq was called "The Holy Land," "Palestine," or "the Levant" in Anglo American tracts, pamphlets, books, and travelogues. Missionaries from England and the United States were convinced that they could help make the desert bloom. Dioramas and lantern shows helped with the removal of spatial distance as audiences learned about the mysteries of Egypt and other "oriental" places (Lant, 1992, pp. 92–99).

In the United States, Arabs were just one of the groups from "Syria" who immigrated to this country between the 1880s and 1920s (Kraut, 1982; Pulcini, 1993). These new arrivals had to deal with "Anglo Saxon" nativist groups, doctors who worried about impure "germplasm," and U.S. American workers who resented the influx of potential competitors. Movies such as *The Sheik* helped maintain the myth that these foreigners had some mysterious powers from the "East."

The changing fortunes of war and altered political alignments transformed allies into enemies. The Arabs who had fought with the Allies during World War I were treated as Nazi allies during the post–World War II years. Haj Amin el Husseini, the "Mufti of Palestine," was accused of being a "war criminal" who conspired with the Axis powers (Sargent, 1946, p. 37). Zionist supporters helped spread the word that Arabs were an irrational, hot-tempered people who dogmatically refused to understand the importance of sharing or political compromise. The arrival of the Arab-Israeli wars—in 1948, 1967, and 1973—simply exacerbated the situation.

By the 1980s and 1990s, the figure of the Arab fanatic or Islamic fundamentalist had become a staple character in Western books, films, newspapers, and other mediums (Jarrar, 1983; Little, 1998; Shaheen, 1985; van Teeffelen, 1994). Saddam Hussein's rise to power made sense in a world that had been configured as filled with the enemies of the Coalition Forces. By 1994, Collier could observe that Islamic fundamentalism was now taking the place of communism "as the principal perceived threat to Western reason and democracy" (p. 395). A few years later, Lind and Danowski (1998) reported that there was still "an overwhelming association in the media between Arabs and violence, threats and war, which serves to foster the stereotypes of 'Arab as barbarian/aggressor/terrorist'" (p. 165). This combination

of symbolic imaging and material conditions helps us understand just why Arabs and Moslems worried about the potential cultural impact of *The Siege*.

A Textual Analysis of *The Siege*

Most of the action in *The Siege* takes place in New York City, and it is there that we see how various "terrorists" from the Middle East organize their underground "cells." Early on in the movie, there is an indication that most of the plot is going to center around the conflict between the forces of goodness (the FBI and assimilated Arabs) and the Islamic fundamentalists who bring their foreign problems to U.S. shores. In the first several minutes of the film, we learn that the FBI director in this region, Anthony Hubbard (Denzel Washington), is a caring person who is not overtly prejudiced against Arabs. To drive this point home, the producers of the movie brought an interesting twist to the film when they added the character of Frank Haddad, a Lebanese American FBI agent. "The character of Haddad," notes Glass (1998), "is meant to be a breakthrough" in cinematic representations of Arabs (pp. 9–10). Haddad is a complicated figure because he appears to be an assimilated Arab who still has strong feelings for his "homeland" in Lebanon. Audiences learn that his children speak fluent English, they attend American schools, and celebrate American holidays. Eventually, other governmental operatives, like Elise Kraft (Annette Bening), work with Hubbard and Haddad in organized efforts to end terrorist violence in America.

In the first half of the movie, audiences are presented with some scenes that might suggest that alliances between assimilated Arabs and civil authorities can help contain the occasional terrorist threat from the foreign "other." FBI agents Hubbard and Haddad are portrayed as conscientious professors who respond quickly to the threats that are posed by a bus hijacking. These are culturally sensitive individuals who understand the importance of compromise and negotiation. Not all Arabs, Arab Americans, or Moslems should be labeled as terrorists, because the vast majority of those who live in the United States are law abiding and understand the need for order. Viewers know this because at one point in the movie Hubbard is allowed to talk about how the "Arab community" works with the FBI because "they love this country as much as we do" (Hooper, 1998, p. A-29).

It is at this point in the movie that we begin to see how the plot sometimes works to undermine some of the more positive representations that might exist in the production. In combating terrorism, even good officials sometimes have to take shortcuts and violate societal norms. For example, when Samir Nazhde, one of the suspected terrorists, is arrested for being an accessory to the Bus 87 murders, Haddad hits him and screams obscenities in Arabic (38:02). Before this time, Haddad may have appeared as a model Christian Arab, but beneath the surface lurked a more malevolent personality. Haddad's apparent rage simply reinforces the image of the angry Arab or Moslem who has no appreciation of the need for diplomacy and control. Sharif (1998) observed about Haddad:

> To justify the vicious treatment of a sector of the Arab American population in this film as being a sophisticated warning that extremism may cut both ways is too simple a thesis. For the history of Arab roles in film is so littered with negative portrayal, trivialization and dehumanization that the sentiment clearly does not ring true. It is at best a history of tactless misrepresentations of Islam. Indeed, it is not lost on many that the sympathetic Arab character in this film is not a Muslim. . . . (p. F-3)

Such tactics may be problematic and offensive, but they are presented as effective. The information that is gathered by Haddad and the other FBI agents is used by a SWAT team to eliminate one of the terrorist cells that contributed to the violence. For a time, viewers are invited to celebrate this victory over the forces of darkness.

Unfortunately, this "victory is short-lived" (Hunter, 1998, D-1), as viewers begin to realize that this cell is merely one of many terrorist cells, and both politicians and FBI agents become frustrated when the violence escalates. Dark clouds gather as we watch how the "ritual washing before prayer is used to cue the audience to the impending bloodshed" (Hooper, 1998, p. A-29). Perhaps the fundamentalists are more powerful than we were initially

led to believe. Several explosions contribute to the screen deaths of some 600 Americans (108:20).

By the second half of the movie, audiences are beginning to see one of the underlying messages of the film: Perhaps civil authorities are not always equipped to deal with Islamic fundamentalism. Perhaps America's military might need to be used in this escalating war between innocent civilians and foreign terrorists. The producer of the movie admitted that one of the messages he wanted to get across in the film was that in the "new war against terrorism," planners need to respond "prudently, and with conscience" (Zwick, 1998, p. A-29). One critic (Hunter, 1998) pointed out that the "whole movie might be construed as a policy essay in which the merits of freedom vs. order are weighed judiciously" (p. D-1).

This issue, of course, is how producers like Zwick allowed actors in the movie to perform this "prudence" when they confronted the demonic terrorists. The escalation of violence brings the internment of tens of thousands of Arabs and Arab Americans, reminding us of the "necessity" of the internment of Japanese and Japanese Americans during World War II (Irons, 1983). The fanaticism of those who go on suicide missions because of their beliefs in Allah means that both Congress and the U.S. president have to seriously consider bringing in military troops and imposing martial law.

Near the end of the movie, New York City is depicted as being in such chaos that the federal government has to send in a military detachment under the leadership of General Devereaux (Bruce Willis). Devereaux is portrayed as a reluctant general who begs his superiors to do everything that they can before deciding to call in the armed forces. He then makes it clear that his tactics and strategies, though harsh, are effective. Within hours of taking command, Devereaux imposes martial law and rounds up potential suspects, puts them in camps, and tortures some of them. The negotiating tactics of the FBI are giving way to "images of tanks and paratroopers and Bradley Fighting Vehicles moving down American streets" in the same way that "they have moved down so many foreign streets" (Hunter, 1998, p. D-1). The message: You can't take shortcuts or compromise with terrorists. Realists must recognize that even good Arabs and Arab Americans need to admit that some of their brothers and sisters are simply "fundamentalists" or "terrorists."

Eventually, Haddad and Hubbard are able to use the powers of civil authority to rein in Devereaux; so in the end, goodness triumphs over evil. Civil law returns as the last of the terrorists are killed. Yet we leave the theater wondering, Was the general right? Should international terrorism be treated as a problem so significant that it can be dealt with only by those who see the "necessity" for martial law? Have we assiduously avoided looking for the signs of Arab or Islamic terrorism in our own backyard?

Conclusion

On first glance, one could make an argument that *The Siege* does help eliminate negative stereotyping, in that the movie at least recognizes the presence of millions of Arabs and Arab Americans in the United States. Haddad may not be the best of messengers, but we do get the sense that the directors, writers, producers, promoters, and other defenders of the film at least respected the importance of cultural pluralism. For example, Zwick (1998) responded to his critics by arguing that the "Arab-American community is as diverse and divided against itself—politically, religiously, socially—as any vibrant community in the United States. And this film portrays Arab-Americans as cops, landlords—and yes, terrorists" (p. A-29).

The inference here is that audiences learn about both the Islamic and the Arab worlds when they are presented with multiple characters and the supposed realities of international politics. After all, haven't representatives of these ethnic groups been complaining for years about their invisibility? Why attack producers who take the risk of including characters from marginalized communities? A puzzled Zwick (1998) told reporters:

> What the critics are saying, as best as I can understand it, is that any portrayal of the life of Muslims that includes representations of violence—no matter how well documented—is not only offensive, but also inflammatory. Forget the World Trade Center and the embassy bombings in Kenya and Tanzania, their position, simply put, is that all one billion Islamic people in the world can be portrayed only in their most positive aspect. (p. A-29)

This of course assumes that the "documented" violence accurately represented the causes of violence in the world, that the collectors of this information were impartial and accurate, and that these cinematic representations are authentic disseminators of this information. Zwick acts as if his film is a transparent purveyor of unmediated realities, a producer whose work is a blend of photojournalism and entertainment. As far as he is concerned, the Arabs, Arab Americans, and Moslems who complain about these stereotypes are playing "the new American hurt game"—if "you're not offended by somebody, you're nobody" (p. A-29).

What critics of these films need to point out are the ways in which the negative stereotyping in the film overwhelms any attempts at casting Arabs or Moslems in a favorable light. Given the Islamic rituals that proceed the acts of international violence, the implied argument is that this portrayal of Moslem prayer could be the signal that some form of violence is about to begin. Both elites and lay persons can leap to the conclusion that we need to keep in mind the mental associations between Arabs or Moslems and terrorism. The "good" members of these ethnic communities are the ones that accept the American way of life, who understand the need to leave behind the devastation that comes with foreign wars. The overarching message of the film, that we need to do more about controlling domestic and international terrorism, is itself an argument that brackets many of the social, economic, political, legal, and religious dimensions of some complex situations.

Given the existence of pernicious stereotypes that were already circulating in America's popular culture, it should come as no surprise that many of the millions of Arabs, Arab Americans, and Moslems living in the United States protested the opening and viewing of *The Siege*. Sherrine Eid, a graduate student in public health at George Washington University, told one reporter for the *Washington Post* that this "hits close to home . . . I hear it when somebody tells me, 'Camel jockeys go home' . . . I have seen the previews and when you see a person praying and then see a building blow up. It feels like the same message" (quoted in Waxman, 1998, p. A-18). "We cannot say there are no Arab and no Muslim terrorists," complained Akkad (an Arab American producer/director), but at the same time there is a need to "balance it with the image of the normal human being, the Arab American, the family man" (Goodstein, 1998, p. 17). Sharif (1998) echoed these views when he noted that such "irresponsible representations can only aggravate and further alienate our already maligned culture and peoples" (p. F-3).

To be fair to the producers and defenders of the film, *The Siege* is not the only rhetorical artifact that can be blamed for perpetuating such stereotyping. These images are tied to material conditions, social ideals, and religious differences that circulate outside of cinematic representations. Moreover, if movies contribute to these dense rhetorical situations, then we need to realize that *The Siege* was only one of dozens of films that cast Moslems and Arabs in the role of villains. During the 1980s and 1990s, audiences were presented with *Executive Decision, Navy SEALS, Not Without My Daughter, True Lies, Voyage of Terror,* and *Terrorist on Trial* (Goodstein, 1998, p. 17; Waxman, 1998, p. A-18).

Obviously, banning such movies may not be the best solution to this stereotyping, especially when we can see the pervasiveness of these images. Ibrahim Hooper, a spokesperson for the Council on American Islamic Relations, suggests that "people ought to go in [to these movies] sensitized to the issue of stereotyping and bias" (quoted in Waxman, 1998, p. A-18). Providing positive role models is an important first step, but cultural critics also need to remind us of the material and symbolic complexities that are involved in cinematic representations of Arabs, Arab Americans, and Moslems. This rhetorical analysis of *The Siege* shows how even well-intentioned producers may be walking into a prefigured world, filled with "terrorist" demons and irrational "fundamentalists."

References

Adelson, R. (1995). *London and the invention of the Middle East.* New Haven: Yale University Press.

Barnes, J. E. (1998, November 7). Protesters say a new movie likens Islam to terrorism. *New York Times,* p. B-3.

Belkaoui, J. M. (1978). Images of Arabs and Israelis in the prestige press, 1966–1974. *Journalism Quarterly, 55,* 732–738, 799.

Collier, J. F. (1994). Intertwining histories: Islamic law and Western imperialism. *Law & Society Review, 28,* 395–408.

Dawson, J. (1999, January 1). Screen: How did a sensitive guy like Ed Zwick get labelled a bigot? (*The Manchester Guardian*), T-8.

Glass, C. (1998, November 20). A prejudice as American as apple pie. *New Statesman, 127,* 9–10.

Goodstein, L. (1998, November 1). Hollywood now plays cowboys and Arabs. *New York Times,* pp. II–17, 20.

Hollings, K. (1999, February). Film Review: *The Siege. Sight and Sound, 9,* 54.

Hooper, I. (1998, November 10). Again, Islam is an easy villain. *New York Times,* p. A-29.

Hunter, S. (1998, November 6). "The Siege": The enemy within. *Washington Post,* pp. D-1, D-8.

Irons, P. (1983). *Justice at War.* New York: Oxford University Press.

Jarrar, S. A. (1983). The treatment of Arabs in U.S. social studies textbooks: Research findings and recommendations. In E. Ghareeb (Ed.), *Split vision: The portrayal of Arabs in the American media* (pp. 369–380). Washington, DC: American-Arab Affairs Council.

Kraut, A. M. (1982). *The huddled masses: The immigrant in American society, 1880–1921.* Arlington Heights, IL: Harlan Davidson.

Lant, A. (1992). The curse of the Pharaoh, or how cinema contracted Eygptomania. *October, 59,* 86–112.

Lind, R. A., & Danowski, J. A. (1998). The representation of Arabs in U.S. electronic media. In Y. R. Kamalipour & T. Carilli (Eds.), *Cultural diversity and the U.S. media* (pp. 157–167). Albany: State University of New York Press.

Little, G. D. (1998). Representing Arabs: Reliance on the past. In Y. R. Kamalipour and T. Carilli (Eds.), *Cultural diversity and the U.S. media* (pp. 261–272). Albany: State University of New York Press.

Ludmerer, K. (1972). *Genetics and American society: A historical appraisal.* Baltimore, MD: Johns Hopkins University Press.

Maslin, J. (1998, November 6). New York as battleground of terrorists and troops. *New York Times,* p. E-15.

Muravchik, J. (1999, January). Terrorism at the multiplex. *Commentary, 107,* 57–60.

Pulcini, T. (1993). Trends in research on Arab Americans. *Journal of American Ethnic History,* 27–60.

Rehman, S. N. (1992, January/February). Media: Muslim images in American cinema. *The Minaret, 14,* 39–42.

Sargent, H. J. J. (1946, October 6). Mufti defends actions; Rabbi Stephen S. Wise calls him war criminal. *New York Times,* p. 37.

Shaheen, J. G. (1984). *The tv Arab.* Bowling Green, OH: Bowling Green State University Popular Press.

Shaheen, J. G. (1985). Media coverage of the Middle East: Perception and foreign policy. *The Annals of the American Academy of Political and Social Science, 482,* 160–175.

Sharif, M. (1998, November 16). "Siege" portrayal furthers trend of ridiculing Arabs. *Los Angeles Times,* p. F-3.

Stack, P. F. (1998, November 7). Arabs protest portrayal in "The Siege." *Salt Lake Tribune,* p. C-3.

Twentieth Century Fox. (1998). *The Siege.*

van Teeffelen, T. (1994). Racism and metaphor: The Palestinian-Israeli conflict in popular literature. *Discourse & Society, 5,* 381–405.

Waxman, S. (1998, November 6). Hollywood's "The Siege" besieged: Film's portrayal of Arab-Americans protested as harmful. *Washington Post,* pp. A-1, A-18, D-1, D-8.

Zwick, E. (1998, November 10). In the hurt game, honesty loses. *New York Times,* p. A-29.

Key Terms

Arab

Arab American

Moslems

popular culture

The Siege

Discussion Questions

1. How have Arabs and Moslems been historically represented in the Western media?

2. What are some of the cultural norms that influence the creation of these stereotypes of Arabs and Moslems?

3. How did the producers and directors of *The Siege* portray Arabs and Moslems?

4. Are all stereotypes of marginalized groups inherently problematic?

5. How can citizens and media representatives counter the negativity of some of these portrayals of Arabs and Moslems?

Activities for Skill Development

1. Media Analysis

For 1 week, keep track of what you watch and read in the mass media. Choose one movie or television show, and one magazine or newspaper. For each of these, identify who is represented in terms of age, gender, race, ethnicity, and other social categories. How are they represented? For example, how many different ethnic groups are portrayed in a given episode of your favorite TV show? What roles do each ethnic group represent? What kinds of intercultural interactions occur? Record your observations, then discuss as a class.

2. Aliens

Imagine that you are an alien from outer space, assigned to do research about Earthlings based on their satellite transmissions. Observe a movie or television show produced in Hollywood (the planet's cultural capital), and write up your observations of Earth culture based on the show. Include anything that might help comrades from your planet integrate effectively into Earth culture, especially characteristics about its inhabitants and how to communicate with them. Then attend an intercultural communication class populated by actual Earthlings. Read your findings to them, and solicit their corrections or clarifications. (This may be done in alien-Earthling pairs in front of the class, and then discussed as a whole group.)

3. You're the Producer

What kind of world would you like to see portrayed by the mass media? If you were a media executive, how would you make choices about what to produce or publish? What outside pressures might you face, and how would you deal with them? With three classmates, role-play a production meeting involving a magazine editor (or studio executive), a writer, an audience opinion poller, and an advertiser. What perspectives might each bring, and how do they, together, shape media content?

4. Culture in Your Closet

Conduct an inventory of your consumption of popular culture. What brand names or pop culture icons are represented in what you wear, use, and place as decoration on your walls? Are there things you refuse to buy

for social or political reasons? Compare notes with your classmates.

Web Sites

1. Mass communication scholars Sut Jhally and Jackson Katz have done some provocative analyses of masculinity and how it is communicated in popular culture. Check out some of their articles and other links at *<http://www.sutjhally.com>*.

2. Have you heard of Bollywood? Did you know that India produces more movies than any other country? Check out *<http://worldfilm.about.com/movies/worldfilm/cs/bollyresources/index.htm>* to learn about India's movie industry.

3. Interested in the latest African American and Black popular culture? Visit *<http://everythingblack.com>* for links to music, television, cable, and film.

Additional Readings

1. Budgeon, S. (1998). "I'll tell you what I really, really want": Girl power and self-identity in Britain. In S. A. Inness (Ed.), *Millennium girls* (pp. 115–143). Lanham, MD: Rowman & Littlefield Publishers, Inc.

2. Ríos, D. I. (2000). Latina/o experiences with mediated communication. In *Our voices: Essays in culture, ethnicity, and communication* (pp. 105–112). Los Angeles: Roxbury.

3. Kamalipour, Y. R. (1998). *Images of the U.S. around the world: A multicultural perspective.* New York: State University of New York Press.

Others

Gorham, B. W. (1999). Stereotypes in the media: So what? *Howard Journal of Communications, 10,* 229–247.

Hall, A., Anten, T., & Cakim, I. (1999). Perceived typicality: American television as seen by Mexicans, Turks and Americans. *Critical Studies in Mass Communication, 16,* 436–456.

Matabane, P., & Merritt, B. (1996). African Americans on television: 25 years after Kerner. *Howard Journal of Communications, 7,* 239–337.

Merskin, D. (1998). Sending up signals: A survey of Native American media use and representation in the mass media. *Howard Journal of Communications, 9,* 333–345.

Communication and Intercultural Transitions

Intercultural communication takes place when we go from our home environment to a host, or foreign, culture. Those who travel from one culture to another often have to adapt to the new norms and rules in the host culture, and this adaptation can influence identity and sense of self. Part Seven explores communication and identity in various types of intercultural transitions, including short-term international travel and work, readaptation to home, long-term immigration and acculturation, as well as international adoptees growing up in the United States.

Although communication and identity are central themes in all these readings, a range of different approaches to adaptation and transitions is presented. The first three essays address communication of individuals in overseas contexts. In "Cross-Cultural Adaptation: An Integrative Theory," Young Yun Kim outlines a systems approach to cultural adaptation. She identifies three outcomes of cultural adaptation: psychological health, functional fitness, and intercultural identity. She sees adaptation as a fairly linear process involving a stress-adaptation-growth cycle. She emphasizes the important role of the individual stranger's (immigrant) communication with host culture members and other ethnic members, but sees ethnic communication in the long term as a barrier to successful adaptation.

Along the same line, Shelley L. Smith, in "The Cycle of Adaptation," addresses the question of how sojourners adapt to their host cultures overseas and how they readapt to their home environment upon return. She points out that these two experiences are very similar and both influence identity development. She also gives practical guidelines for making the overseas adaptation and reentry process easier.

In contrast, "Translated Enactments: The Relational Configuration of the Asian Indian Immigrant Experience" questions the traditional notions of culture as static and acculturation as a taken-for-granted process. Radha Hegde suggests that in today's global world, many immigrant groups find that their cultural boundaries are blurred and that their sense of home and identity is confused. It no longer makes sense to refer to cultural groups as homogeneous groups of individuals residing in one place. Her ethnographic study of Asian Indian immigrants stands in contrast to Y. Y. Kim's essay in that Hegde emphasizes the importance of maintaining relationships with other immigrants. Hegde shows how these relationships provide a sense of grounding and identity for individuals living "on the borders."

In the final essay, "South Korean Adoptees Growing Up in White America," Etsuko Fujimoto examines how these adoptees deal with race and identity issues. While the adoptees themselves are not biologically multiracial, their socialization in White U.S. American families makes it necessary for them to face issues of being physically marked as Asian. Through interviews with Korean children adopted by White parents, Fujimoto describes the struggles that these children face because they are physically different from their parents. She points out that understanding their experiences and views of society provides insight into the changing face of America.

26 Cross-Cultural Adaptation
An Integrative Theory
YOUNG YUN KIM

Millions of people change homes each year, crossing cultural boundaries. Immigrants and refugees resettle in search of a new life, side-by-side with temporary sojourners finding employment overseas as artists, musicians, writers, accountants, teachers, and construction workers. Diplomats and other governmental agency employees, business managers, Peace Corps volunteers, researchers, professors, students, military personnel, and missionaries likewise carry out their work overseas for varying lengths of time. Individuals such as these are, indeed, contemporary pioneers venturing into an unfamiliar cultural terrain where the "business-as-usual" ways of doing things quickly lose their relevance. Even relatively short-term sojourners must be at least minimally concerned with building a healthy functional relationship to the host environment in a way similar to the native population. They confront their cross-cultural predicaments and engage in new learning for an improved "goodness-of-fit" to handle their daily transactions with a greater ease and heightened sense of efficacy. Accompanying this process is an increased self-awareness, which, in time, facilitates the development of an identity that reaches beyond the original cultural perimeters.

Organizing Principles: An Open-Systems Approach

The present theory is predicated on a set of "open-systems" assumptions about the nature of humans as adaptive living entities. . . .

Assumption 1: Humans have an inherent drive to adapt and grow. Adaptation is a fundamental life goal for humans, something that people do naturally and continually as they face the challenges from their environment (Slavin & Kriegman, 1992). The introduction of every new experience, particu-

larly one that is drastic and disorienting, leads to transformation throughout one's life. From the first frustrations of early childhood to the later changes in life circumstances, people go through a series of graduated sink-or-swim situations. For the most part, such challenges are successfully handled by people without a complete breakdown in their internal system. . . .

Assumption 2: Adaptation to one's social environment occurs through communication. Adaptive changes in individuals continue as long as they are engaged in a given sociocultural environment with which they send (encoding) and receive (decoding) messages. In this process, communicators continually engage in generating "information output" to the environment as well as generating meaning for the "information input" or "feedback" internally (Geyer, 1980). . . . This also means that individual adaptation activities occur as long as one lives in a given social environment (Dance & Larson, 1976).

Assumption 3: Adaptation is a complex and dynamic process. Because the person and the environment coparticipate in the person's adaptation through a continual give-and-take, adaptation . . . consists of multiple dimensions and facets.

The Process of Cross-Cultural Adaptation

How, then, do strangers adapt to new cultural challenges? . . .

DECULTURATION AND ACCULTURATION

Throughout the socialization process, children become adapted to the fellow members of their cultural group, which, in turn, gives them their status and assigns to them their role in the life of the community. Culture, indeed, is imprinted in its members as a pattern of knowledge, attitudes, values, mind-sets, perceptions, and behaviors that permeate all life activities. The mere fact that children grow up to be cultural beings bears witness to the fundamental fact of human pliability and the pervasive role of culture in shaping individual behavior.

Upon entering a new and unfamiliar culture, strangers set in motion the process of enculturation all over again. But this time, they are faced with situations that deviate from the familiar and internalized original cultural script. . . .

The process of *learning* and acquiring the elements of the host culture is commonly called *acculturation* (Shibutani & Kwan, 1965). . . . As new learning occurs, *unlearning*, or *deculturation*, of at least some of the old cultural habits occurs—at least in the sense that new responses are adopted in situations that previously would have evoked old ones. The cost of acquiring something new is inevitably the "losing" of something old in much the same way as "being someone requires the forfeiture of being someone else" (Thayer, 1975, p. 240).

THE STRESS-ADAPTATION-GROWTH DYNAMIC

Because cross-cultural adaptation necessitates both acculturation (learning) and deculturation (unlearning), and because a stranger's cultural identity and attributes are placed against the backdrop of the systemic forces of the host culture, the cross-cultural experiences of newcomers are unsettling indeed. The experiences of acculturation and deculturation inevitably produce forms of temporary personality disintegration, or even breakdown in some extreme cases. As parts of their internal organization undergo small changes, the strangers are, at least temporarily, in a state of disequilibrium, which is manifested in many emotional "lows" of uncertainty, confusion, and anxiety.

. . . Such disruptive experiences of a person reflect *stress*, . . . Indeed, the challenges of handling daily activities are most severe during the initial phases, as has been shown in many culture shock studies. . . . Under stress, a so-called defense mechanism is activated in strangers to hold the internal structure in balance by some form of protective psychological maneuvering. They attempt to avoid or minimize the anticipated or actual "pain" of disequilibrium by selective attention, self-deception, denial, avoidance, and withdrawal as well as by hostility, cynicism, and compulsively altruistic behavior (Lazarus, 1966, p. 262).

Defensive (or protective) stress reactions such as these, however, are generally temporary and counterproductive to the strangers' effective functioning in the host environment. They must, and generally do, accompany *adaptation* responses as well. . . .

What follows the stress and adaptation responses is a subtle internal transformation of *growth*. The periods of stress will pass in time as the strangers work out new ways of handling problems through sources of strength in themselves and in their social environment. A crisis, once managed by the strangers, presents an opportunity for a strengthening of their coping abilities. The stress-adaptation experiences bring about change and growth—the creative responses to new circumstances. Over time, the stress-adaptation-growth dynamic plays out not in a smooth, linear progression but in a cyclic and continual "draw-back-to-leap" pattern similar to the movement of a wheel depicted in Figure 1. Each stressful experience is responded to by strangers with a "draw back," which then activates their adaptive energy to help them reorganize themselves and "leap forward." It presents a dialectic relationship between push and pull, or engagement and disengagement, in the psychological movements of strangers.

INTERCULTURAL TRANSFORMATION

As strangers experience a progression of internal change, they are likely to undergo a set of identifiable transformations in their habitual patterns of cognitive, affective, and behavioral responses. Through the processes of deculturation and acculturation, some of the "old" cultural habits are replaced by new cultural habits. They acquire increasing proficiency in self-expression and in fulfilling their various social needs.

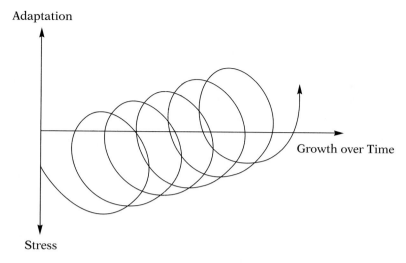

FIGURE 1 • Stress-Adaptation-Growth Dynamics

Three interrelated aspects of the strangers' intercultural transformation are specified in the present theory as the key outcomes of the cross-cultural adaptation process. The first aspect is an increased *functional fitness*. Through the repeated activities resulting in new cultural learning and internal reorganizing, strangers in time achieve an increasing "synchrony" (Hall, 1976; Y. Kim, 1993) between their internal responses and the external demands in the host environment. Successfully adapted strangers have accomplished a desired level of proficiency in communicating and developing a satisfactory relationship with the host society—particularly with those individuals and situations that are of direct relevance to their daily activities.

Closely associated with the increased functional fitness is increased psychological health in relation to their host environment. The *psychological health* of strangers is directly linked to their ability to communicate and the accompanying functional fitness in the host society. . . .

The development of functional fitness and psychological health in strangers is likely to accompany an emergent *intercultural identity*. Adversarial cross-cultural experiences bring about the experiences of what Zaharna (1989) calls "self-shock," a

"shake-up" of the strangers' sense of connection to their original cultural group and an accompanying growth. . . . In Adler's (1976) words, this emergent intercultural identity is based "not on 'belongingness' which implies either owning or being owned by a single culture, but on a style of self-consciousness that situates oneself neither totally *a part of* nor totally *apart from* a given culture" (p. 391).

The Structure of Cross-Cultural Adaptation

PERSONAL COMMUNICATION

The successful adaptation of strangers is realized only when their personal communication systems sufficiently overlap with those of the natives. The capacity of strangers to appropriately and effectively receive and process information (decoding) and to design and execute mental plans in initiating or responding to messages (encoding) is labeled here as *host communication competence*.

By definition, the strangers' host communication competence facilitates their cross-cultural adaptation process in a most direct and significant way. It serves as an instrumental, interpretive, and expressive means of coming to terms with the host environment. It enables strangers to develop their understanding of the way things are carried out in the host society and the way they themselves need to think, feel, and act in that environment. Until strangers have acquired a sufficient level of host communication competence, they are handicapped in their ability to meet their physical, psychological, and social needs and goals.

SOCIAL COMMUNICATION

The strangers' host communication competence is directly and reciprocally associated with their participation in the interpersonal and mass communication activities of the host society. . . . [E]very host social communication event offers the stranger an opportunity for cultural learning.

Host interpersonal communication, in particular, helps strangers to secure vital information and insight into the mind-sets and behaviors of the local people, thereby providing them with points of reference for a check and validation of their own behaviors. Most strangers in a new culture must begin to form a new set of relationships as they find themselves without an adequate support system when they are confronted with highly uncertain and stressful situations. The crucial importance of host interpersonal communication activities in facilitating cross-cultural adaptation has been acknowledged and demonstrated widely and repeatedly across the social sciences (Kim, 1986). In some cases, the degree of host interpersonal communication has been accepted as an indicator of cross-cultural adaptation itself (e.g., Gordon, 1973; Nagata, 1969; Spicer, 1968).

Similarly, *host mass communication* has been observed to facilitate the adaptation of strangers (Subervi-Velez, 1986). While the interpersonal channel of communication offers opportunities for more personalized and thus "meaningful" involvement with members of the host culture, mass communication channels help them participate in vicarious learning through "para-social interactions"

with the host environment at large beyond the ordinary reaches of their daily lives (Horton & Wohl, 1979, p. 32). Compared with interpersonal communication activities, mediated communication activities may be governed by a lesser sense of mutual obligation and effort. Thus, while host mass communication renders less opportunity for feedback than do interpersonal communication situations where a quick exchange of information is maximal (Rogers, 1979; Schramm, 1979), it serves as an important source of cultural and language learning, particularly during early phases of the adaptation process when strangers have less direct access and less likelihood to succeed in communicating with the natives face-to-face.

In many countries today, most strangers' interpersonal and mass communication activities involve their coethnics or conationals and home cultural experiences as well. Whether we speak of British compounds in India, American military posts in West Germany, Puerto Rican barrios in New York City, Chinatown in Tokyo, or a Japanese student association in a Canadian university, ethnic communities provide strangers with access to their original cultural experiences. Many aliens have organized some form of mutual aid or self-help organizations that render assistance to those who need material, informational, emotional, and other forms of social support (DeCocq, 1976). In the case of many larger ethnic communities, mass media (including newspapers, radio stations, and television programs) perform various informational, educational, entertainment, and social services for their members.

These *ethnic interpersonal* and *mass communication systems* serve adaptation-facilitating functions for new immigrants and sojourners during the initial phase of their adaptation process (Kim, 1987). Because many strangers initially lack host communication competence and do not have access to resources to become self-reliant, they tend to seek and depend heavily on ethnic sources of informational, material, and emotional help and thereby compensate for the lack of support they are capable of obtaining from host nationals. Due to the relatively "easy" or stress-free communication experiences in dealing with their own ethnic individuals and media, intraethnic communication experiences offer temporary refuge. In the case of certain temporary residents, such as American military personnel stationed overseas, their daily duties confine their social communication activities almost exclusively to other Americans at the military base.

Beyond the initial phase, however, ethnic social communication has been found to be important for group identity maintenance (Boekestijn, 1988) and negatively associated with adaptation into the host culture (J. Kim, 1980; Kim, 1976, 1977, 1980, 1986, 1989, 1990; Shah, 1991; Walker, 1993; Yang, 1988). Whether by choice or by circumstance, the strangers' heavy and prolonged reliance on coethnics sustains their original cultural identity and limits their opportunities to participate in the social communication activities of the host society (Burgess, 1978). Implied in this observation is that strangers cannot remain strongly ethnic in their communication activities and, at the same time, become highly adapted to the host cultural environment. They are likely to remain poor in their functional fitness in the host environment, which, in turn, hinders their intercultural transformation.

ENVIRONMENT

To the extent that strangers participate in the social (interpersonal, mass) communication activities of the host society, the host society exerts influence on their adaptation process. The nature of such influence, in turn, is shaped by the various characteristics of the host society and, for many, their social environment includes fellow coethnics as well.

Given the mixed nature of the environment in which many strangers find themselves, three environmental conditions are identified . . . as affecting the individual stranger's adaptation process: (1) host receptivity, (2) host conformity pressure, and (3) ethnic group strength. *Host receptivity* . . . refers to the degree to which a given environment is structurally and psychologically accessible and open to strangers. Different locations in a given society may offer different levels of receptivity toward different groups of strangers. For example, Canadian visitors arriving in a small town in the United States are likely to find a largely receptive host environment. On the other hand, the same small town may

show less receptivity toward visitors from a lesser known and vastly different culture such as Turkey or Kenya.

Along with receptivity, *host conformity pressure* (Zajonc, 1952) varies as well across societies and communities. Here, *conformity pressure* refers to the extent to which the environment challenges strangers to adopt the normative patterns of the host culture and its communication system. In particular, the conformity pressure of a host environment is often reflected in the expectations the natives routinely have about how strangers should think and act. . . . Different host environments show different levels of tolerance to strangers and their ethnic/cultural characteristics. For example, heterogeneous and open host environments such as the United States generally tend to hold a more pluralistic political ideology concerning cultural/ethnic differences and thereby exert less pressure on strangers to change their habitual ways. Within the United States, ethnically heterogeneous metropolitan areas such as Los Angeles and Miami tend to demand less that strangers conform to the dominant Anglo-white cultural practices than do small, ethnically homogeneous rural towns. Further, even within a city, certain neighborhoods may be more homogeneous and thus expect more conformity from strangers.

The degree to which a given host environment exerts receptivity and conformity pressure on a stranger is closely influenced by *the strength of the stranger's ethnic group* relative to the host environment at large. . . . In the long run, however, a strong ethnic community is likely to exert stronger social pressure to conform to its own cultural practices and to maintain the strangers' ethnic group identity. This, in turn, discourages their participation in the host social communication activities that are necessary for their adaptation to the larger society. . . .

PREDISPOSITION

Along with the above-described host and ethnic environmental conditions, the process of cross-cultural adaptation is affected by the internal conditions of the strangers themselves prior to resettlement in the host society. . . .

First, strangers come to their new environment with differing levels of *preparedness,* that is, the mental, emotional, and motivational readiness to deal with the new cultural environment including understanding of the host language and culture. Affecting their preparedness are a wide range of formal and informal learning activities they may have had prior to moving to the host society. Included in such activities are the schooling and training in, and media exposure to, the host language and culture, and the direct and indirect experiences in dealing with members of the host society as well as the prior intercultural adaptation experiences in general. In addition, the strangers' preparedness is often influenced by the level of positive expectations toward the host society and of willingness to participate in it voluntarily. Voluntary, long-term immigrants, for example, are more likely to enter the host environment with a greater readiness for making adaptive changes in themselves compared with temporary sojourners who unwillingly relocate for reasons imposed on them.

Strangers also differ in cultural, racial, and linguistic backgrounds. The term *ethnicity* is used here as an inclusive term to refer to various characteristics of strangers pertaining to their distinctiveness as a people. As such, the Japanese sojourners and immigrants bring to a given host society common physical, linguistic, and cultural features that are different than, say, Mexicans or the French. Such ethnic characteristics play a crucial role in the cross-cultural adaptation process, as it affects the ease or difficulty with which the stranger is able to develop communication competence in a given host society and participate in its social communication activities. For instance, many of the Japanese business executives in the United States are likely to face a lesser amount of host receptivity in overcoming their physical, linguistic, and cultural barriers than are their British counterparts. This suggests that strangers of different ethnic backgrounds embark on their cross-cultural journey with different levels of advantage or "handicap" (Phinney & Rosenthal, 1992, p. 145). . . .

Along with ethnic backgrounds, strangers enter a host environment with a set of more or less enduring *personality* traits. They begin the challenge of the new environment within the context of their existing personality, which serves as the basis upon which they pursue and internalize new experiences with varying degrees of success. Of particular interest to the present theory are those personality resources that would help facilitate the strangers' adaptation by enabling them to endure stressful challenges and to maximize new learning, both of which are essential to their intercultural transformation.

Openness is such a personality construct. . . . Openness minimizes resistance and maximizes a willingness to attend to new and changed circumstances. Openness further enables strangers to perceive and interpret various events and situations in the new environment as they occur with less rigid, ethnocentric judgments. . . . Also, the present meaning of openness includes the optimism and affirmative orientation in the strangers' basic outlook on life as well as their fundamental "self-trust" in the face of adverse circumstances. It is a dimension of personality that enables strangers to continually seek to acquire new cultural knowledge and to cultivate greater intellectual, emotional/aesthetic, and behavioral compatibility with the natives.

Strength is an additional personality trait that is vital to cross-cultural adaptation. Like openness, personality strength is a broad concept that represents a range of interrelated personality attributes such as resilience, risk-taking, hardiness, persistence, patience, elasticity, and resourcefulness. Personality strength thus means the inner quality that absorbs "shocks" from the environment and bounces back without being seriously damaged by them. Low levels of personality strength are seen in tendencies to be shy, fearful, and easily distressed by uncertain or stressful situations. On the other hand, individuals with high levels of personality strength tend to be stimulated by new challenges and remain effervescent and confident (Lifton, 1993).

The above two broad concepts, openness and strength, help define the strangers' overall personality predisposition to "push" themselves in their adaptation process. Strangers with greater openness and strength are less likely to succumb and more likely to take on the challenging situations in the

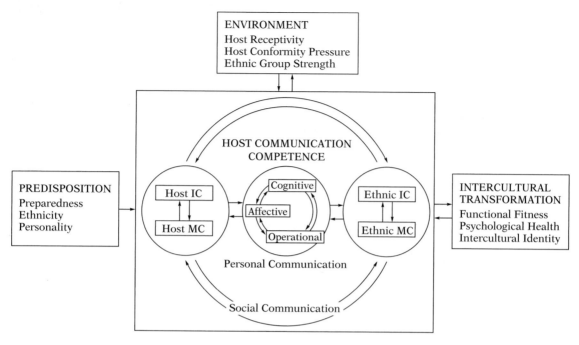

FIGURE 2 • A Communication Model of the Structure of Cross-Cultural Adaptation
(NOTE: IC = interpersonal communication; MC = mass communication.)

host society. Their personality predisposition serves as an inner resource for working toward developing the host communication competence, so as to facilitate their own intercultural transformation and growth. A serious lack of openness and strength, on the other hand, would weaken their adaptive capacity and would serve as self-imposed psychological barriers against their own adaptation.

Conclusion

The present theory portrays cross-cultural adaptation as a collaborative effort, in which a stranger and the receiving environment are engaged in a joint venture [see Figure 2]. As such, one cannot overemphasize the important role that the host society can play to embrace the stranger and facilitate his or her adaptive effort. Ultimately, however, cross-cultural adaptation is, and must be, "the gift of the individuals" (Steele, 1990, p. 171). It is neither reasonable nor practical to expect any large population to

significantly modify its own cultural habits with the sense of urgency that is required of a newcomer. The main power and responsibility for change has to reside in the stranger who, in the end, is responsible for his or her own psychological and social welfare.

Indeed, most strangers under most conditions appear to understand this reality and to accept their cross-cultural predicaments as part and parcel of living in an unfamiliar cultural milieu. They are not only willing but also able to make necessary self-corrections, recognizing that doing so is in their own self-interest (Cornell, 1988). Such is the case in the experiences of many of the former Peace Corps volunteers, diplomats, missionaries, and exchange students, not to mention the countless immigrants and refugees who have ventured through experiential territories seldom thought possible or even desirable. Their successful adaptation experiences are represented by Japanese American writer Jeanne Wakatsuki Houston (1981), who offers a personal intercultural transformation:

Now I entertain according to how I feel that day. If my Japanese sensibility is stronger, I act accordingly and feel OK. If I feel like going all American, I can do that too and feel OK. I've come to accept the cultural hybrid of my personality and recognize it as a strength, not as a weakness.

Personal testimonials such as this bear witness to the remarkable human capacity to carry on life even under the conditions of an extreme cultural estrangement. Cross-cultural adaptation as depicted in this theory thus is not an extraordinary phenomenon that only exceptional individuals achieve. Rather, it is simply an incident of the normal human mutability manifesting itself in the work of ordinary people "stretching" themselves out of the old and familiar. In their individual stories, the present theory finally rests.

Selected References

Adler, P. S. (1976). Beyond cultural identity: Reflections on cultural and multicultural man. In L. Samovar & R. Porter (Eds.), *Intercultural communication: A reader* (2nd ed., pp. 362–378). Belmont, CA: Wadsworth.

Boekestijn, C. (1988). Intercultural migration and the development of personal identity. *International Journal of Intercultural Relations, 12*(2), 83–105.

Burgess, M. (1978). The resurgence of ethnicity: Myth or reality? *Ethnic and Racial Studies,* 1(3), 265–285.

Cornell, S. (1988). *The return of the Natives: American Indian political resurgence.* New York: Oxford University Press.

Dance, F., & Larson, C. (1976). *The functions of human communication: A theoretical approach.* New York: Holt, Rinehart & Winston.

DeCocq, G. (1976). European and North American self-help movements: Some contrasts. In A. Katz & E. Bender (Eds.), *The strength in us: Self-help groups in the modern world* (pp. 202–208). New York: New Viewpoint.

Geyer, F. (1980). *Alienation theories: A general systems approach.* New York: Pergamon.

Gordon, M. (1973). Assimilation in America: Theory and reality. In P. Rose (Ed.), *The study of society* (pp. 350–365). New York: Random House.

Hall, E. T. (1976). *Beyond culture.* Garden City, NY: Anchor.

Horton, D., & Wohl, R. (1979). Mass communication and para-social interaction. In G. Gumpert & R. Cathcart (Eds.), *Inter/media: Interpersonal communication in a media world* (pp. 32–55). New York: Oxford University Press.

Houston, J. (1981, May). *Beyond Manzanar: A personal view on the Asian-American womanhood.* Audiorecording of a lecture delivered at Governors State University, University Park, IL.

Kim, J. (1980). Explaining acculturation in a communication framework: An empirical test. *Communication Monograph, 47*(3), 155–179.

Kim, Y. (1976). *Communication patterns of foreign immigrants in the process of acculturation: A survey among the Korean population in Chicago.* Unpublished doctoral dissertation, Northwestern University, Evanston, IL.

Kim, Y. (1977). Inter-ethnic and intra-ethnic communication: A study of Korean immigrants in Chicago. *International and Intercultural Communication Annual, 4,* 53–68.

Kim, Y. (1980). *Research project report on Indochinese refugees in Illinois: Vol. 1. Introduction, summary and recommendations. Vol. 2. Methods and procedures. Vol. 3. Population characteristics and service needs. Vol. 4. Psychological, social and cultural adjustment of Indochinese refugees. Vol. 5. Survey of agencies serving Indochinese refugees* (Based on a grant from the Department of Health, Education and Welfare Region V, pp. 95–549). Chicago: Travelers Aid Society.

Kim, Y. (1986). Understanding the social context of intergroup communication: A personal network approach. In W. Gudykunst (Ed.), *Intergroup communication* (pp. 86–95). London: Edward Arnold.

Kim, Y. (1987). Facilitating immigrant adaptation: The role of communication and interpersonal ties. In T. Albrecht & M. Adelman (Eds.), *Communicating social support: Process in context* (pp. 192–211). Newbury Park, CA: Sage.

Kim, Y. (1989). Personal, social, and economic adaptation: The case of 1975–1979 arrivals in Illinois. In D. Haines (Ed.), *Refugees as immigrants: Survey research on Cambodians, Laotians, and Vietnamese in America* (pp. 86–104). Totowa, NJ: Rowman & Littlefield.

Kim, Y. (1990). Communication and adaptation of Asian Pacific refugees in the United States. *Journal of Pacific Rim Communication, 1,* 191–207.

Kim, Y. (1993, May). *Synchrony and intercultural communication competence.* Paper presented at the annual meeting of the International Communication Association, Washington, DC.

Lazarus, R. (1966). *Psychological stress and the coping process.* St. Louis, MO: McGraw-Hill.

Lifton, R. (1993). *The protean self: Human resilience in an age of fragmentation.* New York: Basic Books.

Nagata, K. (1969). *A statistical approach to the study of acculturation of an ethnic group based on communication oriented variables: The case of Japanese Americans in Chicago.* Unpublished doctoral dissertation, University of Illinois, Urbana-Champaign.

Phinney, J., & Rosenthal, D. (1992). Ethnic identity in adolescence: Process, context, and outcome. In G. Adams, T. Gullota, & R. Montemayer (Eds.), *Adolescent identity formation* (pp. 145–172). Newbury Park, CA: Sage.

Rogers, E. (1979). Mass media and interpersonal communication. In G. Gumpert & R. Cathcart (Eds.), *Inter/media: Interpersonal communication in a media world* (pp. 192–213). New York: Oxford University Press.

Schramm, W. (1979). Channels and audiences. In G. Gumpert & R. Cathcart (Eds.), *Inter/media: Interpersonal communication in a media world* (pp. 160–174). New York: Oxford University Press.

Shah, H. (1991). Communication and cross-cultural adaptation patterns among Asian Indians. *International Journal of Intercultural Relations, 15*(3), 311–321.

Shibutani, T., & Kwan, K. (1965). *Ethnic stratification: A comparative approach.* New York: Macmillan.

Slavin, M., & Kriegman, D. (1992). *The adaptive design of the human psyche.* New York: Guilford.

Spicer, E. (1968). Acculturation. In D. Sills (Ed.), *International encyclopedia of the social sciences* (pp. 21–27). New York: Macmillan.

Steele, S. (1990). *The content of our character: A new vision of race in America.* New York: St. Martin's.

Subervi-Velez, F. (1986). The mass media and ethnic assimilation and pluralism. *Communication Research, 13*(1), 71–96.

Thayer, L. (1975). Knowledge, order, and communication. In B. Rubin & J. Kim (Eds.), *General systems theory and human communication* (pp. 237–245). Rochelle Park, NJ: Hayden.

Walker, D. (1993, May). *The role of the mass media in the adaptation of Haitian immigrants in Miami.* Unpublished doctoral dissertation, Indiana University, Indianapolis.

Yang, S. (1988, June). *The role of mass media in immigrants' political socialization: A study of Korean immigrants in Northern California.* Unpublished doctoral dissertation, Stanford University, Stanford, CA.

Zaharna, R. (1989). Self-shock: The double-binding challenges of identity. *International Journal of Intercultural Relations, 13*(4), 501–525.

Zajonc, R. (1952). Aggressive attitude of the "stranger" as a function of conformity pressures. *Human Relations, 5,* 205–216.

Key Terms

adaptation

ethnic communication

growth

host environment

intercultural identity

interpersonal communication

stress

Discussion Questions

1. Why is cross-cultural adaptation so stressful?

2. Do you think it ever happens that sojourners do not ultimately adapt and grow in cross-cultural transitions?

3. Can you identify groups of sojourners or migrants for whom cross-cultural adaptation is particularly difficult?

4. Do you think this theory would hold true for sojourners and migrants everywhere in the world? Why or why not?

5. What kinds of research methods might one use to gather information that would prove or disprove Kim's theory?

27 The Cycle of Cross-Cultural Adaptation and Reentry

SHELLEY L. SMITH

All travel is circular. I had been jerked through Asia,
making a parabola on one of the planet's hemispheres.
After all, the grand tour is just the inspired man's way of
heading home.

—Paul Theroux, *The Great Railway Bazaar*

Shall we ever cease our explorations
So that the end thereof will be
To arrive where once we started—
And know the place and the people
For the first time?

—T. S. Eliot

Introduction

I was excited to see my family, my friends, eat certain foods that I hadn't been able to eat, and do activities that I hadn't been able to do. But terror was still underlying because I knew that I had changed a lot, that certain ideas and attitudes had changed and that at times my reactions would be really different than what people would be expecting. I think that was the main source of my terror, knowing that I had changed and trying to figure out how I would fit back into the place that I had left. It was like I was a piece that had been taken out of a puzzle, but I was a different shape now and I didn't know whether I was going to be like an amoebae and just ooze back into it or if I was going to have to cut pieces of myself off and reapply them. That was the terror.

This U.S. student is describing how she felt before returning from study abroad. Her feelings about having changed, and her expression of fear and confusion about how that change would affect her life at home, are not unusual among sojourners who have lived, worked, and shared the lives of people in another culture. It draws attention to the fact that cross-cultural adaptation is a cyclical process that begins with entry into the new culture and continues well after the sojourner has returned home. It also makes apparent the deeply personal, identity-altering nature of the changes that result from significant experience in another culture.

This essay focuses on the nature of cross-cultural adaptation, its effect on the identity of the sojourner, and the reasons that reentry into the home culture constitutes an important part of the process. Although adjustment and adaptation are often used interchangeably, they are separate processes. *Adjustment* involves the need for making short-term changes in order to become comfortable in a new environment. Most sojourners who travel abroad for a relatively short period of time will need to "adjust" to the new culture if they are to be comfortable and productive, but they know that these changes need only be temporary and they are able to make choices about what they will and will not do. As one sojourner put it:

It's hard when you're somewhere different not to kind of try to adapt. It took me a long time to get to the point where I realized, "No matter what I do . . . I'm still going to be American, I'm still going to be this person . . . so, it's okay . . . It's not going to really change; it's still going to stand out." And so it got to the point where *I just had to use that instead of try to hide it.*

However, because we assume that (1) most people must return home; (2) returning home requires sojourners to make choices about how they will integrate their experience abroad into their lives and identities; and (3) *adaptation* is used to describe the need to make long-term value, behavior, and identity changes; we use adaptation to describe the changes brought on by the cyclical process of cross-cultural contact and reentry (Anderson, 1994, p. 300). Examples and quotes from returnees are used to illustrate the theory.

This discussion deals specifically with voluntary sojourners who have spent significant time (more than 6 months) abroad, had meaningful interactions in their host culture, and returned home. Their experiences are likely to be different from those of tourists, people who are isolated from their hosts (i.e., military personnel, guest workers in countries such as Saudi Arabia), and refugees and immigrants.[1] The term "abroad" is used to describe a significantly different culture. It is understood that it is quite possible to experience profound cultural difference without leaving the United States; for instance, a middle-class Anglo American who spent significant time living in an Amish community or on a Navajo reservation might experience changes as profound as someone going to Mexico or Japan.

Cross-Cultural Adaptation

In order to understand how this process of adaptation influences identity, it is important to understand how closely *culture, communication,* and *identity* are intertwined. To do this, we need to view the three as interconnected parts of a *system*. A system is generally defined as "any person or whole that consists of interdependent parts" whose function assumes "dynamic interactions among its parts and with its environment" (Kim & Ruben, 1988, p. 307). In other words, who we are (our internal systems or identities) and what we believe to be right and true about the world and the people in it are profoundly influenced by our environment—our families, the social circles in which we travel, and cultural influences. Further, these same personal, cognitive, social, and cultural systems are interrelated and interdependent. For instance, as U.S. Americans, the ideas of individual freedom, independence, and personal choice are cultural values taught to us and reinforced by our families, friends, and educational systems. Our parents expect us to make our own decisions about our friends, romantic partners, careers, and lifestyles based on the values they have taught us. Our peers encourage us to experiment and find our own ways of expressing

ourselves. We respect those who we believe have "earned" our respect by what they have accomplished and what they know. A "good" student is one who is able to express his or her opinions, ideas, and confusions. Small class sizes are valued because they allow teachers to give each student individual attention based on the student's unique needs. Students from Japan, on the other hand, are more likely to have learned to seek support from and feel obligated to family, friends, and the institutions to which they belong. They are taught to respect hierarchy—those who are older or in positions of higher status. Japanese students are expected to obey parents and teachers because of *who* they are. Good students listen and remember what they are told; they seldom speak out in class or question their teachers. The Japanese prefer larger classrooms because students must depend on one another rather than on the teacher for support.

It is important to remember that these are only generalizations, not stereotypes. Most Americans are not totally self-absorbed or devoid of feelings of obligation to family and friends any more than most Japanese are devoid of individual desires, needs, and opinions. Within any cultural system, you can find great variety and a constant tension as people seek to balance individual and group needs. But in any system, there is significant cultural pressure to maintain the basic social order, however it is defined. That order is maintained through rules of interaction specific to the culture and regulated by a constant flow of communication among the people who make up the culture. Further, culture exists, for all intents and purposes, only to the degree to which it has been internalized by the people who are part of it (cultural identity). This is made even more complex by the realization that people internalize and draw important aspects of their identity and behavior from multiple, overlapping cultural systems associated with ethnicity, religion, race, gender, and the like. As a result, the very nature of a "culture," as it is experienced and expressed by the people in it, is fluid and variable. It is these people, with all their different talents, personalities, and experiences, who have internalized the most significant rules for behavior and interaction within their social and cultural systems. This is what brings

---

[1] Adaptation experiences of refugees and immigrants are colored by the fact that these people will probably never return home; therefore, their experiences appear to have a cycle of their own.

order to a culture's diversity and allows all members of the culture to interact with one another with minimal amounts of confusion and misunderstanding. Culture, then, is not the thing that makes us all the same, it is *the processes that organize our diversity.*

In spite of all this effort to remain stable, people and cultures are constantly changing and adapting to new information, ideas, environments, and people. This particular aspect has become increasingly important as ease of travel and shared media have caused cultures to become more interconnected. As a result, people and cultures are constantly trying to "cope" and readjust to these changes. Further, there can be a profound difference in how much an individual or culture resists change. In the United States, change is generally viewed as "good," and lack of change is seen as "old-fashioned," "hidebound," or "stagnation." However, other cultures may see their realities as more fixed or fragile, and view change as a threat to cultural traditions, values, and beliefs. This can be seen in Amish communities that avoid contact with "the English," pueblos in the southwestern United States that have pulled back from contact with Whites, and fundamentalist Arab cultures that view Western influence as "Satanic."

Finally, *communication* is the process by which all culture is learned and through which all cultural interactions take place. Through communication, people learn to relate to their environments, learn not only how to navigate their cultures but also who they are and how identity is defined (Kim, 1988, pp. 44–46). Communication, therefore, is at the core of culture learning, and this applies both to learning one's own culture and to learning and adapting to a new culture. Living in another culture requires people to interact in meaningful ways with others whose cultural experience and beliefs are different from their own. To be successful, individuals will inevitably need to make adjustments in their behaviors and assumptions about people and relationships. Changing or altering these assumptions is almost always accompanied by changes in identity as well. The greater the difference between the cultures, the greater the potential disruption in the cultural identity system. This is the core of the psychological work that individuals must do as they struggle to integrate new cultural patterns into their own identity systems during the cross-cultural adaptation process.

It is also crucial to understand how important the cultural context is in influencing interactions and relationships. The host or dominant culture has a powerful influence on what is viewed as "normal" behavior in any given situation, and it is the sojourner who must do the adjusting. While this may cause an individual to change, it is only in reentry that those changes can be fully evaluated and accepted or rejected in one's long-term identity. As a result, an intercultural relationship that works in one partner's culture may not always work in the other partner's home country. This doesn't mean intercultural relationships can't succeed, but they require work and often need to be tested in both cultures before they can be put in perspective:

> It was also a good transition for me to have French friends come visit because it allowed me to show them the States and acknowledge and get to deal with and talk about the differences. . . . And it was also nice because they were reminding me of things I really liked about France and *it legitimized all of the differences that I'd really noticed when I came back that my friends and family hadn't really been able to understand.* . . . It helped to have them be here and understand . . . *there were differences I think that I didn't verbalize or didn't even acknowledge* but that made me a little . . . not tense but just . . . I remember being tired a lot when I got back and I think it was just that I was doing all this processing that I wasn't even aware of . . . and that helped me because *it brought some things clearly out in the open.*

In the fact-based movie *Not Without My Daughter,* the plot turns on just such a phenomenon. The U.S. American wife is astonished to find that her loving and "reasonable" (by U.S. standards) husband changes when in the presence of his fundamentalist Muslim family on a visit to Iran. She is surprised and appalled that he behaves like a fundamentalist Muslim male and expects her to behave like a fundamentalist Muslim wife. Yet if we consider that the husband's behavior is related to, influenced by, and consistent with the social and cultural context in which it occurs, it becomes much more logical—even predictable.

Intercultural experience, therefore, does not happen simply by being in another culture (place), but through communicating and building relationships with culturally different others in that culture. In short, *we experience other cultures deeply only by experiencing other people deeply.* In the deepest sense, culture lies *within* and *between* people. The external setting may reflect, reinforce, and trigger certain cultural responses in the people who are part of a given culture, but without the living representatives of that culture to respond to those cues, a place is little more than an archeological oddity.

Adapting to Another Culture

Given the previous discussion, it is logical to assume that better communication skills would lead to better adaptation, better adaptation to more frequent and satisfying interaction, which in turn leads to greater adaptation, and so on. This does not mean the process is always easy. While intense interaction with host nationals and participation in host culture activities can cause initial adjustment difficulties, it also correlates highly with better overall satisfaction with the international experience (Kealey, 1989; Rohrlich & Martin, 1992). As one sojourner said:

> I couldn't imagine a better way to live in Senegal than to be embraced by friends and to *be a part of the community* and part of a project, to be in a work environment, a home environment . . . all of us including the village. I wouldn't trade that for anything.

Since successful adaptation is related to one's ability to communicate in a given cultural environment, adaptation is possible only when one's *internal* communication patterns sufficiently overlap with others within the culture. The degree to which the patterns of the sojourner differ with those of the host is the degree to which the sojourner must adjust or adapt. As one sojourner said of her stay in Algeria:

> At first I remember being really offended by the separation between men and women. It seemed demeaning and insulting. But over time I learned to love and understand the culture and I remember feeling *proud* to be sitting in the back seat with

the other women—they were amazing people those women . . .

Since there is an inseparable relationship between these cultural patterns and an individual's cultural identity, and because this interaction between the individual and the environment is so essential to the process of identity creation and maintenance, *identity maintenance and change become key components in the discussion of cross-cultural adaptation.* Adaptation involves the development and internalization of host cultural patterns of perception, communication—the creation of what Kim (1988) has called an *intercultural identity*—that is, a sense of self that results from the individual having internalized and integrated aspects of the host culture into the self. The individual's experience of the process involved in this transformation of identity has been referred to by many as "culture shock," a term that conjures up the rather unpleasant image of sojourners being attacked by the cultural equivalent of cattle prods. However, many believe that culture shock embodies a cycle of growth and learning that is the very essence of cross-cultural learning and the intercultural adaptation experience:

> The culture shock process is regarded as fundamental in that the individual must somehow confront the social, psychological, and philosophical discrepancies one finds between his or her own internalized culture disposition and that of the new environment. (Kim, 1988, p. 304)

Because the stress, discomfort, and confusion that can result from this process of adaptation and identity change is brought on by meaningful and significant internalization of other cultural patterns, I feel it is more appropriately described as a *deep learning* experience. While potentially difficult, even painful, it is the result of the sojourner achieving the essential goal of voluntary cross-cultural interaction—learning about another culture. In this way, encounters with other cultures help a person come to terms with "the roots of his [or her] own ethnocentrism . . . gaining new perspectives and outlooks on the nature of culture" (Adler, 1975, p. 22). More important, one must also come to terms with one's *self.* By resolving the intrapersonal conflicts that result from this transition process, new levels of personal understanding are realized, and the potentials for creativity, actualization, spontaneous expression of humor, and openness to new situations become part of the communicative response. This journey into self-knowledge is apparent in the statements of these two returnees:

> . . . the first two months or so, the experience was *grappling with myself* and sort of fighting myself. And it was really intense for me because I was very very shy and . . . very very introverted before I went. And that was amazingly difficult for me— it took a lot of intense looking at myself and wondering if I could do this and contemplating should I just get a ticket and go home tomorrow, can I do this—pushing my own limits.

> It was very enriching and rewarding and I learned a lot of things about where I live and where I came from and *who I was and who I am.*

The cross-cultural learning experience is seen in large part as a transition experience reflecting "a movement from a state of low self- and cultural awareness to a state of high self- and cultural awareness" (Adler, 1987, p. 35); that is, there is a change in the sojourner's basic identity constructs. The identity-altering nature of cross-cultural adjustment can be linked to communication between one's self and others in four ways:

1. Our identities (as are our meanings and realities) are largely created through our interactions with others.

2. Our behavior (including our communication) reveals our attitudes, emotions, and values.

3. We use others to validate our perceptions of self, our behavior, and our sense of what is "right." This is done by and large through feedback and perspective-taking.

4. The links between our sense of self, our behavior, and our reliance on others to ground our realities are largely out of awareness (Zaharna, 1989).

The changes resulting from the stress of being in an environment where the expected responses and interactions with others do not occur results in changes at *affective*, *behavioral*, and *cognitive* levels.

At the affective level, sojourners experience a loss of their sense of communication competence. That

is, they seek to meet the goals of others in their interactions, but the outcomes are not always what they expect. As a result, they begin to feel disoriented and incompetent.

> For about two weeks I must have called my parents every single day. I was just crying all the time because I didn't have any friends.

At the cognitive level, sojourners find that their attempts at perspective-taking to determine how and why others will respond to their communication behaviors are uncertain and ambiguous. The process of trial and error in communication attempts is interspersed with attempts to give meaning to the new behaviors by observing the response of others.

At the behavioral level, sojourners begin to change *identity-bound* communication and relationship behaviors in order to achieve better communication and improve relationships. Paradoxically, this behavior, precisely because it has been *adjusted* to the expectations of the other culture, creates a greater strain on the sojourner's sense of identity. This double bind is at the root of adjustment difficulty and the forces at work to create identity change. Only by altering one's sense of identity to accommodate the behavior adjustment can the person move forward into adaptation and ease that stress.

This process results in changes that affect the sojourner's sense of self and perspective, often creating new ways of seeing the world:

> I think I see the world differently. I mean . . . as far as my vision . . . my *lens has changed* for looking at things to pull out different insights . . . I think that those are related to spending a long time in another culture.

It is critical to stress that all or most of these processes occur *out of awareness*. This realization impacts the intensity of the adjustment in-country because the person is essentially unaware of why he or she is feeling confused and disoriented. The reentry experience is also impacted because the perceptual and identity changes that take place are likely to make the person feel essentially more "normal" in the new culture. Therefore, the depth of the change people experience while abroad is not fully realized until they return home. As one sojourner said:

> I expected just to . . . go home . . . you're home. Everything will be the same. Not everything will be the same because I knew that . . . there will be some changes but *I didn't expect that there would be this readjustment process to such a great extent.*

Returning Home

On reentry into the home culture, sojourners finally confront the changes in their identity and perceptual and behavioral frameworks, creating a whole new set of adaptation issues. Many returnees feel that they have become "strangers" in their own culture:

> I found it *harder coming back than going,* just because with everything to look forward to and coming back . . . everything was just the same; nothing had changed, and I felt like I had changed so much.

> It's almost like you're being a visitor again with your own family.

> It was visually very shocking at first . . . I felt really uncomfortable and just really strange . . . really unfamiliar with my surroundings . . .

> What I remember from their impressions from like the first day was that . . . I was just not reacting. I was just going . . . I don't know how I felt . . . I guess I just felt kind of weirded out . . . just kind of disoriented.

As a result, returnees need to *renegotiate* their identities and position within the home culture in ways that raise communication and adjustment issues very similar to the cross-cultural adaptation process (Martin, 1994).

> Coming back from Morocco . . . even after I had gotten back into this secure routine of my life; even after I had assimilated back into my own culture, *there was this constant attempt to deal with and understand this whole experience I'd just gone through.* Here it was my first time out of the country. I had been to a radically different place. It's influenced me tremendously, *I've grown tremendously from it, where is it going to take me, how is it going to define my life.* So, coming back . . . *I was*

very aware that I had just gone through a major transformation. It was going to take a long time to sort it out, how it's affected me and how it's going to continue to affect me and so on

Key among these dynamics is the need for meaningful communication with friends and family regarding the returnee's intercultural experience and identity-related changes. If successfully accomplished, this communication leads to improved relationships, greater social and emotional support, and ultimately the refinement of one's intercultural identity and that identity's orientation to the home culture. But the process is challenging, and many returnees struggle with how and when to talk about their experiences abroad—because in many cases, they still don't fully understand what happened to them.

> You've had this great experience . . . or even if you haven't had a great experience . . . you've just had this *immense* experience . . . regardless . . . and you come back and of course you want to talk about it . . . *because you want to continue the experience* and you want to have people that you can talk with and people get so sick of it . . . like, "I don't want to hear about that anymore!"

> In a lot of ways, I'm not the way I used to be. And I feel like I still am—I still am going through reentry. It's got to be . . . I haven't, *I haven't picked up my life to where I'm a normal American.* And I do, I feel comfortable, I feel relaxed but I still am out of sync. I can't play the mainstream role.

> . . . and so coming back, I have to start over and in some places I'm trying to figure out where to re-orient myself . . . I'm going to be graduating. I'm entering a new stage of life and thinking about my future and career and . . . there's [sic] a lot of transitional things that are going on . . . people are moving away . . . it's just . . . so . . . I feel very ungrounded right now. *I feel like I'm floating around and I don't really know what to hold on to . . .*

The dynamics of this process will be affected by the cultural context in which it occurs. That is, the forces on an individual to readapt, and the freedom he or she is given to express new cultural identities, can vary greatly from culture to culture. For instance, within the United States, the value of *individualism* places the focus more strongly on a person's sense of belonging, and assumes that one has the ability or the power or both to "make a place for oneself" that will meet his or her unique needs. U.S. American returnees, for example, often abandon relationships with friends and romantic partners who are perceived to be unresponsive to the returnees' needs to express their new cultural knowledge (Martin, 1986a, 1986b). The following returnees all expressed an inability to reconnect with people who did not share their experience:

> I had a lot of friends that afterwards *we just never really connected again.* Just because my life had changed and their life had gone in really different directions. There was one friend in particular, I was really sad to not really have anything more in common with her but it was on both ends. It wasn't just that I didn't have any commonality with her, she no longer . . . *we both had moved in such opposite ways.* It was really hard.

> . . . *I am finding it hard to relate to Americans* . . . it is very hard to form good solid friendships in America where they're going to last for a long time . . . because we're such a transient society . . . I find it terribly frustrating to get . . . to make friendships with some Americans . . . how do you get past the "Hi how are you doing" subject and get down to what do you think?

> . . . and my friends . . . I couldn't relate to them. . . . I would go to coffee, but I would have nothing to say to them . . . *we couldn't connect on the same level* anymore. We can now a little bit better, but nothing like we did.

The more collectivist the culture, the more likely reestablishing one's sense of belonging *to others* will be an issue. In cultures where a strong sense of community exists, group goals (family, community, class, etc.) may be seen to take precedence over individual goals or needs. One Japanese student, recently returned from a stay in the United States, described an incident that occurred while she was walking home with her mother after buying groceries. Hungry, she began to eat something they had just bought. Eating on the street is not done in Japan, and her mother chastised her profoundly. What people in the United States would likely see as a small, even humorous, deviation from the norm,

prompted this Japanese student to say, "I was *afraid*! What had happened to me?!"

This highlights the idea that communication in reentry is often "intercultural." Because cultural identity is tied to particular communication competencies and behaviors, and returnees have adopted a repertoire of other cultural competencies and behaviors, it is reasonable to assume that at least some of the time, they will be operating in interactions with this "different," or intercultural, identity. With identity confusion comes confusion in one's ability to relate to others. Research on returnees supports this idea. Returnees relate frustrations and concerns about lack of opportunity to use competencies acquired abroad, a sense of alienation from their peers, and an inability to communicate their experience to others (Martin, 1986b; Uehara, 1986; Werkman, 1980). And the inability of others to understand this process of identity confusion or the returnees' need for validation of intercultural identity and experience, or both, adds to the intercultural nature of their interactions:

> I wanted to just ramble on and just tell people about certain things . . . and I think the most frustrating thing for me was when I was trying to communicate to people how something was, *they just couldn't understand* . . . they just couldn't have an idea of what that was really like because they had never been there . . . they had never seen it . . . they had never tried it and when you're *trying to communicate to someone how something was, you really can't put it in words* . . . you just can never get it as close to how you'd like them to understand it because they have just not a clue . . . they really don't.

> I think because I was working on a different framework . . . I had just moved to a different level . . . because for me studying abroad . . . wasn't just "I go abroad, I come back," *it was something that became such an important part of me* and . . . if someone's not willing to try to relate to that . . . I wasn't willing to be hanging out with someone and not say "Oh, that reminds me of when I was in 'X' country." I wasn't willing to do that, and maybe they weren't willing to keep hearing that.

> . . . that's why Morocco was so important; *it really changed everything about who I was.* It forced me

to do so many things that I never really felt comfortable with before . . . *as a result, personal friendships changed a lot* . . . people that I had been friends with since high school . . . really began falling out after that. None of it negative but *finding it unproductive.*

As the previous discussion suggests, returnees are likely to be juggling a variety of cultural and intercultural identities as they struggle to renegotiate a viable sense of self that is inclusive of their international experience and yet still allows for fulfilling relationships in their home culture. Returnees are actively engaged in a process that requires *creative integration* of their "old" (predeparture) and "new" (host country) perceptual frameworks. The experience abroad, whether positive or negative, whether the sojourner is eager to return or experiences a sense of loss on leaving the host culture, can result in *growth and change that need to be integrated into the person's life* on returning home.

> *I can't even imagine what my life would be like if I had never gone abroad.* I think from the moment I went abroad and came back *there was no way to ever go back to what I was.* Certain things I remember about myself that I know I'm not anymore. Had I not gone away I would have continued along a different path. *But my whole life now revolves around having been an exchange student once.*

> *Going to Morocco was utterly life-changing.* It *completely* changed who I was and who I hoped to be. . . . I came home and . . . *changed my major* and what I chose to do for graduate school which is Middle Eastern studies . . . *the experience of going there has basically dictated what I want to become in every sense.*

Maximum growth and learning occurs when the individual experiencing transition has an *awareness* of the process and some form of *emotional support* from friends, family, mentors, and others who have been abroad in processing that experience—the idea that *you can't do it alone.* The work that needs to be done in reentry seems to require discourse within supportive relationships or environments.

> I didn't really know how to share with anyone because I didn't really have anyone who had similar

experiences to me. And then *it was really helpful to me to be able to find other people who had been abroad.*

> *You really need someone to talk to.* You can't expect someone to think that you're that different . . . that your mind is that far gone . . . and so I think it's absolutely essential . . . for a person going and coming between two cultures . . . that *there's some sort of bridge. There's got to be a bridge* . . . there's got to be something to step on in between to take care of it all.

Strategies for Facilitating Growth

Although long-term living, working, or studying abroad can be difficult at times, it can also provide sojourners with some of the most challenging, growth-producing, and rewarding experiences of their lives. The following suggestions are designed to help sojourners navigate those experiences as wisely as possible. The phrase "coping strategies" is often applied to such suggestions, but because that term seems to infer that one needs to make the best of a bad experience, I prefer to call these suggestions "strategies for facilitating growth." They are not exhaustive, but have been chosen as a place to start as a sojourner undertakes the very personal journey of negotiating and renegotiating cultural adaptation.

WHILE ABROAD

1. *As much as possible, it is important to understand your own cultural assumptions.* Because cultural assumptions remain essentially invisible until they are challenged, this is much easier said than done. It requires sojourners to examine their own culture and values before leaving home, while recognizing that during their stay abroad, some of those values will become apparent only when challenged. A woman who spent time in Greece gives a perfect example:

> I had been told that Greece was a male-dominated country and that they would follow you down the street in groups making noises and teasing you. As a feminist, I found this extremely difficult to put up with. No matter how many times I told myself they were harmless, my guts just tied themselves

into a knot every time it happened—especially at night . . . I just didn't feel safe. Other [foreign] women I knew had even worse reactions—they would yell, argue, one, out of frustration because none of these strategies had worked, even got down on her hands and knees and started barking like a dog to get rid of them—which actually worked, but I wouldn't recommend it as a strategy!

2. When your cultural assumptions are challenged, *you need to try to suspend judgment until you understand the reasons for your reaction.* The reaction is emotional and sometimes very intense. It is the time when it is hardest to be rational, and yet it is important to be able to stop, take a deep breath, and figure out why you feel as you do. This is much easier to do if you already have an awareness of your own values. The advice frequently given to sojourners is "keep an open mind" and accept the other culture's values and behaviors as not good or bad but "simply different"—advice that takes on a whole new weight when you are actually confronted with differences that strongly contradict your deeply held values. This requires that, at the most difficult times, sojourners need to exercise a willingness to try to understand not only what people do and believe, but also why they do it. The narrative in strategy #1 continues:

> Finally, in frustration, I went to talk to a Greek friend and asked her, "*Why* do they follow you?" Her response was, "They do this to Greek women too, but they really like to follow foreigners because it's more fun. I don't know if you will understand this, but it's all I can tell you, they have been there all my life and if they were gone, I would miss them." I kept thinking about that and after a while it actually did soak in that their behavior was "normal" for them. I just stopped being bugged and scared by them and was finally able to walk down the street comfortably.

3. When attempting to understand other cultures, it helps to recognize that *not all values are created equal.* Many differences can be accepted, embraced, and enjoyed over time, but others remain inviolable. I refer to the moment when people confront the places where they simply can't accept a cultural difference as "the cockroach in the soup" metaphor. This rather unforgettable image comes from a friend who was in the Peace Corps in Korea. Following an immersion orientation during which she lived with a Korean farm family, was given a Korean name and Korean clothes, spoke the language, ate the local food, and worked on the farm as a member of the family, she was given a weekend leave in Seoul. In a restaurant there, she ordered a bowl of soup. When served, the soup had a large cockroach floating in it. She remembered thinking, "If this cockroach fell off the ceiling, I can send it back, but if it's supposed to be in this soup, I need to eat it." Then she realized it didn't matter if it was supposed to be there or not, she wasn't eating the soup! It turned out, of course, that it wasn't supposed to be there, and she was given a new bowl of soup. There are always going to be things that sojourners simply can't accept—for example, my friend had no problem eating in a place that had cockroaches, but she was unwilling to consume food that had become their final resting place. Being able to engage in the *mindfulness* that allows you to understand that this is a personal choice, and that it is okay that others embrace behaviors you cannot accept, is an essential part of making those choices.

4. *Be willing to engage the culture.* This requires genuine interest, curiosity, and a willingness to take risks. Risks, in this sense, involve the possibilities of making mistakes, failing, and occasionally looking foolish. And looking foolish at some point is almost an inevitable part of the process. An example from another Greek sojourner highlights the very common issue of language mistakes:

> We were talking to a friend in a shop about what we were doing that weekend, and we meant to say we were going to a wedding, but the word for wedding and the word for orgy are the same— only the stress is different—so we said we were going to an orgy in otherwise pretty understandable Greek and everyone gasped and then started laughing at us, and we just didn't know what had happened.

5. *A sense of humor is vital.* The mistakes one makes invariably make the best stories later, and if people can laugh at themselves at such times, adjustment becomes much easier. While most people will give "foreigners" a reasonable amount of space

to make mistakes, some errors can have serious relational consequences.

6. Therefore, *it is also vital to be willing to explore misunderstandings* with your hosts in order to prevent reoccurrences, and to *be willing and able to apologize when necessary.*

7. *Be patient.* Adjusting to a new culture takes time and happens in increments. Overcoming the initial surprises, adjusting to the stresses involved in mastering language and daily tasks, and finally entering a place where you can deeply engage and understand the most invisible aspects of cultural difference are all parts of the process.

8. *It's okay to temporarily retreat and embrace your emotions.* In fact, it is a good deal better to take a break than to explode needlessly in front of your hosts. Almost all sojourners experience moments of anger, frustration, confusion, and occasionally even contempt for their host culture. All transitions require time and space to reconnect with yourself, examine what is happening, and allow integration of the old and new to take place (Bridges, 1980). This process can be enriching if it is embraced rather than repressed as a sign of "weakness" or "inflexibility." Use the time to relax, explore your feelings, journal, write poetry or letters home.

> I loved Japan and my Japanese family very much and I was extremely busy teaching English and taking ikebana classes and everyone was so nice . . . and then I remember becoming really stressed because I just felt suffocated. It was partly the group orientation and partly the "guest" thing—but no one let me go anywhere or do anything alone—I was so well taken care of that I felt like I'd hit the next person who was nice to me. My individualism was under assault—I felt like I was being treated like a child. Somehow I had enough presence of mind to know that I couldn't tell my Japanese family how I felt—No matter how I put it, it would have hurt them so I called a Japanese friend and she said, "You need a bath!" And she took me to a hot springs, and we took baths and drank saki and she explained a lot of things to me very indirectly and by the end of the day I was fine. I just really needed a time out.

9. *When things are most difficult, try to reframe your situation as positive.* Remind yourself that this is part of the adjustment process, that it likely results from achieving meaningful contact with the other, and is part of the deep learning process.

10. *Successful cultural adjustment is also likely to involve identity change, and that change will impact reentry.* One of the key issues returnees deal with is trying to explain their experience to family and friends at home. Returnees struggle with how to distill highly personal emotional and sensory experience into a coherent response when asked, "How was your trip?" Many find that keeping close contact with significant others at home and sharing with them the people, events, changes, and emotions as they happen makes talking about experiences much easier upon returning home.

> I would say that I always kept in close contact with all my friends and my family. I think a lot of times when people study abroad, sometimes they distance themselves. Maybe not on purpose—some people on purpose. And that doesn't help the readjustment back here either because you lose time—*you lose contact with those people, in just little everyday things*—those count also. I always kept in close contact with them so I felt like I wasn't missing out on a lot of things.

> . . . I had kept really close contact with my family and with a couple close friends and so when I got back it didn't seem like there was a huge gap . . . they wanted to hear about things.

11. *Finally, make meaningful closure with people in the host culture.* As much as a sojourner wants, or even intends, to see people again, it will likely be years (or perhaps never) before that happens. This reality makes saying goodbye a necessity. Telling hosts how much they mean, how much they will be missed, and celebrating the time spent together before leaving can ease the grief and pain of separation by eliminating guilt over the failure to do so.

> my host sister . . . who I shared my bed with and was probably my closest friend there, avoided me at the very end. The last few weeks she slept at her friend's house . . . she couldn't even really be around me very much . . . it was that hard . . .

because she would . . . go crying . . . I was really pretty emotional about it, but I think it might have even been harder for them because . . . I have another life here . . . I was looking forward to something *whereas they were watching someone leave . . .*

. . . When I left, . . . all the host families were all in tears . . . and I remember that my family said they wanted me to wave good-bye before I got on the plane and I thought I'm not going to . . . I just want to get out . . . leave them . . . say good-bye . . . hug them and all that and just leave *and never look back.* But I had an 8-year-old host brother and he and I had bonded quite nicely and so I thought I'd better say good-bye to him so I turned around and I waved, but I didn't make any eye contact . . . because I never really showed my emotions toward them. . . . But the first 3 hours I spent in the bathroom of the plane and I had the flight attendants knocking on the door asking if I was okay, but *I had no idea what to do because I was sobbing in the bathroom.*

ON REENTRY

In general, the greater the change, the more likely a returnee is to experience difficulty in readapting to life at home. In part, this is because the perceptual and identity-altering changes a sojourner can experience abroad change how he or she views relationships, events, and behaviors both abroad and at home. Initially, things may seem strange to returnees, and they may notice things about people and have cultural expectations that they previously ignored or accepted as "just the way it is." This can result in a surprisingly critical view of the home culture that can strain relationships with family and friends and further increase the stress of readjusting to the home culture. This initial discomfort can be compounded by an inability to express or explain how they are feeling or what exactly their experiences abroad meant to them. Sojourners can benefit from taking the following steps to prepare themselves for coming home, and thus avoid much discomfort:

1. *Think about the people and events that have impacted you during your experience abroad.* Reflecting on what you have learned and how you have changed can help put your experience into perspec-

tive. It can also help you begin to explain to significant others what you are going through.

When I came back from Guatemala, I felt something was missing from me and I still do . . . and it's almost to be complete now . . . *I have to integrate those two things* . . . my trip to Guatemala and here because I did leave that part of me there. . . . I envision myself walking down the streets of Guatemala and that makes me feel complete.

2. *Have realistic expectations about returning home.* Expect it to be difficult and confusing at times. It's normal.

People need to realize that things *aren't going to be the same,* to not expect to go back to friendships as they were . . .

. . . *relationships are going to change* . . . people are going to change how they relate to you . . . it's going to be different than it was before you left . . . and you really can't put the same expectations on people when you walk out of their life for a year.

3. *Recognize that, like adjustment to the new culture, reentry adjustment takes time and occurs in stages.*

I don't think I was all that happy about being back for really long at all. I don't think that lasted really. I've always been kind of like rational about it and I knew it was going to be like this . . . "this is okay . . . I know it's going to be hard. I know it's going to be hard to be in class again. I know it's going to be hard to do this." And I think I've just kind of been in this constant state of, "Okay, I'm not really excited about it right now."

4. *Allow yourself to embrace your feelings and take the necessary time to reflect and reintegrate.* Rereading journals and letters, and continuing to journalize and keep in touch with people abroad can help in this process.

5. *Let the sharing of experiences be a mutual process of give and take.* People at home have undergone different kinds of changes, and expressing interest in their lives helps them take an interest in what you, the sojourner, have gone through.

. . . I try to explain why a certain thing they might say would be happening and try to look at social, economic and cultural aspects of it and the history of it and why that would be possible and one of the harder things is that I often try to incorporate how the U.S. and its government and its policies and ideals have directly influenced what happens in another country . . . So that's a battle—to educate people.

. . . I got a lot of "How was Spain?" and I always try to give them a general view . . . I try to tell them that it was very difficult the first time because the culture is very different. But after a while, it turned out to be one of the best experiences that I've ever had. I always try to encourage people no matter what age . . . just to get over— not even to study abroad—just to be in a different country for even a week just to see how things are. So . . . I try to get on some of the important points that I thought happened to me when I was there—the difficulty when I first got there, the transition period, keeping it short so I don't bore them! But I don't want to give them the sense that anyone can go over there and it's going to be a piece of cake . . . So I always tell them "It's just— it's a great experience. It's very eye-opening. But it wasn't easy."

6. *Be prepared to do the necessary "relationship work"* that results from the internal tension of realigning and integrating your identity. People who care for you want to understand and share your experience, but need to be given information and contexts that they can relate to over time. On the other hand, some relationships may be abandoned if there is too much distance created between the returnee and the old friend.

. . . *I had to be the instigator of some thoughts and theories into my family . . . I was looking for how to explain to them that I had changed . . . and what the reasons are that I changed and how I had changed. I was trying to look for a foundation to give them and say "OK, here's what so and so says" or "this is what this type of research says, this is what's going on with me."*

7. In adjusting to your home culture, *apply the same skills you learned when adjusting to the host culture* (patience, empathy, genuine interest, curiosity, and concern).

I can engage in discussions that are multi-level . . . rather than saying, "This is what I think, this is what you think . . . okay, now we know what each other thinks . . . it's over." It's more "This is what

I think . . . this is why . . . I understand how you think" because I can look at it through those perspectives and having looked at it through your perspective, I can say, "I think your perspective is more important." Or I can say, "I'm still right because . . ." *It's almost an ability to be more empathetic and to understand situations from a different point of view.*

8. *Find some degree of structure with which to organize your activities on return.* This doesn't mean "losing yourself in activity," but having a reasonable number of tasks or things that need to be done and doing them.

When I came back from France my life was . . . laid out for me and I had fewer choices that I had to make or that I could make . . . choices were made by people other than myself . . . and that makes it easier . . . *there was this clear structure to go back into . . .* for me it's easier to have a structure and not be able to fit into it than to have almost no structure at all . . . because *having that structure at least gives you a framework to rebel against.*

9. *Seek out others who have similar experiences.* This can help you create a safe and comfortable identity community in which to process your experiences both at home and abroad.

I went to the undergraduate anthropology conference a couple of weeks ago and I met a woman who went to Tanzania on the Fulbright scholarship program, and I didn't know her before . . . we had a lot of talks . . . and *she had a lot of similar experiences . . .* so, I think that I could relate to her in some ways, . . . and so it's very good for me because she can relate . . .

10. *Find opportunities at home to use the language, knowledge, and skills you learned abroad.* Many returnees find it particularly rewarding to mentor others who are involved in international experiences— for example, U.S. Americans who will be going abroad, especially to the returnee's host country, or internationals who are new to the United States. Find opportunities to talk about important political, cultural, or social aspects of the country visited (schools, churches, business groups, etc.), or work as a translator or language tutor for someone who speaks the language you learned abroad. In Japan, where women have traditionally been excluded

from the corporate management structure, Japanese women who have been educated in the United States have created a place for themselves as corporate trainers for executives who need to do business with the West. Along with expatriate U.S. Americans, these women constitute the bulk of the cross-cultural training force.

11. *Recognize that consciously realigning your goals and desires to be congruent with your new skills, experience, and sense of self can be tremendously satisfying and empowering.* One middle-aged professor profoundly changed his life following a research trip to Central America. After a year of soul-searching and reflection to integrate the experience, he made a career change that took him away from the university and to full-time work with national and international social justice groups. Abandoning a career in which he had invested 30 years to take an entirely new direction took incredible courage and force of will. But he has never regretted his decision. While few returnees undertake such an extreme change, facing what needs to be done to integrate your experience remains an important task that is the first step to beginning a new adventure.

Conclusion

Having a significant experience in another culture is never a discrete event that begins and ends with entering and leaving the culture. The experience is deeply affected by the preparation the sojourner takes before departure, the nature of the experience abroad, and the degree to which the returnee is able to integrate that experience after returning home. That integration is, for many, the start of new beginnings and adventures, constituting a cycle of growth and change that impacts the sojourner's identity, career, and life for years to come.

References

Adler, P. S. (1975). The transition experience: An alternative view of culture shock. *Journal of Humanistic Psychology, 15,* 13–23.

Adler, P. S. (1987). Culture shock and the cross-cultural learning experience. In F. Luce & E. C. Smith (Eds.), *Toward internationalism* (pp. 24–35). Cambridge, MA: Newbury.

Agar, M. (1994). The intercultural frame. *International Journal of Intercultural Relations, 18*(2), 221–238.

Anderson, L. E. (1994). A new look at an old construct: Cross-cultural adaptation. *International Journal of Intercultural Relations, 18*(3), 293–328.

Bridges, W. F. (1980). *Transition: Surviving life's changes.* Boston, MA: Addison-Wesley.

Kealey, D. J. (1989). A study of cross-cultural effectiveness: Theoretical issues. *International Journal of Intercultural Relations, 13*(3), 387–428.

Kim, Y. Y. (1984). Searching for creative integration. In W. B. Gudykunst & Y. Y. Kim (Eds.), *Methods for intercultural communication research* (pp. 13–30). Beverly Hills, CA: Sage Publications.

Kim, Y. Y. (1988). *Communication and cross-cultural adaptation.* Philadelphia: Multilingual Matters, Ltd.

Kim, Y. Y., & Ruben, B. D. (1988). Intercultural transformation. In W. B. Gudykunst & Y. Y. Kim (Eds.), *Theories in intercultural communication* (pp. 299–322). Beverly Hills, CA: Sage Publications.

Martin, J. N. (1986a). Communication in the intercultural reentry: Student sojourners' perception of change in reentry relationships. *International Journal of Intercultural Relations, 10*(1), 1–22.

Martin, J. N. (1986b). Patterns of communication in three types of reentry relationships: An exploratory study. *Western Journal of Speech Communication, 50*(1), 183–189.

Martin, J. N. (1994). Intercultural communication: A unifying concept for international education exchange. In G. Althen (Ed.), *Learning across cultures* (pp. 9–30). New York: NAFSA.

Rohrlich, B. F., & Martin, J. N. (1992). Host country and reentry adjustment of student sojourners. *International Journal of Intercultural Relations, 15,* 163–182.

Uehara, A. (1986). The nature of American student reentry adjustments and perceptions of the sojourn experience. *International Journal of Intercultural Relations, 10,* 415–438.

Werkman, S. L. (1980). Coming home: Adjustment of Americans to the U.S. after living abroad. In D. Cohelo & M. Ahmed (Eds.), *Uprooting and development: The dilemma of coping with modernization* (pp. 118–139). Boston, MA: Plenham Publishing Corp.

Zaharna, R. S. (1989). Self-shock: The double-binding challenge of identity. *International Journal of Intercultural Relations, 13*(4), 501–525.

Key Terms

adaptation   reentry
communication   sojourner
culture   system
identity

Discussion Questions

1. The author suggests that international experience is a cycle of growth and change that continues long after the return home. Can you think of experiences that have changed you in significant ways?

2. Does the idea that people and cultures are interacting human systems make sense to you?

3. Does the idea of culture as an *internalized* system of values make sense to you? Can cultures exist independent of the people in them?

4. Does the discussion of "culture shock as deep learning" make sense to you? How do you feel about the term? Can you think of a better way to describe it?

28 Translated Enactments
The Relational Configurations of the Asian Indian Immigrant Experience

RADHA S. HEGDE

"Migrants—borne-across humans—are metaphorical beings in their very essence; and migration, seen as a metaphor, is everywhere around us. We all cross frontiers; in that sense, we are all migrant peoples."

(Rushdie, 1991, p. 278)

Migrants, as Rushdie suggests, cross far more than just national borders. In fact, the migrant experience is characterized by an oscillation between the past and present, the exterior world and the interior, the self and other. These tensions take on a complex and urgent turn in the lives of immigrants, who face a disruption in their sense of cultural coherence and continuity. A sense of loss and a desire to rebuild are frequently evoked by immigrants like myself from India. In the process of forging a new life on the borders, these 'borne-across' individuals redefine the very meaning of community, identity, and culture. The contestation of these taken-for-granted ideas takes place in the context of everyday interactions. This essay elaborates on the ways in which the realities of the Asian Indian[1] immigrant experience is constituted relationally.

Consider this weekend scenario in an Asian Indian immigrant home: The aroma of Indian cooking replete with cinnamon, cardamom, saffron, and ginger rises in the air as friends arrive. The colors of Indian saris stand out, making a statement of embodied difference. The afternoon warms up with an array of appetizers—a tantalizing multicultural spectacle ranging from salsa and chutney to tahini! The conversation also spans a vast geographical and cultural terrain. We hear Raj commenting on the food: "You've really managed to get the taste of these samosas exactly as in India. It reminds me of eating hot samosas and chutney as a college kid in Delhi." "But we must watch the cholesterol," says Sunil. "Did you hear the rate of heart attack among Indian immigrants has gone up leaps and bounds? My cardiologist friends gave me this statistic. I tell

---

[1] "Asian Indian" is a term used by the U.S. Census to refer to immigrants from South Asia—that is, India, Pakistan, Sri Lanka, Bangladesh, Nepal, and Bhutan.

you, it's all the tension in this country." When this morbid topic runs out, a suggestion for Indian music is made. "Any old-time music? I can't stand this new music from India." A raga, a classical melody, begins to waft melodiously and rather sonorously in the background. "So what is the election news in India? Do you get the ethnic channel on your cable network?" Some channel surfing finally yields the football game.

In another part of the house, Priya and Mohana are sharing their feelings about mothering—"It is so hard to parent in this bicultural world. I know my daughter thinks I don't understand her, and she is convinced I don't understand American life either." They share stories of sons and daughters, of workplace politics. Someone changes the subject to an ethnic event at the local Hindu temple—"Oh, by the way, did you hear about that Indian temple that was stoned?" A heated discussion ensues. Just then a new batch of samosas arrives from the kitchen, ready to be savored. There is a roar from the adjoining room. The football game gets intense. "American football is where the action is. What did you say, cricket? Can't take it anymore—just too long drawn out."

This scenario shows you how Asian Indian immigrants collapse cultural worlds even as they socialize and talk about seemingly mundane things from food to raising children. Questions of change, the past, perception of difference by the world outside, and images of hybridity weave in and out of the conversation. The articulation of these issues arises directly from the critical location of these immigrants at the confluence of two cultures. A number of social questions and individual pressures arise from having to adapt to new norms while simultaneously adhering to older, more familiar ways. These experiences of new immigrants are marked by the multiple issues of race, class, gender, and varied historical positionings. The migrant experience is a very visible subject in the current context of increasing globalization and border-crossings (Bammer, 1994). This essay addresses the processes by which Asian Indians locate themselves and create meanings within the bicultural patterns of their ethnic lives.

Clustered in the large urban centers of the United States, Asian Indians represent a fast-growing and new Asian minority group. The major influx of immigrants from the Indian subcontinent came in the 1960s when changes in the immigration law made it possible for the entry of professionally trained people. Asian Indian immigrants represent the rich linguistic, religious, and cultural diversity of India and are very visible for their high levels of education and training in scientific and technological fields (Saran, 1985).

These immigrants actively maintain close connections with India and attempt to preserve Indian traditions by forming ethnic networks in their transplanted contexts (Fisher, 1980). In fact, there is quite a proliferation of Indian social organizations in the United States whose main mission is to promote traditional culture. Recently, there has also been an increase in the number of professional organizations, political groups that strive to provide a voice for the Asian Indian population, including organizations with a strong activist agenda.

Of Disruption and Reconstructions

In the process of traveling between worlds, migrants like the Asian Indians face disruptions in their historical roots, their language, and the social conventions they know and have practiced. Rushdie (1991), who writes with great sensitivity about the migrant sensibility, calls this the triple dislocation. The loss of the three most important parts of self-definition compels immigrants to find new ways of describing self. These disruptions are not just a passing phase or a cultural gap that will be filled in time. Rather, they continually arise and are reproduced in the communicative realities of migrant lives.

The tales of immigrants about their experiences in adopted worlds reveal how the triple dislocations acquire multiple forms. In my conversations with other immigrants from India, certain themes arise with an alarming regularity: a questioning about self, the meaning of immigrant existence, the uncertainty of the future. To immigrants who come from a culture where kinship and a sense of ancestry are important, the loss of historical roots is a deeply disturbing reality to confront. In this context, it is evident that the triple dislocation of roots, language, and societal connections that subsume the individuals and their relational world is not about to be remedied with a handbook on cultural dos and don'ts or a course in accent reduction. Acculturative change is not about exchanging or replacing behaviors. It is imperative to think of these ethnic transformations as a process and not as a simple, one-stop phenomenon. The dislocations identified by Rushdie permeate into the very core of existence—definitions of selfhood, communal bonds, the fabric of culture and what it means. These repercussions are not isolated, psychological reactions but are part of individual and collective migrant narratives that shape reality. The next section discusses the concepts of culture, self, and community and shows how they are interrelated and constituted in the everyday lives of Asian Indian immigrants.

Anchoring Culture

Culture has never been an easy concept to grapple with. Now with globalization, the spectrum of cultural forms has grown exponentially. An old church in Houston is renovated to be a Hindu temple. A street in Queens, New York, feels like and exudes the aura of Bombay. There are areas in Chicago, Cleveland, and Los Angeles where saris and curry make an authentic cultural statement. On August 15, a veil of Indianness covers New York's Times Square to celebrate Indian Independence Day. Each fall, South Street Seaport in New York City is transformed into an Indian *mela,* or festival, with crafts, art shows, music, and dances from India to celebrate Deepavali, the Hindu festival of lights. Through these experiences of food, music, and entertainment, it is possible to experience Indian culture as a collage. As a visitor from India told me in total surprise after being at one of these ethnic public gatherings, "You immigrants are more into 'Indian stuff' than we are in India." That "Indian stuff" is what migrants conjure up as ethnic culture.

What happens to culture when it loses its moorings, its connections to geographical space? Until recently, it has been taken for granted that each country or geographically defined space embodies its own distinctive culture. In a world of mobile communities and interconnectedness, this view of culture is highly problematic because it assumes culture to be a static and discrete category. In the context of Asian Indians, the distance between India and the United States collapses and the lines between here and there blur. As any ethnic neighborhood demonstrates, we now have transplanted or translated cultures. As Little Indias crop up side by side with Chinatowns and Little Italys, one can actually feel the unexpected fusion of culture and place. As Gupta and Ferguson (1992) write, "'cultures' and 'peoples' however persistent they may be, cease to be plausibly identifiable as spots on the map" (p. 10).

It is the fear of assimilation and total cultural absorption that drives Asian Indian immigrants, as it drove earlier groups of other immigrants, to passionately recreate their culture of origins. These hybrid cultures that emerge hold a precarious position and often face violent opposition. History offers many illustrations of immigrant groups surviving hostility and rejection—for example, the building of Hindu temples in New Jersey by Asian Indians has met fierce opposition from local communities who felt their environments had changed with the "invasion" of new immigrants. Neighborhoods that have changed in character as a result of their new ethnic definitions have also aroused similar feelings. Hybrid cultures, therefore, are not always a romantic return to the homeland; they are also cultures that develop and survive as a form of collective resistance.

These experiences of ethnic communities call into question traditional notions of cultures as authentic and homogeneous. These immigrants, who are not only transplanted but translated, simultaneously inhabit the space of two cultures. In this process, they not only are transforming both cultures but at the same time are inventing a space of fusion and hybridity. Globalization and technological advances have so accelerated the interconnectedness of cultures that it seems archaic to think of cultures in any singular insular frameworks. As people are walking in and out of multiple cultural contexts, Chow's (1993) question seems timely: "Where have all the natives gone?" (p. 27). Extending this argument, one could ask, "Who is the authentic native?" What counts for authenticity in this contemporary age of globalization? The Asian Indian immigrants I meet consistently speak about their ambivalence, of being partially at home in two cultures and feeling part of none. What is it then to be an Indian in India and an Asian Indian in the United States?

Simplistic notions of culture have directed our attention to details such as clothing, food, and rituals. Although this total lifestyle view of culture is an important aspect, it is at best superficial. To understand the construction of hybrid cultures, we need to critically revisit the descriptive approach to the study of culture. Is it still a wrap that is superimposed on a community? Do Asian Indians form ethnic organizations only to take shelter under this remembered cultural rubric of the past? Why is it one hears of hybrid musical forms developing, such as Bhangra music among the Asian Indian diaspora that fuses the rhythms of traditional Indian folk music and rock? I am suggesting that we begin to think of cultures, particularly in this context of transitional movements, from the point of view of the processes through which communities render themselves distinct. You can study Indian culture in Delhi or in Queens, New York—which one constitutes the real "Indian stuff"? Cultures and natives travel in and out of familiar frames. You cannot contain culture for very long, not even in a pithy textbook definition.

Locating Identities

In this world of intersections, migrants are irrevocably the products of several interlocking histories and cultures (Hall, 1992). Consider the Singh family from Punjab in northern India whose family migrated to California to work in the orchards in the early 1900s. Take the example of Dr. Chandra, a renowned scientist who emigrated from India in the early 1930s and could not find a place to live because of his color. Meet the more recently arrived Mr. and Mrs. Sethi who run a chain of motels in Alabama and Tennessee, or Mr. Chadda who pumps gas on the New Jersey turnpike and longs for his family left back in India. Consider the second generation Asian Indian student in an Ivy League college who is being pressured by her parents to study engineering. Then there is Neeta, the computer scientist from Bombay who works for a major corporation in San Francisco and battles the glass ceiling as an Indian woman. Here are people who have taken different paths and many turns to reach their particular locations. You can see in each case how the individual is located within multiple points of cultural intersections. It is but inevitable that the narratives of self undergo a significant transformation under these contexts of relocation.

The key question to ask at this juncture is the one articulated by Clifford (1988): "What does it mean at the end of the twentieth century, to speak . . . of a native land? What processes, rather than essences, are involved in present experiences of cultural identity?" (p. 275). Identities, like culture, can no longer be viewed as self-contained, fixed, and stable but rather are constituted with the process of communication (see Gergen, 1994). This fluid conceptualization of identity is particularly relevant for understanding migrants whose coordinates of identity are being repositioned by multiple cultural narratives.

In the multiple crossings encountered by migrants, identity becomes a very salient topic. Identity becomes an issue only when it is in crisis, "when something assumed to be fixed, coherent and stable is displaced by the experience of doubt and uncertainty" (Mercer, 1990, p. 43). Identity is enacted and negotiated in the everyday world of relationships. Traveling between cultures, Asian Indian immigrants are defined and define themselves in shifting patterns of inclusion and exclusion. For example, my Asian Indian respondents tell me of how they squirm when they hear the words "you people" hurled about the ethnic group. They talk with pain about the sense of helplessness when confronted by violent racial slurs. In this way the external world provides a frightening push to migrants to engage with questions about their identity and place in the world.

There is an infinite and complicated process of identity construction that accompanies migration and movement between cultures. It seems to make sense to talk of identities in the plural, or of identities as being constantly invented and negotiated between the self and the external world. For example, as Asian Indians move between varying performative contexts, they develop narratives of self that combine the past and open up a trajectory for the future. These narratives evolve as a quest for self, a process of making meaning of life in the cultural in-between. Ethnic identities have to be seen as a production in which the scripting is contested, negotiated, and transformed from particular cultural and relational locations. There are multiple cultural communities with which one identifies. The sense of belonging being so fluid, immigrants show remarkable creativity in constructing new communities.

Translated Communities

The homeland is a very powerful symbolic anchor around which a sense of community is established for migrants. In a context of the triple dislocations mentioned earlier where culture and roots have lost their moorings, relationships to the homeland assume imaginative and powerful dimensions. Asian Indians build very strong ethnic bonds around points of commonality such as language and place of origin. The ethnic community becomes the new context of connections where an aura of distilled "Indianness" can be recreated.

In this process of forming new relationships within the community, Asian Indian immigrants have created a vast organizational infrastructure. There are religious institutions, temples, and cultural organizations all over the United States. Weekends for Asian Indians are typically crammed with ethnic activities. Dances, plays, religious ceremonies, musical events, and group celebrations of Indian festivals provide the opportunity for Asian Indians to mingle and socialize. These occasions provide an occasion for immigrants to wear special Indian clothes, speak an Indian language, and enjoy the sensuous thrill of India almost as a fantasy.

In a world where Asian Indians are continually aware of being the cultural "other," the need for establishing communal anchors is intense. The past offers the terrain on which to construct community, and solidarity is built around memories. The past acquires significance as a cultural anchor and a point of reference in the context of dislocation. Immigrants create surrogate communities where remembered dimensions of time and space are collapsed into the present. These ethnic communities survive to a large extent on nostalgia and reconnect to places that often have changed or disappeared in reality. The past assumes multiple forms and meanings in the conversations, activities, and rituals of Asian Indians.

These ethnic communities thrive on reviving a spirit of Indianness, an imagined authenticity of tradition. The social mores, rituals, and customs of the past are maintained with self-conscious discipline by many Asian Indians. "Unless we teach our practices to our children, who will? What will happen to them? Will they continue to be Indian at least in their outlook?" asked Nitin, a computer engineer who believes in exposing his children to "Indian ways." This usually means taking oftentimes reluctant youngsters to Indian gatherings, making them familiar with the norms and mores of interaction, and most of all, enforcing on the children a yardstick of Indian cultural propriety.

The home usually represents the untouched Indian cultural space. It is here that the mask can be let down and the social protocols of the outside world can be dismissed. Migrants tend to describe and bracket their lives in cultural binaries such as east/west, tradition/modernity, American/Indian. Mona, who has faced the pressures of growing up in an immigrant home, raised this issue: "My parents use the term 'modern'—they say we have to remember our traditions, kids from India are getting too modern." Or hear Bala, a professor who has lived in the United States for over 20 years: "I expect my kids to wear Indian clothes when we go out to ethnic gatherings and guess what I saw in Delhi? My friend's children who have grown up in India are more Americanized, wearing jeans, dancing to Macarena . . . the whole bit." To migrants, tradition is freezing a memory of Indian culture and a way of life that in all probability has changed even in India.

The ethnic community provides the cultural repository to fuse the narrative disruptions that migrants face in their transplanted lives. The building of ethnic communities represents a retreat into a perceived unity, a quest to bring together individuals who have the seeming potential for establishing solidarity. There is a great deal of time and energy that goes into building and maintaining relational ties within the ethnic group. In order to get at some everyday accounts of community, I asked some Asian Indians to talk about friendships and why they needed Indian friends. Their comments were insightful. The two worlds, inter- and intra-ethnic, were treated as completely different domains. The interethnic world represented the relationships and associations of the workplace. In contrast, their Asian Indian friendships were characterized as more spontaneous because there was no fear of doing something culturally amiss. An Asian Indian woman told me emphatically, "Even though the Indians I mix with are so different from me, in America, we are just Indians and I need them." In this way, even real differences among Indians are overlooked for the common bond of cultural origins. There we have it, the triple dislocations of social norms, roots, and language being healed in a sense by the cohesive power of the ethnic community.

The reproduced community also gains an old-world flavor and charm of its own. The active involvement in each other's lives, a characteristic of older and more cohesive societies, makes a reappearance. For example, Venu, who cherished his privacy, complained about the Indian community: "There is too much gossip, they want to know everything about you and then it's all out in the open." His friend Vasu was quick to retort: "Indians are changing, too. They are becoming as private and individualistic as Americans are, don't you think? You can't just walk into an Indian home in the United States as you can in India without calling or announcing yourself. It's not the same anymore."

The need and definition of community does shift even as the metaphorical distance from "home" changes. What is home to a migrant? The word is elusive to define and tantalizing to pin down. As Mohanty (1993) wonders, "Is home a geographical space, a historical space, an emotional, sensory space?" (p. 352). For those who live on the borders, home is an imaginary construct that shifts between all these spaces. Much as the ethnic group tries to fix the cultures of their origin, what they recreate asserts its own character. The hybrid culture of the Asian Indian community has an individual energy and identity of its own. How do we as scholars of intercultural communication study these cultures that are continually reinventing themselves without fixing them in narrow definitional straitjackets? The next part of the essay deals with this question of representing the complexity of the experiences of people in transition.

Remapping the Frontier

"Modes of representation that legitimated a world of strict cultural separation, collective identities, and rigid boundaries seem hopelessly outdated as the urban landscape is being rewritten within new and shifting borders of identity, race and ethnicity" (Giroux, 1994, p. 40).

The realities of displaced people provoke the reevaluation of some very important social issues. The experiences of the Asian Indian immigrants that you met in this essay exemplify the complex processes by which identities and social participation are constructed. Immigrant lives are constituted at the confluence of multiple realities. Contradictions are synchronous with life on the borderlands. The boundaries between concepts such as rooting-uprooting, local-global, here-there, past-future, national-international blur and are resurrected almost instantaneously. Ambiguity paves the "routes" of immigrants and their hyphenated lives—". . . the realm in-between where predetermined rules cannot fully apply" (Trinh, 1991, p. 157).

These large-scale demographic movements associated with globalization have challenged many traditional ideas regarding the acculturation of ethnic groups. Traditional models of immigrant behavior are based on the assumption of the self-defined autonomous individual who assimilated over time.

This adaptation was considered to be dependent solely on individual behavior patterns. However, the process of culture and identity constructions is by no means so clearly linear and straightforward. Negotiations of ethnic identities do not take place in a neutral, value-free environment. We need to be sensitive to the fact that difference and identities are framed within a complex web of factors, deep-set perceptual biases, and power systems that dictate social hierarchies.

It is unrealistic to recreate the ethnic condition as one of eternal longing for origins or as transitory stage to assimilation. Ethnic identity and culture are far more than frozen spectacles of the past. They are about changes and the multiple ways in which immigrants connect themselves in a social world and articulate their difference. Identity, community, and culture are so intertwined that even setting up boundaries between these concepts seems artificial in the everyday practices of migrant life. So our models have to be more messy and get multidimensional. They need to capture more lines and circles to represent the complex experiences of immigrants.

The experiences of displacement provide a spectacle of human drama. The Asian Indian examples reveal that narratives of self and configurations of culture are products of social interchange and take many curious turns. For example, I was deeply struck when a friend told me, "I went to this old neighborhood back home near Bangalore and some man who runs a store asked me about my grandfather. Can you believe it? Who would ever associate me with my grandfather in this country?" After 20 some years in the United States, where he is bereft of spatial and historical coordinates, this simple episode was emotionally overpowering and empowering in the connections it provided.

It is important to point out that the community of Asian Indians has grown enormously since the 1960s, and it is difficult to generalize about the experiences of diverse groups of immigrants. For example, the lives of Sunil the computer scientist, Raj who works at the docks in Newark, and Shetty who runs the Indian grocery store in the Midwest are caught up in completely different rhythms. Or consider the lives of Asian Indian women whose reali-

ties are appropriated by the sexist structures of multiple cultures. The simultaneity of race and gender further complicate the narrative trajectories of self for many immigrant women (see Hegde, forthcoming). Generational differences also impact the construction of ethnic realities. The famous "What will happen to our tradition?" question provokes an important issue to study and ponder: How will cultures of hybridity get reconstituted over time?

The translated lives and relationships of Asian Indian immigrants provide an enactment of the complexity of not-belonging or belonging partially to a new environment. The hybrid culture of Asian Indians demonstrates the problem of viewing cultures as homogeneous and static. Ethnic identities are the products of interlocking cultures and complex forms of identification. The memories of the past and the ambivalence of the present and the uncertainty of the future are woven together in complex relational configurations. It is in the communicative realities of their everyday world that the intertwined meanings of self, community, and culture are constituted for Asian Indian immigrants.

References

Bammer, A. (1994). *Displacements: Cultural identities in question*. Bloomington: Indiana University Press.

Chow, R. (1993). *Writing diaspora*. Bloomington: Indiana University Press.

Clifford, J. (1988). *The predicament of culture*. Cambridge, MA: Harvard University Press.

Fisher, M. P. (1980). *The Indians of New York City: A study of immigrants from India*. New Delhi: Heritage.

Gergen, K. J. (1994). *Realities and relationships: Soundings in social construction*. Cambridge, MA: Harvard University Press.

Giroux, H. A. (1994). Living dangerously: Identity politics and the new cultural racism. In H. A. Giroux & P. McLaren (Eds.), *Between borders: Pedagogy and the politics of cultural studies* (pp. 29–55). New York: Routledge.

Gupta, A., & Ferguson, J. (1992). Beyond culture: Space, identity, and the politics of difference. *Cultural Anthropology, 7*(1), 6–23.

Hall, S. (1992). New ethnicities. In J. Donald & A. Rattansi (Eds.), *Race, culture and difference* (pp. 252–260). Newbury Park, CA: Sage.

Hegde, R. S. (forthcoming). Swinging the trapeze: The negotiation of identity among Asian Indian immigrant women in the U.S. *International and Intercultural Communication Annual 21.* Newbury Park, CA: Sage.

Mercer, K. (1990). Welcome to the jungle: Identity and diversity in postmodern politics. In J. Rutherford (Ed.), *Identity, community, culture, difference* (pp. 43–71). London: Wishart.

Mohanty, C. T. (1993). Defining genealogies: Feminist reflections on being South Asian in North America. In Women of South Asian Descent Collective (Eds.), *Our feet walk to sky: Women of the South Asian diaspora* (pp. 351–358). San Francisco: Aunt Lute Books.

Rushdie, S. (1991). *Imaginary homelands.* New York: Penguin.

Saran, P. (1985). *The Asian Indian experience.* Cambridge, MA: Schenkman.

Trinh, T. M.-H. (1991). *When the moon waxes red.* New York: Routledge.

Key Terms

Asian Indian	hybridity
community	identity
culture	migrants
displacement	

Discussion Questions

1. Select any urban landscape, trace its growth spatially and symbolically, and see how it has been reconfigured with new borders of race, identity, and ethnicity.

2. Hegde talks about the construction of hybrid cultural forms as being an expression of migrant cultures. Talk to members of an ethnic group from varying age groups and see how they construct the meaning of these cultural forms.

3. Hegde describes globalization as a very significant contemporary issue. In what way does it make an impact in your everyday life? Is globalization in fact collapsing the categories of local and global, of the here and there?

4. Hegde's essay seems to suggest that Asian Indians maintain two distinct relational worlds—the inter- and intraethnic. Talk to people from different ethnic groups and see if their friendships and socializing differ along ethnic lines.

5. How do experiences of racism and discrimination affect the sense of community in an ethnic group? Direct your comments around a specific issue or news event.

29 South Korean Adoptees Growing Up in White America
Negotiating Race and Culture
ETSUKO FUJIMOTO

In his powerful essay "Secrets and Anger," David Mura (1994), a third-generation Japanese American writer and poet, reflects on the challenges he and his White wife, Susie, face as an interracial couple and as parents of a "hybrid" daughter, Sam. He writes that strangers often approach Susie when she is in a grocery store with Sam and ask her *where* she got the beautiful baby. In contrast, no one asks Mura the same question when he is out with Sam, whose physical features define her more as Asian than as White. People just assume that he is her father. The grocery store episode has become such a recurrent scenario that Susie "swears she's going to teach Sam to say: "Fuck you. My genes came all the way over on the *Mayflower,* thank you'" (Mura, 1994, p. 368).

Most of us in academia have come to endorse the sociohistorical construction of race and racial categories (Omi & Winant, 1994). However, as illustrated in the different ways in which strangers interpellate Mura, Susie, and Sam, physical traits (as manifestations of biological explanations of race) still serve as a dominant source of information and are the basis on which we make judgments and presumptions about who should belong to what racial group, who might be biologically related to whom, who may or may not form romantic and familial relationships, and so on. The increasing numbers of multiracial and multicultural families defy these faulty assumptions, and instead assert their self-chosen labels and claim their cultural crossings as valid experiences. There are now publications devoted to this mission (i.e., Root, 1992, 1996).

Multiracial and multicultural families are created not only through interracial and other types of intercultural marriages, but also through international and domestic transracial adoptions. Intercultural adoptees cross a number of social and cultural borders to become part of U.S. American families. Their experiences, perspectives, and feelings provide many insights into the multiculturalizing of families and race relations in the United States. In this essay, I discuss various ways in which South Korean adoptees do or do not establish relationships with their adoptive families and relevant communities.

South Korean adoptees have been one of the largest groups since the beginning of international adoption to the United States. Beginning in 1953, the Seventh Day Adventist church arranged the adoptions of a few South Korean children by U.S. Americans (Koh, 1981). In 1956, Harry Holt, an Oregon farmer, established an adoption program to place biracial children, war orphans, and abandoned South Korean children with U.S. American, Canadian, and Western European families (Koh, 1981; Register, 1991; Wilkinson, 1995). The success of Holt's programs led to the emergence of social agencies in South Korea to provide care and adoption services for homeless children, and these agencies remain active today. In the last 40 years, more than 50,000 South Korean children were adopted by U.S. Americans (Cox, 1996).

In the summer of 2000, I interviewed 20 Korean adoptees of widely diverse demographic backgrounds about their experiences growing up in White U.S. American families and in U.S. society in general. Aged 19 to 32, the group included college students, small-business owners, full-time mothers, a graphic designer, salespersons, and others. Their ages at adoption ranged from 5 months to 12 years. Their adoptive family makeups varied greatly: Some families had both biological and adopted children; some had only adopted children; and others were multiracial, including races other than White and Asian.

Just as their backgrounds are diverse, the adoptees' responses include a number of issues and perspectives, a full discussion and analysis of which cannot be covered in this essay. Therefore, I will share with you just a few things I learned about how the adoptees view their relationships with respective groups and people. First, I briefly discuss how they view their relationships with relevant communities such as Korean Americans and other Korean adoptees. Then, I focus on the relationships and communication within the families. The themes I present were recurrent across several adoptees but were not mentioned by *all* adoptees that I interviewed. All names in this essay are fictional.

(Non)identification with Korean Americans and Asian Americans

All of the adoptees I interviewed grew up in predominantly White neighborhoods and went to schools where the majority of students were White. This encouraged several adoptees to identify with Whites, while avoiding contacts with Asians when growing up. For example, Stephanie, whose childhood friends were all White, says she used to have a lot of self-esteem issues because she was not White. When she would look in a mirror with her White friend beside her, she felt that "this isn't right. She is so much prettier." David, who was adopted at age 12, says that he consciously avoided all Asians because he wanted to assimilate into the family and U.S. society. During his adolescence, he felt that his

Asianness was a handicap, because it was difficult for him to meet girls. Another adoptee, Molly, mentioned that she never wanted to be caught with another Asian in high school because she felt that it attracted more attention to her and that she did not want to be mistaken for the recent immigrants, or "FOB" (fresh out of boat), whose accents and mannerisms seemed very different from those of U.S. Americans. Molly said that she could always identify the adopted Koreans in her school because "all Korean adopted kids would hang out with White kids."

What is interesting about the adoptees who dissociated themselves from Asians during their childhood and adolescence is that now the majority of their close friends are Asian Americans, particularly Korean adoptees and Korean Americans. While their earlier schooling was predominantly with White children, many of the adoptees became friends with other Korean adoptees at their university campuses and found them to be invaluable sources of support and comfort. Several interviewees emphasized that they can share with other adoptees their most intimate feelings about and experiences with race and adoption, which they find difficult to discuss with their parents.

One view that the adoptees shared about their relationships with the Korean American community is that of dialectic and ambivalence. On one hand, they felt that they could very much relate to their non-adopted Korean American peers (and Asians and Asian Americans in general) because of some similar experiences they had as Asians in the United States. For example, several adoptees felt close to other Koreans and Asian Americans when they learned that they were not alone in experiencing racial slurs and struggling with being mistaken for foreigners. As many scholars have pointed out, the U.S. society continues to regard Americans of Asian descent as "foreigners" and "Orientals" regardless of their presence in the society for generations (e.g., Kondo, 1996; Nakayama, 1997; Yep, 1998). Korean adoptees are also subject to this racist ideology, because it is the product of physical foreignness more than anything else, and the adoptees' bodies—just as all Asians' bodies—signify an antithesis to "Americanness." The shared struggles seem to serve as a locus of the adoptees' sense of belonging to Korean American and, more generally, Asian American communities.

Yet, as they get to know non-adopted Korean Americans, many also struggle with the question, "How Korean am I?" Part of the struggle may stem from the fact that the majority of their non-adopted Korean American friends are not U.S. American–born generations whose culture and values are Americanized (Tessler, Gamache, & Liu, 1999), but are what is called "the 1.5 generation," or Koreans who immigrated with their parents when they were younger. According to the adoptees, their 1.5 generation friends are Americanized and yet follow Korean mannerisms when they communicate with their parents and other Korean Americans. Compared to the 1.5 generation, the adoptees feel apprehensive about their competence in "acting Korean." Tom, who has both adopted and non-adopted Korean American friends, expresses such apprehension:

> I know a lot of adoptees that are very very Korean. They can speak awesome Korean, they can write Korean, they can, uh. But I know that they still have authenticity issues, and it's just because of the fact that they *don't know* if they are Korean enough because of the nature of how you grew up. So it *is* a source of friction for adoptees. And for myself, it is a source of friction. If I speak Korean, is my Korean good? Am I Korean enough? Am I acting Korean? Did I bow enough? Did I shake two hands? Am I supposed to shake one hand? All those issues, which of course if you are Korean American or Korean, you don't have them because you just grew up and you just know that you are doing it right. Or you probably are not even thinking about those things.

The dialectic feeling of simultaneously being a part of a group and being excluded may also be evoked when the group assumes your foreignness, while the larger society assumes your membership to the group. Studies of interracial adoptions have shown that adoptees experience negative reactions by people of the same racial background (Simon, Alstein, & Melli, 1994; Tessler, Gamache, & Liu, 1999). My interviewees had also experienced some unpleasant comments. For example, a couple of adoptees mentioned that non-adopted Koreans and Asians had told them, "You must be *really* White" and "You must be Whiter than all of us." At the same time, the mainstream U.S. society treats the adoptees as Koreans, Korean Americans, or Asian Americans, regardless of the adoptees' self-identifications and these communities' views of the adoptees.

As Tom observed, a large part of the ambivalent, conflicting relationship with the larger Korean American community seems to be about authenticity. But is there an authentic identity? An authentic way to act out a culture? Wong (1998) is correct in concluding that questioning who is more authentic is a "grave mistake" (p. 129), because authenticity is a social, historical construction and therefore is dynamic. When we share ideas, we discover that there are multiple subjective understandings of what a culture looks like, depending on the social and cultural locations and status we engage. Perhaps a more meaningful question is, Why are some definitions granted more authenticity than others?

Relationship Issues within Families

While their relationships to communities are significant, many adoptees spoke primarily about their relationships with their families. Studies indicate that international and interracial adoptions are successful, emphasizing that racial minority adoptees grow up psychologically healthy in White families (Gill & Jackson, 1983; McRoy & Zurcher, 1983; Register, 1991; Simon & Alstein, 1992; Simon, Alstein, & Melli, 1994; Tessler, Gamache, & Liu, 1999; Tizard, 1991). In these studies, however, the "success" has been determined from the points of view of adoptive parents. When adoptees were involved in the surveys or interviews, it was generally during their early years of adoption. South Korean adoptees now compose the majority of the adult internationally adopted population, and their adoptive experiences encompass childhood, adolescence, and young adulthood. Their words reveal life experiences that are not necessarily "detected" by their parents.

TALKING ABOUT ADOPTION AND KOREAN CULTURE

Molly, a 24-year-old woman who describes her relationship with her parents as open and very close, said that talking about issues relating to adoption was never difficult in her family. Any time she had questions about being adopted, her parents were willing to talk about it. This was the case with other adoptees as well. When I asked them to tell me how adoption was or was not part of their family dialogues, many responded that their parents were willing to share the information they had about the birth mothers and pre-adoption. Brandi, whose parents adopted two children from South Korea, says, "Whenever I wanted to look at my adoption papers, they'd show them to me, and I'd just sit in the basement and look at them." Similarly, Paul, who also has a Korean adopted sister, felt that his parents were always open to talk about adoption, although he never felt the need to do so.

The adoptees also felt that their parents were very supportive of giving them opportunities to learn about Korean culture. This happened in a number of different ways. Many of the adoptees remembered their parents giving them Korean dolls and books about Korea when they were small. Some parents also sent their children to Korean cultural camps where adopted children can experience a taste of Korean culture, such as music and food, and can talk with other adopted children. Half of the adoptees I interviewed attended those cultural camps at least a couple of times during their K–12 years, and indeed a couple of the adoptees' parents were co-founders of one of the camps. Did the adoptees find these cultural camps beneficial? Yes and no. A few of the adoptees attended the camps until they were too old to be participants, and they now serve as camp counselors. Others quit attending camp after a while. A few of them said that they quit when they were in the fourth or fifth grade, because by that time they had grown tired of talking about being adopted and being Korean.

During the transitional years from childhood to adolescence, children in general begin to form their needs independent from their parents and become more interested in being accepted by their friends. Those who quit attending camp found little meaning in the camps since their daily groups of friends consisted largely of Whites. Bethany, who now counsels at one of the camps, summarizes the conflicting emotions she felt about the camp when she was younger:

> I know for some adopted kids, that was the last thing they wanted to do . . . even acknowledge being Korean and all that, but I think it's important that it's introduced and it's talked about it. Try to instill some pride into who you are and where you came from. I'm fortunate that I've had that, but at the same time I would hide it from my Caucasian friends. I was not embarrassed to go out with my Korean friends but I didn't wanna have to explain what it was. So at the camp, there was "a bring your friend" day, and I would never bring my Caucasian friends, because I felt that they would think it was stupid or whatever. So, I took a pride in being Korean, but at the same time, I kept it at distance so that people wouldn't think that I was really different.

What is noticeable about those who quit the camps is that they are now very interested in exploring their cultural identities, whether it is about being adopted, being Korean, being a Korean American, being an Asian American, or a combination of these identities. However, not all adoptees are interested in exploring their ethnic identities. Michelle, who has always had very little interest in her Korean roots, feels that people—not her parents—always expect her to be interested in her cultural heritage and think that she is in denial of who she is when they discover that she is not interested in it. "I'm not in denial of who I am," she says. "Who I am is I've grown up here since six months old." Although Michelle's parents always gave her the opportunity, she never felt a desire to learn about Korean culture.

In contrast, Kristin, who has been slowly exploring her cultural roots for the past few years, felt that she did not have opportunities to learn about Korean culture and being Korean while growing up. Her mother told her about a picnic they attended when Kristin was about 5 years old—a gathering of families that had adopted Korean children. At the picnic someone talked to Kristin in Korean,

and she turned away from the person. Her parents then decided that she did not want to be associated with anything Korean. Kristin does not remember this picnic. She feels that she was always interested in Korean culture, but was not presented with opportunities:

> My mom has a co-worker who has an adopted son who's 19. And I guess he is getting in a lot of trouble. And so they are talking about it together, and so my mom told me that her friend had said, "Oh, he's just starting to get interested in being Korean." And my mom said, "Kind of like the way you are, you know. He didn't really care about being Korean until just recently." And I thought, "Where have you been? I've been interested in being Korean for as long as I can remember."

So, is there a "right" way to approach teaching adopted children about their birth cultures? Obviously not. What these stories may suggest is that it is important for parents to encourage their adoptive children to get involved in activities relating to the national culture of the child's origin. Yet, it is hasty to assume that adoptive children *want* the opportunities. The age of the child, the racial makeup of the neighborhood (i.e., whether they have daily interactions with other Koreans, other Asians, and other children of color), and the child's personality, among others, are important considerations for determining how much immersion is necessary and when it is appropriate. The literature of international and interracial adoptions suggests that parents usually take one of three approaches to their adoptive child's racial and cultural background (Koh, 1981; Simon & Alstein, 1992; Tessler, Gamache, & Liu, 1999). Some parents immerse the child into his or her ethnic or racial culture; other parents take some variation of the "color-blind" approach; and still others take a bi-cultural, bi-racial socialization approach. All of these approaches may or may not be effective; it is important that parents mindfully listen to their child's needs and interest, whether communicated verbally or nonverbally, rather than make the decision without the child's input. Moreover, adoptive parents need to remember that the child's needs and interests change over the years.

TALKING ABOUT RACE AND RACISM

Read the following scenarios. What would you do in these situations if you were a parent of interracially adopted children? What would you feel if you were the adoptee?

Scenario One You are the mother of three children—two biological to you, and one that you adopted from South Korea. Your 8-year-old adoptive daughter goes to a school that is predominantly White. She comes home from school and tells you that some kids called her racial names, that they stared at her and giggled. She tells you that this has happened several times in the past. Another time, you and your husband take the children shopping at a mall. Your adoptive daughter says, "Mom, they are looking at us. I just hate it when they look at us. I know they are thinking 'she doesn't belong with them.'"

Scenario Two You are the father of an 18-year-old daughter whom you and your wife adopted from South Korea when she was 6 months old. She is your only child. One day you and your daughter take a walk and stop at a nearby store to buy sodas. Your daughter puts the sodas on the counter, and you pay the clerk. He grins as he takes the money from you. As you walk toward the door, he says, "Where did you get a pretty young thing like that?"

Scenario Three You are a social worker and mother of four grown children—one biological to you, and three adopted from India, Columbia, and South Korea. Your parents and your husband's parents live in other states, and your family sees them only a few times a year. Both your parents and your husband's parents hold negative attitudes toward racial minorities, especially African Americans, and over the years they have made rude comments about minorities. However, they tell their grandchildren—your children—that they love them. The last time your husband's parents came to visit, you told them about your current work with international special needs children. Your father-in-law

said, "I don't understand why we are bringing those kids over, and my taxes are gonna pay for them." But in the same breath, he said to his grandchildren, "But I'm really glad that you came."

How do you interpret the scenarios? Do you find any of them disturbing? How would you, as a parent, handle the situations? I will come back to the scenarios after I discuss some views held by the adoptees in my interviews. They found that it was much more difficult to talk about racial issues with their parents than to discuss adoption or Korean culture. As previous studies of transracial adoptions have shown (McRoy & Zurcher, 1983; McRoy, Zurcher, Lauderdale, & Anderson, 1984; Register, 1991), race was one of the most conscious aspects of the Korean adoptees' everyday experience, because they were constantly reminded of their physical dissimilarity to their family. The racial difference between them and their parents has led many of the adoptees to feel that they cannot talk to their parents about racism and related issues. It is important to note that this feeling does not imply that the adoptees have negative views of their relationships with their families. Indeed, all of the adoptees expressed to me that they were fortunate to be adopted in the United States and were happy to be part of their adoptive families.

Nevertheless, the adoptees have learned experientially and intellectually that their parents have privileges as White persons that they do not have. As a number of people, both Whites and those of color, have observed, part of the White privilege is its normative status; it is unnamed and unchallenged (Chambers, 1997; Frankenberg, 1993; Harris, 1995; Martin & Nakayama, 1999; Young, 2000), and the adoptees have learned that this privilege places some barriers between them and their parents. For example, Molly said that until she reached college age, she was unable to talk about race issues and her racially marked physical differences:

> I didn't wanna go to my parents because I *knew* that they've never ever gone through what I go through. They are White. Because they are White, they have a very privileged life. They don't get

looked at and stared at. They get treated like the norm of how people should be treated. But unfortunately not everyone gets treated that way. So, I didn't feel like I could go to them because I felt that they couldn't really comfort my emotions and feelings and stuff like that. I just felt that they would say "Oh, well, that's too bad. Just stand up for yourself" or whatever. And I was like I need someone to tell me that they've been through that. And so during that time I never really heard anyone else's stories or experiences of what it's like to be a minority.

Several other adoptees made comments similar to Molly's. What can White parents do about this situation? Obviously, they have no control over the racial difference that exists between them and their children, and the adoptees are of course aware that this is an unresolvable issue because many international adoptions are transracial. As much as the adoptees mentioned the significance of racial difference, a further examination of their words reveals that it is not the difference itself that becomes an issue to them as far as their family relationships are concerned. Rather, they took issue with the ways in which their family members communicated and responded to the difference.

All three scenarios I presented earlier are from the adoptees I interviewed. In the first scenario, the daughter, Kristin, says that her mother used to tell her that she was "too sensitive about everything," or "oh, that really didn't happen," or "I'm sure they really didn't mean that." After a while, she learned to not share with her family when she got teased or offended by strangers.

In the second scenario, Emily was very offended by the clerk's comment. She says being mistaken for her father's girlfriend is a recurrent incident. She believes the assumption comes from the stereotype of "hypersexualized" Asian women (Allman, 1996). Emily is a very assertive woman who makes sure to let others know that she wouldn't accept inappropriate comments. What disturbs her, however, is her father's silence. When Emily challenges him about it, he says that he doesn't want to waste time explaining because the strangers who make rude, insensitive remarks would not deserve it. Emily does not agree with this; she believes that her father

should make sure that people understand that she is his daughter.

The last scenario comes from Bethany, a 25-year-old social worker. She also talks about her frustration about her parents not standing up for her, although she loves them very much. Different from Emily's situation, however, the source of disturbing comments is not a stranger but her grandparents. Bethany's grandparents tell her, "Oh, we are not talking about you. We are talking about those people." But she feels that their attitudes are also directed toward her because what they say about the minorities does not exclude her. What fuels this struggle with her grandparents is her mother's silence about the grandparents' racial attitudes.

If we are talking about work issues, we are very similar in thinking. But talking about her parents or my dad's parents, it's very difficult for her to be a good advocate for me. And that's very hard for me, because I think I have very high expectations for her because of what she does, and because of the kind of person she is. So, that makes it very hard for me when she doesn't say something. So race is a very hard subject for me to deal with in my family, and it still is. . . . And even though my mom is a social worker, I think she is a daughter before she is a social worker. So she has her parents to answer to and her fears about the way she was raised and what's proper and what's not in her family. But at the same time she chose to do this, she chose to adopt interracially. And as a duty to us, she needs to be able to speak up.

The experiences of the adoptees shed different light on the "success" of international and interracial adoptions. Much research on interracial and international adoptions focused on behavioral, emotional, and intellectual adjustment and performance within families and school, and concluded that adoptees have adjusted successfully and that the ethnic and cultural differences caused little problem to the adoptees and their families (Bartholet, 1994; Simon, Alstein, & Melli, 1994). Those conclusions constitute an important argument for those who support international and interracial adoptions that involve racial minority children and White adoptive parents.

In appearance, the Korean adoptees in my interviews support the research finding; they are all successful in their work and schools, and they are generally happy with their families. The "success," however, should not be rashly understood to mean that the adoptees had little problem with race and ethnicity. The three scenarios are only a few among many that the adoptees shared with me. One strong and persistent message I received from them about dealing with racial issues in family relationships is the need for the parents to understand that their children are likely to face racist and racialized experiences that the parents will not face. Connie, a recent college graduate who feels strongly about race, sums up the message in passionate words:

> [W]hen White parents adopt, a lot of times they only go through what's called cultural training. They say, "Oh, teach our kids about Korea, give them traditional dress, buy them a Korean doll." But to me, that's such a problem in adoption. You need to talk about race. You need to talk about what it's gonna be like for your kids to grow up in America not White, because that's such an issue. But they don't talk about that. And my parents never went through even the cultural training. They don't know anything about Korea. So, when I would talk to them about race, I was really disappointed, because they didn't give what I was looking for. I wanted them to be more supportive of me, or give me words to fight back.

Can White parents give their children words to fight back? In my opinion, yes. But parents must do homework and be educated about minority experiences and about some possible scenarios that may come up. You cannot be ready for something that you are oblivious to. I can see, for example in a case such as Emily's, how a parent may not see the clerk's comment as racist, but rather a humorous misunderstanding, if the parent is not familiar with the troublesome stereotypes of Asian women. I can see how a parent can be caught between two roles, as Bethany sees her mother. As the adoptees mentioned, they know that their White parents have not had and will not have the same racial experiences that their children go through. It is crucial that parents not disconfirm their children's signals for help

and that they let their children decide what is or is not disturbing. And it is also important that parents help their children to connect with other Korean adoptees, who are invaluable sources of support for the children.

The parents' homework needs to include learning about themselves, too, because being White in the United States is more than a color; it comes with a lot of fringe benefits *and* costs. David Mura (1994), although he is not a White parent, asks important questions that are very relevant here:

> When I address the question of raising my daughter, I address the question of her identity, which means I address the question of my identity, her mother's, our parents' and so on. But this multiplication of the self takes place along many lines. Who knows where it stops? At my grandparents? At the woman in the grocery store? At you, the imagined reader of this piece? (p. 369)

I do not know if Mura posed the questions in a rhetorical sense, but I believe that there is really no end to this multiplication. I believe that the multiplication is imperative for people to see how the formations of their identities are interconnected to the formations of others' identities and perspectives. It is the realization of the interconnections that allows us to see the possibilities of making alliances across seemingly rigid cultural and identity borders.

The Changing Face of U.S. Americans

> Whether we are White or Color, we need to know the stories of change agents. They are a renewable source of energy and courage for the long haul of interrupting oppression. (Tatum, 1999, p. 63)

Most of this essay may be thought of as directed toward parents. However, it is for everyone who is concerned about enhancing intercultural relationships. South Korean adoptees participate in the larger scheme of the need for understanding the multivocality and multiculturality of racial and ethnic minority communities. For Asian Americans, physical differences as racial signifiers have been a salient site of struggle, because it is precisely their bodies that mark them outside the circle of "American." The mainstream U.S. society tends to lump

Asian Americans together as a single entity and refuse to acknowledge that Asian Americans *are* U.S. Americans with *diverse* voices, histories, and cultures. It is for this reason that many works by and for Asian Americans challenge the formation of U.S. American identity and history. The adoptees' stories illustrate how these rigid and heedless categorizations are preposterous.

Asian adoptees growing up in White families have dealt with the issues of race and identity. An increasing number of multiracial individuals contest the rigidity of the racial categories and demand that the state grapple with the issue of classifying multiracial people. The Asian adoptees themselves are not biologically multiracial, and yet their socialization in White American families forces them to face issues of being physically marked as Asian while simultaneously dealing with multiracial issues as someone who crossed the uncrossable racial borders in their formation of multiracial families. Understanding the adoptees' experiences and views of themselves and society provides insights into the changing face of America—into a broader understanding of the experiences and identities of Asian Americans and multicultural people.

References

Allman, K. M. (1996). (Un)natural boundaries: Mixed race, gender, and sexuality. In M. Root (Ed.), *The multiracial experience: Racial borders as the new frontier* (pp. 277–290). Thousand Oaks, CA: Sage.

Bartholet, J. (Ed.). (1994). *Race matching in adoption: An American perspective*. London: Free Association Books.

Chambers, R. (1997). The unexamined. In M. Hill (Ed.), *Whiteness: A critical reader* (pp. 187–203). New York: New York University.

Cox, S. (1996). *The birth of intercountry adoption.* <www.rtc.pdx.edu/fp/spring96>.

Frankenberg, R. (1993). *White women, race matters: The social construction of whiteness*. Minneapolis: University of Minnesota.

Gill, O., & Jackson, B. (1983). *Adoption and race*. London: Batsford Academic and Educational Ltd.

Harris, C. I. (1995). Whiteness as property. In C. West, K. Crenshaw, N. Gotanda, G. Peller, & K. Thomas (Eds.), *Critical race theory: The key writings that formed the movement* (pp. 276–291). New York: New Press.

Koh, F. M. (1981). *Oriental children in American homes*. Minneapolis: East-West Press.

Kondo, D. (1996). The narrative production of "home," community, and political identity in Asian American theater. In Lavie & T. Swedenburg (Eds.), *Displacement, diaspora, and geographies of identity* (pp. 97–118). Durham, NC: Duke University.

Martin, J. N., & Nakayama, T. K. (Eds.). (1999). *Whiteness: The communication of social identity*. Thousand Oaks, CA: Sage.

McRoy, R., & Zurcher, L. (1983). *Transracial and inracial adoptees: The adolescent years*. Springfield, IL: Charles C. Thomas.

McRoy, R., Zurcher, L., Lauderdale, M., & Anderson, R. (1984). The identity of transracial adoptees. *Social Casework, 64*(1), 34–39.

Mura, D. (1994). Secrets and anger. In J. Zaitchik, W. Roberts, & H. Zaitchik (Eds.), *Face to face: Readings on confrontation and accommodation in America* (pp. 367–374). Boston: Houghton Mifflin.

Nakayama, T. K. (1997). Dis/orienting identities: Asian Americans, history, and intercultural communication. In A. Gonzalez, M. Houston, & V. Chen (Eds.), *Our voices: Essays in culture, ethnicity, and communication* (2nd ed., pp. 14–20). Los Angeles: Roxbury.

Omi, M., & Winant, H. (1994). *Racial formation in the United States: From the 1960s to the 1990s* (2nd ed.). New York: Routledge.

Register, C. (1991). *Are those kids yours? American families with children adopted from other countries*. New York: Free Press.

Root, M. (Ed.). (1992). *Racially mixed people in America*. Thousand Oaks, CA: Sage.

Root, M. (Ed.). (1996). *The multiracial experience: Racial borders as the new frontier*. Thousand Oaks, CA: Sage.

Simon, R. J., & Alstein, H. (1992). *Adoption, race, and identity*. New York: Praeger.

Simon, R. J., Alstein, H., & Melli, M. S. (1994). *The case for transracial adoption*. Washington, DC: The American University Press.

Tatum, B. D. (1999). Lighting candles in the dark: One black woman's response to white antiracist narrative. In C. Clark & J. O'Donnell (Eds.), *Becoming and unbecoming white: Owning and disowning a racial identity* (pp. 56–63). Westport, CT: Bergin & Garvey.

Tessler, R., Gamache, G., & Liu, L. (1999). *West meets East: American adopt Chinese children*. Westport, CT: Bergin & Garvey.

Tizard, B. (1991). Intercountry Adoption: A review of the evidence. *Journal of Child Psychology and Psychiatry, 32*(5), 743–756.

Wilkinson, H. S. (1995). Psychological process and issues in international adoption. *American Journal of Family Therapy, 23*(2), 173–183.

Wong, K. (1998). Migration across generations: Whose identity is authentic? In J. N. Martin, T. K. Nakayama, & L. A. Flores (Eds.), *Readings in cultural contexts* (pp. 127–134). Mountain View, CA: Mayfield.

Yep, G. A. (1998). My three cultures: Navigating the multicultural identity landscape. In J. N. Martin, T. K. Nakayama, & L. A. Flores (Eds.), *Readings in cultural contexts* (pp. 79–85). Mountain View: CA: Mayfield.

Young, G. (2000). Leonard's Yard: Pulling at the roots and responsibilities of my whiteness. In M. W. Lusting & J. Kroester (Eds.), *AmongUs: Essays on identity, belonging, and intercultural competence* (pp. 161–171). New York: Longman.

Key Terms

authenticity
interpellation
multiculturality
multivocality
racialized
  experiences

sociohistorical
  construction
transracial adoption
White privilege

Discussion Questions

1. Fujimoto explores the problem of racial classification in the United States through the experiences of South Korean adoptees. Why is racial background so important to the ways that U.S. Americans categorize people?

2. The experiences of these adoptees demonstrate the importance of race in U.S. American society. Why is it wrong for the White parents to take the position that they don't see racial differences? How does this worldview fail to serve the interests of the adoptees?

3. Some adoptees do not identify as Korean Americans or Asian Americans. What is the importance of the groups we identify with? What is the significance of the groups that we do not identify with?

4. Fujimoto focuses on South Korean adoptees who were adopted into White families. How might the experience of a South Korean adoptee be different if adopted by a Chinese American family?

5. Many of the parents of adoptees encouraged them to learn about Korean culture. How important do you think it is to raise children in contact with their ethnic culture?

Activities for Skill Development

1. Imagine you have decided to relocate to another country to spend the rest of your life. Make a list of concerns that first come to mind (e.g., language, food, weather). What if you were allowed to bring just one large suitcase? What would you take with you?

2. Interview a couple of people who have lived in another country for an extended period of time. Ask the following questions: What was the experience like? What were the challenges? When they returned, did they experience a reentry culture shock? If so, ask them what it was like.

3. Check out your college or university's International Students Office Web site. Learn how many students from other countries study in your school. What are their countries of origin? Also, see how many international students' organizations exist on campus. Do they host any cultural events?

Web Sites

1. What does it imply to become an American citizen? What does the word "assimilation" mean? Go to "Assimilation and Citizenship" on the Center for Immigration Studies Web site <http://www.cis.org/topics/assimilation.html> and list some of the critical issues that surround immigration within the United States.

2. Have you ever thought of what it is like for an individual from another country to visit the United States? Go to <http://www.edupass.org/culture/> and see through a different lens what it would be like to follow new social rules and customs in your daily life.

3. What is it like to adopt a child internationally? Read some of the family stories compiled by International Adoption Resource, Inc., <http://www.iaradopt.com/story.shtml>. What insights do these stories have to offer? What are your thoughts on international adoption?

4. Go to <http://www.peacecorps.gov/essays/index.html> and read the stories of former Peace Corps volunteers. What did they experience when they worked in Africa, Inter-America, the Caribbean, the Pacific, Europe, the Mediterranean, Central and East Asia?

Additional Readings

1. Clifford, J. (1992). Traveling cultures. In L. Grossberg, C. Nelson, & P. Treichler (Eds.), *Cultural studies* (pp. 96–116). New York: Routledge.

2. Gillan, M. M., & Gillan, J. (Eds.). (1999). *Identity lessons: Contemporary writing about learning to be American.* New York: Penguin Books.

3. Selmer, J., & Shiu, L. S. C. (1999). Coming home? Adjustment of Hong Kong Chinese expatriate business managers assigned to the People's Republic of China. *International Journal of Intercultural Relations, 23,* 447–466.

4. Hall, E. T. (1981). Hidden culture. In *Beyond culture* (pp. 57–69). New York: Doubleday.

PART EIGHT

Communication and Intercultural Relationships

Essays in Part Eight highlight the importance of intercultural communication in family, acquaintance, friendship, romantic, and marital relationships across sexual orientation. Not all families look alike any more than all marriages look like the romantic images we see in mainstream film and television. The intercultural nature of the family is often overlooked, despite its tremendous importance in the development of cultural roles and socialization. Different kinds of families and different kinds of relationships require sensitivity to intercultural communication. These essays offer different ways to think about relationship and culture as well as practical suggestions for developing intercultural relationships.

In "The Role of Family and Macrocultures in Intercultural Relationships," Carley H. Dodd and John R. Baldwin explore how two levels of culture—family and national, or ethnic (macrocultures)—influence intercultural relationships. Specifically, they show how family and macrocultures shape identity and also influence the communication styles of individuals in intercultural relationships, including notions of supportiveness, cohesion, adaptability, receptivity, and availability. They also provide cross-cultural perspectives on these various aspects of intercultural relationships.

In "I, We, and They," social psychologist Geert Hofstede discusses how one core cultural value (individualism-collectivism) influences interpersonal relationships. This essay is based on his extensive cross-cultural studies in IBM subsidiaries worldwide. Hofstede shows how the cultural preference for individualism or collectivism is reflected in family, education, and work relationships in many cultures around the world. He also discusses the implications of these cultural differences for building relationships across cultures.

To further explore intercultural relationships, Mary Jane Collier discusses "Intercultural Friendships as Interpersonal Alliances." Based on her ethnographic research, she identifies three issues central to intercultural friendships: (1) power and unearned privilege, (2) acknowledgement of history, and (3) emergent orientations toward cultural differences. She shows how identity and communication are intertwined as individuals work through these three issues in intercultural relationships.

In "Performing Commitment," Jacqueline Taylor describes commitment in her family relationships with her partner and two daughters. For her, commitment in a lesbian relationship can only be understood by considering current social, political, and legal forces. She explores how commitment is performed communicatively in bridging the gap between her family's lived experience and the laws and customs within which family commitments are traditionally organized and performed. Her family's public and private rituals of commitment include a "marriage of addresses," anniversary celebrations, and rituals of adoption. She describes how ritual, ceremony, language, custom, and laws all interact to construct and constrain conceptions of family.

30 The Role of Family and Macrocultures in Intercultural Relationships

CARLEY H. DODD and JOHN R. BALDWIN

Baldwin and Lindsley's (1994) listing of 206 definitions of culture demonstrates many competing notions of culture today. Much of the literature about intercultural relationships has looked at "culture" in a traditional way, as relatively large groups of people who share the same way of life (Gudykunst & Kim, 1992). However, many scholars, such as Collier (1997), are now suggesting that *any* size group can share a way of life, and for that group, this becomes a culture. Thus, in this essay, we refer to the "large groups of people" who share a way of life, even if those are ethnic co-cultures within a nation, as *macrocultures*.[1] But, as we will suggest shortly, each family comes to develop its own way of life. We suggest in this essay that partners in a relationship bring both the elements of their macrocultures and the elements of their family cultures into the relationship.

In recent years, intercultural specialists have looked at "culture" and "intercultural" communication at a variety of levels, from the culture shared by large groups (Gudykunst & Kim, 1992) to that shared by cultural, regional, age cohort, and even family groups (Collier, 1997; Dodd, 1998). This expanded view, including numerous co-cultures, also involves several relationship dynamics that together with the larger culture help explain intercultural and intergroup communication. Indeed, the impact of relationships on culture and of culture on relationships—and of both on human communication—is an area of growing interest.

Gudykunst and Kim (1992) discuss intercultural encounters using the metaphor of meeting a stranger. They propose that such meetings create a cognitive "head-response" of uncertainty (trying to understand the other's behavior) and an affective "heart-response" of anxiety (fearing some negative outcome). Dodd (1998) combined this approach with a "Third Culture Perspective" to propose that as partners resolve their anxiety and uncertainty, they develop a new, common culture. By initiating positive attitudes, images, and actions invested in building a relationship climate, the partners achieve functional outcomes including accurate information, friendship, mutual goals, and respect.

These writers and others conclude that intercultural communication occurs when people experience or perceive some group-level difference. As we encounter someone different, this intuitive perception of sameness or difference shapes the resulting relationship. This internal classification, resulting from a perceived level of difference, can be accurate or flawed but, regardless, frames attitudes and actions toward others.

This essay explores how intercultural relationships are linked with one of our deepest sources of intercultural perception and emotion, the family. In effect, the family intersects with "culture" in at least three ways. First, the family of each partner in a relationship reflects to some degree the culture of origin of that family. Gushue and Sciarra (1995) note that this influence is one of the major new waves in multicultural counseling:

> Different cultures [have] different ways of understanding "appropriate" family organization, values, communication, and behavior. Although the family perspective had revolutionized the individual view of the client by taking the family context into account, it now needed to understand its own unit of analysis (i.e., the family) in light of an even larger context: culture. (p. 588)

Also, Rohrlich (1988) referred to family communication as an extension of intercultural communication. From her vantage point, the metaphor of culture accurately describes family and is a major influence over intercultural communication.

Second, as noted above, after two partners decide on more than just a casual acquaintanceship, they begin to adjust to one another, to develop

279

rules and behaviors in some ways unique to them. Thus, the communication partners become, in some sense, a *culture*.

Third, the family itself comes to be seen as a "culture" much as organizational researchers have treated organizations as cultures. Family therapists have long looked at families as *systems*—with interrelated parts whose behavior influences one another. But with the emergence of broader definitions of culture that include *any* "historical system of symbols, meanings, and norms" (Collier, 1997, p. 36), families can be said to be *cultures* in that, through family norms, rituals, rewards, and communication, each family develops its own sense of functioning, its own way of life. One family may resolve conflict by arguing or physical aggression; another may use inuendo and moodiness; and another may subterfuge the conflict by moving on to some other activity. In this regard, Falicov (1986) suggests that "strictly speaking, we all intermarry, even if we marry the boy next door" (p. 429).

Thus, family cultures are fundamental perceptual frameworks influencing relationships. Relationships, in turn, are pivotal arenas for intercultural encounters. What happens when a family's culture provides an acceptable set of rules, roles, norms, symbols, social style, stories, myths, and interpretive framework to see the world for Person A, while Person B comes from a family quite opposite? This essay attempts to answer that question along with cultural differences.

Family as Culture: Identity Through Family

First, we must again underscore the nature of family as culture. The case of Maria and Richard's struggling marriage illustrates our core position:

> "You never believe a thing I say!" said 28-year-old Chilean-born Maria to her 29-year-old American husband, Richard. "Every time I talk, all you do is turn on the TV. You're always paying attention to television, or your newspaper, or your friends far more than to me." After another one of their long, drawn out arguments, Maria concluded that the only thing to do was to dissolve their 5-year mar-

riage. Despite the fact that they were so much in love when they first met, barriers seemed all too apparent. As Maria sat in the therapist's office, tears streamed from her eyes as she recounted their dating, courtship, and the 5 years of their marriage. "It seemed so promising," she said, "for Richard and I both knew we were in love. My heart told me and led me to this relationship." Both revealed their missed expectations of how each other's families "always were the perfect pattern" for their marriage, and how disappointed they were of each other.

Maria's story presents many aspects of intercultural marriages. While Richard was paying much more attention to his friends, football games on television, and his computer, cultural factors and family tradition factors also became apparent. He complained of value differences and how Maria never did things like his mom. These perceptions overlooked the comparative richness of Maria's culture and its contrast of time, relationship building, and emotional expectations. The therapist originally overlooked culture and its link within the family system as a cause of their difficulties, but the conditions soon illustrated to the couple and to the therapist that indicators associated with both culture of origin (macroculture) and family culture explained their difficulty.

Maria and Richard's situation reminds us of family culture's powerful ability to frame events and relationships. According to intergroup theory, if there is a significant, positive identity development—that is, if a person has a group that he or she can rely on as a primary group—then there is social identity (Gudykunst & Gumbs, 1989). Families clearly provide this social identity. I am a McClintoch. I am a Johnson. I am a Martinez. I am a Schleyermacher. I am from the family of Lin Chan. My father is Professor Ito. In this sense, family is a cultural unit defining *identity qualities* such as security, intimacy, self-worth, and confidence.

Second, not only does family culture serve to instill these identity qualities, but it is a source of norms regarding interaction and communication style. Each family culture generates ways of thinking, feeling, and acting. For example, Elizabeth

Stone (1996) interviews men and women from different ethnic cultures to find out how the stories families tell, be they about maternal sacrifice, male heroes, or sibling rivalries, teach family members how to act in relationships, influencing family members to communicate a certain way. This "way" often develops into a pattern or a linguistic norm that becomes a preferred and expected communicator style. While families are not the only cause of individual communicator style, family, other cocultures, macroculture, personality, education, and other experiences contribute to linguistic norm development in communities.

Families are made up of people in relationship. Wood (1996) suggests that *relational cultures* are "privately transacted system[s] of understandings" that include the partners' (or family members') identities, attitudes, and actions. As relational cultures, families demonstrate and engage varying interaction patterns, norms, rules, attitudes, values, space, time use, dress, systems of reward, tools, and roles. They have stories, special symbols, myths, and images. They live within an external environment such as a town, a state, and a nation. A family can be characterized as having a unique personality and a resulting communicator style. Some families have an aggressive, assertive style, while others are laid-back and easygoing. Some families are meditative; some are active and fun loving. Some families encourage total dependency, others encourage autonomy.

Therefore, when family culture interfaces with one's macroculture, an enriched source of intercultural communication emerges. To conclude our case example, Maria's family culture (with all its assumptions, procedures, etc.) and her macroculture (Chile) are jointly part of the interaction "package" with Richard. Richard's family habits and outlooks interlocked with his U.S. culture in his talking and listening to Maria. There were at least two cultures influencing their communication and relationship. Her cultures (macro and family) emphasized people first and task accomplishment second, whereas his cultures underscored task orientation above all else. She tried to nurture the relationship, but he seemed to take her for granted

while he advanced his career. Relationship expectations were missed, and the marriage was dissolved.

Still other writers on intercultural marriage, such as Romano (1988) or the various writers in Tseng, McDermott, and Maretzki (1977), give countless instances of misunderstandings. The father (from a Polynesian island culture) rewards conformity in the children, while the mother (an Anglo American) rewards independent thought. The man from one culture defines the marriage (in terms of mutual sexual fidelity) differently than the woman from another. The man from a Central Asian culture wants to fulfill financial obligations to extended family, but the woman from a Western culture sees the nuclear family as having sole ownership over time and financial resources.

Elements of Family Culture Impacting Intercultural Communication

What specific aspects of family culture imprint upon intercultural communication and relationships? Earlier we stated that family is identified as a culture. As a system it can be tightly woven or loose, functional or dysfunctional, adaptable or not adaptable, but unmistakably a system composed of contributing elements and people. If Dad loses his job, certainly the attitudes and actions of all family members can be affected. If an unmarried daughter becomes pregnant, the siblings and parents often change. In other words, what happens to one affects the whole family system. To understand these relationships, a number of systemic elements can be analyzed that help us better understand the nature of this culture. Since intercultural studies involving extensive use of categories of family culture are in development, we will select foundational elements from classic literature focusing on such elements.[2]

SUPPORTIVE COMMUNICATION

Some families encourage various degrees of what family researchers term *supportive communication,* defined here as the quality of affirming family members during crisis. We can illustrate from the case of a family in central Mexico where the father, upon learning of his 16-year-old daughter's pregnancy, literally abandoned her, ordering her out of the house and refusing to talk with her. Although this case is extreme, family rigidity during crisis can take many more subtle forms where families freeze relationships and increase distance. Some silently nurse grudges, ruling out the possibility of healing or happiness. As a result, a person from a nonsupportive family may "act out" in a way that creates dysfunctional communication (Galvin & Brommel, 1996).

It is not hard to see how people from two diverse family systems can experience group clash: one from a supportive family culture and the other from a nonsupportive family culture, each acting from a vantage point modeled by family. Affirming families are able to engage in a number of important communication behaviors. Among those behaviors is the ability to provide reassurance, forgiveness, nurturing, competency, accomplishment, and understanding. Sadly, not every family capably assures affirmation expected in that culture. For example, one father in therapy, over a period of several weeks, refused to look at his teenage son during the sessions. He literally looked straight across the room, craning his head around his son to be able to look at the therapist, despite repeated efforts to encourage father-son communication. As a result, the son failed to resolve his aberrant behavior and remained in an adolescent facility isolation unit until the family's communication source of the problem was corrected.

In addition to the influences of the family culture, macrocultural influences may impinge upon a couple in two ways. First, different cultures may not only define *supportiveness* differently but place a different value on it. For example, Hecht, Collier, and Ribeau (1993) cite much research suggesting that for African Americans goal attainment (in a sense of social support) is a primary goal both in interpersonal interaction and in friendships. This seems to correspond with the values of the African American *Kwanzaa* festival of *ujima* (collective work and responsibility) and *ujamma* (cooperative economics) (Bowers, 1997). African American families might,

according to these principles, highly value *supportiveness,* but in a different way from Caucasian families. Although the latter might define supportiveness in terms of "open communication," the former might define it in terms of goal accomplishment, especially in terms of accomplishing tasks together in the face of an unequal power structure.[3]

The second way that family-culture supportiveness may impinge on intercultural families is in the way the support of extended family is expressed in cases of intercultural or interethnic marriage (Baldwin, 1992). Graham, Moeai, and Shizuru (1985) find that interculturally married couples in Hawaii perceive more of their problems to be caused by "external" factors such as cultural differences and pressure from family, rather than "internal" factors such as personal differences. We hold that, as in all intercultural interaction, two main influences might be present in intercultural romantic relationships: The first is *real cultural differences* brought from the macro or family cultures; but the second, pertinent here under a discussion of supportiveness, is the support from the surrounding family and community. Writers in Tseng, McDermott, and Maretzki (1977) suggest that the success of an intercultural family goes up as the distance from either family of origin increases! Falicov (1986) suggests that boundary management (keeping the in-laws out of nuclear family business) is one of the major issues for intercultural families.

COHESION

Another important family system variable is cohesion. Cohesion refers to a feeling of closeness, and includes two dimensions. The first dimension is a sense of separation or independence, in which family members feel the freedom or desire to "do their own thing," to spend time alone or with friends apart from the family. The second dimension is a sense of connection or interdependence, in which members want to spend time together. Wood (1996) suggests that relationships exist in "dialectic"—or tension between various extremes. She and other dialectic writers would suggest that all relationships have both extremes constantly in tension with one another. "Healthy" relationships (including families) have a balance of the two extremes (Olson, 1976, defined these extremes with combinations across axes of cohesion and adaptability). Often, difficulties arrive when the family members are trying to emphasize different ends, such as when the parents want a *family* vacation and the teens want to go off with their friends and increase their autonomy.

Family cultures characterized by either extreme can be considered potentially unhealthy. On one hand, family members can develop extreme patterns of exclusivity in relationships, expectations of autonomy, and lack of teamwork. Partners and other family members become *isolated* from one another. In contrast, other family cultures might become what some family-system experts refer to as "enmeshed." In this case, interdependence is so extreme that an individual cannot be extricated from his or her family network. Thus, when autonomy is needed, an individual is not able to draw upon independent dimensions of thought. In fact, the evidence indicates that enmeshment can create learned dependency and helplessness (Lewis, Dodd, & Tippens, 1992).

However, notions of connection, enmeshment, and isolation must be reconsidered also from the standpoint of other cultural standards. Shon and Ja (1982), for example, suggest that "Asian cultures"[4] are more "collective." As such, the connections that are important to a particular Asian culture might be as much to the father's family, to society at large, or to some other collective rather than to the nuclear family; and, within the Buddhist or Confucionist cultural framework, this would be "natural" rather than "unhealthy." Such an orientation toward connection influences even verbal and nonverbal patterns, leading Asian Americans to frequently prefer more indirect means of conflict (preserving connection), whereas Caucasians might prefer more direct conflict styles (preserving autonomy). In similar fashion, Gaines (1995) notes the *familism* (a high value on the family) in Latino American relationships and the *collectivism* (preference for the group) in African American families. As familism or collectivism increases, he suggests, Latino American and African American mates would express more respect and affection for their partners. In the cases of any such collective culture, functioning alone, without consultation of the "collective" with which the partner identifies, is rare.

In these and other cases, even the definition of "attachment" or "cohesion" differs. For example, Sprecher et al. (1994) discuss several different types of love that partners may feel for each other, such as *ludus* (game-playing love), *eros* (romantic, passionate love), and *storge* (friendship love). They found that couples in America, Russia, and Japan differed not only in which form of "love" they preferred, but also in the way they approached attachment in general. Thus, we can see how levels and definitions of connectedness impact intercultural relations and communication where two individuals come from very different family or macrocultural traditions.

FAMILY RULES AND CULTURAL ADAPTABILITY

Family rules are the teachings of obligations and expectations of behavior, the dos and don'ts within the family. Family rules can include anything from what you should or should not do at a family reunion to what you should or should not do in cleaning up your room. Every family has its methods of doing things, sometimes taught explicitly, sometimes by example. For instance, an older student returning to college tells a story that illustrates family rules:

> My parents were very rigid. Everything we did had to be done just as they had done them. On one occasion, after I had married and had a baby, I had to move home for a short while because my husband was stationed with the air force in Morocco. My parents had no washer or dryer, and all of our clothes were washed at a laundromat and hung up. To save folding time, I hung the baby's diapers already folded in half. My parents thought this practice was absolutely ridiculous! Their ridicule helped me decide it didn't matter anymore, as long as the job got done. At least I wasn't being called "lazy" anymore.

As this case underscores, rules are not always deliberate, well-thought-out, consciously placed guides to action. Whatever their source, rules guide family norms, influence thinking, feeling, and behavior, and affect relationships in intercultural communication. We have shown that persons A and B experience different family rules that lead to areas of difference in expectation and communication. Sometimes the rules are particular to a family culture, and sometimes they are products of the larger macroculture, such as our earlier example about rewarding children's independence or conformity.

From an intercultural vantage point, Shon and Ja (1982) suggest that shame, or the reflection an action makes on the collective, is more important to collective Asian American cultures than guilt, or the personal responsibility one feels for an action. Thus, an "external" accountability in a collectivist culture may be more motivational in this situation than an individually grounded "internal" application of rules.

Based on our cultural assumptions, we recommend "mindfulness" (Gudykunst & Kim, 1992) about rules—rules should be thought about, considered, and often treated with some flexibility. Children who have rules and are taught "why" understand a sense of permeability. They see why the rules exist, and when conditions change, they can adapt based on the principles involved. In contrast, children raised in families where the reasons for the rules are rarely explained may be at risk in relationships where intercultural communication is needed. As adults, they may experience less ability to cope with adaptation in intercultural environments. One family's rules of cleanliness were so well ingrained that their daughter suffered in her adaptability in New Guinea where village cleanliness standards were very different. Despite her other excellent intercultural skills, this inflexibility about cleanliness impeded her adjustment in the new environment. In sum, many of our intercultural communication encounters can be explained by family rules: decision-making routines, everyday procedures, methods of interaction, finding the right time to talk, who takes responsibility for which task, gender-role expectations, how much to talk and listen, and so on. We learn from this idea to examine the many unconscious rules that define and structure our relationships.

CULTURAL ADAPTABILITY

Family specialists often view adaptability as a family system's characteristic to change its power, roles, and rules based on situational stress or developmental conditions experienced by one or all of the family members (Galvin & Brommel, 1996; Pearson, 1992). Cultural adaptability is important for the intersection of family and culture in two ways. First, families from nondominant cultures must learn to adapt to their new culture or to a culture that marginalizes or discredits their way of life.[5] Gudykunst & Kim (1992), for example, suggest that a major factor in cultural adaptation (which we extend to families) is the receptivity of the new environment.

The second way in which cultural adaptability is important is in dual-culture relationships or multicultural families. Whether the differences in rules are based on family culture or on macrocultures, the family must make a choice of which cultural pattern to follow. Tseng (1977) suggests five possible patterns for adaptation: (1) *One-way adjustment,* in which the family consistently adopts the cultural standards of one of the spouses—"a total capitulation to the culture" of one member (p. 99). For example, a Filipina wife married to an Anglo husband might speak only English, learn to cook hamburgers, and so on, giving up her own culture. (2) In *alternative adjustment,* the partners or family adopt first one culture, then the other—Filipina food tonight, American food tomorrow night (this example is simplistic and ignores deeper underlying value differences that are not so easily reconciled or alternated!). (3) *Mixing* has partners adopting elements of both cultures at the same time. A family might practice Chinese acupuncture or Native American herbal medicine while still consulting the local (Western medical system) doctor. An example of (4) *midpoint compromise* would be to give money to extended family members but negotiate the amount. Finally, Tseng discusses (5) *creative adjustment,* in which "both partners decide to give up the cultural behavior of both sides and invent a completely new behavior pattern" (p. 100). This is similar to the Third Culture Perspective we mentioned earlier.

Rohrlich (1988) suggests that in all dual-culture marriages, *power* might be an issue. We suggest that in issues of cultural adjustment, this is especially the case. Partners from dual cultures (including dual family cultures) must ask themselves questions such as: Who determines *which* rule we follow? (For example, Should we automatically adjust to the husband's culture?) How are such decisions made? Do they treat all family members equitably? Mutual agreement to these questions can facilitate adaptation.

COMMUNICATION RECEPTIVITY

Another major category in understanding family culture is *communication receptivity,* defined here as each family's degree of openness to communication and ability to incorporate and apply new information into family member relationships. When this quality is present, family members are "askable." They are open and they listen. Their communication conveys the attitude, "It is OK to ask any question, or express any feeling. No issue is off-limits in this family. I will not condemn. I will listen with understanding."

When receptivity is absent from a family's culture (avoidance), family members respond differently depending on one's macroculture. For instance, low communication receptivity among U.S. American Caucasians is often viewed as "unhealthy." Failure to be receptive in dealing with taboo subjects illustrates how some children will find relevant information and may experiment outside the family culture. It should not be surprising that communication and family experts assert that avoiding communication may be the worst possible strategy, particularly in sensitive family topics. For example, clinical experience points to Roberta, who remembers her innocent questions about sex when she was 8 years old. Out of his own discomfort, her father responded, "We don't talk about that here." When she was 9, she was sexually abused by an uncle. She tried again to talk to her father, this time about the uncle's abuse. Her father's only response, "We don't talk about that here." At 10, she was molested by her grandfather and once more heard from her dad, "We don't talk about that here." At 34, as a patient in a psychiatric hospital, trying to cope with the trauma of a recent rape, she painfully shared with her father four other instances of sexual abuse. She remembers her father saying the same words, "We don't talk about that here." Today she is a psychotic, locked in a fantasy world, in part because of her father's denial.

In addition, macroculture influences communication receptivity. For example, Rohrlich (1988) suggests that cultural self-disclosure differences should be considered in intercultural marriages. Indeed, much research on initial conversations and developing relationships suggests that different cultures see different topics as intimate or taboo. For example, whereas the "only two subjects you shouldn't discuss are politics and religion" in many American circles, Friday (1997) suggests that for U.S. Americans interacting with Germans, politics, philosophy, and even religion are very appropriate topics. In the same manner, our personal experiences suggest that for many South Americans, death is not a taboo topic.

Communication receptivity is not simply a matter of revising daily schedules. Rather, it may be a deep-rooted cognitive, emotional, and behavioral construct expressed in a pattern of interaction habits affecting intercultural communication. In a study in five Latin American countries, Norton (1984) found that the degree of interpersonal openness was a major contributor to U.S. expatriates' intercultural adjustment. While this study did not examine family culture in detail, many respondents said that family interaction, viewed as a by-product of family culture, helped them adjust to a new country.

A related feature associated with communication receptivity is *availability.* It is one thing to be culturally approachable and appropriately open, but still another to be available. Alex, a rather enterprising young man, was frustrated by having so little time to talk with his very busy father. Under an assumed name, he made an appointment with his father's office. When Alex appeared at the arranged time, his dad quizzed, "Why are you here, Alex? I have an appointment with someone else. Sorry." The teen replied, "Dad, I had to make an appointment under a fictitious name or you never would have seen me. We really have to talk." Time allotted to family members thus contributes to the nature of family and its expectations.

We value these communication characteristics and think they would improve families cross-culturally. At the same time, we recognize that other cultures might have different means of expressing communication receptivity. The family-systems perspective, discussed above, has an element called *equifinality*—that is, a system can reach the same end-state or goal through different means. Although our research suggests that approachability and availability *within the family system* are a key way to have positive family relations and outcomes for individual members, other cultures might meet this goal through other means. For example, some West African cultures expand communication receptivity to significant—and culturally prescribed—roles outside the nuclear family. The Ashanti culture (Ghana) expects a communication receptivity role through a person's maternal uncle.

So, on one hand, low communication receptivity (or avoidance) on the part of an intercultural family member can work against the resolution of cultural and individual differences in the family. On the other hand, conflict literature suggests that many cultures around the world deliberately avoid conflict in order to "preserve the face" or protect the public self-image of the people in the interaction (Ting-Toomey, 1988). The intercultural family must be aware not only of the usefulness (from the U.S. American standpoint) of "open discussion" but also of the need to culturally preserve the "face" of the others in the family.

Overall, we learn here that a lack of communication receptivity can be associated with a number of other communication issues: perception of communication accuracy, contributing to a positive communication climate, risk taking, understanding, encouragement, and listening. What we experience in intercultural communication as negative stereotyping, poor empathy, inadequate relationship development skills, ethnocentrism, stress reactions, and the like can grow from deep taproots related to family culture. Further, conflicts can arise through our assigning negative *personal* characteristics to partners who come from conflict-avoiding macrocultures.

Conclusion

This essay focused on two mutually important levels of culture and their roles in intercultural relationships. First, family culture is a rich source of unexplored social interactions that serve to affect intercultural communication. The family system incorporates rules, roles, myths, customs, communication style, expectations, and the like that alter intercultural relationships.

The macroculture of partners and family members in intercultural relationships offers a second and parallel level of culture affecting intercultural relationships. Thus, outcomes within intercultural relationships such as bonding, nurturing, affirming, cohesion, autonomy, adaptation, codes, rules, social identity, self-worth, and adjustment are defined differentially in the intercultural relationship, from the perspective of *two* cultural units. By blending these two forces, family culture and macrocultural differences, this essay offers a more robust explanation of intercultural relationships.

Notes

1. We do not here intend to present the *only* definition of culture, or a definitive definition. It is merely that this "communicative" definition works more for the purpose of our essay.

2. This list of factors is not intended to be all-inclusive, but rather to provoke thought on the part of the reader. We recognize that our discussion may reflect the biases of our own cultural identities (we are both Caucasian American males) and of the traditional social science framework from which this essay is written, such as the citation of Olson's often quoted categories and his FACES instrument, which has influenced major streams of thought in the family literature.

3. Our cultural examples here are primarily from African, Latino, and certain East Asian ethnicities. This is not to "privilege" these ethnicities, but because these are some of the ethnicities most represented in the United States. The various authors of McGoldrick, Pearce, and Giordano (1982) give extensive discussion of families from 19 different cultures, sometimes even noting regional value and communication differences between co-cultures of a given background (e.g., "British Americans").

4. We recognize that there are vast differences between and within the various Asian American groups (Filipino Americans, Japanese Americans, Korean Americans, Chinese Americans, etc.). We adopt this label here only following the authors we are citing.

5. This sort of adaptability is a major theme of cross-cultural counseling books such as McGoldrick et al. (1982).

References

Baldwin, J. R. (May, 1992). *Dual-culture marriages: An annotated bibliography.* Presented at the annual conference of the Society for International Training, Education, and Research (SIETAR), Montego Bay, Jamaica.

Baldwin, J. R., & Lindsley, S. L. (1994). *Conceptualizations of culture.* Tempe, AZ: Urban Studies Center, College of Public Programs, Arizona State University.

Bowers, D. L. (1997). Capturing the spirit of *Kwanzaa.* In A. González, M. Houston, & V. Chen (Eds.), *Our voices: Essays in culture, ethnicity, and communication* (2nd ed., pp. 121–124). Los Angeles: Roxbury.

Collier, M. J. (1997). Cultural identity and intercultural communication. In L. A. Samovar & R. E. Porter (Eds.), *Intercultural communication: A reader* (8th ed., pp. 36–44). Belmont, CA: Wadsworth.

Dodd, C. H. (1998). *Dynamics of intercultural communication* (5th ed.). New York: McGraw-Hill.

Falicov, C. J. (1986). Cross-cultural marriages. In N. S. Jacobson & A. S. Gurman (Eds.), *Clinical handbook of marital therapy* (pp. 78–90). Rockville, MD: Aspen Systems Corporation.

Friday, R. A. (1997). Contrasts in discussion behaviors of German and American managers. In L. A. Samovar & R. E. Porter (Eds.), *Intercultural communication: A reader* (8th ed., pp. 297–307). Belmont, CA: Wadsworth.

Gaines, S. O., Jr. (1995). Relationships between members of cultural minorities. In J. T. Wood & S. Duck (Eds.), *Understudied relationships: Off the beaten track* (p. 88). Thousand Oaks, CA: Sage.

Galvin, K., & Brommel, B. (1996). *Family communication: Cohesion and change* (4th ed.). Glenview, IL: Scott, Foresman.

Graham, M. A., Moeai, J., & Shizuru, L. S. (1985). Intercultural marriages: An intrareligious perspective. *International Journal of Intercultural Relations, 9,* 427–434.

Gudykunst, W. B., & Gumbs, L. I. (1989). Social cognition and intergroup communication. In M. K. Asante & W. B. Gudykunst (Eds.), *Handbook of international and intercultural communication* (pp. 204–224). Thousand Oaks, CA: Sage.

Gudykunst, W. B., & Kim, Y. Y. (1992). *Communicating with strangers* (2nd ed.). New York: McGraw-Hill.

Gushue, G. V., & Sciarra, D. T. (1995). Culture and families: A multidimensional approach. In J. G. Ponterotto, J. M. Casas, L. A. Suzuki, & C. M. Alexander (Eds.), *Handbook of multicultural counseling* (pp. 586–606).

Hecht, M. (1984). Satisfying communication and relationship labels: Intimacy and length of relationship as perceptual frames of naturalistic conversations. *Western Journal of Speech Communication, 48,* 201–216.

Hecht, M. L., Collier, M. J., & Ribeau, S. A. (1993). *African-American communication: Ethnic identity and cultural interpretation.* Newbury Park, CA: Sage.

Lewis, D., Dodd, C. H., & Tippens, D. (1992). *Dying to tell.* Abilene, TX: ACU Press.

McGoldrick, M., Pearce, J. K., & Giordano, J. (Eds.). (1982). *Ethnicity and family therapy.* New York: Guilford.

Norton, M. L. (1984). *The effects of communication effectiveness and cognitive complexity on culture shock.* Master's thesis, Abilene Christian University, Abilene, TX.

Olson, D. (1976). *Treating relationships.* Lake Mills, IA: Graphic.

Pearson, J. (1992). *Communication in the family* (2nd ed.). New York: Harper & Row.

Rohrlich, B. (1988). Dual-culture marriage and communication. *International Journal of Intercultural Relations, 12,* 35–44.

Romano, D. (1988). *Intercultural marriage: Promises & pitfalls.* Yarmouth, ME: Intercultural Press.

Shon, S. P., & Ja, D. Y. (1982). Asian families. In M. McGoldrick, J. K. Pearce, & J. Giordano (Eds.), *Ethnicity & family therapy* (pp. 208–228). New York: Guilford.

Sprecher, S., Aron, A., Hatfield, E., Cortese, A., Potapova, E., & Levitskaya, A. (1994). Love: American style, Russian style, and Japanese style. *Personal Relationships, 1,* 349–369.

Stone, E. (1996). Family ground rules. In K. M. Galvin & P. Cooper (Eds.), *Making connections* (pp. 59–67). Los Angeles: Roxbury.

Ting-Toomey, S. (1988). Intercultural conflict styles: A face-negotiation theory. In Y. Y. Kim & W. B. Gudykunst (Eds.), *Theories in intercultural communication* (p. 213). Newbury Park, CA: Sage.

Tseng, W.-S. (1977). Adjustment in intercultural marriage. In W.-S. Tseng, J. F. McDermott, Jr., & T. W. Maretzki (Eds.), *Adjustment in intercultural marriage* (pp. 93–103). Honolulu: University of Hawaii.

Tseng, W.-S., McDermott, J. F., Jr., & Maretzki, T. W. (Eds.). (1977). *Adjustment in intercultural marriage.* Honolulu: University of Hawaii.

Wood, J. T. (1996). Communication and relational culture. In K. M. Galvin & P. Cooper (Eds.), *Making connections* (pp. 11–15). Los Angeles: Roxbury.

Key Terms

affirmation	enmeshment
approachability	family
availability	family culture
cohesion	family systems
communication	intercultural
avoidance	relationships
communication style	roles
cultural adaptability	rules
cultural adjustment	social change
cultural identity	supportiveness

Discussion Questions

1. What is the difference, according to Dodd and Baldwin, between family culture and macroculture? What is the relationship between these two? (How are they alike and different? Do they influence each other in any way?)

2. How can people from diverse family backgrounds and cultures develop balance and harmony in their relationships?

3. It is easy to lapse into comfortable "restricted" codes in our relationships, codes that only you and a few others understand. Unfortunately, restricted code usage lacks overlap in experiences, buffer, explanation, and other relationship-building features badly needed for relationship development. How can language and code be an effective beginning point for cultural differences perceived from family differences?

4. Imagine that you and your partner are from different types of cultures (family or macro): one culture values direct conflict ("laying the cards on the table") and the other prefers avoiding conflict ("saving face"). How might you resolve a conflict, say, over household chores or how to spend time together?

5. Interview couples from two different macrocultures and family cultures and ask them to comment on each person's perception of how they are alike and how they are different from one another.

6. If you were to interview a couple from two different cultures (family or macrocultures) where there were *cultural* reasons for doing something, how might one partner understand and explain the other's behavior ("attribution")? What are the implications of these internal explanations on resolving family differences?

7. What role(s) do you find yourself playing in your family system? How do those roles affect other family members? Your friends and significant others?

31 I, We, and They

GEERT HOFSTEDE

A medium-size Swedish high-technology corporation was approached by a compatriot, a businessman with good contacts in Saudi Arabia. The company sent one of their engineers—let me call him Johannesson—to Riyadh, where he was introduced to a small Saudi engineering firm, run by two brothers in their mid-thirties, both with British university degrees. Johannesson was to assist in a development project on behalf of the Saudi government. However, after six visits over a period of two years, nothing seemed to happen. Johannesson's meetings with the Saudi brothers were always held in the presence of the Swedish businessman who had established the first contact. This annoyed Johannesson and his superiors, because they were not at all sure that this businessman did not have contacts with their competitors as well—but the Saudis wanted the intermediary to be there. Discussions often dwelt on issues having little to do with the business—like Shakespeare, of whom both brothers were fans.

Just when Johannesson's superiors started to doubt the wisdom of the corporation's investment in these expensive trips, a telex arrived from Riyadh inviting him back for an urgent visit. A contract worth several millions of dollars was ready to be signed. From one day to the next, the Saudis' attitude changed: the presence of the businessman–intermediary was no longer necessary, and for the first time Johannesson saw the Saudis smile, and even make jokes.

So far, so good; but the story goes on. The remarkable order contributed to Johannesson being promoted to a management position in a different division. Thus, he was no longer in charge of the Saudi account. A successor was nominated, another engineer with considerable international experience, whom Johannesson personally introduced to the Saudi brothers. A few weeks later a telex arrived from Riyadh in which the Saudis threatened to cancel the contract over a detail in the delivery conditions. Johannesson's help was asked. When he came to Riyadh it appeared that the conflict was over a minor issue and could easily be resolved—but only, the Saudis felt, with Johannesson as the corporation's representative. So the corporation twisted its structure to allow Johannesson to handle the Saudi account although his main responsibilities were now in a completely different field.

The Individual and the Collective in Society

The Swedes and the Saudis in this true story have different concepts of the role of personal relationships in business. For the Swedes, business is done with a company; for the Saudis, with a person whom one has learned to know and trust. As long as one does not know another person well enough it is convenient to have present an intermediary or go-between, someone who knows and is trusted by both parties. At the root of the difference between these cultures is a fundamental issue in human societies: the role of the individual versus the role of the group.

The vast majority of people in our world live in societies in which the interest of the group prevails over the interest of the individual. I will call these societies *collectivist*, using a word which to some readers may have political connotations, but it is not meant here in any political sense. It does not refer to the power of the state over the individual but to the *power of the group*. The first group in our lives is always the family into which we are born. Family structures, however, differ between societies. In most collectivist societies the 'family' within which the child grows up consists of a number of people living closely together; not just the parents and other children, but, for example, grandparents, uncles, aunts, servants, or other housemates. This is known in cultural anthropology as the *extended family*. When children grow up they learn to think of themselves as part of a 'we' group, a relationship which is not voluntary but given by nature. The 'we' group is distinct from other people in society who belong to 'they' groups, of which there are many. The 'we' group (or ingroup) is the major source of one's identity, and the only secure protection one has against the hardships of life. Therefore one owes lifelong loyalty to one's ingroup, and breaking this loyalty is one of the worst things a person can do. Between the person and the ingroup a dependence relationship develops which is both practical and psychological.

A minority of people in our world live in societies in which the interests of the individual prevail over the interests of the group, societies which I will call *individualist*. In these, most children are born into families consisting of two parents and, possibly, other children; in some societies there is an increasing share of one-parent families. Other relatives live elsewhere and are rarely seen. This type is the *nuclear family* (from the Latin *nucleus* meaning core). Children from such families, as they grow up, soon learn to think of themselves as 'I'. This 'I', their personal identity, is distinct from other people's 'I's, and these others are not classified according to their group membership but to individual characteristics. Playmates, for example, are chosen on the basis of personal preferences. The purpose of education is to enable the child to stand on its own feet. The child is expected to leave the parental home as soon as this has been achieved. Not infrequently, children, after having left home, reduce relationships with their parents to a minimum or break them off altogether. Neither practically nor psychologically is the healthy person in this type of society supposed to be dependent on a group.

Measuring the Degree of Individualism in Society

The new dimension is defined as follows. *Individualism* pertains to *societies in which the ties between individuals are loose: everyone is expected to look after himself or herself and his or her immediate family. Collectivism* as its opposite pertains to *societies in which people from birth onwards are integrated into strong, cohesive ingroups, which throughout people's lifetime continue to protect them in exchange for unquestioning loyalty.*

Degrees of individualism obviously vary within countries as well as between them, so it is again very important to base the country scores on comparable samples from one country to another. The IBM samples offered this comparability.

The dimension to be identified with individualism versus collectivism was most strongly associated with the relative importance attached to the following 'work goal' items. For the individualist pole:

1. *Personal time* Have a job which leaves you sufficient time for your personal or family life.

2. *Freedom* Have considerable freedom to adopt your own approach to the job.

3. *Challenge* Have challenging work to do—work from which you can achieve a personal sense of accomplishment.

For the opposite, collectivist pole:

4. *Training* Have training opportunities (to improve your skills or learn new skills).

5. *Physical conditions* Have good physical working conditions (good ventilation and lighting, adequate work space, etc.).

6. *Use of skills* Fully use your skills and abilities on the job.

If the IBM employees in a country scored work goal (1) as relatively important, they generally also scored (2) and (3) as important, but (4), (5), and (6) as unimportant. Such a country was considered individualist. If (1) was scored as relatively unimportant, the same generally held for (2) and (3), but (4), (5), and (6) would be scored as relatively more important. Such a country was considered collectivist.

. . . The factor scores for the individualism dimension were multiplied by 25 and a constant number of 50 points was added. This puts all scores in a

TABLE 1 • Individualism Index (IDV) Values for 50 Countries and 3 Regions

SCORE RANK	COUNTRY OR REGION	IDV SCORE	SCORE RANK	COUNTRY OR REGION	IDV SCORE
1	USA	91	28	Turkey	37
2	Australia	90	29	Uruguay	36
3	Great Britain	89	30	Greece	35
4/5	Canada	80	31	Philippines	32
4/5	Netherlands	80	32	Mexico	30
6	New Zealand	79	33/35	East Africa	27
7	Italy	76	33/35	Yugoslavia	27
8	Belgium	75	33/35	Portugal	27
9	Denmark	74	36	Malaysia	26
10/11	Sweden	71	37	Hong Kong	25
10/11	France	71	38	Chile	23
12	Ireland	70	39/41	West Africa	20
	(Republic of)		39/41	Singapore	20
13	Norway	69	39/41	Thailand	20
14	Switzerland	68	42	Salvador	19
15	Germany F. R.	67	43	South Korea	18
16	South Africa	65	44	Taiwan	17
17	Finland	63	45	Peru	16
18	Austria	55	46	Costa Rica	15
19	Israel	54	47/48	Pakistan	14
20	Spain	51	47/48	Indonesia	14
21	India	48	49	Colombia	13
22/23	Japan	46	50	Venezuela	12
22/23	Argentina	46	51	Panama	11
24	Iran	41	52	Equador	8
25	Jamaica	39	53	Guatemala	6
26/27	Brazil	38			
26/27	Arab countries	38			

range from close to 0 for the most collectivist country to close to 100 for the most individualist one.[1]

The individualism index (IDV) scores can be read from Table 1. . . . The scores represent the *relative* positions of countries. What can immediately be recognized by inspecting Table 1 is that nearly all wealthy countries score high on IDV while nearly all poor countries score low. There is a strong relationship between a country's national wealth and the degree of individualism in its culture; it will be further explored later in this chapter.

Sweden scores 171 on IDV and the group of Arab-speaking countries to which Saudi Arabia belongs scores an average of 38, which demonstrates the cultural roots of Johannesson's dilemma. Of course, the Arab countries differ among themselves, and impressionistically the Saudis within this region are even more collectivist than some other Arabs like Lebanese or Egyptians. In the IBM sample the latter were more strongly represented than the Saudis. Sweden's rank among 53 countries and regions is 10–11 and the Arab countries' rank

26–27, so there are still a lot of countries scoring more than the Arab average. As stated above, collectivism is the rule in our world, and individualism the exception.

Individualism and Collectivism in the Family

At the beginning of this chapter individualism was associated with a nuclear family structure and collectivism with an extended family structure, the latter leading to the distinction between ingroup and outgroups. The relationship between the individual and the group, like other basic elements of human culture, is first learned in the family setting. The fact that Japan scores halfway in Table 1 (rank 22/23, IDV 46) can at least partly be understood from the fact that in the traditional Japanese family only the oldest son continues to live with his parents, thus creating a 'lineal' structure which is somewhere in between nuclear and extended.

There is a correlation between the degree of collectivism in a society as measured by the IDV and the likelihood that sons will share the occupation of their fathers (Hofstede, 1980, p. 257; 1984, pp. 169–170). In more individualist societies the chances are greater that sons of fathers in manual occupations will move to nonmanual occupations and vice versa. In more collectivist societies this happens more rarely, an obvious outcome of sons staying within the extended family sphere.

The child who grows up among a number of elders, peers, and juniors learns naturally to conceive of itself as part of a 'we'; much more so than the nuclear family child. An extended family child is seldom alone during the day or at night. An African student who came to a Belgian university to study told us that this was the first time in her life she had ever been alone in a room for any sizeable length of time.

In a situation of intense and continuous social contact the maintenance of *harmony* with one's social environment becomes a key virtue which extends to other spheres beyond the family. In most collectivist cultures direct confrontation of another person is considered rude and undesirable. The word 'no' is seldom used, because saying no *is* a confrontation; 'you may be right' or 'we will think about it' are examples of polite ways of turning down a request. In the same vein, the word 'yes' should not necessarily be seen as an approval, but as maintenance of the communication line: 'yes, I heard you' is the meaning it has in Japan.

In individualist cultures, on the other hand, speaking one's mind is a virtue. Telling the truth about how one feels is the characteristic of a sincere and honest person. Confrontation can be salutary; a clash of opinions is believed to lead to a higher truth. The effect of communications on other people should be taken into account, but it does not, as a rule, justify changing the facts. Adult individuals should have learned to take direct feedback constructively. In the family, children are told one should always tell the truth, even if it hurts. Coping with conflict is a normal part of living together as a family.

A former Dutch missionary in Indonesia (a country with IDV 14, rank 47/48) told about his parishioners' unexpected exegesis of the following parable from the Bible: 'A man had two sons. He went to the first and said "Son, go and work in the vineyard today"; he replied "I will go, sir", but he did not go. The man went to the second and said the same to him. He replied "I will not", but afterwards he changed his mind and did go. Which of the two did the will of the father?' (St. Matthew 21: 28–31; Moffatt translation). The biblical answer is 'the last', but the missionary's Indonesian parishioners chose the first; for this son observed the formal harmony and did not contradict his father. Whether he actually went was of secondary importance.

In the collectivist family children learn to take their bearings from others when it comes to opinions. 'Personal opinions' do not exist: they are predetermined by the group. If a new issue comes up on which there is no established group opinion, some kind of family conference is necessary before an opinion can be given. A child who repeatedly voices opinions deviating from what is collectively felt is considered to have a bad character. In the individualist family, on the contrary, children are expected and encouraged to develop opinions of their own, and a child who only ever reflects the opinions of others is considered to have a weak character. The behavior corresponding with a desirable character depends on the cultural environment.

The loyalty to the group which is an essential element of the collectivist family also means that resources are shared. If one member of an extended family of 20 persons has a paid job and the others have not, the earning member is supposed to share his or her income in order to help feed the entire family. On the basis of this principle a family may collectively cover the expenses for sending one member to get a higher education, expecting that when this member subsequently achieves a well-paid job the income will also be shared.

In individualist cultures parents will be proud if children at an early age take small jobs in order to earn pocket-money of their own, which they alone can decide how to spend. In the Netherlands, as in many other individualist Western European countries, the government contributes substantially to the living expenses of students. Recently the system has been changed from an allowance to the parents to an allowance directly to the students themselves, which stresses their independence. From now on the government will consider both boys and girls as independent economic players from age 18 onwards. In the USA it is quite normal for students to pay for their own study by temporary jobs and personal loans; without government support they too are less dependent on their parents and not at all on more distant relatives.

Obligations to the family in a collectivist society are not only financial but also ritual. Family celebrations like baptisms, marriages, and, especially, funerals are extremely important and should not be missed. Expatriate managers from individualist societies are often surprised by the family reasons given by employees from a collectivist host society who apply for a special leave; the expatriates think they are being fooled but most likely the reasons are authentic.

In an individualist culture when people meet they feel a need to communicate verbally. Silence is considered abnormal. Social conversations can be depressingly banal, but they are compulsory. In a collectivist culture the fact of being together is emotionally sufficient; there is no compulsion to talk unless there is information to be transferred. Raden Mas Hadjiwibowo, an Indonesian businessman from a Javanese noble family, recalls the family visits from his youth as follows:

'Visits among Javanese family members needed no previous appointment. Actually that could easily be done, for although the telephone had not come into common use yet, one could always send a servant with a letter asking for an appointment. But it was not done, it never occurred to one that a visit would not suit the other party. It was always convenient. Unexpected visitors did not exist. The door was (and still is) always open.

The visitors were welcomed with joyful courtesy and would be asked to take a seat. The host and hostess hurriedly withdrew to change into more suitable attire than their workaday clothes. Without asking, a servant brought in coffee or tea. Cookies were offered, while in the meantime the host and hostess had joined the party.

There we sat, but nobody spoke. We were not embarrassed by this silence; nobody felt nervous about it. Every now and then, thoughts and news were exchanged. But this was not really necessary. We enjoyed being together, seeing each other again. After the first exchange of news, any other communication was utterly redundant. If one did not have anything to say, there was no need to recite platitudes. After an hour or so, the guests would ask permission to leave. With mutual feelings of satisfaction, we parted. In smaller towns on the island of Java life is still like this.'[2]

US anthropologist and popular author Edward T. Hall distinguishes cultures on the basis of their way of communicating along a dimension from 'high-context' to 'low context' (Hall, 1976). A high-context communication is one in which little has to be said or written because most of the information is either in the physical environment or within the person, while very little is in the coded, explicit part of the message. This type of communication is frequent in collectivist cultures; Hadjiwibowo's family visit is a case example. A low-context communication is one in which the mass of information is vested in the explicit code, which is typical for individualist cultures. Lots of things which in collectivist cultures are self-evident must be said explicitly in individualist cultures. American business contracts are much longer than Japanese business contracts.

Next to harmony another important concept in connection with the collectivist family is *shame*. Individualist societies have been described as *guilt* cultures: persons who infringe upon the rules of society will often feel guilty, ridden by an individually developed conscience which functions as a private inner pilot. Collectivist societies, on the contrary, are shame cultures: persons belonging to a group from which a member has infringed upon the rules of society will feel ashamed, based upon a sense of collective obligation. Shame is social in nature, guilt individual; whether shame is felt depends on whether the infringement has become known by others. This becoming known is more of a source of shame than the infringement itself. Such is not the case for guilt, which is felt whether or not the misdeed is known by others.

A last concept bred in the collectivist family is *face*. 'Losing face', in the sense of being humiliated, is an expression which penetrated into the English language from the Chinese; the English had no equivalent for it. David Yau-Fai Ho, a Hong Kong social scientist, defines it as follows: 'Face is lost when the individual, either through his action or that of people closely related to him, fails to meet essential requirements placed upon him by virtue of the social position he occupies' (Ho, 1976, p. 867). The Chinese also speak of 'giving someone face', in the sense of honor or prestige. Basically, 'face' describes the proper relationship with one's social environment, which is as essential to a person (and that person's family) as the front part of his/her head. The importance of face is the consequence of living in a society that is very conscious of social contexts. The languages of other collectivist cultures have words with more-or-less similar meanings. In Greece, for example, there is a word *philotimo;* Harry Triandis, a Greek–American psychologist, writes:

> A person is *philotimos* to the extent in which he conforms to the norms and values of his ingroup. These include a variety of sacrifices that are appropriate for members of one's family, friends, and others who are 'concerned with one's welfare'; for example, for a man to delay marriage until his sisters have married and have been provided with a proper dowry is part of the normative expectations

> of traditional rural Greeks as well as rural Indians (and many of the people in between). (Triandis, 1972, p. 38)

In the individualist society the counterpart characteristic is 'self-respect', but this again is defined from the point of view of the individual, whereas 'face' and 'philotimo' are defined from the point of view of the social environment.

Collectivist societies usually have ways of creating family-like ties with persons who are not biological relatives but who are socially integrated into one's ingroup. In Latin America, for example, this can be done via the institution of *compadres* and *comadres* who are treated as relatives even if they are not. In Japan younger sons in past times became apprentices to craftsmasters through a form of adoption. Similar customs existed in medieval Central Europe.

Individualism and Collectivism at School

The relationship between the individual and the group which has been established in a child's consciousness during its early years in the family is further developed and reinforced at school. This is very visible in classroom behavior. In the context of development assistance it often happens that teachers from a more individualist culture move to a more collectivist environment. A typical complaint from such teachers is that students do not speak up in class, not even when the teacher puts a question to the class. For the student who conceives of him/herself as part of a group, it is illogical to speak up without being sanctioned by the group to do so. If the teacher wants students to speak up, she or he should address a particular student personally.

Collectivist culture students will also hesitate to speak up in larger groups without a teacher present, especially if these are partly composed of relative strangers: outgroup members. This hesitation decreases in smaller groups. Personally I obtained broad participation when teaching a collectivist class by asking students to turn around in their seats so that groups of three were formed. I asked the students to discuss a question for five minutes, and to decide who would report their joint answer to the class. Through this device students had an opportunity to develop a group answer and felt comfortable when speaking up before the class because they acted as the small group's representative. I also noticed that in subsequent exercises the students arranged for the spokespersons to rotate. Taking turns in group activities is a habit which exists in many collectivist cultures.

The desirability of having students speak up in class is more strongly felt in individualist than in collectivist cultures. Because most collectivist cultures also maintain large power distances, their education tends to be teacher-centered with little two-way communication. . . .

In the collectivist society ingroup–outgroup distinctions springing from the family sphere will continue at school, so that students from different ethnic or clan backgrounds often form subgroups in class. In an individualist society the assignment of joint tasks leads more easily to the formation of new groups than in the collectivist society. In the latter, students from the same ethnic or family background as the teacher or other school officials will expect preferential treatment on this basis. In an individualist society this would be considered nepotism and intensely immoral, but in a collectivist environment it is immoral *not* to treat one's ingroup members better than others.

In the collectivist classroom the virtues of harmony and the maintenance of 'face' reign supreme. Confrontations and conflicts should be avoided, or at least formulated so as not to hurt anyone; even students should not lose face if this can be avoided. Shaming, that is invoking the group's honor, is an effective way of correcting offenders: they will be put in order by their ingroup members. At all times the teacher is dealing with the student as part of an ingroup, never as an isolated individual.

In the individualist classroom, of course, students expect to be treated as individuals and impartially, regardless of their background. Group formation among students is much more *ad hoc*, according to the task, or to particular friendships and skills. Confrontations and open discussion of conflicts is often considered salutary, and face-consciousness is weak or nonexistent.

The *purpose* of education is perceived differently between the individualist and the collectivist society. In the former it aims at preparing the *individual* for a place in a society of other individuals. This means learning to cope with new, unknown, unforeseen situations. There is a basically positive attitude towards what is new. The purpose of learning is less to know how to do, as to know *how to learn*. The assumption is that learning in life never ends; even after school and university it will continue, for example through recycling courses. The individualist society in its schools tries to provide the skills necessary for 'modern man'.

In the collectivist society there is a stress on adaptation to the skills and virtues necessary to be an acceptable group member. This leads to a premium on the products of *tradition*. Learning is more often seen as a one-time process, reserved for the young only, who have to learn *how to do* things in order to participate in society.

The role of diplomas or certificates as a result of successful completion of study is also different between the two poles of the individualism–collectivism dimension. In the individualist society the diploma not only improves the holder's economic worth but also his or her self-respect: it provides a sense of achievement. In the collectivist society a diploma is an honor to the holder and his or her ingroup which entitles the holder to associate with members of higher-status groups; for example, to obtain a more attractive marriage partner. It is to a certain extent 'a ticket to ride'. The social acceptance that comes with the diploma is more important than the individual self-respect that comes with mastering a subject, so that in collectivist societies the temptation is stronger to obtain diplomas in some irregular way, such as on the black market.

Individualism and Collectivism in the Workplace

Employed persons in an individualist culture are expected to act according to their own interest, and work should be organized in such a way that this self-interest and the employer's interest coincide. Workers are supposed to act as 'economic men', or as people with a combination of economic and psychological needs, but in either case as individuals with their own needs. In a collectivist culture an employer never hires just an individual, but a person who belongs to an ingroup. The employee will act according to the interest of this ingroup, which may not always coincide with his or her individual interest: self-effacement in the interest of the ingroup belongs to the normal expectations in such a society. Often earnings have to be shared with relatives.

The hiring process in a collectivist society always takes the ingroup into account. Usually preference is given to hiring relatives, first of all of the employer, but also of other persons already employed by the company. Hiring persons from a family one already knows reduces risks. Also, relatives will be concerned about the reputation of the family and help to correct misbehavior of a family member. In the individualist society family relationships at work are often considered undesirable as they may lead to nepotism and to a conflict of interest. Some companies have a rule that if one employee marries another, one of them has to leave.

The workplace itself in a collectivist society may become an ingroup in the emotional sense of the word. In some countries this is more the case than in others, but the feeling that it should be this way is nearly always present. The relationship between employer and employee is seen in moral terms. It resembles a family relationship with mutual obligations of protection in exchange for loyalty. Poor performance of an employee in this relationship is no reason for dismissal; one does not dismiss one's child. Performance and skills, however, do determine what tasks one assigns to an employee. This pattern of relationships is best known from Japanese organizations. In Japan it applies in a strict sense only to the group of permanent employees which may be less than half of the total work force. Japan scores halfway on the IDV scale. In individualist societies the relationship between employer and employee is primarily conceived as a business transaction, a calculative relationship between buyers and sellers on a 'labor market'. Poor performance on the part of the employee or a better pay offer from another employer are legitimate and socially accepted reasons for terminating a work relationship.

Christopher Earley, a management researcher from the USA, has illustrated the difference in work ethos between an individualist and a collectivist society very neatly with a laboratory experiment. In the experiment, 48 management trainees from southern China and 48 matched management trainees from the USA were given an 'in-basket task'. The task consisted of 40 separate items requiring between two and five minutes each, like writing memos, evaluating plans, and rating job candidates' application forms. Half of the participants in either country were given a group goal of 200 items to be completed in an hour by 10 people; the other half were given each an individual goal of 20 items. Also, half of the participants in either country, both from the group goal and from the individual goal subset, were asked to mark each item completed with their name, the other half turned them in anonymously.

The Chinese, collectivist, participants performed best when operating with a group goal, and anonymously. They performed worst when operating individually and with their name marked on the items produced. The American, individualist, participants performed best when operating individually and with their name marked, and abysmally low when operating as a group and anonymously. All participants were also given a values test to determine their personal individualism or collectivism: a minority of the Chinese scored individualist, and these performed according to the US pattern; a minority of the Americans scored collectivist and these performed like the Chinese (Earley, 1989).

In practice there is a wide range of types of employer–employee relationships *within* collectivist and individualist societies. There are employers in collectivist countries who do not respect the societal norm to treat their employees as ingroup members, but then the employees in turn do not repay them in terms of loyalty. Labor unions in such cases may replace the work organization as an emotional ingroup and there can be violent union–management conflicts, as in parts of India. There are employers in individualist societies who have established a strong group cohesion with their employees, with the same protection-versus-loyalty balance which is the norm in the collectivist society. Organization cultures can to some extent deviate from majority norms and derive a competitive advantage from their originality. . . .

Management in an individualist society is management of individuals. Subordinates can usually be moved around individually; if incentives or bonuses are given, these should be linked to an individual's performance. Management in a collectivist society is management of groups. The extent to which people actually feel emotionally integrated into a work group may differ from one situation to another. Ethnic and other ingroup differences within the work group play a role in the integration process and managers within a collectivist culture will be extremely attentive to such factors. It often makes good sense to put people from the same ethnic background into one crew, although individualistically programmed managers usually consider this dangerous and want to do the opposite. If the work group functions as an emotional ingroup, incentives and bonuses should be given to the group, not to individuals.

Within countries with a dominant individualist middle-class culture, regional rural subcultures have sometimes retained strongly collectivist elements. The same applies to the migrant worker minorities which form majorities among the work force in some industries in some individualist countries. In such cases a culture conflict is likely between managers and regional or minority workers. This conflict expresses itself, among other things in the management's extreme hesitation to use group incentives in cases when they are the only things that really suit the culture of the work force.

Management techniques and training packages have almost exclusively been developed in individualist countries, and they are based on cultural assumptions which may not hold in collectivist cultures. A standard element in the training of first-line managers is how to conduct 'appraisal interviews': periodic discussions in which the subordinate's performance is reviewed. These can form part of MBO [management by objectives] . . . , but even where MBO does not exist, conducting performance appraisals and the ability to communicate 'bad news' are considered key skills for a successful manager. In a collectivist society discussing a person's performance openly with him or her is likely to clash head-on with the society's harmony norm and may be felt by the subordinate as an unacceptable loss of face. Such societies have more subtle, indirect ways of communicating feedback: for example by the withdrawal of a normal favor or verbally via an intermediary. I know of a case in which an older relative of the poorly performing employee, also in the service of the employer, played this intermediary role. He communicated the bad news to his nephew, avoiding the loss of face which a formal appraisal interview would have provoked.

The Sensitivity Training (T-Group) fashion of the 1960s, the encounter group fashion of the 1970s, and the transactional analysis fashion of the 1980s have all been developed in the USA, the country with the highest individualism index score in Table 1. Each of them is based on honest and direct sharing of feelings about other people. Such training methods are unfit for use in collectivist cultures. There, sensitivity training is felt to be training in *in*sensitivity; daily life is filled with encounters so that no special groups have to be formed to this purpose. Relationships between people are never seen as 'transactions' between individuals: they are moral in nature, not calculative.

The distinction between ingroup and outgroups which is so essential in the collectivist culture pattern has far-reaching consequences for business relationships, beyond those between employers and employees. It is the reason behind the cultural embarrassment of Mr Johannesson and his Swedish superiors in Saudi Arabia related at the beginning of this chapter. In individualist societies the norm is that one should treat everybody alike. In sociological jargon this is known as *universalism*. Preferential treatment of one customer over others is considered bad business practice and unethical. In collectivist societies the reverse is true. As the distinction between 'our group' and 'other groups' is at the very root of people's consciousness, treating one's friends better than others is natural and ethical, and sound business practice. Sociologists call this way of thinking *particularism*.

A consequence of particularist thinking is that in a collectivist society a relationship of trust should be established with another person before any business

TABLE 2 • Key Differences Between Collectivist and Individualist Societies. . . .

COLLECTIVIST	INDIVIDUALIST
People are born into extended families or other ingroups which continue to protect them in exchange for loyalty	Everyone grows up to look after him/herself and his/her immediate (nuclear) family only
Identity is based in the social network to which one belongs	Identity is based in the individual
Children learn to think in terms of 'we'	Children learn to think in terms of 'I'
Harmony should always be maintained and direct confrontations avoided	Speaking one's mind is a characteristic of an honest person
High-context communication	Low-context communication
Trespassing leads to shame and loss of face for self and group	Trespassing leads to guilt and loss of self-respect
Purpose of education is learning how to do	Purpose of education is learning how to learn
Diplomas provide entry to higher status groups	Diplomas increase economic worth and/or self-respect
Relationship employer–employee is perceived in moral terms, like a family link	Relationship employer–employee is a contract supposed to be based on mutual advantage
Hiring and promotion decisions take employees' ingroup into account	Hiring and promotion decisions are supposed to be based on skills and rules only
Management is management of groups	Management is management of individuals
Relationship prevails over task	Task prevails over relationship

can be done. Through this relationship the other is adopted into one's ingroup and from that moment onwards is entitled to preferential treatment. In Johannesson's case this process of adoption took two years. During this period the presence of the Swedish businessman as an intermediary was essential. After the adoption had taken place it became superfluous. However, the relationship was with Johannesson personally and not with his company. To the collectivist mind only natural persons are worthy of trust, and via these persons their friends and colleagues, but not impersonal legal entities like a company. In summary: in the collectivist society *the personal relationship prevails over the task* and should be established first; in the individualist society *the task is supposed to prevail over any personal relationships*. The naive Western businessman who tries to force quick business in a collectivist culture condemns himself to the role of outgroup member and to negative discrimination.

Table 2 summarizes the key differences between collectivist and individualist societies described so far.

Individualism, Collectivism, and Ideas

Individualist societies not only practice individualism but also consider it superior to other forms of mental software. Most Americans feel that individualism is good, and at the root of their country's greatness. On the other hand, the late Chairman Mao Tse Tung of China identified individualism as evil. He found individualism and liberalism responsible for selfishness and aversion to discipline; they led people to placing personal interests above those of the group, or simply to devoting too much attention to one's own things. Table 1 contains no data for the People's Republic of China but the countries with a predominantly Chinese population all score very low on the individualism index (25 for Hong Kong, 20 for Singapore, 17 for Taiwan).

Economics as a discipline was founded in Great Britain in the eighteenth century; among the founding fathers Adam Smith (1723–1790) stands out. Smith assumed that the pursuit of self-interest by individuals through an 'invisible hand' would lead to the maximal wealth of nations. This is a highly individualist idea from a country which even today ranks near the top on individualism. Economics has remained an individualist science and most of its leading contributors have come from strongly individualistic countries like the UK and the USA. However, because of the individualist assumptions on which they are based, economic theories as developed in the West are unlikely to apply in societies in which not individual interest, but group interests prevail. Unfortunately there are few alternative economic theories yet to deal with collectivist economies. The Dutch sociologist Cas Vroom, describing the situation of Indonesia, contrasts the Western orientation towards 'return on investment' with an Indonesian 'return on favors' (Vroom, 1981).

The French Revolution, the bicentennial celebration of which took place in 1989, had as its slogan *'liberté, égalité, fraternité'*: freedom, equality, brotherhood. This was the slogan of political idealists who wanted to have their cake and eat it, for it does not recognize that in politics there is an inescapable trade-off between freedom and equality, and very little brotherhood. Not much of the revolutionary ideal was realized in France, as we know: it led to the Reign of Terror and subsequently to the dictatorship and military adventures of Napoleon. . . .

———————

The degree of individualism or collectivism of a society will affect the conceptions of human nature produced in that society. In the USA the ideas of Abraham Maslow (1908–70) about human motivation have been and are still quite influential, in particular for the training of management students and practitioners. Maslow formulated his famous 'hierarchy of human needs' in 1943. It states that human needs can be ordered in a hierarchy from lower to higher, as follows: physiological, safety, belonging-

ness, esteem, and self-actualization. In order for a higher need to appear it is necessary that the lower needs have been satisfied up to a certain extent. A starving person, that is, one whose physiological needs are not at all satisfied, will not be motivated by anything other than the quest for food, and so forth. At the top of Maslow's hierarchy, which is often pictured as a pyramid, there is the motive of self-actualization: realizing to the fullest possible extent the creative potential present within the individual. This means 'Doing one's own thing', as it was called in the US youth culture of the 1960s. It goes without saying that this can only be the supreme motivation in an individualist society. In a collectivist culture, what will be actualized is the interest and honor of the ingroup which may very well ask for self-effacement from many of the ingroup members. As the interpreter for a group of American visitors to China remarked, the idea of 'doing your own thing' is not translatable into Chinese.

Maslow's main book in which he explained his theories (Maslow, 1970) is based on a concept of personality which is common in Western thinking, but which is not universal. The Chinese–American anthropologist Francis Hsu has shown that the Chinese language has no equivalent for 'personality' in the Western sense. Personality in the West is a separate entity, distinct from society and culture: an attribute of the individual. The closest translation into Chinese is *jen* (*ren* in the modern transcription), which stands for 'person' as a 'human constant', which includes not only the individual but also his or her intimate societal and cultural environment which makes his or her existence meaningful (Hsu, 1971).

———————

The Future of Individualism and Collectivism

The deep roots of national cultures make it likely that individualism–collectivism differences, like power distance differences, will survive for a long time. Yet if there is to be any convergence between national cultures it should be on this dimension. The strong relationship between national wealth and individualism is undeniable, with the arrow of causality directed, as shown above, from wealth to individualism. Countries having achieved fast economic development have experienced a shift towards individualism. Japan is an example: the Japanese press regularly publishes stories of breaches of traditional family solidarity. Care for the aged in the past was considered a task for the Japanese family, but provisions by the state have become necessary for cases where the family stops fulfilling its traditional duties.

Nevertheless, even at a level of per capita income equal to or larger than Western countries, Japanese society will very likely conserve distinctive collectivist elements in its family-, school-, and workspheres. The same holds for differences among Western countries themselves. Next to a noticeable convergency towards individualism under the influence of a common economic boom, relationships between the individual and the group continue to differ between, say, the UK, Sweden, and Germany. The cultures shift, but they shift together, so that the differences between them remain intact.

As far as the poor countries of the world are concerned there is no reason why they should become more individualist as long as they remain poor. The IBM data bank allowed for measurement of the shifts in individualism during the four-year period from 1968 to 1972. Out of 20 countries which had been surveyed in both periods, 19 had become richer, and all of these had shifted towards greater individualism. The only country in the set that had become poorer, Pakistan, shifted slightly towards the collectivist end of the scale.

Differences in values associated with the individualism–collectivism dimension will continue to exist and to play a big role in international affairs, for example in negotiations between rich and poor countries. Individualism versus collectivism as a dimension of national cultures is responsible for many misunderstandings in intercultural encounters. . . .

Notes

1. Using factor scores as a basis for country indices was very easy for the initial IBM study but makes it difficult to compute index values in later follow-up studies. The scoring guide for the 1982 values survey module issued by the Institute for Research on Intercultural Cooperation (IRIC) therefore contains an approximation formula, in which the individualism index value can be computed by simple mathematics from four of the 'work goals' mean scores.

2. From a speech by R. M. Hadjiwibowo to Semafor Senior Management College, the Netherlands, September 1983. Translation from the Dutch by GH with suggestions from the author.

Selected References

Earley, P. C. (1989). Social loafing and collectivism: A comparison of the United States and the People's Republic of China. *Administrative Science Quarterly, 34,* 565–581.

Hall, E. T. (1976). *Beyond culture.* Garden City, NY: Doubleday Anchor Books.

Ho, D. Y.-F. (1976). On the concept of face. *American Journal of Sociology, 81,* 867–884.

Hofstede, G. (1980). *Culture's consequences: International differences in work-related values.* Beverly Hills, CA: Sage.

Hofstede, G. (1984). *Culture's consequences: International differences in work-related values,* abridged edition. Beverly Hills, CA: Sage.

Hsu, F. L. K. (1971). Psychological homeostasis and *jen:* Conceptual tools for advancing psychological anthropology. *American Anthropologist, 73,* 23–44.

Maslow, A. H. (1970). *Motivation and personality* (2nd ed.). New York: Harper & Row.

Triandis, H. C. (1972). *The analysis of subjective culture.* New York: Wiley-Interscience.

Vroom, C. W. (1981). *Indonesia and the West: An essay on cultural differences in organization and management.* Jakarta: Catholic University.

Key Terms

collectivism	organizational
cultural values	communication
family	power distance
individualism	work

Discussion Questions

1. In what ways are your relationships with your friends more or less individualist or collectivist?

2. What advice would you give international students from collectivist cultures about making friends at a U.S. university?

3. How do you think individualist-collectivist behavior might vary from context to context? For example, might your behavior be more collectivist in family contexts, less so in work contexts?

4. Hofstede's research was conducted from a social science perspective. How might an interpretive or critical researcher investigate national values?

5. What are the dangers (limitations) of making generalizations about behaviors based on nationality?

32 Intercultural Friendships as Interpersonal Alliances

MARY JANE COLLIER

In the United States, as in many countries, anti-immigration laws are being debated and Affirmative Action policies are being reconsidered. In several states, laws barring discrimination against gays and lesbians are being challenged, and membership in self-proclaimed racist groups such as the KKK and militia organizations is increasing (Southern Poverty Law Center Report, March 1996). Racism has become a part of our everyday language, as have other forms of "isms" toward many groups.

It is in this sociohistorical, cultural milieu that we find ourselves today. All of us must manage a series of identity dialectics or seemingly contradictory tensions. At the national level, we struggle to manage the tension between the need to be international citizens and the need to maintain a unique national identity. Paradoxically, we have increased our technological abilities and access to international sites and, at the same time, increased our need for defining and protecting our group boundaries.

As ethnic group members we struggle to manage the tension between being U.S. Americans and being, for example, Cuban or Japanese. We recognize that men and women aren't limited to a particular sexual orientation, or a gendered style of speaking, and that families and friendship relationships take many forms. As individuals, we are members of many groups and relationships, yet we maintain some degree of individual uniqueness.

My purpose in this essay is to explore how individuals who have satisfying friendships with people from different cultural backgrounds maintain their friendships as well as demonstrate respect for one another's cultural differences. I am proposing that some intercultural friendships become interpersonal alliances. The word "ally" connotes partner, advocate, collaborator, and supporter, and "alliance" means to be associated, connected, pledged, and joined in a united front. Although most commonly we think of alliances in contexts of war or violence, they arise in different contexts and take various forms within and between many national, ethnic, sex, class, religious, and political groups.

Our everyday talk includes numerous explicit and implicit references to ingroup and outgroup distinctions. We define our own identities in comparison to other groups. Frequently, an "insider" comes to think of and describe others as "outsiders," one of "them" instead of "us." Insider-outsider boundaries are constructed, defended, and challenged through communication; our words and actions create the borders and shared spaces of our world. We become who we are as well as negotiate power through communicating within and across such boundaries.

In an alliance, the insider-outsider distinction becomes open to question and critique. Alliances require at least two people who are both responsible for and dependent upon the quality of their relationship. Often, in regions torn by violent conflict and war, women form alliances to work for peace. When Palestinian and Israeli women march together for peace in the streets of Jerusalem, an observer can't identify who is an insider and who is an outsider; one can see only the alliance.

Intercultural friends must manage not only feelings of being both the insider and outsider at different times but also various tensions. Such relationships are often filled with paradox and dialectical tension between contradictory forces—toward being both separate and together, unique and divided, independent and interdependent.

In the remainder of the essay I describe my orientation to intercultural communication in friendships by explaining an approach based in cultural identity(ies). First, I explain how four group identities—race, sex, ethnicity, and nationality—are formed. Second, I describe how cultural identities become the basis of intercultural friendships. Finally, I identify three critical components important in developing and maintaining intercultural friendship alliances.

Developing Cultural Identities: Race, Sex, Ethnicity, and Nationality

Rather than studying culture as the *place* where people come from, or as an independent variable from which researchers and scholars can predict specific conduct, I focus on the communication processes through which people construct culture and their identities. I define culture to be an enduring and changing, situated and transcendent, co-constructed set of communicative practices and interpretive frames shared by a group. Membership occurs when people self-identify as group members, their membership is bounded and salient, and members of the group confirm the membership (Carbaugh, 1990). In addition, the communicative practices and interpretations must endure to some degree and be invoked for new members while simultaneously being re-constructed and changed.

According to the criteria outlined here, not all groups have a culture. When a culture does emerge,

the particular character of the communicative system that individuals, friends, and group members enact is cultural identity. In this essay, I focus on cultural groups whose members self-identify on the basis of biological characteristics (male, female, skin color), shared ancestry and heritage (ethnicity) or nationality (birth or naturalization), and social and historical construction.

Membership in some cultural groups is more involuntary than voluntary. An individual's sex and race are designated at birth for most people and thus membership is more involuntary. In general, scholars conceive of race in one of two ways. The first focuses on physically inherited characteristics based on generations of geographical and climatic adjustment. But being born into a group and sharing race, for instance, does not mean that each group member will communicate in similar ways or have a similar group identity. The second, more recent approach, is to define race as a social/historical construction. Scholars in this tradition argue today that because of intermarriage and changes in the definitions of racial categories, one can no longer base categories of race on biological or genetic conceptions. They maintain that race as a categorization system has been used throughout history to identify outsiders in order to exert and maintain power. From this perspective, race is a way of creating an identity hierarchy and ascribing to others an identity that allows members of the group in power to keep their power.

Sex is another primarily involuntary group category. Sex, like race, is determined at birth (or is very difficult to change). It should be pointed out, nonetheless, that women (and men) do not all share the exact same identities or even assumptions about how to be women (or how to be men). Men and women in many countries adopt aspects of a masculine or feminine style.

Gender identity is socialized, contextualized, and emergent. Although male children are taught to use a masculine style and female children are taught to be feminine in many countries and contexts, and gender is still a basis for discrimination against women all over the world, gender identity variations are increasing for both sexes.

Race and sex are important because outsiders often use these categories to apply stereotypes of group members, attribute values and beliefs, allocate resources, determine policies, and pursue or avoid relationships. Media examples of such stereotypes and attributions abound. Insiders also use race and sex as markers of group identity and to teach the young norms of expected conduct for males and females within the group. Sex and race categorizations frequently result in different standards for evaluation and often affect the self-concepts of men and women in different groups.

In addition to race and sex, ethnicity and nationality are two other categories of group membership. Ethnicity refers to one's ancestry and heritage from a different nation-state of residence, or to residence in the current nation-state from a time preceding the creation of the nation-state (Banks, 1987). Nationality refers to the nation in which one is born or holds citizenship. Ethnicity designates not only the group of ancestors with whom one shares a sense of history and place of origin but also the history and association with a group in the current nation-state of residence. This is why many ethnic groups choose labels that include both places from which their group identity is constituted, for example, Mexican American.

Ethnicity tends to be involuntary in that one's ancestors cannot be changed. Unlike race and sex, however, some individuals such as White U.S. Americans have the choice of "putting on" or "taking off" their British or German U.S. ethnicity so that others cannot identify their ethnic heritage. In that sense, then, ethnicity, for some, may be a more voluntary group affiliation than sex or race.

Although nationality still commonly refers to the nation in which an individual is born, increasing numbers of people change their citizenship and hold dual citizenship. We can generally think of nationality as an affiliation that is more voluntary than race, sex, or ethnicity (recognizing that there are some circumstances in which a group of people opt to leave a country involuntarily to escape persecution or violence).

Although individuals may share membership in national or ethnic groups, they may not share the intensity with which they enact their national or ethnic identity, or the importance they place on that identity relative to other identities (Collier & Thomas, 1988). For example, Collier and Bornman (in press) found that South Africans of Dutch and British descent talked about their national identity in very different ways. Afrikaners focused on pride in their families, clear standards of acceptable behavior to which any respectable South African should hold, and optimism regarding the "new South Africa." In contrast, the British Whites talked more about Black-White crime and individual responsibility for behavior and had less optimism about the future.

In addition, interpretations of what it means to be a member of an ethnic group may differ dramatically in different regions of the country. For example, individuals of Mexican descent in New Mexico often see their origins as more Spanish; those in Oregon are more closely tied to Mexico. Members of ethnic groups may have different preferences for identity labels (e.g., African American, Black American, or Black) because of what each connotes about political standpoints and history of the group. Dolores Tanno (1997) points out that categorizing her ethnicity with one label misrepresents the complexity of the cultural identity process in that in some situations she is Chicana, in others Mexican American, and in still others, Spanish. Age and generation may also affect perceptions of the language and codes that are viewed as appropriate. For example, third-generation Chicano/a college students may view speaking Spanish with their friends as being more important than do their Mexicano/a grandparents.

In summary, race, sex, ancestry, and citizenship are used by ingroup as well as outgroup members as one set of markers about identity. Such characteristics are often the basis of stereotypes by outgroup members and can be one of the initial criteria used to determine membership for insiders. But these criteria can be very limiting. They may falsely presume a relationship between the inherited or ascribed category and cultural conduct; they may be gross overgeneralizations that include neither the group members' experiences of what it means to be a member of the group nor the historical, social, and contextual variations in how the group membership is constituted and reinforced. Perhaps most important, these criteria ignore the role of power and privilege in determining the categories and outcomes of being assigned to particular categories. Some people, for example, are formally registered as Indians in the United States but may not be considered to be "real" Indians by most of the group (Weider & Pratt, 1990).

Understanding the difference between the involuntary, ascribed group membership and emergent, enacted identity of the group at a particular time and place may help you in several ways in building intercultural relationships. First, it can help you recognize when you are making unwarranted assumptions and applying stereotypical expectations to members of groups. Second, knowing that we are socialized through institutions such as education and religion, and through multiple channels and forms of media as well as messages from parents and friends, can help you understand how others come to know how to be who they are. Third, it can help you understand the origins of *your* own cultural identities. What can also be useful to you is coming to understand the differences in what it takes to be an accepted member of your and others' cultural groups and what it takes to behave appropriately and effectively with people whose cultural identities are different from yours.

Now that I've explained how several group identities are developed and maintained, let's examine Cultural Identity Theory. This theory is one of many useful theories to help us build our knowledge about intercultural friendship communication, and it is the primary theory that I apply in my research on intercultural friendships. It is based on several assumptions about how we come to know who we are and what to believe (epistemological premises) as well as how to be an accepted, competent member of the cultural group (ontological premises).

Cultural Identity Theory

The main premises of the theory are that people have multiple cultural identities and the identities are constituted through discourse with others. We come to know who we are in relationship to others through our talk with others (Hecht, Collier, & Ribeau, 1993). For example, a respondent interviewed for a course project on interethnic friendship said, "If someone says '*Yo soy Chicana*' then we can talk politics. If she says 'I am Mexican American,' I know we may have different views about politics and the importance of history, but we can acknowledge that our people share a history and our ancestors come from the same place."

Next, I outline nine properties of Cultural Identity Theory helpful to build understanding of how cultural identities are defined with one another (Collier & Thomas, 1988; Hecht, Collier, & Ribeau, 1993). The first and second properties relate to avowal and ascription processes.

Avowal, or subjective identity, consists of the perceived identity enacted by the self or group members in a particular context. A Cuban American in a recent study said, "I am always Cuban American, I can't ever not be Cuban American; I am a successful Cuban businessman who holds American citizenship." In sum, avowal is evident in self-perceptions of the discourse "this is who I am as a member of my cultural group(s) in this context" (Collier, Thompson, & Weber, 1996).

Ascription of identity is the individual's perception of the identity attributed to self by other. Ascription is evident in self-perceptions of others' discourse when individuals note, "this is how you are seeing me as a member of my cultural group(s) here and now." We all hold ascriptions about others, and such ascriptions include prejudices and stereotypes. Such stereotypes and prejudices often serve to reinforce ingroup solidarity (our group is better than they are), but negative ascriptions from others can also affect self-esteem and evaluations of one's cultural group.

Avowal and ascription processes are important to recognize in intercultural friendships because when two people are avowing different cultural identities, inaccuracies can lead to misunderstandings and conflict. Avowal and ascription affect relationship tone, content of what is talked about, and desire to continue the friendship. Ascription is particularly important to many U.S. ethnic groups designated as minorities because who they are is strongly affected by ascriptions by socioeconomically dominant European Americans.

Typically, avowals are individually framed, whereas ascriptions are communally framed. Even when questions are asked of the "other," they are posed to the group because that is how we most easily understand others—as group members. There is also a trend to use labels that make fine and more detailed distinctions among members of our own group and to use a broad, overgeneralized label to designate members of the outgroup. For example, outsiders might label a group's members as Latino/a, but insiders may make distinctions and refer to Chicano/a, Mexican, Mexican American, Spanish, Puerto Rican, or Nicaraguan.

Cultural identities are *enduring* and *changing*—the second and third properties relevant to intercultural friendships. They are enduring because they are group identities that are handed down to new members. What is handed down reflects a history and, for national and ethnic groups, a past orientation. However, cultural identities are also changing and affected by context. How young adult Navahos define their ethnic identity as Indians in Denver, for example, may be different from how older Navahos living on the reservation define theirs.

The fifth and sixth properties of cultural identity relevant to intercultural relationship processes are *content* and *relationship* dimensions. What is talked about in the way of topics discussed and information shared as well as themes and core symbols in the talk are all content dimensions. Members of cultural groups are taught norms about what topics to discuss with whom. Collier & Shimizu (1993) found that Japanese and U.S. friends differed in that U.S. friends talked more openly about their family, were more likely to criticize family members or friends, and were more likely to share positive accomplishments with their friends.

Relationship issues include connection, inclusion, coordination, interdependence, emotional attachment, and quality of contact. Relationships are constructed through the changing quality of nonverbal and verbal messages, and power is one of the most critical relational dimensions for intercultural relationships. Members of ethnic "minority" groups are aware of European Americans' unearned privilege, whereas many European Americans are unaware of such privileges. Perhaps the friends develop explicit ways of dealing with their unequal privilege, or perhaps they negotiate power and control in more implicit ways. This is a question that warrants more attention and research.

Because they are members of multiple groups with shared histories and bounded codes and norms, individuals have a range of cultural identities that can become salient in any given context. Thus, a seventh property of cultural identity relevant to the study of thriving intercultural friendships is *multiple types of identity*—national, ethnic, gender, religious/spiritual, regional, professional, and so on. Some identities have broad scope, that is, numerous people share national identity; others have narrow scope—fewer persons share the cultural identity, such as in a regional or corporate affiliation. Acknowledging each individual's range of identities may help limit our tendencies to overgeneralize about the group members.

Context and power affect which identity(ies) is(are) enacted. European Americans, one of the groups having the greatest socioeconomic and sociocultural power in the United States, are highly individualistic and may have the most flexibility in featuring national identity or gender identity or ethnic identity. Members of ethnic groups with lower socioeconomic and sociocultural power, such as African Americans, U.S. Indians, and Latinos, do not have the same freedom of choice because of the frequency and absoluteness with which European Americans or other outgroup members ascribe negative stereotypes and set up expectations for conduct. A Lakota Indian explained, "I can't be Lakota at work. I cut my hair, I wear the tie" (Collier, Thompson, & Weber, 1996).

Salience and *intensity* of avowal are the eighth and ninth properties relevant to the study of intercultural friendships. Salience refers to relative importance of one or two identities to others. One reason salience is so important is that when allies begin enacting ethnic distinctiveness and perhaps move toward conflict, they may remind each other, in explicit or implicit ways, that the friendship is the most salient identity. From that frame of reference or shared assumption, cultural differences can be accommodated or accepted. In South Africa, Asians recommended that all groups needed to first learn about and then accept cultural differences in order to form lasting intercultural relationships (Collier & Bornman, in press).

Another reason salience is so significant is because it may be possible for individuals to enact multiple identities at once. Perhaps friends are both friends and ethnically different at the same time. Identity enactment probably isn't a matter of making choices between polar opposites; it may be a matter of dialectical tensions between ethnic identity and friendship identity. Further, the intensity with which people avow particular identities may change as topics change or as others enter a conversation. As people become proud or threatened, they may more or less intensely avow a particular identity. Iranian Americans talked about the effect of stereotypes during the Persian Gulf War and their resulting desire to correct misperceptions by speaking up (Collier, Thompson, & Weber, 1996).

An African American male interviewed for a course project related that he doesn't think his ethnic identity is important in his friendship with a Japanese American, whereas when visiting his family in the neighborhood where he grew up, he feels less choice about how to be. "At home I'm surrounded by Blacks, so I'm Black." An African American woman said that she is a "proud Black woman" wherever she goes, whomever she is with, and the only thing that changes is how others respond to her.

Enacting Different Cultural Identities in Friendships

As stated earlier, what we say and do constitutes who we are. When we constitute our relational partner as "other," as a member of a different ethnic group or sex, we are constituting our relationship in a particular way. Intercultural relationships are not experienced or constituted in the same way as intracultural relationships. A South African noted in discussions of politics, "my White friends and I have to work harder at understanding each other . . . maybe compromise . . . another Coloured can understand the situation perfectly well because her upbringing was the same" (Collier & Bornman, in press).

What does it take to be a good relational partner in intercultural friendships? Intercultural competence involves two friends who are avowing different cultural identities behaving appropriately and effectively for their friendship in the particular context. This means that friends can benefit from acknowledging that communication is a problematic and dynamic process and that the most appropriate and effective conduct requires some flexibility and negotiation.

Collier & Thomas (1988) suggest that intercultural competence is the continuing match between avowed and ascribed cultural identities; in other words, both people treating each other appropriately and effectively for the particular cultural identity(ies) being enacted throughout the conversation. Thus, allies must develop the knowledge and ability to track and sometimes adapt to their partner's cultural identities. Certainly, people do not shift arbitrarily or necessarily frequently from identity to identity in each conversation in chameleonlike fashion, but they may change the intensity with which their ethnic identity is being advanced.

While friends are negotiating their cultural identities in intercultural communication, they are also negotiating their relationship as friends. Let's look more closely at intercultural friendship.

Although individuals have their own ideas and unique experiences about what friendship is, generally, good friends have relationships characterized by warmth, affection, trust, self-disclosure, commitment, and an expectation that the relationship will grow and endure. Cross-cultural investigations of friendship show that friendships include helpful, supportive behaviors more than fighting or avoidance, asking for advice rather than offering criticism, intimate rather than role-governed behaviors, and overt, visible, rather than covert, hidden, behaviors. In addition, Argyle and Henderson (1984) found that privacy was respected and that debts, favors, and compliments were repaid, in the United Kingdom, Japan, North America, Hong Kong, and Italy.

However, relationships are inherently filled with contradictions, or dialectic tensions. That is, friends usually want both independence and interdependence, openness and privacy, and novelty and predictability. Such contradictions are simultaneously present in friendships, and the presence of opposing forces creates change and the potential for dynamic relationships. Communication scholars Leslie Baxter and Barbara Montgomery (1996) explain that taking a dialectical perspective also includes recognition of praxis, wherein individuals are both actors and acted upon by the partner through the totality or full range of dialectic tensions.

A key to interpersonal alliances across cultures is that while all the aforementioned dialectics are present, there is an additional one—in that both partners maintain a mutually satisfying *relational* identity while simultaneously maintaining *divergent cultural* identities. The relational alliance does not mean that distinct cultural identities lose their importance. It may be that friends with different ethnic identities prefer to simultaneously be friends and be culturally different, rather than seek to develop intimacy based on individual or personal selves. This is different from the process described in more traditional models of interpersonal relationship development predicting that the message content and predictions about the other develop from intercultural to intimate (Taylor & Altman, 1987). Given the important dialectic of autonomy and connection, perhaps in intercultural relationships, friends are able to simultaneously be autonomous in their cultural distinctness and be connected in their relationship.

Emergent Issues in Intercultural Alliances

Three broad issues have emerged from past research that I propose may be central to intercultural friendships: power and unearned privilege; acknowledgment of history; and orientations to affirm differences in cultural identities and the importance not only of the relationship but of the "other" as an individual.

POWER AND UNEARNED PRIVILEGE

Power differences are a salient and ever-present issue for ethnic group members as they negotiate their cultural identities through avowal and ascription processes. Collier & Bowker (1994) concluded that

unearned privilege and unstated power were evident in the talk of European American women describing their own and ideal intercultural relationships. This unstated power was identified by women who were classified as ethnic minorities in the United States, who read the responses of the European American women. They observed that European Americans advising all friends to "be open" included a tacit presumption of power. That is, they noted that the "White women risked less with openness than did the women of color or immigrants." These women of color questioned whether their European American friends *really* wanted them to be open and to voice what they might in the way of anger and rage.

Recognition of power differences is also consistent with acknowledging the dialectic tension between being open and vulnerable and being closed and protected. Understanding how members of intercultural relationships with ethnic, gender, and class differences manage their power issues may help you understand why conflict emerges and why some conflict-management processes may be more competent than others.

IMPACT OF HISTORY

In addition to recognizing power differences and unearned privilege, it may also be important for intercultural friends to recognize the impact and relevance of history and past experiences of discrimination. In South Africa, Afrikaners and British both recommended that in order to build relationships with people from diverse race groups, the Blacks in particular were going to have to "forget the past" and "recognize that this is not 1964, Sharpeville, or Soweto, anymore" (Collier & Bornman, in press). In contrast, the Blacks and Coloureds recommended acknowledging the impact of history and apartheid and said, "All people in South Africa live with the results—the legacy of the past." This suggests that the importance of history is seen differently by the relatively powerful and powerless.

Standpoint theory may be very useful in helping us understand how these differing perspectives evolve and affect interpersonal relationships. Standpoint theory points out that by regulating members' experiences, a culture reproduces distinctions (hierarchies) among groups. "Through this process, societies sustain social hierarchies and, with those, distinct standpoints of individuals in different groups" (Wood, 1995, p. 37). For example, the different experiences of Blacks and Whites in South Africa led to clearly different standpoints from which they view the relative importance of history. Another important requirement for intercultural alliances, thus, may be recognizing the standpoints for self and other and the processes through which such standpoints are developed and maintained.

ORIENTATIONS OF AFFIRMATION

A third theme in intercultural alliances is an orientation or type of conduct that demonstrates positive regard. What characterized successful intercultural friendships for the women studied by Collier and Bowker (1994) was the women perceiving an intention to value differences *and* affirm the other person as a member of a culturally different group. Such intentions were often evident in the discourse and were explicitly addressed in requests to be taught about an aspect of the other person's culture, storytelling, historical accounts of experiences, talk about family, or in conflict.

Another example of an orientation to affirm the other's cultural identity can be seen in Latino friends' descriptions of norms of appropriate behavior in their friendships, showing respect for and the desire to learn more about, the other person's ethnic identity (Collier, 1996). One respondent talked about how much he enjoyed spending time with the friend's family: "I go to his house and get to hear his family talk about their country." An African American male respondent said, "He knows that we show respect for our history." A female noted, "She appreciates that we take pride in our roots."

Friends in intercultural alliances also affirm the value of their relationship. Such affirmations occur within the norms of what the two friends consider appropriate for the friendship. Some friends may have more need for privacy or autonomy, and affirming messages may occur less frequently than in other friendships. Such messages may be explicit

verbal messages, such as this comment from a Latina: "She tells me I am a good friend." The messages may take the form of nonverbal support, as with as an Asian American friend who said, "We always listen to anything and everything, and show we care" (Collier, 1996).

Sometimes, perceiving an intention to affirm may be strong enough to compensate for conduct that has a negative impact on one of the friends. For example, an African American woman noted that she continued her friendship with a European American woman—even when the European American friend "has no clue about how much privilege she has every day, and why I object when she says something like, 'Doesn't everyone want their kids to get a college education, be president of their own company, and live in a nice house?'" She explained that she maintained the friendship because her European American friend kept "coming back for more" and showing that "she was committed to the friendship and wanted to be able to hear my anger and frustration in being Black in the U.S." (Collier & Bowker, 1994).

Friends are more likely to maintain their friendship when their self-concept as well as the value of the relationship is similarly affirmed. It is also important that this affirmation occurs throughout the history of the relationship. For instance, Planalp (1993) found that friends can be distinguished from acquaintances by their mutual knowledge and their sense of continuity—their ability to refer to their past, to a future together, and to a continuous present.

Wrestling with the issues of power, history, and intention to affirm may help you better understand your friend's points of view and conduct and your own reactions, and may perhaps help you to manage conflict when it arises. Making these issues explicit and talking about them with friends may be ways to show respect for the other person's cultural identities and the contextual factors affecting salience and intensity of avowal, thus increasing the potential that your intercultural friendship will endure.

References

Argyle, M., & Henderson, M. (1984). The rules of friendship. *Journal of Personal and Social Relationships, 1,* 211–221.

Banks, J. A. (1987). *Teaching strategies for ethnic studies* (4th ed.). Boston: Allyn & Bacon.

Baxter, L., & Montgomery, B. (1996). *Relating: Dialogues and dialectics.* New York: Guilford Press.

Carbaugh, D. (1990). Intercultural communication. In D. Carbaugh (Ed.), *Cultural communication and intercultural contact* (pp. 151–176). Hillsdale, NJ: Lawrence Erlbaum Associates.

Collier, M. J. (1991). Conflict competence within African, Mexican, and Anglo American friendships. In S. Ting-Toomey & F. Korzenny (Eds.), *Cross-cultural interpersonal communication* (pp. 132–154). Newbury Park, CA: Sage.

Collier, M. J. (1996). Communication competence problematics in ethnic friendships. *Communication Monographs, 63,* 314–336.

Collier, M. J., & Bornman, E. (in press). Intercultural friendships in South Africa: Norms for managing differences. *International Journal of International Relations.*

Collier, M. J., & Bowker, J. (1994, February). *U.S. American women in intercultural friendships.* Paper presented at the Speech Communication Association conference, New Orleans, Louisiana.

Collier, M. J., & Shimizu, M. (1993, May). *Close friendships: A cross-cultural comparison of males and females in Japan and the United States.* Paper presented at the International Communication Association conference, Washington, DC.

Collier, M. J., & Thomas, M. (1988). Identity in intercultural communication: an interpretive perspective. In Y. Kim & W. Gudykunst (Eds.), *Theories of intercultural communication* (pp. 99–120). International and Intercultural Communication Annual, XII. Newbury Park, CA: Sage.

Collier, M. J., Thompson, J., & Weber, D. (1996, November). *Identity problematics among U.S. ethnics.* Paper presented at the Speech Communication Association conference, San Diego, California.

Geertz, C. (1973). *The interpretation of cultures.* New York: Basic Books.

Hecht, M. L., Collier, M. J., & Ribeau, S. (1993). Ethnic identity. In *African American communication* (pp. 59–81, 114–158). Newbury Park, CA: Sage.

Planalp, S. (1993). Friends' and acquaintances' conversations II: Coded differences. *Journal of Social and Personal Relationships, 10,* 339–354.

Schneider, D. (1976). Notes toward a theory of culture. In K. Basso & H. Selby (Eds.), *Meaning in anthropology* (pp. 197–220). Albuquerque: University of New Mexico Press.

Southern Poverty Law Center Report, Vol. 26, Number 1, March 1996. Montgomery, AL.

Tanno, D. (1997). Names, narratives and the evolution of ethnic identity. In A. González, M. Houston, & V. Chen (Eds.), *Our voices* (2nd ed., pp. 28–34). Los Angeles: Roxbury.

Taylor, D., & Altman, I. (1987). Communication in interpersonal relationships: Social penetration processes. In M. Roloff & G. Miller (Eds.), *Interpersonal processes: New directions in communication research* (pp. 257–277). Newbury Park, CA: Sage.

Weider, D. L., & Pratt, S. (1990). On being a recognizable Indian among Indians. In D. Carbaugh (Ed.), *Cultural communication and intercultural contact* (pp. 45–64). Hillsdale, NJ: Lawrence Erlbaum.

Wood, J. (1995). *Relational communication.* Belmont, CA: Wadsworth.

Key Terms

alliance
ascription
avowal
cultural identity
friendship
intensity of avowal

intercultural
    communication
relationship
salience of avowal
standpoint theory

Discussion Questions

1. What are examples of defining culture as place, as a predictor of communication conduct, and as a system of discourse? What are strengths and weaknesses of each approach?

2. Why is it important to talk about involuntary aspects of membership in groups based on race, sex, nationality, and ethnicity? How might you respond to someone who argues, "Why don't we treat each person we meet as a unique individual, and do away with these kinds of group categories?"

3. How can you apply the properties of cul-

tural identity outlined in the essay to your own intercultural friendships? How can discussing such processes as avowal and ascription, having multiple identities, or differences in salience and intensity help friends understand each other and perhaps manage conflict differently?

4. How do you know when an intercultural friendship is an interpersonal alliance? How do intercultural allies manage the dialectical tensions in their friendship? For instance, when and how

should allies explicitly talk about differences or prejudices or historical oppression?

5. To what extent do you agree that giving attention to the three issues of power, history, and intention to affirm can improve intercultural friendships? Specifically, how might friends demonstrate their intention to affirm each other as an individual, a person with a different cultural identity that is valuable to know, and the salience of the friendship?

33   Performing Commitment

JACQUELINE TAYLOR

I grew up in a small southern town, where I lived right smack next door to the large Baptist church my daddy pastored. Although the role of preacher's daughter was often trying, one advantage was that I was almost always invited to any wedding my father performed. As a result, I became something of a professional wedding guest.

Saturday afternoons often found me racing around the church parking lot on my second-hand green Huffy bicycle. Moments before the music was scheduled to begin, I clattered into the parsonage to exchange Keds, shorts, and shirt for my Sunday best. As the first organ notes began to sound, I settled myself in the front row of the church balcony, leaning perilously over the rail to scrutinize the flowers, the guests, the ushers, the music, at last the bridesmaids, and then finally, climactically, the bride. My father stood facing the important couple and intoned the words that transformed them mysteriously and abruptly from two separate people into one flesh. The power to transform was vested in him by church and state. "I now pronounce you husband and wife," he would say, and the ceremony

was complete.[1] The bride and groom kissed, and the happy sounds of the recessional burst from the organ pipes.

I drank in all this lovely, lavish ritual from my aerial perch, evaluating each facet of the performance, dreaming myself into the starring role. After the ceremony, I headed to the basement of the church to partake of the typical Baptist wedding reception fare: gooey white cake, salted nuts, pastel mints, and sweet, oh-so-sweet punch laced with nothing stronger than ginger ale.

---

[1] In the fifties and sixties, when I was watching all these weddings, most wedding ceremonies used the language "man and wife." My father, then and now unlikely to be identified as a feminist, was nevertheless more thoughtful than most of his contemporaries about male and female roles. He used the language "husband and wife" because he wished to stress the equality of the marriage partners. Indeed, his boiler-plate language for wedding ceremonies talked about God's creation of Eve from Adam's rib: "from under his arm, that she might be protected by him, from out of his side, that she might be equal to him, and from near his heart, that she might be loved by him."

If the day was sunny, I sometimes grabbed my cake and nuts and ran. But if the weather was bad or the bride was especially beautiful, I stayed until the uncontested star of this extravaganza had changed into her "going-away outfit" and run hand in hand with the groom down the steps of the church toward a car fitted with tin cans, signs, and streamers. We untied the ribbons on our little satin packets of rice and pelted the lucky pair as they shrieked and giggled past us. We Baptists didn't recognize the ritual shower of rice as an invocation of the favors of an ancient fertility goddess who would bless their union with children; we just found it good fun and unquestioned custom to rain rice on the giddy couple.

I'm 35 years away from that preadolescent girl who leaned over the balcony rail to watch wedding after wedding. But I got another glimpse of her a few years ago during a visit with my parents. My daughters, Lucy and Grace, began complaining of the lack of toys. From the top shelf of a bedroom closet, I pulled down a small, round, yellow suitcase. I flipped the catch with a satisfying snap that recalled to me the hundreds of times I had opened this case as a child. Inside was Charlene, my Miss Revlon doll, a 1950s precursor to Barbie. She rested on the vast wardrobe lovingly sewn for her by Grandmama and Aunt Clarice. As I began to unpack my doll, Lucy's and Gracie's wide dark eyes grew wider and darker. Grace began to brush Charlene's gorgeously flipped red hair, while Lucy combined lounging pajamas and a lace stole in a one-of-a-kind outfit. The doll wardrobe included evening gowns, dresses, purse, heels, coats, jeans, hats, nylons, bra, girdle, petticoats—in short, everything a well-dressed young woman of those days would require. Most particularly, she had not one but two wedding gowns. Grandmama had made her a white voile summer gown, trimmed in lace. From Aunt Clarice she had a full-skirted satin gown for winter. Both gowns included veils.

At the bottom of the case we found Tom, the only male doll near enough Charlene's size to make a suitable groom. I remembered it all. Obsessed with weddings and wedding plans, I determined to make Charlene a bride. Tom came from the dime store

dressed in a gray jumpsuit of the sort garage mechanics wore. With his painted-on hair and too-large head, Tom was not the same calibre doll Charlene was, but the groom was only a minor player in these events, anyway. Aunt Clarice was enlisted to sew him a black suit. We couldn't find shoes to fit him, so we covered his feet in black tape. My sister and two friends were invited for the event. We procured or improvised flowers, cake, punch. I probably preached.[2] In any case, the bride and groom dressed up, said "I do," and then changed into their "going-away clothes" and headed off for a honeymoon.

Of course, a girl wouldn't have to grow up as the preacher's daughter in order to develop an acute interest in weddings. Growing up female in this culture is sufficient to produce this common preoccupation. But the frequency with which I attended wedding ceremonies and the role my father played in the marrying gave me frequent cause for reflection on the nature and meaning of this ritual.

Weddings as Rituals

Cultural anthropologists direct our attention to the ways in which weddings reinforce the traditional social ties between individuals. A wedding is not simply a celebration. Through this event the actual status and relationship of the couple within the community is altered. The participation of family and friends enacts their investment in the success of the relationship. Community ties and beliefs and cultural values are communicated and solidified. Clifford Geertz (1973, pp. 168–169) reminds us that the ritual does not always merely replicate and reinforce the cultural structure. Particularly at times of social change or at points of intercultural contact

---

[2] I have written elsewhere about my gradual discovery of the extent to which I have come, as an adult, to emulate my preacher father. My text, of course, is somewhat different from his, but even these essays function as a variation on testimony that we Baptists were encouraged to practice. See "On Being an Exemplary Lesbian: My Life as a Role Model," unpublished essay and performance piece.

and influence, rituals can reveal tensions between the cultural framework of meaning and the patterning of social interaction.

Put simply, the variations from the traditional script in the performance of wedding ceremonies may highlight the disparity between convention and actual social practice. Such rituals employ a range of communicative acts to both strengthen the social structure of the community and perform the evolution of that social structure. Often, through the highly symbolic communication that characterizes weddings, the couple engages in a process of identity negotiation. Bride and groom may come from different cultural backgrounds. Or marriage partners may stake out a cultural terrain that differs from either family's traditional practices. Ting-Toomey (1993) defines effective identity negotiation as "the smooth coordination between interactants concerning salient identity issues, and the process of engaging in responsive identity confirmation and positive identity enhancement" (p. 73). This process of effective identity negotiation within novel communication episodes is essential to Ting-Toomey's definition of intercultural communication competence. Because each couple desires to put their own stamp on this familiar ritual, each wedding is both familiar and novel. Richard Schechner (1985, p. 120) draws our attention to the way ritual performances engage in a continuous process of rejecting and replacing. The wedding becomes interesting not only because of the mastery with which a familiar cultural script is performed, a mastery that reveals communicative competence, but also because of the ways in which the familiar script is altered. These alterations may, as we shall see below, communicate intercultural conflict and cultural transformation.

NEGOTIATING IDENTITY WITHIN THE CONTEXT OF RITUAL

I married for the first time in 1970, at the age of 19, on a Saturday morning in August. (The time was 10:30. It was important to have the wedding on the half hour, so the hands of the clock would be headed up rather than down.) The antimaterialist and anti-traditionalist impulses abroad in the land in 1970 influenced the plans for what my young man and I intended as a simple wedding. The voile dress I wore was one my mother-in-law-to-be and I made ourselves. My sister was my only attendant. We sewed her long skirt and peasant blouse. I insisted on decorating with and carrying wildflowers— Queen Anne's lace, daisies, black-eyed Susan's, baby's breath—picked and arranged by my mother and me. We wrote our own vows, which I no longer remember, and no one gave me away. I took my husband's name. The church was packed.

Each choice was freighted with meaning and symbolic value. Family and friends from near and far assembled to participate in this ritual that marked my passage from girl to woman and our passage as a couple from private sweethearts to public kin. Unfortunately, the passage was rocky. Before our third anniversary, we were divorced.

A full decade went by and my second marriage began with hope and promises and ended in divorce before I came to understand that no man would ever fill the empty place in my heart. Raised within a culture of compulsory heterosexuality and primed with images of wedding ceremonies that led inevitably into happily ever after, I have a heart that yearns toward women. All those sleeping princesses in the fairytales of my childhood made sense to me at last when the touch of a woman awakened me to a dimension of life that I had thought existed only in dreams.

Crossing Cultures

For over 13 years I have created family within the context of my commitment to Carol, my partner and longtime companion. The law says we are not a couple, but two single women. No church or state has blessed or ratified our union. Although our property and our finances are by this time as entwined as our hearts and lives, the state does not apply its joint-property laws to us or give us the right to inherit from each other in the absence of a will. I cannot include her on the family insurance benefits my university offers. The only place we can purchase a family membership is at the women's bookstore.

Eight years ago we became mothers together, with the adoption of our first daughter, Lucy. One year later we adopted Grace. The law recognized us not as one family, but as two—two single mothers living in the same house with our two adopted children. No blood ties unite any of the four of us. We are a family not because but in spite of the social and legal structures that refuse to name us so. Because our status as a family has been ignored or denied by the laws and customs of our society, our existence as a family can never be taken for granted but must be constantly created and recreated. That our family differs in some significant ways from conventional notions of what constitutes a family means that our creation of family must simultaneously affirm and critique familial structures.

Although the field of intercultural communication has given scant attention to gay culture (see Majors, 1994, for an exception), Martin (1993) argues that "the notion of culture needs to be extended . . . beyond national culture" (p. 28). When gay men and lesbians break cultural norms in their communicative practices, they do so not because of a lack of communicative competence but because the dominant communicative practices erase or deny the existence of gay people. So what happens to the performance of commitment when the family operates outside the legal and social definitions of family? And what happens to intercultural communication when the culture where one finds oneself most at home is not the culture of origin? (Most gay men and lesbians grow up in heterosexual families, sometimes experiencing a substantial degree of alienation in contexts that are quite literally familiar.) In what follows, I describe some of the strategies our family has developed to communicate our commitment and connection and the contexts within which we perform this commitment.

IDENTITY NEGOTIATION WITHIN THE WEDDING RITUAL

Because the dominant culture defines marriage as necessarily heterosexual, gay and lesbian weddings become an important site for the negotiation of identity. Gay and lesbian couples create commitment ceremonies both within and against the grain of the wedding ceremonies that sanctify and legitimate heterosexual unions. Our ceremonies become engaged in the continuous process Schechner (1985) identified as rejection and replacement of these more familiar, and certainly more public, spectacles of heterosexual privilege.

Gay and lesbian weddings have become increasingly common in the nineties. Common enough, in fact, that a 1996 episode of the situation comedy *Friends* portrayed a lesbian wedding. They were almost unheard of in 1985, when Carol and I moved in together. We were already in a committed relationship by the time we set up housekeeping. Living together signified a deeper commitment to our shared life; we wanted to mark this passage with a celebration. We decided to throw ourselves a party.

The party mimicked a wedding reception. We issued weddinglike invitations announcing the "marriage of our addresses" and inviting the recipients to a party in celebration of this union. We followed the Baptist traditions of my youth by having a three-tiered cake, pastel mints, salted nuts, and a guest register, but we also served a catered buffet (my tastes had gone uptown, or at least upstairs, since the basement wedding receptions of my youth). Yet, in our mimicking of tradition, the cultural critique appeared, for the cake was topped by two brides rather than the traditional heterosexual pair.

The question of what to wear occupied a good deal of our attention. The choices we made signaled our connections both to traditional wedding celebrations and to our lesbian community. We also used clothing to reveal the playful approach we took to the whole event. We wore tuxedo shirts, bow ties, and casual pants (one pair black, the other pink). One of us donned high-top sneakers; the other wore black flats and lace socks.

On the appointed day our friend Diane arrived early, wearing a pair of white tennis shoes and an aqua chiffon mother-of-the-bride number she had found at the nearby Goodwill. She played the piano for the event. A lush rendition of "Feelings" had Carol and me whirling around the living room in our best version of the happy couple's first dance. Lesbian friends, work friends, my sister, and one of Carol's sisters ate and drank and celebrated together for hours.

Our "marriage of addresses" party was both a thoroughly camp send-up of wedding receptions and a public performance of the commitment Carol and I so deeply felt. The structure of the party allowed us to make the reference to heterosexual ceremonies explicit while its tongue-in-cheek tone provided us with a technique for distancing ourselves in some ways from the very ritual we were invoking. The differences between our "ceremony" and heterosexual rituals became as telling as the similarities. The fundamental difference, of course, was that the party celebrated the union of two women rather than a man and a woman, a union the state refuses to acknowledge. Perhaps the staging of a reception that was its own reason for being rather than a postceremony party was the most significant variation of all. The event was an allusion to our permanent commitment, but that commitment was deliberately not spelled out or defined in permanent terms.

If I am honest, I must admit that we felt uncertain about the response our heterosexual friends, families, and co-workers would make to our celebration. It is telling that neither of us invited our parents. We did not think they would come and did not want the pain of a refusal. I warned a woman I worked with that she would be getting an invitation from me and should remember that it had been issued with tongue planted firmly in cheek. I felt I had to give her permission not to take us seriously at the same time that Carol and I were both in absolute earnest about the life we were creating together.

FAMILY RITUALS

In the wedding ceremonies of my youth, the showers of rice augured for and foreshadowed the children that would issue from these unions. In the event Carol and I created, nothing foretold the children who would transform us publicly and irrevocably into a family. When we joined our lives together in 1985, the social and legal definitions of family had sufficiently influenced my dreams that I assumed that we would not, rather than that we would, have children. I, who had always dreamed of motherhood, had come to believe that this was a loss in my life with which I must make my peace. So there were no little satin packets of rice when Carol and I performed our commitment to a permanently shared life.

But 4 months after that party, Carol's sister gave birth to a daughter with whom Carol fell hopelessly in love. Carol had never really pictured herself as a mother, but I believe now it was her love of Ardy that caused her to dream of a child of her own. As Carol tells the story, she stood in the airport one day, waiting to board a flight to join me in New Orleans. She saw a mother with a baby, and suddenly she realized that she did not want to go through her life without mothering a child. Within a few weeks we were researching and then initiating the adoptions that made us mothers.

In 1989 in Illinois two unmarried adults could not apply together to adopt. In order to create our family, we each adopted one of our daughters, acting as separate single parents. The pledge we made to each other to parent our two daughters together was belied by the entire adoption process, which with each adoption recognized only one mother. The other mother was at best regarded as good friend, at worst, disregarded altogether.

The process of knitting ourselves into a family has taken years and has been characterized more by daily and, yes, mundane performances of commitment than by rituals and ceremonies. Yet we have also participated in public rituals that have helped us to construct ourselves.

The arrival of our babies was greeted by four different showers thrown by friends. Each of our workplaces and two sets of friends organized parties. The various communities we participate in have worked hard to fill the gap between what the law and convention define as family and what our experience reveals. The four of us create our own rituals, as well.

On the occasion of our 10th anniversary, Carol and I planned a modest celebration in the form of an intimate dinner at a nearby Indian restaurant. The babysitter was scheduled to arrive at 6:00. At 5:15, her mother called to say, "Nina has the flu. She can't sit for you tonight." I quickly called four other sitters, none of whom, of course, were available. Our anniversary celebration appeared doomed. In an exuberant attempt to resuscitate it, Lucy suggested that she and Grace come along. Before we knew it, we were working with a whole new dress code. Our daughters decked themselves out in party shoes and party dresses almost before I had finished dialing the last babysitter. "Wear dresses," they instructed us, and so we did—probably the first time we had both been so dressed up for an anniversary in 10 years.

The girls grew giddy at their inclusion in this anniversary of "the day Mama-Jackie and Mama-Carol fell in love." We toasted 10 years by clinking our ice-water together and passed the Tandoori drumstick to Grace. For the umpteenth time, we told the story of the night I opened the door to the newcomer at my lesbian book group and fell under the spell of Carol's twinkling eyes and devilish smile. Our young daughters capped our celebration by leaping from the table and bursting into a rousing improvised floor-show rendition of "Cruella Deville," the theme song from their then-favorite *101 Dalmations*. This was certainly not the romantic anniversary celebration we had anticipated. Nor was it an anniversary we even in our wildest dreams could have predicted at the beginning of our relationship. Yet after it had happened, we recognized it as exactly the most appropriate of celebrations imaginable for this children-dominated period of our lives. In any case, it was as unforgettable an anniversary as we are ever likely to have.

We have not come effortlessly to the space we now occupy, the space in which we name ourselves family and perform our commitment for one and all. When we brought Lucy home from Peru, she was only 5½ months old. We did not yet realize how soon this bright-eyed little gal would be repeating, commenting on, and questioning everything she heard us say. We knew we were both mothers to this daughter; we knew she would call us Mama-Jackie and Mama-Carol. We just didn't know how quickly it would all become public.

Within a few months we perceived that unless we were going to begin our children's lives with impossible explanations about how wonderful our family was but how embarrassed we were about it in public, we would have to get ourselves entirely out of the closet and stay there. Small children don't understand homophobia, and they don't make refined distinctions between what you tell to your best friend and what you tell to the meter reader, but they do understand when they have a mother who is not claiming them or a mother who seems ashamed of her family.

As the importance of educating people in our community became clear to us, we began to welcome opportunities to let the world know that families like ours not only survive but thrive. So when someone from WBEZ, the Chicago affiliate of National Public Radio, called to invite our participation on a program covering single parent adoption, we accepted without hesitation.

During our interview, we told stories about the discrimination we faced as lesbians wishing to adopt. We also talked about how we worked with and against the grain of the systems put in place to support heterosexual parents' adoption.

For Carol and me, that radio interview was an important coming-out ritual. We left the station with a deeper sense of commitment. In the absence of other defining rituals, it helped us in the ongoing project of defining ourselves as a family. For the next several days, we encountered neighbors and coworkers who had heard us on the radio. We're out now, we said to ourselves and each other. We agreed that out is right where we have to be if we're going to make our family strong and the world safe for our daughters.

Carol reminds me that the most important performance of commitment is the daily care and love we give to our daughters. Parents communicate commitment every day through the constant and repetitive tasks that children's survival depends on—changing diapers, wiping up spills, kissing "owies"—and later on, supervising homework, chauffeuring to sports and music lessons, listening to their stories. For heterosexual families perhaps this is enough. But we gay and lesbian (and adoptive) families create family outside the context of the social and legal structures that allow traditional families to take themselves for granted, and so we must do more.

Thus, we have learned to use language consciously, carefully, and repetitively to define ourselves to each other and our social world. "*Family*" we say, over and over. "Thank you for carrying that package. You are helping our *family*." "This party is just for our *family*." "In our *family*, we don't hit."

Each time we choose a pediatrician, a school, a church, we take care to introduce our whole family and to make sure the relationships are clear. Lucy and Grace are now 7 and 8. For as long as possible, we want them to be surrounded by people who accept and support their family as it is. The forms we fill out have spaces for mother and father. Again and again, we cross out "father" and write in "mother," then complete the form. We always feel nervous when we do this. Will there be someone on the staff who will refuse to treat our family with respect? Each public definition of our family is an act of faith.

So far, we have been blessed with teachers and administrators who have valued Lucy's and Gracie's family as it is. Yet the culture's norms and assumptions bombard us. At 3½, Lucy worked with her preschool class on a special Christmas program. Carol and I sat with all the moms and dads. Along with several dads, I trained my camcorder on my talented child. Lucy hopped by right on cue, fluffy bunny tail attached to her bright green pants. We clapped and clapped.

That night in the kitchen, Lucy announced, "My mom and dad came to see my Christmas program today." I swallowed my surprise. "Oh yeah? It looked like your mom and mom to me." "No," said Lucy. "Carol was my mom but you were my dad." I smiled. "Lucy, honey," I said, "anytime you need a dad, I'll be your dad, you just say the word."

LEGAL TIES

On a sizzling day in July 1995, I picked up a copy of the *Chicago Tribune* and started to toss it into the back seat. Suddenly, my eye caught on the headline—"State court says gays have right to adopt" (Fegelman, 1995). I quickly called Carol and then Rosemary Mulryan, our attorney. Rosemary assured us that with our long history as a couple and as mothers, and with home studies from our original adoptions long since complete, we made what she considered an ideal test case of the new ruling. Within days, Rosemary entered our petition for co-parent adoptions on each of our daughters—a petition that, if successful, would convert our two single-parent adoptions into two-parent adoptions.

We knew we were family before we arrived at the Daley Center shortly after lunch on that hot August afternoon and made our way to family court. Yet when we entered Daley Center dressed in our best, it was with a powerful sense of excitement and anticipation, and, yes, anxiety. What if the judge saw our petitions for co-parent adoptions and decided to block them?

We gathered, along with several other families awaiting their turn, in a toy-filled waiting room that adjoins the Family Court. After 20 anxious minutes we heard our names called. We stepped into the courtroom, each mom holding a daughter by the hand. The judge was a kind and intelligent looking woman about our age. After a brief conversation with me and Carol, she turned to the girls. To get the conversation started, she asked them what school they attended. "Inter-American Magnet School," they answered solemnly. "Are you girls sisters?" she asked next. Carol and I stopped breathing. She was trying to find out whether they understood themselves to be related to one another. "Yes," Lucy and Gracie answered clearly and firmly. Of this answer both girls were comfortably, happily certain, so certain, in fact, that a year later Lucy recalled the judge's query with the words, "What a ridiculous question! Why would a judge ask such a ridiculous question?" And yet it was not until we walked from the court a few minutes later with our temporary custody orders, that the law began to catch up with these sisters' lived reality.

The power of these legal ties and public rituals of commitment can be measured in part by the feelings of exuberance that Carol and I shared as we left Daley Center with our temporary custody orders. Six weeks later, we experienced a similar rush of emotion, when the final adoption decree arrived in the mail.

Carol and I are married in all the ways that matter most. After 13 years and two children together, we don't need a piece of paper to strengthen or cement our commitment. What we do need are the legal benefits and protections that the state provides to families. We also share with other families the longing to perform our deepest commitments and connections through public and private rituals and to have our family supported and embedded within a rich web of kin and community.

In our early years together, we feared the response of family and friends and so gave ourselves a tongue-in-cheek celebration that simultaneously asserted and denied our real commitment. The children in our family have consistently led us toward more public performances of the ties that bind us.

Ritual, ceremony, language, custom, law—all of these interact to construct and constrain our conceptions of family. To the extent that one's family goes against the grain of traditional definitions of the nuclear family, to that extent one must work to make a space for that family.

A couple of years after Carol and I became mothers, I was ranting to one of my lesbian friends about the ignorant, insensitive, and sometimes downright obnoxious and offensive things that strangers say to us—regarding adoption, skin color, ethnicity, or the curious spectacle of two mothers mothering together. My friend gave me an indulgent smile. "Jackie," she said, "you're exactly right. But you must admit you are asking them to take in an awful lot all at once." Well, yes. Even as I write about performing commitment, I realize that writing about these issues as they pertain to our lesbian-parented family leads me into writing about performing commitment within our adoptive and interethnic family.

Our family doesn't fit anybody's mold. But we are a family, held together by ties of love, loyalty, commitment, and daily life. Because our family does not conform to traditional definitions of family, the performances that connect us to the social fabric and to one another take on even greater importance. Through the anniversaries, ceremonies, rituals, and holidays that mark our years and the repeated mundane actions of commitment that mark our days, we perform the bonds that make us kin. Meanwhile, we dream and struggle toward the day when the laws of the land and the expectations in people's hearts and minds catch up to our reality— that family is a group of people who live together and love each other, bound by their shared commitment to the health, growth, and welfare of all.

References

Fegelman, A. (1995, July 19). State court says gays have right to adopt. *Chicago Tribune*, pp. 1, 15.

Geertz, C. (1973). *The interpretation of cultures*. New York: Basic Books.

Majors, R. (1994). Discovering gay culture in America. In L. Samovar & R. Porter (Eds.), *Intercultural communication: A reader* (7th ed., pp. 165–171). Belmont, CA: Wadsworth.

Martin, J. (1993). Intercultural communication competence: A review. In R. Wiseman & J. Koester (Eds.), *Intercultural communication competence* (pp. 16–29). Newbury Park, CA: Sage.

Schechner, R. (1985). *Between theater and anthropology*. Philadelphia: University of Pennsylvania Press.

Taylor, J. (1995, January). On being an exemplary lesbian: My life as a role model. Performance presented at the University of Texas at Austin.

Ting-Toomey, S. (1993). Communicative resourcefulness: An identity negotiation perspective. In R. Wiseman & J. Koester (Eds.), *Intercultural communication competence* (pp. 72–111). Newbury Park, CA: Sage.

Key Terms

adoption

coming out

culture

family

gay

gay and lesbian weddings

homophobia

lesbian

marriage

ritual

wedding

Discussion Questions

1. This essay is predicated on the notion that there is a dimension of cross-cultural communication in the communication between this lesbian-parented family and their community. What characteristics of cross-cultural communication do you see illustrated here? In what ways do these experiences differ from models of cross-cultural communication?

2. What sorts of rituals or performances has your family used to define itself as a family? How is culture embedded in and negotiated through those rituals?

3. Consider the argument that weddings can serve as sites for the negotiation of identity. Can you think of examples from your experience of such identity negotiations?

4. If you did not grow up in a household with gay or lesbian parents, imagine that you are one of the estimated 6 million to 10 million children in the United States who are living in such a household. What communication problems do you think you might encounter? What sorts of changes (legal, social, cultural) would make communication easier for you and your family?

5. It's easy to see that this family encounters some struggles. Can you see any advantages that flow from their ongoing efforts to communicate and perform family relationships?

Activities for Skill Development

1. Movie Review

Watch a movie that addresses intercultural relationships, such as *Mississippi Masala*, *Jungle Fever*, or *The Joy Luck Club*. What barriers do the couples face? Do you think the film is an accurate portrayal of contemporary race relations in the United States? Write a one-page review of the movie that focuses on these issues.

2. Interview the Experts

Interview someone you know who is, or has been, in an intercultural marriage or romantic relationship. What drew the couple together? What difficulties, if any, did they face?

3. Intercultural Friendships

Think about your own circle of friends. How diverse is it in terms of race, ethnicity, and nationality? What conditions do you think encourage or discourage intercultural friendships where you live? With a small group of classmates, make a list of 10 ways to meet and make friends with people of different cultures.

Web Sites

1. What do multicultural families look like? Gigi Kaeser and Peggy Gillespie have interviewed and photographed a wide variety of interracial families. Check out their book and other related projects at *<http://www.familydiv.org/ofmanycolors/>*.

2. For a wide variety of information and perspectives on race relations, including everything from Affirmative Action to slavery to interracial marriage, check out *<http://racerelations.about.com/newsissues/racerelations/mbody.htm>*.

3. Child-raising among gay and lesbian families has come under social critique. Support for gay and lesbian families can be found at *<www.anglefire.com/co/GayFamilyValues/index.html>*.

Additional Readings

1. Romano, D. (1997). *Intercultural marriage: Promises and pitfalls* (2nd ed.). Yarmouth, ME: Intercultural Press.

2. Houston, M. (2000. When Black women talk with White women: Why dialogues are difficult. In A. González, M. Houston, & V. Chen (Eds.), *Our voices: Essays in culture, ethnicity, and communication* (pp. 98–104). Los Angeles: Roxbury.

3. Allen, B. (2000). Sapphire and Sappho: Allies in authenticity. In A. González, M. Houston, & V. Chen (Eds.), *Our voices: Essays in culture, ethnicity, and communication* (pp. 179–183). Los Angeles: Roxbury.

4. Hannassab, S., & Tidwell, R. (1998). Intramarriage and intermarriage: Young Iranians in L.A. *International Journal of Intercultural Relations, 22*, 395–408.

5. Collier, M. J., & Bornman, E. (1999). Core symbols in South African intercultural friendships. *International Journal of Intercultural Relations, 23*, 133–156.

6. Fiebert, M. S., & Karamol, H. (2000). Interracial dating: Attitudes and experiences among American college students in California. *Psychological Reports, 87*, 1059–1064.

PART NINE

Conflict, Communication, and Culture

The following essays explore various intersections among culture, communication, and conflict in domestic and international contexts. In conflict situations, people often experience physiological reactions that may lead them to overlook the intensely cultural aspect of conflict. Yet, conflict—how it is experienced, maintained, negotiated, and avoided—is highly cultural. These cultural differences can often lead to further conflict rather than to resolution.

The authors of these essays offer insights about how cultural groups vary in approaches to conflict and how best to manage intercultural conflict. In these readings conflict is seen as interpersonal conflict or mediated, as causally related to national and ethnic cultures or as dynamically negotiated, and as occurring in international or domestic contexts

In "Intercultural Conflict Competence," Stella Ting-Toomey provides a useful overview and framework for thinking about broad cultural differences in conflict management and resolution. She addresses two questions: How do various cultural groups deal with conflict? How can individuals deal effectively with intercultural conflict? She shows how basic cultural values (individualism-collectivism, personal self-construals, high-context/low-context communication) can influence how individuals approach interpersonal conflict. She points out a fundamental problem—we all approach conflict with ethnocentric lenses. Finally, she identifies components of conflict competence (knowledge, motivation, and skill) and gives practical suggestions for dealing with intercultural conflict.

Peter Ogom Nwosu, in "Negotiating with the Swazis," provides an interesting case study of conflict resolution that stands in contrast to most North American models. In a study based on personal experience and participant observation, Nwosu describes the important characteristics of Swazi negotiation, including credibility, relationship-building, and indirect communication. This study is a good example of Ting-Toomey's description of a collectivist cultural approach to conflict resolution.

Shifting to interethnic conflict in domestic contexts, Karen Lynnette Dace and Mark Lawrence McPhail, in "Crossing the Color Line," provide a way to think beyond interracial conflict. In narrative form, these two authors each explore how empathy has impacted their understanding and behavior as they relate to "the gulf that exists between African and European Americans." They examine their relationships with European Americans and emphasize the importance of resisting "racial reasoning," the tendency to see Black-White interactions in Black and White terms. They present a new way of thinking about empathy—where empathy is more than rational understanding. It is rather *implicature,* or thinking *and* experiencing, both objectively and subjectively, the worldview of others.

In "Mass-Mediated Communication and Intercultural Conflict," Fernando Delgado challenges us to think about conflicts beyond interpersonal contexts. He examines broad international and mediated contexts where power inequities lead to cultural conflict. He provides two examples: The first concerns debates about control and domination over media technology in which Third World nations express concern over the rapid growth of technology and control of media by First World nations. The second example is an analysis of cultural dominance debate. In this conflict, non-U.S. cultural critics express concern over the dominance of U.S. popular culture, its ubiquitous nature, and its influence on other cultures.

34 Intercultural Conflict Competence

STELLA TING-TOOMEY

Intercultural miscommunications and misattributions often underscore intercultural conflict. Individuals coming from two contrastive cultural communities bring with them different value assumptions, expectations, verbal and nonverbal habits, and interaction scripts that influence the conflict process. Intercultural conflict is defined as the *perceived incompatibility of values, norms, processes, or goals between a minimum of two cultural parties over identity, relational, and/or substantive issues.* Intercultural conflict often starts off with different expectations concerning appropriate or inappropriate behavior in an interaction episode. Violations of expectation, in turn, often influence the effectiveness of how members of two cultures negotiate their interests or goals in the interaction. If inappropriate or ineffective negotiation behavior continues, the miscommunication can very easily spiral into a complex, polarized conflict. The following dialogue between two intercultural strangers trying to get acquainted in the Los Angeles International Airport lobby illustrates this type of conflict.

Example 1

MR. GASS (a young, enthusiastic Euro-American businessman, shaking hands with Mr. Lim vigorously): Welcome to L.A., Mr. Lim. Nice meeting you, finally. My name is William Gass. Just call me Bill. Here is my business card. [*Bill forwards the card with his right hand.*]

MR. LIM (an elderly Korean businessman): Nice meeting you, Mr. Gass. I'm Peter Pyong Gap Lim. Here is my business card. [*Mr. Lim forwards his card with both hands.*]

MR. GASS: Please, call me Bill. I hope we'll be doing a lot of business together here in L.A.

MR. LIM: Yes, I hope so too.

MR. GASS (glancing quickly at Mr. Lim's card): Pyong Gap, I'll give you a call tomorrow after you get some rest in your hotel. Maybe we can have lunch together.

MR. LIM (with a polite smile): Yes, maybe, Mr. Gass. Please call me tomorrow. I will await your phone call.

When members of different cultures greet one another in an initial encounter, they often draw on their own cultural scripts to guide their behavior. In Example 1, Mr. Gass is very pleased with the initial encounter with Mr. Lim. He is especially pleased that he called Mr. Lim "Pyong Gap"— his client's Korean name rather than his American name. Mr. Gass feels that he has succeeded in building an informal, symmetrical relationship with Mr. Lim by addressing him on a first-name basis and paying attention to his Korean ethnicity. Mr. Gass believes that they will be able to work well together, since Mr. Lim departed with a smile and a firm handshake.

Mr. Lim, on the other hand, is very uncertain about the initial meeting with Mr. Gass. First, Mr. Lim feels uncomfortable that Mr. Gass forwarded his business card using only one hand. In the Korean culture, a business card represents the face, or public self-image, of an individual. It should always be treated with proper respect and dignity. Mr. Gass should have forwarded his card with both hands and received Mr. Lim's business card with both hands. Second, Mr. Gass should have taken the time to read and admire Mr. Lim's card carefully before putting it away in his wallet. Third, Mr. Lim was uncomfortable and insulted when Mr. Gass addressed him by his Korean name. He would have preferred that Mr. Gass address him more formally as "Mr. Lim"; after all, Mr. Lim is the client and is much older than Mr. Gass.

As an older Korean businessman, Mr. Lim would like to see more asymmetrical deference and respect from Mr. Gass. If Mr. Gass insists on being informal, he should at least address Mr. Lim as "Peter" rather than "Pyong Gap," since Mr. Lim created his western name "Peter" just for the sake of informal interaction in American business transactions. Mr. Lim smiled because he was embarrassed by Mr. Gass's imposed intimacy. His smile was to cover his own embarrassment for the "face loss" incurred in the first few minutes of the initial encounter.

Both Mr. Gass and Mr. Lim have been conditioned by their own cultural norms or standards to behave in a certain way. While Mr. Lim is already anticipating difficulty in working with this "overbearing" American, Mr. Gass has no idea that he has offended his client in so many ways in the first few minutes of interaction. Although no explicit, interpersonal disagreement took place in Example 1, the seeds of potential disagreement or perceived incompatibility were sown. If similar miscommunication between Mr. Gass and Mr. Lim becomes a pattern in subsequent interactions, Mr. Gass may not be able to secure the business contracts he wants from Mr. Lim. Even though both Mr. Gass and Mr. Lim attempted to be sensitive to each other's cultural background, their effort created a cultural chasm.

Not all intercultural conflicts are caused by miscommunication or misunderstanding. Some intercultural conflicts arise because of deep-seated hatred, centuries of antagonism, and clear understanding. However, most everyday intercultural conflicts that we encounter can be traced to cultural miscommunication or ignorance. As cultural beings, we are socialized or "programmed" by the values and norms of our culture to think and behave in certain ways. Our family, peer groups, educational institutions, mass media system, political system, and religious institutions are some of the forces that shape and mold our cultural and personal values. Our learned values and norms are, in turn, expressed through the way we communicate.

The study of intercultural conflict in contemporary U.S. society is especially critical today for several reasons. First, in the United States, immigrants (many of whom are non-English speakers), members of minority groups, and women represent more than 50 percent of the present workforce. Second, by the year 2000, 85 percent of the *entering* workforce in the United States will be new immigrants, minority group members, and females (Loden & Rosener, 1991). Third, four out of every five

new jobs in the United States at present are generated as a direct result of foreign trade (Lustig & Koester, 1993). As the global economy becomes an everyday reality in most societies, we will inevitably encounter people who are culturally different in diverse workplace and social environments. Learning to manage such differences, especially in intercultural conflicts, can bring about alternative perspectives and multiple solutions to an existing problem. Competence in intercultural conflict means managing cultural differences appropriately, effectively, and adaptively.

This chapter examines some of the cultural background factors . . . that influence face-to-face intercultural conflict. . . . First, the cultural variability perspective of individualism/collectivism, in conjunction with self-concept and low/high-context communication, is presented; second, some underlying factors that contribute to intercultural conflict are identified; third, a competence-based approach to intercultural conflict management is discussed.

A Cultural Variability Perspective

Culture refers to a group-level construct that embodies a distinctive system of traditions, beliefs, values, norms, rituals, symbols, and meanings that is shared by a majority of interacting individuals in a community. Simply put, culture refers to a patterned way of living by a group of interacting individuals who share similar sets of beliefs, values, and behaviors. A complex frame of reference influences our thought patterns, our feelings, and our everyday functioning. In order to understand differences and similarities in the assumptions and behaviors in conflict across cultures, we need a perspective or framework to explain in depth why and how cultures are different or similar.

Although there are many potential dimensions in which cultures differ, one dimension that receives consistent attention from intercultural researchers around the world is *individualism/collectivism*. Individualism/collectivism explains group-level differences between cultures. . . . A value-based dimension such as individualism/collectivism, can provide us with a more in-depth understanding of why members of two contrasting cultures (for example, American and Korean cultures) approach conflict differently. In addition to this dimension are the dimensions of self-concept and low/high-context communication. The former explains individual-level approaches to conflict; the latter explains cultural differences in conflict style.

As a whole, a cultural variability perspective emphasizes the following three dimensions: individualism/collectivism, self-concept, and low/high-context communication. These three dimensions influence the values we hold in approaching or avoiding conflict, the way we attribute meanings to conflict events, and the way we communicate in specific conflict episodes.

INDIVIDUALISM/COLLECTIVISM

Individualism refers to the broad value tendencies of people in a culture to emphasize individual identity over group identity, individual rights over group obligations, and individual achievements over group concerns. In contrast, *collectivism* refers to the broad value tendencies of people in a culture to emphasize group identity over individual identity, group obligations over individual rights, and group-oriented concerns over individual wants and desires (Hofstede, 1980, 1991; Triandis, 1995). Individualism is expressed in interpersonal conflict through the strong assertion of personal opinions, the revealing of personal emotions, and personal accountability for any conflict problem or mistake. Collectivism is manifested in interpersonal conflict through the representation of collective opinions or ideas, the restraint of personal emotional expressions, and group accountability, if possible, for the conflict problem. . . .

. . . we can also find "both individualistic and collectivistic elements in *all* . . . countries, in different combinations" (Triandis, 1995, p. 2). In addition, considerable differences within cultures have been uncovered in many pluralistic societies. For example, within a pluralistic society such as Canada or the United States, different ethnic communities can display distinctive individualistic and group-oriented value tendencies. Cultural miscommunication and conflicts often arise because of our ignorance of different value priorities and modes of behavior in different cultures. Moving beyond the general discussion of culture-level differences, we can examine individual-level differences within and across cultures.

SELF-CONCEPT

An alternative way to understand individualism and collectivism focuses on how individuals within a culture conceptualize the sense of self. . . . Individuals with a strong sense of *independent self* tend to see themselves as autonomous, self-reliant, unencumbered agents of change, and as rational choice makers. Individuals with a strong sense of *interdependent self* tend to see themselves as group-bound, role-based, interconnected, obligatory agents, and as harmony seekers. Both types of self-concept exist within a culture. Overall, however, whereas independent concepts of self are more common in individualistic cultures, interdependent concepts of self are more common in collectivistic cultures.

Independent-self people tend to make sense of their environment through autonomous-self lenses; interdependent-self people tend to make sense of their surroundings through group-bound–self lenses. Independent-self individuals tend to worry about whether they present their individualistic self credibly and competently in front of others. Interdependent-self individuals tend to be more reflective of what others think of their projected face image in the context of in-group/out-group relations (which are discussed later in the section on *Conflict Norms*). Finally, while independent-self individuals tend to practice direct verbal communication, expressing their own thoughts and feelings, interdependent-self individuals tend to practice responsive communication, anticipating the thoughts and feelings of the other person. Direct verbal communication is a low-context way of communicating; responsive communication is a high-context way of communicating. . . .

LOW/HIGH-CONTEXT COMMUNICATION

According to Hall (1976), human interaction can be divided into low-context and high-context communication systems. Low-context communication emphasizes expressing intention or meaning through explicit verbal messages. High-context communication emphasizes conveying intention or meaning through the context (for example, social roles, positions) and the nonverbal channels (for example, pauses, silence, tone of voice) of the verbal message. In general, low-context communication refers to communication patterns of direct verbal mode, straight talk, nonverbal immediacy, and sender-oriented value. In low-context communication, the speaker is expected to construct a clear, persuasive message that the listener can decode easily. In contrast, high-context communication refers to communication patterns of indirect verbal mode, ambiguous talk, nonverbal subtleties, and interpreter-sensitive value. . . . In high-context communication, the listener or interpreter of the message is expected to read "between the lines," to infer accurately the implicit intent of the verbal message, and to observe the nonverbal nuances and subtleties that accompany the verbal message. High-context communication emphasizes the importance of multilayered contexts (for example, historical context, social norms, roles, situational and relational contexts) that frame the interaction. . . .

As Barnlund, in commenting on the communication style differences between Japanese and Americans, observes:

> Conflict is far less common in Japanese society for a number of reasons. First, the emphasis on the group instead of the individual reduces interpersonal friction. Second, an elaborate set of standards emphasizes "obligations" over "rights," what one owes to others rather than deserves for oneself. Third, the value attached to harmony cultivates skill in the use of ambiguity, circumlocution, euphemism, and silence in blunting incipient disputes. The ability to assimilate differences, to engineer consensus, is valued above a talent for argument. (1989, p. 39)

Individualism and independent-self concept in the United States promote the need for verbal self-assertion, and verbal self-assertion often promotes individual differences and competitions. In contrast, collectivism and interdependent-self concept in Japan promotes the need for verbal circumspection, and verbal circumspection often promotes face preservation and relational harmony.

To summarize, while independent-self individualists engage in low-context styles of conflict management, interdependent-self collectivists engage in high-context styles of conflict negotiation. Overall, the cultural variability dimensions of individualism/collectivism, independent/interdependent-self concept, and low/high-context communication patterns help guide us toward a general understanding of conflict between members of individualistic and collectivistic cultures.

Factors in Intercultural Conflict

Drawing from the key ideas of a cultural variability perspective, this section identifies the underlying factors that create intercultural frictions and conflicts between individualists and collectivists. These factors include differences in conflict assumptions, conflict rhythms, conflict norms, conflict styles, and ethnocentric lenses.

CONFLICT ASSUMPTIONS

The values of individualism versus collectivism, and how these values are linked to individual self-concepts and low/high-context communication patterns, affect our assumptions about conflict. Cultural assumptions about conflict color our attitudes, expectations, and behaviors in the conflict episode. Different cultural assumptions toward conflict are one factor contributing to intercultural miscommunication and conflict.

For individualists, the resolution of interpersonal conflict follows an outcome-oriented model. For collectivists, however, the management of interpersonal conflict follows a process-oriented model. An *outcome-oriented model* emphasizes the importance of asserting individual interests in the conflict situation and moving rapidly toward the phase of reaching tangible outcomes or goals. A *process-oriented model* emphasizes the importance of managing mutual or group face interests in the conflict process before discussing tangible outcomes or goals. "Face," in this context, refers to upholding a claimed sense of positive public image in any social interaction (Ting-Toomey, 1994a). From the collectivistic perspective, face is not about what one thinks of oneself, but about what others think of one's worth, especially within the in-group/out-group context.

For individualists, effective conflict negotiation means settling the conflict problem openly and working out a set of functional conflict solutions conjointly. Effective conflict resolution behavior (for example, emphasizing the importance of addressing incompatible goals or outcomes) is *relatively* more important than appropriate facework behavior. For collectivists, on the other hand, appropriate conflict management means the subtle negotiation of in-group/out-group face-related issues—pride, honor, dignity, insult, shame, disgrace, humility, trust, mistrust, respect, and prestige—in a given conflict episode. Appropriate facework moves and countermoves are critical before tangible conflict outcomes or goals can be addressed.

In commenting on face issues in collectivistic cultures, Cohen observes, "For the representatives of interdependent cultures the experience of international negotiation is fraught with considerations of face. The very structure of the situation, in which competing parties pit their wills and skills against each other, is uncongenial to societies that see social harmony, not confrontation, as the desired state of affairs" (1991, p. 132).

To summarize, independent-self individualists tend to operate from the following outcome-oriented conflict assumptions:

1. Conflict is perceived as being closely related to the goals or outcomes that are salient to the respective individual conflict parties in a given conflict situation.

2. Communication during conflict is viewed as dissatisfying when the conflict parties are not willing to deal with the conflict openly and honestly.

3. Communication during conflict is viewed as satisfying when the conflict parties are willing to confront the conflict issues openly and share their feelings honestly (that is, assertively but not aggressively).

4. Conflict is perceived as unproductive when no tangible outcome or plan of action is reached or developed.

5. Conflict is perceived as productive when tangible solutions are reached and objective criteria are met.

6. Effective and appropriate management of conflict means that individual goals are addressed and differences are dealt with openly, honestly, and properly in relation to timing and situational context.

Interdependent-self collectivists follow the conflict assumptions of a process-oriented model:

1. Conflict is weighed against the threat to face that is incurred in the conflict negotiation process and is interpreted in the webs of in-group/out-group relationships.

2. Communication during conflict is perceived as threatening when the conflict parties push for a discussion of substantive issues before properly managing face-related issues.

3. Communication during conflict is viewed as satisfying when the conflict parties engage in *mutual* face-saving and face-giving behavior and attend to both verbal and nonverbal signals.

4. Conflict processes and outcomes are perceived as unproductive when face issues are not addressed and relational or group feelings are not attended to properly.

5. Conflict processes and outcomes are defined as productive when both conflict parties can claim that they have "won" with respect to both face-related and substantive issues.

6. Appropriate and effective management of conflict means that the faces of both conflict parties are saved or even upgraded in the interaction, and the parties have dealt with the conflict episode strategically in conjunction with substantive gains or losses.

Thus, while individualists are concerned with resolving conflict problems, collectivists are concerned with the dynamic issues of in-group/out-group face. These implicit conflict assumptions are superimposed on the rhythms and pacing of intercultural conflict resolution.

CONFLICT RHYTHMS

The consciousness of conflict management rhythms varies along the individualism/collectivism divide. Differences in conflict rhythms are the second factor contributing to intercultural conflict between individualists and collectivists. Individualistic values tend to foster *monochronic-time rhythms,* and collectivistic value tendencies tend to cultivate *polychronic-time rhythms.*

As Hall and Hall explain: "In monochronic cultures, time is experienced and used in a linear way—comparable to a road . . . M-time [monochronic time] is divided quite naturally into segments; it is scheduled and compartmentalized, making it possible for a person to concentrate on one thing at a time. In a monochronic system, the schedule may take on priority above all else and be treated as sacred and unalterable" (1987, p. 16). Hall and Hall identified Germany, Scandinavia, Switzerland, and the United States as prime M-time examples. In contrast, they note: "Polychronic (P-time) systems are the antithesis of M-time systems. P-time is characterized by the simultaneous occurrence of many things and by a great involvement with people. There is also more emphasis on completing human transactions than on holding schedules. . . . P-time is experienced as much less tangible than M-time, and can better be compared to a single point than to a road" (Hall & Hall, 1987, pp. 17–18). Many African, Asian, Latin American, Eastern European, Caribbean, and Mediterranean cultures are prime examples of P-time systems.

M-time people prefer to deal with conflict using a linear approach; P-time people prefer to handle conflict from a spiral viewpoint. For M-time individuals, conflict management time should be filled with problem-solving or decision-making activities. For P-time individuals, time is a "being" idea governed by the smooth implicit rhythms in the interactions between people. When two P-time individuals come into conflict, they are more concerned with restoring the disjunctive rhythms in the interaction than with dealing head-on with substantive issues.

M-time people tend to emphasize agenda setting, objective criteria, and clear time schedules to accomplish certain conflict goals. P-time people, in contrast, tend to work on the relational atmosphere and the contextual setting that frame the conflict episode. For M-time individuals, effective conflict negotiation means reaching and implementing tangible conflict outcomes within a clearly established timetable. For P-time individuals, the arbitrary division of clock time or calendar time holds little meaning if the relational rhythms between people are out of sync. For M-time people, a signed contract or written agreement signals joint explicit agreement to the solution of the conflict problem. For P-time people, however, once the appropriate level of relational rhythm or rapport is established, their words can mean more than a signed contract. Likewise, if they perceive that the relational rhythms are disjunctive, renewed face-related negotiation is needed to restore that delicate, face-honoring point. M-time people tend to define conflict using a short-term time line; P-time people tend to view time from a long-term, historical process. For P-time members, "deadline" is always subject to renegotiation, and human deadlines should be dealt with flexibly and patiently.

People move with different rhythms in conflict negotiation. Intercultural conflict between individualists and collectivists is magnified when the implicit rhythm of time plays a decisive role in the encounter. M-time individuals want to move faster to address substantive problems and resolve the conflict. P-time individuals prefer to deal with relational and contextual issues before concrete, substantive negotiation. M-time persons want to establish a clear timetable to achieve specific conflict goals and objectives. P-time people want to spend more time building trust and commitment between the conflict parties. Different rhythms of monochronic time and polychronic time thus can further polarize the individualists and the collectivists in the intercultural misattribution process.

CONFLICT NORMS

Differences in norms of conflict interaction are the third factor compounding intercultural conflict. Norms are standards or guidelines for behavior. They are reflected in our expectations of what constitutes proper or improper behavior in a given setting.

. . . The *equity norm* emphasizes the importance of individual reward and cost calculations, and of obtaining equitable rewards in resolving the problematic issue. The *communal norm* stresses the importance of taking in-group expectations into account in the calculation, and of satisfying the face needs of the in-group members that are involved in the conflict.

While the equity norm reflects the individualistic, outcome-oriented model in conflict, the communal norm reflects the collectivistic, process-oriented model. In addition, in collectivistic cultures different norms govern conflict interaction with in-group and out-group members. According to Triandis, *in-groups* are groups of individuals "about whose welfare a person is concerned, with whom that person is willing to cooperate without demanding equitable returns, and separation from whom leads to anxiety" (1995, p. 9). In-groups usually consist of people who perceive a "common fate" or shared attributes. *Out-groups* are groups of individuals "with which one has something to divide, perhaps unequally, or are harmful in some way, groups that disagree on valued attributes" (Triandis, 1995, p. 9). For very important conflicts, collectivists (similar to the individualists) prefer to use the equity norm when competing with out-group members (for example, people from another company) for needed resources (Leung & Iwawaki, 1988). However, for less important conflicts, collectivists prefer to use the communal, smoothing norm with either in-group or out-group members. Each culture also has different rules and meanings for proper or improper conflict behavior in dealing with in-group or out-group members in different situations.

By the norms of emotional expression, conflict is an emotionally distressing experience. In two extensive, detailed reviews of culture and emotions (Mesquita & Frijda, 1992; Russell, 1991), clear cross-cultural differences in emotional expression and interpretation are uncovered. On the basis of these reviews, we can conclude that there are cultural norms that regulate displays of aggressive or negative emotional reactions in conflict interaction such as anger, fear, shame, frustration, resentment, and

hostility. For example, in many individualistic western cultures, open expressions of emotions in conflict are viewed as honest, engaging signals. In many collectivistic Asian cultures, however, restrained emotions are viewed as self-disciplined, mature signals in handling conflict. Thus, while basic emotions such as anxiety, shame, and fear can be viewed as pancultural conflict emotions, cultural display rules of when to express which nonverbal emotions (to whom and in what context) differ from one cultural community to the next. For example, for collectivists, the masking of negative emotions is critical to maintain a harmonious front during conflict. When collectivists feel embarrassed or perceive face threat in conflict, they may sometimes smile to cover up their embarrassment or shame.

Thus, different norms and rules govern the way individualists and collectivists deal with specific conflict issues. When an individualist prefers to use the equity norm to deal with a conflict issue and a collectivist prefers to use the communal norm, the hidden factor of normative expectations further splinters intercultural communication. In addition, the nonverbal/verbal dimension of emotional expression in conflict can vary along the individualism and collectivism schism, creating further tensions and gaps.

CONFLICT STYLES

. . . Differences in conflict styles are the fourth factor in intercultural conflict negotiation. Cultural differences in conflict style generate intergroup attribution errors and biases. For example, the following dialogue between Ms. Gumb (an African-American supervisor) and Mr. Lee (a recent Chinese immigrant) in a U.S.-China joint-venture firm illustrates differences in conflict styles and attribution processes.

Example 2

MS. GUMB (in the main office): Lee, where is your project report? You said you'd get it done soon. I need your part of the report so that I can finish my final report by the end of this week. When do you think you can get it done? [*Attribution: Lee is very irresponsible. I should*

never have trusted him. I thought I was giving him
a break by putting him in charge of this report.]

MR. LEE (hesitantly): Well, Ms. Gumb . . . I didn't
realize the deadline was so soon. . . . I will try
my best to get it done as soon as possible. It's
just that there are lots of details I need to cross-
check. . . . I'm really not sure. [*Attribution:
Ms. Gumb is sure a tough lady. Anyway, she is
the supervisor, why didn't she tell me the exact
deadline early on? Just last week, she told me to
take my time on the report. I'm really confused.
In China, the supervisor always tells the workers
what to do.*]

MS. GUMB (frustrated): Lee, how soon is soon?
I really need to know your plan of action right
now. You cannot be so vague in answering my
questions all the time. I believe I've given you
plenty of time to work on this report already.
[*Attribution: Lee is trying to be sneaky. He does
not answer my questions directly at all. I wonder
if all Chinese are that sneaky? Or maybe he is
not comfortable working for a black female? Anyway, I have to press him to be more efficient and
responsible. He is in America; he has to learn the
American way.*]

MR. LEE: [*a long pause*] . . . Well, I'm really not
sure, Ms. Gumb. I really don't want to do a bad
job on the report and disappoint you. I'll try
my best to finish it as soon as possible. Maybe
I can finish the report next week. [*Attribution:
Ms. Gumb is sure a pushy boss. She doesn't seem
to like me and she is causing me to lose face in front
of all my peers. Her voice sounds so harsh and
blunt. I have heard American people are hard to
work with, but she is especially rude and overbearing. I better start looking for a new job tomorrow.*]

In Example 2, while Ms. Gumb is assertive and
direct in dealing with the problem, Mr. Lee is hes-
itant and indirect in answering her questions.
Ms. Gumb has a "straight-talk," low-context approach to dealing with the work problem; Mr. Lee
has a "face-talk," high-context approach. If both
understand concepts such as low-context and high-
context communication styles, they may arrive at a
better understanding of each other's behavior.

Conflict style differences between cultural or
ethnic group members profoundly influence the

meanings we attach to each other's behavior. We
typically use our own habitual scripts and interaction styles as a baseline to judge and evaluate others'
behavior. While Mr. Lee is using his high-context
scripts to evaluate Ms. Gumb's behavior as rude and
overbearing, Ms. Gumb is using her low-context attribution (for example, "Lee is trying to be sneaky")
and historical script (for example, "maybe he is
not comfortable working for a black female") to
make sense of Mr. Lee's high-context approach. If
Ms. Gumb and Mr. Lee understand the cultural
and historical conditioning of their own and the
other's behavior, they may learn to be more culturally sensitive in their attribution process. They
may learn to respect each other's stylistic scripts
and work more adaptively in achieving a common
ground in their interaction.

Ms. Gumb may learn to talk privately to Mr.
Lee rather than to engage in such direct face-
threatening behavior in public. Mr. Lee may learn
to be more direct and open in answering his supervisor's questions and to pause and hedge less in their
interaction. On the strategy level, individualists in
conflict appear to prefer direct verbal assertions, direct verbal questioning, direct requests, and direct
clarifications and answers in conflict. In contrast,
collectivists prefer qualifiers (for example, "*perhaps
we should meet this deadline together*"), tag questions (for example, "*don't you think you'll feel better
if you finish it and get it out of the way?*"), disclaim-
ers (for example, "*maybe I don't understand what's
going on here*"), and indirect requests (for example,
"*if it's not too much trouble, let's try to finish this report together*") to convey a softened approach to
working out differences.

. . . Silence is a critical strategy in dealing with
both in-group and out-group conflicts in collectivistic cultures. Silence may signal approval or disapproval in collectivistic conflict interaction. In
silence, the conflict parties incur no obligations. Silence may also be interpreted as an ambiguous
"yes" or "no" response. On the other hand, silence
may be viewed as an admission of guilt or incompetence in an individualistic culture.

Finally, several researchers indicate that collectivists tend to prefer an *informal* third-party conflict
mediation procedure (such as seeking help from
relatives or from wise teachers or gurus) more so

than individualists (Cohen, 1991; Leung, 1987, 1988; Ting-Toomey, 1985, 1988). In mediated conflicts individualists prefer objective advice and facilitation from an impartial, formal third-party mediator . . . , and collectivists prefer to seek help from someone who already is informed about the conflict and whom they can trust and respect.

Different cross-cultural conflict styles create different attribution biases and tensions. In attributing meanings to collectivistic, indirect conflict styles, individualists tend to view collectivists in the conflict as trying to sidestep genuine issue discussions. Conversely, collectivists tend to perceive individualists as pushy, rude, and overbearing because of their confrontational conflict style.

ETHNOCENTRIC LENSES

Although we often rely on the knowledge of our own cultural approach, rhythms, norms, and styles to explain the behavior of other people from our culture, the same criteria may not be applicable to another culture. Being unfamiliar with the other party's cultural norms creates problems that can exacerbate an already tense intercultural conflict episode. An examination of such problems is a natural extension of the discussion on differences in conflict styles.

Ethnocentrism is defined as "the view of things in which one's own group is the center of everything, and all others are scaled and rated with reference to it" (Sumner, 1940, p. 13). When members of different cultures believe that their own approaches are the correct or natural ways to handle conflict, they tend to see the conflict behaviors of other cultures as deviant from the standard. . . .

Individualists with strong ethnocentric tendencies tend to view the outcome-oriented model as superior and more efficient in conflict resolution than the process-oriented model. Conversely, collectivists with strong ethnocentric lenses tend to view the process-oriented model as more desirable and personable than the mechanistic outcome-oriented model. Ethnocentrism reflects our comfort with familiar cultural habits and practices. Individuals are often unaware of their own ethnocentric behaviors and evaluations. They have internalized the standards and norms of their culture as the "proper" and "right" ways of behaving.

Individualists and collectivists also may engage in different attribution processes during interpersonal conflict. Overall, individualists tend to use more dispositional attributions than do collectivists to explain the conflict problem. Individualists might explain conflict by making negative personality statements such as "She's late because she's lazy" or "He's just too dumb to get it." Collectivists, on the other hand, tend to use more situational attributions than do individualists to explain problems. For example, they make statements such as "Maybe she's late because the traffic is really bad" or "Maybe he's confused because the manager did not explain the project clearly." Individualists tend to hold the person accountable for the conflict; collectivists tend to emphasize the context that contributes to the conflict.

Individualists and collectivists sometimes use similar attributions in making sense of conflict. Stewart and Bennett, in commenting on how ethnocentrism leads to more intensified intercultural miscommunication, observe: "When communicators engage in mutual negative evaluation, the recriminatory interaction may be enough to block communication. If the communicators then attempt to overcome the difficulty through ethnocentric procedures, the communication event may deteriorate even further. . . . With each turn of this regressive spiral, negative evaluations are intensified" (1991, p. 165). The lack of specific information about each other's conflict assumptions or styles often creates negative interaction spirals that deepen the cultural schism. The lack of communication skills to handle such problematic intercultural episodes appropriately and effectively also compounds the miscommunication chasm.

Our ethnocentric lenses push us to judge the behavior of another culture evaluatively and negatively. Ethnocentrism creates biased attributions and expectations in intercultural conflict. Thus, cultural differences in conflict assumptions, conflict rhythms, conflict norms, conflict styles, and ethnocentric lenses act as invisible barriers that widen the gap of intercultural conflict. Individualists and collectivists typically collide over their use of an outcome-oriented model or process-oriented model in dealing with conflict. They also collide over the rhythms, the norms, and the styles of how to approach conflict appropriately and effectively. Ethnocentric lenses creep into our attribution process and create further evaluative biases and binary mind-sets (that is, my way is the *right* way and your way is *wrong*).

Competence in Intercultural Conflict

. . . *Knowledge* is the cognitive or experiential understanding that helps one communicate effectively and appropriately in a given situation. *Motivation* is the cognitive or affective readiness, or mind-set, to communicate effectively and appropriately with others. *Skill* is the ability to perform behaviors that are considered effective and appropriate in a given situation. This section examines the effectiveness and appropriateness criteria of competence in intercultural conflict and concludes with some recommendations for enhancing our knowledge, motivation, and skill in managing intercultural conflicts competently. . . .

KNOWLEDGE, MOTIVATION, AND SKILL IN INTERCULTURAL CONFLICT

To act effectively and appropriately in interactive conflict, individuals have to enhance their cultural knowledge and motivation in applying adaptive interaction skills. Of all the dimensions of managing intercultural conflict, knowledge is the most important and underscores the other dimensions of competence.

Without culture-sensitive knowledge, parties cannot learn to uncover the implicit ethnocentric "lenses," or assumptions, they use to interpret and evaluate events in different intercultural conflict situations. "Knowledge" here refers to in-depth understanding of certain phenomena via a range of information gained through conscious learning and personal experiences and observations.

In addition to individualistic and collectivistic value tendencies, individual differences within cultures, such as independent-self versus interdependent-self concept, contribute to the interpretation of intercultural conflict. To manage intercultural conflict competently, we must take other people's cultural perspectives and personality factors into consideration. If others are interdependent-self collectivists, we may want to pay extra attention to their process-oriented assumptions about conflict. If others are independent-self individualists, we may want to be sensitive to their outcome-oriented assumptions about conflict. Although this chapter provides general knowledge for understanding individualistic and collectivistic cultures, knowledge concerning cultural and ethnic conflict assumptions and styles should also be pursued. This chapter emphasizes intercultural conflict differences rather than ethnic differences (for example, African-American versus Mexican-American interaction style in the United States) in conflict. However, the general concepts (that is, differences in conflict models, rhythms, norms, styles, and ethnocentric lenses) should serve as a good working basis in managing any kind of group-based difference in conflict. Both general and specific knowledge of other cultures and ethnic groups can increase our motivation and skill in dealing with people who are culturally and ethnically different.

In addition, while individualists and collectivists have different frames of reference in conflict negotiation, it is important to remember that most conflicts involve some common interests. Rather than harping on positional differences in conflict, parties to intercultural conflict should learn to uncover or cultivate common interests that bind them in the conflict (Fisher & Ury, 1981). Learning about cultural differences and moving toward mutual interest–based negotiation (for example, we both want the computer project to be on time, even though we have different ways of approaching this problem) can serve as the first step toward competent intercultural conflict management. If conflict parties do not develop in-depth knowledge of the implicit theories or scripts that drive intercultural conflict, the root causes of the intercultural conflict may remain unresolved.

"Motivation" in intercultural conflict competence refers to our cognitive and affective predispositions with regard to communicating with people who are different from us. Motivation is a conflict *mind-set* issue. To have an open mind-set in dealing with people who are different, we need (1) to suspend judgment of unfamiliar behavior, (2) to develop a mindful attitude in conflict, and (3) to engage in ODIE (observe, describe, interpret, evaluate) analysis.

Suspending evaluative judgment in intercultural conflict requires us to accept the fact that we engage in ethnocentric evaluations of culturally unfamiliar behavior. Ethnocentrism colors our attitudes and behavior in any intergroup conflict. To act competently in intercultural conflict, we must first acknowledge the ethnocentric lenses we put on in interpreting and judging unfamiliar behavior. As Stewart and Bennett comment:

> Participants in a cross-cultural situation need to consider first the possibility that a negative evaluation might be based on unrecognized cultural difference rather than the result of astute cross-cultural analysis. Each person needs to be aware that he or she is evaluating the other, often on similarly ethnocentric grounds, and seek to suspend these kinds of evaluations until the potential spiraling effects of the action have been considered. . . . swift evaluation is likely to be ethnocentric and detrimental to effective intercultural communication. (1991, p. 167)

Acknowledging our own ethnocentric biases and suspending our reactive evaluations are critical aspects of managing intercultural misattribution. By withholding our gut-level negative judgments about unfamiliar behavior, we are giving ourselves and others a chance to understand the cultural nuances that exist in a problematic situation.

Mindfulness is a motivational concept in managing intercultural conflict competently. Langer's (1989) concept of mindfulness encourages individuals to tune in consciously to their habituated mental scripts and expectations. According to Langer, if mindlessness is the "rigid reliance on old categories, mindfulness means the continual creation of new ones. Categorization and recategorization, labeling and relabeling as one masters the world are processes natural to children" (1989, p. 63). To engage in a mindfulness state, an individual needs to learn (1) to be open to new information, (2) to create new categories, and (3) to be aware that multiple perspectives typically exist in viewing a basic phenomenon (Langer, 1989, p. 62).

To acquire new information in conflict interaction, conflict parties must listen responsively to each other even when they are disagreeing. In intercultural conflict, disagreeing parties have to learn to listen attentively to the cultural perspectives and assumptions expressed in the interaction. They have to learn to listen responsively, or *ting* ("聽," the Chinese character for "listening" means listening with our "ears, eyes, and a focused heart") to the sounds, tones, gestures, movements, nonverbal nuances, pauses, and silence in the conflict situation. They must mindfully notice the verbal, nonverbal, and meta-nonverbal contexts that are being conveyed in conflict negotiation. Creating new categories means learning to create or apply culturally sensitive concepts such as low/high-context communication styles in making sense of variations in conflict behavior. Finally, being aware that there are multiple perspectives means that individuals can apply different frameworks (for example, both individualistic and collectivistic perspectives) in analyzing and interpreting conflict and can come up with a creative, synergistic solution.

The third aspect of motivation is *ODIE analysis* (observe, describe, interpret, and then evaluate). Rather than making snapshot, evaluative attributions, we should first learn to *observe* attentively the verbal *and* nonverbal signals that are being exchanged in the conflict process. We should then try to *describe* mentally and in behaviorally specific terms what is going on in the conflict situation (for example, "she is not maintaining eye contact when speaking to me"). We should then generate *multiple interpretations* (for example, "maybe from her cultural angle, eye contact avoidance during conflict is a proper behavior; from my cultural angle, this is considered an improper signal") to make sense of the behavior we are observing and describing. Finally, we may decide to accept or respect the differences as genuine cultural differences and to adapt ourselves by integrating the differences or by *evaluating* them (for example, "I understand that eye contact avoidance can be either a cultural or a personal habit, but I still don't like it, because I feel invalidated by the person's lack of eye contact"). The idea of the sequence observe-describe-interpret is to allow ourselves a more open-ended evaluation or judgment of unfamiliar behavior. We may realize that the discomfort we experience in the conflict negotiation process is based, in part, on communication style differences. We may want to sample a wide range of people (in a wide variety of contexts) from this cultural group to determine whether eye contact avoidance is a cultural or individual habit. Or we may decide to approach the person (with the low/high-context styles in mind) directly or indirectly to talk about such differences.

Interaction skills, abilities that help us communicate effectively and appropriately in a given situation, are useful in promoting competence in intercultural conflict. The three skills that appear to be most pertinent are face management skills, trust-building skills, and communicative adaptability.

Parties to intercultural conflict should learn to cultivate *face management skills* in order to deal competently with intergroup conflicts. Face management skills address the fundamental issue of social self-esteem. Most human beings like to be respected and affirmed in their daily interaction with colleagues and loved ones. However, the behaviors that reveal the need for self-respect and that show respect and dignity to others differ from one culture to the next.

Individualists may want to learn to "give face" to the collectivists in the conflict negotiation process. Giving face means not humiliating or embarrassing the collectivists in public, and acknowledging collectivists' in-group concerns and obligations. Collectivists, on the other hand, may want to reorient face maintenance concerns and learn to pay more attention to the substantive (or task-relevant) issues. Collectivists may also want to recognize that individualists often separate substantive issues from socio-emotional issues in conflict. Conversely, individualists may want to pay more attention to the link between substantive issues and facework or relational issues when negotiating disagreements with collectivists. Thus, although the concern for face maintenance is universal, how we manage face issues is culture-specific.

Critical to competent management of intercultural conflict are *trust-building skills*. If parties in conflict do not trust each other, they tend to move away (cognitively, affectively, and physically) from each other rather than struggle side by side. According to Fisher and Brown (1988), trust is often viewed as the "single most important element of a good working relationship" (1988, p. 107). When we do not trust someone's words or actions, we tend automatically to turn off our listening devices in conflict. We may hear the words, but we are not listening. Trust building is both a mind-set and a communication skill. Especially in intercultural conflict situations, when we are experiencing high anxieties with unfamiliar behavior (for example, accents, nonverbal gestures), we may automatically withhold our trust. Well-founded trust is critical in any effective and appropriate management of intercultural conflicts. Trusting someone, however, entails risks.

In emphasizing the importance of developing a good working relationship as a base for conflict management, Fisher and Brown (1988) recommend that we learn to be "trustworthy" but not necessarily "wholly trusting." We should also learn to carefully analyze the risk of trust in an intercultural conflict situation. To be trustworthy means we should make our behavior more reliable so that others can depend on our words or actions over time. To avoid wholly trusting someone, we should be neither more nor less trusting than the risks dictate. Well-founded trust is based on a mindful analysis of risk. For individualists, such analysis probably is based on the conflict situation at hand. For collectivists, such analysis is often based on a long-term, contextual view of the layers that enwrap the conflict situation. Well-founded trust, in short, is a mind-set, an attitude. It is also a behavior that is developed via consistent, competent communication skills of managing differences.

Communicative adaptability is one of the key interaction skills in the negotiation of intercultural conflict. Communicative adaptability is the ability to change conflict goals and behaviors to meet the specific needs of the situation (Duran, 1985). It signals our mindful awareness of the other person's perspectives, interests, and/or goals, as well as our willingness to modify our own interests or goals to adapt to the conflict situation. Communicative adaptability can also imply behavioral flexibility. By mindfully observing what is going on in the intercultural conflict situation, both parties may modify their nonverbal and/or verbal behavior to achieve more synchronized interaction.

Summary

Competence in intercultural conflict requires that we communicate effectively and appropriately in different intercultural conflict negotiation situations, and effective, appropriate communication requires adaptation. To manage conflict competently, we must understand and respect different world views and ways of dealing with conflict. We must be sensitive to the differences and similarities between individualistic and collectivistic cultures. We must also be aware of our ethnocentric biases and culture-based attributions in making snapshot evaluations of other conflict management approaches.

Competent conflict negotiation promotes flexible, adaptive behaviors in attuning to both the process and the outcome of an intercultural conflict episode. Although intercultural conflict is complex, understanding conflict along the individualism/collectivism continuum is the first step toward understanding cultural variations on conflict.

Selected References

Barnlund, D. (1989). *Communicative styles of Japanese and Americans: Images and realities.* Belmont, CA: Wadsworth.

Cohen, R. (1991). *Negotiating across cultures: Communication obstacles in international diplomacy.* Washington, DC: U.S. Institute of Peace.

Duran, R. (1985). Communicative adaptability: A measure of social communicative competence. *Communication Quarterly, 31,* 320–326.

Fisher, R., & Brown, S. (1988). *Getting together: Building relationships as we negotiate.* New York: Penguin Books.

Fisher, R., & Ury, W. (1981). *Getting to yes.* Boston: Houghton Mifflin.

Hall, E. T. (1976). *Beyond culture.* New York: Doubleday.

Hall, E., & Hall, M. (1987). *Hidden differences: Doing business with the Japanese.* Garden City: Anchor Press/Doubleday.

Hofstede, G. (1980). *Culture's consequences: International differences in work-related values.* Beverly Hills, CA: Sage.

Hofstede, G. (1991). *Cultures and organizations: Software of the mind.* London: McGraw-Hill.

Langer, E. (1989). *Mindfulness.* Reading, MA: Addison-Wesley.

Leung, K. (1987). Some determinants of reactions to procedural models for conflict resolution: A cross-national study. *Journal of Personality and Social Psychology, 53,* 898–908.

Leung, K. (1988). Some determinants of conflict avoidance. *Journal of Cross-Cultural Psychology, 19,* 125–136.

Leung, K., & Iwawaki, S. (1988). Cultural collectivism and distributive behavior. *Journal of Cross-Cultural Psychology, 19,* 35–49.

Loden, M., & Rosener, J. (1991). *Workforce America! Managing employee diversity as a vital resource.* Homewood, IL: Business One Irwin.

Lustig, M., & Koester, J. (1993). *Intercultural competence: Interpersonal communication across cultures.* New York: HarperCollins College Publishing.

Mesquita, B., & Frijda, N. (1992). Cultural variations in emotions: A review. *Psychological Bulletin, 112,* 179–204.

Russell, J. (1991). Culture and the categorizations of emotions. *Psychological Bulletin, 110,* 426–450.

Stewart, E., & Bennett, M. (1991). *American cultural patterns: A cross-cultural perspective.* Yarmouth, ME: Intercultural Press.

Sumner, W. (1940). *Folkways.* Boston: Ginn.

Ting-Toomey, S. (1985). Toward a theory of conflict and culture. In W. Gudykunst, L. Stewart, & S. Ting-Toomey (Eds.), *Communication, culture, and organizational processes.* Beverly Hills, CA: Sage.

Ting-Toomey, S. (1988). Intercultural conflict styles: A face-negotiation theory. In Y. Kim & W. Gudykunst (Eds.), *Theories in intercultural communication.* Newbury Park, CA: Sage.

Ting-Toomey, S. (1994). Managing intercultural conflicts effectively. In L. Samovar & R. Porter (Eds.), *Intercultural communication: A reader* (7th ed.). Belmont, CA: Wadsworth.

Triandis, H. (1995). *Individualism and collectivism.* Boulder, CO: Westview Press.

Key Terms

collectivism	high context
conflict	individualism
conflict competence	low context
conflict style	self-construal
ethnocentrism	

Discussion Questions

1. Individualism and collectivism promote two rather different orientations to conflict. How are these differences reconciled in an intercultural conflict? One person could completely adapt (conform) to the other person's orientation. For example, a collectivist could take on an individualist orientation during conflict with an individualist. Would this approach be communicatively competent? Why or why not? What are some alternative ways for reconciling differences in values so that conflict can be managed successfully?

2. Think of a difficult conflict you've had with a relative stranger (possibly someone from another culture). Can you explain any of the difficulty in the conflict as being due to the fact that you and the other person had (1) different conflict assumptions, (2) different conflict rhythms, (3) different conflict styles, or (4) different ethnocentric lenses? What happened that leads you to infer any of these differences?

3. Among the dimensions that facilitate communicative competence, knowledge is the most important for managing intercultural conflict. What is meant by knowledge? Do you agree or disagree? Why or why not? Can knowledge about another's culture ever lead you to be incompetent? If so, how? (Hint: If you meet a Chinese man and presume he possesses collectivistic values and treat him accordingly, do you run the risk of unduly stereotyping him?)

4. The desire to maintain face seems to be culturally universal, even though face issues are managed differently in different cultures. Does this universality suggest any general guidelines that would help communicators seek common ground when managing intercultural conflict?

5. How might power differentials come into play in cross-cultural conflicts?

35 Negotiating With the Swazis
PETER OGOM NWOSU

I feel like a man sitting in my house facing a poised snake. I am trying to be very calm and avoid sudden movement. Meanwhile, my friends outside the door are throwing rocks at the snake. I am the one endangered, not they.

—Late King Sobhuza of Swaziland

Negotiation

Negotiation or bargaining[1] has been defined as a process in which two or more players with different needs, different interests and perspectives "attempt to settle what each shall give and take, or perform and receive in a transaction between them" (Rubin & Brown, 1975). Since the players involved in the process are interdependent, they use proposals, counterproposals, and compromises to reach agreements based on mutually acceptable terms (Putnam & Jones, 1982).

In their article "Reciprocity in Negotiations: An Analysis of Bargaining Interaction," Putnam and Jones (1982) note that:

> Although we typically associate bargaining with labor-management disputes, the process of negotiating occurs in a number of settings. Specifically, companies bargain with suppliers, customers bicker with sales personnel, politicians and diplomats make international trades [or agreements], and lawyers bargain case appeals with clients and judges. In effect, we rely on bargaining as a dominant mode of conflict managment in a variety of interpersonal and organizational contexts. (p. 171)

Noting that negotiation [in some cultures or situations] "employs trade-offs as the dominant modus operandi for managing conflict or resolving issues," Putnam and Jones (p. 172), however, warn that negotiation involves more than an assimilation of trade-offs. More important, "it is a communicative process involving persuasion, and is characterized by the exchange of information, arguments, and strategic maneuvers." Shelling (1960) shares a similar view. According to him, communication allows players in a negotiating encounter "to discover patterns of individual behavior that make each player's actions predictable to the other, to test each other for a shared sense of regularity [and] to exploit . . . impromptu codes for signaling intentions and for responding to each other's signals" (p. 4).

However, when the players have become socialized in different cultural milieu—when they "do not share the same ways of thinking, feeling, and behaving"—the process of negotiation at either the domestic or international level becomes much more complex. As Fisher (1980) puts it, the "potential for misunderstanding will be greater [here]; more time will be lost in talking past each other. More complete explanations of positions may be needed, or a special kind of persuasive skill called for" (p. 1). And Fisher warns that "it is naive indeed to venture into international negotiation with the untempered self-assurance that after all people are pretty much alike everywhere."

In fact, no two nations actually negotiate in the same way. Each country's style of negotiation is shaped by [its] culture, historical circumstance, political ideology and its place in the international community (Binnendijk, 1987). Adler (1986), for instance, notes that "countries vary on such key aspects as the amount and type of preparation for a negotiation, the relative emphasis on task versus interpersonal relationships; the use of general principles versus specific details; and the number of people present and the extent of their influence" (p. 152). The ability of an individual, therefore, to understand a country's negotiating style, including the nuances, enhances that individual's effectiveness as a negotiator, and *ceteris paribus*, the atmosphere for the peaceful resolution of issues.

This paper describes the negotiating style of the Swazi, a Bantu-speaking[2] people inhabiting a small but strategically located kingdom in Southern Africa. The paper is based on interviews conducted with Swazi nationals and government officials, as well as on selected literature on the country, and on the subject of negotiation in general. Among issues addressed are the players and the social situation, the negotiation process including strategies and tactics, style of decision making, as well as the impact of national character and cross-cultural "noise" on negotiations.

Swazi Approaches to Negotiation

The story is told of a prominent British evangelist who had come to Swaziland to negotiate a piece of land where he would build a church for his Christian ministry. He was brought before the *Ngwenyama*[3] (King Sobhuza) by an intermediary. The intermediary, while introducing the evangelist to the king, eulogized the evangelist's healing power. He told Sobhuza that the evangelist had come to seek the king's support so that he could live in Swaziland and perform the same miracle works he had carried out in Britain. King Sobhuza listened attentively. After a long pause, he responded by first welcoming the evangelist. He thanked him for his interest in the kingdom and the people. He then turned to his officials after another pause and remarked, "Go and find out if there are people in Britain who still need healing. If there are no such people, then give this gentleman every support that he needs, including a piece of land!" Strong words. Of course the evangelist went back home and never returned. Several months later, reports had it that this evangelist had been jailed for defrauding the government! (M. Dlamini, personal communication, April 14, 1988).

This story underscores a key, but often overlooked, aspect of Swazi negotiation style—the assumption that the Swazis bring to the bargaining encounter. To the Swazis, the other party is guilty of deception until proven innocent. The American notion that a person is innocent or trustworthy until proven guilty does not prevail during negotiations.

Hilda Kuper (1986), a noted authority on Swazi history, remarks that most Swazis prefer that the *umlungu* (a term used for a foreigner, particularly a white person) must prove himself before he could be received as *umuntfu* (a person). Another scholar explains:

> Swazis are very skeptical of foreigners—in whatever form. They want to know by whose authority you come. They want to know why that authority is not personally present. And they want to know whom to go to if a problem arises. Someone has to be accountable for your presence.
> (M. Dlamini, 1988)

The cautious, or perhaps suspicious approach of the Swazis toward negotiations, notes Carlton Dlamini, Acting Ambassador of the Kingdom of Swaziland to the United States, is a reflection of the country's historical past as well as its geopolitical position in Southern Africa. "Our open approach to issues in the past, and our acceptance of people on the face value have created problems for us. In addition, we are sandwiched between two systems of government that are completely different from ours. Such situations dictate that we maintain some form of caution" (C. Dlamini, personal communication, April 21, 1988).

Traditionally, when visitors come to a Swazi homestead or any part of the countryside, the Swazi family is obliged by custom to let the visitor in, even if they do not know the person. In most cases, they allow the visitor to occupy a bedroom, even if it means having the occupants of the household sleep in the living room or in the kitchen. This African concept of hospitality, or the "spirit of accommodation" as it is called, which has been extended to the negotiating encounter, formed the basis for the acceptance into Swaziland of many foreigners (mostly Europeans) during and after the nineteenth century. But as Booth (1983) notes, the European's appetite for Swaziland's resources (particularly the land and its wealth) turned the kingdom into a pawn in the scramble for Africa and eventually into a British protectorate. By 1968, when the country became independent, over fifty percent of Swazi Nation Land had been expropriated, and some ceded to South Africa, under dubious land deals. Today, modern-day Swaziland, a small landlocked kingdom (slightly larger than the state of New Jersey in the United States), and certainly one of the smallest countries in Africa, finds itself bordered on three sides by the Republic of South Africa, and by Mozambique on its eastern side. Negotiations are still continuing with South Africa to recover some of the lost lands.

The Swazis believe that the first step in the negotiation process, either at the domestic or international level, is to establish the legitimacy or credibility of the negotiators. What this entails, for instance, is that a foreigner coming to conduct negotiations, particularly business negotiations, for the first time in Swaziland must develop "legitimate contact." Legitimate contact, according to Martin Dlamini, a member of the Swazi Royal Family, implies an "intermediary," or "go-between," who will be responsible for "clearing the road" for the foreigner before the actual negotiation begins. Usually the intermediary is a prominent person within the community, and his responsibility involves taking the foreigner to meet the "right" people at the "right" time. In the process, the intermediary helps build the credibility or legitimacy of the foreigner, prior to the negotiations. Ambassador Dlamini remarks that the use of intermediaries, or go-betweens, during negotiations is a highly valued aspect of Swazi culture. "In a sense, it shows the seriousness of the issue" (C. Dlamini, 1988).

Generally, the Swazis do not like to be taken by surprise, and by using an intermediary, the negotiation path is smoothed and the element of surprise removed. In the same manner, when a Swazi official is coming to another country, for instance, the United States, to conduct business either at the World Bank, the International Monetary Fund, or the State Department, "we prefer to send a person who makes the initial contacts, thus making things easier for our negotiators" (C. Dlamini, April 21, 1988).

An intermediary may not necessarily be a Swazi national but could be someone from another culture who has spent some time in Swaziland and understands the culture and the people. It could, for instance, be the U.S. Ambassador to Swaziland or any top member of the diplomatic corps; or the director of Peace Corps activities in Swaziland. The subject matter determines the choice of the intermediary.

While intermediaries may clear the way or smooth the negotiation path, they do not necessarily guarantee the success of a negotiation. As the story of the British evangelist suggests, the foreign negotiating team must convince the Swazis of the authenticity of their mission. According to Martin Dlamini, "the Swazis will receive a foreigner given their traditional concept of hospitality, but we know we do not have to agree with you until we have verified your authenticity."

Martin Dlamini recalls the negotiation that took place in 1980 during the hiring of a national soccer coach for the country. Two foreigners—one from Poland and the other from Hungary—had been invited for discussions. While the Polish coach engaged in much self-praise, the Hungarian (Coach Ted Dumitru), on the other hand, was reportedly very low-profile, soft-spoken, less abrasive and less pushy in his comments. He was consequently chosen, even though it would cost the Swazi Government more to hire him!

The Swazis are quick to attribute motives when a person, during negotiations, is very pushy, engages in too much self-praise, or acts like he or she knows everything. "People who talk a lot are not welcome. Be calm, but not too calm that they suspect you are up to some mischief," remarks an official of the Swazi Embassy in Washington, D.C. Indeed, there is such a thin line between talkativeness and calmness, that it is difficult for a foreigner to understand when one is being "too talkative" or "too calm." Hence, Swazi insistence or suggestion that an intermediary be used.

Typically, Swazis employ what Adler (1986, p. 149) calls an "affective approach" to negotiating. An affective approach to negotiations emphasizes the development of a strong sense of relationship. To the Swazis, it is not the piece of paper, the contract, the agreement, or the substance of the negotiation that necessarily counts, but rather the relationship of trust that is developed with the other party.

Thus, prior to the negotiations, they treat the foreign negotiating team to a number of events or ceremonies, including, in some instances, courtesy calls on the *Ngwenyama* (the king) or the *Ndlovukazi* (The Lady Elephant or Queen Mother), or other relevant functionaries of the government.

Swazis use such events or occasions to get to know more about the other negotiators. In fact, the development of a fairly strong relationship at the early stage of the negotiations or bargaining process reduces the element of suspicion. It also provides a basis or context for further interaction or deliberations. While many Americans may downplay these ceremonies and protocol, Swazis cherish them. For them, it is simply not appropriate to sit down to discuss business without, at least, some form of social interaction taking place first. Many foreign negotiators, frustrated by the delays, have actually marred the negotiation process by their impatience and the insistence that they "get down to business immediately" (M. Dlamini, April 14, 1988).

Swazis do not like to be rushed or be expected to negotiate within a specific time frame. A Swazi embassy official remarks that "the worst thing you can do in terms of negotiating with the Swazis is to place a time limit upon them." The issue has to be of national significance and immediacy to require a rush or a time limit. The official advises foreign negotiators to "be prepared to spend a lot more days during negotiations. Come there, knowing that the first day is for protocol and socializing" (personal communication, April 20, 1988). Where the issue is of a certain magnitude, he adds, it may require the final approval of the *Ngwenyama*, or the Ngwenyama-in-council, and this may take more days.

In a sense, Swazi concepts, structure, and perceptions of time, like those of all Africans, are dictated by nature. This is not the situation in case-particularistic societies such as the United States, where time has been reified, and placed at the center of all social, economic, political, and personal activities. Time, as Burgoon and Saine (1978) remark, is the master, Westerners [Americans] its slaves. In Swaziland, as in the rest of Africa, time is the slave, Swazis its masters. As Awa (1987) notes, if a person comes to a meeting "late," he or she does not feel obligated to apologize. And when a paramount chief, for instance,

> summons his cabinet, through a messenger,
> to convene at daybreak [i.e. at the crow of the
> cock] and some arrive at 5:30 a.m. and others at
> 6:00 a.m, none of them will be perceived as late.

Decisions by "chiefs-in-council" require full representation and participation of all section heads, and such decisions are generally preceded by a social event—the ritual breaking of Kola nut, a prolonged libation ceremony—deliberately calculated to allow time for a quorum to be attained.

(Awa, this volume p. 139)

Strategies

During the actual negotiations, the Swazis employ a "traditional" negotiating style. In essence, it is not a give-and-take approach but, instead, it is based on what Martin Dlamini calls the "concept of listening." "We do not throw out all our cards on the table. We first listen to what the other party has to say. If we do not have an immediate response, we may then ask for adjournment to enable us to put our heads together and prepare one."

This may take a few hours or even days, and this could be frustrating to the foreign negotiator. Throughout the negotiating encounter, waiting and silence, as is the case with the Barai of Papua New Guinea (near Australia) or the Japanese, become frequent. To the Swazis, long pauses and silence during negotiations provide an opportunity for them to analyze the implications of what is being said by the other party. Where the language of the negotiation is English, French, or any foreign language other than *SiSwati* (Swazi language), silence enables the Swazis to "think through" the information given by the other party. To Westerners, however, gaps of silence during negotiations can be a terribly discomforting cultural "noise." As Olsson notes, such noise could indicate a lack of interest in the issue being discussed.

Generally, Swazi culture does not allow for open confrontation or disagreement with the outsider. Such would be seen as a negation of the idea of relationship-building which the Swazi prize so much. So when Swazi negotiators become too uncomfortable or have misgivings about an issue, they may ask for an adjournment, rather than engage in an argument.

During the negotiation process, Swazis express disapproval over an issue by looking at each other without saying a word. This non-verbal eye-to-eye

contact message is interpreted or decoded by the Swazi negotiating team as a time to call for adjournment. Meetings could resume the same day or the following day by which time the Swazi team may come up with responses, new strategies, or concessions.

Indeed, the vocalization of this intent (that is the adjournment) is one of five of the verbal tactics used by the Swazis during negotiations. The other four are: to postpone the negotiation *indefinitely,* in order to make a point; to provide alternative suggestions or counterproposals; to employ the concept of sympathy; or to use the notion of a small but powerful country. (personal communications with M. Dlamini, April 14, 1988, and C. Dlamini, April 21, 1988).

Although postponing negotiations *indefinitely* is a tactic in the bargaining arsenal of the Swazis, it is rarely used, except in circumstances where they feel very strongly about certain principles. One example is the question of publicity during negotiations. The Swazis are a very low profile people; hence press coverage of negotiations when, in fact, the negotiations have not been concluded, are frowned upon.

Hilda Kuper (1986), in her book *The Swazi: A South African Kingdom,* notes the national consternation that resulted in 1982 when the South African press reported a controversial land deal between the Republic of South Africa and the Kingdom of Swaziland. The South African press had reported, albeit wrongly, that the government of Swaziland was negotiating with South Africa for the incorporation (into South Africa) of territories inhabited by ethnic Swazis. The truth of the matter was that the Swazi government was negotiating with the government of South Africa for the return to Swaziland of *Ka Ngwane*—the areas inhabited by ethnic Swazis in South Africa and which the South African government had granted the status of *Bantustans* or dependent homelands.

Negotiations for the return of these areas had started long before South Africa formulated its policy of Bantustans. According to Kuper, following the establishment of the Union of South Africa in 1910, Swaziland had negotiated the territories through the British. In 1966, when *Ka Ngwane* was pronounced a Bantustan, the *Ngwenyama,*

King Sobhuza, requested the British to ask the South Africans "to hold the matter in abeyance." Direct negotiations were resumed soon after Swazi independence in 1968. These negotiations, spanning several years, were highly secretive. Sobhuza operated in the background, acting through emissaries, especially his minister of Foreign Affairs, R. V. Dlamini. Most Swazi officials, according to Kuper, were neither consulted nor kept informed. All dealings were with accredited representatives of the South African government "on the grounds that international boundaries could only be negotiated by heads of independent states, not leaders of Bantustans or dependent homelands" (Kuper 1986, p. 156). While it is not exactly clear why the South Africans released their version of the negotiation to the press, that version evoked a feeling of betrayal and outrage in Swaziland.

Sobhuza responded by postponing the negotiations *indefinitely,* and calling a meeting later (March 19, 1982), at his *Lozitha* palace to clarify the position of his government. In attendance were heads of diplomatic missions in Swaziland, as well as all of Swaziland's ambassadors and high commissioners called home from abroad, and by members of parliament, permanent secretaries, and the Swazi National Council. He also dispatched a team of top-level officers to different African countries to explain the position of his government to African leaders.

Another verbal strategy that the Swazis employ during the bargaining process is to provide alternative suggestions or counterproposals. As Adler (1986, p. 176) notes, counterproposals involve negotiators responding to their opponents' proposals by simply offering their own proposal. Counterproposals are frequently used by the Swazis especially when the concept of sympathy, or appeal to emotions, as a verbal strategy fails. In some instances, notes Martin Dlamini, Swazis have occasionally, even in a subtle manner, prefixed their responses to negotiations with emotion-laden appeals. For example, a Swazi negotiator may refer to Swaziland's small size or that it is a disadvantaged developing country, as a tactic for winning concessions from the other party. However, as Fisher (1980) discovers in his study of Mexican negotiating styles (and this

applies to Swaziland as well), "where this approach crosses the line from being a sincere position to calculated tactics is not easily determined" (p. 25). Ambassador Carlton Dlamini further remarks that while the concept of sympathy may not be as pervasive as other strategies during negotiations, the Swazis may play, in a positive way, on the size of their country, the strength of their economy, their geographical location, and their peaceful coexistence with their neighbors as a basis for winning concessions. In reality, Swazis describe their country as the "Switzerland of Africa." Clearly that notion of its peace and stability in a region of great conflict, in addition to its large deposits of natural resources, make it a more important country in Southern Africa than its size would indicate. These factors embody the concept of a small but powerful country, which the Swazis often bring to the negotiating table as a strategy for influencing the bargaining process and outcomes.

Swazi verbal responses to requests sometimes leave the other party wondering what they have said or what they mean. When he is not sure how he wants to respond, a Swazi negotiator, as Martin Dlamini reveals, may use such phrases as, "Oh, I see, I see," while at the same time nodding his head. The nodding of the head does not necessarily indicate that he agrees with what the other party is saying. This behavior often creates problems for the foreign negotiating team. Again, when he is not sure of what responses to provide, a Swazi negotiator may use the phrase, "Well, I think this may need the approval of the king."

Negotiators

We turn now to the negotiators themselves. How are they selected? In general, a Swazi negotiating team is composed mainly of a wide range of officials appointed because of their status and loyalty to the *Ngwenyama,* their experience in the bureaucracy, and their technical expertise. Because Swaziland is traditionally a monarchy, there is a conscious effort to include a symbolic representative of the king in the negotiating teams. The king's representative is selected on account of his age, wisdom in traditional precedence, and loyalty to the royal family.

He is perceived as the *Ngwenyama's* "ears" and "eyes" at the meetings, even though he may have no knowledge of the subject matter. Usually the official chief negotiator is a senior person with sufficient status and experience to serve as a symbolic representative of the domestic consensus. He could be a cabinet minister or a permanent secretary, for example. Then there is a person(s) with the technical expertise—usually a younger person. While the chief negotiator may know and say little about the subject matter, he usually refers the matter to the younger person with the specialized knowledge. As a rule, many of these younger specialists have acquired their education and training at colleges and universities in the United States, the United Kingdom, or at the University of Swaziland. In dealing with foreigners, particularly whites, Western education is recognized as an asset, and young people with this qualification are occupying important positions within the bureaucracy (Kuper, 1986, p. 35).

Like the selection process, the process of decision making is highly centralized in Swaziland. Swazi negotiators do not have a wide latitude to commit the country to certain deals, without the approval of higher authorities. Certain issues, for example, the land negotiations with South Africa, require the final approval of the *Ngwenyama* or the full *Ligogo* (the inner council).

In general, trying to influence the process of decision making in Swaziland is a delicate issue, as the Swazis are suspicious of attempts by foreigners to manipulate them or to goad them into making precipitous and costly decisions. The story is told by a prominent observer of Southern Africa that he was conversing with the late King Sobhuza about the problem of South African political refugees—and even freedom fighters—using Swaziland as a base for operations. Although Swaziland did not allow its territory to be used as a base by the freedom fighters, there was considerable pressure from other African leaders for it to do so. Sobhuza, an aging but astute politician, commented, "I feel like a man sitting in my home facing a poised snake. I am trying to be very calm and avoid sudden movement. Meanwhile my friends outside the door are throwing rocks at the snake. I am the one endangered, not they" (Grotpeter, 1975).

While caution predominates the Swazi approach to bargaining, it must be noted that increasing contact with the outside world, both economic and political, means that Swaziland must adjust certain aspects of its "traditional" negotiating style. "The status quo is already losing its touch," says Martin Dlamini. He recalls several negotiations with the World Bank and the IMF for loan agreements, pointing out that "Swazi negotiators are abandoning our traditional approach to negotiations, and instead, are throwing their cards first on the drawing board, without first *listening* to what the other party has to offer. In the final analysis, too little is achieved, too much concessions are made to the detriment of Swazi national interests."

We have already noted certain aspects of protocol and formalities in negotiations with the Swazis, but suffice it to state (and this is important) that the American custom of addressing people (negotiators) by their first names is not accepted by them. During the December 1987 Reagan-Gorbachev meeting in Washington, D.C., President Reagan informed the American audience that he and Soviet General Secretary Gorbachev have agreed to call each other by their first names—Ronnie and Mikhail. But this egalitarian behavior has long been recognized as a threat to international protocol. Swazis frown at such cross-cultural noise. Nobody ever addresses the *Ngwenyama* by his first name; only by his official title. Both the *Ngwenyama* and the *Ndlovukazi* receive elaborate deference during official ceremonies. Royal speeches, according to Kuper (1986, p. 158), are punctuated with flattering titles: "He is 'The Lion,' 'The Sun,' 'The Milky Way,' 'Obstacle to the Enemy.' She is 'The Lady Elephant,' 'The Earth,' 'The Beautiful,' 'Mother of the Country,'" and so on. Other Swazis, as a rule, prefer to be addressed formally during negotiations.

Also, when shaking hands with Swazi officials prior to the actual negotiations, the Swazis prefer that the foreign negotiators do so the "Swazi way," using both hands, with the left hand holding the arm very close to the wrist of the extended right hand. Swazis consider this a sign of respect, and the behavior comes from Swazi philosophy that in receiving something from a person, you must do so fully and sincerely. Putting one hand in one's pocket while shaking hands with the other, notes Martin Dlamini, is considered noise, a mark of disrespect, and could create a barrier to effective communication during negotiations.

Finally, as a people steeped in tradition, the Swazis like their culture to be esteemed. Knowledge of a few Swazi words places the foreign negotiator at an advantage. It opens up the door to relationship building, an important aspect of Swazi negotiating style. In the final analysis, a foreign negotiator must learn to be patient, and gradually build the trust that is needed for negotiating successfully with the Swazis.

Notes

1. The terms *negotiation* and *bargaining* are used interchangeably in this paper. This position is supported by some theorists such as Shelling (1960) and Putnam and Jones (1982), who argue that the processes and characteristics of bargaining and negotiations are similar to one another. The difference, however, may be in the degree of interactions. While bargaining may involve interactions among small units, negotiations often involve interactions among large social units. But such differences do not obviate the fact that at both levels of interaction, the interactants may use similar approaches or strategies to argue their cases.

2. *Bantu* literally stands for "People," in SiSwati, the Swazi language. It is a linguistic label derived from the root *ntu,* meaning "person," and the plural prefix *ba.* For a detailed analysis of the Swazi people and their history, see, for example, Kuper, Hilda, *The Swazi: A South African kingdom. Case studies in cultural anthropology, 1986.*

3. *Ngwenyama* is a Swazi word for "The Lion." It is a title used for all Swazi kings, including the current one—twenty-year-old King Mswati III.

References

Adler, N. (1986). *International dimension of organizational behavior.* Boston, MA: Kent Publishing Company.

Awa, N. (1987). *Communication in Africa: Implications for development planning.* Paper presented at the 37th Annual Convention of the International Communication Association, Montreal, Canada.

Binnendijk, H. (Ed.). (1987). *National negotiating styles.* Washington, DC: Foreign Service Institute, Department of State.

Booth, A. (1983). *Swaziland: Tradition and change in a southern African kingdom.* Boulder, CO: Westview Press.

Burgoon, J., and Saine, T. (1978). *The unspoken dialogue. An introduction to non-verbal communication.* Boston: Houghton-Mifflin Press.

Fisher, G. (1980). *The cross-cultural dimension in international negotiation.* Rev. discussion paper prepared for the Foreign Service Institute, Washington, DC.

Grotpeter, J. J. (1975). *Historical dictionary of Swaziland.* Metuchen, NJ: Scarecrow Press, Inc.

Kuper, H. (1986). *The Swazi: A South African kingdom.* New York: Holt, Rinehart and Winston.

Olsson, M. (n.d.). *Meeting styles for intercultural groups.* Washington, DC: Society for Intercultural Education, Training and Research.

Putnam, L., and Jones, T. (1982). Reciprocity in negotiations: An analysis of bargaining interaction. *Communication monographs, 49,* 171–191.

Rubin, J., and Brown, B. (1975). *The social psychology of bargaining and negotiation.* New York: Academic Press.

Shelling, T. (1960). *The strategy of conflict.* Cambridge, MA: Harvard University Press.

Key Terms

Africa	emic
bargaining	negotiation
communication style	Swaziland
conflict resolution	

Discussion Questions

1. How does the Swazi style of conflict resolution compare with U.S. conflict resolution styles?

2. What is the role of intermediaries in Swazi negotiation?

3. What advice would you give Swazi students studying at a U.S. college about how to best deal with conflicts they may have with U.S. friends?

4. Nwosu researches from an interpretive perspective. How might a social science researcher investigate negotiation styles?

36 Crossing the Color Line
From Empathy to Implicature in Intercultural Communication

KAREN LYNNETTE DACE and MARK LAWRENCE MCPHAIL

In 1903 the African American historian W. E. B. DuBois (1982) argued that "the problem of the Twentieth century is the problem of the color line" (p. xi). When DuBois died three score years later, the line that divided African and European Americans seemed finally to be at a point where it would be erased, where individuals would be judged not by skin color but by character. As we approach the beginning of the 21st century, however, Blacks and Whites in this country continue to live in different emotional, intellectual, and material worlds, divided as much by psychological separation as by physical segregation. "It's sad," writes Nathan McCall (1994) in his best-selling book *Makes Me Wanna Holler*, "this gulf between blacks and whites. We're so afraid of each other" (p. 349). McCall's autobiography tells an emotionally powerful story of an African American man's personal growth and transformation, of a journey from the streets of a working-class neighborhood to prison, and finally to a position working on one of America's most prestigious newspapers, the *Washington Post*.

It is in the culmination of McCall's (1994) journey and in his own ambivalent feelings about racism that he articulates an important recognition of the problems and possibilities created by the color line in American society: "I have come to believe two things that might be contradictory," he writes. "Some of our worst childhood fears *were* true—the establishment *is* teeming with racism. Yet I also believe whites are as befuddled about race as we are, and they're as scared of us as we are of them. Many of them are seeking solutions, just like us" (p. 414). Although he frames his understanding in a language of difference, in the terms of "us" and "them," McCall's belief that both Whites and African Americans experience the fear and sadness of racial divisions, and that both may be seeking the same solutions, illustrates an attempt to cross the color

line by finding common ground, an attempt to establish what psychologists and communication scholars call "empathy," the ability to "feel with" another human being. It is in the psychological concept and communicative practice of empathy that, we believe, students and scholars of intercultural communication will find a strategy for addressing the difficulties of human difference and division, and for facilitating interracial identification.

This essay will present the perspectives of two African American communication researchers, one male and one female, both of whom have focused on issues of interracial communication and interaction, and both of whom believe that the concept of empathy holds significance for communication theory and practice in general and addresses issues of interracial interaction in particular. First, we discuss how the concept of empathy has been examined in various areas of communication scholarship, and how it might be usefully extended to the discussion of interracial communication. Then we each present personal narratives that illustrate, in our own voices, how empathy functions in our lives not only as a theoretical concept but as a practical strategy for understanding and dealing with racial differences. Finally, we extend the concept of empathy beyond its cognitive and affective emphases to suggest its potential as an ontological and epistemological principle that holds transformative possibilities for human consciousness, communication, and culture.

Empathy as Understanding and Sharing: Addressing the Problem of Being Human

Webster's New World Dictionary (1987) defines empathy as "intellectual or emotional identification with another" (p. 201), and the concept is generally seen as the psychological capacity to "feel with" another human being. Psychologist Carl Rogers (1967) defines empathy as the ability to understand another's "inner world of private personal meanings as if it were your own, but without ever losing the 'as if' quality" of the experience (p. 89). At its best, then, empathy encourages individuals to respect and appreciate cultural differences instead of simply erasing or ignoring them, and encourages communication that is nonjudgmental and accepting of others. Numerous scholars have considered how empathy might be useful in addressing rhetorical, interpersonal, intercultural, and performative aspects of communication. Charles Kelly (1973) offers a rhetorical consideration of "empathic listening," which involves "participation in the spirit of an environment as receiver" (p. 264) and "full attention to total communication environment" (p. 270). Brant Burleson (1983) discusses the concept of "emotional empathy," noting that "in emotionally empathizing with another, one does not merely recognize another's emotions, but also *shares* these emotions" (p. 297). He suggests that it is not sufficient to simply possess empathic skills, but that one must also be motivated to understand and share the experiences and feelings of others. The emphasis on both understanding and sharing exemplified in the rhetorical and interpersonal approaches to empathy also emerges in its intercultural and performative considerations.

Benjamin Broome (1991) explains that empathy is "a central characteristic of competent and effective intercultural communication" (p. 235), and Larry Samovar and Richard Porter (1995) echo Broome's findings when they note that "empathy can be increased if you resist the tendency to interpret the other's verbal and nonverbal actions from your culture's orientation. Learn to suspend, or at least keep in check, the cultural perspective that is unique to your experiences" (pp. 286–287). Samovar and Porter suggest that, in addition to its conceptual aspects, empathy also involves specific communicative behaviors. Myron Lustig and Jolene Koester (1996) offer an explanation of empathy similar to that presented by Rogers in that it emphasizes the "as if" dimension of empathy, noting that although it is impossible to put oneself in another's place, it is possible to "behave as if one

understands the world as others do" (p. 331). Empathy, they believe, contributes to intercultural awareness and understanding and is an important indicator of communicative competence.

Empathy also plays an important role in the study and practice of performance, as Jill Taft-Kaufman (1985) points out: "Through an understanding of theories of empathy, interpreters seek to explain the subtle process by which a performer becomes involved in a text and an audience becomes involved in an experience" (p. 171). Taft-Kaufman notes that the concept of empathy has evolved over time to reflect both its complexity and its importance for human interaction. Ronald Pelias (1982) considers this evolution in terms of the directions it offers for the field of performance and presents an integrative approach to understanding the concept. For Pelias, empathy is "a qualitative, developmental process in which individuals not only come to share and understand another's feelings but also consider the reasons and context that inform the other's feelings" (p. 527). Pelias calls for further amplification of the concept of empathy, both beyond its affective and cognitive dimensions and toward its implications for human being and knowing.

Such an amplification involves extending the concept of empathy beyond abstract psychological experience to the concrete emotional and intellectual practices of communicative behavior. We attempt to facilitate this amplification through personal narratives that illustrate how empathy has impacted our own understanding and behavior as they relate to interracial communication. Both narratives address the "gulf" that exists between African and European Americans and offer strategies and insights to suggest ways in which the conceptual and cultural divisions that separate us might be bridged. Karen Dace's narrative addresses the interpersonal and intercultural implications of the color line, and Mark McPhail considers how the study and practice of performance might enable us to cross that line. Together, they illustrate how the communicative practice of empathy can be extended to inform our theoretical understanding of difference through the idea of "implicature"—the notion that human beings are linguistically, materially, psychologically, and spiritually interrelated and interdependent, or "implicated" in each other. The move from empathy to implicature, we believe, represents a transformative evolution of the symbolic and social possibilities of dealing with dissonance and difference in communication between European Americans and African Americans.

Karen Lynnette Dace: Empathy as an Escape from Racial Reasoning

Before reading McCall's *Makes Me Wanna Holler,* I had never spent a great deal of time analyzing my friendships with European Americans, but I had always been aware that these friendships fell into at least three distinctions or categories. One relationship type is best characterized by our ability to discuss anything pertinent to our existence, including race and culture. A second relationship type consists of "guilty liberals" who pity my oppression more than they value my culture. Although these friendships provide an opportunity for an open and frank discussion of race, class, and gender, the tone is often apologetic—that is, these "guilty liberal" European Americans recognize what McIntosh (1986) identified as their "white privilege" and accept blame for every oppressive act perpetrated against people of color since the beginning of time. The third intercultural relationship type includes those European American friends with whom I can discuss anything, except race and culture. The fact that an essential part of who I am (and who they are) is taboo is a constant source of frustration. Similar feelings result when I am not allowed to discuss my concerns as an African American woman in my relationships with some African American men. Other than being aware of these distinctions, I gave very little thought to what makes these relationships work. On some level, they did work. That was all I needed to know.

That changed when I read the short but powerful chapter "Danny" in McCall's autobiography. I began to see similarities between McCall's relationship with the European American man after which the chapter is named and my relationship with a European American man named Bill. McCall's Danny lives in an African American neighborhood and is well-read in African American literature. Bill lived on Chicago's North Side in a predominantly European American neighborhood and was well-versed in blues. Although McCall does not talk about developing respect for Danny explicitly, as I read his narrative, that is what comes through. I developed respect for Bill when I learned that on two nights a week he coached a basketball team of kids from the Cabrini Green Housing Project. They played other "Green" kids every Saturday. The neighborhood is infamous, and certainly there are European Americans and African Americans who refuse to go anywhere near the area. The fact that Bill worked with these kids was not what impressed me. The fact that he kept his coaching a secret for some time, coupled with the knowledge that he was not required to do any type of community service by our employer or any other entity, moved me. I loved the fact that he never bragged about his participation in that league as if what he was doing deserved special recognition. When asked why he participated, Bill explained that he loved the kids and the sport.

I believe my respect for Bill and trust in the sincerity of his motives for friendship grew out of what I perceived as his empathy for the children at Cabrini Green. Unlike so many do-gooders from all cultures, Bill never asserted himself as a savior the kids should worship and be grateful to have in their lives. He was not condescending and neither looked for nor expected recognition. Bill was most concerned with understanding the kids' needs and being available to them at times and in ways that were important to them. He worked hard not to impose himself and his beliefs on the kids and their families. Bill's relationship with the children of the Cabrini Green Housing Project created the space for our relationship to grow.

McCall (1994) writes of Danny, "whenever he said something to me, there was a straightforwardness, a childlike honesty, that I didn't get from most other white people" (p. 343). The first time I read that passage, Bill came to mind. A few years ago, after I left the firm for graduate school and Bill left to work at a local radio station, he called me, deeply concerned. His new employer, a nationally recognized industry giant, instituted a service program in which a group of European American men worked as softball coaches for another group of inner-city, mostly African American, kids. This new program included weekly talks and workshops to help these men interact with the children. The night Bill called, their guest speaker had been an "angry African American woman." Bill explained, "everything she said was full of anger and fury. It was like she hated us." What separated Bill from the other men in the group, many of whom vowed not to return, was that he genuinely wanted to "understand her anger." We spent several hours that night discussing the source of that fury.

"Are *you* angry?" he wanted to know.

"Yes," I explained, quoting Toni Morrison's (1970) observation in *The Bluest Eye,* that "anger is better. There is a sense of being in anger. A reality and presence. An awareness of worth. It is a lovely surging" (p. 43). We talked about all major social movements resulting from anger. He tried to understand. What was most important to me was his wanting to understand. He tried to understand the source of African American anger, and he was willing to suspend his own preconceived notions and judgments in an effort to permit space for another point of view and experience.

My relationship with Bill has taught me three important things. First, all of my friendships with people outside of African American culture are initiated by those people. There are no instances where I did any of the preliminary work. Although I understand why this might be the case for most people of color, I am also struck by the problematic nature of this truth. Second, these relationships are characterized by sincerity on both our parts. Neither of us is out to prove we are exceptional because we have friendships across cultural lines. Instead, an empathic understanding drew us together and was sufficient to keep us interested in one another long enough for the development of deeper bonds. Finally, there has always been a certain sense of freedom on the part of those European Americans with whom I have developed friendships—that is, they feel comfortable enough to ask uncomfortable questions. Like Danny, these friends often ask "the damnedest things out of the blue." McCall (1994) recalls that Danny asked the questions most European Americans wanted to ask but refused to out of fear of being labeled racist:

But Danny didn't seem to care. I concluded it must have been because he was secure in his mind that he wasn't racist, and he had nothing to hide. He was simply curious. He didn't know, so he did what any intelligent person should have done: He asked rather than assume. I respected that about him and found that, in spite of myself, there was something about this dude I really liked. (p. 343)

When Danny left the newspaper where he and Nathan McCall once worked, he informed his African American friend that "you may not believe this, but there are several white people in the newsroom who are *really* good people. You should give them a chance before writing them off as racists. Get to know some of them. You might be pleasantly surprised" (pp. 348–349). There are times when I wonder if I might open myself up more and be more pleasantly surprised. My friendships with European Americans like Bill, though valuable, are also outnumbered by equally enduring relationships with African Americans. I am often curious about whether I have refused—out of fear—to admit others who are different (not just European Americans) to my circle of friends.

Understanding and addressing this fear may be the most important lesson that I have learned from my relationship with Bill. He has helped me deal with what Cornel West (1993) describes as "racial reasoning," the tendency to see interactions between European and African Americans in rigidly Black and White terms (pp. 37–38). McCall (1994) explains racial reasoning to Danny when he informs him that race "affects every facet of my life" (p. 346). Although Danny has the luxury of not having to think or feel about race, McCall does not: "I can't get away from it, man. I stay so mad all the time because I'm forced to spend so much time and energy reacting to race. I hate it. It wearies me. But there's no escape, man. No escape" (p. 246). As an African American woman, I can certainly empathize with McCall; yet, I can also appreciate Danny's recognition that the feelings of hate often reflected in reacting to race "ain't healthy" (p. 346). Danny, like my friend Bill, confirms that relationships between European and African Americans, like relationships in general, are seldom Black and White. Indeed, both these European American men give me some hope that there may be some escape from the prison of racial reasoning, and that empathy might just be the key.

Mark Lawrence McPhail: Unlocking the Self Through Empathic Performance

I teach a course called "African American Experiences" in the ethnic studies program at our university, and in it I require a final performance from a selection of African American literature. I relate performance to the African American experience through exploration of the oral influences on the culture, and also through a discussion of how the act of performance offers the opportunity to "get us out of our own heads," and experience—if only for a moment—what it might be like to be in someone else's. One student, a young European American man, performed a selection from the conclusion of the chapter entitled "Danny" in McCall's (1994) *Makes Me Wanna Holler* and stated in his introduction that it gave him "some sense of what it must be like to be a Black person." The section that he performed clearly illustrated the empathic potential of performance for both the writer and the reader: "The notion that one of them cared, really cared, about what I thought moved me. Danny was the first white person I met whom I actually saw trying to understand," recalls McCall. He also explains that his relationship with Danny helped him "better understand the fear and ignorance behind prejudice" and realize "that the education system in this country has failed white people more than it's failed anybody else. It has crippled them and limited their humanity" (p. 347). This failure reflects what is perhaps the greatest pitfall of racial reasoning.

In considering my own encounter with the difficulties of racial reasoning, I wish to reflect on the influence that two White men, the poet Robert Penn Warren and the rhetorical scholar Richard Lanham, have had on my personal and professional development. Their work has had particular impact on my own writing and performance. Warren's poetry has stayed with me throughout my educational and professional career and influenced my own writing

perhaps most powerfully in a piece I authored in college entitled "Between Two Cities." The poem attempted to imitate the aesthetic qualities I admired in Warren's (1978) "American Portrait Old Style," which ends with the statement that "love is a hard thing to outgrow" (p. 7). Lanham's (1976) discussion of "the rhetorical ideal of life" (pp. 1–35) helped me come to grips with what it meant to be "between two cities," not only in relation to the "double-consciousness" that W. E. B. DuBois (1982) saw as an essential aspect of the African American experience (p. 45), but also in terms of the human struggle between emotion and reason, between what Lanham (1976) calls the "social" and "central" selves (p. 6).

I wrote "Between Two Cities" as a tribute to Warren when I was a junior in college, and it continues, to paraphrase the late James Baldwin (1974), to "spell out the language of my life" (p. 65). It embodies the experience of the intersections between communication and culture that have shaped my life since high school, where I was first introduced to the writings of an elderly southern White man whose words spoke to me in powerful ways, influencing my writing of poetry in college and my study of performance in graduate school. Perhaps more important, the poem reflects the tensions that occur when one chooses to live emotionally and intellectually between the opposing poles of Whiteness and Blackness that circumscribe racial reasoning, to accept and embrace one's Africanness as well as one's Americanness. Critics on both sides of the color line might view the acceptance and embracing of both Blackness and Whiteness as indecision at best, or "collaborating with the enemy" at worst, but I choose to view this as a manifestation of the "two-ness" spoken of by DuBois (1982, p. 6), a two-ness that is paralleled in the personality of what Richard Lanham (1976) calls "Homo Rhetoricus": rhetorical man (p. 6).

The distinguishing characteristic of that personality is, in Lanham's (1976) account, the love of language and performance. "Rhetorical man is an actor; his reality public, dramatic. His sense of identity, his self, depends on the reassurance of daily histrionic reenactment. He is thus centered in time and concrete local event" (p. 4). This performative quality of existence emphasizes emotion and empathy. As Lanham explains, rhetorical man "usually has the sense of humor to know that he—and others—not only may *think* differently, but may *be* differently. He pays a price for this, of course—religious sublimity, and its reassuring, if breathtaking, unities" (p. 5). The "rhetorical ideal of life" offers a way of knowing and being that recognizes interdependence and interrelatedness. It is, like love, a hard thing to outgrow. Yet it is a way of knowing and being from which racial reasoning attempts to free us. But, as Lanham states, we cannot be free from it:

> If truly free of rhetoric, we would be pure essence. We would retain no social dimension. We would divest ourselves of the very mechanism of forgiveness. For what is forgiveness but the acknowledgment that the sinner sinning is not truly himself, but plays a misguided role. If always truly ourselves, which of us shall scape hanging? (p. 8)

We would, in short, rid ourselves of the capacity for emotional connection, of empathy. We would be trapped in, as Lanham describes it, "the nightmarish prison of unchanging essence" (p. 8), and we would lose what Vincent Crapanzano (1985) calls "that small space of freedom that is at the heart of humanity and enables us to engage in a vital manner with those about us" (p. 20). Our ability to connect to one another would indeed be crippled, and our humanity limited, and our differences would continue to divide us from one another, in the segregated cells of a prison of our own making.

What I have learned from Warren and Lanham, however, is that performative empathy—the rhetorical ideal of life—may be the key to unlocking these cells. Embracing Warren's aesthetic influence and performing his poetry have taught me that the spaces that connect us, a young African American and an old southern American, are potentially just as powerful as those that separate us. Lanham's criticism has shown me a transformative vision of language, life, and method, one that transcends material realities and touches the spiritual ideals of our humanity, despite our differences of race, age, or ideology. These two White men have taught me important and lasting lessons about the problems and possibilities of racial identity, and had I not been

willing to listen to and experience their words, I would not be who I am today. Perhaps the young European American student who encountered McCall's words will be similarly moved and will become another in the chorus of voices speaking into being a more coherent understanding of human interaction, one that resists racial reasoning. Such an understanding is certainly needed, for as Cornel West (1993) observes: "Either we learn a new language of empathy and compassion, or the fire this time will consume us all" (p. 8).

From Empathy to Implicature: Creating a New Language of Compassion

The concept of empathy provides an important touchstone for transforming how we think about and enact language practices, and its significance for communication cuts across the various divisions within the discipline. Although empathy has been explored in terms of its emotional and intellectual dimensions in rhetorical, interpersonal, intercultural, and performance studies, we might look beyond the surface of the concept to consider its larger implications for human knowledge and existence. Empathy, as traditionally conceived, assumes a view of the world in which self and other are essentially separate and distinct. This view of the world, however, has been challenged dramatically in a number of disciplines, from philosophy to physics, by the notion that our separateness is an illusion, and that *in reality,* we are all essentially implicated in each other. From this perspective, empathy is a state of mind that reflects an underlying state of being, an experience of reality that is defined not by separateness but by wholeness, or what we have chosen to call "implicature."

One of the most powerful expressions of implicature is seen in the writings of the late David Bohm (1987), a physicist who explains how our prevailing beliefs about existence and knowing separate us from one another psychologically, physically, and spiritually. Bohm contends that this view of reality deals only with its "explicate" manifestations, and that another view, one that recognizes the "implicate order" of existence, will enable us to better deal with the divisions and fragmentation that affect human individual and collective experience. The implicate order reflects "the unbroken wholeness of the totality of existence as an undivided flowing movement without borders" (p. 7). It represents an empathic connection not only with human beings, but with reality itself, because it assumes that just as we all are implicated, at a fundamental level, in one another's lives, so too are all aspects of existence implicated in one another.

Implicature extends the notion of empathy from the psychological to the physical by acknowledging that self and other are never separate and distinct, but are always interdependent and interrelated. Whereas empathy reflects psychological aspects of human experience and understanding, implicature reflects the lived, "dialogic" experience of otherness in which, according to Mikhail Bahktin (1986), "I realize myself through others." Bahktin's conceptualization of dialogue points to the intersection of experience and consciousness that undergirds implicature: "Just as a body is formed initially in the mother's womb (body), a person's consciousness awakens wrapped up in another's consciousness" (p. 138). Implicature intimates that the separation of self and other that begins at birth can be attenuated in those intimate spaces of interaction in which separation and division is transformed through a conscious and embodied embracing of difference.

Recognizing and cultivating implicature is a critical task for students and scholars of communication, and the exploration of the significance of empathy for human symbolic and social interactions is certainly a step in the right direction. Still, we believe that more theoretical and practical work is needed, especially if we are serious about healing the divisions created by differences of communication, culture, and consciousness. In the realm of interracial relations, the need for continued inquiry and action is clearly evident. If, as Karen Dace (1994) suggests, the present state of African and European American symbolic interaction "leads one to wonder if there can ever be a different kind of communication between these two groups" (p. 18), then it is imperative that we begin to examine existing concepts, as well as to articulate new

ones, that will enable us to reframe our interactions and relationships. In this essay, we have attempted to suggest through theoretical insight and practical experience that the move from empathy to implicature might facilitate such a reframing. If we are correct, then perhaps the problem of the 21st century will no longer be the problem of the color line.

References

Bahktin, M. M. (1986). *Speech genres and other late essays.* Austin: University of Texas Press.

Baldwin, J. (1974). *If Beale Street could talk.* New York: Dial Press.

Bohm, D. (1987). *Wholeness and the implicate order.* London: Routledge and Kegan Paul.

Broome, B. (1991). Building shared meaning: Implications of a relational approach to empathy for teaching intercultural communication. *Communication Education, 40,* 235–249.

Burleson, B. (1983). Social cognition, empathic motivation, and adult's comforting strategies. *Human Communication Research, 10,* 295–304.

Crapanzano, V. (1985). *Waiting: The whites of South Africa.* New York: Random House.

Dace, K. (1994). Dissonance in European-American and African-American communication. *Western Journal of Black Studies, 18,* 18–26.

DuBois, W. E. B. (1982). *The souls of black folks.* New York: New American Library. (Original work published in 1903)

"Empathy." (1987). *Webster's new world dictionary.* New York: Warner Books.

Kelly, C. (1973). Empathic listening. In J. Trent, J. Trent, & D. O'Neill (Eds.), *Concepts in communication* (pp. 263–272). Boston: Allyn and Bacon.

Lanham, R. (1976). *The motives of eloquence.* New Haven, CT: Yale University Press.

Lustig, M., & Koester, J. (1996). *Intercultural competence: Interpersonal communication across cultures.* New York: HarperCollins.

McCall, N. (1994). *Makes me wanna holler: A young black man in America.* New York: Random House.

McIntosh, P. (1986, April). *White privilege and male privilege: A personal accounting of coming to see correspondence through work in women's studies.* Paper presented at the Virginia Women's Studies Association Conference, Richmond, VA.

Morrison, T. (1970). *The bluest eye.* New York: Pocket Books.

Pelias, R. (1982). Empathy: Some implications of social cognition research for interpretation study. *Central States Speech Journal, 33,* 519–532.

Rogers, C., & Stevens, B. (1967). *Person to person: The problem of being human.* New York: Simon & Schuster.

Samovar, L., & Porter, R. (1995). *Communication between cultures* (2nd ed.). Belmont, CA: Wadsworth.

Taft-Kaufman, J. (1985). Oral interpretation: Twentieth century theory and practice. In T. Benson (Ed.), *Speech communication in the 20th century* (pp. 157–183). Carbondale: Southern Illinois University Press.

Warren, R. P. (1978). *Now and then: Poems 1976–1978.* New York: Random House.

West, C. (1993). *Race matters.* Boston: Beacon Press.

Key Terms

color line
dialogue
double-consciousness
empathy
implicate order

implicature
racial reasoning
rhetorical ideal of life
wholeness

Discussion Questions

1. Discuss how the move from empathy to implicature might be achieved in any of the following arenas of interaction: religion, gender, class, ability.

2. What are some of the barriers that exist between African Americans and European Americans that make empathy difficult? How might implicature help us understand these barriers?

3. How might we think of implicature in terms of the intimate relationships we have with others in our lives? Is it possible, or desirable, to extend the type of intimacy we experience with those who are close to us to others who are significantly different?

4. Karen Dace suggests that the present state of race relations between African Americans and European Americans "leads one to wonder if there can ever be a different kind of communication between these two groups." Respond to Dace's suggestion by discussing your perceptions of existing communication between African and European Americans as well as what a "different kind of communication" would look like.

5. Mark McPhail suggests that performance can provide opportunities for people from different backgrounds to experience "otherness" in positive and productive ways. Do you agree or disagree? Give concrete examples from your own experience to support your answer.

37 Mass-Mediated Communication and Intercultural Conflict

FERNANDO DELGADO

Conflict has typically been conceptualized and examined by communication scholars as an interpersonal issue. For example, communication scholar Mary Jane Collier (1991) suggests that "conflict occurs when *relational partners* perceive incompatibility in such diverse areas as ideas, values, emotions, needs, access to resources, and constraints on action" (p. 132). Intercultural communication textbooks also tend to reinforce this in-

terpersonal perspective (Gudykunst & Kim, 1992, pp. 84–87; Lustig & Koester, 1993, pp. 268–271).

This essay takes a different approach to intercultural conflict. I share with intercultural scholars the perception that conflict is an integral part of intercultural contact, and that it often results from clashes between dissimilar cultural experiences and meaning-making systems. However, I also believe that culture transcends the dyad and exists at all levels of communication, from the interpersonal to the mass-mediated. Therefore, I argue that intercultural conflict should be examined in contexts other than interpersonal communication, specifically in mass-mediated and popular culture forms.

In what follows I review and assess the interpersonal emphasis in intercultural communication study. I then describe and discuss two forms of conflict related to the transmission and reception of mass-mediated and popular culture. Such moves are important if we are to enrich what we do in intercultural communication research.

Interpersonal Emphasis in Intercultural Communication

As I have already noted, intercultural scholars mainly study interpersonal contact. The intimate relationship between interpersonal and intercultural communication has developed principally because of the theoretical, methodological, and disciplinary biases of many intercultural researchers. For example, William Gudykunst (1984) has noted several shortfalls of intercultural research; nevertheless, he bases his perspective of intercultural communication on the presumption that *dyads* are the ground for intercultural inquiry.

Nwankwo (1979) has written that "some communication scholars have tried to limit intercultural communication to the interpersonal level of interaction and to distinguish it from such other forms of communication as interracial, interethnic, international, and cross cultural communication" (p. 325). Nwankwo suggests that these tendencies among intercultural scholars reflect personal and collective research biases rather than actual human (and cultural) contact or behavior. Intellectual choices are often made to delimit an area of inquiry and justify teaching activities, but in this case they reduce our understanding of culture in the context of intercultural contact.

Therefore, when intercultural communication scholars examine conflict, it is not surprising that they envision an interaction between two people of dissimilar cultural backgrounds with different motivations, goals, behaviors, and symbol systems. For example, Ting-Toomey (1988) explains that "conflict is a pervasive phenomenon that penetrates all forms of social and personal relationships in all cultures. Partners in a conflict situation typically bargain over many facets of the conflict process" (p. 213). This perspective, however valid, provides only a partial view of culture, communication, and conflict. If conflict is a clash between cultures' values, norms, symbols, ideologies, and political autonomy or national sovereignty (as in the cases of the former Yugoslavia or Soviet Union), then the interpersonal perspective is too restrictive.

On the other hand, if we take culturalist approaches (Hall, 1959) literally—that communication is culture and vice versa—any symbolic activity that crosses or links cultures can be defined as intercultural contact without distinguishing or privileging levels or even contexts of interaction. Let us look at how intercultural conflict can be seen as something more than a clash between dissimilar interactants of a dyad.

Culture, Conflict, and the Media

Most intercultural scholars share the perspective that communication and culture are dynamically interrelated. Robert Shuter (1998) argues that practical concerns—economic, political, technological, social—should inform a return to the study of culture by communication scholars: "Compelling global conditions require intercultural researchers to alter their research agenda and return culture to preeminence in their studies" (p. 42). Such research could involve interpersonal, small group, and organizational as well as rhetorical, media, and political research.

Intercultural communication can include more than two people, and conflict often involves a level of cultural contact beyond the dyadic interaction. For example, when nations negotiate in diplomacy, they do so with political and national concerns in mind but through members who reflect cultural perspectives and imperatives. Such contact is clearly more than interpersonal communication. Moreover, when we broadly consider the exchange of symbols and meanings from one group to another, the possible interactive contexts and levels expand to include peace (and diplomacy) communication (see Korzenny & Ting-Toomey, 1990) as well as the interrelated areas of mass-mediated communication inquiry, which include developmental communication, global and world communication, and international communication (Mowlana, 1986; Nordenstreng & Schiller, 1993).

The reality of international politics, the development of communication and transportation technologies, and the expansion of globalized economics mean that cultural contact through various forms of mediated and unmediated forms of communication is a given. Nations must negotiate to reach agreements, develop alliances, and engage in and resolve international conflicts. The prevalence and power of mediated forms of communication (computer technology, telephone, television, film, even radio) make intercultural contact—communication that crosses cultural and national borders—all the more pervasive. But such contact can lead to intercultural conflict because of economic and political conflicts as well as clashes over values.

In the following sections, I examine two interrelated aspects of intercultural conflict at the macrolevels: First, I survey debates over media domination related to information and media flows. Second, I examine ideological and cultural critiques of American culture based on structural rather than interpersonal contact.

INTERNATIONAL COMMUNICATION: NEW WORLD INFORMATION AND COMMUNICATION ORDER DEBATES

In this first example I examine how mass communication can be understood as a form of cultural, and hence intercultural, contact that leads to conflict. More specifically, by surveying intellectual and ideological debates regarding media domination (or imperialism) and a world information order, we can see that intercultural conflict is a reality beyond interpersonal contact. Sean Macbride and Colleen Roach (1993) explain that "[r]esolutions, meetings, and manifestos [often involving UNESCO and the United Nations] calling for a 'new order' in international information structures and policies became a feature of the world scene in the early 1970s and generated intense dispute" (p. 3). The debate re-

garding the control and domination over media technology and cultural forms, and the broader arguments over media imperialism, are examples of macrolevel intercultural conflict.

Briefly, the New World Information and Communication Order (NWICO) debates arose from nonaligned and developing (Third World) nations' concerns over the pattern and speed of national and international communication systems; the role of the mass media in the international sphere (with special emphasis on the political and economic impacts); and potential for egalitarian and democratic restructuring of international information systems (Kleinwachter, 1993, pp. 15–17). These abstract concerns are more concrete when seen from a communication perspective. Much of the debate centers on (1) the unequal distribution of and control over means of communication; (2) the related imbalance or inequity of the flow of media products; and (3) the distortion of media coverage regarding developing regions by more powerful First World nations (Galtung & Vincent, 1992, pp. 1–24; Kleinwachter, 1993).

The United States, with its vast technological resources and economic development, is at the forefront of these debates and conflicts. As *the* communication power, the United States dominates global cultural and entertainment markets. As former president Ronald Reagan approvingly noted:

> [O]ur culture is as powerful and transcendent as our military. In 1989, America made the top five movies in Greece, Ireland, Italy, the Netherlands, Norway, Switzerland, Hungary, Bolivia, Brazil, Australia, and Japan. In October 1991, almost half of the top fifty T.V. entertainment programs in Italy and Spain were American—including programs like *Cheers* and *Golden Girls*. (Cited in Lincoln, 1994, p. 152)

Such cultural dominance, though celebrated at home, can spark intercultural conflicts because it inhibits the development of other nations' indigenous popular culture products, stunts their economic development, and foists U.S. values and perspectives on other cultures. These effects, in turn, often lead to resentment and conflict. For example, Henry Comor, in defending Canadian cultural products, has observed that "American television has made the development of a Canadian cultural identity almost impossible" (in Schiller, 1992, p. 123). Comor's sentiments are reflective of nations' desires to defend their industries and culture from undue outside influence.

Although a critique of technological control or of the dominance over the economic benefits related to media and entertainment industries is valuable, several scholars have also focused on the impact of the ideas and values that international media flows can transmit (Tunstall, 1994). Taken as a whole, the elements of mass media can pose a threat to national sovereignty as well as cultural development and identity (Garnham, 1993). For example, the economic needs of a commercialized television network alter the relationship among entertainment product, corporate entity, audience, and consumption values in ways that may not be typical or "natural" to a culture; though, retrospectively, these relationships appear natural to Americans.

Herbert Schiller (1992) argues that U.S. mass-media corporations are part of a military-industrial complex that seeks world domination by pursuing pocketbooks as well as minds, as reflected in Reagan's remarks. This is achieved, for example, when American media companies pursue a strategy similar to that of Japanese electronic companies allegedly "dumping" their products in the United States. Media scholar Jeremy Tunstall (1994) describes how this happens:

> [T]he standard American practice in all media fields is to initially undercut the opposition through price competition; this follows from the enormous numbers of publications and broadcast outlets in the U.S.A. The policy is wide sales at low prices. (p. 42)

The effect of such practices is that products from Hollywood and New York dominate the markets in Europe, Asia, Latin America, and Africa. It is this kind of market domination that has sparked the conflict and debate over the control of information and communication technology.

Critical and Marxist scholars such as Schiller note the interconnectedness between our global economic and political domination and the diffusion and penetration of our cultural products. In short, what we might consider a TV sitcom in the United States might be considered, or function as, propaganda elsewhere. Joseph Straubhaar (1991) argues that there is an asymmetrical interdependence among most nations when it comes to popular and media culture forms. In practicality what that means is that movie houses, television stations, and record stores in faraway lands display many of the cultural products we experience here. The reverse, although possible, is not nearly as prevalent or obvious. For example, India produces many more films than Hollywood, but few Indian films are available in the United States. Although American films (or television programs) are arguably aesthetically pleasing, they indisputably transmit cultural perspectives and values that often clash with and overrun local cultures.

The New World Information and Communication Order debates are fundamentally about access, equality, and flow of communication, and hence culture. It is clear that multinational entities, which do not respect national borders, are increasingly paying for the expansion and diffusion of media technologies and content. The domination of technological markets and entertainment industries has political as well as economic and cultural effects. Cultural groups who feel that they are being economically and culturally dominated predictably react with feelings of resentment. The rise of multinational corporations and alliances shifts the debate somewhat, but experience tells us that the United States, along with its culture and ideology, will remain a leader in the hierarchy of popular and media culture dissemination. At the same time, it is also clear that developed and developing nations will resent that presence and dominance.

CULTURAL CRITICISM: UGLY AMERICA, UGLY AMERICANS

Indirectly related to the New World Information and Communication Order debate, another form of intercultural conflict is reflected in the work of cultural critics. These cultural critics include academicians, journalists, and politicians who speak and write about issues affecting their respective cultures. They often write about the preservation of the best of their home cultures and at the same time are highly critical of other cultures. As a highly visible cultural superpower, the United States has been on the receiving end of several such satirical and scathing critiques. These critiques often reflect intercultural conflict in mediated rather than interpersonal levels of conflict.

As a teenager, I spent time in Europe and was able to see how American media and culture existed in a foreign context. In one instance I was struck by the incongruity of seeing street graffiti admonishing "Yankees go home!" and the same day seeing *How the West Was Won* dubbed in Spanish for Spain's national network. The incongruity grew as my Spanish friends and I sat around in our Rolling Stones t-shirts, Levi's, and Adidas tennis shoes and drank Coca-Cola. It was during this time that French cultural minister Jack Lang began to criticize media imperialism; these critiques turned into protectionist policies with respect to the culture industries of France (issues revisited during the 1993 General Agreement on Trade and Tariffs [GATT] negotiations). Lang's rhetoric was both protectionist in defending France's cultural autonomy and chauvinist in attacking the cultural value of U.S. cultural products. In both of these examples we can see mediated, rather than interpersonal, intercultural contact and conflict.

During a recent trip to Europe, I again noticed the presence of anti-American sentiments. For example, graffiti, newspapers, and television programs in Spain and France disparaged the U.S. policy toward the former Yugoslavia and continued to label the United States as an imperial power. At the same time, youth fashions, popular music, television, film, and now automobiles bore the unmistakable imprint of U.S. products. Only fast-food outlets, perhaps the ultimate sign of American cultural exportation, seem to be out of fashion or in decline. Yet, a palpable sense of resentment, frustration, and disdain among the locals coexisted with an amazement at the penetration of U.S. popular culture.

Politics, economics, and technology clearly accelerate networks for intercultural contact while blurring national borders and cultural boundaries— consequently provoking intercultural conflict in many instances. European scholars, grappling with the cultural dilemmas caused by the European Union, continue to note the presence and impact of U.S. culture and products on foreign soil. Whether we call it internationalization or globalization, political and economic forces are bringing cultures together. During my stay in Spain, I was also struck by the availability of American television there, now in network form via cable systems rather than dated reruns. Indeed, in Madrid one could catch Conan O'Brien, in English, through the National Broadcasting Company's (NBC) feed. But television watchers could just as easily choose from programming offered by ESPN and CNN. Satellite and cable communications have indeed shrunk the physical space of the world. But a shrunken global village does not necessarily make for a global community or foster a sense of unity.

Three noted European critics—Umberto Eco, Jean Baudrillard, and Vicente Verdú—have assessed American culture with varying degrees of vitriol, amazement, and shock as they analyze various forms of cultural conflict brought on by the forces of globalization. Eco (1986), often in cautious terms, finds ways to compare (rather unfavorably) European popular and "high" cultures with the cultural activities and life found in the United States. Exemplars of European popular culture are often described by Eco as "subdued, [and] diffident [whereas] their American counterparts are loud and aggressive" (p. 12). Indeed, Eco's assessment of American popular culture is peppered with adjectives such as "crude," "loud," "fake," and "violent." It is as if Eco were shocked by the sheer scale and intensity of U.S. popular culture. Noting a culture rife with imitations, illusions, and the absence of authenticity, Eco writes that "the ideology of this America wants to reestablish reassurance through Imitation. But profit defeats ideology, because the consumers want to be thrilled not only by the guarantee of the Good but also by the shudder of the Bad" (p. 57).

In his book *Travels in Hyperreality,* Eco (1986) visits the United States and finds a world of playgrounds, wax museums, zoos, and amusement parks and observes reconstructions of environments that never were. We too can see the incongruity in American culture: a resort in Las Vegas that purports to recreate the physical structures and inner soul of New York; a Disneyland that gives tourists "a small world" to cavort in while elsewhere reconstructing a politically correct "Pirates of the Caribbean" ride. Or perhaps we could look at department stores touting "genuine virgin acrylic" or "authentic reproduction" in order to sell blankets and collectibles. Between the lines of his writing we can almost hear Eco, the Italian intellectual, noting that Europe retains its experience while the United States copies just enough so that what was real can be marketed to those who seek safe, sanitary, and entertaining approximations.

In a direct indictment of the restructuring and recontextualizing of experience that is at the heart of American popular culture, Eco (1986), promoting and hoping for an alternative path for Italian culture, asks "what could happen when we attain the levels of institutionalized cultural showmanship that have been reached in the United States?" (p. 155). Eco answers his own question and simultaneously delivers a devastating critique of American culture:

> If cultural performance is going to follow this road, then we have little to be content about. Not because the show is "cultural," but because it is a "show" in the worst sense of the word: a false life depicted on the stage so that the witnesses, in silence, may have the illusion of living, through an intermediary. (p. 156)

It is clear that Eco is concerned about cultures, specifically European, becoming infected by the corrosive inauthenticity and crass commercialization he sees in American popular culture. The cultural conflict is insinuated, the European communities, more sensitive to history, are contrasted with the constructed and commodified audiences of the United States.

If Eco worries about the simulations that mark American popular culture, Jean Baudrillard revels in them. In his travelogue, *America,* Baudrillard (1988) picks up on Eco's themes: "America ducks the question of origins; it cultivates no origin or mythical authenticity; it has no past and founding

truth. Having known no primitive accumulation of time, it lives in a perpetual present" (p. 76).

Baudrillard (1988) is amazed at what Americans have created in the United States, yet there is also a sense of mocking, a subtle and stinging critique of U.S. culture, in his work. Baudrillard is clear to distinguish, as Eco did, Europe from America: "[T]he confrontation between America and Europe reveals not so much a rapprochement as a distortion, an unbridgeable rift. There isn't just a gap between us, but a whole chasm of modernity" (p. 73). It is as if Baudrillard is suggesting that Europe grew with all the ugliness, dirtiness, and naturalness that is human existence whereas America is like a test-tube baby subsequently raised in a sterile environment with no past, only brilliant present and future, and Utopia within its grasp. But reading Baudrillard, one is also led to believe that if Americans could not find Utopia, they would manufacture a close approximation of it and sell tickets to the attraction.

As with Eco, Baudrillard (1988) seems to be descriptive, assessing what he sees but not being overly judgmental. That is deceptive. In Baudrillard's work we can observe the seeds of cultural conflict between the old and new worlds. The old world evolved, learned, and matured; its weaknesses documented, its strengths to be protected. The United States has different origins and elements, "America is neither dream nor reality . . . America is a giant hologram" (pp. 28–29). Baudrillard respects the technical acumen and commitment that has created America, appreciates the success that Americans have achieved in short order, and notes the sheer egoism of our culture. But he does not see these achievements and values as possible or desirable in other cultural contexts. In fact, Baudrillard can be read as particularly disdainful of Americans: "For me there is no truth of America. I ask only of the Americans that they be American. I do not ask them to be intelligent, sensible, [or] original" (p. 27).

If Eco and Baudrillard are seductive, even playful in their critiques, Vicente Verdú (1996), in his *El Planeta Americano* (The American Planet), is blunt. Verdú finds the United States and the American people easy to critique as boorish, vulgar, overly prideful. His text is a polemic against the United

States' global economic, ideological, and cultural hegemony. In short, his work is a warning to Europeans to avoid all that is culturally American. Briefly, several examples illustrate Verdú's position. On the U.S. secondary education system Verdú writes,

> [A]t that level we are talking about a vocational education that, more than anything, attempts to form determined citizens, with a strong dosage of self-esteem and self-confidence. Strong and apt to develop within the United States, where they not only are but where they believe the world will come to be. (p. 15; Verdú's work is in Spanish, all translations are mine)

Verdú perceives a destructive cultivation of individual ego and collective ethnocentrism among Americans that is also present in our culture and social institutions.

Verdú (1996) finds much to criticize. Whether it be our incongruent celebration of religion and obscenity or our anti-intellectualism, Verdú perceives American culture to be of questionable value. The incongruity of the church next to the porn palace, cultural elites complaining about nudity in film while celebrating rapacious violence, and the denigration of educated people as "impractical" confuses and dismays Verdú. For example, if Americans were to say they have the best cinematic resources, Verdú would ask then why are Arnold Schwarzenneger and Sylvester Stallone films so popular? Any culture that makes Beavis and Butthead cultural icons is difficult to defend against Verdú's thesis. Indeed, Verdú even finds a way to critique our core value of individualism by noting our related tendency toward exhibitionism (exemplified in reality, tabloid, and talk television) (pp. 96–97). The combination of exhibitionism and individualism suggests to Verdú that American culture is immature, egotistical, and not something to be invited in or emulated by other cultures.

From Verdú's perspective as a Spanish intellectual, the United States is a nation to be interrogated for its excesses, sanctimony, and greed. When Verdú (1996) is critiquing Americans' approach to capitalism, he might also be talking about our politics and culture as well, noting that "the history of the United States is constructed of winners of a certain style, opportunistic, audacious, and aggressive" (p. 65). In sum, these characteristics are what Verdú finds to be at the core of American culture and, consequently, why he feels compelled to warn the world away from us. Verdú shares with Eco and Baudrillard an appreciation for America's accomplishments, but a disdain over what effect U.S. values and habits might have in other cultural contexts. For these critics it is enough to experience our culture, but one gets the sense they would not live here.

Returning to the issues of conflict, these three European scholars are engaging in mediated forms of communication rife with conflict. Each is demonstrating his own biases toward the United States, reflecting on meanings, values, and identities (of another culture) that trouble them, and ultimately arguing against U.S. culture and for their own. In short, the content of these three writers' respective efforts are examples of intercultural conflict—a clash over ideas, values, and norms.

Conclusion

In this essay I have briefly surveyed a series of debates and perspectives that demonstrates how cultural conflict is not simply found in, or processed through, interpersonal communication. Intercultural conflict is based on a clash over competing and opposing systems of symbols, meanings, and values carried by multiple channels and forms of communication. If intercultural communication scholars are going to meet the challenges of the next century, we must expand our conceptual repertoire and become more creative in examining conflict. Intercultural scholars must attend to conflict in its many contexts and many levels of interaction.

I have no doubt that intercultural communication is complex and confounding to researcher and student alike. But as the examples in this essay demonstrate, we might likely face greater complications before we find the answers. As Robert Shuter's essay indicates, culture is the key concept in intercultural communication. As illustrated here, culture and communication coincide in various forms that affect our daily lives. We are each emblematic of our own cultures; we are created by and subsequently re-create the structures of cultures and societies. But if Baudrillard (1988) is correct in noting that "New York and Los Angeles [and therefore the United States] are at the centre of the world" (p. 23), Americans owe it to themselves to understand how cultures relate and how conflict is generated culturally.

References

Baudrillard, J. (1988). *America.* (C. Turner, Trans.). New York: Verso.

Collier, M. J. (1991). Conflict competence within African, Mexican, and Anglo American friendships. In S. Ting-Toomey & F. Korzenny (Eds.), *Cross-cultural interpersonal communication* (pp. 132–154). Newbury Park, CA: Sage.

Eco, U. (1986). *Travels in hyperreality.* San Diego, CA: Harcourt Brace Jovanovich.

Galtung, J., & Vincent, R. G. (1992). *Global glasnost: Toward a new world information and communication order?* Cresskill, NJ: Hampton Press.

Garnham, N. (1993). The mass media, cultural identity, and the public sphere in the modern world. *Public Culture, 5,* 251–265.

Gudykunst, W. B. (1984). Intercultural communication: Current status and proposed directions. In B. Dervin & M. J. Voigt (Eds.), *Progress in communication sciences 5* (pp. 1–46). Norwood, NJ: Ablex.

Gudykunst, W. B., & Kim, Y. Y. (1992). *Communicating with strangers: An approach to intercultural communication* (2nd ed.). New York: McGraw-Hill.

Hall, E. T. (1959). *The silent language.* New York: Doubleday.

Kleinwachter, W. (1993). Three waves of the debate. In G. Gerbner, H. Mowlana, & K. Nordenstreng (Eds.), *The global media debate: Its rise, fall, and renewal* (pp. 13–20). Norwood, NJ: Ablex.

Korzenny, F., & Ting-Toomey, S. (Eds.). (1990). *Communicating for peace: Diplomacy and negotiation.* Newbury Park, CA: Sage.

Lustig, M. W., & Koester, J. (1993). *Intercultural competence: Interpersonal communication across cultures.* New York: HarperCollins.

Macbride, S., & Roach, C. (1993). The new international information order. In G. Gerbner, H. Mowlana, & K. Nordenstreng (Eds.), *The global media debate: Its rise, fall, and renewal* (pp. 3–12). Norwood, NJ: Ablex.

Mowlana, H. (1986). *Global information and world communication: New frontiers in international relations.* New York: Longman.

Nordenstreng, K., & Schiller, H. I. (Eds.). (1993). *Beyond national sovereignty: International communication in the 1990s.* Norwood, NJ: Ablex.

Nwankwo, R. L. (1979). Intercultural communication: A critical review. *Quarterly Journal of Speech, 65,* 324–346.

Reagan, R. (1994). Remarks by President Ronald Reagan at the National Association of Broadcaster's 70th Annual Convention, 13 April 1992. In B. Lincoln, *Authority: Construction and corrosion* (pp. 147–153). Chicago: University of Chicago Press.

Schiller, H. I. (1989). *Culture Inc.: The corporate takeover of public expression.* New York: Oxford University Press.

Schiller, H. I. (1992). *Mass communications and American empire* (2nd ed.). Boulder, CO: Westview Press.

Shuter, R. (1998). Revisiting the centrality of culture. In J. Martin, T. Nakayama, & L. Flores (Eds.), *Readings in cultural contexts* (pp. 38–47). Mountain View, CA: Mayfield Publishing.

Straubhaar, J. D. (1991). Beyond media imperialism: Asymmetrical interdependence and cultural proximity. *Critical Studies in Mass Communication, 8,* 39–59.

Ting-Toomey, S. (1988). Intercultural conflict styles: A face-negotiation theory. In Y. Y. Kim & W. B. Gudykunst (Eds.), *Theories in intercultural communication* (pp. 213–238). Newbury Park, CA: Sage.

Tunstall, J. (1994). *The media are American: Anglo-American media in the world* (2nd ed.). London: Constable.

Verdú, V. (1996). *El planeta americano.* Barcelona: Editorial Anagrama.

Key Terms

developing nations

First World nations

globalization

ideology

imperialism

intercultural conflict

international communication

Discussion Questions

1. Delgado argues that intercultural communication and conflict can be seen in different ways. How can conceptions of intercultural conflict vary?

2. Delgado discusses debates relating to the flow of communication products and technology. What

are these debates called and what are the key issues involved in them?

3. Delgado's essay makes a case for a way to examine intercultural conflict. What are the benefits of looking at conflict in this way? What are the limitations of his perspective?

4. Given Delgado's perspective, how are culture and communication linked in mass-mediated communication?

5. Delgado introduces three critical thinkers—Eco, Baudrillard, and Verdú. Of the three, who is the most vigorous critic of American culture? Why? Who is the kindest critic? Why?

Activities for Skill Development

1. Conflict Scenario Exercise

Based on your study of intercultural communication and personal experience, develop a case scenario where an "individualist" and a "collectivist" (a) encounter a conflict and (b) successfully manage the conflict. Fully describe the situation and specific behaviors of each communicator to illustrate how conflict arises and is managed. Then ask your friends from other cultures whether they have encountered a similar situation. Ask them whether your scenario sounds "realistic," and, if not, what changes they have to offer.

2. Intercultural Conflict Management Interview

Ask a couple of people from other cultural backgrounds the following questions: In a conflict situation with your friend, how do you like to solve or manage the problem? Do you like to "talk things out" or do you avoid confrontation? What communication styles do you prefer for conflict management, for example, open, direct styles or silence?

Make a list of a variety of expectations and communication behaviors (verbal and nonverbal) associated with conflict management. Then compare your findings with your classmates.

Web Sites

1. "We lost our country in 1991 . . . since September 9, 1999, this is our home . . . not a geographically visible country." Cyber Yugoslavia <*http://www.juga.com/*> is "Home of Cyber Yugoslavs" since they have lost their own geographically visible country. Visit their homeland and see the independent country they are constructing with constitutions, registered citizens, and the like.

2. What is it like to see a doctor or other health practitioner in a foreign country? What issues do you think today's health practitioners face in this diverse society? Check out some of the voices from underserved populations <*http://www.xculture.org/home/no barriers/index.html*> and also learn some of the lessons that health care providers have learned about intercultural competence from their health care practices.

Additional Readings

1. Kivel, P. (1996). *Uprooting racism: How White people can work for racial justice.* Gabriola Island, BC: New Society Publishers.

2. Lindsley, S. L., & Braithwaite, C. A. (1996). "You should 'wear a mask'": Facework norms in cultural and intercultural conflict in maquiladoras. *International Journal of Intercultural Relations, 20*(2), 199–225.

3. Mura, D. (1999). Responses: Explaining racism to my daughter. In T. B. Jelloun, *Racism explained to my daughter* (pp. 91–137). New York: New Press.

PART TEN

Ethics and Intercultural Communication

Ethics is an important series of considerations in any intercultural interaction. Because we live in a world that is increasingly hostile, violent, and conflicted, the study of ethics has become much more significant in intercultural communication. The following readings address questions of how to behave ethically in an increasingly complex and hostile world. Although there is no one correct way to be ethical, it is vital that you think about ethical considerations. The essays in this section explore various ethical issues involved not only in being competent intercultural communicators but also in studying "others."

In "Ethical Issues in Intercultural Communication," Judith N. Martin, Lisa A. Flores, and Thomas K. Nakayama outline a theoretical framework for developing a metaethic of intercultural communication. They first define ethics and issues of concern for ethical communicators. Then they propose three principles to guide ethical intercultural interaction: humanness, dialogic, and speaking "with" and "to." Finally, they identify and discuss everyday dilemmas in intercultural communication practice and study.

In "Joint Performance Across Cultures," Mary Catherine Bateson describes how the canon of humanness may be applied in actual intercultural encounters. She recounts the story of taking her daughter to a religious celebration in Iran that involved the ritual killing of a sheep. Bateson describes this intercultural encounter as a "joint improvisation" in which, as is often the case, the scripts are not written for intercultural interaction. Instead, individuals participating in the ritual together create a common script. She also describes the culture-learning that occurred in that encounter for her daughter and herself, and she emphasizes the importance of *experience* in understanding intercultural communication.

We then turn to ethical issues in studying about intercultural communication and learning about others.

Dolores V. Tanno and Fred E. Jandt join this discussion and address the challenge of how to study "others" ethically. In "Redefining the 'Other' in Multicultural Research," they suggest that cultural communities should not be seen as research objects, but as co-learners. They offer ways in which participants can play a more active role in research.

Finally, in "Painting the White Face Red," María Cristina González provides a good example of a researcher who meets the ethical challenges of studying "others." Her interpretive ethnographic study investigates how some White Americans appropriate Native American spirituality. Her study, from methods to analyses, reveals an ethical commitment to the community involved. Her "Four Seasons" methodology—based on Native American thought—assumes that the researcher is not in charge, that research is instead the natural unfolding of experience. Her concern for ethical issues leads her to present her findings through poetry rather than through traditional academic writing. Her poems reveal the complexity and intensity of this intercultural contact between Indians and non-Indians.

38 Ethical Issues in Intercultural Communication

JUDITH N. MARTIN, LISA A. FLORES, and THOMAS K. NAKAYAMA

How do we decide what is right and what is wrong for ourselves and others? We usually rely on our personal sense of ethics or morals to guide us in making important decisions and in evaluating our own actions and the actions of others. We learn a sense of right and wrong by explicit teaching and by implicit example from our families, religion, and other cultural experiences. However, what is considered right in one cultural context may be considered wrong in another.

These different ethical systems sometimes collide in intercultural interactions. A common example in international business is that of taking bribes. What is considered just compensation in many Asian countries is considered unethical bribery for U.S. managers (Howell, 1982). Another example is absolute honesty versus relative honesty. In some countries it is more ethical to save face than to tell an unpleasant truth (Kras, 1989). Or it may be unethical to date, even casually, without a promise of commitment to marriage.

There is currently no accepted metaethic, no universal guides for ethical communication in intercultural encounters. Perhaps this is not surprising, given the complexity of the challenge. As communication scholar Dean Barnlund (1982) predicted more than 15 years ago:

> The ethical systems we know are each tied to and reflect the premises of a particular body of people. . . . Until a metaethic . . . can be articulated in ways that gain wide allegiance, or until a common one emerges from the thousands of daily confrontations, confusions, and antagonisms that characterize such encounters, we shall continue to conduct intercultural affairs in a moral vacuum. (p. 381)

Based on an assumption that there are no easy answers, this essay seeks to join the search for ethical guidelines in intercultural encounters. In the first section, we define ethics and describe the relationship between culture and ethics. We then review four common ethical models in communication. Finally, we propose several principles to guide ethical intercultural communication and explore how these principles might work in everyday life.

Culture and Ethics

Ethics or morals have to do with what is considered right and wrong, "the practical, specific, generally agreed-upon, culturally transmitted standards of right and wrong" (Johannesen, 1990, p. 1). Some scholars distinguish between morals and ethics, reserving ethics to mean the study of morals, but in this essay we use the two terms interchangeably.

Ethics tells us what is right and wrong, and our cultures tell us what is right and wrong. They both provide frameworks for assessing others' behavior and for guiding us in important choices. However, not all cultural patterns are ethics statements. Cultural values are those fundamental beliefs that tell us what is "good" and what "ought to be"—for example, individualism, desirability of material wealth, equality, hard work, efficiency. Although these may motivate us and function as criteria for making choices and judging others, communication scholar Richard L. Johannesen (1990) suggests that ethical judgments focus more precisely on *degrees of rightness and wrongness* in human behavior than do cultural values (p. 1). For example, we may criticize someone for being inefficient, conformist, extravagant, lazy, or late, but we probably would not also claim that he or she is unethical.

However, some value standards such as honesty or directness, promise-keeping, fairness, and humanness *are* used in making ethical judgments of rightness and wrongness. So there is some overlap between cultural values and ethics standards. Put simply, all values standards are not ethics, but most ethical decisions are probably related to cultural values.

Different cultural ethics are not much of a problem when cultural groups are isolated. For example, it isn't of great consequence if cultural groups have two different ethics of telling the truth. Each system can be understood within its cultural contexts. However, if members of those cultures are trying to communicate "truthfully" to one another, then a more universal metaethic would be helpful. What we are searching for are some principles that can guide everyone—regardless of cultural background—in intercultural interactions. Continuing the explorations of culture and ethics, let's review contemporary communication models of ethics.

Review of Ethical Models in Communication

Communication scholars Janet Metzger and Jeffrey Springston (1992) argue that the lack of insight on intercultural ethics arises from the limitations of accepted communication models. They review four common communication models and describe how each addresses ethical issues.

The traditional mechanistic model represents communication as composed of several distinct components (e.g., sender, receiver, channel, message, and noise). In this model, good (successful) communication occurs when the message received is the same as the message sent. That is, there is good communication when there is no noise, for example, cultural differences in the channel. A related psychological model views cultural differences as conceptual filters that influence the encoding or decoding of messages. In both the mechanistic and the psychological models, the skillful (ethical) communicator is one who understands, deals with, and minimizes the impacts of cultural differences. Both these models take an individual-centered approach and do not specifically address ethical issues. We could surmise, however, that ethical guidelines in these models would involve trying to understand other cultural patterns as well as developing empathy and other skills that lead to maximum understanding. For example, understanding different definitions of truth and dishonesty would go a long way in resolving conflicts about truth-telling. How-

ever, as we know, people can understand each other very clearly and still behave unethically in doing violence and harm to one another and to society.

Moving from the individual-centered models to social ethics, Metzger and Springston (1992) review models based on a systems approach to communication. A systems model of communication emphasizes the interconnectedness of human communicators to each other and to their environment (the cultural context in which communication occurs). Any change in one element of the system affects other elements and ultimately the entire system. In this model, ethical communication occurs when there is a fit between communicators and the cultural environment. Change agents may adapt a systems approach in helping resolve ethical dilemmas across cultures—by helping individuals or organizations adapt their communication to meet the challenges of the cultural environment.

In symbolic interactionism, the locus of communication is in role-taking, and culture is viewed as an outworking of ideas. Good communication needs to be looked at on a case-by-case basis, either as what participants define as good or as what the researcher, using her or his own frame, determines to be good. Intercultural communication consultants often use this approach in helping individuals learn to take various roles and perspectives and work for the good of the group. However, ethical, moral, and class concerns are not specifically addressed and are generally brought in by other means of analysis.

Metzger and Springston (1992) argue that what is needed for intercultural communication is an integration of the individual level, which is relatively amoral and acultural, with the concerns of social ethics for justice. In a case study of fishing rights concerns in Wisconsin, they show how each of the previously mentioned ethical systems is limited in capturing and resolving the individual, social, historical, political, and religious complexities of this case (pp. 79–81).

Three Principles for Ethical Intercultural Communicators

In our search for a metaethic, it may be useful to apply a dialectical approach, where ethical communication must be both individually and socially oriented. There are three principles that might provide the foundation for such a framework.

1. THE HUMANNESS PRINCIPLE

Although proposed by several scholars, the following description of the humanness principle is from philosopher Christopher L. Johnstone:

> to be human suggests that one's conduct is guided by a respect for and a tenderness toward others' beings. . . . a humanist ethic requires that the individual be responsive in his or her actions to the impact they might have on the humanity of those affected by the act. It demands, finally, that one conduct oneself so as to maximize opportunity for cultivating in oneself and in others an awareness and appreciation of humanness. (Johnstone, quoted in Johannesen, 1990, p. 56)

This principle seems sound and has led to other general ethical principles such as the peace principle (Kale, 1994). This metaethic, the peace principle, prescribes addressing others with respect, describing the world as accurately as possible, recognizing the uniqueness of all groups, and trying to identify (empathize) with others. We can ask ourselves what violating these principles of humanness might mean for us in our everyday lives. Might violating the ethic of peace mean denying access to discourse in public settings? Another violation might be to make fun of others' communication styles or cultural beliefs, or to portray cultural groups as stereotypical caricatures in conversations or in media representations. However, we need to search for more specific communication guidelines. A more specific principle is the dialogic principle.

2. THE DIALOGIC PRINCIPLE

This principle concerns specific attitudes of communicators toward each other and is particularly apt for intercultural communication. It is based on many different strands of philosophical thought. It stresses the centrality of *relationships* in the human experience, that we become most human in the "betweenness" of relationships. This principle is both in contrast and complementary to the more self-centered principle of humanness (see Buber, 1958; Friedman, 1960). Applying the dialogic principle to

communication means turning outward, reaching for and developing relationships with others. Particularly appropriate for intercultural communication is the emphasis on trying to understand and share the lived experience of another—which implies developing empathy with others. Benjamin Broome (1991) refers to *relational empathy,* which is dynamic and provisional and allows two individuals to move toward *varying degrees* of understanding (p. 241). He also stresses that relational empathy takes time. It develops when people are willing to open themselves to new meanings, to engage in genuine dialogue, and to respond to new meanings emanating from the situation (p. 243).

A related notion is the ethics of caring. The ethics of care extends the ethic of justice because it promotes seeing the world as "a web of relationships, or circles and chains of people" (Metzger & Springston, 1992, p. 81). This means that using other principles of ethics may result in good but not necessarily moral communication. This is quite striking when we consider that from this ethic, communication without a sense of relationship may be immoral, that reaching out is not just a nice thing to do, but an ethical obligation. This challenges much of our individualistic way of thinking.

There are specific guidelines for following this relationship-centered dialogic principle, for example, authenticity, inclusion, confirmation, presentness, a spirit of mutual equality, and a supportive climate. However, these seem to be limited in that they reflect cultural biases of Western individualism and as such, do not provide a metaethic (Johannesen, 1990, pp. 62–63). We can see again a strong emphasis on empathy. The practical implications of following the dialogic principle in intercultural encounters lead to three challenges: cultural constraints of empathy, power differentials, and considerations of contexts.

Cultural Constraints Scholars have pointed out that empathy, central to the dialogic principle and the individual-centered communication ethics model, is culture bound. That is, empathy works best among people who share similar cultural backgrounds and experiences. In order to meet this challenge, communication scholar Milton Bennett (1979) suggests replacing the Golden Rule of "Do unto others as you would have them do unto you" with the platinum rule "Do unto others as they themselves would have done unto them" (p. 422). How do we truly understand what others would want done unto them? How do we learn about "others"? In many ways, this is the crux of success in intercultural encounters—knowing about others' experiences. It is easy to imagine learning about other cultures in an intellectual way, but as Karen Lynnette Dace and Mark Lawrence McPhail suggest in their essay in Part Nine, we must go beyond empathy to implicature. Implicature is a fusing of both knowledge about *and* feelings for in reaching out empathically across cultural boundaries. Like Broome's (1991) notion of relational empathy, implicature can happen only when individuals take time and make the effort to nurture and develop intercultural relationships.

We are bombarded daily by messages about others' behavior, and we often make ethical judgments about these behaviors. Although contrasting worldviews sometimes stand in the way of empathy, there is another challenge that must be considered: the role of power.

The Role of Power Power is an omnipresent but often hidden part of all intercultural interactions. What does power have to do with empathy and understanding others? One of the characteristics of power relations is that those with less power usually understand those with more power rather than the other way around. For example, women often direct more energy toward understanding men (e.g., those articles in "women's magazines" telling women how to understand and be successful in relationships with men) than men direct toward understanding women. Individuals from ethnic minority groups often know more about White experiences in the United States than vice versa (Miller, 1992).

For example, studies contrasting various ethnic groups' notions of effective communication show that U.S. Whites approach communication assuming equality, whereas African American models include elements of power and powerlessness (Martin, 1993). The point is, in order to approach an empathic understanding or to understand the limits of empathy, we have to (1) understand how power

works and (2) examine our position(s) with respect to power (Collier, this volume). Ethical dilemmas require an analysis of power relations. For example, Metzger and Springston's (1992) analysis of the fishing controversy in Wisconsin showed how different groups had different access to power (pp. 82–85).

Understanding Contexts A third challenge in following the dialogic principle is that we cannot understand the human experience (or human communication) without understanding the contexts in which this experience is lived. For example, to study communication between Whites and Blacks in the United States without a firm grounding in the historical contexts of slavery and African diaspora is limiting. In studying interaction between Arabs and Jews, we must incorporate historical events of the Middle East.

In order to develop empathy and really learn about others, we interculturalists need to understand how our own contexts have shaped our lives and discourses as communicators. If we are White Americans, we may approach intercultural interactions with little distrust or apprehension, assuming that if we are nice and polite that others will like us. If we are African American or members of another U.S. ethnic minority, we may approach some intercultural interactions with mistrust. The challenges of cultural constraints, power differentials, and considerations of contexts lead to questions of how to ethically learn about others and of who can speak for others. Our third principle provides some answers by extending the relational dialogic principle to *communication*.

3. THE PRINCIPLE OF SPEAKING "WITH" AND "TO"

Given the challenges identified in the previous section, perhaps it seems discouraging to learn about others and to pursue ethical intercultural relationships. Yes, intercultural understanding is challenging, but the answer is not to stop learning about others or to say that only members of a particular group can speak for this group (e.g., only White women can speak for White women). This can be a cop-out because if you speak only for yourself, no one can criticize your position and you don't have to reach out to others. Linda Alcoff (1991/1992), a cultural studies scholar, proposes a *"speaking to"* position, which promotes the practice of speaking *with* and *to* rather than speaking *for* others (p. 23). This promotes "listening to" others as opposed to speaking for others. She equates speaking "for" others with speaking "about" others and suggests that the impetus to speak for must be carefully analyzed and approached carefully. What does this mean for students of intercultural communication?

It may mean that one should *approach scholarly descriptions of others with a critical eye.* Intercultural communication students are often asked to read descriptions of various cultural groups. However, scholars are relatively privileged people and, like anyone else, cannot transcend their own location easily. Alcoff suggests that when scholars speak for (or describe) cultural patterns of less privileged people, they sometimes reinforce the oppression of the group spoken for (p. 7). These descriptions are coming more and more under criticism from members of those oppressed groups (Rosaldo, 1989).

Be Self-Reflexive In order to recognize and understand contextual influences and the role of power, ethical intercultural communicators should examine the "location" from which they are speaking (Rosaldo, 1989). So we, the authors of this essay, as middle-class academicians must think carefully about how our social position influences the way we see the world. What do we know about working-class life? Or student life, for that matter? How do our experiences influence our descriptions and our understanding of intercultural communication?

These are not easy questions to answer, but they *form the foundation* of an ethical approach to intercultural interactions. We must think about the bearing and location and context on what we are saying—to first articulate the possible connections between our location and what we are saying (but not as a disclaimer). Also, our speaking about others should carry an accountability with it.

Listen One of the most difficult things to do is to truly listen. We are often struck by the resistance of

people to really listen, particularly on the part of people who speak from relatively privileged positions. Power and listening are related. People who are privileged are often less motivated to listen. Oppressed groups always know more about the lives, motivations, and desires of the powerful than vice versa. This is unfortunate for both (Miller, 1992).

Perhaps a crucial part of listening is not only asking but educating ourselves and not waiting for others to educate us. Gloria Yamato (1995), in "Something About the Subject Makes It Hard to Name," emphasizes that we shouldn't expect others to educate us. She suggests that especially for U.S. Whites who want to be allies of people of color,

> Do not expect that people of color should teach you how to behave non-oppressively. Do not give in to the pull to be lazy. Think, hard. Do not blame people of color for your frustration about racism, but do appreciate the fact that people of color will often help you get in touch with that frustration. Assume that your effort to be a good friend is appreciated, but don't expect or accept gratitude from people of color. Work on racism for your sake, not "their" sake. Assume that you are needed and capable of being a good ally. Know that you'll make mistakes and commit yourself to correcting them and continuing on as an ally, no matter what. Don't give up. (p. 73)

For people of color:

> Remember . . . various groups have been oppressed in a variety of ways. Educate yourself about the ways different peoples have been oppressed and how they've resisted that oppression. Expect and insist that whites are capable of being good allies against racism. Don't give up. (p. 73)

Engage in Dialogue Just listening is limiting. If individuals are committed to stronger intercultural relations, they need to commit to those relationships, and that means both listening to and dialoguing with others across cultural boundaries. But, how to engage in dialogue that is guided by a speaking with and to ethic? It's tricky to know when to speak and when to listen. Sometimes it's important to speak up—to engage others. If one can remember that *speaking with and to* builds on the principles of self-reflexivity and listening, it is possible to avoid a *speaking for.* Tanno and Jandt (1994 & this volume) provide very specific guidelines for reaching across cultural boundaries to engage "others" in collaborative culture-learning.

Ethical Dilemmas in Everyday Intercultural Interaction

Our insistence on the relative nature of ethics is not meant to argue that any behavior can be ethical. Instead, we insist that the character of ethics is deeply embedded in cultural ways of living. Cultural differences take on heightened significance in the realm of ethics. The old saying, "When in Rome, do as the Romans do," is only a partial guide to navigating the tricky waters of intercultural communication ethics.

Given the enormous number of cultural differences around the globe, we cannot hope to be able to offer any reasonable lists or guides to ethics in culture-specific contexts. Instead, we offer the following examples to help you think about ethics and intercultural communication. As you unpack the ethical issues in each of these examples, think about the ways that people deal with these intercultural situations in everyday life. Intercultural communication takes place on a number of levels, and our examples highlight different aspects of that interaction. Ethical issues arise in interpersonal intercultural interactions with tourists, businesspeople, refugees, and migrants. They also arise in newspaper and television reports and popular culture representations. They occur in ingroup jokes and other interactions that are not directly addressed to members of another cultural group. Ethical concerns also arise both in the way intercultural communication is studied and in the way different cultural groups are characterized in those studies. Finally, intercultural communication students should be concerned with how they (and others) use the results of those studies. Let's look at some examples.

Example 1: In his class in intercultural communication, John learned that, when shopping, Japanese often consider it insulting to count the change given by the cashier. Counting change in front of the cashier is often taken as an accusation of either mathematical incompetence or deliberate shortchanging. John works in a tourist-related industry with many Japanese clients. He surmises that they are often well-to-do, as low-income Japanese do not have the luxury of leisure travel. How unethical is it for him to shortchange these clients? Does it depend upon his financial needs? What if he feels the tourist-related company is underpaying him?

Example 2: Maria is interested in studying a particular cultural group, but she is not interested in being very involved in that cultural community. She does not read their ethnic newspaper; she does not participate in any of their community activities. She only interacts with members of that cultural group as students in her courses. She uses her courses to recruit these students as respondents in her studies. Her use of intercultural concepts is derived from journal articles, not from the community she is studying. Is this kind of intercultural communication research ethical? In what ways is it ethical? In what ways is it unethical?

Example 3: The concept of X is important in Mark's cultural group. He utilizes this concept to study another cultural group. In interviewing members of this other group, he finds that they have difficulty expressing how the concept of X functions in their group. He concludes in his study that this other cultural group is less developed and less sophisticated and needs to learn how to enact X more effectively, if it is going to compete effectively on the world market. Is he being unethical in his assessment of this other cultural group? How might his methods of gathering information (interviewing) influence his conclusions about cultural behavior?

Example 4: Diane has read studies about the aggressive nature of men in the country she is visiting. She is wary when she is there, particularly as she is traveling alone. She consciously avoids intercultural communication with men in that country. Is she being sexist? Racist? Is she using her intercultural communication knowledge ethically?

Although these examples are hypothetical, they illustrate the kinds of issues in intercultural communication that call for ethical judgments. By returning to the framework we provided earlier and the ethical challenges we presented, we can examine these issues from an ethical perspective.

First, let's consider John, who was deciding how much change to give to the Japanese tourists he helped. The cultural constraint of empathy requires us to position ourselves within the other culture as we decide how to act. Bennett's revised Golden Rule asks that we "do unto others as *they would have you do unto them.*" With this as an ethical guide, what should John do? It is likely that the tourists he is helping, regardless of their financial position, would like all of their change. For John to short-change them violates an ethical norm of empathy.

However, the answer may not be quite so simple. Empathy and ethics in intercultural communication also hinge on power. Who has greater power in this situation? From one perspective, John can be seen as having power. He is a member of the host culture, and he has the knowledge of cultural customs that allows him to consider the possibility of shortchanging the tourists. And yet, there may be other factors that are important here. If John is dependent on his job for his living and the tourists seem to have greater resources, enough to allow for this trip, might his "miscalculation" of a dollar here or there help to level the power difference?

John's musings here, on the Golden Rule and on power differences, might require him to remember another ethical guide—self-reflexivity. Before John makes any decisions, he should think about his thought processes. What cultural values are influencing John's decision? Does John's own class position affect his attitudes about international travel? Is he operating from a dualistic perspective, thinking that *either* you have enough money to travel *or* you have to work hard for your living? John's notions of right and wrong develop out of his cultural location. However, if he wants to make an ethical decision in this intercultural interaction, his recognition of the cultural influence on his decision can help him assess the situation in a more complex manner. As you first read Example 1, you may have had an immediate response, such as, "Well, that's a simple question; of course John should. . . ." The ethical guides that we are proposing here suggest that before we go for the "easy answer," we stop and think about the intercultural implications of the situation.

What happens if we turn to Maria, whose interest in a particular cultural group is based on her research interests? To what extent is she, as an intercultural communication scholar, obligated to the cultural community she studies? One consideration she might want to make is to use a critical eye when reading scholarly research on this cultural group. She might want to consider whether the research that is available on the cultural group has been done by members of that group or by nonmembers. If the scholars she is reading are not members, she might want to think about power differences—are they members of a more dominant group? Why is this an important ethical consideration? As we mentioned, the growing body of research being done within African American, Asian American, and Latino/a studies, gay and lesbian studies, and women's studies, by members of those groups, calls into question much of the existing research. Because even intercultural scholars have to reflect on the biases we bring to our research, Maria should use the available research carefully, so that she does not impose meaning on the group she is studying. Does this mean Maria should not read scholarly literature on the cultural group? Or should she read only research that has been done by members of the group? No. But it does mean that Maria cannot accept the conclusions of the existing research without thinking about the subject positions of the authors and of herself. This critical lens should also be used when she reads work that has been written by members of the group. Biases exist in all of us and affect all the work that we do.

In addition to thinking critically about the work, Maria can also extend her knowledge by turning to individual members of the group. By listening to the members talk about their community, their interests, their goals and needs, Maria can balance her background in the scholarly literature with the knowledge that comes from people who can tell her about daily life. This moving toward listening can then lead to dialogue between Maria and members of the group. If Maria begins by speaking with and to the members of the group she is studying, she can gain a whole new perspective on the ethical issues that surround her research. She can identify the kinds of knowledge that would benefit the members of the group, and she can merge her scholarly interests with those of the group so that both she and the community she is studying can benefit from her research.

Think now about Mark and Diane. What questions should they consider as they decide how to act? We leave you to unpack these last two examples. How might Mark follow suggestions of listening, being self-reflexive, and engaging in dialogue in order to more ethically communicate in these unfamiliar intercultural contexts? Similarly, how might Diane use these suggestions to more ethically learn about and understand the cultural group she is visiting?

As you can see from our discussion, the ethical principles and challenges offered here provide a beginning. They are offered to help you think in more complex ways about ethical dilemmas in intercultural encounters. The intercultural situations faced in everyday life are often difficult and cannot be answered easily or quickly. Cultural differences in what is considered right and wrong, good and bad, mean that as we think about ethics, we must approach situations from many perspectives. The place to start is by reflecting on the humanness of others, establishing and nurturing dialogic relationships, and speaking with and to others across cultural boundaries.

References

Alcoff, L. (1991/1992). The problem of speaking for others. *Cultural Critique*, 5–32.

Barnlund, D. C. (1982). The cross-cultural arena: An ethical void. In L. Samovar & R. E. Porter (Eds.), *Intercultural communication: A reader* (3rd ed., pp. 378–383). Belmont, CA: Wadsworth.

Bennett, M. J. (1979). Overcoming the Golden Rule: Sympathy and empathy. In D. S. Nimmo (Ed.), *Communication yearbook* 3 (pp. 407–422). New Brunswick, NJ: Transaction Books.

Broome, B. J. (1991). Building shared meaning: Implications of a relational approach to empathy for teaching intercultural communication. *Communication Education, 40,* 235–249.

Buber, M. (1958). *I and thou* (2nd ed., R. G. Smith, Trans.). New York: Scribners.

Cooper, T. W., Christians, C. G., Plude, F. F., & White, R. W. (Eds.). (1989). *Communication ethics and global change.* New York: Longman.

Friedman, M. S. (1960). *Martin Buber: The life of dialogue.* New York: HarperTorchbook.

Grice, H. P. (1978). Logic and conversation. In R. J. Fogelin (Ed.), *Understanding arguments* (pp. 329–343). New York: Harcourt Brace Jovanovich.

Gudykunst, W. B. (1980, November). *Communication, ethics, and relativism: The implications of ethical relativity theory for intercultural communication.* Paper presented at the annual meeting of the Speech Communication Association, New York City.

Hatch, E. (1983). *Culture and morality: The relativity of values in anthropology.* New York: Columbia University Press.

Howell, W. S. (1982). *The empathic communicator.* Belmont, CA: Wadsworth.

Johannesen, R. L. (1990). *Ethics in human communication* (3rd ed.). Prospect Heights, IL: Waveland Press.

Johnstone, C. L. (1981). Ethics, wisdom, and the mission of contemporary rhetoric: The realization of human being. *Central States Speech Journal, 32,* 177–188.

Kale, D. W. (1994). Peace as an ethic for intercultural communication. In L. Samovar & R. E. Porter (Eds.), *Intercultural communication: A reader* (7th ed., pp. 435–441). Belmont, CA: Wadsworth.

Kant, I. (1949). *Fundamental principles of the metaphysics of morals* (T. Abbott, Trans.). Indianapolis, IN: Library of Liberal Arts/Bobbs-Merrill.

Kras, E. S. (1989). *Management in two cultures: Bridging the gap between U. S. and Mexican managers.* Yarmouth, ME: Intercultural Press.

Martin, J. N. (1993). Intercultural communication competence: A review. In R. L. Wiseman & J. Koester (Eds.), *Intercultural communication competence* (pp. 16–29). Newbury Park, CA: Sage.

Metzger, J. G., & Springston, J. K. (1992). The skillful, the loving, and the right: An analysis of ethical theories and an application to the treaty rights debate in Wisconsin. *Howard Journal of Communications, 4,* 75–91.

Miller, J. B. (1992). Domination and subordination. In P. S. Rothenburg (Ed.), *Race, class and gender in the United States* (pp. 20–26). New York: St. Martin's Press.

Rosaldo, R. (1989). *Culture and truth: The remaking of social analysis.* Boston: Beacon Press.

Tanno, D. V., & Jandt, F. E. (1994). Redefining the "other" in multicultural research. *Howard Journal of Communications, 5,* 36–45. (Reprinted in this volume)

Wellman, C. (1988). *Ethics and morals* (2nd ed.). Englewood Cliffs, NJ: Prentice-Hall.

Yamato, G. (1995). Something about the subject makes it

hard to name. In M. L. Andersen & P. H. Collins (Eds.), *Race, class, and gender: An anthology* (2nd ed., pp. 71–75). Belmont, CA: Wadsworth.

Key Terms

cultural values   ethics
dialogic   humanness
ethical issues

Discussion Questions

1. What ethical dilemmas have you encountered in intercultural relationships?

2. How might one go about researching a universal metaethic for intercultural communicators?

3. In what ways does cultural background constrain development of empathy?

4. How might power differentials constrain the development of empathy in intercultural relationships?

5. In applying Bennett's platinum rule, how can you discover how others want to be treated in intercultural relationships?

39 Joint Performance Across Cultures
Improvisation in a Persian Garden
MARY CATHERINE BATESON

Often when I speak I start with a story or example that I can turn at different angles, a story that fits with my subject in multiple ways. Today I want to begin by describing an episode that happened in a Persian garden. Before you let your imagination go too far in thinking of what that garden might be like, let me warn you that it is winter. But still we are dealing with a classic walled garden, full of fruit trees and rosebushes, with a watercourse down the center. I have just arrived in Tehran with my husband and our two-and-a-half-year-old daughter Vanni for the beginning of a period of research, teaching, and institution building. It is twenty years ago, pre-revolutionary Iran.

The day before, we had gone to drink tea at the home of the landlord and landlady of the apartment we had just moved into. When they heard that I was an anthropologist and that I would be learning about Iranian culture, they invited us to come with them the following day to the garden where we are now gathered, on family land in a village near Tehran, to celebrate Eyd-e Qorban, the Feast of Sacrifice.

At the same time of year that pilgrims are going to Mecca and going through the ritual steps of the Meccan pilgrimage, Muslims around the world are also celebrating some of the steps of that multi-day ritual, one of which is the sacrifice of a sheep or a camel. They tell me that in Saudi Arabia there are so many sheep and camels slaughtered by pilgrims, as part of their observance, that they are simply plowed under the ground by bulldozers. Originally they were given to the poor, but this has become unmanageable given the numbers involved. In any case, many families in Iran do sacrifice a sheep on the Feast of Sacrifice, and when our landlady invited us, although my husband couldn't come, well of course I said yes. That's my business. Then I stopped and thought briefly and I said, "I'm afraid I'll have to bring my daughter Vanni with me." And they said fine.

Then, in the car, on the way to the village, it suddenly occurred to me to wonder what I had gotten myself into. I am taking my two-and-a-half-year-old daughter to see a sheep killed. What am I going to say? How bloody will this be? How am I going to handle this so that it is not disturbing to her? What I thought about in the car was motherhood, not anthropology. It seemed to me that the key was going to be to keep her close to me and to give her a running commentary. This is the advice that is given about some of the horrors that children see on television: they are not so horrifying if they are watched in the company of an adult who provides a model for how to respond. So given that set of ideas it seemed to me I knew how to deal with the slaughtering of the sheep.

So there we were: myself and Vanni, our host and hostess, their gardener, who would do the slaughtering, and his wife who was wearing a coarse village *chador* (veil), and their three children—all gathered outdoors in the cold for this ritual. My landlady had the most elegant high-heeled French boots on, and a fur coat. You have a sense of the contrasts of all this.

Such a garden, you know, is a cosmological statement. Most of you have not seen a Persian garden, but you have seen models of them if you have seen a Persian carpet, for there is a metaphorical relationship between them. A garden is bounded, walled. Inside, it is fertile and hospitable, and there is always an awareness of an outside world that is not so fertile and hospitable. Water is part of every garden. The Shah used to have a palace in the northern part of Tehran, at the high edge of the city, where there was a garden with a fountain, and the water from that fountain symbolically went down through the city to his subjects. A garden is also a model of the paradise to which the faithful will go after death.

To be in that garden was to stand in the middle of a complex statement about the world. There was also a statement there about the social structure of Iran at that time. The sophisticated, affluent Westernized urbanites, the villagers, the performing of a ritual that rooted them in the past—all of these things going on implicitly and explicitly in that setting.

The gardener gave the sheep a drink of water, turned it to face toward Mecca, prayed in the name of God the merciful and the compassionate, and slit its throat in the ritually correct manner. He then proceeded to clean and dismember the sheep. The way he removed the fleece from the sheep was by making a little cut next to one of the hind hooves, and blowing through it to separate the skin from the body. Then he put the fleece down and started laying the different organs out side by side. I was holding Vanni, figuring that body contact was going to be important here, and giving her a running commentary: "You see, that's the sheep's *heart*. You have a heart, and the heart is pumping blood around the body. Put your head here and you can hear my heart beating. See, that's a liver. And those are intestines."

And then I had one of those moments when you notice what you are doing: I was taking advantage of the visual aids to give a little mini-lecture about each organ in a vocabulary appropriate to a very verbal two-and-a-half-year-old. But just at the point when I was saying, "That's a lung . . ." I realized: it's HUGE. Then it occurred to me that although I could identify it as a lung, I had never actually seen the lung of a substantial-sized mammal. The knowledge that was allowing me to recognize a lung was entirely theoretical—as for many of the other organs I was giving a commentary on. What I was passing on to her was not knowledge based on previous experience of the dissection of large mammals, but an entirely abstract set of labels, the theoretical character of which was not accessible to me, until I was shocked by a feature that I had failed to anticipate.

And you know, just as I could say, "That's a heart, that's a lung," we go through life, and we say: "I must be in love," "Oh, this is an orgasm," "This is a midlife crisis," "This is seasickness." We are provided with the labels, the culturally-constructed labels, long before we encounter the realities—up to the point even of saying: "This is a heart attack," "I must be dying."

Now, I became aware of this because of the dissonance of my different roles in that situation. To be an anthropologist is a complicated role anyhow, because one is a participant—a performer—and an observer at the same time; and quite often the dissonance there will break through. It may pull you closer to the experience when you've distanced it and thought of yourself as an observer. Or it may push you away again when you have identified with what was happening. So I was there as a learner, as an observer, as an outsider. And yet because I was there as a mother, I was simultaneously a teacher, an authority on what was happening, trying to establish an interpretation that would be intelligible and *educational* for my daughter. And out of that dissonance, I believe, came the possibility for an extra layer of awareness.

This is one of the things that I have been writing about in relation to women—that the effect of being under multiple simultaneous role demands is to stretch awareness and to force you out of particular stereotyped interpretations of what is going on in a particular situation. This is not something that is unique to women, of course, but it has been experienced by most women through history for two reasons: because they are subject to multiple demands of spouse and children at different developmental stages who require different kinds of attention and response in the same setting, and because women's work includes all those things that can be done simultaneously with something else, namely caring for a child. Women must be one thing to one person and another to another person simultaneously, and must see themselves through multiple eyes and in terms of different roles. This is something that women have experienced that leads to a kind of multiple vision which, if you limit roles to separate contexts, you may not have.

One of the things that has struck me as I look back on that day in the Persian garden is that it has come to represent for me what is wrong with much of our thinking about education. We tend to think of classrooms as places in which there are teachers who know and students who don't know, instead of seeing education and learning as a two-way process all the way through, in which all the participants often have to play multiple roles as both teachers and learners.

Furthermore, what I was forced to do in that setting was to improvise, and, incidentally, to improvise responsibly. I did not know the rules. I had just arrived in Iran. I had no way of knowing what was

going to happen. I had indeed no real sense of the depth of my own ignorance of the situation. But even so I was trying to put together a way of performing in accordance with what I believed to be the nature of my relationship with my child and my relationship with my profession. And this was improvised: there was no previously-given set of rules for that improvisation. What I was doing was stringing together elements of previous knowledge in accordance with patterns that I did have in advance.

This, you know, is how improvisational art works. I do think one of the most important things that Noam Chomsky ever pointed out is that most of the sentences that most of us speak day in and day out have never been spoken before. We have the components and we have the rules for combining them, but we generate novel performances.

Vanni of course was generating a novel performance too. Let me not get so preoccupied with my own navel that I forget that she was also facing something she had never seen before, having an experience she'd never had before, and trying to figure out who to be and how to react. And those of you that have had much to do with children will know that she got some of her cues from me, but she also kept a watchful eye on the children of the Iranian gardener. She picked up from them their sense of occasion combined with their sense that this was an ordinary, unfrightening, matter that was taking place in front of them.

So there we were, eight or nine people, differing in at least three dimensions: adults and children, Iranians and Americans, affluent urbanites and villagers, with differences of language and religion falling along the same cleavages. We were sustaining a joint performance in spite of the fact that, as performers, we did not share a common code. What was happening had different meanings to us according to where we fell in these different categories. The contrasts were as great between the sophisticated urban people and the villagers, who were all nominally Muslims and Iranians, as between the American outsiders and our hosts. We were going through the performance of a ritual, with a beginning and an end, and a certain festive but serious quality to it. We were sharing in sustaining that joint performance without working from the same codes or the same systems of meaning.

I had, at that point, come from a period of research on mother-infant communication. When my daughter was born, I had decided that since I was going to be distracted for some time to come, I would arrange my professional work in such a way that the distraction would be beneficial. I had been working at the Research Lab of Electronics at MIT where another researcher, Margaret Bullowa, had collected a corpus of films of mother-infant interaction, and I was studying those films and tapes and then dashing home to nurse Vanni when the babies on the film reminded me that it was time. I had set my work up that way, working on infants between one and two months old, because I was convinced that I would see and be able to document interactions in the film that I was seeing and responding to in my own relationship with my daughter. And indeed I found myself describing a pattern of playful vocalizations between mother and infant that I spoke of in terms of the epigenesis of conversation.

What interested me about these proto-conversations was that whereas the mother was speaking sentences to the infant, using the words and grammatical patterns of adult language, the infant was responding with little coos and gurgles, so that the internal structure of the infant's behavior was quite different from the internal structure of the mother's behavior, but together they were collaborating in sustaining a joint performance that looked like a conversation. And that joint performance preceded the differentiation of linguistic structure—learning words or grammar or rules of sentences. Just as, in this later scene in the Persian garden, Vanni was able to be a participant in a scene with a very complex history and set of cultural references which she knew nothing about and did not need to know in order to be a participant.

This relates to another line of thought about the classroom. Classes, like the giving of speeches and the presentation of papers at conferences, involve joint productions shared in by people with only partially overlapping systems of meaning, constructing in the process the categories with which they subsequently work. Vanni was also, I suppose, learning something about my stance in a situation of that

sort. She doesn't remember this occasion now, but she would have remembered it over the next few months, and other experiences would have been matched with it and sorted out in her learning process. She was going through experiences of immersion in a new culture and having to learn not only the things that adults can tell you about being a guest, but also the things they don't know about how children are expected to behave in that setting. And even as a two-year-old she was playing multiple roles.

I was struck, several years later, when my daughter was about twelve, with a comment of hers: "Gee, Mom, it must be awfully hard on you and Daddy that I'm not interested in any of the things you're interested in." Now what do I say? Because she was coming up on adolescence, maybe she needed that sense of distance and contrast: on the other hand, maybe she didn't. So I asked, "How do you mean?" She said, "You're social scientists, and I'm an actress." Which she is, in fact; this is an interest that has continued. She said, "I'm not interested in writing books or giving lectures or being in a university or any of that stuff; I'm interested in acting." And I said, "Well, it does seem to me that to be a good actress you have to be good at observing people and trying to understand their motivations and the meanings they're working with—trying to empathize with them. It seems to me that you use a lot of the same skills that your daddy and I use, in a different setting." I was praying that this was the right response, and I think it was, because she's been repeating a version of it to people ever since. It gave her a reframing, a way of connecting the meaning of what she cared about doing with a relationship that she cared about. That reframing was based on a true connection between observation and performance. Vanni subsequently joined an improvisational theater group and got me thinking about improvisation as central to the way we really behave. What I didn't know enough to mention that day was that we, the social scientists, are also performers—actors—not only in classrooms and lecture halls, but in our conduct as we find our way into the settings and relationships from which we learn most.

As I look at the anthropological literature, I find discussions of enculturation that seem to imply that the knowledge of a culture is packed into children in childhood, and then they know it. You find a little more in sociology, in terms of discussions of adult socialization as you enter a new institution or a new role, and in recent years there's been discussion of how one learns to be a widow, how one learns to be a retired person, of learning new roles as these come up in different stages of the life cycle. But even so, the assumption is that you first learn a role and then you perform it. Now I'm arguing that this often happens the other way around. You have to begin performing a role before you learn it, and the learning never ends.

There are moments when one experiences this very sharply, like the moment of arriving home from the hospital with a new baby. You're in the role, and you're learning it as you go along, and improvising. As time goes on you get a little more skilled. As for the father, depending on the era he belongs to, he knows he's supposed to pace in the waiting room or to count breaths in the delivery room, but he too has to make it up as he goes along. You have to improvise, you have to invent, all the way. The available scripts are fragmentary at best. The invention of how to be the person you are at a moment in time takes place in a social and communicative context where you are also instructing the other person, like most teachers, in something you don't know too much about yet yourself.

Recently, I've been experimenting with a phrase that may help address some of the issues that we live with at the moment: the notion of a canon of human experience, as contrasted with a canon of great books. On the one hand, there are the experiences represented in this story by the sheep's liver and pancreas and heart—the realities of biological life: learning one's own body, one's maturation, sexuality, illness, the biological possibilities of being human. But you can't even begin to think about these commonalities without encountering cultural differences, because the world—and even the body—is experienced differently through the interpretive systems of different cultures. When you encounter (let us say) the body in the context of cultural difference, in the context of the contrasting patterns that we've seen in that garden, you attend in a new kind of way. This is true even of death. If you go to

the funeral of an immigrant, there will be present at the funeral relatives from the old country who mourn in a different way. When you mourn in your Anglo-Saxon-influenced American way while someone else is there wailing, the juxtaposition of the two reactions to the same biological phenomenon offers a deepening of your sense of that experience. This is the "canon" we need exposure to.

We have gotten ourselves into a terrible pickle today, where the term "multiculturalism" has apparently come to mean we ought to have (in the classroom) a dose of role models and historical figures for every ethnic group, and then each cluster of people can refuse to learn about other people's traditions. That's not what multiculturalism is about at all. I would hope "multiculturalism" would mean everyone in that classroom being exposed to the traditions of the others. Multiculturalism refers to a situation in which the world is not fixed because of this or that customary arrangement, like the 1950s vision of domesticity. A husband and wife in the suburbs with two children, a station wagon, and a puppy is not a model of "family" given by the laws of nature, but one of several ways of doing things and by no means the healthiest or most adaptive; so we can all benefit from exposure to alternative models, not one but several. If you look at "family" cross-culturally, you are liable to conclude that children are better off with more than one caretaker, but a household with only two adults is also pretty skimpy, and children may be best off with five or six caring adults, in all sorts of possible arrangements. This is what multiculturalism should mean: access to a very wide range of experiences.

Anthropologists get away with murder, you know. One day we claim, rightly, the status of a science, and the next day we apply to the National Endowment for the Humanities for a grant. There's a great deal to be said for this, because the divisions are artificial. One reason I like to talk about the canon of human experience is that when you expose yourself to the culture of another human community, you are exposing yourself to a masterpiece, to a work of art, to the invention of a form of humanness that has been made over a long period of time. This then allows the thinking of ways to connect, to share, in spite of disparate codes. We hear all this concern at the moment about what we are going to do if we don't have all the same central ideas, if we haven't read all the same books, if we don't have a core on which we agree. Well, you know, we may do what mothers and infants do. We may do what often enough strangers do. We may work together to sustain joint performances, joint institutions, joint conversations in the larger sense, including the entire process of political discourse, in spite of not sharing a single, uniform code. And do everything we can to make those shared performances contexts for learning.

Somebody once described to me what used to be called "the U.N. gesture": you are walking down the hall and you sort of move your right hand part way forward because you are trying to figure out whether the person walking toward you comes from a culture where people shake hands; you're ready to shake hands if shaking hands is the appropriate thing to do. That search for cues, that willingness to improvise, is not a bad starting point in human relations.

After I got married, my husband and I went on our honeymoon to Beirut to visit his family. There are a lot of good stories about that but I'm only going to tell you one, which happened at the airport on our last day. It is quite interesting learning to be a Middle Eastern daughter-in-law. My husband's family is Armenian, and there they were at the airport saying goodbye to us. And I thought, oh dear, I forgot to ask Barkev whom I'm supposed to kiss. Well, there was his mother: easy, I was sure I should kiss her. And there was his brother. I wasn't absolutely sure, but I figured, let's do it. There was the other brother, I kissed him. There was his sister: easy. There was his sister's husband, and next to him was the sister's husband's brother. Well . . . the question was, *how many people to kiss?* There was not much to go on in this process because they were also having to work out how to deal with a foreign daughter-in-law. You have to meet a situation like that with the sense that the traditional frameworks within which individuals repeat traditional patterns are themselves works of high art, but that the improvisations are also works of art. So I kissed the sister's husband, and I could feel in the set of his shoulder muscles that I had done the wrong thing,

and at least I knew better than to kiss his brother. I was only a little off in this particular improvisation, and there was good will to spare.

This is really the kind of issue we all face, not always with sufficient good will. We are only going to be able to feel comfortable in this world of multiculturalism, in this world where we struggle to sustain joint performances with disparate codes, if we combine with the improvisation that has to go on a sense of the aesthetic values involved in this process: the sense that the traditional frameworks within which individuals carry on their improvisations are themselves works of high art and of improvisation as an art form.

Improvisation is central to living in periods of change, when it is very hard to prepare for a specific future and you have to find ways of combining skills that are not given in existing models. The roles of women are changing, at the moment, faster than the roles of men, which means that there are some contexts in which, willy nilly, women are the pioneers. It is women who are figuring out how to adapt to a very different shape of life cycle, in ways that I believe will be true of men as well. But of course it is women and men together who have to learn to sustain joint performances, both learning and teaching at the same time. I see an analog between my situation as a bride, newly arriving in another country, and that of a child newly arrived in a particular society, or the situation of refugees, as there are today many refugees from Iran, trying to reconstruct their lives. These issues arise for people dealing with other discontinuities too: lost jobs, changing technologies, political upheaval; the need to re-invent constantly, and therefore to improvise. But you see, we have a library we can draw on, the canon of human experience that teaches as much by its diversity as by its specific details.

Sometimes it is helpful to have a fresh metaphor that changes the way you are focusing your attention in a given situation. A lot of women have talked about "juggling" their multiple roles. Just thinking of that metaphor makes me uncomfortable, because it does have a truth but it primarily conveys the sense of anxiety about whether one will in fact be able to sustain the performance: whether one of these many balls in the air is going to fall down. Real jugglers are highly skilled, and they perform with great grace, yet the metaphor evokes anxiety. By contrast, the metaphor of an improvisational art form, putting together different elements, dealing with the unknown in a way which sustains performance and connects it with other systems of meaning, can make us celebrate the uncertainties with which we are beginning to live.

For some reason, which is not fully clear to me, I have been recycling this episode in the Persian garden which has recently come to seem pregnant with the meaning that can be drawn out of it. I should tell you how the story ends, to the extent that such a story ever does end. The theoretically correct behavior is to give the meat of the sacrificed sheep to the poor. In fact, the fleece and the internal organs were given to the gardener as a reward for his work, and the landlord and landlady packed up the meat to take back to Tehran to share with family members. We got in the car and drove to the city, with Vanni falling off to sleep on my lap. I went on with trying to learn Persian and Iranian customs. By now, as you know, it is quite likely that the landlord and landlady are outside of the country. Perhaps one or two of that gardener's sons died in the war with Iraq. A lot of time has passed, a lot of changes. But the revolution that eventually occurred was present in that garden. It was present in the class differences, and in the ambivalent relationship to tradition of the wealthy urban landowners, the cultural disparities between them and the villagers they were employing. Even the presence of a foreigner, I think you would have to say that Iran was a society in which the codes did become unmanageably disparate, so I cannot use that episode only to say that it is possible to sustain a joint performance across vast differences. But I can use it to make people aware that when we talk about multiculturalism we are talking about the opportunity to learn, and that multiculturalism is only viable if we combine it with the expectation of life-long learning. When we talk about going beyond the traditional canon, we are talking about opening up a library not of great books, but of versions of humanness—some of them never written down in any form at all. A lifetime is long enough for multiple versions without, in the end, scanting one's own tradition.

My emphasis on improvisation and on learning going on all the time is a way of escaping from the notion that you are supposed to get something under your belt, some fixed body of knowledge: control it, have it, be educated and then live a life. If we can get away from that we may be able to reshape the current, very badly shaped, debate about education in such a way that we have some sense of the resources available for learning and of how life can keep on unfolding as an artistic performance, as a graceful and creative improvisation, for people of every age.

Key Terms

culture learning	performance
experience	Persia
Iran	ritual

Discussion Questions

1. According to Bateson, how is intercultural communication a "joint performance"?

2. Bateson writes from an interpretive perspective. How might a social science scholar investigate this topic of intercultural learning?

3. How do you think the different power positions of the people present in this Persian garden (e.g., male-female, U.S.-Iranian) might influence their communication with each other?

4. Do you think the international relations between the United States and Iran would have influenced the intercultural relationships of the people in this essay? Do you think this kind of interaction would be different today?

5. To what extent does Bateson think experience is important in intercultural learning and scholarship?

40 Redefining the "Other" in Multicultural Research

DOLORES V. TANNO and FRED E. JANDT

Science may date from human prehistory, but at least since the time of Aristotle we have believed that to explain an event we must give its causes. However, societies differ in the extent to which science is an accepted way of knowing, as Malinowski (1948) has pointed out. Science, as a methodology as well as a body of knowledge, has influenced Western thought since the 17th and 18th centuries. Its impact has been so strong that it is still often perceived as the only legitimate way to determine what constitutes knowledge.

The position that very little in social science exists without a parallel in physical sciences has given rise to fierce debate. One side argues that by the nature of social data, physical sciences cannot serve "as a model, observing that social scientists have not succeeded in confirming any laws. The other side argues that it is not the physical science model per se but rather the underlying reasoning that is significant: that is, establishing facts as empirically verifiable observations about social relations.

This paper does not continue the debate over the adequacy of the physical science model for studying human society, a debate described by Maulana Karenga (1993) as one of "power and place" in which power is given exclusively to the researcher as definer and evaluator. Rather, this paper examines the *consequences* of research based on the physical science model in the *multicultural context*, in which concerns about the production and ownership of knowledge lead to questioning who is the "other" in the multicultural research process. Any research model based on the physical sciences will, by definition, lead the researcher to consider and talk about "others" as objects who are subject to observation and manipulation. In addition, this model assumes a monologic, monocultural perspective through which the "other" is studied, a perspective that underscores the researcher's position of power and authority.

Before we proceed further, we want to provide the rationale for our specific focus and to define our terms. We have chosen to focus on multicultural communication studies because they offer a unique research opportunity insofar as other cultures have generally been understood by superimposing on them the accepted epistemological, ontological, and methodological assumptions of another, more dominant culture.

We have used the word *multicultural* for two reasons. First, it serves an inclusive function, since it subsumes all the communicative acts previously defined as occurring in intercultural, cross-cultural, and international contexts. Second, because the common emphasis in these contexts is the study of communication as it is affected by cultural traditions, rituals, and so forth, we adhere to Prosser's (1978) definition of culture as "the traditions, customs, norms, beliefs, values, and thought-patterning which are passed down from generation to generation" (p. 5). We define the multicultural "other" broadly as including all participants in any multicultural study, as well as the cultural collectives to whom study conclusions are often generalized. We agree with McPhail's (1991) argument that the language of research should be "a *rhetoric of coherence,* one that defines and constructs reality in such a way as to resolve the problem of privileging one position at the expense of another" (p. 10). The idea of dialogue here implied is articulated by Broome (1991) in his study of empathy in the intercultural context; Broome argues that "instead of trying to understand the other as a separate objective entity, the focus is on co-creating with the other a shared reality" (p. 247).

Redefining the multicultural "other" is an attempt to humanize research through a multidisciplinary effort that seeks empowerment through dialogue with those previously labeled and perceived as subjects for observations. For example, in the field of communication studies, Altman and Nakayama (1991) address empowerment by arguing that it is essential to have "difficult dialogue" about the ways "differences . . . are constructed in social interactions and in public discourse" (p. 116). Nakayama and Altman (1992) also advocate dialogue as one critical strategy whereby we can "emphasize multivocality and inclusiveness" in multicultural studies (p. 10).

The researcher can be empowered in new ways. Anthropologist Dan Rose (1990) suggests the need for researcher empowerment by calling attention to graduate schools' strong conformist ideology that constructs our research persona, as well as the persona of the "other" whom we study. This socialization not only creates a gap between the "expert" and the "other" but also inculcates the fixed belief that our true audiences, the ones for whom our knowledge is produced, are fellow experts.

Buchler (1955) recounts that philosopher Charles Peirce argued there are four general ways of "fixing belief": tenacity, authority, a priori, and science. *Tenacity* refers to firmly held truths; *authority* refers to established beliefs; *a priori* refers to self-evident assumptions; and *science* refers to the method by which beliefs are determined by "nothing human, by some external permanency, by something upon which our thinking has no effect," by which all can reach the same ultimate conclusion (p. 18). Clearly, the research persona has resulted from socialization according to the scientific way of inculcating ideas.

Over 30 years ago, Thomas Kuhn's book *The Structure of Scientific Revolutions* (1962) challenged the scientific community to examine its perceptions of an objective reality as resulting from socially accepted beliefs that he called "paradigms" (p. 10). Kuhn argued that science progressed by way of paradigm shifts or changes in scientists' beliefs. A new paradigm is created when the old paradigm fails to provide solutions for critical problems. In early times, for example, the Ptolemaic paradigm in astronomy was replaced by the Copernican paradigm when the increasingly complex understanding of the heavens did not lead to a concomitant increase in predictive accuracy. Kuhn's thoughtful analysis clearly showed that paradigms act as filters that screen our experiences and our perceptions. Kuhn asserted that advocates of differing paradigms cannot communicate with one another because the meanings of their respective concepts can be contradictory.

More recently, Bohm and Peat (1987) have contended that the break in communication between persons holding different paradigms calls for the establishment of a true dialogue, a dialogue that acknowledges any point of view "as it actually is whether one likes it or not" (p. 241) and that requires exploring the other's point of view. Bohm and Peat describe the major barrier to this dialogue as the rigidity in the tacit infrastructure of rules governing how interactions should occur. This rigidity is also in place in the research process, and it often prevents us from engaging in a dialogue. Bohm and Peat thus help explain why various marginalized groups are increasingly challenging the adequacy of the science-based research paradigm to provide truly accurate and complete understanding of their respective cultures.

Clearly, our attempts at understanding our diverse society have not been as successful as we hoped. Our studies have provided great amounts of information, but they do not seem to have resulted in the self-reflection, self-definition, and self-understanding that can lead to the empowerment of those we study. While the discovery of the boiling point of water at various elevations does not change the *nature* of water, multicultural studies have the potential of changing the *nature* of how groups perceive themselves: discovering contributing factors to school dropout rates among different marginalized groups, for example, has the potential of forever changing group identity whenever members internalize and act on that information. Klaus Krippendorf (1989) has argued that "we have to take *responsibility for the kind of image . . .* we portray in our theories of human communication and human participation in social affairs" (p. 79).

Even as our studies have failed to empower multicultural research participants, our approaches to research have largely reflected our unwillingness as researchers to work outside the constraints of a science-based model. One notable exception is Kenneth Bancroft Clark's body of work, which challenged the paradigm that led to the "tendency to replace notions of biological inferiority with notions of cultural inferiority" (Steinberg, 1989, p. 118). That Clark's challenge contributed to civil rights reform and thus to some degree of empowerment is evidenced by the extensive citation of his work in the 1954 *Brown v. Board of Education* decision. Other examples of questioning the science-based model include some feminist, ethnographic, performance-based, and critical studies.

It seems we are operating under a dominant paradigm that can no longer deal with the complexities of a multicultural society. Once we accept that proposition, the characteristics of a new paradigm should be sought. We want to argue that the "others" in multicultural research should be perceived as being co-owners and co-producers of knowledge, as having the ability to ask questions and assist in gathering and validating data, and as becoming the primary audience to whom our findings should be addressed. In attempting to redefine the "other," this essay represents a beginning point. We have organized it around three paradigmatic issues, the first epistemic and the latter two ontological, as well as methodological: "The 'Other' as Co-Producer/ Owner of Knowledge," "The 'Other' as Participant," and "The 'Other' as Audience."

The "Other" as Co-Producer/ Owner of Knowledge

The first characteristic of the new paradigm concerns the epistemic issue of production and ownership of scholarly knowledge. We have long been accustomed to the idea that once publication occurs, we move on to more and we hope, better studies. We presume that the academic community owns the knowledge that results from such studies. But what if the "other" participated in all aspects of the research process and thus could claim co-ownership? We offer here three examples that suggest such participation can and should occur: the first describes shared production of knowledge, the second addresses the purpose of research, and the third raises the question of owning knowledge.

Shared production of knowledge that approaches research as dialogue or co-production of

knowledge is found in Alberto González's (1989) study of WMEX-FM radio in Ohio. González wanted to understand the role played by this Mexican-American radio station in simultaneously helping to maintain cultural identity and reducing intercultural distance. Of particular significance in this study is the way González made the DJs active participants:

> Throughout the study, I attempted to make my observations accessible to and understood within the social world encompassed by the site. Periodically during the two-and-one-half years of research, I explained my observations and interpretations to the DJs and gave them opportunities to clarify their perceptions. . . . In the summer of 1985, the original DJs met a final time . . . to retell their experiences with WMEX and to respond to my interpretations. (p. 399)

González and Peterson (1993) reiterate the importance of real participation when they address feminism and intercultural communication: "Rather than *determining* whether the lot of women has improved or worsened, feminists studying intercultural communication should demonstrate their respect for those women they study by *asking them*" (p. 268).

Both González's radio study and González and Peterson's admonition demonstrate that understanding how discourse is used to promote ethnic pride, as well as participation in the larger society, occurs at two levels. Thus in the former case we see *intracultural* understanding occurring because the DJs were intimately involved in the study from beginning to end, as well as the *intercultural* understanding that adds to the collective knowledge of how a particular marginalized group perceives itself in the greater society. Together these two levels of understanding suggest a degree of empowerment.

The second example, taken from an anthropological study, points to the attitudinal stances of researchers that we will have to recognize, define, and reassess before we can move toward a research-as-dialogue process of understanding. In *Living the Ethnographic Life*, Rose (1990) makes a compelling argument "urging a more radical democratization of knowledge" that "deprivileges our academic inquiry while serving to help recover ideas and practices from other points of view—whether of marginal or oppressed people, whether close to home or geographically and culturally remote" (p. 11). Rose urges researchers toward self-study, toward questioning why we do research and what is the impact of the knowledge we find. If knowledge about cultures is to be richer and truer, the logic of inquiry demands that our methodologies must mirror cultural realities and needs. This understanding will occur when we acknowledge that "people have the right to define their own reality, establish their own identities, name their history" (hooks, 1989, p. 42).

Concerning the ownership of knowledge, we offer our third example: the Maori. Biculturalism was asserted in the 1840 Treaty of Waitangi between the British Crown and the Maori of New Zealand. But since the signing of the treaty, the relationship between the two cultures has been one of domination and marginalization of the Maori people (Walker, 1990). To cite one significant example, schools were established on the English model, which valued the written over the oral in marked contrast to the Maori-preferred modes of knowledge transmission.

Social-science research *on* the Maori has concentrated on identifying the characteristics that contribute to "subcultural" and "dysfunctional" behaviors of group members in the dominant majority culture (Smith, 1991). Much research has belittled or otherwise adversely affected the Maori and their history even as it benefitted the researchers and the non-Maori academic community. Academic theory even has the Maori crossing the Pacific by the winds of chance, thus effectively denying their skills as navigators.

Today a growing number of Maori insist that Maori research should be done by Maori people only. From a more moderate position, Ohia (1989) argues that the place of Maori in the research is as initiators of the process; it is the Maori who best understand what is necessary to promote their own improvement and empowerment.

Maori opposition to traditional social science research raises questions about the initiator, the controller, the interpreter, and the owner of research. It is not difficult to project this scenario onto cultures represented in the Americas. Unless we change our attitudes and practices, we may have no "participants" at all.

The "Other" as Participant

The second characteristic of the new paradigm is a redefined role of the participant. Over the years, many small steps have been taken away from thinking of individuals as passive sources of data. One example is the informed consent requirement, which resulted from concern voiced about the possibility of harm to those being studied. Another example is rhetorical in nature and signals an understanding of the power of language. We have largely replaced *subjects* with *participants,* hoping to establish the idea of a more dialogic approach to research. Yet the language of the American Psychological Association's 1982 Code of Research Ethics still assumes an authoritative position of power on behalf of the researcher: "The investigator always retains the responsibility for ensuring ethical practice in research," or "The investigator protects the participant," or "After the data are collected, the investigator provides the participant with information." A clear separation of the "expert" and the "nonexpert" serves to dehumanize the "other." Moreover, the use of *subjects* still finds favor in recent publications. In *Planning Ethically Responsible Research,* Sieber (1992) argues for the use of the term as follows:

> Many have argued that the term *research participant* is more respectful than the term *subject.* For some purposes, I would agree. For the purposes of this book, however, I would prefer to use the term that continually reminds the reader that the person being studied typically has *less power* than the researcher and must be accorded the protections that render this *inequality morally acceptable* [italics added]. (p. 13)

We italicized language in this quotation to demonstrate the deeply rooted assumptions underlying the traditional research paradigm. Understanding the power of language, Karenga (1993) argues that to replace "slave trade" with "the holocaust of enslavement," for example, permits greater insight into African American culture, and to replace "colonization" with the "holocaust of colonization" allows for a perceptual stance that would allow researchers to see Latino and Native American cultures in a different light.

The examples taken from the Code of Ethics and those provided by Karenga illustrate Kuhn's contention that different paradigmatic stances lead to different perceptions. More important, these examples illustrate that ultimately the words that shape the paradigms possess transformative power. In a multicultural context, such transformation can lead either to generally empowering those involved or to maintaining a power schism between the expert and the so-called nonexpert.

To diminish the gap between researcher and participant, we must begin thinking of the "other" as someone who possesses the ability, means, and willingness to participate in creating and understanding knowledge. We must acknowledge that the "other" can contribute not only the data upon which we impose our methodologies but also the questions that guide our research, the interpretation of data, and the validation of conclusions. As Karenga (1993) suggests, we need to generate research questions from within cultures. According to anthropologist Renato Rosaldo (1989), the postmodern view of participants is that they can and do "critically interrogate" (p. 2). Furthermore, as Anthony Giddens (1989) observes, participants are human agents, and "all human agents know a great deal about the conditions of their activity" (p. 57). Thus the idea of passive subjects or participants is an illusion that offers us a comfortable intellectual distance because of "our sense of possessing intellectual control . . . [and] a reliance on ourselves to interpret [studies] successfully by appropriately modifying our framework of anticipations," as Michael Polanyi (1962, p. 103) has stated. Instead, Polanyi gives us a new definition of the "other" as knower when he writes of "personal knowledge," or the "*personal participation* of the knower in all acts of understanding" when "comprehension is neither an arbitrary act nor a passive experience" (p. vii). Perceived in this way, the redefined "other" in multicultural research can be invited to become the co-originator of research questions and the co-validator of research results.

Clearly, if we begin talking about the research process using terms such as *true participation* and *dialogue* and the "other" as *expert* about his or her life conditions, these rhetorical changes may help us synchronize the multicultural research process with the multicultural social reality.

The "Other" as Audience

A third characteristic of the new paradigm is the incorporation of research participants and cultural communities into our concept of *audience*. This particular change can occur if we ask ourselves questions proposed by Bishop (1992): Who needs to have access to research findings? To whom is the researcher accountable?

Currently, we are accountable only to one another, and thus our research is directed at a specialized few—in the language used to formulate the questions we ask, in the methodologies we use to answer those questions, in the language of the conclusions themselves, and in the dissemination of those conclusions.

There is the sense that participants become constructed *before* the research begins. This perception can happen when the results of earlier studies on particular ethnic groups are unquestioningly accepted as accurate and truthful representations of their cultures (the Maori are a case in point). We ask research questions and accommodate the methodology on the basis of *a priori* construction. But we know that answers are often embedded in the questions we propose; therefore, we end up finding that which we seek. Such commitment to the received view at the expense of true understanding is "unconscionable," as Krippendorf (1989) argues:

> By making an objective and observer-independent reality the principal ruler over the constitution of scientific knowledge, *this dominant paradigm in effect absolves scientists from taking responsibility for their constructions.* (p. 78)

The question then becomes: what can we do to take responsibility? One answer is that we can begin making conscious efforts to turn the "other" into the audience of our research results.

If research questions and data collection are co-designed by the "other" and if results are owned by the "other" as well, researchers become consultants or participants in a dialogue. Viewing the "other" from within this new paradigm has the potential to change study results in important ways. For example, if we use a traditional approach to the problem of birth control in a society, we may assume that a public medium is the most appropriate channel for disseminating information and thus may conclude that radio or television programming would be the most effective means. However, by redefining the "other" and inviting true participation, we may discover that birth control is viewed as so personal an issue that more private channels of information dissemination not only are perceived as more appropriate but also are more effective. The multicultural "other" might, for example, recommend messages on calendars because not only are they inexpensive but also they are more private and are consulted daily in every home.

Another aspect of making the "other" an audience is to stop writing only for each other, beginning instead to communicate our knowledge back to participants. We know very few people outside any given discipline who regularly read academic journals. A first step would be to identify the primary information outlets of each culture we study and attempt consistently to use them in conveying information about studies. To publish in other than "legitimate" journals is professionally risky, but to take the risk is to take responsibility for our part in the social construction of cultural images.

We recognize the paradox of publishing these ideas in an academicians' journal. In fact, a reviewer astutely asked, "Aren't you, the authors, by publishing an essay in an academic journal, merely perpetuating the very practice that you are criticizing?" At this time, the only honest answer to this question is "Yes." But we perceive that two trends are developing in multicultural research. The first is that the "other" is increasingly becoming more actively critical about the process of sharing knowledge about his or her culture. The second is that a growing number of researchers and critics[1] are actively examining the role of traditional research in the multicultural context to find, as Broome (1991) argues, that it has "offered more confusion than inspiration and more discouragement than motivation" (p. 245). We can add only that the traditional research paradigm has largely failed to acknowledge the power of the other. We raise the possibility that

what we describe here is a need to reduce uncertainty between the researcher or critic and the multicultural "other." We hope that as the need for a paradigm shift becomes more obvious and as more researchers conduct studies that adhere to these new definitions, we will increasingly find access to a wider variety of information outlets, while at the same time becoming more comfortable with our roles as participators in a research dialogue.

Conclusions

In effect, we argue for closing the gap between the expert and the presumed nonexpert. William Foote Whyte (1991) has proposed the label *participatory action research* (PAR) to describe studies that involve participants in the entire research process, from initial design, to data-gathering and analysis, and finally to conclusions and actions arising out of the research. Whyte's *Street Corner Society,* published in 1943, was a precursor in using this methodology. In 1991, Whyte continued to promote PAR as "the alternative view . . . that it is important, both for the advancement of science and for the improvement of human welfare, to devise strategies in which research and action are closely linked" (p. 8). Although PAR has been used primarily in industrial and agricultural studies, PAR-like methodologies are appropriate to multicultural research because of the approach's concern for improvement and empowerment through participation. PAR is clearly different from "applied research" as it is commonly understood: the researcher is the professional expert who controls the design, the collection of data, and the interpretation of findings, and who ultimately makes the recommendations. With methodologies like PAR, the gap between participant and researcher is considerably lessened as they work together throughout the research process.

The dialogue between researcher and participant is clearly one of the most important benefits gained when we redefine the "other." Through research dialogue, the empowerment of both participant and researcher is potentially increased. But other benefits may be gained, most notably the shared production and ownership of knowledge and the promise of a deeper understanding.

We will encounter obstacles, however, as we re-define the "other" in multicultural communication research. The most obvious is that the research enterprise we have described will be much more time consuming. The less-obvious—but perhaps the most difficult—obstacle is the uncertainty we will experience about the different roles we must play in the research process. Ultimately, the clearest evidence of our willingness and ability to change how we view the multicultural "other" will be the willingness and ability to change how we view our role as researchers and critics.

Note

1. In addition to those cited, other examples include B. Broome (1991), "Bridging the Gulf Between Two Realities: Personal Reflection and Essay," *International Journal of Intercultural Relations, 15,* 323–326; B. Broome (1993, November), "Collective Design of the Tribal Future," paper presented at the annual meeting of the Speech Communication Association, Miami Beach; A. Mirande & D. V. Tanno (1993), "Labels, Research Perspective, and Contextual Validation: A Commentary," *International Journal of Intercultural Relations, 17,* 149–155; A. Mirande and D. V. Tanno (1993), "Understanding Interethnic Communication and Research: 'A Rose by any Other Name Would Smell as Sweet,'" *International Journal of Intercultural Relations, 17,* 381–388. In addition, the 1992 SCA convention included a seminar, "New Agenda in Intercultural Communication," that addressed new ways of thinking about intercultural communication.

References

Altman, K. E., & Nakayama, T. K. (1991). Making a critical difference: A difficult dialogue. *Journal of Communication, 41,* 116–128.

American Psychological Association. (1982). *Code of research ethics.* Copyright 1973, 1982.

Bishop, R. (1992, July). *Toward a paradigm for participant driven empowering research in a bicultural context.* Paper presented at the Summer Workshop for the Development of Intercultural Coursework at Colleges and Universities, East-West Center, Honolulu.

Bohm, D., & Peat, F. D. (1987). *Science, order, and creativity.* London: Routledge.

Broome, B. (1991). Building shared meaning: Implications of a relational approach to empathy for teaching intercultural communication. *Communication Education, 40,* 235–249.

Buchler, J. (Ed.). (1955). *Philosophical writings of Peirce.* New York: Dover.

Giddens, A. (1989). The orthodox consensus and the emerging synthesis. In B. Dervin, L. Grossberg, B. O'Keefe, & E. Wartella (Eds.), *Rethinking communication: Volume 1, Paradigm Issues* (pp. 53–65). Newbury Park, CA: Sage.

González, A. (1989). "Participation" at WMEX-FM: Interventional rhetoric of Ohio Mexican Americans. *Western Journal of Speech Communication, 53,* 398–410.

González, A., & Peterson, T. R. (1993). Enlarging conceptual boundaries: A critique of research in intercultural communication. In S. Bowen & N. Wyatt (Eds.), *Transforming visions: Feminist critiques in communication studies* (pp. 249–278). Cresskill, NJ: Hampton Press.

hooks, b. (1989). *Talking back: Thinking feminist, thinking black.* Boston: South End Press.

Karenga, M. (1993, April). *Multiculturalism in the university: The multidimensional challenge.* Paper presented at the Second International East Meets West Conference in Cross-cultural Communication, Comparative Philosophy, and Comparative Religion, Long Beach, CA.

Krippendorf, K. (1989). On the ethics of constructing communication. In B. Dervin, L. Grossberg, B. O'Keefe, & E. Wartella (Eds.), *Rethinking communication: Volume 1, Paradigm Issues* (pp. 66–96). Newbury Park, CA: Sage.

Kuhn, T. S. (1962). *The structure of scientific revolutions.* Chicago: University of Chicago Press.

Malinowski, B. (1948). *Magic, science and religion, and other essays.* Glencoe, IL: Free Press.

McPhail, M. L. (1991). Complicity: The theory of negative difference. *Howard Journal of Communications, 3,* 1–13.

Nakayama, T. K., & Altman, K. E. (1992, October). *Rhetorics of culture.* Paper presented in New Approaches to Intercultural Communication (W. S. Lee & P. Wander, Chairs), seminar conducted at the meeting of the Speech Communication Association, Chicago.

Ohia, M. (1989, Summer). *Research for Maori education.* Paper presented at New Zealand Association for Research on Education Conference, Trentham.

Polanyi, M. (1962). *Personal knowledge: Towards a post-critical philosophy.* Chicago: University of Chicago Press.

Prosser, M. H. (1978). *The cultural dialogue: An introduction to intercultural communication.* Boston: Houghton Mifflin.

Rhetorics of culture. Paper presented in New Approaches to Intercultural Communication (W. S. Lee & P. Wander, Chairs), seminar conducted at the meeting of the Speech Communication Association, Chicago.

Rosaldo, R. (1989). *Culture and truth: The remaking of social analysis.* Boston: Beacon Press.

Rose, D. (1990). *Living the ethnographic life.* Newbury Park, CA: Sage.

Sieber, J. E. (1992). *Planning ethically responsible research.* Newbury Park, CA: Sage.

Smith, T. L. (1991). Te Rapuna I Te Ao Marama: Maori perspectives on research in education. In R. Morss, Jr., & T. J. Linzey (Eds.), *The politics of human learning: Human development and educational research* (pp. 46–55). Dunnedin, New Zealand: University of Otago Press.

Steinberg, S. (1989). *The ethnic myth: Race, ethnicity, and class in America* (rev. ed.). Boston: Beacon Press.

Walker, R. (1990). *Ka Whawhai Tonu Matou: Struggle without end.* Auckland, New Zealand: Penguin.

Whyte, W. F. (1943). *Street corner society.* Chicago: University of Chicago Press.

Whyte, W. F. (1991). Introduction. In W. F. Whyte (Ed.), *Participatory action research* (pp. 7–15). Newbury Park, CA: Sage.

Key Terms

multicultural research	researcher responsibility
"other"	researcher role
ownership of knowledge	

Discussion Questions

1. Tanno and Jandt suggest that dialogue should be a central feature of intercultural communication research. Can we use their notion of dialogue in our daily intercultural interactions?

2. If we follow Tanno and Jandt's suggestion that the "other" be redefined in multicultural research, how will this new direction in research change the way we think about and do intercultural communication?

3. What responsibilities do we have as researchers in intercultural communication to the field we are studying? To the people we are studying? If these responsibilities come into conflict, what guidelines should we use to negotiate that conflict?

4. What should be the primary goal of intercultural communication research? Does our conception of the participants in the research affect that goal?

5. If we follow Tanno and Jandt's redefinition of the "other," and see the "other" as co-producer and owner of knowledge, as participant, and as audience, how might our research change? What strengths and limitations would there be in doing the participatory action research that Tanno and Jandt advocate?

41 Painting the White Face Red
Intercultural Contact Presented Through Poetic Ethnography

MARÍA CRISTINA GONZÁLEZ

It is claimed that the Native American spiritual leader Sitting Bull once stated that "if the Great Spirit had wanted me to be a white man, he would have made me one." Each of us is born into a particular set of circumstances, familial and cultural, racial and historical, that despite the changes in our lives, we can never really escape. Phenomenologists call this phenomenon "thrownness"—that great inexplicable sense of not having had any "say" over certain aspects of our experience. In the "great United States," we live with the myth that we can do, say, or be whatever or whomever we wish. In many ways, this myth allows us as individuals to challenge the thrownness of our social experience. It provides a belief system by which we can reject the undesirable or personally unacceptable in favor of a preferable reality.

Intercultural contact provides us all with opportunities to get to know how others view the world, how they experience day-to-day realities and differences in personal cultural identities. When this happens, we are able to examine our own worldview, experiences, and identities. Sometimes the boundaries we have established for our own identities are rigid and impermeable, not allowing for the changes that intercultural contact invites. Many of our efforts to improve intercultural relations focus on the negative attributions of "others" that occur and interfere with the potential for good relations when persons of different cultures meet. What is different is seen as bad, threatening, or offensive. As long as these views of the "other" remain, it is unlikely that good relations can develop between cultures.

Having a belief system that allows people to create their own identities creates the potential for a different sort of intercultural challenge. If for some reason an individual is unhappy with his or her social experience or personal identity, meeting people who live a different cultural reality can become a door of opportunity. New routines, values, forms of language, and norms for personal relationships can offer someone a "way out" of a lifestyle or cultural experience that is "not working" for one reason or another. When the social and cultural myths we live by support the idea of freedom to shape one's own identity, the potential for this possibility is increased.

The emphases on postmodern identities in contemporary social research, which allow for the simultaneous existence of many different identities, can also work to enable individuals to believe identity is something that can simply be chosen, as from a menu. The idea that all of our realities are socially constructed is often used as a philosophy for methodology and research. If we are not careful, such philosophies can lead to intercultural research that doesn't take into account the importance of the meaning of identities and realities that are constructed by particular cultural groups.

Often, contact with a different culture opens us to see possibilities for our own existence. By deconstructing our current identities and identifying the multiple forces that have influenced the "way we turned out," it is possible to imagine the ways we would have turned out if we'd had more freedom to be ourselves "naturally." The idea of returning to a more organic source of identity can be empowering.

These ideas create an interesting backdrop for the study that captured my attention for a 3-year period. In a nation where the freedom of personal choice is valued (if not practiced), and where cultural studies are leading us to see that no aspects of our social experience are by nature fixed, some people decide to choose to consciously reject aspects of their selves, to change who they are, to become "new persons," even if it means assuming a totally different ethnic identity. Some make new families, recreate histories, and even go so far as to alter their biological features of gender, race, and ethnicity.

For this study, I became interested in people who were deciding to "become Indian" (native American), even when they had no legitimate claims to the identity. Specifically, I was interested in those non-Indians who began practicing native American spirituality,[1] sharing with and learning from native Americans engaged in indigenous spiritual traditions.[2] In the United States it is common for people to acquire artifacts and features of many of the cultural groups who make up the U.S. society, to share in rituals and traditions as part of a multicultural experience. This is not the phenomenon that caught my attention. Rather, I was interested in people who gradually rejected their everyday ways of life in favor of an "Indian" lifestyle, transforming their living environments, adjusting their schedules, and altering their personal relationships in order to live in accordance with how they perceived the native American spiritual traditions they were learning and practicing.

In my personal experience of learning about my own family history of Lipan Apache and Tarahumara origin, I remembered that I was often asked if I was tribally enrolled to prove my claims of Indianness. I learned that there was a trend of "ethnic fraud" and cultural appropriation sweeping "Indian country" in the United States, and that it often showed itself most vividly in the arena of spirituality. This theme recurred throughout my ethnographic study of non-Indians sharing and learning native American spirituality.

Somehow, although identities are socially constructed and in many ways arbitrary, the phenomenon of people deciding to acquire new identities rooted in cultures not indigenous to their own experience or history can create an experience of violation. In this study, the respect of boundaries for ownership of and access to their own cultural experiences was integral to the cultural identity of the native Americans who shared (either voluntarily or involuntarily) their spiritual traditions.

This concept of respect for indigenous cultural experience and identity seemed to be vital to the understanding of what it was to "be Indian." It was a concept held to be central to the personal identity

and spiritual and emotional harmony of all peoples. As such, the non-Indian desire to become Indian was a mystery and perplexing. As each individual's life was by nature complex, it was baffling for anyone to want to add to that complexity. Why would someone want to add to the confusion of personal identity by attempting to take on an identity judged to be inauthentic, or as many asked, "why would someone want to be who they're not?"

As a scholar of human communication, the questions were equally as intriguing as they were perplexing. If I were to study this phenomenon of identity-shaping through the sharing of spirituality, what would I find? It was truly an intercultural process, one in which some seemed to be participating voluntarily, of which others claimed to be victims. As I read books and talked to people involved with native American spirituality, I found some to take a disciplined, studious approach, others to be undoggedly faithful to their teachers and traditions, and still others who seemed guided by an invisible and spurious intuition and sometimes by powerful personal preferences. Given this array of participants, how could an understanding of the boundaries of identity ever be reached?

As an ethnographer, my purposes were to eventually write about the intercultural experiences I witnessed, attempting to build understanding. I used the methods of participant observation and conversational interviewing over a period of $2\frac{1}{2}$ years, devoting another half year to writing the ethnography. For this work, I encountered many who were seeking to learn and practice Native American spiritual traditions. I found them in sweat lodge ceremonies, craft supply stores, New Age bookstores and workshops, public lectures, college campuses, museums, on and off Indian reservations. They were an international lot, prevalently from the United States, but with a growing interest and presence of European inquirers. A smaller contingent of Latin Americans were present. Also included in the groups were Native American and Chicana and Chicano individuals attempting to regain their own cultural identity through a commitment to practicing ancient traditions.

Although there was a largely intertribal "Indian" population involved, the traditions that I saw shared were primarily Lakota (which many non-Indians referred to as "Sioux"[3]). Because of the Lakota influence, much of my field immersion took place at sites and ceremonies to which I was invited on the Pine Ridge and Rosebud Reservations in South Dakota. I also attended ceremonies and gatherings in both private and public locations throughout the southwestern United States. I did not attend any private events to which I was not invited by a participant, family, or tribal member.

Because much of my work was done during actual ceremonies and in the events that surrounded these ceremonies, I did not choose to record in any traditionally academic way the experiences I witnessed. Instead, I chose to make impressionistic notes that triggered my recall of what I witnessed. For example, instead of recording verbatim the prayers or taking photographs of a ceremony, I would jot down phrases that captured the images for me. More ritualistic forms of expression, or the words used "every time" by "everyone," I would use in their verbatim form. In the few instances in which I conducted more formal interviews or attended lectures, I did make tape recordings and write notes.

As I proceeded with the study, I used the Four Seasons (González, 1996) as the guide for methodology, employing a combination of traditional ethnographic methods with introspective, reflective techniques. These methods, familiar to all ethnographers, I organized around a cycle of naturally occurring seasons of activity and based them in an ontology (assumptions of what is real) that privileges natural experience as determinant of action.

From the Four Seasons approach, natural experience is seen as having a powerful "say" in how one's research is done. It is therefore possible that the study you start out doing will look significantly different when you finish, based on what develops as you engage in the study. The validity of a study is based on its groundedness in real experience that determines its form and outcome, even if not preferred professionally or personally by the researcher or his or her discipline.

So, although the "four seasons" may seem on the surface to simply be a scheme for organizing methods in which others already engage, it is actually a worldview for doing research, one that says that the

researcher is not in charge; rather, it is the natural unfolding of experience that determines the process and outcomes of the study.[4] This powerful role of naturally occurring experience, both personal and social, was infused into the study by regularly asking the following questions throughout observation, interviews, analysis, and writing:

- Do I know why am I doing this study, both personally and professionally? (purpose, motives)
- Is this the right time for engaging in the method I choose to use, or is there a better time—or none—for doing what I want to do? (appropriateness)
- Am I open to all available sources of information in my data, even if it is not in agreement with my "hypotheses" and preconceived notions and wishes for this research? (rigor)
- Will my study accomplish what I intend without distorting the nature of what others have shared with me, or the relationships I developed? (ethics)
- Should I change my study or its focus given what I have learned? (adaptability)

It is the openness to radical change in direction or purpose of one's study that characterizes methods that reflect the ontology of natural experience. It is much the same as the unexpected late frost that thwarts a farmer's plans for a particular harvest, or a fire starting from a lightning bolt forcing whole natural populations to migrate. In this study, the passage of the seasons resulted in a nontraditional report of my "findings" through poetry.

Most ethnographies are written in prose. I chose to report through poetry for various reasons. Among those reasons was the growing awareness of the culture and personal experience involved in the phenomena I was studying. As I maintained my discipline of the Four Seasons and repeatedly asked myself the questions related to my study, I was concerned with the anonymity of the actual persons about whom I wrote, as well as respecting the sacredness of the ceremonies and spiritual practices shared. I would often remember how as a child raised Roman Catholic, I had been taught to revere the chalice at Mass; no one except those specially designated could touch it—the wine and crumbs from communion had to be disposed of in a special manner and in a special place. I chose to remember this type of reverence when dealing with traditions equally sacred to the people who were sharing them, and it allowed me to learn very much.

It also led me to realize that traditional academic writing would distort what had been shared with me in ways that would very likely offend or hurt. As I sifted through my notes and recollections, photographs and recordings, and discussed what I had experienced with participants, it also became increasingly obvious to me that to write the ethnography in prose that purported to express intercultural "facts" about the groups I observed, both Indian and non-Indian, would not capture the integral nuance of the phenomena. The dialectic tension would be removed by reporting units of knowledge, rather than by presenting both the positive and negative, the strong and the weak, the admirable and shameful, as it existed in the real experience. It was during this "fall harvesting" of my ethnographic process that I realized I would write the ethnography in poetry because poetry enabled the dialectic tension to be maintained and allowed for the experience of the spiritual through poesis.

I wrote almost 60 poems as the record of my study and shared these poems with members of the groups with whom I had shared experiences. I gave them the opportunity to respond to the versions of their experience I had represented poetically. In traditional ethnographic language, this is the process of "member-checking," of validating one's report through a checking of its content with members of the cultural groups. Had they disagreed with the versions I presented, or protested in some fashion, the required ethical response would have been to either change the poems or omit them entirely from the final ethnographic collection. Two poems were thus eliminated, being poems that reflected more my own editorial opinions and reflections than actual experiences. Others were deleted because of ambiguity resulting from the way in which they were written.

The 52 poems that resulted all describe phenomena that are based on actual situations that occurred during the 2½ year period of my participant observation; in other words, they are about "things that really happened." The names were all changed except when they referred to actual places and public gatherings, or when a dedication was made to a specific individual. Dedicated poems were shared with the persons to whom they were dedicated or with family members, if the person was deceased.

Many of the poems contain a composite of similar situations; as such, they are functioning as textual categories of field experience. The poems are able to give us the sense of an entire category of experience without the use of hierarchical outlines or axiomatic structures. Rather, they are contextually situated in a poetic form that allows for a simultaneous manifestation of emotion, spirit, intellect, and description.

Each poem contributes a piece toward a "whole" experience. They mirror the actual feelings and experiences of the events I observed. Some of the poems seem to reflect an attitude of support for the sharing of spirituality; others seem to oppose it; still others seem to have no opinion. Although my personal agenda as an individual may lean more in one direction or another, as an ethnographer in this study it was to be descriptive. By choosing to write the text in poetry, decisions could be left to the readers, in much the same way that they would be left to decide if a part of the situations was described. Any opinions expressed in the poems were actual opinions expressed in conversations in the field.

The following poems are selected from the 52 poems in the ethnography to demonstrate how they represent aspects of the intercultural experience of sharing culture through the sharing of spirituality. I hope you will come to understand aspects of what occurs within the intercultural arena of the sharing of native American spirituality by reading these poems. I further hope that you will recognize that each poem presents small holograms of the entire experience, which although expressing the nature of the phenomenon are not as accurate alone as when read with others. Finally, I hope that you will find in these glimpses of this particular intercultural context evidence of what characterizes intercultural communication across other contexts in which traditions are being shared, learned, protected, or challenged.

She Sees No One

When I look in the mirror
   I see no one
she said.
no legacy
no traditions known or treasured
nondescript mousy brown hair
pale skin the color of silly putty
I see no one.

And so she puts on feathers
and turquoise
and feigns a downward glance
when she talks to friends
They think something's bothering her
because she doesn't look at them anymore
she pretends it is a noble tradition
she has always practiced
though she still has to concentrate
when she catches herself looking
into somebody's
Eyes.

So when a well-meaning friend asks
"what's up?"
she can voice defiance
anger
disgust with *the System*
with white supremacy
with European culture
why do we have to look at each other?
it's so invasive.
it's a Native American tradition . . .
to look . . .
inward.

And somehow she feels noble
for defending an Indian way
when her friend only wondered if she was okay.
yesterday she was white.

When she looks in the mirror
she sees feathers
and turquoise
fringe and frill around the
nothing
she saw before
and she is frightened to take them off
because even in her noble
lack-of-eye-contact
newfound Indian ways
she still sees
No One.

Getting Smudged [5]

What's that smell?
is someone burning something in here?
it smells just like . . .
just like what?!
getting purified smells
like it's against the law
to your citified nostrils
and intellectualized senses
illicit Indian smells
trigger fear.
getting clean
feels like getting dirty.

Seminar Lady

Calls herself Starfeather Woman
and runs these seminars
on walking the sacred road
they cost a couple of hundred dollars
and people actually pay for it.
Starfeather Woman
man, she was nobody but little
Jane Doe
when she first came around here
who gave her that name anyway?

The "Open" Sweat [6]

They hovered around the firepit
with towels and
t-shirts and gym shorts
fluorescent white legs with
curly golden brown leg hair
the women in big baggy dresses
towels draped over their breasts
some less modestly over their arms
standing, watching
watching each other—

He has his towel *on*
he *doesn't*
I wonder which is *right?*
her dress has sleeves
hers is short
Hers is a solid color
I thought
you weren't *supposed* to wear jewelry
why are they holding sage
why are they wearing sage on their ears?
do I need some?

Have you ever noticed
how the air feels like

it's tangled
when everyone is busy
watching everyone
trying to learn
from others trying to learn
   . . . from others trying to learn
      . . . from others trying to learn

They say it is "traditional"
to learn by watching.
but was there ever a tribe
where only a couple of people
knew *how*
and the rest didn't?

Loop Hole

You guys could probably
make lots of money
if you sold
sweat lodge kits
tobacco prayer tie[7] kits
just put in everything for them
some little squares of cloth
some string
a package of tobacco
a little bit of sage
some matches
sell it for ten dollars
if you put it in a basket
you could sell it for fifteen
then the sweat could be free
and you wouldn't have to
worry about charging
for ceremonies.

Feminist Friends

Stop cooking so much!
don't feed the men first!
be liberated!
They come to help the women
to see their oppression
they want to show them a better way
a way to come out
from under
Male
oppression
so they instigate
motivate
tempt
and disrupt
leave a mess
in the same place

they found them
and go home
to their liberated condos
and nine-to-five jobs.

Indians Only

With a sense of entitlement
he walks into the meeting.
"I want to help;
I understand you."
No words uttered in response
a mass of pursed lips
as he takes a seat
amongst their circle
about to *help* them.

I understand you
he says.
I am glad to be here
I am not Indian
but I understand you.

Perhaps in saying it a *fourth* time
he will understand
that if he understood us
he would understand
that part of helping us
is to stay away
and let us help ourselves
decide
when *we* want to
invite others
into our circle.

Questions Like Speeding Bullets

Your desire to know
has a speed all its own
a speed that is so fast
it often surpasses my ability
to tell you
in the right way
what it is I have
what it is I know
what it is I have inherited
from my grandfathers.

Asking in a Good Way

If you want to know something
you don't have to ask any questions.
the Grandfathers know
and if we are the ones to tell you
then you will learn from us

but more likely
you will learn from you
and only *think*
that you are learning from us.

When you ask your questions
peering over our shoulders to
watch what we are doing
you act as if knowledge is something
that is scheduled
and your deadline for knowing is now.

In our ways,
there is no problem
when there are no answers
when we ask questions
you cannot force water
from a cloud
that is not a rain cloud.

The rain will come when it comes
or when it is asked
in the right way
in a good way

And no, we cannot tell you what that means.

Unwelcome Visitor

I really don't know what the problem is
or if there *is* a problem
or if there should *be* a problem
am I really not welcome here?

I know you've told me about *others*
but I thought that meant—
I thought that meant
I was different
I thought that meant
you trusted me
I thought that meant
you saw more than
the color of my skin

You gave me an Indian name
you stayed at my house
I bought your groceries
and I fixed your car
you taught me about spirit
and that we are all related
but right now
right now I feel like
you want me to go home.

I feel something
something that feels like

hatred
disdain
I'm confused
can't you see
that I changed my whole life
to be with you?

Moment of Truth

Generations
and Imposed Borders
separate *me*
from the people around me
always
forcing me to be stronger
to stand more firmly
in my place
Wherever I am,
in my place.
Always a visitor—
in my place.
Learning to be present
with self-respect
even when there's no
invitation.

The Talking Stick

Feeling respect
in a new way
they hold the Talking Stick
reverently
fingering the beadwork
the smooth sanded knots
gripping it solidly
like "Warriors."

Head warrior explains
it is an old tradition . . .
nodding solemnly
no one dares smile
and they pass the stick.

Each man speaks once
it moves in a circle
from man to man
warrior to warrior
each sharing words
feelings
thoughts
from the depths of his
feminine masculinity
each focusing on words

speaking poetry
and feeling good when all have
Spoken.
feeling good *that*
all have Spoken.

Not realizing that the true wonder
was that they all had
listened.

Painful Screams

Make tobacco ties
and pray.
face the Spirits of the
    West
    North
    East
    South
send smoke to the sky
touch your fingers to the earth
know that the pain in your heart
is good.

Learn to feel comfort
from
the pain
do not avoid it.

It is the voice of your spirit
sending health
and help.

Listen.

Your pain is the screaming voice
of spirit
telling you how to heal.

Inipi[8] Pain

I do not think
that until we see clearly
as in the sweat lodge
Inipi
as when we smoke the pipe
Chanunpa[9]
or offer up our ties
black
    red
        yellow
            white
blue and green

I do not think
that until that begins

that we know
what we are doing.

My pain now
is like the pain of the sweat lodge
I have chosen it.
crawled to my place
seated in revealing darkness
burning
because it will purify me
because it will heal me
because it is good.

Mundane Medicine Men

Who are the medicine men
who are the healers
that are placed on sacrificial altars
and granted special status

Some would have it that they are
somehow
more than human
somehow
somehow
men who have transcended
what it is to be human
what it is to be mundane on the earth.

Placed on pedestals
so that all can hear
so that all can see
that his feet no longer
touch the ground
and when we no longer
walk on the ground
we do indeed escape
what it is to be human
what it is to be mundane.

So we help medicine men healer gurus
to leave the ground
out of respect
we do this to them
out of respect
and awe
we take away their source of power.

A Spirit People

Everything we have
and have had
have had for ages
and will have—

everything
is Good.
Good.
we are Good.
no power on earth could make me claim
    otherwise.
no power in heaven would make me try.
the united spirit of us
a people
is stronger than you
or
me.
the united spirit of *us*
a people
will live on forever
they cannot kill our spirit.

Sitting Bull Freedom

Thousands of you came
hundreds of years ago
and keep coming today
like scurrying ants
that have forgotten
where the farm is
fleeing religion
fleeing oppression
fleeing family distress
and because you never dealt with it
came and created the same things here
invited us along for the ride.

They say Sitting Bull
sat in the middle of a battle
bullets and arrows flying past
and around him
never touching him
just sat there.

If you came here to escape
you're in the wrong place
turtle island[10] freedom
Is not about moving
Turtle Island freedom
being Indian
is about staying put
even when you are moving.

Notes

1. Readers are encouraged to read the work of Ed McGaa (1990, 1992) for treatment of the tradition of spir-

ituality that was shared, as well as commentary from the perspective of those who support it.

2. A note on my terminology: I am calling "Indian" those with legitimate claims to Indianness, whether through tribal enrollment, family history and tradition, or acknowledgment by an Indian community. Those I call "non-Indian" are those who cannot make these claims. I also include within the category of "non-Indian" those who claim to have "rumors" of a past Indian ancestry but whose families have no proof of this fact, more significantly, no incorporation of Indian culture into the accepted ways of the family. The term "native American" is used at times to refer to the traditions.

3. Many attribute the incorporation of Lakota spiritual practice into other tribal "traditions" to the Lakota spiritual leadership of the intertribal American Indian Movement, especially in the early 1970s, inspiring a resurgence and return to traditional spiritual practices nationwide by many "urban" and culturally displaced (through adoption into non-Indian families) native Americans. For more history and cultural context, readers are directed to Peter Matthiessen's (1991) treatment.

4. "Spring" focuses on the preparatory phases of the study, heavily emphasizing personal introspection, relevant reading, increasing one's awareness of assumptions and motives, and striving for appropriate access to the phenomena of interest. "Summer" then serves as the season of one's actual immersion in cultural phenomena, with much emphasis on the lessons derived through interpersonal contact, conflict, and personal dilemmas and stress. "Fall" is the season of harvesting one's efforts, celebrating the findings with the persons who supported the study, preparing for the isolated task of writing, and recognizing the resources available (including data) for the actual report. "Winter" is then the season of figurative hibernation, of writing one's report and determining its best form and purpose, based on the experience and knowledge gained in the previous seasons. Each season emphasizes its own activities, but several questions are asked constantly. They are based on the awareness that the research does not control the seasons; rather, the seasons will determine the research.

5. "Smudging" is the practice of burning herbs such as sage, sweetgrass, cedar, or pine in order to use the smoke as a form of purification or vehicle for prayer. This is done at many times, but routinely at the beginning of ceremonies or prior to important meetings or discussions.

6. "Sweat" is the name used for a purification ceremony in which steam is used to purify individuals. An "open" sweat was one to which non-Indians were allowed.

7. "Prayer tie" is the name used by some to describe the small pouches filled with tobacco and tied together with string as offerings of prayer.

8. *Inipi* is the Lakota word for what is, in English, referred to as a sweat lodge.

9. *Chanunpa* is the Lakota word for the pipe used in ceremony and prayer.

10. Turtle Island is the reference made by many indigenous (native American) peoples to the lands that make up what is known as North America.

References

González, M. C. (1996, February). The four seasons of ethnography. In Martin, J. (Chair), *Ethnicity and Methodology.* Symposium conducted at the 1st Conference on Ethnicity and Methodology at Arizona State University, Tempe.

Matthiessen, P. (1991). *In the spirit of Crazy Horse.* New York: Viking Penguin.

McGaa, E. (1990). *Mother Earth spirituality.* New York: Harper.

McGaa, E. (1992). *The Rainbow Tribe.* New York: Harper.

Key Terms

contact	Native American
cultural myth	postmodern identities
ethnic fraud	spirituality
ethnic identity	thrownness
ethnography	tradition
indigenous	

Discussion Questions

1. According to the author, why is the form of a research report important? What does poetry contribute to a report on intercultural communication?

2. Select one poem that you believe demonstrates how intercultural contact heightens the awareness of a person's cultural identity. Based on the insights of the poem, what could be done to increase the quality of intercultural communication?

3. How likely is it that individuals would have a totally positive response to a culture very different from their own? How do the poems reflect the struggles between two such cultures?

4. Based on these poems, what should people be aware of when they begin to learn about another culture?

5. Do you think it is possible to become a member of another culture by choice?

◀◤ Activities for Skill Development

1. Code of Ethics for Research

(from Robert McPhee, Arizona State University, 2000)

Write a code of ethics for intercultural communication researchers. List several principles that researchers should try to follow. For each one, give an example of a situation in which a tension or dilemma might come up, and recommend a way to handle it.

2. Code of Ethics for Intercultural Contact

Suppose you are approached by a multinational company who, knowing your expertise in intercultural communication, asks for your advice in creating a code of ethics for international business. How would you respond?

3. Advice Columns

Collect several columns by advice columnists such as Ann Landers or "Dear Abby." Analyze them by identifying the values behind each response. How might a columnist with a different cultural viewpoint respond? Discuss your views with your classmates.

Web Sites

1. What ethical dilemmas might you face working in international conflict resolution? See what the professionals are talking about at <*http://www.brandeis.edu/ethics/coexistence/dilemmas/dilemma.html*>.

2. Many people think it is wrong to intervene in the cultural practices of others, even when they seem to be oppressive to women or other groups. Others feel it is unethical *not* to intervene in the perpetuation of practices such as female genital mutilation (FGM). Check out the Web site of one such organization at <*http://www.fgmnetwork.org/eradication/orgs.html*>.

3. As we continue to move toward a global village, questions of what it means to be an ethical global citizen are sure to arise. For some thoughts, visit <*http://www.globalethic.org/*>.

Additional Readings

1. Paige, R. M., & Martin, J. N. (1996). Ethics in intercultural training. In D. Landis & R. S. Bhagat (Eds.), *Handbook of intercultural training* (2nd ed., pp. 35–60). Thousand Oaks, CA: Sage.

2. Bennett, M. J. (1998). Overcoming the golden rule: Sympathy and empathy. In M. J. Bennett (Ed.), *Basic concepts of intercultural communication* (pp. 191–214). Yarmouth, ME: Intercultural Press.

3. Shuter, R. (1999). Ethics, culture, and communication: An intercultural perspective. In L. A. Samovar & R. E. Porter (Eds.), *Intercultural communication: A reader* (pp. 443–450). Belmont, CA: Wadsworth.

Credits and Acknowledgements

Reading 6 Spellers, Regina E. Happy to be nappy! Embracing an Afrocentric aesthetic for beauty. Opening quotation from *Untitled* by Me'shell N'Degeocello. © 1993 WB Music Corp. (ASCAP), Askia Music (ASCAP), & Maverick Music Company (ASCAP). All rights administered by WB Music Corp. All rights reserved. Used by permission of Warner Bros. Publications U.S. Inc., Miami, FL 33014.

Reading 9 Baldwin, James. (1955). Stranger in the village. From *Notes of a Native Son* by James Baldwin. © 1955, renewed 1983, by James Baldwin. Reprinted by permission of Beacon Press, Boston.

Reading 13 Giles, Howard, & Noels, Kimberly A. (1977). Communication accommodation in intercultural encounters. FIGURE 1: Some increasing variants of convergence and divergence. Adapted by permission from H. Giles, R. Y. Bourhis, & D. M. Taylor (1977). Towards a theory of language in ethnic group relations. In H. Giles (Ed.), *Language and intergroup relations* (p. 324). London: Academic Press. FIGURE 2: Degree, direction, and mutuality of accommodation. Adapted by permission from C. Gallois & H. Giles. Accommodating mutual influence in intergroup encounters. In M. Palmer (Ed.), *Mutual influence in interpersonal communication: Theory and research in cognition, affect, and behavior,* vol. 20 of Progress in Communication Science Series. Greenwich, CT: Ablex Publishing.

Reading 15 Carbaugh, Donal. (1995). "I can't do that!" but I "can actually see around corners": American Indian students and the study of public "communication." In Jaakko Lehtonen & Leena Lahtinen (Eds.), *Critical perspectives on communication research and pedagogy* (pp. 215–234). St. Ingbert, Germany: Röhrig Universitätsverlag. Reprinted by permission of the publisher and the author.

Reading 16 Fitch, Kristine L. (1990–1991). A ritual for attempting leave-taking in Colombia. *Research on Language and Social Interaction, 24,* 209–221, 223–224. Reprinted by permission of Lawrence Erlbaum Associates, Inc., and Kristine Fitch, University of Iowa.

Reading 18 Hall, Edward T., & Hall, Mildred Reed. (1990). Key concepts: Underlying structures of culture. In E. T. Hall & M. R. Hall, *Understanding cultural differences* (pp. 3–31). Reprinted with the permission of Edward T. Hall Associates.

Reading 20 Kim, Min-Sun. (1992). A comparative analysis of nonverbal expressions as portrayed by Korean and American print-media advertising. *Howard Journal of Communica-* tions, 3, 317–339. Excerpted by permission of the *Howard Journal of Communications.*

Reading 21 Philipsen, Gerry. (1976). Places for speaking in Teamsterville. *Quarterly Journal of Speech, 62,* 15–25. Used by permission of the National Communication Association and the author.

Reading 22 King, Janis L. Cultural differences in the perceptions of sports mascots. Excerpts from Tim Giago, Notes from Indian country, *Indian Country Today,* reprinted by permission of Tim Giago.

Reading 23 Seiter, Ellen. (1990). Different children, different dreams: Racial representation in advertising. *Journal of Communication Inquiry, 14* (no. 1): 31–47. Reprinted by permission.

Reading 26 Kim, Young Yun (1995). Cross-cultural adaptation: An integrative theory. In R. L. Wiseman (Ed.), *Intercultural communication theory* (pp. 170–193). Excerpted by permission of the National Communication Association and the author.

Reading 31 Hofstede, Geert (1991). I, we, and they. In *Cultures and organizations: Software of the mind* (pp. 49–79). McGraw-Hill U.K. Reprinted with the permission of the author and copyright holder.

Reading 34 Ting-Toomey, Stella (1997). Intercultural conflict competence. In William R. Cupach & Daniel J. Canary (Eds.), *Competence in interpersonal conflict* (pp. 121–147), Prospect Heights, IL: Waveland Press, Inc. Reprinted with the permission of Waveland Press, Inc. All rights reserved.

Reading 35 Nwosu, Peter Ogom (1988). Negotiating with the Swazis. *Howard Journal of Communications, 1,* 145–154. Used by permission of the *Howard Journal of Communications.*

Reading 39 Bateson, Mary Catherine. (1993). Joint performance across cultures: Improvisation in a Persian garden. *Text and Performance Quarterly, 13,* 113–121. Used by permission of the National Communication Association and the author. Portions of this material were included in Chapter 1 of Mary Catherine Bateson, *Peripheral Visions.*

Reading 40 Tanno, Dolores V., & Jandt, Fred E. (1994). Redefining the "other" in multicultural research. *Howard Journal of Communications, 5,* 36–45. Used by permission of the *Howard Journal of Communications.*

Index